Culture

Culture War

*How the '90s Made Us
Who We Are Today
(Whether We Like It or Not)*

TELLY DAVIDSON

McFarland & Company, Inc., Publishers
Jefferson, North Carolina

LIBRARY OF CONGRESS CATALOGUING-IN-PUBLICATION DATA

Names: Davidson, Telly R., author.
Title: Culture war : how the '90s made us who we are today
(whether we like it or not) / Telly Davidson.
Description: Jefferson, North Carolina : McFarland & Company, Inc., 2016. |
Includes bibliographical references and index.
Identifiers: LCCN 2016021606 | ISBN 9781476666198 (softcover : acid free paper) ∞
Subjects: LCSH: Political culture—United States—History—20th century. |
Political culture—United States—History—21st century. | Nineteen
nineties. | United States—Politics and government—1989– | United
States—Politics and government—1989–1993. | United States—Politics and
government—1993–2001. | United States—Civilization—1989–
Classification: LCC E839.5 .D38 2016 | DDC 306.20973/0904—dc23
LC record available at https://lccn.loc.gov/2016021606

BRITISH LIBRARY CATALOGUING DATA ARE AVAILABLE

ISBN (print) 978-1-4766-6619-8
ISBN (ebook) 978-1-4766-2570-6

Front cover images: (top) © 2016 iStock; (bottom, left to right)
Bill Clinton (White House), Newt Gingrich (Gage Skidmore)
and O.J. Simpson (Department of Defense)

Printed in the United States of America

*McFarland & Company, Inc., Publishers
Box 611, Jefferson, North Carolina 28640
www.mcfarlandpub.com*

*To Adam Frisch and Brent R. Simon—two unusually
talented colleagues and brothers-from-other-mothers,
my East and West Coast "bookends" on the shelf of life*

Such as it is, the [mass-media] press has become the greatest power within the Western world, more powerful than the legislative, the executive, and the judiciary. One would like to ask, by whom has it been elected—and to whom is it responsible?

　　　　　　　　　　　　　　　　　　—Aleksandr Solzhenitsyn

Those who do not learn from the past are condemned to repeat it.

　　　　　　　　　　　　　　　　　　　　—George Santyan

Table of Contents

Acknowledgments

Chuck Donegan has been a great friend of mine since the 1990s decade was still under way, and his lovely family including his wife, Jaye, parents Carol and Charles, and his sister Jacqui and niece Carole Ann Ross have been like an East Coast annex family for me whenever I've visited. Chuck is an accomplished media man in his own right, hosting and engineering marvelous radio shows for WVOX in Long Island (on which I have had the privilege of being interviewed by him), and he is one of the leading video archivists of TV game/reality and talk shows, while also having authored his own coming-of-age novel, *Struggle of the Big Man*. Chuck's built-in talent is only exceeded by his native intelligence, unflappable good nature, and wit, and his compassion and empathy for others is only that much more obvious in that he never makes a big show of it—it's just always there when you need it. The real winners in the game show of life are the ones who know him.

Sean Hunter (formerly of Nielsen and currently of The CW) also goes back to the late '90s, when I was a just-outta-school baby researcher/writer and he was a super-young exec (at least we've aged gracefully, I think)—a friendship has been longer-running than most TV series and of infinitely higher quality. Ditto the rockin' and rulin' music historian extraordinaire Brent Mann, of New York and San Francisco (and Boston), a true chart-topper. And Gary Snyder's talents are only exceeded by his kindness and class.

For support in the truest sense of the word, I must deeply thank a family that I grew up with and alongside, headed by Barbara and Wallie Granger, their lovely daughter Rhonda Agnew, and her husband, the late Doug Agnew (a true "compassionate conservative" and everyday hero, as a proud Marine during the last days of Vietnam, who went on to be the perfect father to an adopted child), and to that now-grown daughter, Rhonda and Doug's lovely daughter Tess.

As always, I could never have accomplished this book, let alone so much else in the theater of life, were it not for my mother, and for my late grandparents, Jack H. Wartenberg (1918–94) and Lauryl M. Wartenberg (1923–2000), who laid the foundation for everything that this book (and so much in its author's life itself) rests on. And to my extended family—the Dantzlers and Froehles—my best regards, always.

Special shout-outs to friends and colleagues like the wildly multi-talented and handsome young actor/photographer/stuntman/TV host/multi-instrumentalist/is-there-anything-he-can't-do Peter Newman and his brilliant and beautiful writer partner, (Miss) Casey Greenberg; to Dave Sklar, a terrific New York-based musician and performer, teacher and friend; and to the book's unofficial science-rabbi, Dave Zobel, the finest and funniest "science guy" this side of Bill Nye—check him out on the Web.

LA Weekly, Vogue, and NPR giant John Powers, to whose wonderful 2004 book *Sore*

Winners this is sort of an unofficial prequel, has been nothing but wonderful to this project and its author.

Toni Lopopolo of Lopopolo Literary provided the confidence and the support necessary to get it off the ground.

Much love to Gary and Kathy Young, Flo Selfman, Robin Quinn, Ina Hillebrandt, Roberta Edgar, Libby Slate, James F. Mills, the late Pam Leven, and so many other regulars (and ir-regulars) of the marvelous and most worthwhile Independent Writers of Southern California (www.iwosc.org), of which I have been blessed to have been a part since 2003. Shout-outs to Eddie Pietzak, ace literary agent and all-around "Renaissance" man in every sense; my ace author and filmmaker friend (and deserving Oscar nominee) Dana Adam Shapiro; to the marvelous, generous, and ultra-talented media maven and HuffPo columnist Gary Snyder; and to longtime pal Tyson Cornell, a rare friend and CEO/founder of Rare Bird Literary Events (and Barnacle Books).

Kind thoughts and regards to those wonderful and essential pillars of LA literary life, Carolyn See, the queen bee and inspiration for so many who've come after her (including her bestselling daughter Lisa), and especially those like myself who've been lucky to meet and talk with her; and to Dr. Dianne De La Vega, a charming, insightful, and brilliant retired psychotherapist and author in her own right. And to Ohio's Larry James Gianakos, one of (and still) my earliest and greatest influences as a film and TV critic and historian, someone who shattered the glass ceiling for writing about the political/cultural context of pop-entertainment back in the '70s with his seminal reference guides and Midwestern movie reviews, and provided an example to so many other writers (particularly those others outside the NY/LA/DC/San Fran/Boston/Toronto media treadmill) on what to look *for* when you're looking *at* cinema and television.

And of course, sincerest thanks and respect to David Frum, whose book on the 1970s, *How We Got Here,* set the standard for all modern pop-political retrospective books of this nature, and whose *Dead Right* anticipated the Gingrich, Cheney, and Tea Party eras way back in early 1994, like a veritable reading from The Mentalist. Writing for the late and sorely missed FrumForum.com made you write smarter, better, and forced you to up your game—such a blessing from the shorter, dumber, "hotter," senselessly sensationalized, "We don't want it good—we want it by 5 o'clock!" mentality at so many other magazines and websites of all and any stripe. And to David's co-pilots during the FF's three years of existence—in particular the classy, ultra-smart, and friendly Meghashyam Mali, Tim Mak, and Noah Kristula-Green, the hippest of all so-called "nerds" and a pollster *par excellence* in Washington.

To two very important Jeffs in my life—screenwriter Jeffrey Berman, of RDRR Productions, for whom I helped produce *The WRITE Environment,* and Jeff Porter, president and CEO of the marvelous full-service producers' services and film sales agency, Porter Pictures of Beverly Hills, whom I've had the privilege of working with over the past nearly four years.

The late journalist and author Ron Kenner, who left us in 2013 just as work on this book had begun, and his marvelous wife, Mary, have served as constant inspirations and social conscience to this book, as well as a literary aunt-and-uncle to its author. A veteran of the *Los Angeles Times, Orange County Register,* and numerous award-winning books and editing gigs, Ron once suggested to me towards the end of his column on the newspaper of life that we measure a nation's GND—Gross National Decency—(to the comfort and quality-of-life of its citizens), as well as its bottom-line Gross National Product. I vote heartily in favor.

Preface

It was the media, stupid.

When Sen. Lindsey Graham announced that he was quitting the 2016 Republican race for president, Graham said archly (in a thinly disguised attack on rivals like Donald Trump and Ted Cruz), that running for president is "not a reality show."

Oh, but it IS, Sen. Graham, in so many ways—and it first truly became a "reality show" because of a youngish (by political standards, at the time) Boomer couple, who made a concerted effort to draw a media distinction between themselves and a fading, aging, out-of-touch, Greatest Generation President, against a backdrop of rising new technology. And an overheated, 24-hour spin cycle of cable news and opinion journal/editorial "punditoc-racy," as Eric Alterman correctly called it, morphing into online magazines and websites before the decade was through. Though these new styles and platforms brought us many advantages in the '90s (and beyond), it was also the era when, in Ezra Klein's wise words, the media collectively "lost its mind for eight years."

So many of the issues that define us today—immigrants and people of color and LGBT persons demanding full equality and diversity against people who fear what they repre-sent.... Islamic and Middle Eastern terror being the focus of foreign policy ... an out-sourced, downsized, electronics-and-education based New Economy that tears down obsolete business models as mercilessly as a torture-porn killer, no matter how many decades or centuries they had worked before ... a ballistically hostile Red State/Blue State divide. It was all there, as the 1990s progressed. It was also the decade-long coming out party for almost all of the modern political figures who shape today's narratives, from Clin-ton and Gingrich to Bush and Gore, from Karl Rove and James Carville to Rush Limbaugh and Bill O'Reilly, from Michael Moore and Bill Maher to Chris Matthews and Ann Coulter, and from Barack Obama's first book to Osama bin Laden's first terror attacks.

Some people might think that someone whose main writing credits are as a film and TV critic hasn't the right to pass serious historical judgment on a decade. To them I say that perhaps a media critic is the *best* possible person when it comes to the 1990s decade (and the ones that came afterward). It would be possible, if not exactly complete, to write a "serious" or academic study of most other periods of history and their behind-the-scenes palace intrigues and politics, while just glossing over what we would call pop culture—the pop songs, movies and TV shows, books, and so on that were current at the time. It would be utterly impossible to do that about the O.J. Simpson-Monica Lewinsky-*Bush vs. Gore* 1990s. The era of grunge and gangsta, indie films and the dawn of TV's "second golden age," plus tabloid TV and Internet news, the era when *South Park, Survivor, The Real World,* Fox News, Rush Limbaugh, Spike Lee, Quentin Tarantino, Eminem, Kurt Cobain, Jon Stewart, Bill Maher, and Conan O'Brien first made their biggest marks, and when Oprah, *The Simpsons, Entertainment Tonight,* David Letterman, Jerry Seinfeld, Michael Moore, and Oliver Stone were at their height.

As important as Bill and Hillary Clinton, Newt Gingrich, Al Gore, George Bushes (both Senior and Junior), Dick Cheney, Tom DeLay, Bill Gates, Steve Jobs, and Rush Limbaugh were, none of them were the truly central figure of the 1990s decade. That honor would go to the mass media itself (including a rising Internet) that interpreted, filtered, parsed, distributed, and largely created the feelings and perceptions that Americans had of the times in which they were living—a media that went from merely covering the parade to making itself the unquestioned star of it—to paraphrase the late Marshall McLuhan, the era when "the Media *became* the Message." It was the decade when pop culture and politics melded into one another so much that it was sometimes impossible to tell where one ended and the other began.

The dust jackets of some of my favorite mid-century "existentialist" novels (and even showbiz potboilers like *Valley of the Dolls*) would say things like, "She lived in a world that was beyond Good and Evil." And what strikes me perhaps the most about looking back on the pop culture, as well as the politics, of the 1990s, is how little actual truth mattered, as opposed to the larger and perhaps more important truths of optics, context, and coded appeals. Whether or not Clarence Thomas or Anita Hill was telling the truth during Thomas' confirmation hearings ... whether or not O.J. actually "did it" ... whether or not Clinton illegally obstructed justice or sexually harassed Monica Lewinsky and Paula Jones— the "right" and "wrong," the who-dun-it aspect, became entirely *beside the point*. The real "truth" was that Anita Hill spoke for millions of women who *had* faced the ugliest kinds of gender discrimination and harassment at work. That O.J. was as guilty as sin, and yet so was the often unfair and sometimes openly bigoted "system" prosecuting him. And that if Bill Clinton were punished for Monica and Paula, it would be war-on-women fundamentalists who hated Clinton for his sexual and racial liberalism—not Gloria Steinem feminists—who would score the biggest victory.

Those were the only "truths" that now mattered, once the smoke of these culture wars had cleared. And while Bill Clinton claimed the same "hope" and "change" mantra in 1992 that Barack Obama would claim 16 years later—when it was all over, the American public was so racially, sexually, and religiously polarized that most people weren't "hoping" that George W. Bush or Al Gore would WIN, so much as they were *praying* that "the other guy" would LOSE.

Before closing, a final note as to my own personal politics and so-called "agenda": One of the many great memories I have of working as the Culture Columnist for David Frum's *New Majority* and *FrumForum* from 2009 to early 2012 was how many readers would often try to play a game of ideological "Where's Waldo?" with me (and with several of his other relatively young columnists), trying to box us down as quack-quack doctrinaire "liberals" or "conservatives," and then wondering how and why we could keep going off-message the way we did. (To David's great credit, while insisting on certain ideological basics, he also insisted on racial, gender, preferential, and generational diversity among his many columnists and contributors.)

In short, if you're searching for ideological consistency or a clear, fixed point of view— here it is, one that transcends my loyalties to "liberal" or "conservative" or "Republican" or

"Democrat": I have a REAL attitude problem with hypocrites, double-standards, and bullies, no matter what "side" they claim to be on. And unfortunately, all three of those things were in definitive supply during the 1990s decade. It was the 24-hour decade when talking points memos, rigged question-and-answer rallies, staying resolutely "on message" and appealing to your "target demo" became THE standard of success.

I have enclosed a bibliography of books and websites used in the writing of this one, and have attempted to quote magazine, newspaper and Internet sources on the spot in the body of the text. Few books have been written yet on the impact of the 1990s decade—and almost none examining the media of the era (as opposed to historical biographies and/or glorifications of Bill, Hillary, Gore, Bush, Gingrich, Cheney, etc.). However, by far the most essential were *A Complicated Man* (Takiff, 2010), *What's the Matter with Kansas?* (Frank, 2004), *What Liberal Media?* and *Sound and Fury* (Alterman, 2003 and 1992), and *Dead Right* (Frum, 1994). I also owe something of a "debt" to the Michael Kinsley/Andrew Sullivan/Marty Peretz era *New Republic* for a treasure-trove of material most writers could only hope to plumb from.

The late, great Pauline Kael once said to the effect that writing about history that one has actually lived through forces you to do reconstructive surgery on your own past. As I finish my attempt at this do-it-yourself face lift, with any luck, you'll find a running through-line of even-handed fairness (or at least the sincere attempt at such). And a humanistic attempt try to explain, if not justify, why both sides of a contentious or inflammatory issue felt the way they did (and how and why things turned out) as you read along. I sincerely hope that you will enjoy the ride!

Introduction:
Postcards from the Edge

Once upon a time, not so very long ago, and in a land not so very far away....

A controversial, game-changing president has just been elected in one of the ugliest contests in American history. He lost mature white Americans by a considerable margin, but his election was almost entirely due to bringing new, young first-time voters into the game by virtue of his personality and New Media hip sophistication—along with unprecedented support from African Americans and Latinos. His radicalized opponents, meanwhile, refused to even recognize him as legitimate, as he was far younger and more assertively liberal and activist than any Democrat in recent memory. They launched total war on both him and his family, retaking the Congress just two years into his government with never-before-seen religious and Tea Party–type radicalism, after a bruising healthcare and budget battle. The economy was in a punishing recession—with massive working-class unemployment, rising crime, and huge deficits—though just a few years earlier, it had seemed like the good times would never end. And even as the economy climbed back towards prosperity, it underwent the biggest game-changes in postwar history, transforming itself from old-fashioned, predictable business models into an uncertain, technology-and-outsourcing-based future. Right-wingers were declaring a culture war—but liberated women and minorities were now fighting back, as were newly visible gays and lesbians. Cable TV and independent films were rewriting the storytelling landscape, while Internet bloggers and talk-radio titans were becoming more powerful and influential than major newspapers and magazines. Lower-middle-class white and senior voters were frightened like never before, of a demographic destiny they didn't understand and had never anticipated.

Sound just like today?

Try the 1990s.

The 1990s were not only, as the 2000 election demonstrated, the beginnings of Red and Blue America—they were essentially the opening salvo of what we now think of as the Tea Party. The presidential candidacies of figures like Sarah Palin, Ted Cruz, Michelle Bachmann, Rick Santorum, and Donald Trump would have been unimaginable were it not for the hard core religious and racial warfare that came to light with Pat Buchanan's famed "culture war speech" in 1992 and the so-called "Republican Revolution" of 1994, as well as the rise of conservative talk radio (Rush Limbaugh, Dennis Prager, Sean Hannity, Dr. Laura, Larry Elder, etc) and right-versus-left cable TV screamers. Not to mention the demagogic, "plain speakin,'" Aunt Blabby candidacy of Texas computer CEO Ross Perot in 1992—the

5

first to truly fetishize the whole "private sector experience" thing as being superior, even preferable, to Big Guv'mint experience and to advertise for the "CEO President" ideal. (Even that scourge of big government, Ronald Reagan, had been a successful two-term governor of the nation's largest state before becoming president. And his successor and partner in power, George Bush, Sr., was said to have the longest resume in Washington— Congress, CIA, Republican National Committee, ambassador, and of course, vice president.)

Think the Obama-style shaming and disrespect of a sitting president is something new? How about military veterans turning their backs on Clinton at a Memorial Day salute. Virulently racist cartoons and Photoshop images (Obama as a monkey or ape, or a bone-wearing witch doctor)? How about talk radio stars calling teenage Chelsea Clinton "the White House dog," Hillary a "femi-Nazi," and a sculptor putting up a statue of "Hitlery" Clinton. Black Lives Matter, immigrant-bashing, and the controversies over police violence and "war on crime" laws? Paging Rodney King, Willie Horton, O.J. Simpson, and the "Three Strikes" laws and the 1993–94 "Crime Bill," plus numerous statewide affirmative-action repeals and California's noxious Proposition 187. The fight for gay civil rights? While Defense of Marriage and Don't Ask Don't Tell were hardly positive milestones, they were proof that at least gay issues were being brought to the center of the American conversation—as well as Ellen coming out, the premiere of *Will & Grace,* Tom Hanks winning an Oscar for playing a gay man with AIDS in *Philadelphia* (and if early 2001 counts, the start-offs of *Queer as Folk* and *Six Feet Under*).

The late 1980s and '90s was the time when words like "diversity" and "political correctness" first really went mainstream, and true to form, the people who lived in and affected (and were affected) by that tumultuous decade were as diverse and different as day and night. The story of the 1990s was the story of how a country coped with the often very painful and traumatic birth pangs of a completely rebooted new reality—a New Economy based on microchips, information, education, and market bubbles, instead of labor, production, and tangible goods. A New Media, deregulated beyond Ronald Reagan or George Bush, Sr.'s wildest dreams, with the Internet and cellular technology opening up never-before-dreamed-of opportunities—and also posing a direct threat to newspapers, magazines, and traditional book publishing that movies and TV never could. And an atomized New Attitude, paradigm-shifting from "broadcasting" products, services, films, music, TV shows, books, and political campaigns, to "narrowcasting" them to zeroed-in, sweet spot target audiences and key demographics—where who WASN'T watching, buying, voting was as important as who was.

It was the era when "independent films" were officially transformed from drive-in slasher and blaxploitation cheapies into the most challenging, artistic, and literate story-telling on the silver screen, and when cable dramas and upscale comedies first started doing the same thing for network TeeVee. It was when the music business encompassed everything from booming ballads from Whitney, Mariah, and Celine to performance art by Madonna, k.d. lang, Morrissey, and Marilyn Manson, and from sweaty and smelly alienated white boys in Seattle to black gangsta-rappers bulging with bling and fly girls from South-Central, north Vegas, and Harlem.

The things that most greatly shape our world today, technologies like the Internet, cell phones, reality TV, and social networking, all came out of the closet in the 1990s. From the instinctive, automatic raised-eyebrow "irony" of Jon Stewart and Conan O'Brien to the 24/7 celebration of in-yo'-face attitude from Bill O'Reilly to Bill Clinton, from The Notorious B.I.G. to Donald Trump—all came alive to their zenith in that era. It was the time when the barriers between tabloid news and "real" news collapsed, when the 17-year-old college kid who was good at indexing web pages could become almost as hot and influential a "film critic" or "political commentator" as Roger Ebert or Bob Woodward. And it was a decade that started with one epic collapse (that of the Berlin Wall) and the end of the Cold War, with the fall of the Soviet Union—and ended with the collapse of the Twin Towers, and the beginning of today's "war on terror."

In recent years, there have been many look backs on the politics and popular culture of postwar history, from *Mad Men* and *That '70s Show* to *Capitalism: A Love Story* and several bestselling books. Rick Perlstein would write a 2008 bestseller called *Nixonland,* which posited that Richard Nixon and the political tricks and treats he'd invented (the so-called "Southern Strategy" of getting Dixiecrats and the urban white working class to vote Republican) had made for the definitive presidential administration of the modern era. David Frum and Dominic Sandbrook countered that it was Gerald Ford and Jimmy Carter who had done the trick, with the first abortion-gay-feminist and busing/affirmative action culture wars, plus the "Me Generation" self-empowerment of the late '70s, in their books *How We Got Here* and *Mad as Hell.* Our fellow Gen-Xer David Sirota said that it was the Reaganautical '80s that ruled the roost, in his book *Back to Our Future.* And most persuasively of all, perhaps, historian Sean Wilentz would counter that the years from 1974 to 2008—a timeline which very much included the Clinton government from start to finish—were *The Age of Reagan.*

And the one thing they almost all agreed upon was that it was Barack Obama, not Bill Clinton, who truly began bringing the Reagan/Bush era to a close (not to mention being the "first black president" for real). Not for nothing was Obama pointedly anointed the "Game Change" of modern American politics, as John Heilemann and Mark Halperin put it in their January 2010 bestseller. Indeed, when it came to the raw exercise of power and force to get his way—whether the public wanted it or not—to put it crudely, the opinion-poll-addicted Bill Clinton couldn't even hold Barack Obama's basketball uniform.

Within little more than a year of taking office, Obama signed into law (and later defended and won in the Supreme Court) a ballistically controversial requirement that every self-employed person or small businessman buy private, if sometimes partially subsidized, for-profit health insurance, whether they could afford to or not. (And if they couldn't, they'd have to tell their troubles to the IRS.) Obama continued more-or-less full throttle with the Bush/Cheney wiretapping and domestic spying programs that he had earlier run against, as Edward Snowden and Bradley Manning would reveal. Obama oversaw the top-down, Bush bailouts of Wall Street and their "Too Big to Fail" banking mega-mergers and takeovers, plus mounted a sequel for the auto industry—all while rewriting the rules for borrowing business and home loans in his spare time!

And when it came to the social issues, as the real first black president, Obama was all about the reboot button. He sent Clinton's two signature '90s "triangulations" on LGBT issues, Defense of Marriage and Don't Ask Don't Tell, to history's dustbin, refusing to even defend or enforce them and successfully encouraging the Supreme Court and the (pre-2011) Democratic Congress to strike them down. (For this, columnist Andrew Sullivan half-jokingly anointed Obama the "First Gay President.") Obama signed the Lily Ledbetter Equal Pay Act into law, and appointed not one but two female Supreme Court justices— one a self-described "wise Latina," and the other a never-married (or even engaged), child-less Jewish woman of indeterminate lifestyle preference. He defended illegal immigrants against Arizona and other would-be tough states' excesses, while overseeing nationally legalized gay marriage to boot. And above it all, it was Barack Obama who made Osama bin Laden rest in pieces, during the midnight "Zero Dark Thirty" raid, in Pakistan in 2011.

For better or worse, whether you loved them or hated them, the record is inarguable: Bill Clinton was a *manager*—but Barack Obama was a *leader*. There was no doubt about who was in charge, who the decision-maker and agenda-setter was at the Obama White House, in sharp contrast to the committees and panels and warring egos of Clinton's George Stephanopoulos vs. James Carville, Madeleine Albright vs. Colin Powell, Janet Reno vs. Kenneth Starr, Hillary vs. Al Gore kitchen cabinet. In shocking contrast to how Bill Clinton was viewed by conservatives and Republicans at the time—as the epitome of draft-dodging, smarmy, self-indulgent narcissism—today Bill Clinton is now historically looked back on by many as merely the most colorful Democratic supporting actor in the 28-year Republican miniseries that ran from 1980 to 2008, by both Wall Street Republicans and left-wing Democrats alike!

Yet on closer inspection, that in no way, shape, or form diminishes the historical impact or importance of William Jefferson Clinton, or of the decade of the 1990s. Bill Clinton spent eight years "triangulating" his way through the decade, and while it preserved his and Hillary's power seat, it had also defenestrated the Democratic Party's existing A-list leaders in Congress and the statehouses, in 1994's reactionary "Republican Revolution." Clinton had tried giving Wall Street, Silicon Valley, and Big Media moguls whatever they wanted, whenever they wanted it. Yet the Gingrich-Limbaugh-Rove Republicans, and the Murdoch/Mellon Scaife/Koch Brothers right-wing media, still remained utterly committed to destroying him, whatever it took.

And in his most important legacy by far, Bill Clinton had made a point of hiring the most racially and gender-diverse group of White House officials and cabinet members in then-history, and actually took the trouble to speak to and occasionally include open gays and lesbians, back in an era when Ellen and Elton were still boycott-controversial, when Matthew Shepard and Brandon Teena and AIDS victims still "deserved" to die. But the hard left nonetheless grew to loathe Clinton almost as much as the Republicans did, for "selling us out" with NAFTA, media deregulation, Defense of Marriage, welfare reform, G8, Glass-Steagall's repeal, and all the dismal rest. If "triangulating" and "compromising" only sprayed gasoline on the cultural backdraft, if reaching out to the other side only got you two bloody stumps (one from the opposition party and the other from your own disappointed people), then who needed *that* crap to begin with? As Dick Cheney himself would famously say, from now on, it would be "Full speed ahead!"

During the 1990s, the bestseller lists were jam-packed with right-wing tomes detailing the most mind-boggling conspiracies and hate speech against Bill and Hillary (Clinton brutally murdered Vince Foster, Clinton was a Mafia-connected drug runner, Clinton was a serial rapist and Hillary an insatiable butch lesbian...). And then there were just the garden-variety haters and vessel-bursting outrages: *Slouching Towards Gomorrah. BOY Clinton. Where is the Outrage? Can She Be Stopped? American Evita. HELL to Pay! The Case for Impeachment. No One Left to Lie To. Values Matter Most.*

Yet after he left office, and indeed even as Clinton's reign came to an end, it would be the ultra-*liberal* media royalty—people like Robert Scheer, Christopher Hitchens, Alexander Cockburn, Matt Taibbi, Barbara Ehrenreich, Thomas Frank, and Michael Moore—who would write anti–Clinton screeds that were just as scorchy. They would indict "Clinton Democrats" every bit as blisteringly as "Reagan Republicans" for the decline and helplessness of America's working and middle class. (Indeed, to many of them, Clinton Democrats and Reagan Republicans seemed to be almost one and the same, except for the Religious Right aspect.)

Bernie Sanders—that's your cue!

Starting in the 1990s (especially after the traumatizing 1992 loss of Bush Senior), the Republican and conservative movements veritably canonized Ronald Reagan, as not just a good or inspiring president, but as THE best president of the 20th century, or at the very least the second-best behind Franklin Roosevelt. And after George W. Bush left office in 2008–09, it seemed that the centrist Democrat movement decided "if you can't beat 'em, join 'em!" and began canonizing Clinton as the best president of the postwar era—far better than those black-and-white Cold Warriors Harry Truman and Dwight Eisenhower, and at the very least the equal of John F. Kennedy.

The biggest reason why Clinton hit the top tier was because his term coincided exactly with the historical gap—after the Cold War and before 9/11—and the 1990s stock market bubble-boom. Both working-middle and wealthy Americans had at least *superficially* the best economic conditions since the *Mad Men* era (despite rising educational/credentialing standards and inequality), and African Americans and Latinos, restricted from much of the mid-century economy's prosperity, had some of their best times ever.

Yet instead of rejoicing in the sunshine of their good fortune, the public was as blood-boilingly bitter and polarized alongside class, religious, and racial lines as they were during Vietnam and Watergate—with the O.J. trial, Monica Lewinsky and impeachment, and *Bush vs. Gore* as Exhibits A, B, and C. And it was also that legacy of unfiltered, unmoderated, self-published hate and willful, even proud ignorance, of a "marketplace of ideas" beyond Ayn Rand or Joseph Pulitzer or William Randolph Hearst's imagination, where everybody's opinion carried equal weight and could be equally publicized, which found its perfect incubation period in the 1990s.

Bottom line: if there had been no Bill Clinton—and especially if there had been no Internet/cell phone, New Media revolution, there almost surely would never have been a Barack Obama—and certainly nowhere near as soon as 2008. When Barbara Jordan delivered her keynote address at the Democratic National Convention in 1992, she said that the first ingredient necessary for the Democrats to retake the White House was to have the courage, and the belief that "victory IS possible!" And she wasn't engaging in hyperbole. Before 1992, the Democrats seemed to many voters almost as marginal and headed-for-extinction as the Tea Party-racked Republicans do today—a powder keg of race-warring "quota queens," pretentious and out-of-touch academics, Vietnam-era unreconstructed peaceniks, "humorless" radical feminists and AIDS-era "God is Gay" queer activists, labor leaders quite justifiably terrified by a hyper-driven and outsourced New Economy, politically correct atheists and thought police, and Rose Bird-worshiping, ribbon-wearing, radical chic limousine liberals straight from the ACLU. In the '70s and '80s, it was a recipe that had worked out just about as well as a circular firing squad. All while things went from bad (Nixon, Carter) to even worse (Reagan, Bush I) in the progressive liberal's outside world and mind.

Bill Clinton changed all that. Whether for better or for worse is still in the eye of the beholder, but that was where HE was truly the gold standard "game change." He proved that the Democrats could win the White House (twice!), that they could believe in themselves again as a cultural force and even have "hope and change" for the future. For a generation of liberals who had come of age with LBJ's war in Vietnam followed by Nixon, and then a dozen long years of Reagan/Bush, even as AIDS wielded its bloody scythe across the American landscape, even as "Greed is Good" became the new national motto, seeing Clinton win—at least initially—was an electrifying achievement. It was a triumph akin to the greatest Super Bowl or World Series or Olympic games highlights, a validation, a victory. *Oh my God! We really DID it this time! He actually BEAT them! HE did it! WE WON!!*

But as we said earlier, as important as Bill and Hillary Clinton were to the story, the 1990s decade and its legacies cut far deeper than any one presidential or political couple. To paraphrase the first President Bush's 1989 Inaugural Address reference to the Vietnam War, the legacy of the 1990s "cleaves us still." Despite what the 24-hour interventionist neocons said, it was a decade that was anything but a "holiday from history." Anyone who still thinks that the 1990s marked the "end of history," as historian Francis Fukuyama half-jokingly put it, should ask Arianna Huffington, Craig Newmark, Mark Zuckerberg, or Jeff Bezos how all that end-of-history stuff's been workin' out for ya over the past two decades. There were just as many people who saw the first sneak previews of an economy, a media, and a way of life that would bring nothing but warp speed "creative destruction" of decades, even century-old ways of life and thinking as there were people on the winning side who could literally afford to write the decade off as nothing but "peace and prosperity."

So with that, let us now begin our time-tripping travelogue through the decade that ended one millennium and gave birth to another. A decade where "diversity" and "multiculturalism" were both celebrated and feared, and where—contrary to today's revisions and reimaginings—the people who wove the tattered tapestry of that era were as diverse and under-pressure as life itself. Because the 1990s were many things, but a contented, peaceful, and prosperous holiday from history they certainly *weren't*. Instead, the 1990s were, quite simply, the decade which made us who and what we are today. Whether we like it—or not.

1

Falling Down

The finest day I ever had was when tomorrow never came.
—Kurt Cobain

"I'M the bad guy??"

That was the memorable tag line of the 1993 Michael Douglas vigilante movie *Falling Down,* where Douglas played a fortyish defense engineer (known as D-FENS for most of the movie, based on the vanity license plate to his pathetic, secondhand 1979 Chevy Chevette), who takes ever-increasingly violent revenge on the crack-ed up, gangsta-ridden, racially polarized, urban decayed landscape of early '90s Southern California—a land where euphemisms like "equal opportunity" and "income equality" could only be qualified with the prefixes "un" or "in."

Douglas accepted the role less than five years after his Oscar triumph for the movie that defined the go-go late 1980s, *Wall Street,* and was fresh off the giga-blockbusters *Fatal Attraction* and *Basic Instinct.* And while D-FENS may not have left the same gigantic cultural footprint that Gordon Gekko did, in his day, he was almost as influential. D-FENS' face made the cover of *Newsweek* in early 1993—just after the inauguration of a game-changing, draft-dodging, minority-friendly, ex-hippie president named Bill Clinton—accompanied by the headline, "White Male Paranoia." (For anyone who thinks that the Tea Party vs. Obama atmosphere of the past decade was something new or different, one would best be reminded of the borrowed signature line of another lovable cinematic antagonist, Sister Aloysius of *Doubt:* "There is nothing new under the sun.")

Falling Down's screenwriter, actor Ebbe Roe Smith, said on its 2009 DVD commentary that when he was figuring out what occupation to give Douglas's character, he had been reading one headline after another about the circa-1991 annihilation of defense industry jobs across the West Coast, and Southern California in particular. These jobs, which had boomed ever since Pearl Harbor—and had essentially *built* modern suburban LA, Orange County, San Diego, Sacramento, Portland, Seattle, and non-casino Las Vegas—were now being lopped off at a jaw-dropping rate, as the Cold War (and Gulf War I) came to a close.

By the time of the 1992 election, So Cal's media image was also being redefined, by movies like *Colors, Boyz N the Hood, White Men Can't Jump,* and *Falling Down*—plus the vicious real-life beating of Rodney King by LAPD officers, and the horrifying 1992 LA "uprising" in reaction against it (the worst riots since Martin Luther King or Watts). The same Los Angeles and Orange County "lifestyle" that had been defined a decade earlier by the convertible-driving beach bunnies of *Charlie's Angels* and *Three's Company* now became synonymous with hairnetted Mexican gangstas and musclebound African American youths, belligerently cruising their hip-hop-blaring "hoopty" low-riders around smog-choked traffic jams and graffiti-laden ghettos, in their stanky wife-beater undershirts and floor-to-ceiling tattoos. (Meanwhile, the New York City of *Do the Right Thing* and *Law & Order's* early years, had only gotten worse—now so hopelessly degenerated into AIDS, crack, heroin, meth, drive-by shootings, "wild-ings" in the public parks, *Precious*-style welfare bureaucracy and high school hell-mouths, it made the days of *Kojak* and Charles Bronson look like paradise lost.) The barely suppressed racial, ethnic, and social class pressure-cooker, simmering under the surface during all of the "prosperous" Reagan-Bush era, had finally exploded.

Ebbe Roe Smith went on to say that in D-FENS' mind, he had effectively been fired *for having been too good at his job.* We'd finally won the Cold War at long last, just as we'd earlier beaten Adolf Hitler with our can-do American military might! And the Berlin Wall had come down in no small part thanks to the big, Reaganized weapons programs and buildup from the 1980s, right? But now, instead of a gold watch or a brand new car or even just a thank-you, it was pink slip time. As they say in Hollywood and Broadway, "Love ya—but we gotta lose ya!" And while one didn't necessarily have to feel all that sorry for the doomed D-FENS, both Smith and star Michael Douglas said that *Falling Down,* was above all, a story about a man who'd *played by the rules,* who'd stayed in school, probably served in Vietnam, didn't openly abuse alcohol or drugs, someone who'd married and had a daughter, paid his bills and taxes on time, and cared for his dotty mother. In short, he was someone who'd done everything he was "supposed" to do as a good citizen up to that point—*and he'd ended up being punished for it.*

When one does a psychological autopsy of 2016's Donald Trump phenomenon and the conservative movement of today—who can trace their roots in a straight through-line back to the "Republican Revolution" of 1994 (and Ross Perot's demagogic, reactionary third-party candidacy in 1992)—this dynamic is likely the root of all of their side effects, from racial and religious to economic. Ditto the Elizabeth Warren/Bernie Sanders/Michael Moore style "populist" liberals, still sitting *shiva* for the destruction of Big Labor and consumer advocacy's 1960s and '70s clout, and for the mom-and-pop business, stable income, fixed-salary economy of midcentury America and Canada. As President Obama himself said, at the rock bottom of an even worse Great Recession in 2010, "The rules have changed—in the middle of the game."

That was the one thing that everyone could have agreed upon by then, in post–2008 meltdown America—but by the time Obama got there, the melting pot had already reached critical mass and boiled over, after more hopelessly deferred maintenance than a 90-year-old widow's house.

For further evidence, let's look at the other era-defining movie from the end of the '80s and the start of the '90s, which covered not smoggy and scorching post-aerospace LA and Orange County, but the area that was once the industrial heartland of America—and was now fast on its way to becoming a post-industrial wasteland. Michael Moore's all-too-real (if slightly unfair and unbalanced) 1989 signature epic about the first wave of what would soon come to be known as "outsourcing," *Roger & Me.*

After having survived the late '70s/early '80s "malaise" era of ever-tightening fuel-efficiency and emission standards, 15 percent interest rates, and gasoline lines, by the mid–1980s General Motors was back on top, posting record profits and sales. Top-billed Cadillac set an all-time record in 1985; GMC trucks and soccer-mom minivans were flying off the lots, and Ronald Reagan had officially declared that it was "morning in America" again. As late as 1990, Cadillac sold more cars in the U.S. and Canada than any one of its luxury competitors, foreign or domestic. Life was good in the GM neighborhood—or so it seemed on the surface. But there was trouble brewing beneath the ledgers.

The Japanese imports that had taken hold in the energy-conscious '70s, like Honda, Nissan, and Toyota, along with new Korean counterparts like Hyundai and Kia, were increasing their market share almost every year—especially with Baby Boomers and younger buyers who didn't have any lingering "issues" over World War II or Korea. Toyota was planning to unveil its signature Lexus division before the decade was out, aiming straight at suburban doctor/lawyer professionals and business owners, and those prosperous Greatest Generation seniors who *were* willing to give them a try. In other words—the audience that was high-profit Caddy and Buick's bread and butter.

The result was that GM mercilessly massacred its long-established plants in Moore's hometown of Flint, Michigan, which (after his film) became synonymous for the industry-abandoned, hollowing-out Rust Belt—replete with "bitter" downscale voters who "clung" to their guns and their simple religions (as Barack Obama cruelly but too-truthfully later described this demographic, in 2008). After years of loyal service, the formerly good-paying and easy-to-get jobs now started heading south of the border, down Mexico way. (Or to Guatemala, Honduras, India, China, etc., as time went on.) The message was clear: "Business as usual" was no longer an option. By the early 1990s, just being "good enough" just *wasn't* good enough anymore—if you wanted to keep your job.

The "peace dividend"

Like poor D-FENS from *Falling Down,* these workers (and by the way, many of them were African American) were being given a hard and fast lesson in the emerging "Global Economy," and what it would mean for them and their children—in good times and bad—from that point on.

And what really twisted their boxer briefs was that the early 1990s was when we were *supposed* to be finally cashing in on the "peace dividend" that had been promised to us. Once we finally won the Cold War, like World War II before it, once freedom had triumphed, why, we could plough all that money we'd been spending on nuclear bombs or napalm or Scud missiles, and spend it on our schools, hospitals, and police departments, and on improving our infrastructure. Life would be Easy Street from now on!

Except that Dwight Eisenhower didn't call it the "military-industrial complex" for nothing. And as offensive as many may find Gore Vidal and Howard Zinn's even more provocative "National Security State" moniker, the fact was that when the defense contracts dried up, and the military bases became redundant, and the big General Motors and General Electric–type companies started outsourcing and downsizing, it was the schools and libraries and police departments, the small businesses and hospitals that were the hardest hit—from Akron, Ohio to Anaheim, California, and from Seattle, Washington to Sunnyside, New York. Massive domino-effect unemployment cracked down as working- and middle-class house values collapsed, and tax revenues cratered. Already schools and police departments were crumbling, due to the crack/meth and gang epidemics, record-breaking divorce and unwed parenthood, and legal and illegal foreign-language immigration. There was also the much more fortunate news of Greatest and Silent Generation seniors living longer (on their vested pensions and Social Security and Medicare), thanks to ultra-costly new 1970s and '80s advances in medicine like bypass and open-heart surgery, IVACs, transplants, chemo, MRI scans, life-support respirators, modern-day dialysis, and pacemakers. Things that were barely coming out of Robert Heinlein science-fiction territory when Medicare was founded back in 1965. (And there was also the much *less* fortunate news of the AIDS plague.) All of it costing money ass over elbow. And neither side was willing—or really *able*—to give an inch.

"A strange sort of recession"

"The country was suffering from a strange sort of recession in 1992," noted David Frum, in his definitive psychological autopsy on the post–Reagan/Bush (and immediately pre–Gingrich/Cheney) Republican Party and conservative movement, *Dead Right,* published in early 1994. Indeed, it was perhaps the first recession of its kind in the modern era—but it would certainly not be the last! Just look at the tell-tale symptoms: Residential home prices across America "were tumbling, big corporations were laying off middle managers, engineers were waiting by the mailbox for their unemployment checks, and retirees' income from their certificates of deposit had been cut in half," combined with rampant income inequality and round-the-clock foreclosures and repossessions. *Any of that sound familiar?*

According to the Commission on State Finance in Sacramento, over 800,000 jobs were lost in California between 1988 and 1993. With Russia dissolving and the Gulf War over in a matter of days, 1991 had killed off over 60,000 jobs just in California's defense industry alone. More than half the job loss had occurred in Los Angeles County (with next-door neighbors Orange County and San Diego close behind). Between 1990 and 1994, according to Susan Faludi, nearly 30,000 jobs had been eliminated in Long Beach and northern Orange County, just by the McDonnell-Douglas company *alone!* And it wasn't looking any better anytime soon. In that just-before-the-Internet era of 1993 and '94, the Commission predicted nearly 100,000 more aerospace jobs, plus 35,000 civilian military base jobs—and God only knew how much "collateral damage" of stores, restaurants, bars, banks, Realtors, etc., that served those people—headed for extinction over the next couple of years. In only the first two quarters of 1992, nearly 10,000 separate businesses had failed or gone bankrupt just in California. General Motors was closing its Van Nuys and South Gate Cadillac plants, in addition to the ongoing genocide of redundant Orange County, San Diego, and Sacramento military bases and defense plants.

The economic cancer was hardly confined to the Golden State or West Coast. The deindustrialization and "restructuring" of the post–Carter era had "scythed through vast swaths of industrial America, shuttering steel and auto plants across the Midwest, decimating the defense industry, and eliminating large numbers of workers" in once-untouchable "corporate behemoths," according to Susan Faludi in her 1999 look-back on the early '90s worker, aptly titled *Stiffed.* The downsizing statistics of the early 1990s were dizzying—almost like reading casualty numbers from World War II or Vietnam: 60,000 jobs lost at Chrysler, 74,000 at General Motors, 175,000 at IBM, 125,000 at AT&T. And on and on and on….

By the spring of 1994, when the first pangs of recovery were just barely starting to flit across the New York Stock Exchange's fabled electronic tickertape, Southern California, New York City, and the urban-Midwest Rust Belt were still treading water in the deep end, with the pool drains turned on full-force below. Faludi gives a chilling account in her book of her visit to an Employment Development Department's "Career Transition Center." (Note the same kind of happy-talk euphemism for the human carnage of mass firings and downsizings that George Clooney's efficiency expert in *Up in the Air* might have later recommended using.) In keeping with that theme, the confused and desperate workers there were being "processed" through a sort of "human retooling shop," featuring an "assembly line" of Interview Skills Training and Skills Transference Workshops, plus Resume Development Classes, and Stress and Anger Management sessions. There were also "helpful," uplifting workshops like "Making Transitions Work for You" and "Surviving a Layoff Financially."

Faludi tells the archetypal story of one laid-off defense worker, Don Motta, who received his "R.I.F." (Reduction in Force) discharge papers in early 1993. So traumatized, so humiliated was he by this reversal of fortune that he couldn't even bear to tell his wife until his last week before the proverbial cleaning-out of his desk. "I just…. I just couldn't," he shuddered. The weeks and months to follow "were like an endlessly reeling bad dream," Faludi reported. The loyal, eager worker with years of experience sent out over *one hundred* resumes—and got a grand total of *four* interviews—after those resumes and cover letters made their peristaltic way through all the bureaucratic layers of Human Resources Employment Recruitment Headhunter Screening Equal Opportunity Affirmative Action Process Procedurals.

Meanwhile, the foreclosure reviews and the car repo threats were cracking down. He gave up his health insurance. It took three out of his four weekly unemployment checks just to pay the monthly minimum on the mortgage. His savings evaporated. And worst of all, Motta's wife decided that she'd had it. While it was unfair to blame him, she now guiltily admitted, Motta's now-ex wife Gayle said she herself was so traumatized by what had happened that her "fear of ruin and abandonment drowned out" everything else. Even though she knew that the entire department had been downsized and outsourced, that it wasn't his fault, her justifiable terror of impending economic annihilation, of perhaps sleeping on the relatives' couch (or even bag-lady homelessness and foreclosure) had caused her to become irrational in her panic. "I felt hurt, like I couldn't trust him anymore." She found a new boyfriend who had a stable job, and by her own admission, "threw [Don] out of the house."

"There is no way you can feel like a man" if you're "not capable of supporting your family," Motta recalled. "I'll be very frank with you—I feel like I've been castrated." He wasn't the only one. Faludi also told the equally grim story of Owen Benson, whose marriage also had blown to smithereens following the downsizing epidemic. He was forced to trade away his stable, high-paying, full-benefits Old Economy, Inc., job for a minimum-wage (at the time) night shift desperation gig paying less than $5 an hour, at a factory making plastic video-rental covers. He augmented his meager income (upping the humiliation factor to Keystone Kops level) as a costumed Mister Peanut, petitioning and pantomiming on the sidewalk, but it was all for naught. His stressed-to-the-max wife called the divorce lawyer.

Mike Mulk's marriage of twenty years also fell apart. As he ruefully put it, "When the job fell off, so did she."

A few years later in 1997, *New Yorker* columnist, Clinton aide, and Bill and Hill bestie Sidney Blumenthal wondered why—with the stock-market economy, and brand-new Internet and cell-phone technologies now taking off like a rocket—*why* the fabled "white working class" still hadn't gotten the memo. Why, despite now being surrounded by surpluses "as far as the eye can see," and "irrational exuberance," the memories of the early '90s recession still lingered like body odor in a men's locker room, like grease stink in a fast-food kitchen, when it came to the Norma Raes and Erin Brockoviches, when it came to the NASCAR dads and small-business salesmen.

Well, Mr. Blumenthal—there's your answer! *This* is what the American working and middle class thought about whenever they thought about the "New Economy." And even if it hadn't happened to them, even if *they* had managed to come through relatively unscathed—they certainly *knew* somebody who had been destroyed by this economic genocide, this ultimate "rebooting" process. *There but for the grace of God go I...*

"Moral hazard"

In the run-up to the massively controversial Wall Street and Big Auto bailouts of 2008, much gum-flapping and print-scribbling was given to the concept of "moral hazard"—the climate that results when an irresponsible or corrupt business like Lehman Brothers, Bear Stearns, or Enron thinks that it can be as outrageous as it wants to be, because they're "too big to fail," because they just *know* that Uncle Sammy will always bail their asse(t)s out in the end.

And of course, in the past, recessions had always happened, from comparatively minor blips in 1957–58 and 1971 to savagely cruel ones in 1974–75 and 1979–83. People would lose their jobs or get laid off, and have to shame-facedly go on unemployment and borrow money and cut back—for the time being. But sooner or later, there would be a "morning in America," to use Ronald Reagan's signature phrase. The economy would eventually come back, and so would the jobs.

The SAME KINDS OF JOBS, for the most part.

But as we've seen already, the early '90s recession was different. Big time. Now, people were being fired en masse, hundreds and thousands at a time. And for many of them, especially these blue-collar and low-level white collar workers, the heartbeat of the working middle class, *their* jobs *weren't* coming back. Ever. They might get another job—*but it wouldn't be the same job*, or perhaps even for the same company. Or, if they simply wanted to *keep* their current job or transition to a department within their corporation that was still hiring—then they'd better "retrain" and "re-educate" themselves, and up their game in a hurry! Once again, just being good enough *wasn't*. And this created a sort of trickle-down version of "moral hazard"—one that would debilitate the economic discourse and dialogue from Bill Clinton and George W. Bush right on through to Barack Obama and the Tea Party.

The great lesson that this first wave of Downsizing and Outsourcing "1.0" taught the American work force was that being a "good worker," that being a polite, respectful, professional Dudley Do-Right, didn't mean jack squat when the accountants and lawyers were getting out their red pens. Peter shows up 10 minutes early and leaves 10 minutes late, is always Boy Scout-polite and respectful to the ladies and his co-workers, and says "Whatever you say, Boss!" with a big grin on his face. Meanwhile, Paul is an N-word using, sexual-harassing, dope-smoking smartass who sasses back at the boss and takes 90-minute lunch breaks. But when the downsizing Grim Reaper wielded his scythe, when the outsourcing memo was sent down from Corporate, when the bankruptcy court judge banged his gavel, it didn't make a dime's worth of difference in the end, did it? Both Peter and Paul would be dispatched summarily to the welfare office, to the unemployment line, to beg their friends and relatives for loans, and their banks and landlords for payment extensions and not to repossess or foreclose. In other words, *both the "good" employee and the "bad" employee would get the exact same treatment.*

The Coen Brothers Economy

This unexpected first wave of *Roger & Me* and *Falling Down* metro-suburban economic collapse created a permanent divorce from the laws of cause-and-effect in the working and middle-class mind. (Not to mention the soon-to-come free trade agreements.) It created the suspicious and cynical mentality that Sidney Blumenthal mentioned, which remained stubbornly fixed from the tail end of the early '90s recession, all throughout Clinton and George W. Bush's economic good times, right up until the next bigger-badder Great Recession cracked down again in the fall of 2008. Now, we were living in The Economy as Coen Brothers Movie: a random funhouse where the not-at-all tender mercies of Fate and Luck use hapless mortals as prizes and props, where the other shoe always drops, the last-minute curveball always gets thrown, where the best-laid plans always turn to shit. Where the more people tried to play by the rules that had always worked before—the ones they were raised to believe in the happy-days '50s and early '60s—the more determinedly and ruthlessly the unseen hands of economic and technological change would teach them humility by way of *humiliation.*

And people wondered why Generation Xers, born from 1965 through 1980, the ones who were either coming of age or starting their grownup lives amidst this colossal game-change, became the "slacker" generation, became so "cynical" about politics, spent all their time listening to Tupac and Biggie and Public Enemy, to Alanis Morrissette and Kurt Cobain and Eminem, thinking that life was just an alienated and alienating "whatever." Why the hell shouldn't they have thought that way? In this kind of economic and cultural environment, being cynical and alienated "slackers" with an attitude to match didn't seem like an inappropriate response. It seemed like the only logical one.

"It's Time for a Change"

As Sidney Blumenthal noted, President George H.W. Bush had come into office, after eight years of loyally serving Ronald Reagan, fighting what a particularly vulgar 1987 cover story in *Newsweek* called "The Wimp Factor." This World War II aviator, former congressman and Republican National Committee chief, ex–CIA director, and Cold War vice president was initially thought of as having a "wimp factor" simply because of his old money, grandfatherly prep-school affect. (And some on the hardest ultra-right thought that Old Bush was a "wimp" because he wasn't a fire-breathing culture warrior, like Pat Buchanan, Jesse Helms, or Rush Limbaugh—or the way his son George W would be, for that matter.)

However, as Blumenthal noted, once the Berlin Wall actually fell and the Soviet Union disintegrated (not to mention victory in the first Gulf War), those "wimpy" days were over! But now that Bush had proven conclusively that he *wasn't* a wimp, his lack of aggressive economic leadership and his seeming indifference to the plight of the downsizing victims of the early '90s seemed positively "cruel" to the American public. Not to mention the public school classrooms and colleges that were now crowded to the breaking point, and the record crime rates. New York, California, Detroit, Chicago, and Washington DC's newspapers and nightly news broadcasts were replete with a daily litany of drive-by shootings and never-ending AIDS deaths. *Why wasn't he doing something? Doesn't he care about us??*

Not even the Psychic Friends Network could have predicted that things would turn out this way for George Bush, Sr. Just one year earlier, in the spring of 1991, with the Berlin Wall having freshly crumbled, with Saddam Hussein driven out of Kuwait in the (first) Gulf War, drug lord Manuel Noriega deposed from Panama, and the Soviet Union about to formally disband, Bush's approval ratings topped 90 percent. Not even his old boss, Ronald Reagan, had scored that high a rating! Bush had always touted his expertise as a foreign-policy president—as well he might have, given that the CIA headquarters in Langley would soon rename itself in honor of the first "Chief Spook" (as Bush humorously referred to himself during his 1975–77 reign there) to make the top prize. And Bush had been side-by-side with Reagan, Margaret Thatcher, and reformist Russian premier Mikhail Gorbachev as the Cold War finally thawed in the late '80s.

Queen Elizabeth would famously describe the Year of Our Lord 1992 as an "annus horribilis." And it was just as true for her presidential counterpart "across the pond." As 1992 began, in addition to the crummy economy, there was the leftover smoke of the 1989 "wildings" that had happened in Central Park, where jogger Trisha Meili was raped (allegedly by out-of-control young men of color). Nor had the controversy dissipated over 1988's Tawana Brawley rape fiasco, where a young black woman (falsely, it turned out) accused a gang of six white men of assaulting her. By the end of 1992, a "Spur Posse" of out-of-control high school and college-age white men began vandalizing, assaulting, and attacking young women in the Orange County/Long Beach area, as if they were playing some kind of sexual video game.

Indeed, President Bush had come to office against a smoldering racial backdrop—the infamous "Willie Horton ad," a political ad for Bush/Quayle '88 which told the story of a scary, African American criminal who had been let out on a weekend furlough program by Bush's rival for the presidency that year, Massachusetts' ultra-liberal governor Michael Dukakis. Horton had promptly escaped and committed a home-invasion robbery, brutally raping the wife of his (white) victim. The ad was almost a cartoon of the bug-eyed, ooga-booga, scary You Know What, out to "get" innocent white women and children, and as blatant an appeal to racism and racial stereotyping as anything until Barack Obama's enemies discovered Photoshop.

Two years after that, fundamentalist Dixiecrat Republican Senator Jesse Helms ran an even more provocative ad during his successful 1990 campaign for re-election, called "White Hands." It showed a pair of hands and arms belonging to a white man, angrily and hopelessly tearing up a form rejection letter from a cold, unfeeling human-resources department. The narrator informed viewers that this unfortunate man was the most qualified person for the job he'd just interviewed for—but a diversity quota had mandated that they still hire a minority instead of him. No accident that Helms' soon-to-be-defeated opponent for the Senate seat was black.

And less than a year after that, a young black man with a criminal past named Rodney King was pulled over by LAPD officers for drunken and reckless driving, in early 1991. He resisted arrest (or at least failed to be as compliant as the cops would have wanted), and a small army of police that had been called for backup brutally beat the hell out of King, even after he was lying on the ground. But fatefully—in an early foreshadowing of today's era of cell-phone camera videos—a bystander happened to have a video camera, and recorded the beating on tape, which was quickly picked up by virtually every news broadcast from coast to coast and in Canada. And sensational stills of the beating made front-page headlines from the Los Angeles to the New York *Times*.

When the police officers who had allegedly beaten King were acquitted in April of 1992, the smoldering keg of racial dynamite finally exploded. (It was something of a sneak preview of the furore over today's more recent acquittals of the cops and "self-defending" citizens who killed young black men like Michael Brown, Eric Garner, Oscar Grant, and Trayvon Martin.) The worst race riots in a quarter-century killed dozens of people, as buildings were bombed, display windows were shattered, traffic smash-ups and vandalism were nonstop. And an innocent white Los Angeles truck driver named Reginald Denny sustained permanent brain damage when he was dragged from his stalled rig by hooligans and beaten—with a brick—within an inch of his life. (As a side note, they were in the middle of filming *Falling Down* when this started happening in real life.)

And all the while, "the economy, stupid" (as a famous 1992 campaign slogan would go) wasn't looking any better, especially for working-class voters like military, domestic auto, and aerospace workers. After Reagan and Bush era deregulation, the economy continued to consolidate and globalize at a furious rate. New technology had made workers more productive than ever during the 1980s—but employers could now get more work done with less workers than ever, too. Retirees who'd been used to getting 8, 9, and 10 percent interest all through Reagan and early Bush (and had gotten far more than that during Carter) on their safe money-market accounts were now lucky to get half that, as Fed chief Alan Greenspan began slashing rates to 1950s and '60s levels, to stimulate the automobile and home purchases that were now as stalled as a flat tire.

The warning signs first came when Wall Street had had a mini-crash in late 1987, towards the end of the Reagan boom, but the real crisis started when the Savings & Loan and "junk bond" scandals hit in 1989 and '90. That and the fact that Japan and Hong Kong's economies, which had been shooting for the stars across the 1970s and '80s, were finally slowing down—as were their massive, hand-over-fist investments in California and New York real estate. And when the 50-year gravy train of World War II and Cold War defense contracts dried up—it wasn't just a *crash*; it was the worst economic catastrophe since the Carter era, until the total meltdown of fall 2008. And neither President Bush nor his team had the faintest clue about what to do about it.

When Bush tried to brag about overseeing the Cold War's end, he found out the hard way that this monumental achievement was now, in MTV parlance, "like *so* 10 minutes ago!"—conjuring B&W images of 1950s atom-bomb drills, of Joe McCarthy, and J. Edgar Hoover, instead of the far more recent triumphs he wanted to remind people of. When Bush reminded people how he'd won in Iraq, it looked like a bad joke considering that not only was Saddam still in power (however hobbled for now), but that it was the last hurrah of the now furiously downsizing and job-cutting aerospace industry, and fast-closing Army bases. And Bush's tone-deaf, patrician, "well-meaning" attempts to address the hip-hop gangsta culture and blown-out decay of the whack-on-crack, AIDS-ridden inner cities and the Rodney King riots were downright laughable—considering that Bush had ridden the infamously racist Willie Horton ad to victory less than four years before.

When it came to what Democratic strategy guru James Carville would famously call "the economy, stupid," Bush just didn't have any answers. Or rather, Bush didn't have any answers that could pass muster with the working-class and *petit bourgeois* Republicans who were on the wrong end of downsizing, globalization, immigration, and big-box consolidation—AND the ever-more fanatical "1 percent" check-writers, media mavens, and Establishment donors. Bush had already been drawn and quartered by the Koch Brothers/Richard Mellon Scaife ultra-right for raising taxes on luxury items (Caddies, Lexuses, BMWs, etc., that were bought for cash instead of leased, speed boats and yachts, cigarette sales…) and capital gains rates in 1990–91, as he vainly tried to control the big-spending deficits and pay for Operation Desert Storm. To growling right-wing media watchdogs and top-level donors, the ONLY acceptable answer to the lousy economy was *more* tax cuts, more "incentives" and giveaways to the rich, more S&L and corporate bailouts—and of course, more demonizing of the "welfare queen," "wetback," and "trailer trash" poor. (Again—*any of that sound familiar?*)

The profound anti-incumbent sentiment brewing in the early '90s was hardly confined to Bush alone. A veritable Hurricane Katrina of "mad as hell" voter initiatives and laws were crashing across the state levels during the late '80s and early '90s, requiring draconian "term limits" for all and every elected office wherever the Federal courts would allow it. State legislators and senators, and official-agency regulators would now be forcibly termed out after "X" amount of time in office—regardless of their competence, seniority, clout, honesty, or likability. "Elite" state-level Supreme Court or appeals' judges would need to face the voters for renewal every few years. Many state governors and big-city mayors, in places like California and New York City, would now be limited to two consecutive terms, just like presidents were.

In late 1991, an old enemy of "Texan" President Bush named H. Ross Perot put the frosting on the cake. (Bush was born and raised in New England, but had moved to Texas after World War II to diversify his family's banking concerns and branch out into the oil business.) Perot was a Reagan loyalist and conservative (although he didn't seem to really care one way or the other on culture-war issues like abortion, gay rights, or racial preferences) who'd made zillions of dollars starting in the 1960s. It should also be noted that Perot made his nut mainly off of Big Guv'mint—by running a data-processing company called Electronic Data Systems that utilized then-new computer and mainframe technologies to do Medicare (launched 1965), Social Security/IRS, and other such billing and payment procedures.

While Perot was undeniably technically brilliant, he downplayed that in a just-folks, cracker-barrel, *Hee Haw* persona, and was (like his buddy Sam Walton, founder of Wal-mart) a notorious reverse-snob, wearing off-the-rack suits, driving modest domestic mid-size sedans and trucks, and still sporting his Korea-era graying buzz crewcut. One of Perot's primary reasons for running was his decades-long dislike of Bush, whom Perot had known and hated for years in Texas high society. Perot considered Bush to be an effete, pretentious, preppy Eastern elitist, who had no business carpet-bagging in Houston, let alone "repre-senting" the Lone Star State at the highest levels of government. The more successful that New England–raised, Yale-educated Bush became as a congressman, Republican National Committee chair, CIA chief, and vice president—all while proudly pretending in local TV and newspaper ads to be the veritable "face" of Texas—the more that Perot's jealousy and class resentments ballooned to soap-opera proportions.

Now, he was finally able to get his revenge. Perot's candidacy and plain speakin' persona threatened to strike the very heart of Bush's swing voters, drawing off working-class "Reagan Democrats" and old-fashioned, World War II and Korea-era retirees of Bush's own gener-ation, with Perot's Sarah Palin–like "common sense" solutions to big problems. Perot also threatened to draw an exodus of educated bourgeois mid-level manager types, who voted for the Republicans during the '80s based on their pocketbooks, but who winced at the Religious Right's archconservative positions on social and women's issues.

And the Religious Right itself was by now a pressure cooker waiting to explode. In 1992–93, Kurt Cobain, Madonna, Tupac Shakur, and Ice-T were the biggest hits on the radio. Potty-mouthed sitcoms like *Roseanne, Married with Children, Beavis and Butt-head,* MTV videos, and statutory-rapey new teenage soaps like *Beverly Hills, 90210* and *Melrose Place* ruled the ratings. Quentin Tarantino made his feature film premiere that year with the ultra-violent *Reservoir Dogs,* while Best Picture went to last year's arty slasher movie, *The Silence of the Lambs,* and the number one box-office hit of early '92 was the equally graphic *Basic Instinct.* Radical AIDS-era gay artists stuck their thumb in conservative Chris-tians' eyes with explicit gay S&M photos or dunking crucifixes in urine, to express their rage at the homophobia of the hardcore Religious Right.

A Tale of Two Narratives

Perhaps the best temperature-taking of this bizarre moment was published in David Frum's *Dead Right.* In the liberal imagination, the Reagan years (very much including Old Bush's reign) were a nightmare world of gaudy greed and near-pornographic wealth worship, of purposeful and deliberate ignoring of the poor and of racial discrimination, of 1950s-style Cold War rhetoric and Iran-Contra. Not to mention corporate mega-mergers, lever-aged buyouts, and hostile takeovers, and a forceful turning-back-the-clock on many of the cultural gains that feminists and gays had made in the swinging '70s, plus the deadly onset of the AIDS crisis.

Most of all, the '80s were the era of the "Celebrity CEO" and noveau riche society. Fic-tional tycoons like JR Ewing, Alexis Colby, Blake Carrington, and Gordon "Greed Is Good" Gekko were already national obsessions in the movies and on TV. Now, thanks to super-market tabloids, *People* magazine, and drooling TV shows like *Entertainment Tonight, PM Magazine,* and *Lifestyles of the Rich & Famous,* they were joined by the real-life figures on which those fictional characters were based. Names like Leona Helmsley, Charles Keating, Holmes Tuttle, Ross Perot, T. Boone Pickens, Malcolm Forbes, Lee Iacocca, Roger Smith, John De Lorean, Michael Milken, George Soros, Warren Buffett, Jack Welch, Michael Eisner, Barry Diller, David Geffen, Rupert Murdoch, Ted Turner, and Donald Trump suddenly went from the back pages of the Financial section (where only investors, bankers, and high-ranking Old Society matrons knew or cared who they were) straight to the front pages. Now, every other truck-stop waitress and hairdresser could eagerly follow the Beautiful People's sensational real-life soap operas and fabulous fashion faux pas. This was the "dele-terious environment of the '80s" that civil-rights and feminist icon Barbara Jordan shook her fist at, during the 1992 Democratic convention.

Yet in spite of all this success, on the far-right side of the street, the Reagan-Bush years looked like a farce. Instead of the permanently changed conservative landscape that these think-tankers and evangelicals and free-market fanatics had dared to hope for back in 1980—and which had seemed almost within reach after 1984 and 1988's landslides—they found to their near-existential disappointment that life in America was the same as before. The jacket blurb on *Dead Right* spoke for itself. "The great conservative revival of the 1980s is over. Government is bigger, taxes are higher, family values are weaker.... However heady the 1980s may have looked to everyone else, they were for conservatives a testing and dis-illusioning time" [at least privately, in retrospect]. Conservatives owned the executive branch ... they dominated the Senate for six years, and by the end of the decade they exer-cised near-complete control over the federal judiciary [and Federal Reserve]. And yet, every time they reached to undo the work of Franklin Roosevelt, Lyndon Johnson, and Richard Nixon—work they had damned for nearly half a century—they realized they didn't dare. Their moment came, and flickered."

Walk into a social services office or county hospital in 1992, and you were walking right back into the paisley-wallpaper ghetto of *Claudine* and *Good Times*. No sign of a recession at the local Planned Parenthood clinic, where unwed mothers and young career women walked in, and their unborn babies never walked out. At the 1992 junior high school fashion show, school prayer and creation-science was "out"—but condom demonstrations on bananas and AIDS talk was "in." Affirmative action quotas and set-asides were stronger than ever—with Latinos and working women now included too, as well as African Amer-icans, plus bilingual and multicultural education in *las escuelas*. Every major city now boasted a Gay Pride parade, complete with drag queens deluxe, cross-dressing Mother Superiors, and diesel dykes on bikes.

Despite little trifles like winning the Cold War (and Gulf War I) and beginning to deregulate the economy, to the conservative hard core, the 1980s had been all for naught—because they hadn't gotten absolutely 100 percent of their wildest, nutter-butter fantasies: Flat-out cancelled all welfare to everyone except for the assisted-living disabled, totally blind, and mentally retarded. Privatized Social Security and Medicare. Turned civil service teacher and police retirements and labor union pensions into individual 401(k)s and IRAs. Put prayer and creation science back in schools, and wiped out compulsory sex-ed. Elim-inated any and all affirmative action or diversity quotas and bilingual ed. Repealed *Roe vs. Wade*. Made homosexuality and lesbianism illegal once again, by resurrecting struck-down-in-the-'70s "anti-sodomy" laws in California, New York, Florida, and Massachusetts. Returned movies and TV back to the world of Louis B. Mayer, and pop music back to Sinatra, Elvis, or the Beatles singing about boy-meets-girl—no more rap and punk, or Madonna videos! Put the Ten Commandments back in the town square. Why, if they couldn't accomplish 100 percent of ALL that—*then what difference did it make, anyway?*

"As their coalition broke up before their very eyes, as so many former Republicans suffered extreme economic distress (often for the first time during their lives)," Frum went on, "the old Reagan faith sounded more and more unconvincing." This was only egged on by rising conservative media figures, including a prominent talk radio host who had a syndicated late-night TV show that would run for four years starting in the fall of 1992, plus a *New York Times* bestseller on the charts. (His name was Rush Limbaugh.) "Conservatives were ready for something tougher," and at the notorious Republican National Convention of 1992, they got it!

"Wall to wall ugly"

"From the news reports," Frum bemusedly continued, "you'd think the Republicans had hired Leni Riefenstahl to stage-manage their 1992 convention." *Newsweek* had growled that the "whole week was wall-to-wall ugly." The late, great liberal Texan columnist Molly Ivins accused the GOP, in another *Newsweek* piece, of wanting to mount veritable "pogroms" of minority, Jewish, gay, feminist, and even mainline Christian voters.

As the show opened, Trinity Broadcasting Network superstar Dr. D. James Kennedy, of the enormous Coral Ridge Presbyterian Church of Florida (his was the most conservative branch of otherwise generally tolerant Presbyterianism) delivered a "Sinners in the Hands of an Angry God" invocation that was worthy of a 17th century Puritan: "We have turned our backs upon Thy Laws by every imaginable immorality, perversion, vice, and crime ... and even now a hideous plague [AIDS] stalks our land! ... Oh Lord, we know that there are those who are atheists and secularists here in our midst that would lead us down ... the godless trail to destruction!" That was just the starter course. Pat Robertson served the dessert, warning that when the Democrats talk about "families,'" they're *really* talking about "a radical plan to *destroy* the traditional family!"

But it was Pat Buchanan who delivered the sizzling main course—upstaging both President Bush and even a returning 81-year-old Ronald Reagan as by far the most notable and memorable speaker of Convention '92, when Pat delivered what came to be known as the Culture War Speech. And in so doing, he defined what every game-changing election would *really* be about from here on in—from the Republican Revolution of 1994 and the Tea Party Election of 2010, to Impeachment '98 and *Bush vs. Gore*, to Barack Obama battling it out with Sarah Palin, Michelle Bachmann, Rick Santorum, Newt Gingrich, Ted Cruz, and the Tea Party, in 2008 and 2012.

"There is a religious war going on in this country," Buchanan thundered. "It is a cultural war as critical to the kind of nation we shall be as the Cold War itself—for this war is for the soul of America. And in that struggle for the soul of America, Clinton and Clinton [Bill and Hillary] are on the other side!" After a long litany of eye-poppingly homophobic, racially coded, and anti–Hillary one-liners and accusations, Buchanan finished by asking Right Wing America to have the "moral courage" to "take back our cities, take back our culture, and take back our country—block by block!!" As thousands cheered.

Yet it was "simply childish to imagine that Houston was taken over by crazed Baptists" and Pentecostal tele-evangelists, snarked David Frum. "Political conventions are controlled by the national campaign organization—which is to say, by the man they are about to nominate. Who would speak, in what order, and what those speeches would be permitted to say—these decisions came not from Pat Robertson's headquarters, but from the topmost heights of Bushdom, from almost pathological moderates" coming from the preppy, Ivy League, white shoe country club world of Republican big business and hierarchy.

Clearly, it had been an epic fail. The upper-middle-class and educated swing voters were horrified and offended (as well they should have been) by Buchanan and the convention's antics, while the hard-right base had seen and heard it all before. All talk and no action. And for the most part, the same delicate balancing act occurred on the Left side of the street, too. Yes, you had Barbara Jordan and Jesse Jackson to rally black and "urban" voters. But you also had that year's Democratic nominee for president pointedly "dissing" on female rap star Sistah Souljah, for her insensitive (and meant-as-a-joke, in the Lenny Bruce/Richard Pryor sense of "a joke") routine. (Sistah had said that, with all the black people who'd been killed by whites and other blacks, maybe there could be one day where blacks could get some revenge on Whitey without having to pay. This was around the same time as the horrific LA Riots. Some cynics would say that Sistah eventually got her wish with the O.J. trial, but that's for another chapter to judge.) Clinton compared Sistah to white supremacist leader David Duke, to the fury of civil rights leaders—and then used that rigged fury to "prove" to white America that he wasn't merely a puppet of minority demagogues and civil rights activists.

Robert Bork and Clarence Thomas' America

Just five years before Pat Buchanan's convention craziness, one of the first and highest-profile battles in the modern-day culture war was ignited when Ronald Reagan, a year after elevating William Rehnquist to Chief Justice of the Supreme Court and appointing arch-conservative Antonin Scalia to the vacated seat (and a year before the end of his Presidency) announced what he thought would be his final nomination to the Supremes. His choice was Robert Bork, a high-ranking federal judge, distinguished Yale scholar, Constitutional law professor, published author, and former Nixon-era Solicitor General and "Acting Attorney General" (after Bork's controversial participation in Nixon's famous "Saturday Night Massacre" of independent investigators looking into the Watergate abuses).

There was no question that Robert Bork was indeed "supremely" qualified for the job on paper. There was also no question that if the far-right Bork were appointed to the highest court in the land (particularly if Reagan's popular Vice President George Bush won the 1988 election, as it looked like he would), it could reshape the face of civil rights, women's issues, and civil liberties for years to come—and not in a good way. Bork loathed gay rights, and was opposed not only to *Roe vs. Wade* but to its predecessor, *Griswold vs. Connecticut* (which had finally abolished Edwardian state laws against contraception and non-abortive birth control). Bork was also intolerant of any and all race-based "remedies" like quotas, busing, affirmative action, and whatnot, and he had zippo patience for transgressive artists, Communists, or other unpopular public speakers' First Amendment rights. Bork had openly and viciously attacked the Voting Rights Act of 1964, the only thing strong enough to have finally lynched Jim Crow, and Bork was completely opposed by the ACLU.

Liberals were also just plain running out of patience with Reagan by late 1987, after the Iran-Contra hearings all through the previous months revealed abuses and rampant dishonesty within his government. (Although there was no mainstream political will to impeach or truly punish the much-loved, grandfatherly president.) Democrat and feminist leader Ann Lewis openly acknowledged that if Bork's nomination were carried out as just another routine, internal Senate debate, with the Old White Boys Club discussing academic credentials, theories of *stare decisis,* and strict constructionism over coffee and Pimms Sherries in the Senate cloakrooms, "we would have deep and thoughtful discussions about the Constitution—*and then we would lose.*" Thankfully for her, the liberal lion of the Senate, Teddy Kennedy, pounced on the ultraconservative Bork, delivering the most shocking and damning speech on the Senate floor since George McGovern's famed 1970 "Blood on our Hands" attack against the Vietnam War:

> Robert Bork's America is a land in which women would be forced into back-alley abortions, blacks would sit at segregated lunch counters, rogue police could break down citizens' doors in midnight raids, school-children could not be taught about evolution, writers and artists would be censored at the whim of the government, and the doors of the federal courts would be shut on the fingers of millions of citizens for whom the judiciary is often the only protector of the individual rights that are at the heart of our democracy.... President Reagan ... should not be able to reach out from the muck of Irangate, reach into the muck of Watergate, and impose his reactionary vision of the Constitution on the Supreme Court and the next generation of Americans. No justice would be better than this injustice.

Not surprisingly, after that unprecedented takedown from America's most powerful senator, the Bork nomination spectacularly failed by a margin of 58–42 in the Democrat-dominated chamber, to the utter horror of right wing conservatives. All of Ann Coulter's worst stereotypes of self-righteous liberals—for whom principle meant nothing and "winning" meant everything, even if it involved blatant character assassination—seemed to have come true, in their eyes. Further adding insult to social conservatives' injury, a chastened and on-his-way-out Reagan later nominated the staunchly pro-gay and pro-choice (though also very pro-corporate) California moderate Anthony Kennedy, who sailed through the Senate over the holidays in 1987–88.

Things had only gotten worse four years later, when Supreme Court Justice Thurgood Marshall, the first African American ever to serve on the Supreme Court when LBJ had appointed him in 1967, and the man who'd argued the landmark *Brown vs. Board of Education* case for the NAACP in 1954, finally decided to retire. (Marshall was in very failing health, and had only a year and a half left before he passed, in January of 1993, at age 84.) Even the most reactionary Tea Party-style conservative knew that it would be unimaginable to appoint a white "old boy" to Marshall's seat, and President Bush didn't even try. Bush had no problem, in fact, appointing another African American, so long as he was the most conservative, activist Republican black man that he could get his hands on.

Enter a forty-something conservative black attorney, professor, and jurist named Clarence Thomas. But if Bush and his crew thought that just by appointing a "token" black they would be able to avoid disaster, they had another thought coming! To many civil-rights era African Americans, and virtually all movement liberals of every color, the Marshall "seat" on the court wasn't just for someone of color, but for someone with a decidedly liberal-activist political outlook. Thurgood Marshall was behind only Nelson

Mandela, Malcolm X, Rosa Parks, and Dr. King in the hall of 20th century black heroes, the living embodiment of the civil rights struggle. And he was also the Court's most reliable vote in favor of feminism, choice, and gay civil rights, and for expanding civil liberties. To replace *him* with a melanin-enhanced movement conservative seemed to reduce the entire civil rights and progressive movements to a grotesque self-parody, to the level of a "watermelon joke." Liberals bitterly joked that Clarence Thomas (himself a staunch opponent of race quotas) was the ultimate affirmative-action baby, in the worst sense of the phrase.

And as with Robert Bork, they weren't going to take it sitting down. It wasn't long after the Thomas hearings began that liberals' and women's worst fears of the kind of man Thomas was were realized, with the testimony of a young black female lawyer and professor named Anita Hill, describing what she saw as a veritable locker-room environment of degradation and insults for women staffers under Thomas' supervision. (Many conservatives and Thomas supporters, meanwhile, shot back that Hill was the very stereotype of a humor-impaired, priggish, doctrinaire feminist.)

One will probably never really know which side was telling the whole truth in the Thomas/Anita Hill battle, but what was saddest (and most politically revealing) about it is that, in some sense, the actual truth—the "who dun it" aspect—was almost beside the point. Clarence Thomas and his supporters were right that the hearings became a "high-tech lynching" that pandered to the most disgusting stereotypes of predatory, drooling-at-the-mouth, *Birth of a Nation* black male sexuality. But to a generation of working women who could well remember the days of *Mad Men* and *9 to 5* style workplaces where they were virtually *expected* to either "put out" (or at least put up with) being chased around the desk, pinched on the fanny, criticized on their dress and makeup to their faces, passed over for promotions again and again, and otherwise routinely humiliated and marginalized—Anita Hill became their heroine. *Finally, somebody had the guts to speak up for what we ALL went through!*

Sadly for Anita Hill, if she was indeed telling the truth, the fact that Thomas' opponents were so openly and blatantly looking for something, *anything* to discredit him with, certainly did her no favors—in that it made her completely truthful allegations look to many people as if they had been made up all along for political convenience. "We're going to BORK him!" promised African American civil-rights attorney and feminist icon Flo Kennedy, as she addressed the National Organization for Women, who not surprisingly opposed the anti-choice and rabidly homophobic Thomas' nomination to the max. "We're going to kill him politically," Kennedy resolved, further adding in disgust, "This little creep—where did he come from?"

While Thomas—just barely—made it through the gauntlet, the culture war on both sides "politically killed" a lot more than one judge and one harassed professional woman. Instead of being an ugly exception, Thomas proved that the Robert Bork hearings had now become the rule: nothing but coded appeals and *ad hominem* attacks acting as stand-ins for the Grand Canyon divides between black and white, rich and poor, straight and gay, pro-choice and pro-life, male and female. The only fortunate side effect of the Thomas/Hill hearings was that it motivated a "Year of the Woman" in politics in 1992, where an unprecedented number of female attorneys, judges, and activists ran for Congress and Senate, and many if not most were successful. (And no one profited more from the "year of the woman" than the outspoken, career-holding, and feminist lawyer wife of a certain Democratic presidential nominee that year.)

Still, the damage was done, and the bells could not be un-rung. A year and a half before Judge Bork's death in late 2012, at age 85, the *New York Times'* Joe Nocera recalled that the Bork and Thomas fights "in some ways, [marked] the beginning of the end of civil discourse in politics," at least after the temporary fires of Vietnam and Watergate were put out. "The anger between Democrats and Republicans, the unwillingness to work together, the profound mistrust ... the line from Bork to today's ugly politics is a straight one."

* * *

Yes, by the early 1990s, America truly was "falling down." And like the famous Life Alert TV ads for senior-oriented home security monitoring, to many voters at that time, it seemed as though America had fallen—and it couldn't get up. All of the racial, sexual, crime, gang, and economic tensions that had been papered over during the glossy, *Dynasty, LA Law,* and *Wall Street* "Morning in America" expansion from 1983 to 1990, were now hemorrhaging all over the place like an ER patient, bleeding both political parties out. The script wasn't working out as planned. Everybody had questions, but nobody seemed to have the answers anymore.

Nobody that is, except for a charismatic Southern governor and his liberated, feminist attorney wife, supported by a very different kind of "liberal media" establishment—all of whom finally saw their chance to grab the brass ring of real power, which they had been eyeing for more than a decade.

2

Daddy's Dyin'—
Who's Got the Will?

"Because he's a womanizing, Elvis-loving, truth-shading, non-inhaling, draft-dodging, war protesting, abortion-protecting, gay-promoting, gun-hating baby boomer. That's why!"

—A conservative voter, quoted by author Steven Gillion, explaining why he wasn't exactly president of Bill Clinton's fan club.

Today, our concern must be with the future. For the world is changing. The old era is ending. The old ways will not do....

—John F. Kennedy

"In every presidential election from 1968 to 1988, the Democrats nominated a goody-goody (Hubert Humphrey, George McGovern, Jimmy Carter, Walter Mondale, Michael Dukakis)," wrote an amusedly frustrated columnist named Michael Kinsley in 1996. "And they lost every election" except for one. But in 1992, the Democrats "finally decided they wanted to win this time, so they nominated a man who was no one's idea of a goody-goody. They nominated a slippery politician," who was also "not coincidentally" a "morally flawed character" with serious "personal and (perhaps) financial" baggage to deal with.

The most memorable slogan for the 1992 election may have been "It's the economy, stupid!," as Clinton media strategists James Carville and George Stephanopoulos refocused attention from rival President George H.W. Bush's successful Cold War wrap-up and 1991's Iraq War achievements, to Bush's helpless cluelessness on domestic matters. Behind the scenes, however, Election '92 was about something far more significant and long-lasting. It would prove to be a generational warfare battle that would be the sequel to Vietnam—where a fading, conservative, old-school Greatest Generation President was being forced to step aside for his liberal and liberated 40-ish adult children who, after taking over the culture in the late '60s, '70s and '80s, were now ready to take over the whole thing for real. And 1992 was bent and shaped to the tune of elite Washington opinion journals and their media acolytes—and to a spin-off of those "neoliberal" opinion journals called the Democratic Leadership Council—more than any modern major election before or since.

Arise, Ye Yuppies! (or, Building a New Republic)

As 1992's presidential campaign got underway, Eric Alterman wrote in his book *What Liberal Media?*, a game-changing young Arkansas governor named Bill Clinton "proved a remarkably popular candidate with the media. The affection demonstrated by influential reporters like Sidney Blumenthal, Joe Conason, Joe Klein, Jonathan Alter, Mike Kinsley, and Martin Walker reached such a crescendo that *New York Times* editorial director Howell Raines complained openly about the 'extraordinary burst of journalistic fawning'" over the eventual Clinton-Gore '92 ticket.

By contrast, most of those indeed very influential journalists went out of their way to portray third-party candidate and Texas computer billionaire Ross Perot as a wiggy far-out space nut, and sitting President George Bush, Sr., as just that—a hopelessly out-of-touch and outmoded, seventy-year-old senior citizen, racially and sexually insensitive—the very definition of the grumpy old man. In 1992 at least, conservatives from Rush Limbaugh and Roger Ailes to William F. Buckley and William Safire had every right to be appalled by the shamelessness of the elite Opinion Makers' "liberal bias" for Bill Clinton.

But where they went wrong was in attributing that to liberal bias in the media. What *really* caused all of the above reporters to swoon and croon over Bill and Hill was not that they were liberals, but that they were specifically *yuppie Baby Boomer* liberals—as were every last one of those aforementioned journalists and cable pundits. The Clintons' came with a values system and life experiences that more-or-less completely dovetailed and aligned with those reporters' own lives, careers, and educations—and had no credible corollary among Silent or Greatest Generation liberals, who were almost as outdated and tragically un-hip as Ronald Reagan and George Bush were.

The New Republic famously billed itself as "the in-flight magazine of Air Force One" (and there was more truth than poetry to that phrase, especially in the 1990s). Its circulation never passed much over 100,000 at its zenith, but it wielded almost as much judicial-like power among the People Who Matter in Washington policy as *The New York Times, The Washington Post,* CNN, and *60 Minutes* did. "You can't swing an axe in a major American newsroom without hitting six people who used to work at *The New Republic* or *Washington Monthly*," laughed David Brooks, looking back in 2007. By the 1990s, "influenced by their sensibility, many major news organizations became neoliberal institutions, whether they knew it or not."

"Reporters and editors see Democratic candidates—*Ivy-educated, socially liberal, and economically centrist*—as people very much like themselves," added Eric Alterman revealingly (our emphasis) in 2003. And what he said was certainly true of top reporters and editors *of Alterman's own generation,* the Baby Boom, and those who came afterward. But what is most remarkable about Alterman's statement was just how NOT-true it was of most reporters and editors, until the neoliberal Boomers took over.

Let's take a glance over the Curricula Vitae of Greatest (and early Silent) Generation scribes like TV icons Walter Cronkite, Eric Sevareid, and Dan Rather; or three-martini Bubs like Jack Germond, Bob Thomas, James Bacon, or Robert Novak; or defiantly proletarian and unglamorous, two-fisted working men like Studs Terkel and Mike Royko. Very few of these children of the Depression, almost all of whom grew up in the urban South or Midwest, had upbringings that could be described as "upper-middle class" or "wealthy." Indeed, if you searched for one of them who'd gone to a tony prep school or who'd been "Ivy-educated," you would probably come up empty.

The track record was even worse for their forebears, like Robert La Follette, Walter Lippmann, and Edward R. Murrow—let alone the street-smart but far from intellectual

World War I "Lost Generation" scribes of Hollywood, Broadway, and Babe Ruth/Lou Gehrig era sports—those "columnists" like Walter Winchell and Ed Sullivan. They were lucky to have graduated *high school,* much less gone to a high-end, snob college. The Wikipedia entry for midcentury American columnist Joseph Alsop (who was born to the ruling class) noted how "unusual" it was—in Alsop's day—for an Ivy-educated preppy to pursue a career as a reporter.

Instead, for most of the later 19th and 20th century, the stereotype of the journalist or "newspaperman" was of the eager-beaver, fedora-wearing Front Page Farrell type smart-aleck, tossing off crackerjack one-liners with wisecrackin' film-noir dames right out of a 1930s movie or a James Ellroy novel. Later on, it was the middle-aged, crusty, seen-it-all editor running his newsroom with a heart of gold, a fist of iron, and a belt of booze (think Edward Asner as *Lou Grant,* or William Holden as Max Schumacher in *Network*). Smart, knowledgeable, and dedicated in their profession—but about as far from a silk-shirted, Porsche-driving metrosexual yuppie, or a snooty academic intellectual, as you could get.

But at *TNR* and *Washington Monthly,* the times they were a-changin.' Twenty-something writers fresh out of Harvard, Stanford, Princeton, NYU, USC, Yale, Columbia, Bennington, or Berkeley—who hadn't so much as covered a freeway accident, presidential press conference, city-council meeting, or police beat for the local paper—were now being asked to elucidate "think pieces" with all the answers to knotty issues like inflation, abortion, feminism, homosexuality/AIDS, Iran-Contra, racism, religion, science, atheism, taxes, the deficit, and foreign policy dilemmas.

Without a doubt, the most influential alumnus of both *Washington Monthly* (where he worked in 1975–76) and *The New Republic* (where he worked off and on from 1976 onward, having been appointed executive editor before he turned 30) was Michael Kinsley, who went on to co-host CNN's groundbreaking *Crossfire* in the early '90s, and to found *Slate* magazine for Bill Gates and Microsoft in 1995. (*Slate's* founding was such a high-profile Big Event amongst the political/news glitterati that it scored Kinsley a cover photo on *Newsweek,* dressed in a rain-slicker and carrying a fish, symbolizing his journey from DC to Microsoft's seaside Seattle HQ.)

In his salad days, Kinsley was a surprisingly young and good-looking alternative to the hard-edged, almost exclusively World War II or Korea-vet Greatest Generationers who owned all the major op-ed columns and nightly news shows in the late '70s. But that was only the start of his influence.

Atlantic Monthly doyenne Caitlin Flanagan once said that her idol, Joan Didion, gave young women "a way of being a woman and a way of being a writer that no one else" in the late '60s and '70s could give them. In much the same way, Michael Kinsley gave young political journalists a way of *being* a political journalist that simply no one else in the late '70s or '80s could—or would—have given them. This preppie Harvard Law grad wasn't the usual back-slapping cigar-chomper and martini-drinker, covering the ol' mugs, bubs, and boobys in the smoke-filled rooms of political "bosses." Nor would this whimsical, self-deprecating, nice Jewish boy ever be mistaken for some booming-baritone, "beacon of truth" nightly anchorman, intoning his copy like a Supreme Court Moses making pronouncements from granite. (Indeed, Kinsley came across like some kind of Harold Ramis or Joe Flaherty character from the glory days of *SCTV,* who'd somehow managed to wander onto the real-life set of *Nightline.*) Back when Jon Stewart and Conan O'Brien were still studying for their algebra exams, the lethally sharp-witted Kinsley could be said to have invented modern-day "snark" commentary—transfusing the same needling humor and sarcasm-with-a-smile that *Saturday Night Live,* George Carlin, Mort Sahl, the Smothers Brothers, and David Letterman had brought to topical and political standup comedy.

In the pages of the "liberal" *Washington Monthly* and *New Republic* of the '80s and '90s, writers like Kinsley, Mickey Kaus, and Sid Blumenthal displayed an almost British lack of sentimentality in their coverage of those struggling in blue-collar factories and menial office or sales jobs, and for Social Security seniors. The concern voiced in their pages for the poor and racial minorities often ranged from condescension to contempt— so much so that Kinsley himself joked towards the end of his tenure as full-time editor around 1989–90, that the magazine should change it's name to "*Even The* Liberal *New Republic…*" because of how often Reagan and Old Bush's teams cited articles from *TNR* to "prove" that their most iron-handed conservative policies had "bipartisan" or "liberal" support. Indeed, it was said that the Reagan White House ordered nearly two dozen copies of *TNR* to be messengered over each and every week, for their high-level staff to devour. *TNR's* outspoken and controversial mogul from 1974 to 2011, former Harvard professor Martin "Marty" Peretz, was forthright about his motive to purchase the opinion-making magazine (with money from his high-society heiress wife, Anne Farnsworth): "I bought *The New Republic* to take back the Democratic Party from the McGovernites," Peretz firmly adjudicated, in a 2012 retrospective in *The Wall Street Journal.*

No surprise that his second-in-command Mike Kinsley was almost as brutal to unreconstructed "paleo-liberal" Democrats (as he termed them) as he was to Ronald Reagan and George Bush, Sr. In 1984 and again in 1988's Democratic primaries, Kinsley (and most of the *New Republic* and *Washington Monthly* crowd) abandoned any shred of objectivity in their coverage, plumping and puffing the sleek, chic, upscale neoliberal Colorado Senator Gary Hart at almost every turn—while making campy fun of boring, old-fashioned liberal pander-bears like Walter Mondale and Michael Dukakis. Kinsley wondered aloud if the Democratic platform of 1984, with its oh-so politically correct giveaways to "special interests" (like minorities, strident feminists and gay activists—and of course, Big Labor) was a for-real platform—"or is it social hypochondria?"

Meanwhile, the love affair that the Reagan/Bush right wing was having with the neoliberal yuppies was only getting steamier. Neocon godfather Norman Podhoretz called *The New Republic* "indispensable." Conservative founding father William F. Buckley praised *TNR* in his own directly competing (and equivalent in power-cache) magazine, *National Review,* as did Buckley's number-one protégé, *Newsweek's* George F. Will. A 1984 party for *TNR's* 70th birthday was attended by Republican royalty Henry Kissinger, Jeane Kirkpatrick, and Pat Buchanan.

The liberal wing of liberalism, however, had said "Enough already!" Gore Vidal famously and repeatedly called the Peretz-era *New Republic* a magazine of "the extreme right wing." Liberal legend Robert Scheer wiped up the floor with *TNR* superstar Mickey Kaus in a thumbs-down 1992 *Los Angeles Times* review of Kaus' first book, which Scheer called a "yuppie manifesto" for what he felt was Kaus' thinly disguised racism, elitism, and hypocrisy. A mid–1980s "class picture" of *New Republic* staffers (including such brilliant marquee-intellectual names as Charles Lane, Steve Wasserman, Charles Krauthammer, Hendrik Hertzberg, Michael Kinsley, Morton Kondracke, Fred Barnes, and others) tells an even sadder story. There was not one single black face in the masthead writers' crowd. It may have been the era of *The Jeffersons* and *The Cosby Show* in the outside world, but at "liberal" *TNR? Not even one.*

A decade later, the situation had gotten no better. In the mid '90s, *Post-Newsweek* CEO Donald Graham blistered that *The New Republic's* writing staff was so appallingly undiverse, it should make its slogan, "Looking for a Qualified Black since 1914!" Mexicans, Puerto Ricans, or Cubans, you ask? *Nada, señor.* Or how 'bout a couple of salaried high-profile Asian writers, to give perspective on how Japan, Hong Kong, and South Korea became 1980s economic powerhouses, or the 1990s awakening of China (and 1989's Tiananmen Square horrors). And what about those post–Vietnam and post–Cambodian-holocaust Asian businesspeople who were remaking Orange County, San Francisco, Seattle, the Texas coast, and Hawaii? Look at another fortune, Cookie—there was no Column B on *TNR's* menu. (And among the white staffers, the amount of them who could probably be accused of having had a working- or lower-middle class upbringing, or who didn't graduate from a top-tier school? Take a guess….)

By the 1990s, *The New Republic* had added newer and deadlier weapons for the yuppies' and neo-liberals' war on conventional liberalism. When head honcho Marty Peretz wasn't crooning how "Ivan Boesky is a dear personal friend" (yes, the greed-is-good '80s junk bond felon, who inspired *Wall Street's* Gordon Gekko), Peretz was offering full-throated support to George Bush, Sr.'s early 1991 Gulf War, which had been strenuously opposed by the peacenik wing of the Democrats. Later in 1991, Peretz promoted the observantly Catholic, Margaret Thatcher and Ronald Reagan-admiring, young British "Tory" journalist Andrew Sullivan, as *TNR's* decision-maker editor (after Kinsley went to CNN and Hendrik Hertzberg went on to bigger-better things).

But Sullivan wasn't just another Young Republican, or some Brit-accented Rush Limbaugh—he was openly gay, making him allergic to the blatant homophobia of many high-profile Republicans, and to bigoted Jerry Falwell/Phyllis Schlafly style wars on feminist women. Sullivan was also tech-savvy, racially sensitive to some degree, intellectual—and perhaps most importantly of all, he was only 28 years old and media-hip, right on the "Generation Jones" dividing line between the Baby Boomers and their Generation X young adult kids. (He even famously posed for Gap ads.) Certainly a perfect fit for the more conservative, less atheist-chic or snidely sarcastic branch of neo-liberalism. Looking back on this era, departing *TNR* veteran Franklin Foer wisely and correctly said in November of 2014, that *TNR's* signature 1990s accomplishment was in "gleefully attempt[ing] to overthrow" the "oppressive orthodoxies" of liberalism.

By the 1992 election, as David Brooks alluded to, many of those "star" cub journalists who got their first breaks with *Washington Monthly* or *New Republic*—people like the aforementioned Kinsley, Jonathan Alter, Mickey Kaus, Sidney Blumenthal, plus the likes of Taylor Branch, E.J. Dionne, Nicolas Lemann, and foreign-policy neocons Charles Krauthammer and Leon Wieseltier—had moved on to set the agendas at the New York or Los Angeles *Times, Washington Post, Newsweek, Time* magazine, *The New Yorker*—or to CNN and/or the Big Three network news divisions. And the ones who'd stayed had book deals and lecture gigs practically thrown at them by top literary agents, publishers, and think-tanks.

The Terri Schiavo or Sunny Von Bulow of Politics

It was said that Franklin Roosevelt (and later, Barack Obama, with the bailouts and Obamacare) had "saved capitalism from itself." That is, at times when the situation was so extreme that real revolution would not have been out of the question (or at the very least a Vietnam/Watergate societal breakdown and protest movement), they applied reforms that curbed capitalism's worst excesses—*while still preserving* a capitalist, largely hierarchical system and infrastructure—even as their opponents painted them as wild-eyed socialists and Commies.

Likewise—in their own minds at least—people like Mike Kinsley, Sidney Blumenthal, Mickey Kaus, Joe Conason, Jonathan Alter, and Democratic Leadership Council head Al From, never thought of themselves as country-club conservatives in sheep's clothing, deliberately trying to sabotage the progressive liberal movement from within. The neoliberal yuppies simply seemed to believe that, by the early 1990s, the Democratic Party had become the Terri Schiavo or Sunny von Bulow of politics—its outer shell stubbornly clinging to life and refusing to face up to its own funeral, long after the heart, mind, and soul had gone on to a better place. In the rising New Economy of leveraged buyouts and hostile takeovers, of a booming Japan, South Korea, and Hong Kong, and a beginning-to-wake-up China and India, in an era where their fellow nerd-geniuses like Bill Gates and Steve Jobs were first starting to rewrite the rulebook, these pundits thought that lower-middle-class-centered, New Deal liberalism had become as outdated and bankrupt as a Depression-era S&L. *It simply had to go.*

Now, all these pundits and intellectuals needed was a powerful Democratic politician who was charismatic enough to hit the ball they'd been pitching straight to home plate. And fate was about to hand them one, from somewhere and someplace that seemed to be the least likely source.

Game Change—1.0 Version

With culture-warriors like fundie tele-evangelist Pat Robertson and civil-rights firebrand Jesse Jackson stealing all the thunder at the 1988 Republican and Democratic National Conventions, few people in the pundit class noticed a keynote speech given that year by a charismatic, sexy, and idealistic-seeming young governor from the tiny rural state of Arkansas. And the ones who did had noted that the young man's speech, while entertaining at times, seemed to drone on and on (and on!) forever.

But Johnny Carson noticed it, and he invited that fortyish Arkansas governor named Bill Clinton on to *The Tonight Show*. Playing opposite the King of Late Night, the charming, media-savvy young pol more than rose to the challenge—bantering, allowing himself to be the butt of the joke without being made a fool of, and eliminating all traces of diarrhea-of-the-mouth and un-self-aware awkwardness. Just like Johnny had done for Roseanne Barr, Jerry Seinfeld, Ray Romano, and Ellen DeGeneres, Carson had given the young politician his ticket to the big time. And just like those other stand-up artists, Clinton had been working the political equivalent of the saloon clubs and chitlin' circuits just as long and just as hard, waiting and striving for that big break.

For the past 10 years straight (with only a brief hiatus between 1980 and '82, as Arkansas governors were elected in 2-year intervals), William Jefferson Clinton had been governor of Arkansas, after having been first elected in 1978 to become the youngest then-serving governor in America. (He'd previously been Arkansas attorney general for two years, after having taught graduate law classes for two or three years previously.) His high-powered corporate lawyer wife Hillary Rodham Clinton was even more accomplished than he, a board member of Walmart before leaving her thirties (and involved in numerous other go-go late '70s and '80s economic takeovers and investments, including Tyson Foods, and fatefully, a land development known as Whitewater.) She'd gotten her start as a legal counsel on the Committee to Impeach President Nixon in 1974. The daughter of a prominent society family headed by (staunch Republican) businessman Hugh Rodham, Hillary had already made headlines in 1969 for a famous graduation speech she gave when near the top of her class at Wellesley, en route to her juris doctorate at Yale law school.

While Hillary brought home the bacon as a career woman and raised their young daughter Chelsea (born in early 1980), Bill ran the state from the Governor's Mansion, and along with his fellow Southern Democrats Chuck Robb, Sam Nunn, and Albert Gore, Jr., had helped to found a consortium called the Democratic Leadership Council, headed by longtime DC activist and insider Al From. At that point, Clinton was largely the least experienced or prestigious member of the A-list inner circle of DLC regulars—Robb, Nunn, and Gore were all senators at that point, and from far more powerful and high-profile states. And Gore's father had been the legendary Senator Albert Gore, Sr., who ruled Tennessee in the House and Senate from the Depression-era late 1930s all the way through 1970.

Clinton was also younger than they were, except for Gore (who was younger than Clinton by two years—though Gore always *acted* like the "older brother" of the two.) And Al Gore had embarrassingly just overreached himself, running for the Democratic nomination for president in 1988 against Massachusetts Governor Michael Dukakis, Texas Senator Lloyd Bentsen (the eventual presidential and vice presidential nominees), and Colorado Senator and Hollywood pallie Gary Hart. (Al Gore was younger in 1988 than John F. Kennedy and Barack Obama had been at the point of their announced candidacies for president, and Gore hadn't even completed his first term in the Senate. Needless to say, he was annihilated.) But Bill Clinton was also arguably the best-looking, and certainly the most energetic and charismatic. He had what rock and jazz record execs would call "crossover appeal"—and he'd just proven it with no less than Johnny Carson.

And crossover appeal was what the DLC was all about during the dark days (as they saw it) of the Reagan-Bush 1980s. The Southern-fried flavor of the DLC was no accident—it was largely founded by pragmatic "Blue Dog Democrat" politicians who had watched Richard Nixon's infamous "Southern Strategy" of welcoming Dixie-crats into the Republican ranks. Even more devastating was when the fast-rising Religious Right angrily turned against "born again" President Jimmy Carter, for his failure to thwart the continued activism and visibility of "anti-family" feminists, pro-choicers, "secular humanists," and "the gay agenda" during the *Boogie Nights* late 1970s. That had ensured Ronald Reagan and George Bush, Sr.'s complete triumphs across the Southern and interior Bible Belt states in 1980, '84, and '88—the ones that would become known by the 2000 Election as the "Red States."

When it came to what Bill Clinton would soon sloganize as "the economy, stupid," most of these DLC politicians were resolutely pro-business—and far more so than the so-called "paleo-liberals" who up until then were still clinging to power within the Democratic hierarchy. Like Jimmy Carter before them, these DLC types were mostly tone-deaf to the specifically New Yawk/New Joisey, Boston/Philly, and Detroit-Chicago-Cleveland "machines" of heavily ethnic big labor politics and politicians. (And despite their social liberalism, they were also far more at home in Baptist or Assembly of God surroundings then in the ethnic and ritualized Catholic, Orthodox, and Reform Jewish worlds of the northeast.) The younger and high-techier ones like Al Gore were jokingly called "Atari Democrats," wanting to be on the same page as rising '80s and '90s stars like Bill Gates and Microsoft, Steve Jobs and Apple, Samsung and Sony; the older and more traditional DLC Dems came from land-owning states with textile, coal, and tobacco industries that loathed "Big Guv'mint" over-regulation. And they were all acutely aware of the rock-hard grip of the NRA's gun lobby on macho, huntin-and-fishin' Real Men.

Put simply, the DLC pols (and pollsters) knew that the Democratic Party, as it existed under George McGovern, Teddy Kennedy, Walter Mondale, Michael Dukakis, Gloria Steinem, and Mario Cuomo (let alone Jesse Jackson or Al Sharpton) was simply off the table for their part of the country. It wasn't *even* an option. And that, strangely and interestingly, made them the perfect partner for the overwhelmingly Eastern neoliberal media pundits. They had, after all, already reached the same conclusion, watching image and education-conscious young professionals ditch the blue-collar and/or ghetto-pandering Democrats for Reagan and Bush throughout the '80s. As the not-so-lovely bones of Campaign 1992 began to form in late 1990 and '91, the DLC's Southern-fried down home Protestants, and the sophisticated and mostly Jewish neoliberal pundits, became the ultimate mixed marriage.

For the neoliberal-yuppie opinion gurus, the DLC offered them the first tantalizing whiff of having their opinions and intellectual advice sought after, respected, and actually used *by other Democrats*. How much better than being constantly upstaged by Reagan and Bush stealing their best arguments out from under them, to prove how "bipartisan" the Republican Party was! How thrilling to no longer be shoved to the sidelines by bellowing ghetto activists, or old-fashioned "paleo-liberals" like those semi-literate dumb jocks from Big Labor! The smarter and pop-culturally savvier members of the yuppie opinion class, like Sid Blumenthal, Mike Kinsley, and (the genuinely lefty) Eric Alterman, instinctively understood the possibilities. They might have had the right prescriptions, but they knew they would need a different doctor to actually deliver their treatments. And the DLC just might have their miracle cure.

Like Hollywood Ten screenwriters and playwrights searching for a way back in, the Eastern pundits realized they might need an acceptable "front" to get their submissions past the front office. And like a country star adapting a rock song or jazz melody, they needed someone who could add that all-important "twang" and blue-eyed soulful feeling to their cover versions of neoliberal theme songs. Just as critically for social and academic liberals, they needed someone who could credibly take the edge off of the presumed nose-in-the-air "elitism" and "feminism" and "social engineering" overtones of the Democratic racial and sexual priority list.

"Bill Clinton knows how to speak 'cracker!'" exulted his fellow Southern governor, Florida's Lawton Chiles, wearing the knowing grin of a supporting actor in a movie watching the hero he'd mentored finally take the cockpit. The very sad endings to Southerners Lyndon Johnson and Jimmy Carter's reigns had caused 1980s Democrats to look away from Dixieland, and more and more towards urban and minority voices, and politicians from liberal bastions like New York, Boston, and the industrial Midwest. Now, they would be forced to reassess that strategy. Not only was Bill Clinton proving himself to have almost unprecedented drawing power among African Americans and Latinos, he was also the first Democrat in eons to speak to Southern white males and unpretentious blue-collar "Reagan Democrats" too—and at one and the same time!

Revealingly, the first two people to recognize that it would be Bill Clinton who would pose the biggest threat to a sitting President Bush were the Republican genius "Southern strategist" Lee Atwater, and his best buddy and spiritual kid brother, Karl Rove. After seeing his fellow Southern good-ole-boy-genius Bill Clinton, a-pickin' and a-grinnin' on Johnny Carson, Atwater could name Clinton's tune in one note. He immediately set out to derail Clinton's 1990 re-election as governor of Arkansas, in the obvious hope of making a preemptive strike that would deny Clinton his platform for running for a far more serious office two years later. But two could play at that game, and for the first time in his life, Lee Atwater finally met his match. After years of wiping the floor with clueless paleo-liberal pols and tone-deaf Northeastern "elitists," Atwater's fellow media-savvy Southern baby boomer saw him coming a mile away. And this Friday night football game was on Bubba's home turf. Bill and Hillary's well-oiled Arkansas machine knocked Lee Atwater out of the park. The 1990 mid-terms saw Clinton re-elected stronger than ever, and Atwater and Rove had to figure out how to regroup—and fast.

Unfortunately, Lee Atwater himself didn't have much time left—his campaign against a terminal cancer diagnosis proved to be one that not even he could win, and he left us at age 40 in 1991. Now with the perhaps-exception of Karl Rove, nobody else on either the Republican—or just as fatefully at this early date, the *Democratic*—side of the fence took Bill Clinton seriously. (Not YET, anyway.) Indeed the old-time cigar-chompers and backroomers of the Democratic Party were the very *last* to get the memo.

"No prominent senator or governor in the Democratic Party chose to run for president against Bush in 1991," wrote Sidney Blumenthal. They had become convinced in the aftermath of the (first) Gulf War, the fall of the Berlin Wall, and the impending break-up of the Soviet Union, that Bush had become "impregnable," and these Democratic apparatchiks "wanted the Presidency conferred upon them without struggle." Many of the Democratic A-list (Mario Cuomo, Ann Richards, Geraldine Ferraro, Pat Moynihan, Lloyd Bentsen, Mondale and Dukakis) were also a good bit closer to Bush Sr's generational outlook and age group than to the Baby Boomer, Elvis-rockin', fortyish Arkansas governor. "Snug in their cloakrooms and statehouses, they left the field to someone they thought foolhardy enough to undertake the race."

Even New York Governor Mario Cuomo, to whom many Democratic superdelegates and pundits were ready to hand the nomination on a silver platter, finally refused. Cuomo was captured by the press in a metaphorical picture worth a thousand words—trapped like a cat in the headlights with indecision, waiting for a plane that could take him to the opening of presidential primary season, while in the midst of overseeing a budget battle in New York state, in December of 1991. Ultimately, Cuomo decided to stay home to dither over local taxes in Albany, instead of pursuing the most powerful office in the world. And by doing so, he effectively telegraphed to the media that he himself, and the entire Democratic establishment, privately felt that it would be suicide for any Democrat who would dare to challenge President Bush.

As the fed-up women who were running for office in the 1992 aftermath of Anita Hill would say, "They just didn't get it!" Bill Clinton "was not the kind of Democrat the Republicans were used to deconstructing," said Sidney Blumenthal in his aptly titled memoir, *The Clinton Wars*. For one, Clinton had sex appeal. He was "alive from the waist down," as feminist writer Erica Jong later put it (approvingly) in the *New York Observer*. He had the kind of ruddy virility and Southern charm that couldn't help but turn many women and gay men on, often in spite of themselves. There is a popular if coarse saying in Hollywood that the essential ingredient that separates a true movie, TV, or rock-and-roll STAR (or an endorsement-worthy pro athlete) from a mere worker bee is that "women want to fuck him, and men want to be him." It would be almost redundant at this late date to reveal that many women indeed wanted to fuck Bill Clinton—and to many other dudes, he seemed like a regular guy you'd want to watch *Monday Night Football* with, while having a brewski.

But that didn't mean Clinton was a dummy; he was also an Oxford Law grad who taught law school himself before he was 30, with a Mensa-level IQ and a machine-gun command of facts and figures plus a near-photographic memory to boot. Someone who devoured Harvard-level legal journals and academic history doorstops the way other people read raging romances at the beach. Indeed, Clinton was a near-perfect recipe of all the top-tier Democratic leaders' qualities baked into one delicious cake. He was a card-carrying genius—but he couldn't be dismissed as another depressive, didactic, pretentious academic "intellectual," or some tyrannical "elitist" federal judge or senator who made rulings (that he never abided by himself) by diktat and filibuster. He had the swingin' sex appeal and discriminating yuppie tastes, and he'd certainly done the hippie thing back in the '60s and early '70s, complete with a "radical feminist" wife. But he also had a butter-wouldn't-melt-in-my-mouth, J.R. Ewing-like, "love to hate me" irresistible Southern charm—the one thing that Clinton's own mentor, the preening, smirking, Warren Beatty-wannabe Gary Hart, had conspicuously lacked. Clinton became beloved by minorities like no one since Dr. King and Bobby Kennedy (until Barack Obama himself), yet he was without a doubt a child of the white working class. He was a genuinely Southern Southern Baptist, but he was also far and away the most openly pro-choice, gay-embracing, and pro-feminist candidate for president that either party had yet fielded in American history.

"It's our turn, now!"

All this building drama finally came to a head as the presidential race really got underway in the spring and summer of 1992. It was best summed up in an anecdote that radical-left journalist Alexander Cockburn liked to start off his memories of the Clinton Administration with. He was at a party where he and a colleague allegedly bumped into the wife of Sid Blumenthal, who was now covering Campaign '92 for the even more influential and upscale *New Yorker*. Cockburn asked Mrs. B why her Sidney wasn't even *pretending* to journalistic objectivity in his breathless, adulatory, sycophantic stenography for Bill and Hillary Clinton, and his snide asides towards President Bush. Mrs. Blumenthal shot back the most icy-socialite glare you could imagine, as though the question itself didn't even need to be asked by people as savvy as Cockburn, and "hissed" that it was because "It's *our* turn" now!

Yes, during the last big "game change" election in 1980, the news was still largely the private property of fading World War II generation journos like Punch Sulzberger, Otis Chandler, Ben Bradlee, David Brinkley, and Walter Cronkite. But in 1992, the Boomer neoliberals were finally ready, willing, and *able* to take over—and take over they did, furiously rewriting the all-important media narrative of the first election that would change generations in the White House since sophisticated and sexy Jack and Jackie took over, after the black-and-white, bland, plain-folks Truman/Eisenhower era. It would be just as sharp a contrast.

Bill Clinton's opponents, the aging, patriarchal, Nixon-supporting, World War II-veteran President George H.W. Bush (and the crewcut Korea-era Navy vet, self-made businessman, and reactionary "third party" candidate Ross Perot), were as straight from the 1950s as a black-and-white sitcom. Before 1992, only a small handful of Baby Boomer politicians had truly hit the big time. For the most part, American politics was still firmly in the hands of the Greatest and Silent Generations, people born in the late 1910s, '20s and early to-mid '30s. From the nine Supreme Court justices to Alan Greenspan (b. 1926) or his predecessor Paul Volcker (b. 1933) at the Fed, to fifty-something Speaker of the House Jim Wright (and Tip O'Neill before him), to Presidents Reagan and Bush themselves.

There were only a few truly A-list, card-carrying Baby Boomer national politicians who'd made it to front and center on the world stage before Bill and Hill came onto the scene. Two of them were old-money sons of political fathers, to whom they were both fiercely loyal, who'd both entered Congress in the class of 1976 while still in their twenties (and with no small amount of help from dear old Dad). Both were overtly Christian and devoted family men who had loyally served in the Vietnam-era military, who had long-running marriages to their high school or college sweethearts, had fathered relatively large broods of children, and who advertised their rock-ribbed beliefs in family values. Their names were Al Gore and Dan Quayle.

And as if preordained by the Fates themselves, one was the sitting vice president at the time (Quayle)—and the other one was the Democratic Leadership Council "classmate" and fellow Southern Boomer that Bill Clinton would hand-pick to be his vice presidential running mate in 1992 (Gore). The big difference was that Tennessee Senator Al Gore was known for his insatiable passion for technology and his high IQ—while Dan Quayle was mainly known for having considerably fewer mental gifts. Indeed, it was said that Bush cynically chose the young, strawberry-blond and boyishly handsome Indiana senator mainly because he (or Bush's consultants, including his son George W.) knew that in the 1988 world of *Miami Vice,* MTV, and Tom Cruise, a grey-haired, glasses-wearing grandpa with a white-haired wife and a World War II record simply *needed* a good-looking younger man to back him up. Bush was already older in 1988–89 (at just shy of 65 years old) than Eisenhower, Truman, or anyone except Reagan himself had been when he first took office— a fact that would be devastatingly used against him after four more years.

Unfortunately, Dan Quayle's good looks and so-called youth were the only things he had going for him—that and a sense of puppy-dog, painfully earnest, and hopelessly inarticulate loyalty that bordered on the masochistic. (Quayle was also a hardcore culture warrior, having made outrageously Rush Limbaugh–like innuendoes about gays, AIDS, and safe sex. And he was so radically Right to Life that his famously uptight wife Marilyn was quoted as saying that she'd even *force* their barely teenage daughter to give birth, rather than consent to let her have an abortion, if the girl had gotten pregnant.)

Well-meaning, semi-lovable and hopelessly incompetent, Dan Quayle was a man who apologized for the Holocaust as a disgraceful period in OUR history (maybe he meant the world's history, which it certainly was, but in context it sounded like he meant *America's* own). Quayle pathetically butchered the United Negro College Fund's famous slogan, "A Mind Is a Terrible Thing to Waste," sweat-pouringly turning it into "What a waste it is to lose one's mind!" And in 1992, Danny-boy famously and mistakenly "corrected" an elementary school child at a photo-op, who had correctly spelled the word "potato." ("There's an 'E' at the end of 'potato!'" he cried.) No wonder that Quayle's most infamous moment happened in the 1988 vice presidential debates, where, after Quayle egotistically compared himself to John F. Kennedy, his opponent Lloyd Bentsen, who had known and worked with JFK, shot back "Senator—you're no Jack Kennedy!" The applause from the audience was thunderous. (President Bush himself was known for being tongue-tied in his speaking; Texas Governor Ann Richards memorably called the incredibly rich and powerful Bush "born with a silver *foot* in his mouth!" But Bush looked as articulate and witty as Gore Vidal and Oscar Wilde when compared against Quayle—which may have been the whole point.)

In Dan Quayle's other most eye-rolling moment—when Candice Bergen's top-rated feminist TV sitcom heroine Murphy Brown chose to have a baby without marrying its father—Quayle went on the warpath, accusing the show (and Hollywood in general) of "mocking the importance" of fathers. Quayle might have had a point there, but given that the Republican Party had spent the past 15 years indulging in one high profile anti-feminist and homophobic pander after another (so as to suck up to ultra-right activists like James Dobson, Phyllis Schlafly, Jerry Falwell, and Jesse Helms), the only thing most liberated women heard was yet another tiresome attack on them for not being "submissive" stay-at-home moms. (And what should Murphy have done, Dan, after she found out she was pregnant? Get an *ABORTION?* At least she "chose life!") Indeed, Quayle's speech came just months after the ballistically gender-politicked Anita Hill controversy, and sounded even more tone-deaf because of it. Younger and single women began ditching the Bush-Quayle '92 ticket in droves.

At least Dan Quayle had been consistent in his life pattern. He was just as right-wing, devoutly religious, and personally conservative during the '60s revolution (loyally serving in the National Guard during Vietnam, and grindstone-nosing it through law school) as he would be in his glory years to come. In contrast, Al Gore was known during his Harvard daze for hosting long after-hours hangouts with his Ivy pallies—with plenty of funny cigarettes and "herbal" bowls, while his psych-major debutante sweetheart Tipper Aitcheson played drums in girls' rock bands and go-go groups. Yet when Al and Tipper Gore truly hit the national big-time in 1992, they came across as being almost as conservative as Dan and Marilyn Quayle were, personally if not politically—like the kind of young couple whose favorite Saturday-night pastime back in 1968 was watching *The Lawrence Welk Show.*

That was no accident, but the result of two intervening decades' worth of careful, calculated, and deliberate planning on their part (especially Al's). Until the screaming car-crash conclusion of his political career in the *Bush vs. Gore* debacle of 2000, the defining moment of young Albert Gore, Jr.'s life had occurred back in 1970, when his Senate icon father lost a bitterly contested re-election race against a hard-right, Nixon-backed, 39-year-old Republican businessman. Pioneering the strategy that fellow "Dixie-crat" Republicans like Jesse Helms and Strom Thurmond were bringing to perfection, Gore Sr.'s opponent didn't so much run against Gore himself as he did against the hippie-dippie, picketing and protesting, anti-war and pro-civil rights youth of the late '60s. While no one would mistake 63-year-old Southern aristocrat Albert Gore, Sr., for some kind of flower child, in that kind of revolution, simply being thought of as "too soft" on those kinds of "anti–American" "subversive" "Commie" "radical" youth sealed his doom in conservative, country-music, Bible-belt Tennessee.

It was said that when Al Gore's future nemesis (and fellow political son) George W. Bush lost a close Texas race in 1978, the young Bush groused to himself that from here on in, he would never let anyone else "out-Texan or out-Christian him again!" In 1970, the 22-year-old Gore had just married Tipper after graduating Harvard the year before, and was preparing to ship out for Vietnam—a war he personally despised, but he'd decided to enlist in it anyway because he felt it would help his dad win re-election. (The year before, while studying under his favorite Harvard professor, a young instructor named Marty Peretz, Gore flirted with the protest movement—only to be personally horrified when one of the "peace" activists started talking about the possibilities of robberies or bombings. That was "it" for young Al with the radical Left!) Now, weeping openly at his beloved father's humiliating loss, one can easily imagine a traumatized young Al Gore thinking to himself that if he ever followed in Dad's footsteps, he would never let anyone paint HIM as some kind of anti–American, "ultra liberal," subversive, hippie-Commie radical—*no matter what!*

And he didn't! Young Al Gore finally ran for an open House of Representatives seat in 1976, after a desultory career as a local newspaper journalist and a stab at law school following his Vietnam service. (His hitch ended in 1971.) And when he did, he kicked off a Congressional career almost as far to the reactionary right as his contemporary Dan Quayle's. Cognizant of the rising Religious Right's mood during the *Swingtown* 1970s, in overwhelmingly Southern Baptist and Pentecostal Tennessee, Gore went out of his way to volunteer to a reporter how quote, "abnormal" he thought gays and lesbians were. "I don't believe a woman's right to freedom to live her own life, in all cases, outweighs the fetus' right to life," Gore finger-pointed for good measure. Later on, Gore joined fundie Senate icon Jesse Helms in trying to add an amendment to the Civil Rights Act making the term 'person' include, quote, "unborn children from the moment of conception" (the amendment failed) and again to impose strict restrictions on AIDS funding, during the height of the early gay-rights struggle. He voted for several incarnations of the successful Hyde Amendment to curtail federal funding of abortions, and to deny abortions for poor women.

By 1992, Gore had racked up an 84 percent rating from Right to Life (almost the equal of Quayle), while his record on gay rights was so abysmally bad that the horrific Rev. Fred Phelps—of "God Hates Fags" fame—had actually *endorsed* Gore during his 1984 campaign for Senate! (To Gore's credit, he at least disclaimed *that* particular endorsement.) Indeed in 2000, the leftist journalist Alexander Cockburn said that Gore had been "a gay-basher his entire career" in the Congress. He voted to keep DC's Victorian "anti-sodomy" laws on the books (overruling DC's own city council's wishes), boasted that he would "never accept" money from gay groups, and voted to stop gays and lesbians from being able to file sexual discrimination and harassment suits against homophobic employers (once again, side-by-side with Jesse Helms and his crew). Meanwhile, Tipper first made national headlines calling for strict ratings of sexually explicit and/or violent gangsta rap, hip-hop, and punk rock lyrics on albums and CDs, and crusading against sex and violence in movies and on TV.

On foreign policy, the record was no better, if you were from the progressive Left. Gore distinguished himself as one of Ronald Reagan and George Bush, Sr.'s go-to Democrats, voting proudly for practically every chest-thumping foreign invasion and police action (and bling-bling weapons program and defense giveaway), as well as "greedily" soliciting contributions from "homophobic preachers, tobacco companies, chemical and oil companies, and weapons manufacturers" (to return to Cockburn's colorful words).

Al Gore finally reached his all-time low in cynicism, trying to prove that he wasn't "too liberal," on the eve of Old Bush's early 1991 war against Saddam Hussein. He theatrically gave a self-pitying speech on C-SPAN about how personally "excruciating" it was for him to vote in favor of Operation Desert Storm—*after* he'd asked both sides whether they would play Let's Make a Deal by providing him with prime TV time behind the scenes, as his fellow Senators Alan Simpson and Bob Dole pointed out. (Less than a dozen Senate Democrats agreed with him—the rest, typifying the Democrat Party's post–Vietnam peacenik era, were "apoplectic" as one Gore adviser put it, that Gore would help provide Bush's 52–47 margin to authorize the first Iraq War.) Of course, in reality the consequences for Gore would have been far more "excruciating" (for him, anyway) had he voted with the pacifist wing of his party against a still-popular, Cold War-winning Bush. We don't go for any of that pansy-hippie BS, pardner—not in flag-saluting, John Wayne and *Gunsmoke*-watching, Grand Ole Opry-listening Tennessee, thank you very much! Just ask dear old Dad, who'd come out against Vietnam in the late '60s, and had lost his Senate seat because of it.

The Gores' personal conservatism, and their being the same age as Bill and Hillary, plus being fellow Southerners and fellow members of the DLC, made Al an irresistible choice for vice president once Clinton sewed up the main nomination for himself. (Indeed, Clinton feared Al Gore running against him for the presidential nomination in 1992, more than he did any other Democrat except maybe for Mario Cuomo, who bowed out before the campaign season began.) By picking Gore, Clinton was taking out an insurance policy with "swing voters" who thought he himself was too liberal, while also doubling down on the generational-change message. There would be no gray-haired World War II or Korea-era old pro like Lloyd Bentsen or Pat Moynihan or Cuomo to rein in the young whipper-snapper. The name of the game was Youth vs. Age. Tomorrow vs. Yesterday. All the way, or nothing at all.

Of course, Bill and Hillary Clinton had certainly gone from hippie to yuppie during the '70s and '80s. Hillary long ago had abandoned her shapeless peasant blouses, frizzy hair, and no-makeup for *Dynasty*-style power suits and makeovers, and Bill had his decades-long career as the head of government and law enforcement in Arkansas to point to. But the Clintons had never made anything like the same kind of page by page, line by line attempt to extreme-makeover themselves into a socially conservative, "family values" Democratic couple, or to repudiate the legacy of the '60s, the way the Gores had. (Even if they had, the tabloid revelations about Bill's swingin' sex life and ballistically sexist media rumors about Hillary's supposed lesbianism would have reduced any such attempts to camp.)

Indeed, in the most (in)famous moment of the famously slippery Bill's attempt to "triangulate" the culture wars, Clinton came out of the closet about having smoked pot in college—but, he added, with straight face intact, "I didn't inhale!" (as eyes rolled across America). Indeed, Bill and Hillary Clinton had lived a veritable baby-boom Via Dolorosa, to rival *Forrest Gump* or *The Big Chill*, drawing the through-line from all the major points of the civil-rights and anti-war '60s, to the liberated singles-bar '70s, to the yuppie-executive 1980s.

For better or worse, of all the major politicians out there as late as 1992, only Bill and Hill truly cut a convincing figure of the Baby Boomers' experience and life-passage journey, of the values and ethics of post–1960s society. That is why they were hated and feared by those who hated and feared them, and why they were loved by those who loved them. And that is also, perhaps, why they were *necessary*. In order to have the long-overdue "national conversation," as the academic intellectuals might put it, about post '60s American culture, there would have to *be* a truly authentic child of the '60s and early '70s, a real-deal Baby Boomer in a position of White House power, someone who had actually been there and done that. Someone who *had* inhaled, if you will. Not a Dixiecrat reactionary like Lee Atwater or Karl Rove—much less a personally conservative, borderline Silent Generationer like Joe Lieberman, Newt Gingrich, Paul Tsongas, Jack Kemp, or Dick Cheney. This time, only the real deal would do. Bill Clinton was both the best and the worst person to be elected president in 1992, at one and the same time.

While Andrew Sullivan would go on to become one of Bill and Hillary's most implacable critics in the later 1990s and 2000s, both he and *The New Republic* (which he was now editing) went "all in" supporting and cheerleading for the Clinton ticket in 1992, for the exact same reason that Sullivan would give for his later adulation of Barack Obama, against reactionary Tea Party Republicans in 2008 and 2012. In 2007, Sullivan famously wrote that despite the many old Washington pols who were counseling young upstart Barack Obama to "wait his turn" before running for president, "the fundamental fact of his candidacy is that *it is happening right now*." Sully could just as well have been writing about Bill and Hillary Clinton in 1992. The entire point of Bill Clinton's 1992 candidacy was that it was happening NOW, in 1992. That neither he, nor the Baby Boom generation, were going to "wait their turn" any longer. Ready or not, here they come!

As that avatar of Boomer consciousness Bob Dylan might have put it, "there was something goin' on here—but you just don't know what it is, do you, President Bush?" George H.W. Bush, Pat Buchanan, and Ross Perot (and Mario Cuomo, Paul Tsongas, and Mondale and Dukakis)—indeed, all the other A-list political spokesmodels of 1992 America still looked and talked like the Greatest and Silent Generations that they mostly still hailed from—and pandered to. Their frame of reference was still an industrial age, pre-diversity, mid-century America that just didn't live here anymore. They all looked and sounded like the past. And in 1992, Bill and Hillary Clinton—and ONLY Bill and Hillary Clinton—thrillingly looked like the future. (Or for that matter, even the *present*.)

Bill Clinton did for politics what Hunter S. Thompson, Graham Greene, Carl Hiassen, Don DeLillo, and Thomas Pynchon had done for American literature, and what David Lynch, Charlie Kaufman, and Quentin Tarantino had done for film. Bill Clinton had single-handedly created the Postmodern Presidency. And there would be no going back, no matter how much some people wished there would be. More importantly, it was largely *because of the comparison* to Bill and Hillary that America first began to see just how outmoded and outdated all the other candidates really were—including many Congressional and state-level Democrats. And for the next eight years, neither those candidates, nor their behind-the-scenes loyalists, party infrastructures, and family members, would ever forget that insult.

Bill Clinton, Superstar

As it became more and more clear that Arkansas Governor Bill Clinton was the one to beat, the shocked and awed Republicans dragged Bill (and Hillary) through the mud with the many quote-unquote "bimbo eruptions" from Clinton's obviously '70s-style open marriage, and his insatiable sexual appetite while governor and attorney general in Arkansas. The worst came when his mistress from 1977 to 1990, a dancer and singer named Gennifer Flowers, came out of the closet about their long extramarital affair. Allegations also soon surfaced that Clinton had had sex in limousines and used government officials in Arkansas to arrange and/or cover up "dates" with other women.

Clearly, despite Atwater and Rove's premonitions, the Republican Establishment had still been planning for yet another sad-sack bureaucratic "lifer" like Mario Cuomo or Paul Tsongas or Michael Dukakis as their main opponent. The sex-card had already worked like a charm against Gary Hart in 1987—when his mistress Donna Rice came out against him, ol' Gary's goose was as cooked as a bowl of Minute Rice. When Congressman Bob Packwood and Supreme Court nominee Clarence Thomas were accused of sexual impropriety, it ended the first man's career outright and came within a gnat's lash of destroying the second one's. Both Republicans and many Democrats thought that the "bimbo eruptions" and Gennifer's kissing-and-telling to the supermarket tabloids would be the end of Bill Clinton.

Think again! At that crucial moment, Hillary became the original Good Wife, and went on *60 Minutes* blasting the snoopy media as the villain, sitting right next to her husband and "standing by her man," no matter how much she later tried to downplay it. To put it crudely, in Hillary Clinton's mind, Bill may have screwed around on her—but it was the scandal-mongering, tabloidy media that was *fucking* her, trying to deny her the chance to be First Lady even while having the gall to cast her as a victim. And Hillary knew *exactly* how to fight back.

Then the Republicans tried portraying Clinton as an unreconstructed, Ted Kennedy-Jerry Brown-George McGovern style ultra-libby. But Clinton trumped their ace—he went ahead and executed mentally challenged African American murderer Ricky Ray Rector (then on Arkansas' death row), and publicly dissed the controversial black rap star Sistah Souljah right in front of people like Jesse Jackson and Al Sharpton. A truly doctrinaire liberal or progressive leftist wouldn't have *dared*. Now, that dog just wouldn't hunt anymore, except maybe with Rush Limbaugh's "dittoheads."

Foiled again, the Republicans now upped the Clinton comparison to even more subversive counterculture icons and '60s radicals like Abbie Hoffman and Jerry Rubin—only to find that many Baby Boom voters almost *approved* of the comparison! Finally, here was *one of our own* making it to the winner's circle—instead of some nerdy, resentfully retro reactionary like Dan Quayle or Karl Rove. The Republicans tried resurrecting past nominees

Walter Mondale and Michael Dukakis from the political graveyard, but Mondale and Dukakis didn't have as much pheromone-drenched, effortlessly hip media appeal as Bill Clinton had in his saxophone case.

Finally, the Republicans hit their desperate last-ditch. They tried bringing back memories of the last Southern governor to hold the White House—Jimmy Carter, in his angry and malicious "malaise" meltdown, with his self-righteous, finger-pointing lectures and out-of-control crisis modes, back when all the Democratic wheels were coming off in 1979 and '80. Alas, the more they tried to paint Clinton with that brush, the more aw-shucks, ear-to-ear grinnin', accessibly hand-shaking, and defiantly optimistic Clinton became, pallin' around with voters of all and every color and class. Effortlessly ... eagerly ... cheerfully.

This was what Sidney Blumenthal's wife was talking about when she said that it was Our Turn Now. Only a Clinton Administration could truly mark the arrival of the entire yuppie neo-liberal package, especially as it was defined and deconstructed by the academics and journalists of the Opinion Journals That Mattered: the knowing meta-media hipness and David Letterman-style irreverence; the venturesome sexuality and empowered, liberated career women; the token cracks in the racial diversity glass ceiling (while still running a basically rich-white-straight-male show); and the prestige of high-end college credentials and prep-school secret handshakes replacing the gaudy surface "high society" glitz and glamour of the Reagan-Bush '80s.

Bill Clinton followed up his late '80s appearance on Johnny Carson with the heir to Johnny's throne, Jay Leno, and reached out to young, college, and first-time voters in a way that no candidate had ever done since Vietnam (and no candidate ever *would* do until Facebooker-in-chief Barack Obama in 2008 and '12). His most famous campaign stop was on MTV, where he answered questions no presidential candidate had ever answered before—including the seminal "Boxers or briefs?" (For the record, the basketball-playing and jogging saxophonist preferred tighty-whities.) Just imagine Lyndon Johnson, Richard Nixon, or Jimmy Carter being asked a question like that, though! Better yet, *who on Earth would want to know the answer?*

Clinton continued rewriting the New Media rulebook in a way that was so far out of the league of the "dignified" old-money and old-media George H.W. Bush (as well as Beverly Hillbilly Ross Perot), Clinton wasn't even playing on the same field. Nor for that matter, were any of his fellow Democrats. Clinton's other most famous appearance was when he went on African American comedian Arsenio Hall's late-night talk show, televised mainly on Fox network stations that targeted the 18-to-34 year old age demographic (and had a total command of urban late-night audiences), sportin' a pair of shades and his tenor saxophone, belting out a rendition of his hero Elvis Presley's signature song, "Heartbreak Hotel." He received an ovation, with Arsenio famously beaming at Clinton, as he jammed on the same talent level with Arsenio's Hollywood studio-pro house musicians. It was if Arsenio was saying, "He's the Man!" to his millions of young and diverse viewers—and first-time voters.

The contrast couldn't have been sharper to old President Bush, poised on the edge of seventy, and getting grumpier by the minute. He was so out-of-date that he was photographed expressing amazement at the up-to-the-minute technology of grocery-checkout barcode scanners. Up to the minute, that is, if you were still living in 1975! Bush called environmentalist Al Gore "Ozone Man" and compared Bill Clinton to a frog. He did everything but chase Clinton and Gore off of his lawn with a cane.

As James Carville and Paul Begala had said, in a spreadsheet banner across the fabled Clinton campaign "War Room," *It's the Economy, Stupid.* For the past half century, foreign policy had been the #1 tune on the presidential charts. The end of World War II and the start of the Cold War had defined Harry Truman and General Dwight Eisenhower. The first word in Lyndon Johnson and Richard Nixon's political obituaries would forever be "Vietnam." And even a gasoline-line, 15 percent interest rate economy took second billing in 1980 to the spectacle of terrified American hostages being held at gunpoint in Iran, under Jimmy Carter. For the first time in a half century, now that the Cold War was finally over, the pendulum swung back to domestic issues—and it couldn't have come at a worse time for old President Bush. The deficit was sky high, and so was unemployment, reaching Great Recession levels for most of 1992, as the domestic auto and aerospace industries continued their merciless downsizing and outsourcing campaigns, as overpriced '80s New York and California real estate kept on plummeting, and scads of neighborhood small businesses kept going belly up.

"I feel yer pain"

Bill Clinton delivered that famous (if not infamous) line at a New York City fundraiser in the spring of 1992. In light of today's battles for gay marriage equality, it's worth noting that Clinton said that when addressing an AIDS activist, demanding to know what Clinton planned to do about the plague, after the indifference of the Reagan/Bush era. But in the punishing early '90s recession, Clinton's comment made world headlines, *Saturday Night Live,* and late-night talk faster than an Internet "meme" of today. No one else was talking about "feeling the pain" of the downsized, the foreclosed, the laid-off, the repossessed, and the confused—at least not in that naked, hand-holding, psychological-therapy way. Clinton wanted to brand himself as the Empathizer-in-Chief, underlining a key campaign slogan, "Putting People First." And he succeeded beyond his wildest dreams. If, that is, you were "buying it."

To paraphrase a tasty comment that the legendary author Pauline Kael once made on a different subject, Bill Clinton's style of emotional, lip-biting, tear-shedding retail politics was so shameless and sleazy that it forced us to reconsider our very notions of what shameless and sleazy politics really were. To cynics and traditionalists, Clinton was turning the very real agony of blue-collar and office-worker America into high camp—with every ruddied cheek, bitten lip, and conspicuous teardrop cynically timed for maximum Nielsen ratings impact. His antics turned as many stomachs as it made hearts bleed. To them, Bill Clinton seemed to have all the good taste, restraint, and dignity of a *Newlywed Game* question.

And fatefully, this attitude wasn't limited to Rush Limbaugh and Pat Buchanan's fan clubs. Left-winger Alexander Cockburn said in the *Los Angeles Times* in 1992 that Bill Clinton was such an obvious scammer, just listening to him was "like having a pillow shoved into one's mouth." Less than four years after the Clinton administration ended, lefty author Thomas Frank would best-sellingly express disgust with Clinton's "patently phony compassion" and "obvious contempt for" working and middle-class Americans.

Yet Clinton's emotive and emotional approach was also light years ahead of what any of the other Democrats or Republicans were doing—or were really *capable* of doing. In Peter Morgan's 2006 movie *The Queen,* set during 1997, there is a scene where the anti-monarchist wife of newly elected Prime Minister Tony Blair is watching Queen Elizabeth give a speech (written by Blair aides) on the recent death of Princess Diana. The famous "As a Grandmother" speech, which set out to "humanise" Her Majesty after she initially appeared cold and distant following Diana's shocking car-crash death, was a huge success— but in the movie, Blair's wife was having none of it. "Look at her—she doesn't believe a word of this!" Madam Cherie laughs. But her media-savvy husband, open-mouthed with admiration at the Queen's skillful rebirth, replies, "That's not the point. What she's doing is brilliant!"

What Her Majesty was doing, of course, was trying to seem "accessible," and more like a quote-unquote Real Person in a new media age. And how much more urgent a need was there for that in the 1992 America of Phil Donahue, Larry King, Oprah, Sally Jessy Raphael, Barbara Walters, Dr. Ruth Westheimer, *People* magazine, *Entertainment Tonight,* pop-psychology and self-help bestsellers, and Wayne Dyer and Tony Robbins PBS motivational seminars? (As well as the first initial glimmers of what was then just starting to be referred to as the World Wide Web.)

The fact that Clinton may or may not have been "patently phony" and insincere was no longer the point. *At least Clinton made the effort.* At least he was *willing* to bare all, to make a showy show of crying and commiserating publicly with the people whose lives were being upended by a changed economy and cultural situation over which they had virtually no control. That was sure a helluva lot more than Ronnie and George would ever have done, let alone ball-busting Barbara Bush or Fancy Nancy Reagan! Just look at them riding around in their limos and Rolls-Royces, going shopping at Gucci and vacationing at Kennebunkport or Santa Barbara, and hanging out with their high society friends. It's not like THEY ever had to worry about anything. *They think they're too High n' Mighty! They wouldn't want to "lower themselves." Because they're Just Too Good for people like us, ain't they?*

No wonder that Roseanne Barr delivered a speech on her number-one rated TV sitcom just days before the election, where she repeated point-blank the Clinton campaign's mantra and slogan: "It's Time for a Change!" This, *this* was the real issue. The Clinton campaign's sleeve-wearing emotionalism and "Putting People First!" sloganeering may have been just cynical PR BS and branding strategy all along, but it was so brilliant it hurt. Pedantic, elitist Democrat intellectuals like Pat Moynihan, Paul Tsongas, and Mario Cuomo would have thought that they *shouldn't* have done it. Hopelessly civil service Demo-bureaucrats like Walter Mondale and Michael Dukakis *couldn't* have done it. And dignified, old-school Republican icons like Ronald Reagan and George Bush, Sr., certainly *wouldn't* have done it. But Bill Clinton could. Bill Clinton would. And Bill Clinton DID.

On November 3, 1992, for the first time in over 30 years, the generational torch was passed, from a defeated George Bush, brought down from an administration that looked like one of America's biggest successes from 1988 to early 1991, but had been an epic failure in its final 18 months. Liberals, progressive Leftists, and racial minorities who hadn't dared to dream that the Reagan-Bush era would or could end so soon were weeping in the kind of ecstatic jubilation not seen until Barack Obama in 2008. Meanwhile, the voters that

President Nixon famously termed the Silent Majority, who would neither remain silent (nor much of a majority) for much longer, were open-mouthed in their shock. How could this hippie, this hillbilly, this *nobody,* have beaten Bush? (And by extension, Ronald Reagan?) What did this mean for us? What would this guy DO to us?

And while Bill (and Hillary) Clinton may have won the election, they did it with the lowest voter share of any postwar president—only 43 percent. It was the Herculean strength of Ross Perot's third-party candidacy, drawing off a record 19 percent of voters (millions more than other third-party pros like Ralph Nader or George Wallace ever dreamed of) that had apparently sealed the deal—not Bill Clinton's hopey-changey rhetoric or Southern charms alone. Perot referred to blacks and Mexicans as "you people," had no real interest in feminism, and set the template for other "common sense" demagogues like Sarah Palin and Michelle Bachmann. Hardly a magnet for the progressive or minority Democratic base. Had Perot not run—*at least in the Republicans' opinion*—Bill Clinton would be back in Arkansas, Bush would be back for four more years, and all would be right (or at least right-wing) with the world.

As *Salon's* Steve Kornacki would later underline, in actuality Perot's vote had been roughly 50/50 split between potential Clinton and old Bush voters. But even if Clinton's win was therefore inevitable, the problem Perot had posed (for both parties) was that—while the progressive, feminist, and minority Democratic base was largely repulsed by him—Perot had drawn his first blood from fence-sitting, persuadable "swing voters" from both sides. He'd gotten just enough professional, educated Republicans who were allergic to Dan Quayle, Jerry Falwell, and Pat Buchanan's culture-warring; plus "Reagan Democrats" who were suffering in the worst economic pain since Jimmy Carter (and the earliest of Reagan's 1981–82 recession). And Perot had also captured conservative Democrats who were put off by Clinton's immorality and sleaze, and still wished for someone "honest," like Paul Tsongas or Mario Cuomo, if not a revived JFK or FDR. In other words, Democrats who might have been persuaded to vote for a Ronald Reagan or a Dwight Eisenhower (or even a Richard Nixon), in better circumstances.

One thing *was* crystal-clear: No matter how or why it happened, as legendary Republican Senator Bob Dole would frequently remind voters, 57 percent of America had voted *against* Bill Clinton. And Bill Clinton would be brutally reminded of that fact, over and over again, in the coming two years. Tellingly, on Election Night, every TV broadcast and cable news network's newscasts rocked out to the strains of Bill and Hillary's favorite song, Fleetwood Mac's "Don't Stop." It was only too apt. Liberals and progressives were pinching themselves, dreaming ever-bigger dreams and fantasies about what tomorrow might bring, now that we had a Democrat in the White House—and tomorrow was exactly what a lot of the people who'd voted against Clinton were most afraid of.

Amidst all the elation and euphoria, this was both the hope and the warning for Bill and Hillary Clinton. Because, as that ultimate Southern power couple, Rhett Butler and Scarlett O'Hara had once observed, tomorrow … is another day.

3

"The year that Washington
lost its mind"

"It was cultural as much as it was anything else. It was generational ... he liked modern music, he loved [New Hollywood] movies, he was a playful sort of guy. He was handsome and he liked movie stars. The old-line conservative forces in America didn't know what to make of him. I think the real answer is that this is the first president who reflected the social changes that had occurred in America.... Bill was in the anti-war movement; Hillary did the Watergate thing. [To conservatives] they were the 'culturally elite liberals who looked down on us, and we're going to put them in their place'... It wasn't just political opposition; it was visceral hatred.... The dislike of [Bill and Hillary] was not because of [their] policies...."
—*Clinton-era Cabinet members Dan Glickman, Mike McCurry, and Leon Panetta, as quoted at various times by Michael Takiff, in "A Complicated Man" (2010)*

By 1992, there was a feeling among Republicans of manifest destiny, that they were supposed to rule forever.... How could Clinton have won? Their only explanation was that he must have done something terrible. He must have cheated, because he wasn't supposed to win.

—*Michael Kinsley*

It was the literary icon Truman Capote who said in his final book that there were perhaps more tears shed over "Answered Prayers" than unanswered ones. And a saying as old as folklore itself has warned feckless humans to "Be careful what you wish for." It was advice that Bill Clinton and his "New" Democrats could have used during their first two years at the helm in 1993 and '94. They had finally made the Democratic dream come true, winning back the White House for the first time in a dozen years, and only the second time in a quarter-century. The election of 1992 had been all about "The Man from Hope."

Talk about irrational exuberance! (Indeed, the Obama-mania of 2008 was in many ways just a remake of 1992's "Man from Hope" election—and its disappointing comedown.) "Bill Clinton had not been president more than five minutes before many Democrats began reacting in horror" that their man "wasn't a plaster saint," snarked perceptive Clinton loyalist Michael Kinsley in the spring of 1996, as he looked back on the carcinogenic Washington environment of early 1993. Many of those Democrats had apparently forgotten that it was Clinton's very ruthlessness and less-than-saintliness that had enabled him to stand up and win in the first place, after previous Democrats like Walter Mondale and Michael Dukakis had been eaten for lunch by the right-wing noise machine.

In addition to Republicans, still in post-traumatic denial of what had just happened,

Washington was chock-full of a lot of resentful *old* Democrats, who understood neither Bill and Hillary Clinton themselves nor the very specific reasons why they had been able to win. Before Clinton's first year in office was over, the one thing that united the established political pros in Congress would be this bipartisan sense of jealousy. Now that Bill Clinton's "New Democrats" were actually in the hot seat at 1600 Pennsylvania Avenue, they were about to learn in no uncertain terms that they would need a whole lot less "hope" (and a helluva lot more *audacity*) just in order to survive. And they'd learn that lesson the hard way.

In 2014, *New Republic* contributor Jonathan Chait looked back on the political atmosphere that kicked off while he was a political-junkie college student, twenty years earlier, and correctly noted that the line from 2014's "Obama vs. the Tea Party" politics, to the 1993–94 war between the (then-Democratic) Congress and the Clintons, was a straight one. It was quite simply, in Chait's bluntly honest phrase, "The year that Washington lost its mind."

Fantasy Island

During the 1992 campaign, as we have previously noted, many high-profile journalists (especially Baby Boomer neoliberal opinion-magazine gurus) fell in love with Bill Clinton—or rather, with "the [Bill] Clinton of their imagination," as Eric Alterman noted in his book *What Liberal Media*. Here, they fantasized, was a president who "would call [them] in the middle of the night and ask for advice," when he wasn't "shooting the breeze" with them. Clinton "loved to talk about serious things" gushed Joe Klein—a marked contrast to the let-them-eat-cake, old Hollywood and old money distance of Nancy Reagan and Barbara Bush's husbands. And he "seemed to be up on every social program in America." Alterman hit the bullseye when he said that the Liberal Media—in particular the Baby Boomer, Ivy-educated, *neo*-liberal media, "eagerly awaited the arrival in Washington of a regime that appreciated their vast knowledge of 'the process,' and enjoyed their company at state dinners followed by late-night bull sessions in the Private Residence." Why, it'd be almost like hanging with the cool kids in college (or better—prep school) once again. And Candidate Clinton gave them every reason to fantasize.

But the romance quickly went sour. The charming seducer who loved journalists disappeared on Election Day and was replaced by a president who seemed to hate reporters, when he bothered to think about them at all. Far from regarding or flattering them as his intellectual equals, he now seemed to view the press with contempt. He and his wife knew far more about "the political process" in their little fingers than they ever did. While the elite opinion journos and cable pundits still clung to their ideal role-playing scenarios, Bill Clinton had to actually *deal with* a racially and generationally fractured public, and a furiously reactionary "Tea Party 1.0" building within the Republican Party—with figures like Newt Gingrich, Rush Limbaugh, Tom DeLay, Dick Cheney, Mitch McConnell, Jesse Helms, and Trent Lott now waiting in the wings. (Not to mention a radicalized Religious Right, who viewed the draft-dodging, dope-smoking, Russia-visiting, immovably pro-choice, feminist, and gay-envelope-pushing Clintons as a veritable abomination.)

While some have put this down to a sort of "blame the bitch" school of logic, by most accounts it was actually Hillary who rang down the iron curtain around Team Bill after they were safely inaugurated. And after Gennifer Flowers and the "bimbo eruptions" of the 1992 campaign, can anyone blame her? High ranking conservative moneymen like Carnegie-Mellon banking heir Richard Mellon Scaife, energy gurus like the (in)famous Koch Brothers, and future Fox News topper Roger Ailes were just a few of the high-profile and high-income Right who had been outraged at the nakedly pro–Clinton bias of the elite press in 1992. And they quickly began doing something about it—big time. They lavishly funded new "newsmagazines" and opinion journals of the hard right like *The American Spectator* and *The Weekly Standard* that were to *National Review* and *Atlantic Monthly* almost what *Hustler* and *LA X-Press* were to *Playboy* and *Penthouse.* Pure red meat, filled with anti–Clinton and anti-liberal conspiracy theories, and replete with stories of conservatives as "victims" of Big Government horror shows.

That was only the beginning. Trashy and superficially non-political "magazine" shows like *American Journal, Hard Copy, A Current Affair,* and *Inside Edition* (starring none other than Bill O'Reilly at the time) were always on the lookout, like snarling watchdogs, for any hints of scandal. As were AIDS-era gays and "radical feminist" journalists and academics, who believed in "outing" public figures' private lives to make political statements. The Gennifer Flowers adultery mess that almost smothered Hillary's husband's campaign in its crib was soon followed by former Arkansas staffer Paula Jones coming out of the closet about the sexual harassment and near-rape she'd allegedly suffered at Clinton's hands when he was Arkansas governor. Right-wing media mavens also demanded an inquiry into the Clintons' late '70s and '80s real-estate investments (what ultimately became the Whitewater scandal). After all that, can anybody blame Hillary for adopting a defensive "bad cop" posture with the press?

The same dynamic was true amidst the pillars of Washington high society. *Washington Post* doyenne Sally Quinn, arguably DC's most powerful hostess as the wife of legendary *Post* editor and board member Ben Bradlee, tossed off an article less than two weeks after the Clintons' election. It had a shockingly blunt and in-your-face title: "Welcome to Washington—but Play by OUR Rules!" To underline the point, her next item up for bids at year's end in 1992 was frankly titled, "Beware of Washington."

"Washington is not Little Rock," Quinn scolded. If the Clintons decided that they didn't "need [the] help" of what author Michael Takiff would later term "Permanent Washington," then, Quinn warned, "don't be surprised if you end up with poison darts in your back." Quinn finished by reminding the new First Couple that "when the Clinton Administration is gone and forgotten … the Establishment will remain." Journalist and Washington Establishment pillar David Broder would later echo those thoughts, adding, "He came in here and trashed the place—and it's not even his place!" (A curious way to refer to the president of the United States, sitting commander-in-chief, and leader of the free world. After all, if Washington, D.C., isn't the president's "place," then where or what exactly is? Curious, that is, unless you were reading between the lines.)

Listening to the columnists and Congressional careerists clucking and chattering in the year after Clinton's election, one isn't so much reminded of typical Serious Washington Jibber-Jabber in the Henry Kissinger/Alan Greenspan mode, as of dialogue outtakes from an "industry" party scene in a Julia Phillips or Joan Didion bestseller. Georgetown divas started pointedly using phrases like "This Town" to refer to Washington, in just the same way that Sue Mengers and Ronni Chasen did back in '70s New Hollywood, when referring to the movie and TV biz. (One can easily imagine one of these DC mavens commenting, "We don't go for strangers in Washington!") To put it a bit more charitably, as Eric Alterman wisely said, most of these status-conscious society types were simply "never asked to face the kinds of difficult choices that a president had to make every day." Especially a generationally game-changing Democrat, coming after 12 years straight of Republican rule.

"The man-woman and bitch goddess"

"There's no sin like being a woman," vamped the flamboyantly gay British literary and theatre icon Quentin Crisp, in one of his final interviews. And for twenty years after what was then called "Womens' Lib" first broke open in the early '70s, that was still nowhere truer than if the woman in question didn't happen to be empathetic, maternal, and automatically nurturing.

The power-wielding and power-suited cutthroat female attorney who was now our nation's First Lady (and was rumored to be, with good reason, our nation's Second-in-Command) was about to find herself branded as the biggest and baddest castrating-bitch of them all. But this was not exactly *terra incognito* for Hillary Rodham Clinton.

After graduating law school and marrying Bill, Hillary had put on her shoulder pads (if not her jock strap, some sexist folk might have joked) and essentially supported the Clinton household during the go-go '80s, while Bubba pursued his expensive, campaign-financed political career. While Bill Clinton got to live in the governor's mansion of Arkansas, with chauffeurs, company cars and household help, plus free health insurance paid for by the taxpayers, his actual take-home pay as governor of his small, largely rural state was less than what a relatively experienced police officer, public school teacher, or insurance salesman in a major coastal city would have made back then. It was Hillary who brought down the six-figure income, Hillary who palled around with the boards of big companies like Walmart and Tyson Foods, Hillary who had invested most of the money in what would become the notorious Whitewater land development deal.

This fact already had a lot of Old Boys in Old Washington nervously crossing their legs for protection. It was made even worse when Hillary, in a "show of force" worthy of Dick Cheney himself, opened up a business office for herself in the heart of the White House, complete with her own staff. The shocked gasps and raised eyebrows from Permanent Washington, with its demure debutante wives and on-the-side "kept" mistresses, were worthy of a Broadway comedy. It was so unlike the plain-speakin' reverse snobbery of Bess Truman, and the "I turn the lamb chops while Ike runs the country" self-effacement of Mamie Eisenhower, or the tragic steel-magnolia loveliness of Lady Bird Johnson, Rosalyn Carter, and Pat Nixon. It went beyond even the matriarchal outspokenness of Barbara Bush and Betty Ford, or the society dry ice of Jackie and Nancy. Not since Eleanor Roosevelt herself had Hillary Clinton a true precedent for First Lady.

When post-feminist and out lesbian author Camille Paglia famously (and basically approvingly) referred to Hillary in *The New Republic* as "Hillary the man-woman and bitch goddess," many liberals and feminists took offense—but it was clear that the offense was mainly because of how painfully accurate Paglia was. A butched-up "man-woman" and a nighttime soap opera-style "bitch goddess" was in fact *exactly* how Hillary was perceived, by both friend and foe alike. To many liberated career women, Hillary was the first First Lady whom they could directly relate to as a diva-licious personal role model: a college-educated professional woman who held decision-maker positions with deadline pressure, and balanced a difficult husband, an active social life, and raising a daughter at home.

Yet for every woman who elatedly cheered a "You go, girl!" at Hillary Rodham Clinton, there was another man—and in many cases, another *woman*—who was horrified by this non-maternal, bottom-line businesswoman and ball-busting boss. They felt as insulted by her perceived disdain of their simpler, home-and-family oriented ways of life as they imagined she no doubt felt contempt for people like them. One of the campier moments of Campaign 1992 was when Hillary stirred up a tempest in a tea pot, by saying to the effect that going out and having a fulfilling and lucrative career was a better use of her time and law-school education than staying home and "baking cookies." The Republican spin machine immediately spun this as a coded attack on wife/mother homemakers, and working-class women who had *jobs,* not "careers." (This was especially true among evangelical values voters. Remember, this was *before* the Sarah Palin and Michelle Bachmann era of pit-bulls with lipstick. In 1992, the ideal fundamentalist woman was still living in the world of Anita Bryant, Phyllis Schlafly, Beverly LaHaye, and Tammy Faye Bakker, albeit perhaps with a little less makeup or glamour. "Biblically submitting" to her head-of-household husband, and deriving her main value as a person from her house and home.)

"There's Going to Be a Co-President—But She's Not Al Gore!"

When Al Gore initially started work under Bill Clinton, you couldn't throw a stone in a Washington or New York newsroom without hitting someone who was working on a profile piece about how much "unprecedented" power and authority Bill Clinton was investing in his vice president. But what Clinton gave Gore to do was nothing compared to the power that George W. Bush would invest in Dick Cheney just eight years later—or for that matter, the power that Bill Clinton's outspoken and accomplished wife would have *right now*. An article in the *New York Times Magazine* (quoted again in Sally Bedell Smith's 2007 book, *For the Love of Politics*) summed things up succinctly: "Al Gore hasn't realized yet that there *is* going to be a co-presidency—but *he's* not going to be part of the 'co!'" Longtime Clinton collaborator and adviser Susan Thomases added that Gore "would have to adjust to a smaller role," and Bedell Smith related that many of Clinton's inner circle had nicknamed the stuck-up VP as "Dudley Do-Right" behind his back. (It wasn't exactly meant as a compliment.)

As time went on, Al Gore indeed found a very useful (and as it turned out, very necessary) niche to fill in the new Clinton government. The high-IQ, research-addicted, information-sponging journalism major Gore would become Bill's best intellectual "chess partner," the one Bill would ask for advice, stage debates, and argue with so that he could see all sides of an issue. The one who would keep the famously peripatetic and restless Clinton laser-focused on the proper course. And if Bill was dithering or unsure of whether he should go *this* way or *that,* with the Congress or Federal Reserve or the Pentagon, Al Gore could be counted on to be Bill's GPS.

Except there was one gaping flaw. In both classicist literature and in the movies and on TV, it's usually the older and wiser doctor, lawyer, detective, king, or businessman who has to keep and mould the headstrong young pup into the responsible gentleman that he was always meant to be. In *this* movie, it was the headstrong and self-indulgent Big Dawg who had all the power, clout, and media profile; and it was the mature grown-up who was playing second chair, disempowered and dependent on the Prodigal Son. In Broadway or movie terms, Al Gore was the Salieri—but Bill Clinton was the Mozart.

In 2001, Marjorie Williams wrote the definitive essay on the Clinton/Gore relationship, with the tongue-in-cheek title "Scenes from a Marriage." (The accompanying illustration was as campy as a cross-dressing Bugs Bunny cartoon: a disheveled Bubba schlumpfing in an Archie Bunker easy chair watching TV, while his prissy "wife" Al—complete with lace apron—shot daggers at Bill while doing the dishes.) To use Williams' "marriage" metaphor, Al was playing the role of the bossy wife, constantly nagging on Bill to fix this or that, *kvetching* about her household allowance, putting a wet blanket on the guys' dirty jokes, always telling little Billy to do his homework and clean his room.

In an especially revealing aside, Williams recalled Gore wistfully noting, midway through the Clinton administration's run, that he had never once been invited to Clinton's famous after-hours "movie nights" in the White House projection room. (No doubt they were often jam-packed with glammy celebrity friends of Bill, like David Geffen, Judy Collins, sitcom royalty Markie Post and Linda Bloodworth-Thomason, George Clooney, and Babs Streisand, who were all in and out of the White House practically at will throughout the Clinton years.) One can only feel sorry for Al Gore, as one would towards a bullied Asperger's elementary schooler, or an overweight and acne-ridden high school student wondering why nobody liked him, completely unable to pick up the cues. Bill Clinton would probably no sooner have invited Al Gore to movie night than Al Bundy from *Married … with Children* would have invited his harpy wife Peg to poker night, or out to Hooters with the guys. As valuable and essential a member of Team Clinton as Al Gore was, he had consigned himself (or had *been consigned*) to the "Miss Jane Hathaway" role of efficient office-husband and human resources martinet from 8 o'clock to 6. And movie nights were for friends and play—not for Debbie Downer!

Family Feud

Bill Clinton's campaign slogan in 1992 had been, "It's the Economy, Stupid." Sixteen years later, Barack Obama took office facing an even worse meltdown. The big difference was that Obama's two biggest projects during his first two years (Obamacare and the Wall Street and General Motors bailouts) were at least directly related to the economy, if not to the direct point of job creation. Tellingly, Bill Clinton's first signature policy issue in early 1993 was heavy on culture war—and zippo on jobs.

During the '92 campaign, liberal-ish reporter Andrea Mitchell (though she was married to Republican icon Alan Greenspan) had asked President Clinton if—after reaching out to the LGBT community and speaking out forthrightly for AIDS funding like no other presidential candidate ever dared to—if he was going to keep the military's ages-old ban on gay and lesbian service people. Clinton hemmed and hawed like the politician he was, but basically said to the effect that he wanted to get rid of it. And as it happened, Clinton couldn't have avoided the issue of sexual politics in the military for much longer even if he'd wanted to.

As Clinton took office in early 1993, the sordid details of what came to be known as the Tailhook Scandal were coming to light. During a military post-mortem conference on the seemingly successful Desert Storm (first Gulf War) held in Las Vegas in September of 1991, over 83 women (and seven men) claimed to have been the victims of rape, improper sexual conduct, or gross harassment, by over 100 of the Marine officers in attendance. The Tailhook Scandal would scintillate the front pages of newspapers and magazines and the CNN and nightly news shows like nothing since Anita Hill, and would be used as ripped-from-the-headlines fodder on top TV dramas like *Law & Order* and *LA Law* during 1993–94.

As to the gays-in-the-military issue, it wasn't just Rush Limbaugh or Newt Gingrich who was stirring the pot. The showiest Senate showboat on the gay issue was none other than Bill Clinton and Al Gore's fellow Southern Democratic Leadership Committee founder, Georgia Senator Sam Nunn, pandering to his socially conservative and religious Southern base. (Many high-ranking military figures and Joint Chiefs members, including Colin Powell, also vocally opposed allowing open gays in back then.) Clinton may have been commander in chief, but under Nunn's demagogic leadership, the Senate Armed Services Committee declared jihad on the idea, fearing that it would "demoralize" straight soldiers if they were "forced" to share showers, bunks, latrines, etc., with open gays.

As with everything in post–Willie Horton, post–Rodney King 1990s *politik*, the gay issue was really just a kabuki-democracy "coded appeal" and "dog whistle" for a far more damaging issue, one that would cut to the quick of all of Bill Clinton's foreign and military policies for the rest of his run. As almost everybody knows—and as everybody over the age of 12 not attached to life-support equipment knew back in 1992—Bill Clinton had openly dodged the Vietnam draft.

It was appalling enough that HE was going to be the Commander in Chief of brave men and women in uniform, after he'd taken the so-called coward's way out. But to then use the military itself as nothing more than a politically correct social engineering experiment? *This means war!*

With conservative Republicans up in arms (and not a few "Blue Dog" Democrats from the red states—many of whose states still had "anti-sodomy" laws on the books, making all gay relationships, let alone "gay marriage," an actual crime), the bitterly fought-over compromise deal became known as "Don't Ask, Don't Tell." The military could no longer specifically accuse people ahead of time or screen people out for gay or lesbian tendencies—as long as they remained closeted and/or discreet in their private lives. But if a gay or lesbian officer was "caught" in bed, or holding hands or kissing on their "roommate" or "buddy," it would still be "So long, Soldier!" While not satisfying for the gay community or the military (or fans of equal protection in the Constitution), the important thing was now saving face, and moving this otherwise intractable issue off the agenda, so that Clinton and the Congress could focus on "the economy, stupid." Both sides could walk away and declare victory, or moan about their "defeat," depending on whatever was politically expedient at the time. While Clinton himself would denounce DADT in today's more tolerant climate for LGBT equality, back in the '90s, he could say that at least he had tried, had put himself out on the line for you guys (and gals) in the gay movement—which was more than any other president had ever done, up to that point.

Offensive though many might rightfully find DADT in light of today's more open and visible era, in 1993 at the height of the AIDS epidemic, it was actually a great leap forward for gays in society. Not least of which because the gay community's most intractable enemies viewed DADT as a total win for gay people, and a loss for their beliefs in morality and tradition. At best, the hard right could freely fulminate that, although they had thwarted the decadent Clinton from total victory *this* time, DADT was only proof that *unless we fought him tooth and claw, unless we never give him one inch,* he would surely destroy us all with his godless, button-pushing, vulgar immorality.

Then there was the one other issue that was guaranteed to hit just as raw a cultural nerve as gay rights, religion, the race card, and even abortion. *Gun control.* In February of 1987, a new law called The Brady Act was introduced in the Congress for the first time. The law was named for former Reagan White House press secretary James Brady, who was shot and confined to a wheelchair by John Hinckley in Hinckley's March 1981 attempt to assassinate Ronald Reagan. The Brady Bill would be a computer-era strengthening of the Great Society's "Gun Control Act of 1968," requiring that all legal purchasers of a handgun or firearms be subject to an FBI database background check, to confirm that the would-be purchaser lived at their provided address, and had no felony or mental hospital convictions on their records. (Initially, in mostly pre–Internet 1993–94, this necessitated a "waiting period" of up to five days to clear a subject; however, by the end of the '90s, most Brady checks could be done same-day on the phone or online, while the customer was still in the store.)

Ronald Reagan himself editorialized in favor of the law, two years after retiring from office, and both he and President Bush had indicated that they would've signed the law if it had passed both houses of Congress during their reigns. But that "if" had so far proved to be an impossible dream. The National Rifle Association and many other conservative groups spent millions in lobbying and pressure to stop the bill, fearful of more "big government" and federalized intrusion into people's lives, afraid that if the Brady bill cracked the door open to strict gun control, another law would come barreling in right behind it like an elephant.

They were right. At virtually the same time as the Brady Act was being debated and passed in fall 1993 (to take effect in early 1994), Clinton let loose with his other big gun-control priority: an Assault Weapons Ban, proposed at the height of gangsta "drive-by shootings" in the ghettos and barrios of Harlem, Detroit, Chicago, Baltimore, and South-Central LA. Further impetus came with one of the first modern-day examples of school shootings, the horrific rampage of a homeless young man with a long history of severe mental illness and addiction, outside of a Sacramento-area elementary school in January of 1989. The murderer went on a racist rampage against Asian children, killing five and wounding 30 (before committing his long-overdue suicide), using a semi-automatic rifle capable of firing over 100 rounds in under 3 minutes. In response, California enacted an Assault Weapons Ban, after which President Bush (Sr.) banned the importation of foreign assault weapons. Clinton's Federal Assault Weapons Ban finally passed the Congress and Senate in November 1993, and just after that victory, retired Presidents Gerald Ford, Jimmy Carter, and Ronald Reagan all spoke out in favor of extending the ban to semi-automatic assault guns, which was added to the law by September of 1994.

So to recap: Ford was for it, Carter was for it, Bush Sr., was for it, even Reagan was for it. But the NRA and the rising talk-radio and conservative commentators were against it, not only for the precedent of what they felt would be more federal "Trojan horse" interference into the lives of the vast majority of law-abiding gun owners, but also to deny President Clinton yet another political victory.

While the NRA had been handed one of its few defeats in this instance, the voters for whom "law and order" wasn't just a TV show had scored huge with the overall passage of the Violent Crime Control and Law Enforcement Act in 1993–94—of which the Assault Weapons Ban was a part. The "Crime Bill" was the largest law enforcement act in United States history, taking federalized control of innumerable offenses that used to be handled at the state level. The Olympian reach of the Crime Bill included the first major federal "hate crimes laws" that would became the hot political-correctness item during Clinton's second term and throughout Bush II and Obama—making murder or assault a federal crime if it was found to be motivated by racial or sexual prejudice. 50 new federal offenses were added, and both the death penalty and incarceration terms were vastly expanded. Following the lead of one of California and Nevada's most popular ballot initiatives, the bill included a "3 Strikes" provision making life imprisonment automatic for criminals convicted of certain third offenses.

As for the political optics, the Crime Bill had something for everyone to love—and hate. Conservatives loved that even the dope-smoking Hippie-in-Chief was now taking urban crime and "gangsta" culture seriously—but hated that Big Government was shoving aside state and county district attorneys and judges to handle everything at the federal level. (Social conservatives also fought tooth and claw against the inclusion of LGBT people as a protected class under hate crime legislation.) Liberals loved the federal activism part, especially the Violence Against Women Act, and neoliberals and moderates adored that Clinton had taken one of the Republicans' top talking points away from them: that the Democrats were "soft on crime" and indifferent to the legitimate fears that seniors and suburbanites had. But left wing voices considered the Crime Bill to be a virtual war on African American and Latino youths—and they were incensed at the vast ramping-up of Ronald Reagan's "war on drugs" (and from an ex-hippie president, too!), and at the repeal of Pell Grants for prisoners to receive free college-equivalency instruction and classes while in jail. Liberal journalist and activist JoAnn Wypijewski fumed that "Between Clinton's inaugural and the day he left office, 700,000 more persons were incarcerated," and that they were mostly minority young men, with the least chances in life to begin with.

The Crime Bill. Gun Control. Gays in the Military. Compared to the glacial pace of Congressional and Senate domestic legislation under Ronald Reagan's second term (and all of Bush Senior's), the Clinton Congress seemed to be almost frantic with its laundry list of domestic policies, like the Cookie Monster let loose at a Hometown Buffet, like a screaming contestant on an exciting game show. The 1993–94 Congress was passing more game-changers-per-minute than anything since Lyndon Johnson, Richard Nixon, and Martin Luther King. However, these battles were mere practice sessions compared to the economic main events that would define not only Bill Clinton's first two years in office, but largely the entire trajectory of pre–9/11 domestic politics on all sides. For better, and for worse.

Home Economics

With deficit-mania the hottest tune on the charts in Washington thanks to Ross Perot's constant squaking about "The Daff'cit!" and with Democrats determined to draw a line in the sand separating today's era from Reagan-Bush, inaction on the Federal budget was not an option. This terrified the Republican and conservative Congressional minority (and fat-cat lobbyists on all sides), who had become only more and more adamantine to keep every jot and tittle of Reaganomics intact now that Reagan (and old Bush) were gone. Conservative talk radio and op-ed columns ignited, warning people that Clinton was just another old tax-and-spend liberal in today's up-to-date fashions. There was no question that taxes were going to go up, which settled the "tax" part of the equation right off the bat. And with everyone from pundits and economists like *Newsweek's* Robert Samuelson and CNN's Michael Kinsley, to Federal Reserve royalty like Alan Greenspan and former chair Paul Volcker, flat-out *demanding* cuts in "entitlements" and domestic programs, Clinton's economic Priority One would have to be to *prove* that he wasn't Mr. Big Spender.

As the University of California at Berkeley noted, Clinton's initial proposal included massive investments in infrastructure, technology, and job-retraining education for displaced workers in a new economy. "However, these proposals were largely gutted during Congressional negotiations." And fuggedabout a middle-class tax cut; while most working taxpayers would see their rates stay largely the same (and the poorest households would get an Earned Income Tax Credit—the idea for which started out as a Republican plan under Nixon), they'd get no real tax relief either. But they'd sure share the pain, with more cuts to schools, colleges, libraries, and other state and local services, not to mention a 4-cents-a-gallon increase in gasoline and energy taxes.

The Clinton budget raised top rates from 31 percent to 39.6 percent, for the richest percentage of American households ($250,000 a year in taxable 1994 dollars), as it stood for final passage. (This was still roughly 25 or 30 points lower than the top rates that had prevailed until Ronald Reagan's tax cut package of 1981.) The corporate income tax would rise, though by only 2 percentage points, and only for corporations with profits in excess of $10 million a year. Most unappetizing from a public-relations point of view was that the percentage of Social Security benefits subject to tax would rise dramatically for high-income seniors with "Cadillac" pensions or big investment portfolios. (Rich or not, raising taxes on Granny and Grandpa was no way to win a popularity contest.)

In plainer language, Bill Clinton would have to force people to *pay more money* in tax with one hand—while *cutting back money* on vital services with the other. Even on things like Social Security, Medicare, emergency services, and education. And the military was already reeling from post Cold War base closures and musterings-out of redundant soldiers. It was the worst of worst-case scenarios. And just when the political environment couldn't have gotten any worse or more controversial—it did.

Nebraska Senator Bob Kerrey, a Vietnam veteran who'd been defeated by the draft-dodging Clinton early on in the 1992 primaries (not to be confused with Sen. John Kerry of Massachusetts), was a Jerry Brown-style, more-righteous-than-thou, "era of limits" Democrat who theatrically toyed with refusing to vote for the Clinton budget. Unlike his fellow Dems, this was not because it provided *too little relief* to working-class households trying to claw out of the early '90s recession—but because it *spread too little pain!* "Playing

Hamlet," as several newspapers called him, a quote "anguished" Kerrey crocodile-teared to the press that his heart "ached" because he was about to vote for a bill that "challenges Americans too *little.*"

The tension between the two men had come to a head in a phone call, recalled by journalist Michael Takiff in 2010. Clinton told Sen. Kerrey, "If I don't win this [budget battle], I just might go back to Arkansas." With nary a whiff of deference to the president, Kerrey smugly tossed back, "That's an option. I wouldn't recommend it, but that's an option you'll have if this doesn't pass." Clinton's hanging-up reply was succinct and no doubt heartfelt: "Go fuck yourself!" Kerrey finally voted for Clinton's budget, but he still cruelly rubbed it in, wailing on C-SPAN from the Senate floor like a daytime soap confession, "Get back on the high road, Mr. President, where you are at your best!" As it stood now, Kerrey said, if working and middle class fathers, single moms, and retired seniors "notice, I will be surprised, and if they complain, I will be ashamed."

Get out the dunce cap, Sen. Kerrey, because they noticed all right—and they complained! *The Los Angeles Times* correctly adjudged that "every lawmaker voting for [the budget] was well aware that they were going home to voters who are outraged over the bill's tax increases and spending cuts." "Put down your remote and grab your wallet," warned venerable Republican Senate icon Bob Dole. "I guess the Democrats are going to go out and celebrate. We nailed the rich, we nailed the successful, and we nailed the people who are creating the jobs." As the *Times* further noted, "Republican after Republican rattled off cataclysmic forecasts of massive job losses and warned that the Clinton plan would devastate … an already fragile economic recovery."

Meanwhile, many House Democrats were red with anger at the 1993–94 budget for shredding the social, educational, and fair-pay safety nets during a recession and a weak initial recovery. Former House staffer Lawrence O'Donnell later recalled that he felt Bill Clinton was actually "far more conservative than Ronald Reagan. I don't think there was [truly] liberal governance during the Bill Clinton years. [Newt] Gingrich [later] forced big spending cuts on Clinton, but in '93, Clinton started with what, for Democrats, were *extraordinary* spending cuts. It was actually, as of that time," before George W. Bush, "the most conservative governance we had had."

Of course, that last little line gave away the game that would define the grammar of politics under Clinton, Bush II, and Obama. Clinton might well have been the "most conservative" president we'd had to that point, *economically*—but no one else had been as pro-gay, pro-choice, pro-feminist, minority-friendly, or *culturally* liberal, and no president would be until Obama. As Thomas Frank and others have noted, the Clinton era was when the definition of "liberal" and "conservative" was redefined from being first and foremost about money, taxes, and foreign affairs, to how you voted on sexual, racial, lifestyle, and religious hot buttons. If Hillary was a "man-woman," then Bill Clinton was a conservative-leftist– or really, more like a political Rorschach test. When someone said that Bill Clinton "was" this or that, it revealed a lot more about the person who was *saying* what he was than it revealed what Bill Clinton *actually* was. And it's been that way ever since.

Freshman Pennsylvania Congresswoman Marjorie Margolies-Mezvinsky, swept to power in an otherwise rock-ribbed old line Republican district during post–Anita Hill "year of the woman" power in 1992, was almost one of those House Democrats. She planned on symbolically voting against the Clinton budget because she wished it provided more relief and less discomfort. But realizing the stakes, both for the deficit and the cost of inaction, of maintaining an untenable status quo, she said that she would probably vote for it if it came right down to the wire.

It did. Like a courtroom drama or movie thriller, with the ominous soundtrack thundering away, the vote was neck-and-neck. Once again previewing the Obamacare/Tea Party wars, not a single solitary Republican House representative (or even senator)—from Los Angeles to Louisville, from Manhattan to Muskogee—would vote in favor of the bill. And plenty of Democrats were already voting nay. As if a camera was framing her for history, whether she was ready or not for her close-up, the turn fell upon Congresswoman Mezvinsky...

She said "yes!" The budget deal would pass! Clintonomics was officially underway.

"Bye-bye, Marjorie!!" the Republican congressmen hooted and hollered at her, openly waving their white hankies at her from the floor of the Congress, as she cast her vote and doubtlessly bit back the tears with humiliation, anger, and dread. (Of course, Mezvinsky knew at that very moment that the Republicans would spare no expense to bring her down and make an example of her. After this kind of "betrayal," they would put out a political hit on her as mercilessly as John Travolta and Samuel L. Jackson from *Pulp Fiction*. And they did—Mezvinsky lost her seat in a punishingly cruel defeat the very next year.)

A New World Order

For all their Perot-like emphasis on cutting the deficit and debt, Team Clinton did have one major point of departure with the Perot-istas: the North American Free Trade Agreement (NAFTA), which New Democrats Clinton and Gore supported, and Perot had violently opposed. Perot predicted that free trade with low-wage, often corrupt Latin America would herald a "giant sucking sound" of working and middle class jobs being outsourced.

Charlene Barshefsky was another one of Bill Clinton's glass-ceiling shatterers, acting as Deputy U.S. Trade Representative under Mickey Kantor. (She ascended to the top post in 1996 when Kantor replaced Ron Brown, killed in a plane crash, as secretary of commerce.) "It got nasty," she said in the understatement of the year, when discussing the one signature Clinton law that was just as controversial as gun control and raising taxes would be. NAFTA had originally been written under Ronald Reagan, largely by the right-wing Heritage Foundation, as a way to increase multinational corporate profits and break labor unions. And to try and stop the continuous mass *imigracion* of Cesar Chavez-voting, proletarian, non–English-speaking Latinos that were already tidal-waving across the border by the 1980s, in California, Arizona, and Texas. NAFTA had been signed by Old Bush as he was practically out the door, in December of 1992—but the Clinton-era Democratic Congress of 1993–94 still had to ratify it.

And therein lay the drama. Talk about a lump of coal in the Christmas stocking! Aside from the straight-ahead economic implications, the big question for President Clinton was, "What [would be] the cost to the US of repudiating Mexico?" Barshefsky recalled that the U.S. (under Reagan and Bush Sr.) had "pushed Mexico, 'Do NAFTA, Do NAFTA!'" And after Mexico finally *does* NAFTA, signing the basic agreement, how could America now turn around and renege on its promise, without looking like a traitor—or worse, like a bunch of stark raving *racists*—to Mexico and the Hispanic community as a whole? With the fast-growing Latino population quickly becoming second only to African Americans and coastal Jews as a lynchpin of the Democratic Party in states like California, Texas, Arizona, Nevada, and New York, saying that the U.S. would renounce NAFTA was "almost unthinkable" to Clinton economic guru Lawrence Summers. Let alone to the pro-free-trade Federal Reserve chief Alan Greenspan, then at the summit of his influence.

With the controversy needle already having been turned up to "11" by all the other songs on the 1993 political hit parade, Clinton decided that he needed to sell NAFTA and World Trade to the American public. Using his then-unparalleled media savvy, he arranged for a debate with Ross Perot himself, to be held on Larry King's iconic CNN talk show, in the fall of 1993. CNN and King eagerly agreed, correctly sensing that it would be a ratings needle-breaker for the cable channel. Perhaps showing even more (cynical) media savvy, Clinton decided that instead of him or Hillary debating Perot, he would send Vice President Al Gore in his stead. The information-addicted Gore jumped at the chance, to show off that he was a Partner in Power (just like Hillary), the most "important" vice president in pre–Cheney America. His staff compiled as devastating a stack of statistics and evidence as Marcia Clark or Johnnie Cochran going into a trial. But that was just the beginning.

Gore deliberately baited the tightly wound, temperamental Perot, presenting him with a "gift"—a photograph of his intellectual forbearers, the notoriously isolationist Senators Reed Smoot and Willis Hawley, the namesakes of the Smoot-Hawley Tariffs of the early '30s, widely credited by economists as prolonging the Great Depression. Perot became almost as furious as a Donald Duck cartoon, reducing what had been a serious, 1950s-style issues-and-answers debate to a 1990s or 2000s-style reality show—which was *exactly* what Clinton's media gurus were hoping for! Every salesman, from a door-to-door nobody to Donald Trump, knows the saying: "Sell the sizzle—not the steak." Perot was coming off as irrational and batty, like *Sesame Street's* "H. Ross Parrot" or an SNL parody—totally discrediting him in the eyes of columnists, professionals, and many congressmen.

The debate literally saved NAFTA. It passed before 1993 was out, with GATT and the modern-day iteration of the World Trade Organization conference being set up by the end of the following year. But while the debate was a success for Clinton's policy goals, it was an epic fail for the Democratic brand among both "white working class" voters and left wing firebrands alike. And it would prove to be a public relations nightmare for Al Gore, as he vainly (and very unsuccessfully) tried to go populist when running for president seven years later. All the negative media stereotypes about what a cold-hearted lab geek Al Gore was, about him being a robotic "Al Gore-ithm" or "Gore-acle" (as Rush Limbaugh would joke), began truly crystallizing with this debate, with his smug, provocative, even cruel path to victory over Ross Perot.

Now, Al Gore had become the "face" of NAFTA. When Gore later found himself in the fight of his political life with George W. Bush, it was famously said that Bush Jr., was the guy "you wanted to have a beer with"—whereas Gore was like the horrible boss who came to fire you.

This is what Ralph Nader and Alexander Cockburn and Michael Moore were talking about in 1999 and 2000, when they said there was only "a dime's worth of difference" between Al Gore and George W. Bush, between Republicans and Democrats.

In another play-by-play prequel to when Republicans fiercely turned against the Republican-designed Romneycare healthcare model the minute that Barack Obama plagiarized it for his Obamacare plan, many Congressional Republicans came out hard and strong against the Reagan/Bush-written NAFTA. Although in fairness, the trouble had been brewing amongst Republicans for a full year before Clinton's election. Back in November of 1991, conservative think-tanker Paul Weyrich—who helped turn the Religious Right into the lynchpin of the Republican Party, and co-founded the very Heritage Foundation itself—called a press conference in Washington to denounce NAFTA. "We are here to warn the Republican Party that they had better take this issue seriously!" Weyrich's fellow Religious Right icon and Dixie Senate archconservative Jesse Helms loudly voted a "NO" on NAFTA when it finally came to a vote, as did several of his Southern protégés, including his favorite, Lauch Faircloth. And many more Republicans who ended up voting for NAFTA loudly said that the only reason was in the hope that it would staunch the flow of illegal Latinos (who, just like those ghetto-rapping and hip-hopping blacks before them) were threatening to essentially swamp America with a different culture. Not exactly what progressives (who opposed NAFTA for labor-clout reasons) wanted to hear.

House Minority Leader Newt Gingrich, already planning and plotting his way to the top, quickly voted in favor of the bill (which pleased his rich Republican check-writers no end)—and then booked himself on the lecture circuit and on Sunday and cable news shows to start pointing the finger at China, India, and Japan as the *real* threats. He certainly didn't want any of his "white working class" constituents to think he was for free trade indiscriminately, or just because it served big business interests. *Perish the thought!*

Still, most Clintonites and neoliberals smelled a big one, in the Republicans' two-faced rhetoric. "It would be inconceivable that dozens of Republicans in Congress would be against [NAFTA] if George Bush had been reelected," fumed Michael Kinsley in the *Los Angeles Times*. Kinsley rightly suspected that for as many true paleo-conservatives of the Ross Perot/Pat Buchanan school, there were just as many who were against NAFTA for no other reason than so they could "hand Bill Clinton a defeat, no matter what." Savvier Republicans also realized that the NAFTA vote was about to be the economic equivalent of when the Democrats threw Dixie under the bus during LBJ's Civil Rights era. If Republicans were members of the get-along gang, no one would care; but if the Republicans reached out olive branches and flowers to the "white working class" (and not a few African Americans who might lose their job security as well)—at the same time that Clinton's New Democrats were bidding Big Labor *adieu*—the GOP could potentially sop up millions of disillusioned formerly Democratic voters at the next election!

That little trick had already worked once before, back in 1980. The year before that, Jimmy Carter appointed tight-money guru and Wall Street veteran Paul Volcker to run the Fed, who immediately raised car and home loans to eye-popping 14 and 15 percent interest rates throughout '79 and '80, with interest for short-term credit hitting *Godfather*-levels of 20 percent by Carter's final month, so as to squeeze the runaway inflation of the late '70s. Carter had been just as merciless in prosecuting brand new Corporate Average Fuel Economy (CAFÉ) regulations, passed by the post–Watergate Democratic Congress under President Ford, with candidate Carter's strong agreement—requiring the immediate downsizing and total computer redesign of popular full- and mid-sized car lines. The regulations cost so much money to comply with that Chrysler and Ford almost went into bankruptcy.

No surprise that the domestic manufacturing industry fell into catastrophe, worse than any time since the Great Depression. Bursting with anger and betrayal at Carter, much if not most of Big Labor eagerly took time out from their 20-minute-long gasoline lines to vote for Ronald Reagan in 1980—the fabled "Reagan Democrats." (Alas, Ronnie wasted no time in effectively destroying union collective-bargaining powers, with Volcker's fervent approval, when he mass-fired a bunch of air-traffic controllers for daring to strike against him in 1981.) And now, after all that Campaign '92 noise about how Clinton would Put People First, Bill Clinton was about to deliver the lower middle class an even bigger, badder betrayal—right into the palms of the Republicans' hands!

By now, there was so much inflammatory palace drama in Permanent Washington, it was enough for a full season of *The West Wing, House of Cards,* or *Scandal* later on. The soapy, scandalous atmosphere infuriated plenty of Washington cocktail-party "consensus" types, who now began scheming and plotting like Cruella De Vil to put this uppity upstart couple ruining "their town" in their place. No matter what it took, or who else would get hurt. Healthcare Reform—that's *your* cue!

The Death Panel

The feudin' and fussin' over NAFTA (and its de facto creation of the modern-day World Trade Organization), the 1993–94 budget, and "guns, God, and gays" was only a mere warmup to the definitive political battle of Bill and Hillary Clinton's first half-term. It was no surprise to anyone by now that Bill had appointed Hillary to formulate what he hoped would be his government's signature policy initiative. And the "Hillarycare" bill sent the seethingly jealous Old Boys of the Congress and Senate, and the hard-liners still uncomfortable with women-folk having that kind of power, into coronary country.

After having spent most of 1993 in a closed-and-locked door commission with policy guru Ira Magaziner, Hillary unfurled her blueprint for remaking the nation's healthcare delivery and insurance system in the fall. No doubt many of the senators and congressmen were positively green with sexism, furious to find that this "man-woman bitch goddess" was trying to usurp their "Constitutional authority," that SHE had the temerity to try and tell *them* what to do. (*Someone doesn't know her place. Go back to the washing machine, honey, and iron my shirts!*) In Thomas Frank's book *What's the Matter with Kansas?*, he profiled a Kansan folk artist who, in the mid–1990s, erected a public authoritarian-art statue of Our First Lady, *Hitlery* Clinton. Healthcare Reform was Exhibit A: the artist had Hitlery proudly standing over her healthcare bill, dubbed on the plaque as nothing but, quote, "liberal vomit." (The artist's sentiments were not at all extreme or unusual on the ultra-right at the time. Rush Limbaugh was then making headlines for referring to "humorless" politically correct feminists as "Femi-Nazis.")

Indeed, what probably incited our sculptor's fury was the fact that healthcare was and is a literal "matter of life and death." What could be a bigger or badder expansion of Big Government, after all, *especially if you didn't want to expand Big Government in the first place,* then for it to have seeming control of end-of-life medical decisions? Or the potential power to ration who'll get chemo, bypasses, dialysis, hip replacements, AIDS cocktails—and who *wouldn't.* Whatever your feelings, the Republicans came up with the political line of the year, when they forecast that Hillarycare would deliver healthcare "with the efficiency of the Post Office, and the compassion of the IRS!"

Indeed, if people were still so wary of the spectre of "government run healthcare" in 2009 and '10 that "death panels" and "pulling the plug on Grandma" were major concerns, than just imagine what the atmosphere was like back in 1993 and '94. Healthcare was the smoking gun that "proved" once and for all just how totalitarian and power-hungry and I-know-better-than-you the Clintons and liberals were, in the conservative imagination. The Clintons were besieged on all sides.

After strenuously supporting the media-savvy, neoliberal, and hip Clintons in 1992 against out-of-date Bush Senior, the neoliberals of *The New Republic* now turned on the Clintons with a vengeance. (While then-editor Andrew Sullivan remained unapologetic for having helped defeat Hillarycare in 1994, he was one of the biggest cheerleaders for Obamacare sixteen years later.) In a front-cover article titled "No Exit," a Washington researcher and think-tanker named Betsy McCaughey wrote a lengthy attack on Hillarycare, aimed right at the senators, congressmen, and federal judges who gave *TNR* its nickname as the "in-flight magazine of Air Force One."

But Ms. McCaughey was far from fair or balanced. She had a long history of working with right-wing causes, and had just gotten a grant from the Manhattan Institute to work on a book-length attack on Willie Horton/Rodney King and AIDS-era "identity politics," with the subtitle *Overcoming the Narcissism of Minor Differences.* McCaughey supported the Clarence Thomas Supreme Court nomination, opposed the redistricting of Congressional districts and school systems to increase African American and Latino representation and integration, and supported restrictions on abortion. Still, *The New Republic* went full steam ahead with her—more for the sake of maintaining their all-important Kinsley/Peretz "contrarian" brand than anything else. While he was "aware of the piece's flaws," said then-editor Andrew Sullivan, he still decided to run the spot to "provoke a discussion." (The accent was apparently on *provoke.*) And did he ever!

Earlier, McCaughey had written a *Wall Street Journal* attack on Hillarycare which was published for maximum strategic damage within the same week as Bill's September 1993 national address on healthcare in America. McCaughey claimed the bill would have "devastating consequences" for American consumers, and when she came back for an encore in November 1993, she predicted "price controls" and "rationing" of healthcare services.

Most damningly of all, McCaughey claimed—and in all likelihood she was right on this score—that many Americans would be forced to give up their chosen doctors and be forced into stingy HMO (Health Maintenance Organizations) under Hillarycare. She came right out and said that people would be prevented or punished from going outside The System, in the name of so-called fairness and equality. True enough, but the late 1980s and the 1990s were the initial takeoff point for the rise in HMOs and "preferred provider" (PPOs) with pre-negotiated costs and treatment levels. As such, it was very likely that a lot of people wouldn't have been—*and weren't*—"allowed to keep" whatever local doctor they wanted, or to "make their own decisions" about healthcare for much longer in any case. Insurance companies and HMO's were *already* reviewing, second-guessing, and flat-out overruling "unnecessary" or "little chance of success" treatments, with red pens as busy as a book editor or IRS auditor. Indeed, that was one of the reasons why "health care reform" was such a must among progressives and liberals in the first place.

The real coded dog-whistle was what later became (in Obama-era parlance) the threat of "death panels." Despite the fact that Hillarycare said, in black-letter law, that "Nothing in this act shall be construed, as prohibiting ... an individual from purchasing any health care services," McCaughey (and *Newsweek* fixture George F. Will) speculated that, since the rich would be able to pay out-of-pocket for any services they wanted, whenever they wanted them—which would defeat the whole purpose of "price controls" and governmentally managed care—the civil-rights courts and bureaucrats might deem privately paid healthcare as unfair "bribery" under the new laws. (A poor or minority person probably wouldn't have the same options, would they? And you can't legally buy your way ahead on transplant organ donors' lists, for example.) So what was there really to stop an ACLU-lulu from bringing down the iron curtain on all private-paid healthcare, in the name of "fairness" or equality?

Translation: just like rape, when Big Guv'mint bureaucrats said "no" to a treatment, it would mean NO. If Big Government thought you were too old or too sick or too undeserving of that transplant or that experimental AIDS drug or cancer treatment, better call up Forest Lawn and start putting your affairs in order. (McCaughey frosted the cake by predicting affirmative-action quotas for top-level brain surgery, heart, AIDS, and cancer-type specialists, instead of a blind-audition process based on test scores and internships, if that was what it took to ensure racial balance.)

"No Exit" ramped up the innuendo, speculation, and Tea Party-style worst case scenarios to a point that it became a bitter laughingstock among the truly liberal. Indeed, it was later revealed that McCaughey was working hand-in-hand with Big Tobacco lobbyists opposed to Hillarycare as she wrote her articles. (Part of the mechanism for financing Hillarycare was to have come from a sharp increase in cigarette taxes.) A decade later, *TNR* editor Franklin Foer issued an open-ended public apology for the magazine ever having run "No Exit" to begin with. (This was rather gallant of Frank Foer, as he didn't bear any responsibility for it; the decision to run the piece was made back when he was still in college, under the Peretz-Sullivan administration.)

Another interesting sidelight during all of this wailing and gnashing-of-teeth was that it was Republicans like Senate leader Bob Dole and the conservative Heritage Foundation, who first suggested the dreaded Individual Mandate (that "liberal" Barack Obama would later successfully resurrect) as a *conservative* alternative to what they thought was the more Canadian/British style "government run health care" that awaited under Hillary. If you simply *forced* all U.S. citizens to buy private-only health insurance, whether their incomes or job-benefits allowed them to afford it or not (and if you taxpayer-subsidized the truly poorest and neediest cases, for some semblance of fairness), it would be such a bada-bing jackpot for the private insurance industry that they would be only too happy to offer expanded coverage and better services as a mandated trade-off.

In a strong foreshadowing of the Republican Party of Newt Gingrich and Dick Cheney, the "individual mandate" was actually far more corporate-welfarist and crony-capitalist than it was truly *conservative* or libertarian. But it WAS more superficially conservative (or less overtly "big government") than "Medicare for all" or directly government-administered healthcare. And at this point, the name of the game was to protect against any other game-changing Clintonomic victories, no matter what. Former Dan Quayle staffer and rising neoconservative fixture Bill Kristol wrote the roadmap when he editorialized that instead of dickering and dithering to get a better deal, the conservative-Republican posture should be to become what later pundits would call "The Party of No." They should violently oppose *any and all change* to the status quo. "No Exit," indeed!

Now Hillarycare was on the respirator, and with a lip-smacking flourish, the right wing noise machine reached for the on/off switch. The health insurance industry sponsored a series of top-dollar TV ads, to be run during many of America's must-see shows. Set in the near future, they showed a frustrated, middle-aged, middle-class, swing-voting (do we even need to say white?) couple named "Harry and Louise" who were horrified at the welfare-like bureaucracy and red tape, and the lack of choices or privacy, that had fallen on them now that Hillarycare passed. Furious liberals nicknamed the ads "*Thelma* and Louise," and the comparison couldn't have been more apt. Those ads drove healthcare reform right off a cliff.

It's hardly a spoiler alert to say that if Obamacare was the "Waterloo" for conservatives stunned by its passage in early 2010, Hillarycare became the Hindenburg disaster for reform-minded liberals exactly 16 years earlier. It crashed and burned to a now-inevitable defeat in early 1994. And the political parallels from the Obamacare battle in 2009–10 and the Hillarycare and budget battles in 1993–94 were so similar, if it were a novel or a screenplay, it would have been guilty of straight-up plagiarism. Especially as Hillarycare's main cause of death was not only at the hands of "movement" conservatives—but because quite a few resentful and jealous "Blue Dog" Democrats proved as determined as Rush Limbaugh himself to deny this game-changing, "uppity" new president his biggest political victory.

Ironically, the very same reasons that ClintonCare died in 1994 were exactly the same reasons why Obamacare succeeded sixteen years later. Just enough congressmen and senators finally realized in 2009–10 that there would be (and perhaps *could* be) no "perfect" solution that would have any real chance of passage—at least at first. And the last time both sides had stuck it out with no compromise, they got absolutely nothing in the end. That was not gonna happen a second time, said Barack Obama, Harry Reid, and Nancy Pelosi. (They were eventually seconded by the educated, corporate–Republican, Supreme Court chief justice John Roberts.) The "hostage taking" mentality, as Mitch McConnell and others later put it during the 2011 and 2013 debt-ceiling standoffs—where Congress and President Obama were at such war with each other that the very solvency and international credit rating of the United States was put at risk—can be directly through-lined back to healthcare reform in 1993 and '94.

In retrospect, it was a miracle that Hillarycare had gotten as far as it did. Bill and Hill had already cram-packed so many game-changers—the 1993 tax/budget deal, the gun control legislation, Don't Ask Don't Tell, the Family and Medical Leave Act of 1993 (forcing employers to offer working people a safe harbor of time off for eldercare and parenting emergencies and bereavement)—into less than two years' time, it was bound that something was gonna give. Not even Mickey Mantle and Joe DiMaggio had the kind of batting averages that could have ensured all wins and no losses, with an agenda this aggressively transformative.

Pete Wilson's Blues (or, The Sleeping Giant Awakens)

With all this Washington doom and gloom, it's time for a short side trip to the carefree sunshine of the West Coast. Strangely enough, the major-level politician who was most likely to have felt Bill Clinton's pain came from the very opposite side of the political spectrum—a former San Diego mayor beloved by his conservative hometown, jam-packed as it was with military bases and country-club seniors (just like San Diego's friendly next-door neighbor, Orange County). Pete Wilson had left his safe Senate seat, where he had served with distinction for eight years, when the Republican Party establishment practically *begged* him to run for governor, after 1980s California governor George Deukmejian finished his second term.

Wilson was pro-choice and pro-gay, though he was also immovably pro-death-penalty and corporate. Most of the state's other major Republicans were fruit-loop wingers of the Sarah Palin/Rick Santorum school (like fundie congressman "B-1 Bob" Dornan and his protégé, State Rep. Tom McClintock), or entitled Richie Rich businessmen from the Mitt Romney-Al Gore-Dan Quayle school of charisma and charm, like later (loser) nominee Bill Simon. California's Republican establishment and check-writers (along with interested behind-the-scenes observers like Lee Atwater and Karl Rove) practically *gave* the centrist Wilson the governor's nomination on a silver platter. Despite a razor-close race with Democratic former San Francisco mayor Dianne Feinstein (who would go to the Senate by 1992), Wilson won—but Pete Wilson's victory in November 1990 proved that winning is for losers.

The same fall and winter of 1990–91 that Wilson was elected was the very same fall and winter that California's grotesquely overinflated 15-year-long real estate bubble finally burst, along with the start of the post–Cold War downsizing of Southern California's massive defense industry and military bases. As far as the West Coast (and Nevada) were concerned, even the worst of the Jimmy Carter era was a picnic compared to now. The New York and Los Angeles *Times* and the San Francisco *Chronicle* accurately noted that the early '90s recession was "the worst economy since the Great Depression" for Southern and Central California. Especially given that most of the developing cellular phone and Internet companies of the near future were up north in the Silicon Valley and Bay Area—and they were only beginning to emerge.

With 1994's gubernatorial and Congressional elections looming, California Governor Pete Wilson was facing a yawning 20-point deficit in the polls to Kathleen Brown Rice. (Yes, that was her real name—she was the sister of former and future governor Jerry Brown, and daughter of California's other most influential governor besides Ronald Reagan and Earl Warren, the quintessential Great Society Democrat Pat Brown.) As late as December of 1994, what had once been the most desirable county in America, Orange County, had filed for bankruptcy. It wouldn't be until well into late 1995 and '96 when there would be true signs of gold again in most of the Golden State. (And even then, real estate and median home values largely remained flat as a pancake, except in the richest districts, until the start of Bush II's credit-default-swap era and its real estate bubble, from 2001 and '02 through 2006 and '08.)

And whose fault was that? Pete Wilson might have wondered. He didn't "create" the circumstances of the Great Recession 1.0 in California, any more than Barack Obama created the total meltdown that struck when George W. Bush left office years later. Wilson was *forced* to raise taxes, largely by a ballot initiative passed by *right wing Republican* voices—1979's Proposition 4, which shredded the state's already-flimsy "rainy day fund," required an absolute balanced budget in good or bad years, and required all surplus to be rebated at once to the taxpayers. (It was later amended to half the money to the taxpayers, and half to public schools and colleges—*regardless* of the schools' racial or economic balance, and with NO built-in student or teacher accountability. And let's not even talk about 1978's controversial Proposition 13 property tax limitations!) Wilson wasn't the one who'd halted the 50-year Big Defense Congressional gravy train that had *built* his own San Diego and Orange County, and the greater Los Angeles suburbs, during World War II and the Cold War. Nor was he the one who ended the Nixon-Ford-Carter era of lavish, no-strings federal "revenue sharing" with local schools, colleges, hospitals, and police and fire departments. Why, that was Ronnie Reagan, back in the go-go good times of 1986.

A quarter-century earlier in 1970, California was only 12 percent Latino—which was still an extremely high figure compared to most of the rest of the country then, except maybe for Florida or border Texas and Arizona. (Noting the crucial role that overwhelmingly Democratic and activist Latino voters played in Barack Obama's successful 2012 re-election, wherein Latinos were 10 percent of the national electorate and growing, many pollsters noted that as late as 1992, Latinos were only a mere 2 percent of the American national population as a whole.) So 12 percent back in 1970 was impressively diverse indeed—though it still looks Clorox-white for a state that was once a province of Mexico, or considering the veritable tsunami of Mexican and Central American *imigracion* that came from the '80s and '90s through today. (Today, California's Latino population is essentially neck-and-neck with its white one, and outpaces it in most of Los Angeles and northern Orange County.)

California (along with Hawaii) had also been Ground Zero in the 1970s for the relocated refugees from Vietnam, Thailand, and the Cambodian holocaust, and the surrounding areas in Southeast Asia. Being at the outermost of the Pacific coast, California had always had a strong Asian population, and historically, most of them had done admirably in carving out some of the highest achievement scores and business successes. Indeed, many of the new Vietnamese, Thai, and Cambodian refugees had immediately set to work with beauty salons, donut shops and coffeehouses, convenience stores, real estate offices, video stores, and restaurants. Admirable as their resolve was, to many a native white Californian, this looked like a total all-out "takeover" of their cities. In many sun-baked Asian enclaves, like Cerritos, La Palma, and Westminster in northern Orange County, and Monterey Park and Alhambra in the San Gabriel Valley, cities and counties were actually forced to enact codes requiring that signs for businesses be translated into English. So many of them were written in Asian-only lettering and calligraphy, an un–PC driver from out of town might think they had taken a slow boat to China. Because of the fact that many of these new people were refugees from countries where America had failed on its promise to protect them from Communism, they also enjoyed certain head-start advantages to help them pick up the pieces of their shattered lives.

(Of course, even before the recession, Californians had spent the 1980s and most of the 1970s as a virtual economic protectorate of Asia's first world, as tsunamis of Toyotas, Nissan-Datsuns, Hondas, Hyundais, Wang Computers, Sonys, Hitachis, LG's, Yamahas, Seikos, Daewoos, Samsungs, Kias, and Toshibas poured into its shipping ports from Japan, Hong Kong, and South Korea. And the state's famous 1975 to 1990 real-estate boom would have been utterly impossible without massive Asian speculation and investment.)

Topping it off was the fact that, along with Texas, California had the weakest "weak governor system" of any major state in the union. Pete Wilson couldn't even appoint his own Attorney General, school superintendent, budget controller, or lieutenant governor—all of whom were elected separately (and often came from the opposition party). The state had a full-time, year-round, Washington-style legislature and state senate, and a famously liberal and activist state Supreme Court. And it was the legislature that wrote and passed each year's budget, when the courts weren't ordering this taxpayer-expense "remedy" program or that. Both branches were openly at war with Wilson—bought and paid for by overwhelmingly Democratic teacher, university, and public employee unions, as well as Jesse Jackson/Al Sharpton type racial activists and ACLU types. And that wasn't even *mentioning* California's famous "direct democracy" process of voter referendums and state Constitutional amendments by ballot initiative proposition, which bypassed the legislature and gubernatorial offices entirely.

No, Pete Wilson was not just going to be *defeated* in 1994. He was going to be utterly *humiliated*—forced from his state office in as much disgrace as Herbert Hoover, Richard Nixon, and Jimmy Carter had been, *with the worst approval ratings of any California governor in the state's history,* up to that point. (Sadly and revealingly, Wilson's successors—the impeached-by-recall Gray Davis, and movie legend Arnold Schwarzenegger, who was serving when the 2008 economic meltdown hit—would equal or surpass him on that bottom-barrel score.) Wilson was "the most hated governor in the U.S.," according to polls in late 1993 and early '94. A failure so spectacular that both Ann Coulter and Al Franken might well have joined arm-in-arm to agree that Pete Wilson was the worst of the worst. He could kiss his thinly veiled dreams of the presidency or vice presidency, or getting secretary of state in 1996, a curt good-bye! He was going to take the fall for everything! Like it was all his fault!

Or WAS he? They say that an animal is the most dangerous when it's cornered. Janis Joplin once philosophized that "freedom's just another word for nothing left to lose." And in 1994, Governor Pete Wilson had his back up against a locked iron gate. He had nothing—or really, he had *everything*, left to lose. With the Religious Right already allergic to Wilson's country-club Republicanism, there was only one card left for him to play—from the very bottom of the deck.

In 1994, California's mad-as-hell voters would introduce a ballot initiative so controversial, so lastingly racist and battery-acid toxic, it would make Proposition 13 look like a Hallmark card. It was called Proposition 187. Created by archconservative San Gabriel Valley Republican Assemblyman Dick Mountjoy, and bluntly titled the "Save Our State" (or "S.O.S.") initiative, Proposition 187 would effectively deny all major social services, including public school education and day care, basic physicals and immunizations/blood tests from county public health clinics, and so forth from anyone (or any child whose parents) were undocumented immigrants. Even emergency room cases and pregnancies would be subject to immediate screening for citizenship status.

The law itself was, of course, as doomed to failure as if a state tried to outlaw all abortions in violation of *Roe vs. Wade,* or tried to conduct religious revival meetings in public schools. The Supreme Court had already ruled in black-letter law that school districts were required to provide education to children, whether or not the parents were here legally. (What were illegal children supposed to do—sit at home alone and unsupervised and learning nothing?) And the dread spectre of "racial profiling" was as obvious as the color of your skin. But as was the case with so much of 1990s politics—the era of the Symbolic Gesture, of Speaking in Code—that wasn't the point. The uber-point of Prop 187 was to drum up an army of people who could express and vent their rage to an "elite" system stranglehold by political correctness. And to whip up an army of voters who would vote for Pete Wilson (or at least vote *against* Kathleen Brown Rice). If Prop 187 did get struck down in federal civil-rights court (which, of course, it did), then so much the better from the cynical consultants' and pundits' POV. That would just prove again how dictatorial, out-of-touch, and reverse-prejudiced the system really was against regular, hard-working (Anglo) Americans. Boffo box office at the next election guaranteed. Talk radio and cable TV ratings through the roof. Bestseller bait for sure!

Whitewater, WACO, and WTC Attacks (Take #1)

1993 and '94 would have had enough wall-to-wall trauma if those years' game-changes were confined only to the above domestic policy tussles. Not even close. In February of 1993, just one month after Clinton's inauguration, Middle Eastern terrorists attacked the World Trade Center with a car bomb parked in an underground garage, killing or wounding dozens of people. (Little did we know what a sneak preview this was.) The smoke of the 1993 WTC attack hadn't yet subsided when newly appointed authoritarian Attorney General Janet Reno went after a rural Texas compound run by a self-styled messiah named David Koresh. Koresh had been indoctrinating the underage children of his live-in cult of followers in all sorts of nutty and hateful beliefs, while stockpiling assault weapons for the coming apocalypse. And when Reno's patience ran out, it was Apocalypse Now, when she and FBI director Louis Freeh's agents attacked the Waco compound with flammable tear gas canisters in an invasion. Koresh himself and many of his followers—including many of those innocent children—died horribly at the scene.

Just what Bill and "Hitlery" needed, when they were trying to prove that they were compassionate New Democrats who felt people's pain, instead of high-handed elitists who wanted to control everyone else's lives. Conservative talk radio and conspiracy theorists rocked and rolled from coast to coast. The murder mystery intrigue only got spicier that summer, when the dead body of longtime Clinton associate Vince Foster was found, dead by suicide—or was it MURDER? (In a way, you could make the case that Vince Foster's suicide *was* murder—killed by an irredeemably toxic, mean-spirited, corrupt, and sadistic Washington environment.) But the biggest news was when the Congress, egged on by hard-right magazines and talk radio, demanded that a Special Prosecutor be appointed, as had happened in Watergate and Iran-Contra, to investigate questionable 1980s dealings in an Arkansas real estate and land development known as Whitewater.

Whitewater was the blanket name for a 1978–80 land development that was purchased by then Arkansas Attorney General Bill Clinton and his wife Hillary, then an associate at Arkansas' most prestigious law office, the Rose Law Firm. Bill and Hillary were making a combined total of about $50,000 a year then ($25,000 apiece)—about half of what two Ivy-graduated, Washington-credentialed young lawyers or large-state Attorney Generals might have made on the coasts (or in Chicago or DC) back in the late '70s or early '80s. Acutely aware of this shortfall as Clinton pursued his expensive campaigns for governor, they pooled their resources with old pals and aspiring bankers Jim and Susan McDougal to augment their income, borrowing $200,000 to purchase prime riverfront land on which they hoped to sell vacation and/or retiree homes. Alas, this happened just in time for Jimmy Carter and Paul Volcker to raise mortgage rates to 12 and 14 percent and higher, to try and stem the runaway inflation of the late '70s. "Whitewater" looked as though it had gone over the cliff. But after Jim McDougal lost his place in Clinton's gubernatorial cabinet with Clinton's 1980 loss of the governorship, he parlayed his credentials into starting a Savings & Loan called Madison Guaranty. This time, timing was on the McDougals' side, as they took full advantage of the deregulatory orgy and "greed is good" mentality of the Reagan era, engaging in several suspicious transactions for further real estate and investment schemes—until Madison finally collapsed amidst audits and investigations during the 1989–90 S&L crisis, costing the taxpayers over $73 million.

While Bill and Hillary weren't really involved in these later problems, there were two smoking guns: Hillary and the Rose Law Firm had been on retainer as Madison Guaranty's law firm, and the Clintons had never really officially dissolved their partnership in the Whitewater "resort"—making it look to Clinton enemies as though the Clintons had been "in business" with the McDougals every step of the way.

Right-wing voices were demanding a full-on investigation, with longtime Clinton associate Vince Foster's suicide turning up the volume to McCarthy-era levels. Hillary for her part literally begged her husband not to appoint a Special Prosecutor. Having served on the Committee to Impeach Nixon in 1974, she knew better than anyone what kind of hell this type of inquiry could be, and the potential for abuses that lay within a partisan system. But Bill wanted—needed—to have some chance at passing his shopping list of signature policy game-changers—healthcare, NAFTA, the tax increase, gun control, gays in the military, et cetera. If he refused to go along with the Republicans' insistence, why, it would look as though he and Hillary *did* have something to cover up, that they *were* guilty of something. And it would destroy what little chance there was of any kind of "bipartisan" cooperation on any of those other legislative priorities.

Clinton went ahead and authorized the investigation, in the hopes of proving he had nothing to hide. Soon enough, initial Special Prosecutor Robert Fiske concluded that the Clintons had done nothing provably illegal. Faster than you can cry Whitewater Whitewash, a supposedly independent three-judge panel appointed fundamentalist former judge and law professor Kenneth Starr to continue the investigation, to the delight of the hard right in Congress. (Cynics later said that the Clintons might secretly have been pleased by the Starr choice. If Starr *did* find anything damaging against the Clintons, he would be so obviously prejudiced—both against the Clintons and against core Democratic constituencies like feminist women and gays, the Democrats would unite and fight against him, just like Clarence Thomas and Robert Bork. And sure enough, that's exactly what happened.)

But the move was as toxic as swallowing a bottle of rat poison. Starr had initially been appointed to investigate Vince Foster's so-called "murder" investigation. (He came up empty there, too, of course.) In this same grand tradition, while Starr would come up empty on Whitewater (and later investigations into supposedly stolen White House files—"Filegate"—and "Travelgate," a pointless farrago into unreported travel expenses), he ever-expanded his jurisdiction into looking into former Clinton statehouse staffer Paula Jones' allegations of sexual assault and harassment. Starr used that as his carte blanche to find out what was going on with Clinton and another dissatisfied young woman who'd once worked for him, named Monica Lewinsky, egged on all the way by an army of talk-radio programs and big-donor subsidized, scandal-mongering books and magazine pieces. As legendary White House press correspondent Helen Thomas summed it up, Bill Clinton "never knew a second in the White House when he was not being investigated. The ultra-right gave him no quarter, they were after him from the moment he stepped into the White House. Every second, every breathing moment. He didn't understand how far they would go."

The year 1993 ended as it had begun, with more mindless death and destruction, when a U.S. military helicopter running world-policeman errands with the UN, was shot down by warlord Mohammed Farrah Aidid in the faraway lands of Somalia. Just seventeen days into the new year of 1994, a killer earthquake struck in California's San Fernando valley—the worst North American quake disaster in four and a half years, since the deadly October 1989 collapse in Oakland and San Francisco. LA still had not recovered from the Rodney King riots of 1992, and all of Southern California was still neck-deep in recession, gangs, and crime. And just a couple of months before the quake, a calamitous series of summer/fall wildfires had struck in the Hollywood Hills and towards Malibu, along the Pacific Coast. The Northridge earthquake and the Malibu fires might just as well have been a metaphor for all the pent-up stress, tension, and anger in the air.

The Hypocritic Oath

Now that Sheriff Ronnie and his faithful deputy, Marshal Bush, had ridden off into the senior-citizen sunset, the Republican Party was left without a unifying center of attention—and *with* a power vacuum the size of the Milky Way. Rush Limbaugh and Pat Buchanan (and some of their lesser disciples from the world of conservative talk-radio and book-writers) were trying to insert themselves into that vacuum when it came to info-tainment. But when it came to insider political power, it seemed at first that there was no one left. Until one very ambitious, media and branding-savvy, and even more ruthless congressman seized his big chance.

Unlike the many religiously sincere "values voters" and small-town congressmen and state officials who were looking up to him for leadership during the summer and fall of 1994, House Minority Leader Newt Gingrich was hardly a beacon of morality (unless you qualified "morality" with the prefix "im.") And the very idea that he had any shred of "family values" or genuinely Christian faith, at least back then, was downright laughable. He'd handed one of his wives her walking papers while she was still lying in hospital recovering from *cancer surgery*. (Not exactly What Would Jesus Do…) It was later revealed that at the very same time that he was encouraging the family values firebrands in his Congress to impeach President Clinton for his "sexual immorality" in 1998, Gingrich himself was having a red-hot affair with another on-the-side mistress, cheating on yet another wife.

As a published historian and university professor with a law degree, Newt Gingrich could hardly be accused by even the snobbiest intellectuals of being stupid or unscientific. And that was what truly horrified his high-IQ equals in the liberal-intellectual elite: this brilliant and strategic congressman was emerging as the ablest and most powerful witch-hunting demagogue since Joe McCarthy and Roy Cohn—ready, willing, and able to empower, pander to, and team up with the most bass-ackward dummies and wild-eyed fruitloops out there—if that's what it took to consolidate his power base with a "movement" of psyched-up, right-wing foot soldiers. (Just so long as *he* was the one who got to lead the army!) Like their publicists, the late Lee Atwater and Karl Rove, people like Newt Gingrich, Grover Norquist, and Dick Cheney were much more *reactionaries* and (especially in Cheney and Norquist's cases) *corporatists*, far more than they were ever Buckley-Thatcher-Goldwater principled *conservatives*. They knew the talk and the walk, of course; but their true animating concern was to rebuild the long-dreamed-of "permanent Republican majority" by whatever means necessary, while handing out plenty of corporate-crony giveaways to the top 1 percent. Gingrich folded into this recipe a racialized, nativist, 'phobic jihad against a diverse, polit-ically correct, trash-talk culture that he felt was heading further and further towards Africa, Mexico, and southeast Asia, instead of classical Britain, France, and Germany.

Most importantly, Newt Gingrich was the biggest and closest-in-age (along with Rush Limbaugh and future Vice President Cheney, now off to run Halliburton) opposite cultural number to the Clintons. He was the veritable TV spokesmodel for all of those "red state" and Southern Baby Boomers who never went counterculture. The ones who'd proudly gone to Vietnam (even if Gingrich, Limbaugh, and Cheney themselves hadn't), the ones who'd spent the '70s and early '80s raising their families and serving on the PTA, the ones who showed up to church every Sunday, believed the Bible, and perhaps sent their children to Christian schools. The ones who somehow missed going to key parties, group therapy, disco and punk rock shows, or doing coke with Warren Beatty at Studio 54. Gingrich said that Bill and Hillary Clinton represented the triumph of the "counterculture McGovernicks ... total bizarreness, total weirdness," and were therefore "the enemy of normal Americans."

*   *   *

After forty years, McCarthyism had finally made its comeback. Naked sex discrimi-nation, blatant racism, fire-breathing homophobia, "loyalty oaths" and litmus tests and "party discipline" from the floors of the Congress. Representatives and senators being openly jeered and booed at by their own colleagues. Laws being passed or defeated for no other reason than to "send a message" to this politician or that. Innocent underlings being publicly crushed for the sake of show, some even literally hounded to suicide. Looking back on this first act, it's no wonder that a lot of people thought Bill Clinton was a throwback to the hippie era. The political slut-shaming, systematic humiliation, and complete disre-spect of this president during his first 100 days—not only from his expectable right-wing opponents but from official Washington as a whole—was like nothing since the days of "Impeach Nixon!" or "Hey there, LBJ—how many kids did you kill today?" The brakes were going out, and so far, nobody on either side seemed to have the power (much less the will) to stop it. The marbled halls of the United States Congress and Senate were being reduced to the level of *Geraldo* and *The Jerry Springer Show*.

It had truly been The Year That Washington Lost Its Mind. And the year wasn't over yet. The most important election in the 20 years between Reagan vs. Carter and Bush vs. Gore would not be a presidential one—but a mid-term, one that would change the entire grammar of politics from then right on through Barack Obama and the Tea Party today. Why, some people might have even called it a Republican *Revolution*.

4

Clinton and Gingrich:
A Love Story

Ever since Bill Clinton was elected, conservatives have been acting as though the Oval Office had been festooned with macramé and bongs, as if there were some kind of crazy free-love, war-protesting, pig-hating, Bobby Seale-supporting, Carlos Castaneda-reading, Bob Dylan-grooving hippie running the country. But their notion of a big McGovernick revival has always been hallucinatory. The day-trippers have become day-traders. Dylan is singing in Vegas.
—Maureen Dowd, The New York Times, *April 7, 1999*

"There was [really only] a two-year Clinton Presidency, where if Clinton wanted to do something it would not necessarily get done, but it would get a fair hearing and a lot of legislative energy pushing it," sighed Lawrence O'Donnell, looking back for author Michael Takiff in 2009–10. "And then there was a six-year Gingrich Government, in which Clinton was allowed a small editing function…. What's the legacy? I don't get it. There's no lesson on how to be President—at all."

Oh really? Tell that to Barack Obama, who used the *exact same template* to ensure his successful two-term run. Obama takes office amidst an economic meltdown, after a far more failed president with the last name Bush. He knows that with the House and Senate both in Democratic hands for the first time since he was barely out of law school, this was his only window to force through game-changes like healthcare reform and a for-real LGBT equality agenda—which he proceeds to do with alacrity. The public voted for "change," but the change they got was inevitably processed, blenderized, Mixmastered, watered down, and filibustered by a bought-and-paid-for, bloviating Congress and Senate, a fact which ends up discouraging his base –while empowering his worst enemies. Those worst enemies then take control of the Congress the next year—but their looney-tunes outrageousness and wild-eyed extremism only assures that when Obama faces re-election, the entire Democratic base will surround and protect his presidency like a firewall.

Lesson learned! In fact, it worked like magic!

The "lesson" that Bill Clinton, Newt Gingrich, and Rush Limbaugh taught the political system in 1995–96 was actually THE template for divided government, from then right on through today. Newt Gingrich had been able to do the one thing that platinum-politician Bill Clinton couldn't. It was Newt Gingrich, Jerry Falwell, James Dobson, Jesse Helms and Rush Limbaugh—and the irresponsible fever-swamp wingers and fanatics that they gave unprecedented power, platforms, and visibility to—who'd finally managed to "unite" the Democratic Party. Not Bill or Hillary Clinton or Al Gore. The November 1994 Republican

Revolution and its fallout was nothing less than the birthplace of Red State and Blue State America.

The Quota Queen

The instantaneous dislike that Bill and Hillary Clinton had inspired in much of Establishment Washington might have been overcome quickly enough if this otherwise politically genius power couple had been more willing to play ball when it came to rounding out the rest of their government. By 1992–93, Washington's would-be kitchen "cabinets" were veritably overflowing with House Democrats (and small-state senators and governors) who had been twiddling their thumbs and rubbing their hands with anticipation for a dozen long years, just waiting for the high-profile Cabinet positions and powerful Federal judicial appointments that would be theirs—if only they could get out from under Reagan-Bush!

Knowing full well of this, Bill Clinton still decided to make the most of his high-level appointments outside of the Beltway box—and by doing so, he directly paved the way for Barack Obama, and for true gender and racial diversity in Washington. While Bubba may have compromised and fast-talked his way out of a heckuva lot during his eight-year run, one promise that he was rock-ribbed, immovable, and adamantine on keeping was appointing a Cabinet of advisors and federal judges who truly "looked like America." And by that, he most assuredly did *not* mean the Ward Cleaver America of mid-century and earlier. Clinton was determined to appoint African Americans, Latinos, and plenty of empowered women to top level positions (and even a gay or lesbian or two). This was both to reflect the realities of what 1993 America now "looked like" (especially the ascendant constituencies of the Democratic Party), and to send a message that would symbolize those glass ceilings being shattered, for all other employers to see. Clinton had just broken records for turnout and for voter percentages among people of color, in ways not seen since the heyday of LBJ's civil rights era. He had brought business-minded Asian voters into the loop more than just about any pre–Obama Democrat, and his "gender gap" between female and male voters was one of the biggest on record, up to that point. Now it was time to pay them back.

But amongst those veteran (white male) establishment Democrats who were lip-lickingly craving a piece of the White House action, that meant the political payoff they were coveting would be returned marked "insufficient funds." When it came to congressmen and senators *of color* (let alone women), as late as 1992–93, the cupboard was still practically bare. In many cases, the few who already had cracked the sexual or racial ceiling (like Nancy Pelosi and African American civil-rights hero John Lewis in the House, or Barbara Mikulski in the Senate) were just too indispensable in the Congress, if Clinton wanted any chance of legislatively passing any of his signature policy initiatives. (Other women who went on to become fixtures in Congress, like Dianne Feinstein, Patty Murray, Maxine Waters, Marjorie Margolies-Mezvinsky, and Barbara Boxer, had just been "promoted" from House to Senate or from state governments to the House that very same year, in the post–Anita Hill "Year of the Woman" in 1992. They had barely taken their oaths of office; they could hardly be asked to leave to join the Clinton cabinet.)

Clinton also knew that young people were instrumental not only in his victory, but in establishing his entire "brand" as the youthful, energetic, New Democrat with fresh new ideas, as opposed to tired old President Bush, and Ross Perot's gray crew-cut. That meant that even amongst the white males, young whippersnappers (like George Stephanopoulos) would have a certain amount of "set-asides" as it were, to further underline that a new generation was in town, that the torch had truly been passed.

So instead of going for the old, cigar-chomping "machine politicians," white-ethnic labor leaders and Congressional, Senate, and big-state officials, Bill Clinton largely turned his back on the Old Boys' Club—for the very reason that it *was* an old boys club. Instead, Clinton would appoint (an only barely closeted by many rumors) Florida alligator wrestler's daughter named Janet Reno for Attorney General, while shoulder-padded and always-single Donna Shalala would take over Health and Human Services. A little-known African American woman named Joycelyn Elders, who had served as a health director in Clinton's Arkansas—and who supported sex-ed and condoms in schools, legalization of certain recreational drugs, and encouraging middle- and high-school students to use masturbation as a way of avoiding AIDS and pregnancy—would now sit in the same Surgeon General's chair that patriarchal, *Marcus Welby*–like, world-renowned pediatric surgeon C. Everett Koop had vacated just three years earlier.

Black businessman and political consultant Ron Brown would rule Commerce, and while the conservative African American hero Colin Powell would (temporarily) stay on from the Bush team, he would find himself more and more embroiled in a power struggle with an assertive female appointee (who would eventually become Secretary of State in Clinton's second term) named Madeleine Albright. And Clinton's first Supreme Court appointment would be a Jewish feminist pioneer named Ruth Bader Ginsburg, who'd worked on innumerable abortion, gay rights, and equal pay matters, and helped to cement affirmative action quotas and preferences for women in the workplace and colleges, as well as for racial minorities.

Both George W. Bush and Barack Obama would later follow Clinton's lead to such an extent that it doesn't really seem all that remarkable today. But in 1993, Clinton's appointments were a thrilling example of diversity that was light years beyond what *any* president (of either party) before him had ever attempted. Thrilling, that is, if you approved of the idea in the first place. But if you had wanted things to stay the same—or worse, if you had personally just lost out on an appointment you'd been coveting ever since Jimmy Carter, one that "should have been yours," to a less-qualified or less well-known person who happened to be black or brown or female—then it was something else.

As Bill Clinton's Cabinet nominees attempted to clear the hurdles and stumbling blocks of the Senate, it became clear that the Senate's old white boys had declared a literal "war on women." (Bear in mind that the House and Senate were still in supposedly progressive *Democratic* hands at this point—and that still, they had said Yes to Clarence Thomas and No to Anita Hill eighteen months earlier.) The proceedings started off on the wrong foot when Clinton's original nominee for Attorney General, Zoe Baird, was disqualified for a technicality as flimsy as June Cleaver's lace aprons—because she had failed to pay her share of Social Security taxes for a housekeeper-nanny that was in her employ. (This came within a few years of a check-cashing scandal at the House Bank, and despite the fact that many of these same congressmen and senators had skirted campaign-finance and lobbying laws in ways to gladden a loophole-lawyer's heart.)

Then Clinton nominated another non–Washington woman, Kimba Wood, who *had* paid taxes for her household help—some of whom were undocumented immigrants. (Of course, *no one* in the rich and ritzy Senate would ever *dream* of employing an "illegal" gardener, nanny, or maid! *Perish the thought!*) Kimba Wood got the trapdoor faster than a celebrity guest on an old *Laugh-In* rerun, but apparently Bubba *still* hadn't gotten the message. Instead of taking the cue to nominate one of the senators or congressmen (or some federal judge or governor buddy of theirs), instead of nominating someone from Permanent Washington who'd been drooling over the thought of scoring Attorney General ever since 1980, Clinton once again went outside the box, to get Janet Reno. (At least she—almost miraculously—made it through the gauntlet.)

No easier was the confirmation process when Clinton nominated San Francisco supervisor Roberta Achtenberg for Assistant Housing and Urban Development Secretary. Ms. Achtenberg was even worse than just another ball-busting uppity female; she was an out lesbian, from the most flamingly progressive city in America, and would be the first openly gay member of a presidential cabinet in history. (No doubt, in addition to her qualifications, that was one of the reason the socially liberal Clinton had chosen her—to "send a message" to his many LGBT supporters that he heard them loud and clear.) When fundamentalist Senate fixture Jesse Helms explained why he was voting to quash the clearly qualified and professional candidate, the seventyish Dixiecrat didn't bother mincing any words: "Because she's a damn lesbian!" he disgustedly snarled in *The Washington Times*. (And not just a regular lesbian, mind you, but a "militant, activist, mean lesbian.") Not one syllable was uttered about whether or not she was *qualified* for the job, or indeed about any other aspect of her character—at least not by him.

Without a doubt, however, Clinton's most destructive and damaging appointee battle came with African American female law professor Lani Guinier, who was his choice to run the Justice Department's Civil Rights Commission, and who had been an old pal of his and Hillary's at Yale Law School. Guinier would author the too-truthfully titled study *The Tyranny of the Majority* less than a year after her nomination, and had already written a contemptuous radical-left deconstruction of the Civil Rights Act, called "The Triumph of Tokenism." In her writings, she made the case for affirmative action quota-style "remedies" that would have given votes cast by people of color more weight than white voters' votes, in certain areas and circumstances, and for a "minority veto," so as to secure more proportional representation for people of color. Her writings were termed by the *New York Times* in July of 1993 as "poorly written, provocative, and easy to caricature" as well as "extreme-sounding ... rare and invasive."

Bad enough already—and then, the smoking gun was fired. In the most shocking of her ebony-tower musings, Guinier had said in the *Virginia Law Review* that African Americans who were Republican could only consider themselves quote, "descriptively black." It was one thing to say that people like Colin Powell, Clarence Thomas, and Condi Rice didn't necessarily reflect the broader political views of the African American community. But to effectively *deny* that they had faced the same barriers (or to make fun of them for having done so), to say that black Republicans were essentially traitors to their race, was about as close to a dictionary definition of reverse-racism as you could get. (For example, Sammy Davis, Jr., James Brown, and basketball legend Wilt Chamberlain had all campaigned for Nixon back in 1972—while also being arguably the biggest and most barrier-busting black entertainers in the *entire world* in 1972. Did Ms. Guinier really think that *they* were nothing but a bunch of Uncle Toms?)

Now there was no going back—it was almost as bad as if a white politician were caught saying the you-know-what word in public. Senator Joe Biden, the future vice president to an African American named Barack Obama, told the Clintons point blank, "There is *no way* [Guinier] is going to be confirmed" by the Senate. (And he should know—Biden ran the ballistically controversial Robert Bork and Clarence Thomas hearings.) Clinton told Guinier that he felt for the good of the country and the process, she would be better off withdrawing her name from consideration. But Lani Guinier told Clinton to stick it. No way was she going to give in, let alone play slave for him, so to speak. You're going to have to publicly force me off, she shot back. And force her off Clinton did. Bubba dropped Lani Guinier like a hot potato.

At this critical moment, the lovely Sally Quinn came in to set everything right. In July of 1993, hot on the heels of her "Welcome to Washington" article of eight months before, she tut-tutted at the Clintons, "People who have attained a certain social or political position" in Permanent Washington "do not want to be dissed. They want the new team to respect them" (read: to toady up to them). Instead, in Bill Clinton's very Inaugural address, with its rainbow of diversity epitomized by literary legend Maya Angelou's inauguration poem, it's pre-endorsement by working-class domestic goddess Roseanne Barr, its throngs of blacks and browns and white Norma Raes and Erin Brockoviches out in the crowd, Clinton had publicly damned Permanent Washington. DC was a place that "forget[s] those people whose toil and sweat sends us here and pays our way." With that, Ms. Quinn seethed, "the new president sent a clear challenge to an already suspicious Washington Establishment."

All Politics Are National

Newt Gingrich and his coterie of Congressional colleagues knew that if they wanted to back up their talk with some action, if they wanted results instead of rhetoric, they needed a bulletproof and irresistible game plan in order to win. Something that would be as unstoppable against the Clinton machine as the Clintons themselves were against the Reagan-Bush one. The key, Gingrich knew, was for the Republican Party and conservative movement to create what we would now call a "brand," a unifying and uniform identity—just as the Denny's, McDonalds, or KFC customer in Long Island gets served the same menu as the one in rural Louisiana and the one in Laguna Beach. Everyone from coast to coast would have to know exactly what was on the Republican menu, everybody had to be on the same page.

But how could this be done, especially in an off-year, localized election? What message could a man (or woman) running for governor or senator in a heavy-minority, pro-gay, immovably *Roe vs. Wade*, high-finance powerhouse like California, New York, or Massachusetts, ever have in common with someone running in the rural backyards of Oral Roberts University and *The Old-Time Gospel Hour*? And in Congress? The whole *idea* of a House of Representatives was to have someone who would *represent* the specific demographic, racial, educational, and economic needs of each district and area of the country—needs that almost by definition varied somewhat from area to area. So how can we possibly get 435 candidates for the House on the same page? As well as "deliberative," "elite" Senate candidates, or careerist state governors? It had almost never been done before. And when it had, those exceptions proved the rule of just how extreme things had to be in order to make it happen—a World War II, a Vietnam or Watergate, a Carter-era economic collapse. (Or later on, September 11th or a 2008-style meltdown.)

But what Newt Gingrich had the hopeful audacity to realize was that the roadmap to victory had already been written. A winning strategy that had gone into overdrive at the end of the Reaganized '80s, with the initial rise of national narrative-writers like CNN and prime time "newsmagazines," and was now, under Gingrich's visionary leadership, about to come into full flower. It was for candidates to run for *local* offices—using *national* platforms and issues. As liberal Thomas Frank freely admitted in his brilliant 2004 diagnosis, *What's the Matter with Kansas?*, so much local power and authority had already been Hoovered up by hovering, know-it-all federal courts and state and federal officials during the late '60s, '70s, and '80s, by the 1990s, there was hardly anything of real importance *left* to be decided at those same local levels anymore.

You wanna teach biblical creationism in your science curriculum, or have voluntary prayer at the beginning of class? Tell it to the Supremes, baby. You want to "opt out" your children from sex education classes and gay tolerance? In an era where AIDS, teen pregnancy, and teenage suicide was on every other Oprah, Sally Jessy, Dr. Ruth, and Phil Donahue show? *Fuggedaboudit.* You want to have a free hand in zoning and planning all your town's vacant areas, or allow the local Realtors, developers, and small businesses to do the job? Better check with the Equal Opportunity people, and their low-income housing and "racial balance" mandates, not to mention the Air Quality Control people or the EPA. You want to "censor" those sexy, witchy teenage young-adult novels, or those suicidal, God-is-dead existentialist authors from the city library? Check, please—with the ACLU. You want to put up the Ten Commandments in the town square? Not gonna happen, Cookie!

Robbed of all but the most menial, parking-ticket and code-enforcement powers by snoopy state and federal overseers (or at least, *so it seemed* to the people who most resented this unwanted regulation and oversight), by the 1990s, the grass roots finally found a way to strike back. All right kids, if you can't actually *decide* local issues at the local level anymore—why, we'll start debating *national* issues at the *local* level! School board and city council elections in certain aspects of the red-state hinterlands would now hinge on *Roe vs. Wade*. AIDS funding and *Heather Has Two Mommies*-type children's literature (and later "witchcraft"-promoters like *Harry Potter* and *Buffy the Vampire Slayer*) would be debated in rural-suburban city councils and libraries where the out-and-proud gay population, or those openly outside of Judeo-Christian religious observance, could've been counted on a few hands. Gun control, strict anti-pollution, and carpooling/smog standards would be debated in areas where nobody really wanted them to begin with. "Non-partisan" city council, school board, and county supervisor seats in many interior and Southern states would become ground zero for hand-wringing speechifying about the ongoing degeneracy of movies, music, and TV piped in from Hollywood, or the avant-garde artwork, transgressive plays, and publishing that were the toast of SoHo, TriBeCa, and the Castro—all of them thousands of miles away.

And boy, did it ever work! Across the 1990s, new, rising, and young city-council commandantes and school-board balebosses (with names like Sarah Palin and Michelle Bachmann) would win their first elections at the local level. They would master the arts of petitioning, door-knocking, flyer-copying, and rubber-chicken Chamber of Commerce dinners—all while tossing out surefire Southern Strategy one-liners and honing their Evangelical-ese routines to perfection in front of friendly, hometown audiences. And if it all worked out according to plan, one day they would be ready for prime time, to "go national!"

The esteemed novelist, screenwriter, and literary critic Carolyn See offered an interesting insight into this psychology, in her heartbreakingly funny 1995 memoir, *Dreaming: Hard Luck and Good Times in America*. She noted that in the '80s and early '90s, "people began being Born Again faster and faster, and a belief in a Satan as charming and personable as the young Christ himself also sprang up…. And why not? How else could you explain PCP, gang warfare, methamphetamines, the depletion of the ozone layer, and the mass rape of nursery school kids?" See continued, "If you squint your eyes a little, this search for a new belief system that will once again make us members of a meaningful family might be the thrust behind the Pro-Life movement. The Pro-Lifers, with their relative lack of formal education, have been metaphorically orphaned. They have been tricked; they have been laid off, short-changed, scorned. They know from their own lives what it is to have been *scraped off.* Maybe, they think, there's going to be an end to all the scraping!"

For all those people struggling with the aftermath that "drugs, drink, demoralization, depression, and divorce" had wrought in post–1960s society, See noted, many everyday people were looking for something, anything that could appear to put back the pieces of their shattered lives. "We WILL be a family again! A family like we seem to remember, with pigeons in the backyard, and a tree house and ballet lessons for the kids, and Mother in the kitchen or in the back bedroom, crying. (We don't give a damn where she is, as long as she's *there*.) And Dad still comes home at night."

"Is It a Sin for a Christian to Be a Registered Democrat?" asked a typical flyover-country flier in 1994's coming election. As Thomas Frank ruefully noted, especially after Clinton and Gore went full-throttle on free trade, plenty of economically terrified lower-middle-class Christians "clearly came to believe that it was." Even among the less-religious, there were the *Roseanne* fans and Michael Moore interviewees who'd taken a chance on Clinton '92 because they hoped against hope that he really would "put people first." Now they'd gotten their answer. And while Bill Clinton himself wasn't on the ballot that year—plenty of Democratic congressmen, senators, and governors *were*. When Kansas Democratic Representative Dan Glickman, accurately described by Thomas Frank as a "staunch Clinton loyalist," voted for NAFTA, union painter at Boeing (and part-time Republican Kansas state legislator) Dale Swenson recalled, "I couldn't any longer vote for him. I know a lot of union members were really mad at Glickman when he voted for NAFTA."

On election night 1994, the blue-collar districts of south Wichita voted for Religious Right favorite Todd Tiahrt, a true-blue member of the blue-collar class. The incumbent Representative Glickman was annihilated amongst the lower-middle-class white voters who used to represent his most fervent base—until Clintonomics and a computerizing, outsourcing New Economy had changed the game. Now, the only precincts where Glickman won were in the socially liberal, country club districts (in other words, the rich traditionally Republican ones), which had the most to gain from NAFTA and the World Trade Organization, and from a Wall Street-based, Alan Greenspan economy. Professionals whose doctor-lawyer-CPA jobs were largely immune to outsourcing, recession, or illegal immigration. "The inversion was now complete," noted Thomas Frank. The Democrat could only depend on the professional white-collar Republicans who were embarrassed by the *Praise the Lord* and *700 Club* theatrics, and the "uneducated" background of Todd Tiahrt.

A Contract with America

Now Newt Gingrich closed the deal. With a showman's dramatic flourish, just after Labor Day 1994, he created (along with Rep. Dick Armey) what he called "The Contract with America," to (supposedly) restore honor, dignity, and accountability to the runaway Congress. Written largely by the Rolls-Royce of conservative think tanks, the Heritage Foundation, Gingrich's Contract called for:

1. All laws that apply to the rest of the country to also apply to members of Congress
2. The appointment of a major, outside accounting firm to conduct a floor-to-ceiling audit of federal spending for what Reagan termed "waste, fraud, and abuse."
3. Cut the number of House committees and cut committee staff by ⅓.
4. Term limits for all committee chairs.
5. Ban the casting of proxy votes in committee.
6. Require meetings to be open to the public.
7. Require a 60 percent supermajority to pass tax increases.
8. Implement zero-baseline budgeting.

The Contract also demanded a Balanced Budget requirement, tax cuts for small businesses, working families and seniors, tort and welfare reform, fast-tracks on the death penalty, increases in the war on drugs, and a very un-specific form of "reform" to supposedly protect Social Security and Medicare. It was as brilliant as it was a largely empty gesture, designed to be inflated like the Goodyear blimp into something more than it was, by both friend and foe alike. (The contract also pointedly avoided the Four Furies—God, guns, gays, and abortion, as well as saying virtually nothing about foreign policy.) As a strategy, branding, and marketing ploy, however, it was as brilliant as anything Bill Clinton or Barack Obama ever came up with. Magazines, newspaper op-eds, cable pundits, network news shows, and local news centers were all over it. Photo-ops galore. A "teachable moment" complete with props and signs. The Contract became almost as buzzworthy a trending topic in the mass media as a hot new sitcom, a Grammy-winning CD, or a blockbuster feature film.

Best of all, it served the twin purpose of "branding" the entire election as a national affair as important as the very presidential race, as something everyone everywhere had a stake in—while also enforcing "party discipline" to make all Republicans hew the same party line. All but two of the Republican members of the House, and every last one of the non-incumbent Republican Congressional candidates running for office, signed up.

Even the Contract's enemies would rally around the unifying national "narrative" now established by the Contract of us-versus-them. Indeed, many progressives and liberals took to calling Gingrich's program The Contract ON America—a hit job. While there was nothing especially controversial about allowing greater transparency or term-limiting committee chiefs or even the vague "reform" of entitlements, to liberals and progressives it was the most shameless coded appeal since Willie Horton or the Rodney King video. Nothing but a radical-right battle plan, dressed up and cynically marketed with the *Touched by an Angel* theatrics of home, family, faith, and restoring America's trust.

You Say You Want a Revolution?

Like a hockey player or jazz trumpeter finishing up, or a man who lucked into two girls in one night, after the internecine, intramural, and interminable two-year struggle of 1993 and '94, the Democratic Party was tired and spent, badly in need of a change of clothes, a hot shower and toothbrush, and some bleary-eyed rest. But the Republicans were now as revved up as the Energizer Bunny. They had the righteous anger that many Democrats would later feel after *Bush vs. Gore,* as if the 1992 election had essentially been "stolen" out from under them, what with Clinton's 43 percent three-way victory. Their fury at watching Clinton remorselessly going from gay rights and AIDS to free trade and health care reform to raising taxes and gun control, gave them as much angry momentum as the Democrats had disappointment and disillusionment. And this time, everyone from Establishment fixtures to the talk radio and cable red-meat brigade to the tele-evangelists … *everyone* was cheering, "Go, Team Go!!"

On Tuesday, November 8, 1994, the levees finally broke. It would not be an overstatement to say that the November 1994 mid-term was every bit as game-changing a sneak preview of the future, and almost as important an election, as those of Clinton, George W. Bush, and Barack Obama themselves. The Republicans would assume control of both the House *and* the Senate for the first time since brand-new episodes of *I Love Lucy* were being made, since Elvis battled with Sinatra and Patti Page for chart supremacy. And these were not Eisenhower or Rockefeller Republicans, whom even their opponents generally respected and got along with. These were the fire-breathing culture warriors who would later go on to rally around figures like Sarah Palin and Ted Cruz, the ones who would later form the backbone of the Tea Party, motivated and empowered by talk radio, grass roots, conservative church groups, and ultra-right think-thanks and subsidized magazines. People who thought that Richard Nixon was a liberal and George Bush, Sr., was a flimsy moderate, people who thought that the Reagan Revolution was just for starters.

Hurricane Gingrich's destruction of the Democratic Party power infrastructure was complete, whole, and almost total. Not long afterward, Clinton publicly whined, "The president is still relevant!" as if he were saying it to himself in the mirror, instead of to the news. National icons like New York governor Mario Cuomo and Texas topper Ann Richards were retired from their jobs. (In Richards' case, she lost in favor of a new Texas governor named George W. Bush.) Indeed, the most economically important, big-ticket states, with their Godzilla-sized media, energy, and computer footprints—like California, New York, Texas, and Massachusetts—all had elected or re-elected Republican governors, and largely Republican legislatures. For a dress rehearsal in the summer and fall of 1993, ethnically diverse, heavily Jewish, pro-gay, and pro-choice urban centers like New York City and Los Angeles had also flipped to tough-on-crime, bottom-line Republican mayors like Rudy Giuliani and Richard Riordan. Both of them would still be ruling their respective roosts after the Clinton era ended.

Indeed, more than fifty House and Senate Democrats had lost their jobs in 1994! Democratic pillars like Dan Glickman, Marjorie Margolies-Mezvinsky, and Jim Wright, without whom the 1993 budget (and any Democratic support at all for free trade or chance of healthcare reform) would have been dead on arrival, all were given the exit cue. So was the self-proclaimed "Ayatollah of Sacramento," African American firebrand and California Assembly Speaker Willie Brown. The Democratic Party of Mario Cuomo, Walter Mondale, Michael Dukakis, Jesse Jackson, Marion Barry, Gloria Steinem, and Ann Richards existed no more. Whatever was left post–Reagan of the great Great Society experiment was now over.

Now it was the Democrats' turn for weepin' and a-wailing. Like a Sartre novel or a Charlie Kaufman screenplay, the entire Democratic Party was now thrown into an existential crisis. *Was it really worth it?* Was "winning" the White House in 1992 with Bill and Hillary Clinton worth the complete loss of the Congress, Senate, and almost all the major statehouses and big cities? Did we lose because we were *too* liberal, because we had pushed too far and too fast on raw-nerve issues that middle America wasn't ready to deal with yet? Because we let our atheist-chic ACLU types and our O.J.-supporting, jive-talking African Americans and our outer-than-out Queers to go off the leash? Because we tried to beat the clock? We had *both* houses of Congress AND the Presidency! *How could this have happened to us?*

Reversal of Fortune

In the camp classic *Valley of the Dolls,* Susan Hayward plays an aging Broadway and Golden Age movie queen who has a younger, prettier, and perhaps more talented ingénue fired from a supporting role as her second lead. Not because the younger actress wasn't *good enough* to star alongside her; but because she was *too good*, because she might upstage the insecure veteran, *All About Eve*-style. "The ONLY star that comes out of a Helen Lawson show is Helen Lawson, baby!" she triumphantly bellows at her producer. "And that's *me!*"

No sooner had the mid-terms done their damage than Republican political consultant and strategist (and later Fox News royalty) Dick Morris was swooping in like a sleazy Superman. (He'd already worked with Bill and Hill back in Arkansas.) White House Chief of Staff Leon Panetta said in a 2010 book that he felt like washing his hands after meeting Morris, the guy was so skuzzy. Said one appalled staffer, "He could advise Hitler and Mother Teresa in the same night!" Morris may have been morally bankrupt, but he was also one other adjective: *Effective.* Morris not only *knew* the Republicans' insider strategies; better, he knew how to turn the lemons of 1994 into a refreshing glass of ice-cold lemonade.

Let's have a little reality check, shall we? If the Democratic-run Congress of 1993–94 was supposed to be Bill Clinton's "friend," then who needed an enemy? Morris underlined that the key fact of the post–1994 reality was that Bill (and Hillary) Clinton had suddenly gone from being merely the head of a large, undisciplined, whiny, running-off-at-the-mouth Democratic Party, into becoming the Democratic Party's *sole and singular last best hope.* Now, there was only ONE star (couple) in the Democratic Party, baby—and you're lookin' at em!

Morris and his crew further pointed out that this could be the president's biggest advantage, instead of his worst embarrassment, if he stuck to his guns. Before, Bill and

Hillary had to referee between progressive leftists versus Wall Street-Hollywood-Silicon Valley donors, between gay and feminist academics and Southern Blue Dog Democrats, between civil rights blacks and Jewish neoliberal yuppies. Each group yelling their demands and commands, with no compromise. Clearly, after healthcare reform, NAFTA, the 1993 budget, and Don't Ask Don't Tell, the carrot-versus-stick was not going to be enough for Bill Clinton to be able to govern. In order for Clinton to enforce any kind of "party discipline" on Congressional and statehouse Democrats, every other escape hatch, every alternative power base, *every other power seat besides his and Hillary's* would have to be as brutally foreclosed as a 6-months-behind house in Flint Michigan.

And thanks to Newt and Rush, that's just what had happened. Now, Bubba was the only A-list liberal decision-maker in town. All Clinton had to do was point over at Newt Gingrich and say "Him—or me!" and the Democrats and progressives would have no choice but to instantly whip into line. From now on, Bill and Hillary would tell *them* what to do—not the other way around!

The total defenestration of almost all the other A-list Democratic leaders had actually made Bill and Hill *more* powerful, not less, if you looked at it the right way. Whether other Democrats liked it or not, all their eggs were now in the Clinton basket. All Clinton needed was the audacity to press his advantage. From now on, merely in order to survive, the entire Democratic Party would have no other choice but to become Brand Clinton.

Not surprisingly given these optics, the most irritating, cavity-like problem now lay within many of the surviving Democratic congressmen and women. The ones who had been established in "This Town," in Permanent Washington, long before the two-and-a-half-year-old Clinton government. People who'd been helping to make national policy while Bill and Hill were dithering over local school textbooks and auto license fees back in Arkansas. These people had lost many of their oldest and dearest friends in the 1994 tsunami—now replaced by a bunch of holy rolling, "Bible believing" culture warriors from the hinterlands, or a bunch of survival-of-the-fittest Ayn Randian bankers and proto Tea Partiers. Suddenly, their own power seats seemed to be more vulnerable than ever. According to Sidney Blumenthal, Michael Takiff, Haynes Johnson, and several other historians, many Congressional and Senate Democrats all but openly *hoped* that the Clinton era would be a one-term one-off. That maybe it would be *their* turn to ride to the rescue next time, to set things back to where they "rightfully" belonged. That Brand Clinton would go away and the pre–Clinton Democratic Party would return.

Not a chance.

The Love "Triangle"

With this kind of thinly disguised hostility from his own people, Morris advised (with the eager assent of many Friends of Bill like George Stephanopoulos, Michael Kinsley, Al From, and Sid Blumenthal, plus Morris' fellow Republican crossover David Gergen), the key strategy from now on would be what became known as Triangulation. It was essentially a bigger-badder sequel to the "Third Way" politics of Clinton's own Democratic Leadership Committee: to take back the Southern Strategy themes that Republicans had run on ever since Nixon and Reagan, and then sell them back, after sanding off the harshest and most potentially racist edges. And to use these triangulations, like Muhammad Ali or George Foreman in the ring, to rope-a-dope and jujitsu the Repubs. To leave them sputtering without a message—except for the most extremist wingnuts.

Instead of making coded racial appeals against "welfare queens," antagonizing AIDS-era "Queer Theory" filmmakers and artists, or dissing on hairnetted and hoopty-driving Hispanic youths—talk about Personal Responsibility. Instead of talking about outsourcing or free trade, talk about a New Economy with No Limits. Instead of trying to "take over" everybody's healthcare, pass donut-hole fillers for uninsured children of the working poor, that would be administered by the states. (Who could object to that?) Call for V-chips against violent and sexy TV shows, and for egalitarian public school uniforms. Get out of the way of Wall Street and Silicon Valley, but stand immovable on abortion rights, and give as much leeway to gay people as you can, while continuing to make a point of embracing African American culture and celebrities and athletes, and attending every Latino fiesta and *celebracion* you can get your schedule around.

And once again, *own* up to the fact that the progressive Left will never, ever vote for you with any real enthusiasm—especially after you "lost" healthcare and passed free trade. That ship had sailed like the Love Boat. And the white working class (especially males) will at best be a draw. Your key demo from now on will be "soccer moms"—upper-middle-class moms and career women, coastal and suburban, married to professionals or professionals themselves with stable careers. Women who care about quality of life issues, schools, and security—and their 35-to-54 year old yuppie husbands and boyfriends, who identify with you as one of their own. And those people just don't "do" class warfare, or support race quotas or harp about inequality. They are generally pro-choice (or if they are pro-life, not obsessive about it); they pride themselves on being tolerant (or at least not overtly prejudiced against) gay and minority co-workers, and they don't cling to guns and fundamentalist religion for comfort in a changing world. These people don't want to hear Newt or Rush harping about how Big Guv'mint is out to get them with the black helicopters—so long as Big Government never does anything to poop their party.

Translation: No more busing *their* kids into the ghettos or barrios to achieve racial balance, or mandating anything more than token levels of "low income housing" near *their* upscale gate-guarded suburbs. (And forget about passing healthcare laws that would force them to give up *their* private-practice doctors or insurance!) And don't even think about upping auto-mileage standards! Do you want to be the one to take these people's Chrysler convertibles, mom-car minivans, Jeep and Range-Rover SUVs, or Bimmer 740s and Jaguars away from them? To raise *their* taxes back to "confiscatory," significantly pre–Reagan levels?

In other words, Clinton would base his strategy on courting *traditionally Republican voters*—a sort of tit-for-tat after Nixon successfully recruited all those patriotic, blue-collar, middle-aged Archie Bunker "hardhats" during Vietnam, and after Ronnie grabbed hold of the "Reagan Democrats" of late 1970s Rust Belt workers who'd been thrown to the wolves by Jimmy Carter. And while Triangulation would hit photon-torpedo speed during the last six years of Clinton's reign, the groundwork for it had already been laid by the Clintons' best political friend.

Democratic fundraiser extraordinaire (and future Virginia governor) Terry McAuliffe was proud of his nickname, "Mad Dog McAuliffe," which he'd earned as a teenager for his fearless eagerness in taking on two, three, four older bullies at a time, either to protect himself or defend his best friends and brothers. By the time he was in his thirties, the sports-playing young lawyer from Syracuse had taken more bloody beatings and endured more excruciating pain than Rocky or Mike Tyson, with a cheerful endurance and indefatigable energy level that amazed even hardened Beltway insiders. Having cut his teeth as a campaign aide after college for Jimmy Carter's 1979–80 reelection campaign, where he first rubbed shoulders with A-list corporate Democrats like Hollywood uber-mogul Lew Wasserman, "Mad Dog" prided himself on doing quote, "anything for a check." He was the type of uber-alpha male who would wrestle a live alligator in a "Battle of the Network Stars" type DC publicity stunt, compete in Iron Man marathons, grab a trumpet during a photo op with the University of Virginia's marching band (later on, while Virginia governor) and start playing it on the spot, or stand up on stage and tell *Gong Show*-worthy one-liners and self-effacing jokes at Beltway press shows.

This good-naturedly ruthless Irish guy was an ideal protégé for New Democrat and neoliberal power broker Tony Coelho (the later showrunner of Al Gore's disastrous 2000 presidential campaign). According to lefty journalist Jeffrey St. Clair, under Coelho's tutelage in the greed-is-good late 1980s, the eager young McAuliffe learned that "no enterprise was off-limits [to Coelho] ... weapons makers, oil companies, chemical manufacturers, big banks, sweatshop tycoons. Indeed, McAuliffe made his mark targeting corporations with festering problems." But what about the traditional bulwarks of the Democratic Party from Franklin Roosevelt through Walter Mondale, Michael Dukakis, and Mario Cuomo, you ask? Big Labor? Environmental groups? Teachers unions and college academics? "Not only didn't their objections matter, they actually made McAuliffe's pitch more appealing." After all, the Republicans didn't have any clout with those groups to begin with. "In the early '90s.... McAuliffe recruited robust donations from Arco and Chevron, Entergy and Enron, Phillip Morris and Monsanto, Boeing and Lockheed, Citibank and Weyerhauser. Many of these corporations had all but abandoned the Democrats during the Reagan era, but McAuliffe lured them back with promises of favorable treatment."

As St. Clair's article showed, the reaction from what left-wing wags would later call "the Democratic wing of the Democratic Party" was one of shock and awe. Just as Lawrence O'Donnell had indicted, we now had a Gingrich Government as well as a Clinton Administration. For left-wing liberals and economic inequality watchdogs, the triangulated latter half of the Clinton era was an absolute blood-boiler.

Of course, Dick Morris, Terry McAuliffe, George Stephanopoulos, and both Clintons (and Al Gore) all knew that this Triangulation strategy could *only* work while maintaining the current optics—with a bunch of downscale, bitter, intolerant, war-on-women "dittoheads" from the Deep South and the rural interior ruling the Republican roost. People who were guaranteed to make moderate swing voters think twice, politicians who would horrify progressive leftists and people of color into doing whatever Clinton wanted, so as to protect against this much bigger threat. And savvy political chess player Newt Gingrich must *also* have known on some level that (at least for the time being) he could only hold power if he had an equal and opposite enemy to play off of. Someone whose very presence in the White House infuriated and inflamed his rage-addicted base voters, a couple who symbolized all of the 1960s and '70s worst excesses.

Br'er Rabbit's Budget

After all the sound and fury, the first true test of the Gingrich Congress versus Clinton came exactly one year after the 1994 mid-terms, with the first federal budget to bear a Republican House and Senate's stamp. The 1995–96 budget battle and attendant "government shutdown" was nothing less than the full dress rehearsal for the 2011 and 2013 "debt ceiling" wars between the Obama administration and the "Tea Party" Republican Congress to come.

The Gingrich Congress was demanding one cut after another to what remained of the social safety net and to "giveaway" government programs. (Of course, almost all the spending cuts were domestic ones; the already-downsized military-industrial complex and corporate-welfare recipients wouldn't have to worry about living on beer and skittles just yet.) Plans for a federal level line-item veto (which Bill Clinton supported) were shot down when prerogative-guarding Democratic senators like Robert Byrd sued against it (successfully) in federal court, as a violation of the federal government's separation of powers. The Senate, even after going into Republican hands, wasn't keen on cutting funding for their committees and aides and benefits, and the balanced budget amendment just wasn't gonna happen. (Could Ronnie have won the Cold War, and could FDR have put Hitler in his place, with a balanced budget amendment?) As it was, Clinton and Newt had agreed to balance the budget within seven years—but just how to do it was the trillion-dollar question.

As the impasse went on—to the utter, open-mouthed horror of the sincere left, and what remained of working-class voters in the "New Democrat" party—Clinton began giving in to Gingrich hook, line, and sinker. Again and again and again! Forget about "triangulating" to find a Third Way—he was holding a fire sale! To progressives, the initial budget "negotiations" seemed to resemble some sort of demented *Saturday Night Live* or Carol Burnett skit, where a dictator or Mafia don makes up the rules of a poker game as he goes along, "winning" with every hand. And with each Clinton give-in, Newt Gingrich's already elephantine ego ballooned into Michelin Man proportions. It was working out better than he ever dreamed—or so he initially thought.

But that was just the sweet spot that Clinton had been looking for, once it became crystal clear that Gingrich and his crew never really wanted to deal in good faith in the first place. With his beloved, irrepressible, seventy-year-old nurse mother less than two years dead, and her final husband now eighty years old, Bill Clinton drew the line at Medicare and Social Security, and at cutting the schools a second time. And with that, he set a trap for the Republicans as cleverly as Dick Van Dyke catching who dun it on that week's episode of *Diagnosis Murder*. Insatiable and unwilling to compromise, Newt and the Republicans cried "No deal!" And with no budget in sight and IOUs running out, the federal government actually "shut down" over December of 1995 until January 6, 1996, with almost all nonessential and nonmilitary services closed. The "Ging-Grinch Who Stole Christmas" indeed (as a famous political cartoon claimed). Newt never realized with the warmth of his initial victory, the cold shiv of the switchblade that was now in his back.

By now it was clear that Gingrich and Tom DeLay's "revolutionary" new Republicans never wanted a budget. What they'd wanted was a temper tantrum. Above all, they wanted to do anything to weaken Clinton, to make sure that he would fail, to put him in his place, as Election 1996 got underway. As Mitch McConnell would later say of Barack Obama, the name of the game was *to see that this president failed.* Just like health care reform. As Diana Christensen in *Network* might have said, these Revolutionaries wanted to "articulate their rage" at the fact that HE was still there (along with that castrating b*tch wife of his). Still grabbing all the headlines, still the "face of America" to the rest of the world, still making all the decisions. As the quintessentially liberal Berkeley university's website on the government debt cycle put it, "Republican focus [had now] shifted to limiting President Clinton's ability to govern."

Like a Bart Simpson or Cartman-style big baby—holding his breath, banging and kicking, wetting his pants, and saying the F-word and the N-word in order to get attention—the red-meat "revolutionaries" in this Congress finally got to have their giga-tantrum, banging their heads against the floor until they passed out. And like the overworked teacher finally showing her disbelieving school parents at the conference what kind of little devil their "little angel" turned into behind their backs, this would be the tailor-made "teachable moment" that the Clinton crew was looking for. Something to show the great American public what the reactionary representatives they hastily elected in 1994 were *really* like.

Victory from the Jaws of Defeat

As the brilliantly lovable *Salon* writer and MSNBC star Steve Kornacki pointed out in 2013, the Republican Revolution turned out to be just as much of a gift to the long-term future of the Democrats, as it was a temporary boon to the Republicans. (Especially after the culture war went Chernobyl, during the Monica Lewinsky scandal.) In 1993 and '94, Bill and Hillary's forthright feminism and pro-choice stance, insistence on diversity in their Cabinet appointments, initial pushes for gay equality and AIDS funding, attempt at a national healthcare overhaul, major league gun control laws, and the 1993 tax increase and NAFTA controversies—all had driven home the point that there was simply no place left for social conservatism or old-fashioned values in the Brand Clinton Democratic Party. The fed-up Southern, small-town Midwestern, rural Californian, and upstate New York voters who used to "split" their votes between the president and their local congressmen, senators, and governors, now began voting a straight Republican ticket, to make a statement and send a message. Newt and Rush and Bill and Hillary had successfully nationalized both the Democrat and Republican brands.

Then the anti-science, anti-choice, anti-gay, red-meat congressmen and senators who took over the party during and after '94 got in front of the cable cameras and the news headlines. The college-educated "soccer moms" and "desperate housewives" who lived in The World Where Things Work, the liberated shoe-shopping single gals in the big cities, and the white male yuppie professionals, Hollywood execs, and computer gurus who'd spent the 1980s voting Republican (at least for president) because of their pocketbooks, now recoiled with disdain. They began turning their backs on the party of Newt, Rush, Cheney, Karl Rove, Tom DeLay, and Pat Buchanan—especially as Bill Clinton would soon prove to be just as good for their pocketbooks as Ronald Reagan himself. And the rising African American and Latino populations only doubled down in order to defend themselves.

Newt Gingrich and Bill Clinton, while superficially one another's worst enemy, instead found themselves to be each other's best friend. Locked in a political danse macabre, where one man's fate was inextricably linked to the other, where each one's worst excesses worked as the get-out-of-jail-free (and get-out-the-vote) card for the other. The lead story was now Bill Clinton versus Newt Gingrich. Him, or me. This time, it was *personal...*

The Return of Ronald Reagan

Bill Clinton had used the full faith and powers of his presidential bully pulpit and media-savvy ways to let America know just who was at fault with the budget battle, and boy, had it worked! The budget passed *without* an annihilation of the eldercare and educational safety nets. But savvy seducer to the end, Bill *didn't* rub Newt or the Republican Congress' noses in his victory. Far from it. Instead, just three weeks later during his State of the Union Address, he would utter an all-out love letter to Ronald Reagan, in what many truly liberal politicians—including a young African American lawyer and community organizer named Barack Obama, and the openly gay Rep. Barney Frank of Massachusetts— would consider to be the most signal phrase of Clinton's entire Presidency. On January 27, 1996, New Democrat Bill Clinton took to the microphone and announced in front of the Congress, Supreme Court, Federal Reserve, and world TV, that "The era of Big Government is over!"

Progressives and liberals looked like a Don Knotts or Jim Parsons character might look after getting punched in the face by Arnold Schwarzenegger. They were knocked so far into next week, it was a wonder there weren't little cartoon birds tweet-tweeting around the tops of their heads. Bill Clinton had WON! He had just *beaten* Gingrich and his crew! His popularity was up, and Newt's was going down! The public had blamed Newt for the shutdown, not him, just as they should have. *He* had the advantage, what Yiddish speakers would call the *handl,* the clout and the leverage. Yet instead of using it to crush the Gingrich Congress once and for all, Clinton just gave conservatives a sloppy wet kiss on TV! What was going on here?

What was going on here, of course, was Triangulation 101. And for the next two years, Bill Clinton would finally began to be able to start really passing some meaningful laws with relative ease through the Congress. The kicker is, most of these laws would be basically *Republican-leaning* and conservative in nature.

For one, there was media deregulation. One of the few things that Gingrich and Clinton stood arm-in-arm on was agreeing to take Ronald Reagan's trend towards lazziez-faire in cable, telephones, and motion pictures up to the next level. You didn't need to be Sherlock Holmes to figure out why big-business oriented Republicans wanted media deregulation. And with people like David Geffen, Barry Diller, Lew and Edie Wasserman, Ted Turner and Jane Fonda, Steve Jobs, and Steven Spielberg writing one six-and-seven-figure check after another to the Brand Clinton Democratic Party, it wasn't exactly hard to figure out why Clinton wanted to sign off on media deregulation as well.

Now, with the Telecommunications Act of 1996, the floodgates were opened—much to the horror of left wing progressives, watching the Time-Warners, Rupert Murdochs, Disneys, Viacoms, and the like gobbling up all the book publishers, newspapers, affiliate stations, movie theatres, and whatnot that had survived the Reagan era, like Ms. Pac-Man on an eating binge. By the early 2000s, the situation had gotten so extreme that even pro-corporate Ann Coulter was quoted by Thomas Frank as calling it "the monopoly media" and "the opinion cartel." By the year 2000, Disney would effectively run ABC, numerous cable channels, much of indie royalty Miramax Films, and several book publishers, in addition to its legendary film studio. Time-Warner would control a cable empire from CNN, TNT, TBS, Cartoon Network, and Time-Warner Cable to The WB (now The CW), the MGM library, book publishing, and be the nation's leading supplier of prime time, in addition to Warner-Brothers films and Robert Shaye's indie lynchpin, New Line/Fine Line Features. (Time-Warner also disastrously merged with Internet giant AOL from 2000 to 2003). Both Viacom (which by 1999 included Paramount, Simon & Schuster, and CBS), and Fox's News Corporation would become if anything, even bigger. And the crown jewel went to General Electric, which by 2004 would control not only all of NBC but Universal movie studios and both studios' cable TV offshoots as well, selling half-interest to cable giant Comcast by the end of the 2000s.

Progressive leftists and non–Hollywood liberals were downright horrified. With Internet blogs and "social media" just beginning in the 1996–2000 era (and sites like DailyKos, Firedoglake, and Pam's House Blend still in the faraway future), liberals felt what little access their fellow progressive muckrakers and rabble-rousers had to media megaphones, as well as anything resembling local input in culture and news, was now under house-arrest. And non-corporate conservatives were also livid at more decisions being made, and more cultural "narratives" being written, from the pro-gay, pro-choice, anti-gun, trendy halls of Hollywood and Manhattan, instead of back at the all-American, hometown local level.

But media consolidation was the least of the Clinton-Gingrich agenda in 1995–96. While not one single state in the union had legalized gay marriage by 1996, Hawaii's Supreme Court had recently been in the headlines for flirting with the issue. More to the point, there were ongoing pushes for legal "domestic partnerships" in states like California, Hawaii, New York, Massachusetts, Vermont, and the like, which would grant gay and lesbian couples essentially the same rights as a married couple (with regards to hospital visits, power of attorney, inheritances, pensions and healthcare, and so forth). In the latter Bush II and Obama eras, the fight against marriage equality was framed in the sacredness of marriage as an institution. During the '90s, it was done in much blunter and harsher terms. So what if it wasn't actually *called* marriage? If the law itself puts its Good Housekeeping seal of approval on gay relationships, and allows those so-called "perverts" and "immoral" people the same "domestic benefits" as a married couple, then how long will it be before the hellfire and brimstone starts flowing? Indeed, while the sexual revolution and the Equal Rights Amendment/*Roe vs. Wade* era had wiped away Victorian and Edwardian "anti-sodomy" laws in almost all of the coastal states back in the '70s, many of the interior and Southern "red states" still clung to laws that criminalized homosexuality with all ten fingers—until the Supreme Court finally said enough in 2003's *Lawrence vs. Texas*.

As a preventative measure—and just to underline that those filthy AIDS-mongering gays weren't going to boss around *this* government anymore (in culture-warrior eyes, Don't Ask Don't Tell was a total victory for the gay agenda), the Republican Revolutionaries in Congress began floating a full-on constitutional amendment to "limit marriage to a man and a woman." (Sadly and predictably, the ugliest hysterical arguments were all on dis-play—that gay marriage would inevitably lead to men marrying dogs and cats or their underage children, that three and four people would then be allowed to marry one another, and all the dismal rest.)

By some accounts, this was so extreme that even Newt Gingrich himself was on the run. While a Constitutional amendment stood little chance, the culture war that would surround it would be the worst thing since the *Roe* and ERA battles. It would be a fight where everybody lost. There was only one chance to head it off—a Defense of Marriage Act, that would say that—just on the off chance that a single state legalized gay marriage (as Massachusetts would do in 2003–04), that gay marriage would not have to be recognized in any other state but the one it was issued in.

While being a flagrant violation of the Full Faith and Credit and Equal Protection clauses of the Constitution (by allowing each state to pick-and-choose which legally exe-cuted marriages between consenting adults they would recognize and which ones they wouldn't), DOMA would be a symbolic gesture for an era when tolerant, Obama-voting Millennials were still learning their times tables. For hard-right Republicans, it would be the stunning blow that they were aching to deliver to those uppity "fags," with their "un–Christian" art and their decadent "Queer Cinema" films and their borderline-pedo S&M novels by Dennis Cooper and Bret Easton Ellis and their AIDS plague. And it would prove to everyone who wasn't a total wingnut that Bill Clinton had "matured" from being the sexual-harassing, wife-swapping, pot-smoking hippie that he'd been back in the day. That he also cared about "family values" and moderation in the face of excess.

Interestingly enough, Bill Clinton's signing of the Defense of Marriage Act was so out-rageous in the LGBT world that it ignited the momentum that led to its successful ouster 17 years later. (Ironically, DOMA was killed by the country-club Republican Supreme Court of John Roberts and Anthony Kennedy, at the hands of uber-Republican lawyer Ted Olson, alongside Democratic legal eagle David Boies.) Until the mid-to-late 1990s, the idea of "gay marriage" seemed to many liberal "queers" of the ACT UP activist variety to be campier than the draggiest Bette Davis or Bette Midler impersonation. A burlesque John Waters parody of straight marriage, where once-proud "sexual outlaws" (as gay novelist John Rechy termed his community) would now be reduced to the same bland, boring, Cool-Whip con-formity of the Stepford Wives and *Mary Hartman Mary Hartman*. THAT's why we moved away from our families to Greenwich Village and The Castro, to South Beach and Province-town, to Palm Springs and Las Vegas and Hawaii and WeHo in the first place—to *escape* that stifling so-called "normality!" (Indeed, gay marriage first crossed over into mainstream discussion in 1989 courtesy of *New Republic* "Tory" Andrew Sullivan, who was despised for his otherwise right-leaning politics by the radical gay left.)

But after DOMA (and Don't Ask Don't Tell), the mood in activist gay circles flipped almost as instantly as a price tag on *The Price Is Right*. (Clinton further infuriated gay activists by renewing Old Bush's ban on entry to the United States by anyone suffering from full-blown AIDS.) As outer-than-out literary lions like Edmund White and David Ehrenstein would later note, this final proof that the straight community was still *this* hostile, still *this* threatened by the mere idea of two men or two women slipping a ring on each other's fingers, now galvanized the gay community in favor of marriage. *We want to have it because you DON'T want us to have it.*

But in 1996, all that progress was still in the future. And from a progressive liberal's point of view, the worst was yet to come.

"Welfare queens"

Until the era of Lyndon Johnson and Richard Nixon, the image of someone on welfare "relief" was of a proud, taciturn, Gary Cooper–type farmer whose crops had failed for the year, or a factory worker or coal miner whose union was on strike. Someone who needed some temporary help to see things through to the next season. Or a careworn Whistler's Mother, a Mary Coin, an Auntie Em, a humble and grateful widow-woman whose husband had been killed in a car accident or on the job, who gratefully and prayerfully accepted the money to keep her household safe and the kids in school. There was no need to make being on welfare an object of especial shame, because those proud, rules-playing Americans were already probably ashamed of being on it in the first place, of needing help, of taking a "handout." By the end of the 1970s, though, there was an entirely different narrative at work. The public's perception of a typical welfare recipient now wasn't someone who had been forced into it by extreme hardship, disability, disease, or bad luck, but of a different kind of person. Someone who didn't use the social safety net as a safeguard, as much as they used it as a *hammock*.

Now, the public's image of a welfare "queen" was of an angry, overweight black woman like *Precious'* mother Mary (or perhaps an equally belligerent Latina firecracker, fast-talking and gesturing in mile-a-minute Spanglish), trying to control her brood of unruly, different-father-for-each-one children, surrounding her like a dust cloud. Their white-trash equivalent was the sizzle-toothed, coffee-nerves, meth-crack-heroin Babymama, taking time out from her trash talk shows and trailer park, to chain-smokingly join her sisters of color down at County, in yesterday's halter top and hot pants, with her bruised and unbathed children. Women who didn't humbly *ask* for assistance, looking downward so as to avoid eye contact, but who haughtily *demanded* their welfare *and* their AFDC, *and* their food stamps, *and* their Medicaid, AND their low-income housing, and all the rest … and who wouldn't stop until they got it, too!

These appallingly ugly, racialicious and sexist stereotypes had helped the Republicans win one election after another during the 1980s, from 1978's "tax revolt" to 1980's Carter defeat to 1984 and 1988's Reagan/Bush landslides to 1990's big wins for Pete Wilson in multicultural California and William Weld in Kennedy-backyard Massachusetts. By the time Bill Clinton took the reins, these media stereotypes had become almost an article of faith— for *both* parties.

And at that critical moment in 1996, Marty Peretz's *New Republic* sealed the deal. In August, *TNR* published a cover story featuring a stereotypical Precious-and-Mary-style black welfare queen, threateningly smoking a burning-hot cigarette over her helpless, bottle-nursing baby. (Of course, no man was in sight.) It was bordered by a pulsating shade of blood red with bold black letters headlining, "DAY OF RECKONING." The sub-header beneath the picture read, "Sign the Welfare Bill Now!"

The cover was so eye-poppingly racist, it went beyond even *TNR's* lengthy excerpting of *The Bell Curve* (the 1994 Charles Murray bestseller that argued for genetic inferiorities in intelligence among blacks and Latinos). To many an African American's eyes, they might just as well have published a 1930s cartoon of a bamboozled moon-eyed mammy with her "pickaninnies" talking in jive talk and Ebonics. It was almost as if they'd put minority single moms on a "Most Wanted" or "Public Enemy #1" poster. Ta-Nahesi Coates used this very cover story as Exhibit A when he ruefully and publicly later recalled in 2014, that at the '80s and '90s *New Republic,* "Black lives didn't seem to matter much."

Yet at its core, this was merely standard neoliberal doctrine "unplugged." From Franklin Roosevelt through Lyndon Johnson, Hubert Humphrey, Jimmy Carter, and even Richard Nixon, poverty was seen as primarily being caused by racial and class discrimination, lack of opportunity or education, poor physical and/or mental health, income inequality, and hard-luck people who could just never catch a break in life. Ronald Reagan, Margaret Thatcher, Barry Goldwater, Milton Friedman, and both Bushes had said *au contraire—*poverty was primarily a moral and character failure of the poor person himself, or because of the "culture of poverty" in ghettos, barrios, and trailer parks. People who felt that the world owed them a living, people who were either too shiftless and lazy (or unprofessional and rude) to get or keep a job, people who felt they were "too good" to take unpleasant or demeaning jobs, people who had no motivation or ambition beyond sitting on the couch and watching *Ricki Lake* and *Springer* with their Yoo-Hoos and Ho-Hos.

Liberal Democrats went into post-traumatic stress disorder at the very *idea* that Bill Clinton might sign on the dotted line. Congressman and civil rights hero John Lewis thundered, "Where is the compassion? Where is the sense of decency? Where is the heart of this Congress? This bill is mean. It is base. It is downright lowdown. What does it profit a great nation to conquer the world, only to lose its soul?" Arne Christenson added that the change in welfare from an entitlement to a time-limited program with strict pre-qualifications "was a huge, huge compromise of everything the progressive Democrats had been for, for at least a generation."

This, *this* is what drove the disillusionment of liberal Democrats throughout the latter run of Clinton's term, and set the stage for the final political acts (like Nader for president) of the millennium. Yet there was also another strategic reason why Bill Clinton made welfare reform, big-media giveaways, and curbing gay enthusiasm into the lynchpin of his re-election strategy against 1996's Republican nominee, the outdated Republican Senate fixture Bob Dole.

Christopher Hitchens and Alexander Cockburn were far from the only left-wing pundits who believed that secretly, Al Gore and Bill Clinton actively *wanted* the Republicans to retain control of the Congress and Senate in 1996. Clinton insider Peter Edelman told Michael Takiff that Bill Clinton made a "brilliant political deal for himself. The deal was, implicitly, that the Republicans get to keep the House [and the Senate too, as it turned out] because they can point to this achievement," especially with their loyal-turnout bases. And "Clinton gets reelected president. As far as the Republicans were concerned, he was going to be reelected anyway."

Al Gore had an even bigger motive to go along with this little game of Let's Make a Deal. Once it became statistically clear in October 1996 that Clinton was going to beat Bob Dole, Gore actually *opposed* the release of surplus Democratic National Committee funds to help struggling Democratic congressmen and small-state senators in their re-election campaigns, according to journalist Alexander Cockburn. Gore was reported to fear that if the Democrats retook the House in '96, it would promote his arch-rival, the paleo-liberal Dick Gephardt—who made no secret of his presidential ambitions—to an equally high-profile and prestigious perch (succeeding Newt Gingrich as Speaker of the House) as the one Gore himself would have in 2000. Better to neutralize the threat *now*. Better to, as Michael Corleone and Tony Soprano might say, "take Gephardt out" before things got any further.

And why wouldn't Bill Clinton and Al Gore think that way? Did they really want to risk a *rerun* of the nightmare world of 1993–94, when the Democrats at least nominally controlled both houses of Congress, the year when Washington had "lost its mind?" It may well have been in the *Democratic Party's* best interest to have a Democratic Congress and Senate going forward. But the culture-war hysterics and media optics of the past four years had made it crystal clear that it was in *Bill and Hillary Clinton's* (and Al Gore's) personal best interests to renew everybody's favorite Congressional comedy show: "Leave it to Gingrich!" And to make sure that the entire Democratic Party had no other choice but to remain Brand Clinton.

Al Gore was in hot enough water that fall, as details of his unethical and possibly illegal partisan fundraising on government time came out in the press, as well as his attendance at an Orange County area Asian Buddhist temple, which may have been a cover for illegal campaign contributions from China. In April of 1996, Gore attended a fundraiser at the Hsi Lai Buddhist Temple in Hacienda Heights, California. Critics alleged that this visit was the connection point for an international-intrigue scheme for the People's Republic of China—then seeking Most Favored Nation status in world trade—and several wealthy Chinese citizens, to funnel campaign and legal-defense cash to Gore and Clinton. Gore also was alleged to have made over 60 fundraising calls from his White House office during the 1996 re-election race, which appeared to violate 1883's Pendleton Act, barring fundraising during normal work hours on federal grounds. Gore argued that the spirit of the Act was to bar federal employees from trying to extort money from taxpayers for voters, or from subordinate employees under a patronage system. And since telephones (much less the Internet) weren't around in 1883, Gore delivered the deathless line that there was "no controlling legal authority" stopping him from doing what he did.

An even more blatant and vulgar example of pay-to-play Clintonomics had already happened, when Terry McAuliffe sent a notorious memo just after the Republican Revolution in late 1994. Mad Dog had suggested that the party's "top supporters" be allowed to meet with President Clinton at "meals, coffee games, morning jogs, coffees"—as though the White House had become the Continental Hyatt House or the Biltmore Hotel. And it would be a five-star price tag that those "top supporters" would have to pay for this privilege. McAuliffe said in his 2006 memoir, *What a Party!* that he thought there was "nothing controversial" about the memo—but he still tried to keep it under wraps and worded it with lawyerly precision just the same, because he felt the undisciplined Clinton White House "leaked like a sieve." McAuliffe was right on that score—the letter was soon leaked, and became known as the infamous "Lincoln Bedroom" memo. Critics of the Clintons charged that Bill and Hill were essentially renting out the Lincoln Bedroom to bling-a-ding-ding Democratic donors and celebrities, in exchange for plenty of campaign cash.

By the time the presidential campaign had kicked into maximum overdrive after Labor Day, the Welfare Reform Bill of 1996—largely conforming to the Republican Revolutionaries' wish list—had Bill Clinton's proud autograph on it. It would be Newt Gingrich's biggest and highest-profile triumph ever. After the humiliation of the Christmastime government shutdown nine months earlier, with the ghosts of the 1995 Oklahoma City attacks hanging over fire-breathing anti-government rhetoric, Newt and his team were now as re-energized and refreshed as a pop diva making her comeback. The Democratic Party's power intelligentsia had essentially said "You were right all along!" to Ronald Reagan, Milton Friedman, and Margaret Thatcher's view of poverty and dependence. Total vindication for conservatives!

Meanwhile, the Republican-controlled state houses were doubling down. Fresh off the triumph of the successful passage of Proposition 187 in 1994 (only for it to be inevitably struck down by an "elite" federal court), a conservative African American Republican businessman and University of California regent named Ward Connerly introduced a "sequel" in 1996, a voter initiative which would ban all forms of affirmative action quotas, what little remained of school busing, and racial set-asides and preferences (aside from those absolutely mandated by federal court order) in the state of California. However, the bill's passage, like Prop 187, was a dark victory. From 1996 on, California's booming, activist, and activated African American and Hispanic populations saw to it that almost no Republican would ever again be elected to the Senate, as governor or lieutenant governor, or attorney general, for the next 20 years. (The only truly notable exception was a pro-choice, pro-gay, and minority-friendly Republican movie star named Arnold Schwarzenegger, in his term as California's "Gover-nator" from 2003 through 2010.)

So intense was the anti-affirmative-action furore on the Republican right, three years later in 1999, a newly elected Florida governor named Jeb Bush felt that he couldn't even wait until after his brother's 2000 election race to install an affirmative-action ban in Florida. He did so barely a year after taking office. According to some reports, Jeb feared that impatient right-wing activists would go ahead and put an affirmative-action ban on the November 2000 presidential ballot if he didn't pre-empt them right now, which Jeb thought would result in massive minority turnout to vote against it—and his big brother George W.—at the same time. If so, Jeb needn't have worried. The same thing happened anyway. After the Florida repeal passed in early 2000, outraged African American voters promised to "remember in November!" The NAACP shattered all known records for registering black voters in Florida that year. Strangely, when the 2000 election did happen, a series of mysterious road closures, block-long voting precinct lines, and "mistakenly" purged, overwhelmingly black voter rolls occurred. (But of course, who would ever *dream* that Jebby had anything to do with *that* kind of thing? It was *only his older brother's election for president* that was at stake!)

Once again, all this proved that Dick Morris' media strategy was right on the nose. Allow the extreme right to have their head with culture-war theatrics outrageous enough to motivate an equally outraged reaction from Democrat-base and minority voters—and then cynically use it to build for the future. Subtly encourage the worst Tea Party-style talk radio and radical-right firebrands—not the Beltway Republican moderates—to become the "face" and voice of the Republican Party. The better to brand *yourself* as the only remaining voice of reason.

The Perfect Storm

When the presidential election tally came back on November 5, 1996, it was no surprise that it had the lowest proportional turnout of any post–World War II presidential election in America—the sharpest possible contrast to 1992's booming Rock the Vote record-breaker. Adding insult to injury, the past-their-sell-by-date duo of 73-year-old Bob Dole and 66-year-old "Reform Party" rerun Ross Perot had *still* managed to stitch together a slim "silent majority," if their vote totals were combined. Despite the phenomenal first growth spurt of the Internet and cellular technologies and all their exciting opportunities, despite an economy that had finally turned around and was starting to boom, and a budget heading towards balance, Bill Clinton had won re-election—with only 49 percent of the popular vote. It was the ultimate Whatever, Never Mind election for the cynical, grunge-rock and hip-hop 1990s.

And as expected, both houses of Congress remained in solidly Republican hands, with congressmen of all parties returning to and from their gerrymandered "max white" and "max black" racially redrawn districts. Just as his contortionist consultants and neoliberal cheerleaders had predicted, Clinton's "triangulations" on welfare and gay marriage had robbed those grumpy old white grandpas, like Dole and Perot, of their strongest argument: that Clinton was nothing but an irresponsible, tax-and-spend, 1970s style liberal. Welfare reform in particular could (and did) damage Clinton's standing with some high profile African American leaders like Marian Wright Edelman, who theatrically resigned from office in protest. But really, at the end of the day, where else were people of color going to go? At least, as long as Newt Gingrich or Rush Limbaugh or Pat Buchanan were on the other side! Sure enough, Clinton shattered the records with blacks (as well as with Latinos) in percentage shares of the 1996 vote. Indeed, he owed his razor-thin re-election to them—and to "gender gapping" women.

As *Salon's* Steve Kornacki further elaborated, Bill Clinton had barely won New Jersey and New Hampshire in 1992, and only because of how hard they were hit by the corporate downsizings and real estate crash of the early '90s recession. They hadn't voted Democrat since LBJ versus Goldwater. Yet by 1996, Clinton won them both in a landslide. "In other states where Republicans had won or were at least competitive through the Reagan and Bush Sr. years"—states like California, Connecticut, Vermont, Delaware, Oregon, Washington, Illinois, Pennsylvania, and Michigan—those days were over after the 1994 Revolution took hold. "All [were] once in play at the presidential level—all written off as blue states today," Kornacki rightly noted. The Republicans' biggest short-term triumph would also be their biggest long-term path to death by demographics.

In other words, Dick Morris' triangulated "soccer mom" strategy was working better than a Martha Stewart cake recipe! It's no wonder that this Clintonomic strategy was thought up by veterans of the Nixon era like Morris and David Gergen. As a 2015 "diary" on the liberal website DailyKos article noted, "Nixon got working class whites to vote against their economic interests" due to racial issues and Vietnam-era patriotism against the hippie counterculture. (Though actually, Nixon did very well for working-class whites until the last few months of his run.) Likewise, "Clinton got wealthy [white] suburbanites to vote against their economic interests in the name of being against the far-right social platform that Pat Buchanan and Dan Quayle were pushing, and [he] got the northeast and the west coast to vote Dem permanently." But they wouldn't have kept "voting Dem permanently" unless two things happened: unless Clinton had *also* embraced Wall Street and Silicon Valley's Reagan-lite "economic interests" sooner or later. And unless the Republican brand *remained* inextricably wedded to the "far-right social platforms" of Pat Buchanan, Dan Quayle, the Christian Coalition/Moral Majority, Focus on the Family, and Rush Limbaugh.

*   *   *

As 1996 ended and 1997 began, Brand Clinton was Terminator-strong, soaring like the dot-com stock market. But without Bill and Hillary, the Democratic Party seemed as pencil-necked and bankrupt as a bunch of '80s junk bonds. It wasn't *even* a contest. Yet with that "anti–American degenerate" Bill Clinton (and his hated wife, "Hitlery") now returned to power, whatever sense of victory that the talk-radio and Richard Mellon Scaife/Koch Brothers ultra-right had about successfully keeping all and every other branch of government, now fizzed out like a birthday balloon. More and more, hard core conservatives would no longer turn to Establishment politicians from either side, to try and make sense of this brave new world—but to Rush Limbaugh, Dr. Laura Schlesinger, Dennis Prager and other talk radio titans, plus sizzling bestsellers by Oliver North, Pat Buchanan, William Bennett, and Robert Bork. (And some brand new right-wing hotties named Ann Coulter, Nancy Grace, Michelle Malkin, and Laura Ingraham, plus a new cable network called Fox News, starring former *Inside Editon* anchorman Bill O'Reilly—all of whom and which would come to prominence during Clinton's second term.)

In the early days of *Saturday Night Live*, a young and handsome Chevy Chase played a smart-alecky and almost insanely pompous New York newsman (the first to anchor *SNL's* legendary Weekend Update), who began each broadcast reminding those less fortunate that "I'm Chevy Chase—and you're not!" Whether you were on the Republican Revolutionary right, or on the Michael Moore/Ralph Nader left, as the 1990s decade wound up, there was only one true star in the Democratic Party, baby. He was Bill Clinton—*and you weren't*.

Though he would continue to be sliced and diced for the next four years by talking-heads pundits on CNN, NPR, PBS, *Meet the Press, The Nation, National Review, New Republic, Time, Newsweek, U.S. News* (and brand new venues like Fox News, MSNBC, *Salon*, and *Slate*), that was no longer the main point, either to the Democrats or the Republicans.

The point was that Bill Clinton could get himself successfully elected (and re-elected) as president.

And all those other people *couldn't*.

5

If It Bleeds—It Leads

You're television incarnate, Diana. Indifferent to suffering, insensitive to joy ... all of life is reduced to the common rubble of banality. War, murder, death ... they're all the same to you as bottles of beer! And the daily business of life is reduced to a corrupt comedy. You even shatter the sensations of time and space into split seconds and instant replays. You're madness, Diana, virulent madness. And everything you touch dies with you...

—News division chief Max Schumacher (William Holden) to
programming exec Diana Christensen (Faye Dunaway),
in the movie Network (1976)

Of course, the political environment of the '90s was in no small part the creation of a scandal-obsessed media. The media just lost its mind for eight years, went crazy with class hatred and status-envy and groupthink and scandal-mongering. The Clintons had their problems ... [but most of their] problems are the ones the media created for them.

—Ezra Klein, "The Tony Soprano Approach to Clinton-Hatred" (2007)

In 1996, when *The New York Times* gave his old friend Maureen Dowd a regular column, our old friend Michael Kinsley gave MoDo some tongue-in-cheek advice. From now on, he warned, "You've got to write boy stuff. The future of NATO, campaign-spending reform, throw weights. Otherwise they won't take you seriously." ("They" being the Washington political-news and New York literary-publishing establishments.)

Whether or not those subjects were really "boy stuff" is something on which we'll reserve comment, but Serious Subjects like those—approached from a straight-ahead, largely humorless, just-the-facts-ma'am viewpoint—had been the bread and butter of newspapers, magazines, and nightly network broadcasts from the Depression and Pearl Harbor to the fall of the Berlin Wall. Not anymore. As Kinsley proudly noted, Dowd "wisely ignored me and proceeded to reinvent the political column as a comedy of manners" on the "psychopathologies of power," thereby spicing up the "tired literary form" of dry and flavorless political reporting with a zingy, blingy, magically delicious new Freudian recipe. And before the '90s were over, she would score a Pulitzer Prize for this reinvention, too.

Meanwhile, the mainstream news—both newspapers and magazines, and the nightly TV news broadcasts—now found themselves suddenly forced to compete with the brand new rules of Internet journalism, where the only rule was that *there were no rules*. Instead of CBS worrying about competing against NBC, or *Time* fighting against *Newsweek*, the mainstream media now had to contend with brand-new and mushrooming Internet sites like Slate and Salon.com (both founded circa 1995)—who followed the Peretz-Kinsley-

Sullivan *New Republic* model of grabbing youthful and irreverent Ivy (or near-Ivy) educated Gen Xers (and later Millennials)—turning them loose to write hip, buzzy, and culture-provoking articles in succinct, Net-friendly lean cuisines, rather than turgid 5,000 word essays or humorless anchorman intonations. (And fortunately, it should also be said that Slate and Salon demonstrated at least something of a commitment to gender and racial diversity from the get-go, in the starkest contrast to many of the traditional broadcast and print news organizations at the time.)

However, when the Internet giveth, the Internet also taketh away. For every quality website like those, there were others that ran the gamut from white supremacist neo–Nazis and Holocaust deniers to foaming-at-the-mouth hard leftists, reverse-racists, and Commie mommies. Not to mention more conspiracy crackpots and black-helicopter theorists than the Lone Gunmen on *The X-Files*. All of them proudly unconstrained by the restraints and constraints of "serious" journalism and discourse, let alone good taste. There were also new right wing print magazines, some of them subsidized by far-right moguls like Richard Mellon Scaife and the Koch Brothers, and top-rated talk radio demagogues like Rush Limbaugh and Dr. Laura. On the left side of the street, there were snarky provocateurs like Michael Moore, Al Franken, and Bill Maher. And 24-hour cable news networks with a non-stop rotation of talking (and screaming) heads.

No question about it, the reinvention and rebranding of the news itself was the top news story of the 1990s. The "scandal-obsessed" media, as Ezra Klein rightly remembered it, was desperately trying to both stay ahead of the curve, and to frantically hold on to what they'd got.

Tabloid TV

The yellow-journalism brick road that would lead to the media environment of the '90s took its first baby steps a decade or so earlier. In 1974, *People* magazine launched to sizzling success, while national supermarket tabloids like *The Globe, Star,* and the *National Enquirer* began taking up where the late '50s likes of *Confidential* left off. Then, on September 14, 1981, *Entertainment Tonight* beamed its first broadcast from coast to coast across the skies of the U.S. and Canada, using then-up-to-the-minute satellite technology. It was specifically designed for the 7 to 8 p.m. early evening "prime time access" syndicated timeslot, and it ruled the ratings practically from Day One.

Taking note of *ET's* monumental success, the next big step would occur in 1987–88, at the beginnings of the launch of the Fox network by media mogul Rupert Murdoch. *A Current Affair* debuted in 1987 over the Fox-owned stations, and "went national" in the fall of 1988, starring a prematurely grey newsman who combined a surface sense of reportorial dignity with a hard-edged, Jon Stewart-style attitude, and who was for many a perfect combination of sexy and sleazy. His name was Maury Povich. The show hit a home run within its first year or two, unearthing a "sex tape" of hot young "bad boy" movie and TV star Rob Lowe, not to mention occasional fist-fights between its young male reporters and cameramen and their unwilling subjects. *A Current Affair* ruled the ratings and the buzz right off the bat, and Fox never looked back until the show finally ended in 1996—by which time a slew of equally sleazy imitators had taken the field.

Indeed, as the 1990s dawned, a veritable tabloid-show sweepstakes was hitting the airwaves. By 1994, shows like *Hard Copy, Inside Edition, American Journal, Entertainment Tonight,* and *A Current Affair* were inescapable to anyone who switched on a TV from 7 o'clock to 8. And a funny thing happened because of these programs' scheduling—and their massive popularity. Most of them were shown in the 7pm and 7:30 "access slots" (in the case of top-raters like *ET* and *Current Affair,* their station contracts usually required it)— which meant they *ran immediately after* the "legitimate" national network news shows that were broadcast from 6:30 to 7. Others ran at 11 o'clock or 11:30, immediately after the late local news, as a cheap moneymaking alternative to the otherwise unbeatable Carsons, Lenos, and Lettermans. Here's why that's so important: because of this, to the casual viewer, there was *almost no distinction* in the seamless flow of watching Tom Brokaw, Dan Rather, or Peter Jennings presiding over the "serious" world-political news at 6:30—and the sexy and sin-sational hot stuff that came immediately afterward. Indeed, the only difference was that the entertainment and tabloid magazines were more cinematically produced, faster-paced, wittier, a hell of a lot more fun to watch—and got better ratings, too.

Talking Trash

Pioneering talk show titan Phil Donahue first cracked the door open in the 1970s, tying his legendary daytime show not to what a popular reference book called the "couch-bound showbiz prattle" of Johnny Carson and Merv Griffin. Instead, *Donahue* preferred to focus on serious (and seriously promotable) juicy lifestyle hot-buttons—like menopause, divorce, atheism, abortion, date rape, wife-swapping, interracial romance, child molestation, transsexualism, and other previously taboo TV topics. Occasionally Donahue would devote an entire show to an A-list movie or music legend or a TV icon, but those were the exceptions that proved the rule. For the most part, on his show, regular Real People were the "stars." Or rather, real people who might *seem* regular and "normal," but were often anything but. In an era when going to see an "analyst" or heading off to "encounter group therapy" was becoming an upper-middle-class status symbol, and when books like *Passages, Fear of Flying, I'm OK—You're OK,* and *The Female Eunuch* were flying off the shelves, Donahue tapped into the zeitgeist of late '70s and early '80s society like few others—especially for his target audience of liberated and "finding themselves" female viewers. And if Phil Donahue had opened the door, then an African American anchorwoman and actress who managed to combine being pioneeringly powerful with being big-sister lovable, confidently strode right through it.

Premiering in 1986, hot on the heels of her Oscar nomination for *The Color Purple,* and after a decade in local TV as one of the first black women ever to co-anchor the news or host her own local talk show, Oprah Winfrey shot to the top of the ratings from her first episode to her last (some 25 years later). Feminist and empowering, Oprah soon became as glitzy a Hollywood superstar as Barbra Streisand or Meryl Streep, yet she also seemed as friendly and down-to-earth as your big sister or next-door neighbor.

Yet for all of Oprah's many marvelous and deserving merits and innovations, her show also defined what author and pundit David Frum came to call the "Let's Talk About ME" society.

Two years before Oprah, a radio therapist named Sally Jessy Raphael had become the first female talk show hostess to truly make a ratings impact since '40s big-band and '50s variety-show queen Dinah Shore retired from her bubbly daytime talker in 1980. Sally's show and its subject matter could get pretty dodgy at times, but it was tempered by her no-nonsense temperament and (at least mostly) genuine-seeming concern for her guests. (Sally Jessy's show was also given the questionable honor of being savagely spoofed by Bret Easton Ellis in his signature 1991 novel, *American Psycho*. One of antihero Patrick Bateman's favorite ways to relax when he wasn't raping and killing young women and homeless run-aways, or watching hard core pornography to the tunes of Phil Collins and Huey Lewis, was by viewing a talk show whose hostess bore more than a little resemblance to Sally, and who showcased one maudlin, campy-ghastly feature spot after another—talent shows with seriously disabled children pathetically trying to be "normal" … tragic victims of domestic violence … and so on.)

Ultimately however, Oprah and Sally's forthright feminism and Phil Donahue's touchy-feely "sensitive male" image created an opening. Longtime controversy-baiting ABC investigative journalist Geraldo Rivera (just after presiding over an embarrassing "Secrets of Al Capone's Vault" special, that turned up empty) and talk-radio shock-jock Morton Downey, Jr., launched their shows in 1987. Instead of Donahue, Sally, and Oprah's female fans, they targeted young males with the most in-your-face subject matter yet: white supremacist groups, neo–Nazis, "separatist" African American ministers of the Louis Farrakhan reverse-racist school (often fighting against Jews or Korean shop owners), ACT UP gay activists and "Queer" transgressive artists—and of course the usual selection of pimps, molesters, pornographers, and predators.

Following in the footsteps of his mentor, the late 1960s reactionary talk show host Joe Pyne (who told Commies and hippies to "go gargle with razor blades" and other such friendly greetings), and Downey's old friend, local Orange County talk-icon Wally George, Morton Downey's show was forthrightly conservative in a Rush Limbaugh/Pat Buchanan culture war sense. He attacked identity politics and politicians, ghetto ministers, teachers' unions and snooty professors, and know-it-all liberals like a snarling junkyard dog, as his young male audience fist-pumped and cheered. Pioneering the format that Jerry Springer would soon bring to perfection a few years after the fall 1991 launch of *his* show, yelling, screaming, bleeped profanities, and fist-fighting became commonplace on both programs. Geraldo's most iconic episode saw his nose and face in a bandage following an on-air free-for-all when a KKK-type group was onstage. *Geraldo* ran through 1998, while Morton Downey's show ended in 1989, after it had been revealed he had painted a swastika on his face (in the mirror) while faking a publicity-stunt "attack" by neo–Nazis. (He died of a heart attack in early 2001, no longer at the height of his fame or infamy, but while still maintaining a very visible web-TV-radio presence.)

By the early to-mid 1990s, there were shows like *Ricki Lake,* starring the lovable John Waters movie actress who refashioned herself into a Gen-X icon with her talker, and *Jenny Jones,* the flagship of a former dancer and Vegas backup singer who saw her chance to redefine daytime talk, plus Maury Povich as he exited *A Current Affair* (he was replaced by Maureen O'Boyle and Steve Dunleavy) to launch his own program. And above—or below—them all, was of course, the gold standard of the gutter, *The Jerry Springer Show.*

With these trashy talk shows' low production costs, high ratings, youth demographics, and culture-changing success, it was perhaps only a matter of time before the networks themselves decided that it was time to gussy up these low-budget cheapie formats into something ready for big-budget, prestigious prime time. In just half a decade between 1988 and 1994, the Big Four networks launched *Unsolved Mysteries, 48 Hours, America's Most Wanted, Cops, PrimeTime Live, 20/20 Downtown, West 57th, Saturday Night with Connie Chung, Top Cops, Street Stories, Rescue 911,* and *Dateline NBC*—the last of which ran not *once* a week, but *three times* a week during 1999 and 2000, on Tuesdays, Fridays, *and* Sundays! (By 1999, even the top-notch *60 Minutes* had diluted its brand with a cheesy *60 Minutes II.*) And the rising cable networks of the '90s were hot on their big brothers' heels, in light of the newsmagazines' high ratings and cheap budgets.

Here's a week's listing from a typical Los Angeles/Orange County market *TV Guide* from 1998. During the daytime, there were *Jerry Springer, Jenny Jones, Maury Povich, Geraldo,* and *Ricki Lake.* Then in the "prime access" hours of 6 o'clock to 8, there was *Entertainment Tonight, EXTRA!, Access Hollywood, Inside Edition, American Journal, Real TV,* and *Hard Copy.* After that came the aforementioned prime time biggies: *48 Hours, 20/20 Downtown, Dateline NBC,* and *Prime Time Live.* On A&E Network, there were *American Justice, Investigative Reports,* and *City Confidential,* while the Learning Channel and Discovery had their "Forensic Files" and "Real ER" type shows, which by 1999 were inspiring an edgy young indie-film screenwriter named Anthony Zuiker to whip up a spec script for a dramatic TV series. (It was called *CSI.*) Sandwiched right in between it all was an hour or two of ever-more frantic local news broadcasts, giving the latest updates on local drive-by shootings, daycare molestations, freeway chases, celebrity scandals, panic-attacking health scares, and gory crime scene investigations. And by 1998, not only CNN, but Fox News and MSNBC, were running news programming and political discussions 24 hours a day.

EVERY. SINGLE. DAY.

News Helper

According to the legendary, glass-ceiling-shattering Los Angeles news icon Kelly Lange (Hollywood's first full anchor-woman, who ruled KNBC News from 1971 to 1998, and the local CBS station for three more years, before retiring to her career as a novelist and speaker), it was a proven fact that the two most highly rated [local news] features were diets and relationship advice—in that order. Wanna guess the third and fourth most highly rated? Crime and disease, in most cases. As the media consolidated again and again under both Ronald Reagan and Bill Clinton, local newscasts were under ever more pressure to deliver bigger, better, faster, after one deregulated merger or hostile takeover or big buyout after another. And that was just the beginning; the frenzy would go into maximum overdrive as the full impact of the Internet really hit.

Commenting in 2002 in the London *Observer* on the late 1990s rise of cable news and Internet journalism, Al Gore himself recalled, "The introduction of cable-television news" and blogger-driven "Internet news, made news [into] a commodity, available from an unlimited number of sellers at a steadily decreasing cost, so that the established news organizations"—newspapers, magazines, local TV—suddenly "became the high-cost producers of a low-cost commodity." In order to still be able to pay the bills and attract the eyeballs against this new onslaught, the established newspapers and news programs began "selling a product now that's News plus News Helper; whether it's entertainment or attitude or news that's marbled with opinion." Eric Alterman delivered the death verdict on where this all headed in his book, *What Liberal Media?* "Instead of John Kennedy and Nikita Khruschev as the iconic images of the world of 'news,'" we were now "presented the comings-and-goings of Madonna, O.J. Simpson, Princess Diana, Gary Condit, and Chandra Levy."

TV's First Reality Shows (or, Natural Born Killers)

The Monday morning of June 13, 1994, was a lovely if somewhat smoggy late-spring day in southern California. But southern California wasn't feelin' the love that year. Los Angeles, Orange County, and San Diego were still clawing their way out of a 2008-like real estate collapse, and a post-aerospace recession even more punishing than the Carter era. The smoke of the Rodney King riots of 1992, the October 1993 wildfires, and the deadly January 1994 Northridge earthquake, was only starting to dissipate. But on that very unlucky 13th day of June, all of the rest of the world's problems seemed to suddenly stop dead, when the bodies of a gorgeous blonde 35-year-old Hollywood and Laguna Beach socialite and mother, and a handsome and athletic 25-year-old waiter at Brentwood's trendy Mezzaluna restaurant (who was saving up to open his own restaurant and nightclub), were both found lying murdered, horror-movie style, in the bloody courtyard of the woman's luxury condo, just hours after she had returned from a Sunday-night dinner at Mezzaluna with her mother.

The bodies were, of course, that of Nicole Brown Simpson—the ex-wife of NFL legend, action-comedy movie star, Hertz car rental spokesman, and *Monday Night Football* commentator O.J. Simpson—and her friend Ronald Goldman. A week or so later, the case hit "the whole world is watching" status when O.J. took to the LA freeways in his famous white Ford Bronco with close friend Ron Cowling, while O.J.'s lawyer pal Robert Kardashian (who happened to have a brood of little girls named Khloe, Kourteney, and Kim growing up at home) read on TV what was clearly intended as a suicide note, reeking of guilt. The helicopter coverage of O.J. driving aimlessly and perhaps suicidally on the freeways hypnotized a media-mad, celebrity-obsessed tabloid America—but that was only the coming-out party. Let's cut to the *real* chase: An insanely jealous, hulking black man savagely murders his gorgeous blonde trophy wife, along with the hot young Jewish jock who'd died trying to protect her, and who may or may not have been her boyfriend. It was as if the entire case had been designed by a Central Casting office of ugly racial stereotypes.

And it was just as obvious "who dun it." O.J. was goin' *down*. Nobody in their right mind could think he was innocent after that. *Or could they?* Let's look at the case from the POV of someone whose "Cliff Huxtable" father or uncle was regularly pulled over in his Cadillac, Lexus, BMW, Jaguar, or Mercedes, just so he could be hassled and humiliated by for a "DWB" violation. (You know—Driving While Black). Someone who'd grown up under the police departments of James Ellroy and Walter Moseley novels. Someone who'd watched the cops beat Rodney King's ass within an inch of his life on videotape just three years ago, and still get off scot-free, just as white people had been getting off for victimizing blacks for centuries. (Or worse, someone who'd grown up with the nakedly racist Jim Crow South's police and sheriffs to deal with.) Someone who'd had family members caught in the dragnet of Ronald "Just Say No!" Reagan (and Bill "I Didn't Inhale" Clinton's) "wars" on drugs and crime.

Sadly, that was what a lot of urban Americans first thought of, when it came to the people whom Tyler Perry's immortal Madea would later call "the Po-Po." Ghettos and barrios throbbed to gangsta rap songs like "Fuck Da Police!" and "Cop Killer" in the late '80s and early '90s. Instead of thinking of the cops as their only protection against rape, robbery, gangs, and murder, many urban Americans saw the police as almost an "occupying force" in their communities. Incarceration levels had increased hugely throughout the late 1990s, even as violent crime rates themselves went down. Remember Bill Clinton's famous "Crime Bill," or the "Three Strikes" laws that were all the rage in the 1990s? Where criminals with a magic 3rd offense could be sentenced just like a hard core rapist, murderer, or child molester, even for a drug offense or shoplifting, something comparatively harmless and in many cases non-violent?

Six months into the interminable trial, 61 percent of whites believed that O.J. was guilty—while an equally large 68 percent of blacks believed he was innocent, framed no doubt by the supposedly "racist" LAPD. "In the O.J. case, the public fascination with violent entertainment and courtroom drama" became a "prime example of how media profit-seekers manufacture and exploit a mass audience," journalist and historian Haynes Johnson sighed in his excellent 2001 post-mortem on the Clinton era, *The Best of Times.* "Long before the trial even began, virtually all hope had vanished that it would provide for a watching world an example of the American criminal justice system at its best. It quickly degenerated into a spectacle that demonstrated some of the worst characteristics" of the New Media 1990s. "No one escaped unscathed."

Whether it was embattled prosecutor Marcia Clark and her African American second chair, Chris Darden, or whether it was superstar attorneys Johnnie Cochran, Alan Dershowitz, and F. Lee Bailey over on Team O.J., everyone knew going in that the physical evidence was going to take a clear backseat to the boiling racial and sexual stewpot that the case exemplified. Simply put, whoever won would be the side which furnished the jury with the most compelling "narrative." When ballistically racist homicide cop Mark Fuhrman, who had been amongst the first on the scene to handle sensitive forensic evidence, was found to be captured on tapes (made years before while collaborating with a female screenwriter on a planned movie about the LAPD) not only using the nigger-word—but *bragging* about savagely beating black men so that they wouldn't show bruises, it was virtually all over. Marcia Clark did her very best to arrest the damage, but she couldn't answer the question that Johnnie Cochran asked in his famous closing argument: "Who polices the police?" when they get out of line?

On October 2, 1995, all of the United States and Canada seemed to temporarily stop on its axis, in a way that wouldn't happen again until the 9/11 attacks six years later, when the verdict finally was read. "We the jury find the defendant, Orenthal James Simpson, *not guilty* of the crime of murder," said courtroom clerk Deirdre Robertson, stumbling over O.J.'s given name, allegedly out of her own shock at the verdict. (A gloweringly angry Judge Lance Ito, himself married to a top female LAPD officer, barely concealed his contempt for the jury's decision.) Cameras herked and jerked back to reveal O.J.'s aged mother rejoicing and praising the Lord, while Ronald Goldman and his daughter shrieked and wept openly, shaking their heads in disbelief. Novelist, veteran Hollywood producer, and high-society fixture Dominick Dunne (whose own daughter was beaten and strangled to death by her boyfriend in 1982) all but buried his head in his hands. Their reactions were the perfect stand-ins for how both Black America and White America reacted to the verdict.

As for O.J., Ron, and Nicole themselves, the real truth finally came out—too little and too late—a dozen years after the killings, in O.J. Simpson's own barely disguised confessional, *(If) I Did It,* acquired and published by Ronald Goldman's family to set the record straight once and for all. (After the criminal trial was over, Nicole's parents and Ronald Goldman's family sued O.J. in civil court for wrongful death. He was found liable, but his judgment went largely unpaid as his hefty NFL pension and his home and car, under Florida bankruptcy law—where he had relocated to in his newly won freedom—were immune to the judgment.)

O.J. finally revealed in his own words what had happened on the fatal night, when he found Nicole, clearly waiting up for *someone* if not for Ron Goldman, and picked a fight with her in her courtyard. Just then, Ron came by, sauntering in casually "as if he owned the place," in O.J.'s retelling. O.J. angrily laughed in Ron's face at the idea that a mere head waiter would know the private home address of one of his customers—unless Nicole was getting something from Ron that wasn't exactly on the Mezzaluna menu. As O.J.'s jealousy now reached volcanic proportions with the younger man, and Nicole's furious conversation filled up with more F-bombs than a Quentin Tarantino movie, Nicole finally struck out alley cat style at O.J., and fell down the steps on her porch. Ron courageously reacted to try and defuse the situation, but it was already too late—O.J. himself was starting to blank out, as if something else was taking over—just *after* he'd "remembered" that he had brought a huge survival knife with him....

In other words, it was almost exactly what Marcia Clark had said had happened all along. But by now, it hardly mattered; the trial was long over. (Not long after the book came out, O.J. *was* finally thrown in jail for, ironically enough, trying to "steal back" football memorabilia that had belonged to him, but if recovered, would have probably gone to the Goldman family as part of the wrongful-death judgment that he had so far avoided paying.) In the O.J. case, the truth had become almost irrelevant.

Just as important was the "verdict" that the O.J. case (followed four years later by the even bigger Monica Lewinsky "trial of the century") gave on the status of women in the post Anita Hill years of American culture: "For all the talk of post-feminism, for Nicole and others like her who didn't go to college, who didn't pursue a professional career, the reality is that being Mrs. Somebody often appears a better choice than being Mrs. Anybody or Ms. Myself, especially if one aspires to the benefits of the affluent life," said Haynes Johnson. "In [Nicole's] case, the choice becomes more complicated when compared to the path women of the Nineties were expected, and pushed, to follow: Go to college, have a career, have a family, 'have it all.' Wonder women! Super-moms! For whatever reasons, Nicole becomes one of those exceptions to the nineties' expectations for Ideal American Women. She fills her life with other signs of accomplishment—a tanned and toned body, designer clothes, a celebrity marriage, and abundant funds to maintain the good life."

In Johnson's otherwise worthwhile study, that's the one fluffed note that the elite academic journalist hit. In retrospect, it seems painfully obvious that Nicole was, if anything, a brilliant "career woman" who was *ahead* of her time, instead of a bubble-headed throwback to '40s and '50s gold-diggers. Just look at the TV shows, novels, and feature films that were aimed at college educated, sophisticated, professional, job-holding "ideal American women" in the fifteen or twenty years since Nicole's last tango with O.J.: *Ally McBeal, Sex and the City, Desperate Housewives, Bridget Jones's Diary, American Beauty, Eat Pray Love, The Devil Wears Prada, Will & Grace, Private Practice, Grey's Anatomy, The Good Wife, Real Housewives, Scandal, Girls.* While most of the women who were portrayed in these bestsellers, feature films, and top-rated TV series were indeed "super women" who had exciting careers, college educations, and whatnot—at the end of the day, they were still judged by themselves, their boyfriends, *and by one another* on how "tanned and toned" they were, on what "designer threads" and jewelry they wore, what upscale or luxury cars they drove, and on their New York-San Francisco-London power lifestyles, or their fashionable, all-white suburban addresses.

No, Nicole Brown Simpson wasn't just a dumb blonde who took the only path available to her to cash in. On the contrary; she had apparently realized, with the cost-benefit analysis of a power-suited Hillary MBA doing a leveraged buyout, what the real Rules of Attraction in the "post feminist" game had become, and simply played it as it laid. (Depressingly, if not surprisingly, the likely unfair portrait that O.J. painted of Nicole in his long-after-the-fact 2006 confession *was* of a nymphomaniacal, emasculating, grossly entitled bitch—the kind of person who would bellow lines like, "I can't believe you made me buy my own house, O.J.!" Not to mention allegedly telling him how violent rages and catfights aroused her, and turned her on.)

Haynes Johnson righted himself when he noted that "the mass cultural message relentlessly beamed at the twenty-something [wannabe] Nicoles through television dramas, sitcoms, soaps, films, and seductive commercials and flossy magazines ads" all reinforced the "desirability of following the material-girl path" above all else. Unfortunately, the second-most-outrageous Crime of the Decade contained an even uglier example of someone who was being raised by her posh parents to be a literal "material girl" right from Day One—and we especially emphasize the word *girl* here—and the equally horrific death that awaited her.

The first sight most Americans and Canadians saw of the beautiful little 6-year-old girl named JonBenét Ramsey was after her short six years on this Earth were already all over, after her lifeless body was found, strangled and tortured with sexual overtones, in the basement of her millionaire parents' home on Christmas in 1996. But JonBenét had already left a video legacy that would have put some 25- and 30-year-old supermodels to shame, as people got an after-the-fact eyeful of JonBenét's "career" as the kindergarten queen of America's strange subculture of baby beauty pageants. TV news viewers and those who were on the Internet in 1997 and '98 were treated to the sight of JonBenét in her element, singing and dancing in skin-tight costumes like some kind of kindergarten Vanna White or Barbara Mandrell—dancing the double-hustle with her hips, licking her glossed lips and rolling her eye-shadowed eyes, sticking out her hardly discernible breasts and teasing her bleached Farrah hair, photographed in soft focus close-ups like a Hollywood actress' publicity stills.

In her own way, JonBenét revealed as much of a cultural, feminist, and sexual divide in our country as O.J. had along the most toxically visible racial fault-lines. The JonBenét case was the ugliest example of the sexual schizophrenia that afflicted '90s culture—far worse, considering, than Monica Lewinsky, Paula Jones, or Anita Hill. 1990s America had more of an awareness of incest and molestation than ever, but parents still bought and allowed their pre-pubertal children to dress in Gap Kids and junior-designer clothes that were "modeled" (literally) on sexy and sophisticated adult attire. As the Religious Right (quite correctly) pointed out, 1990s high school and college kids couldn't have been *more* sexualized or encouraged to start having teenage sex, on TV shows like *90210, Party of Five, Buffy the Vampire Slayer,* and *Dawson's Creek,* or in movies like *American Pie, Scream,* and *Bring It On.* (Let alone the middle-school Tweens who never missed those shows and movies, because they were so "mature" and "hawt.") Popular "young adult" literature became ever more cockteasing and titillating throughout the decade, as any family values school board member, librarian, or grandma would be only too unhappy to tell you.

The same '90s teens who were being freely encouraged to hop from one blowjob to the next in their summer blockbuster movies and their Fox and WB soap operas, suddenly became as pop-eyed and innocent as Barney and Elmo from *Sesame Street,* as soon as a Big Bad Grown-Up entered the room. And of course, as any outraged viewer of *The 700 Club* knew only too well, children as young as 12 and 14years old were being taught by their teachers in health class how to put condoms on bananas and have safe sex or masturbate against AIDS and teen pregnancy—whether their conservative parents *wanted* them to be taught this or not. Whether you were Patricia Ireland from the National Organization for Women, or Paul and Jan Crouch from *Praise the Lord,* you had to agree that when it came to underage sex, 1990s culture was a case of multiple-personality disorder.

As to JonBenét's case herself (which remains unsolved), just about everybody in the United States and Canada "tried and convicted" John and Patsy Ramsey of their daughter's murder. And quite understandably, too. The Ramseys couldn't have acted more suspicious than if they were characters from an Alfred Hitchcock movie—hiring media publicists and "lawyering up" before their daughter's body had gotten cold; giving bizarrely bipolar TV interviews where they managed to seem both blankly unmoved by their daughter's torture and murder, yet also freaky and hyper; and they generally seemed to take a hostile and uncooperative position with local law enforcement. The impression that this super-rich, "1 percent" couple gave was that they preferred to handle this amongst themselves, amongst Their Crowd, Their Kind of People.

On one of his last regular shows in 1998, *Geraldo* even invited his studio audience to act as a "jury" after the "evidence" that had come to light by then in the JonBenét case was presented. (Not surprisingly, they found the parents "liable.") In 2000, CBS completely dominated the May Sweeps with a miniseries called *Perfect Murder, Perfect Town,* starring Marg Helgenberger and Ronny Cox as Patsy and John, which also clearly implied that the parents were guilty. (Later that same year, CBS would rule the ratings with a Norman Mailer–scripted miniseries that prefigured FX's recent ratings-ruler *American Crime Story* on the OJ trial.) And in 2008, Joyce Carol Oates published a roman-a-clef about the case, titled *My Sister, My Love.* (Spoiler alert—the mom did it.)

Shockingly, that same year of 2008, DNA evidence came out that proved that an unknown intruder *besides* John or Patsy Ramsey had actually committed the murder. (Perhaps one of the reasons for the long delay and confusion was that a seriously disturbed man, John Mark Karr, "confessed" to JonBenét's murder, only to later be proven innocent! He'd apparently just wanted the media notoriety that serial killers and maniacs were given in the *Dateline NBC* 1990s and 2000s!) Sadly, Patsy Ramsey never lived to see her vindication-of-sorts; the cancer she'd been fighting since even before JonBenét's murder finally caught up to her in 2006. Apparently—and horrifically—an outside killer *did* manage to break into the Ramsey house the night of the murder, and lie in wait in order to kill (and perhaps attempt to rape) little JonBenét. Whoever he was, unless he (hopefully) died or was jailed or mentally institutionalized in the intervening years, is still out there.

The third act of the 1990's trilogy of A-list media and murder scandals happened just months after poor JonBenét was found, and right at the same time as O.J. Simpson's "wrongful death" follow-up trial in Orange County was coming to its climax. And it would be a double feature of senseless death, with a sad ending that would rivet the entire Western world.

Part One began when a brilliant and handsome, but mentally unstable and substance-abusing, young gay Southern California man named Andrew Cunanan finally snapped, in the early spring of 1997. The 27-year-old Cunanan was a very literal "star fucker" and media whore who went on a cross-country murder spree, targeting wealthy and predominantly gay men who were known for being on the fabled "circuit" of the A-list gay male party lifestyle. If O.J. Simpson and Willie Horton exemplified the ugliest, *Birth of a Nation* stereotypes of black men—insanely jealous, woman-beating, out to rape or kill innocent white people—then Andrew Cunanan was the most virulent kind of gay stereotype: shallow, heavily into hard core S&M and bondage, obsessed with working out, physical beauty, the "right" clubs and discos, designer labels and convertibles, status and money. As Maureen Orth wrote in *Vanity Fair,* "Wherever [Cunanan] went, he craved the limelight and aspired to the top, whether through charm or falsehood." He was Patrick Bateman from *American Psycho* come to life.

Needless to say, the media-mad, celebrity-crazed 1990s were the perfect breeding ground for this little creep, and the dark journey he was about to undertake. After Cunanan snapped, following one too many falls off the high-speed merry-go-round of 24-hour party people and the coke/crystal fast lane, he began his spree by killing his best friend, 28-year-old Jeffrey Trail, followed by his (Cunanan's) former lover, 33-year-old David Madson. Having apparently realized that he had no way out, now that he had backed himself into the dark corner of murder, the fame-starved Cunanan began to set his sights on targets that would help him attain the kind of grim "immortality" of past A-list assassins like Mark David Chapman, John Wilkes Booth, John Hinckley, Sirhan Sirhan, James Earl Ray, and Lee Harvey Oswald. Escaping to Chicago, Cunanan brutally murdered the 75-year-old (and apparently straight) real-estate magnate Lee Miglin (the husband of cable cosmetics queen Marilyn Miglin), stealing Miglin's green Lexus and making his escape to New Jersey. He then killed the (straight and middle-class) cemetery caretaker and gardener William Reese, for no other reason than to rob him and "exchange" getaway cars. At least Reese was spared the torture that Cunanan put his first three victims through—slasher-movie murders that exhibited all the telltale signs of a "pathological, sadistic sex offender," and were designed to be so shocking and atrocious that newspapers, TV, and what little existed of the Internet just couldn't resist them.

Cunanan had made little attempt to hide his identity, and by June the marauding maniac who was still at large had made the big-time—the FBI's fabled Ten Most Wanted List. But Cunanan was already planning a grand finale worthy of the kind of "star" he fancied himself as being. In the highlight of his status-crazed life, Cunanan had apparently met his idol, the legendary gay Italian fashion designer Gianni Versace, years ago as a teenager at Versace's villa in Lake Como—and apparently the buff-bodied and handsome Cunanan was, err, 'memorable' enough for Gianni himself to call out and remember his young acquaintance when they met again in 1990, at a San Francisco society ball. Versace epitomized the lifestyle that Cunanan craved, of sex, parties, drugs, movie and TV stars, fashions, cars, jewelry, and Croesus-like wealth and social clout. Like the jealous wife who points a gun at her cheating husband and says, "If I can't have him, no one can!," Cunanan's next stop would be the heart of Miami's ultra-chic gay South Beach—where Gianni Versace kept one of his vacation homes....

The assassination of Gianni Versace made world headlines, as did the eventual and inevitable public suicide of his killer, when Andrew—having achieved his nauseous goal of permanent infamy, with every biography and memory of fashion icon Versace now stained by his assassin's presence—finally and belatedly took himself out. (His work now complete, as it were.) But as if in a twist that Andrew Cunanan himself might have wrought from beyond the grave, although Cunanan and Versace's part of the story was now finished, the drama was a long way from over.

Versace's funeral in July of 1997 attracted the tippity-top of the worldwide A-list, and at the very top of that list was gay rock icon Elton John, and his best friend, Diana, Princess of Wales. Diana had just undergone a world-headlined divorce from Prince Charles after 15 years of marriage, as Charles had been showing no apparent intention of giving up his long affair with Camilla Parker-Bowles (whom he would eventually marry). Diana was now being dragged across the headlines for her new romance with Harrods department store heir Dodi al-Fayed. Diana and Dodi became the '90s answer to Jackie and Aristotle Onassis, as this Middle Eastern Muslim scored the ultimate WASP goddess-diva and symbol of high society beauty.

But Diana and Dodi would be reunited with Gianni Versace all too soon. On the last weekend in August of 1997, the couple were leaving a Paris function in their Mercedes limousine. An army of tabloid photographers, in cars and on motorbikes, were lying in wait for them outside, after which Diana's chauffeur, Henri Paul, the deputy head of security at the Paris Ritz, engaged the paparazzi in a real-life movie or TV-style car chase. Paul was found to have been under the influence of alcohol, and lost control of the heavy Mercedes as they ploughed at top speed into the Pont l'Alma tunnel in Paris. A horrific crash ensued, killing Paul and Dodi Fayed almost instantly, and injuring bodyguard Trevor Rees-Jones, who at least survived. (Of course, there were theories that the crash was caused deliberately, perhaps by MI-5 or the Royal Family themselves, out of either revenge or embarrassment at Diana's divorce and post-divorce society antics.)

Diana died in a Paris hospital not long afterward. Not only Great Britain, but the entire world went into a period of mourning for "The People's Princess," as she was known, with a celebrity-packed state funeral carried by virtually every first-world TV network. A devastated Elton John returned to his second funeral that summer, repurposing his iconic 1973 tribute ballad to Marilyn Monroe, "Goodbye Norma Jean," into "Goodbye England's Rose," in honor of the late Princess. (It was also the week that an even more important symbol of charity, perhaps the 20th century's very synonym for goodness, Mother Teresa of Calcutta, had gone to her great reward at age 87. However, while Teresa's funeral and death weren't entirely forgotten, she was "upstaged" in death by the media frenzy over the much younger, prettier, and more glamorous Diana.)

The money quotes came from Diana's brother, Lord Charles Spencer, when he gave a press conference shortly after Diana's horrific death. "I always believed the press would kill her in the end. But not even I could imagine that they would take such a direct hand in her death, as seems to be the case! It would appear that every proprietor and editor of every publication that has paid for intrusive and exploitative photographs of [Diana] has blood on his hands today." (America would suffer its own sequel to Diana's traffic-accident tragedy, when John F. Kennedy Jr., the former "First Son" and publisher of the political-hipster magazine *George,* as in Washington, died along with his glamorous wife, Carolyn Bessette, in a plane crash off Martha's Vineyard in the spring of 1999. While not achieving the worldwide, round-the-clock media coverage of Diana's funeral, President Clinton's essential takeover of JFK Jr.'s services ensured saturation coverage.)

It would be some comfort to think that if nothing else, perhaps the horrible deaths of JonBenét Ramsey, Gianni Versace, Princess Diana, and Dodi Fayed—all having paid the ultimate price for their media fame—would have been a cautionary warning. Unfortunately and chillingly, they were only the beginning.

What Liberal Media?

As we've already noted, the Ivy educated, neoliberal baby-boomer journalists writing for *Newsweek, Time, Vanity Fair, The New Yorker, The New Republic, The Los Angeles Times, The New York Times,* and appearing on CNN, PBS, and *Nightline,* were mostly in the tank for Bill Clinton during his first go-round of 1992. But though Ann Coulter, William Bennett, and Bill O'Reilly might disagree, this wasn't because Clinton was left-wing—there was nowhere near this kind of ga-ga fawning over genuine liberals like Walter Mondale, Michael Dukakis, or even Mario Cuomo. It was because Clinton was a *media-hip Baby Boomer liberal.* Someone whom these "liberal media" folk could personally identify with, someone they'd like to make friends with.

And nobody noticed this more than right wing moguls like Carnegie-Mellon banking heir Richard Mellon Scaife, energy zillionaires David and Charles Koch (the Koch Brothers), the conservative Regnery book publishing family, and future Fox News founder Roger Ailes. After seeing George Bush, Sr.'s approval rating literally *cut in half,* going from a better-than-Reagan 90 percent in spring 1991, to approaching Carter and Nixon levels in summer 1992 (followed by Bubba's triumph in the fall), they wasted no time in fighting back.

Eric Alterman debunked a lot of the hyped-up '90s myths about how "liberal" the media really was, in his excellent 2003 study (titled, of course, *What Liberal Media*)—but Alterman also gave it away when he freely admitted that the overwhelming majority of A-level journalists were indeed *socially and religiously* liberal. And THAT's what counted in the hearts and minds of much of "red state" America. From Fox News to the *New York Times* (and everything in between), the top journalists themselves were overwhelmingly pro-choice and gay-friendly. Mostly in favor of gun control and evolution and sex-ed, and embarrassed by Pentecostal or Southern Baptist altar-call theatrics. They watched arthouse films, Emmy and cable/PBS shows, edgy comedians, and had devoured existentialist novels, "humanist" philosophers, and Freudian psychology at honors high schools and good colleges.

To someone who felt threatened, even outraged, by the entire cultural "code" that a Bill and Hillary (let alone a Barack) represented, to a sincerely religious and cultural conservative, or to a World War II or Vietnam veteran who'd had it up to here with the reflexively smug and snarky, America-questioning, *Harvard Lampoon/Saturday Night Live* attitude of the Ivy-graduated commentariat—the news media *was* in fact hopelessly liberal. And they had every right to say it was, too. And to a Michael Moore-Barbara Ehrenreich-Ralph Nader style lefty, someone who craved to hear more about income inequality, and less '80s-style blather about the "irrationally exuberant, best economy ever," the mainstream media wasn't "liberal" at all. For someone who opposed military adventurism, whether the "humanitarian" interventions of Madeleine Albright or the hard core later ones of Dick Cheney, the media *was* hopelessly corporate, controlled, and conservative. And *they* had every right to kvetch about it, too.

In reality, the air-quote "respectable" media of the 1990s was pursuing the same kind of tapioca-pudding objectivity and bland moral equivalence in presenting serious news and "think pieces" as it had always done. What *had* changed was just how intractably divided alongside cultural, racial, economic, and religious lines that Diversity America was itself becoming. Now add the do-it-yourself freedom of the growing Internet, where everyone from the wingiest conspiracy theorists, neo–Nazis and white supremacists, to the nuttiest left wingers and academic theorists, could build an insta-platform for themselves.

Author, Author!

To further illustrate: Once upon a time in the late '90s, there were three authors who wanted to write a politically oriented book. Author Number One was a young conservative up-n-comer from your friendly neighborhood right-wing think tank, looking to make his book-industry bones. His book proposal for your consideration was called *The Great Betrayal: How a Liberal Elite Is Destroying America's Family Values!* It would feature his picture on the cover, wearing the same "see, I told you so" expression that Rush Limbaugh and Bill O'Reilly use as their visual signatures. Or if "he" was a physically attractive "she," like late 1990s up-and-comers Ann Coulter and Laura Ingraham (or later on, Sarah Palin), it'll feature her posed hands-on-hips in a discreetly sexy outfit, and a "you bother me" facial expression.

Not to be outdone, Author Number Two—our first author's feminist or gay or economically leftist opposite number—comes from a tragically hip, big-city "alt weekly." He wants to write a book called *The Great Betrayal: How Corporate Crony Capitalists Undermined and Outsourced the American Dream.* Despite being a prep-school alumnus and a USC or NYU Film School grad, he'll pose for the cover in proletarian/slacker chic, denim shirt and baseball cap backwards, while wearing the same kind of smug, self-regarding smirk.

Finally, there's Author Number Three, who simply wanted to write a straightforward account of the economic and cultural trends affecting and afflicting his time. He was trying to play by the rules that his Professor Fifty Year Olds taught him in high school and college, and while interning at the local paper or small-town TV station. (You know, little things like objectivity, reportorial neutrality, "just the facts, ma'am," being unbought and unbiased, truly "fair and balanced," comforting the afflicted while afflicting the too-comfortable...)

Well, in the parlance of *Let's Make a Deal,* guess which two authors were (and still are) likely to get The Big Book Deal of the Day—and which one was probably going to get "zonked!" (You don't have to be Monty Hall, or even Wayne Brady, to figure out the answer.) The superior literary and journalistic merit of the third proposal wasn't—and was no longer—the point. The salient point was that the first two books both had a readily identifiable and easy-to-market-to target demographic, with built-in infrastructures for support. They were both "promotable," and everyone knew exactly who was going to respond to them.

Late 1990s bookstores and bookshelves overflowed with one air-quote 'expose' of the Clintons and their supposedly insatiable lust for power, greed, and perverted sexual habits, even before the Monica Lewinsky scandal. And each insta-bestseller adhered to the same format: "How Dirty Filthy Liberals Are Threatening to Destroy, Undermine, and Ruin Absolutely Everything." They were eagerly lapped up by mailing lists, and hit the jackpot on the launched-in-1995 Amazon.com. And it wasn't long before publishers and bookstore-chain buyers began crafting liberal spinoffs that followed the same format ("Conservative Dummies Are to Blame for Everything and Liberals Are Totally Awesome"...) plus books that said that anyone who truly believed in God or Jesus or an afterlife was a stupid idiot ... and all the dreary rest.

By comparison, the third book—the one that *wasn't* just preaching to the choir, the one that wasn't just a greatest-hits compilation of talking points memos, the one that didn't bend and break facts over its knee to fit its pre-recorded "narrative," the one that didn't stick to as tightly formatted a script as a rigged 1950s quiz show—that one looked as plain and vanilla as a shake from Foster Freeze! Why bother with it, when the first two will create fireworks?

Writing about power brokers exercising their power without meaningful regard to context or to whether their powerful decisions would actually be *good for people* or not was, in Joan Didion's term, "political pornography." If that's true, then these type of pop-political books which began proliferating in the '90s (and continue through to today) were the intellectual world's answer to slasher movies. Verbally violent, filled with self-conscious shock and forced hype, designed to stimulate the reader's limbic regions and raise their blood pressure with a cathartic release—and little else. These kinds of books existed not to educate, inform, or illuminate their readers, *but to do the precise opposite:* to merely validate what the readers *already* felt and knew (or thought they did)—not to challenge or enlighten.

And as hard-edged as they were by their titles and their snarky attitudes, under the hood they really came from the same touchy-feely world as Oprah, Dr. Phil, Wayne Dyer, and Dr. Joyce Brothers. Whether it was Rush Limbaugh or Michael Moore, the books were designed to "empower" their readers to feel better about themselves—to tell the "truthiness," as Stephen Colbert might have put it a few years later. The Sales and Marketing departments of their publishers would identify a large market segment (the Republican Revolution/future Tea Party Right; the frustrated, Old Labor, economic Left) who felt oppressed and ignored—with good reason, too—by the insufferably insular, Beltway cocktail-party elite "consensus."

And then they would pander to that group by giving them the warm fuzzies of personal validation by a big, rich, influential media authority figure. "Finally, someone else 'gets it!'" their readers would say, as they lapped up the copies. "This guy really tells it like it is! You go, Rush/Michael/Bill-O/Ann/Judge Bork/Al Franken/insert-name-here…"

Bottom line: Both the liberals and the conservatives' new media echo chambers were making the hopelessly "centrist" and "mainstream" news look that much more degenerate (to the values-voter right) and *also* that much more corporatist (to the economic/foreign policy left)—at one and the same time. And that made truly "objective" or mainstream reporting look that much more outdated and pathetic—to just about *everybody*.

The Permanent Campaign War Room

"You want a viewer to react emotionally to a contestant. *Whether you react favorably or negatively is really not that important*; the important thing is that you *react*. You should watch a contestant hoping the contestant will *win*—or you should watch a contestant hoping that the contestant will *lose*," to have someone so irritating, irredeemable, and unlikable that people would "watch him, and *pray* for his opponent to win!"

Thus said the wonderful and esteemed TV game and talk show producer Dan Enright, in a fall 1991 interview, nine months before his death at age 74. Unfortunately, the same principle applied too well to people playing the ultimate "TV game show" for the highest stakes. The deservedly acclaimed 1993 documentary on the Clinton-Gore media boiler room, all-too-accurately titled *The War Room*, showed how all of these savvy media principles (though some might say *lack* of principles) were put into deadly action.

After having watched Republican media gurus like Lee Atwater, Karl Rove, Pat Buchanan, and Roger Ailes eat goody-goody Democrats like Walter Mondale, Michael Dukakis, and George McGovern for breakfast in the '70s and '80s, Team Clinton decided to get just as down and dirty—and sophisticated. His nuance-parsing, demographically targeted, media-savvy mavens like George Stephanopoulos and James Carville planned each Clinton media event just like producers of a rigged quiz or reality show, like a bunch of staff writers plotting out tonight's episode of Jimmy Fallon or Stephen Colbert. Who would speak when, what "acts" or messages or constituencies would get the top of the bill and the big finish (the "grabbers" or "showstoppers" in Broadway terms). And which issues and answers would be sent to the back of the bus.

These kinds of stage-produced, rigged rallies only illustrated what a "vassal relationship," as Joan Didion once wisely put it, that most people would now have with those who would govern them. With 24-hour cable TV, talk radio, political bestsellers, and the steady rise of the Internet, the White House realized that while elections would be won or lost in a single day, if Bill Clinton were to govern effectively after winning, he would have to go into what many media pundits very correctly termed as the "Permanent Campaign" mode, especially after the 1994 mid-term Republican Revolution. Team Clinton realized they couldn't afford to give themselves, *or the general public*, a minute's rest. (Their opposition certainly wouldn't!) In Lyndon Johnson's famous phrase, they would have to "sit on the ballot box"—or in this case, the Nielsen ratings box and the newspaper and magazine press boxes—on a 24–7 basis.

Caught in the "Crossfire"

CNN's top-rated *Crossfire* became the essential business model for the cable news showcases of the 1990s. The show, which started in the mid–1980s and became a CNN sensation for the next two decades, had a genius-simple format: Two top opinion journalists or media figures, one representing the "conservative" and one representing the "liberal" side of the street, would battle it out at top volume over the hot button issues of the day, in between interview features with other colorful characters from right and left. And who else but good ol' Michael Kinsley would take the host's chair in 1989, playing the "liberal" against a Who's Who of pre–Tea Party, ultra-right royalty like Robert Novak, Rush Limbaugh, John Sununu, Jerry Falwell, Pat Buchanan, and Oliver North. (Perhaps the only people besides Ann Coulter or the late Joe McCarthy himself who could make a self-admitted "not very liberal" free-trader, labor union foe, austerity fan, and passionate yuppie like Mike Kinsley come across as a doctrinaire, pinko leftist.)

There was certainly a lot of good unclean fun to be had in watching a friendly, bookish intellectual like Kinsley soaking with perspiration, red cheeks, and hyperthyroid eyes— while Jerry Falwell or Pat Buchanan casually rubbed another war-on-women or gratuitously homophobic gobstopper in his face, with all the delight of Roseanne or Andrew Dice Clay saying another dirty word. All that was missing was the laugh track. And seeing a stereotypical African American ghetto demagogue like Jesse Jackson, Al Sharpton, Johnnie Cochran, Marion Barry, or Maxine Waters scowling, preachin', and finger-pointing at Limbaugh, Novak, Sununu, or Bill O'Reilly—as the right-wingers deliberately race-baited and provoked them right back—one might have the same kind of guilt-laughs one would get at watching a politically incorrect "bamboozled" 1940s cartoon, or an *Amos & Andy* rerun. At least the format was fair and balanced. By the time the credits crawled, both black and white, both liberal and conservative guests alike—all looked like hell warmed over.

People like Limbaugh, James Dobson, and Dennis Prager rocked talk radio from coast to coast, followed quickly by the likes of Sean Hannity, Larry Elder, Laura Ingraham, Dr. Laura Schlesinger, and many more. And despite the late 1980s scandals of Jim and Tammy Faye Bakker and Jimmy Swaggart, fundamentalist and dominionist TV networks and radio shows continued booming throughout the '90s, even in "secular" enclaves like southern California and Washington, D.C. Paul and Jan Crouch's Trinity Broadcasting Network, Pat Robertson's *700 Club* and Family Channel, and individual tele-evangelists like Falwell, D. James Kennedy, Benny Hinn, Jack Van Impe, Hal Lindsey, and John Hagee ruled the 1990s cable and UHF-channel alternate worlds, even as *Left Behind* apocalypse thrillers flew off the shelves.

In *What Liberal Media?*, Eric Alterman said that a 1997 National Committee for Responsive Philanthropy report revealed 12 major conservative foundations were awarded over $200 million in grants and subsidies just from 1992 to '94 alone. (These investments paid off big-time, with the Republican Revolution that fall.) And in 1995–96, Rupert Murdoch frosted the cake when he decided to finally answer his fellow media mogul, Southern liberal Ted Turner (who'd inadvertently gotten the whole ball rolling when he founded the center-left CNN way back in 1980). Murdoch hired Nixon and Reagan-Bush media maven Roger Ailes to launch his own 24-hour cable network called Fox News. No surprise that Fox News launched around the same time as President Clinton was passing floor-to-ceiling deregulation of the TV, radio, and motion picture industries—against the hair-tearing objections of progressive Left voices in his own Democratic Party.

Scandals 'R Us

O.J. JonBenét. Andrew Cunanan. Jeffrey Dahmer. Princess Di's car-crash death, and the "*Dallas* at the Palace" atmosphere (as one tabloid put it) at Buckingham that preceded it, with Prince Charles and Camilla Parker-Bowles reigniting their long affair. "Malibu Madam" Heidi Fleiss, who kept a little black book almost as infamous as Monica Lewinsky's little black dress, filled with Hollywood movers and shakers who used her escort service. And Heidi's eastern soul sistah, 17-year-old "Long Island Lolita" Amy Fisher, who shot her 30-something lover Joey Buttafuoco's wife Mary Jo in the face. And their male equivalents, like Vili Fualaau, the 12- or 13-year-old junior-high jock who got a very literal kind of sex education from his teacher Mary Kay Letourneau, and Sam Manzie, the 14-year-old gay teen who started having sex with a 40-year-old man who found him on an Internet chat-room in 1997, and then was forced by the police to give evidence on his (statutory) rapist "lover" against his will—only to have a psychotic break due to the stress, brutally murdering another young boy who was going door-to-door in his suburban neighborhood a few days later.

And let us not forget Whitewater and Gennifer Flowers and Paula Jones, and Vince Foster's suicide—or was it *murder?* Or white-trashy figure skater Tonya Harding, who hired thugs to injure her principal U.S. competitor, America's "ice princess" Nancy Kerrigan, at the 1994 winter Olympics—only for an already under-suspicion Tonya (wearing tear-running Tammy Faye Bakker makeup, no less) to burst into sobs in front of unsympathetic, grim-faced Euro judges when her skates came undone during her big moment. ("Tonya vs. Nancy" set ratings records that were in the same league as the *M*A*S*H* and *Seinfeld* finales, several Super Bowls, and "Who Shot JR?")

And how about Eric and Lyle Menendez, who also tried to play the child-abuse and molestation card in their 1993–94 murder defense for offing their Beverly Hills socialite parents in 1989, only for many of the same legal players to move on to the even more exciting O.J. case right afterwards? And what about John Wayne Bobbitt, whose wife Lorena cut off his favorite body part as a revenge for infidelity? Then there was Susan Smith, the mother who in 1994 added the worst kind of insult (blaming a fictitious African American carjacker) to the worst kind of injury (savagely murdering her two toddler children by drowning them fully conscious, in a locked car driven into a lake, so she could start her life over with a new boyfriend). And if early 2001 still counts as the '90s, you can add a natural-triple jackpot of the murder of Bonnie Lee Bakley, wife of film and TV legend Robert Blake; plus the kidnap-murder of Congressional intern Chandra Levy; and Andrea Yates, the post-partum-psychotic mom who murdered her children because (she thought) Mickey Mouse and Oscar the Grouch were telling her to kill them.

Was there EVER a decade in living memory as 24–7 *obsessed* with the trashiest, goriest, scummiest kinds of scandals and sensations as the 1990s? Why, it's a wonder anybody paid any attention to geopolitics, world affairs, or a fast-changing economy at all, with all those steaming piles of News Helper that we had to tuck into each night!

The Public Has a "Right to Know!"

All this trash TV and cable/publishing culture war might have been expectable to cynical and jaded movie and TV critics looking at the fast-evolving, Internet-era media landscape. What *wasn't* expectable, however, was the full-on veneer of intellectual *respect* that gossip news and innuendo would now be given by the Serious Journalistic establishment. After all, Walter Cronkite and Edward R. Murrow didn't make their careers by dressing up like a couple of garbagemen, hands-rubbingly going through the trash Dumpsters outside some Hollywood star or Washington matron's mansion. As far as we know, Bob Woodward and Carl Bernstein didn't make a habit of asking to use your bathroom so they could raid your medicine cabinet, sniff your jockey shorts and gym shirts, or check the wastebasket for used condoms and drug paraphernalia. (Nor did they take a cigarette boat and a wide-angle camera out on the ocean to see if they could watch Princess Di going topless or having sex with Dodi on her yacht.)

No. That was what *Confidential*-magazine type scumbags, like Danny DeVito's immortal editor in the film adaptation of James Ellroy's masterpiece *LA Confidential,* did to ply their skuzzy trade. That was what tyrants like Joe McCarthy and J. Edgar Hoover sent their hit men out to do for them, so that they could blackmail and "get the dirt" on their victims. And that was exactly who, what, when, where and why *The New York Times, Time* magazine, and *The CBS Evening News* would never be caught dead engaging in that kind of revolting, inexcusable behavior. If a Real Journalist™ lowered himself to that kind of sleazy, tabloid-trash "journalism," it would *reduce* their serious newspapers, magazines, and news broadcasts of record to the level of *The Weekly World News* or *The Ricki Lake Show.* This kind of sleazoid reporting was the "N-word" of journalistic ethics at serious news organizations. There was simply *no excuse* for engaging in anything like it. EVER.

But now, everything had changed. After Anita Hill, Gennifer Flowers, and Paula Jones, didn't American women have a "right to know" whether or not a powerful man had engaged in inappropriate or sexually themed conduct around the office? After the AIDS epidemic, with teen suicide on the rise seemingly every year, radicalized Queer journalists said that closeted gay teens in the hinterlands (with their white-trashy, homophobic parents and coaches) had a "right" to have high-profile gay role models to look up to—whether those high-profile gay people *wanted* to be role models or not! (As Larry Kramer put it, "Silence = Death.") And in the era of Sally Jessy, Oprah, Dr. Ruth, and *People* magazine, what gave a movie star or sitcom queen or pop singer the right to "hide" her breast cancer surgery, tragic eating disorders, childhood molestation, or her battles with the bottle and pills? Especially since, if she came out of the closet about her struggles, she could "empower" and "raise awareness" for those dread afflictions, could help take the stigma off and even save some people's lives?

The right to privacy that had once undergirded all of liberal social tolerance, from reproductive freedom to birth control to the right to gay relationships and marriage, was now ironically being converted into sexist or homophobic "code," if well-known political figures or celebrities actually *wanted* to have their privacy respected for themselves. In January of 1990, the late cultural critic William Henry III popularized the phrase "outing" in a feature story in *Time* magazine, noting the 1989 founding of *Out Week* magazine, whose star columnist, Michelangelo Signorile, was at the forefront of forcing open closet doors that had previously been locked shut. Signorile's colleague in gay journalism, Michael Petrelis, had already publicly claimed that aging (and married) Republican Senator Mark Hatfield was gay, after the moderate Rockefeller Republican went ahead and supported fundamentalist legislation sponsored by Jesse Helms. The seventy-year-old, arch–Republican businessman and publisher (and Elizabeth Taylor boyfriend) Malcolm Forbes had been dead from a heart attack for less than a month, when Signorile exposed his extracurricular life with the boys, in March of 1990. More high-profile figures, from Hollywood icons Anthony Perkins, Raymond Burr, Richard Chamberlain, Robert Reed, and Merv Griffin, to politicians like Illinois Governor Jim Thompson and the venerable retired New York Mayor Ed Koch, would now receive the same unwanted sexual spotlight.

The fact that all of these men came from the Greatest Generation (or were only just a few years younger), that they came from an era where acknowledging gay or bisexual preference would have been instant career suicide for a movie star or politician (and could even have gotten them in trouble with the law)—that mattered no longer to these boiling-over, AIDS-era journos, as they chafed under deliberate Reagan-Bush neglect and fundamentalist hostility. (Already, the formerly shaded truths about Liberace and Rock Hudson's AIDS deaths had been exposed.) Soon, younger stars like Jodie Foster, Richard Gere, Queen Latifah, and Chaz Bono would face the press's scrutiny.

Another Washington scalp to be collected was Dick Cheney's young undersecretary of Defense, Pete Williams, who was said to have sometimes vacationed in gay enclaves like Provincetown, alongside other conservative power-gays like Andrew Sullivan. Williams' closet door was also kicked open by Signorile, which quickly resulted in Williams moving on to pursue other challenges, as the press releases say. (Of course, had Williams been an actual officer in the armed forces, he'd have been out on his keester—this was before even Don't Ask Don't Tell, back when being gay or lesbian itself was grounds for an often *dishonorable* military discharge.) Perhaps the most delicious victory for LGBT radicals was when Religious Right founding mother Phyllis Schlafly, who'd led the fight against the Equal Rights Amendment in the '70s, rallied against *Roe vs. Wade* from day one, and mercilessly fought the so-called "gay agenda" every step of the way, had one of her sons, Fred Schlafly, exposed as gay by radical journalists, in 1992. (Mary Cheney hadn't been outed yet, but her day in the lesbian spotlight would come before the 1990s were over.)

This newfound respectability of "outing" private sexual and dependency/disease/abuse secrets in mainstream news now encouraged the real tabloids and gossip shows to go to the very edge of the envelope. On an episode of the daytime trash talk show *Jenny Jones,* an all-too-typical program taped in March of 1995 focused on Secret (Gay) Crushes. One of the guests, a handsome and buff young man named Jonathan Schmitz, went on the show out of curiosity to have the fun and excitement of being on TV, and to find out who in his small Michigan town might be his "secret admirer"—clearly expecting that it would be a young woman, perhaps the fiancée whom he'd broken up with a few months earlier. He realized he still loved her, and had bought a brand new set of clothes and shoes for the TV taping, eagerly anticipating a reunion.

Not quite. Instead, while Schmitz waited backstage listening to music on headphones, a young local man named Scott Amedure was dishing all the details (alongside his best galpal, a mutual friend of his and Schmitz's). Jenny urged Scott Amedure to tell her oooh-oohing audience about the intense sexual fantasies he'd been having about Schmitz ever since he saw Schmitz's well-endowed lower "hardbody" under a car while repairing it. (These included tying Schmitz to a backyard hammock "with whipped cream, champagne…" "AND??" Jenny egged him on…) Finally Jenny brought out Jonathan Schmitz for what game and talk show producers call "the big reveal"—after which a nervously laughing, rigid with "gay panic" Schmitz was treated to an instant replay of Scott's cutesy sexual fantasies. Later in the show, Jenny would comment on whether kisses between two men were really "errooootttic" or not, in front of her hooting and hollering studio audience.

Unfortunately, just as Jonathan Schmitz didn't know until he was ambushed before the cameras about his gay secret admirer—the contestant or guest coordinators of *The Jenny Jones Show* didn't know (and hadn't bothered to find out) about Jonathan Schmitz's history of suicide attempts and substance abuse. Three days after the taping, after having just barely gotten home and off the plane, Schmitz was confronted on his doorstep with a sexually graphic letter written by Amedure, even though Schmitz had made it clear on the show that he just wasn't into other men—despite Jenny's nonstop gay-baiting and provoking. That did it, and Schmitz snapped, going over to Scott Amedure's home armed with a shotgun. (You can probably guess what happened next.) Paddy Chayefsky's satirical prophecy at the end of *Network* had finally come true. A man had literally *died* … for the sake of ratings.

While the Jenny Jones show murder was one of the ugliest scandals of the 1990s, it was hardly atypical. Many if not most episodes of these talk shows were all but designed to provoke on-air fights and bitch-slapping, amid theatrically "bleeped" cries of "shut the fuck up!" "bitch!" "nigger!," "faggot!," "skank," "cunt," and the like. (And who can forget the Latino gay male prostitute who hip-wigglingly announced on a 1999–00 season Springer show, "I'm a streetwalking 'ho, Jerry!" to thunderous applause and cheers.) Bottom line: whether it was Jenny, Ricki, Jerry, Maury, or Geraldo, whether it was *Hard Copy, Inside Edition,* or *EXTRA!,* all of these shows ran for at least a decade—and none of them lost any money.

With all this snickering and sniveling, the line that separated tabloid trash from serious journalism had now been thinned from one as wide as the San Diego Freeway to one no bigger than a postage stamp. Georgetown icon Sally Quinn (who had famously earlier written the high-handed "Welcome to Washington" articles in *Newsweek*) was busy in 1996 trying to solve the exciting mystery of whether or not Hillary had actually written her book, *It Takes a Village* (To Raise a Child). (A famous, world-traveling celebrity hiring a ghost-writer? *Say it isn't so!*) The book itself became another minor sideshow at the culture war circus, when far-rightists and proto–Tea Partiers saw Commie-statist code in the book's call for communities to show greater communal responsibility towards the rearing and educating of their young. "It doesn't take a village to raise a child," shot back Ward Cleaver-era Republican presidential nominee Bob Dole in 1996. "It takes *parents!*"

In the book *The Clinton Tapes,* longtime confidante Taylor Branch recalls suggesting that Bill and Hillary invite Quinn and her husband, *Washington Post* board member and legendary Watergate editor Ben Bradlee, over to 1600 Pennsylvania for dinner. But while Bubba may have been commander-in-chief, Hillary was still queen of the house, and this time she exercised her veto power. "You know, she has been hostile since the moment we got here. Why would we invite somebody like that into our home? How could she expect us to?" The next thing Bill and Hillary knew, the hot new topic amongst the Ladies Who

Lunch was that Hillary had been "caught" having red-hot lesbian sex with a female veterinarian treating Socks the White House Cat. (It was later gleefully repeated as late as 1999, on where else but Ann Coulter's online message-boards.)

Of course, all this was at the apex of the "Whitewater," "Filegate," and "Travelgate" investigations, where after mega-millions of taxpayer dollars and three years straight of inquisition—err, inquiry—wing-nut prosecutor Kenneth Starr came up virtually empty. (He'd have better luck, so to speak, with Paula Jones' case for sexual harassment, especially after he found out about a White House office worker named Monica Lewinsky. And to the real conspiracy fans, there was the so-called "murder" of Vince Foster, Clinton's "drug running" in Arkansas, and all the rest...)

Meanwhile, *Newsweek* journalist Joe Klein's novel, *Primary Colors*—which was adapted just in time for Monicagate into a John Travolta and Emma Thompson-starring, A-list Hollywood movie—had Hillary's character gettin' it on with a considerably younger press secretary-stud, modeled on George Stephanopoulos. (Klein added spice to the "whodunit" atmosphere by initially crediting his book's byline to "Anonymous." Klein soon came out of the closet, however, proudly basking in all of the "It was ME all along!" free publicity. *Beacoups fantastico*, Joey Baby!)

That same year of 1998, our old friends at Marty Peretz's *New Republic* suffered one of their blackest eyes ever. The venerated magazine's credibility had already taken more beatings than a Quentin Tarantino victim, on the heels of articles like their serious discussion of Charles Murray's abominably racist *The Bell Curve*, and their even more virulent "Day of Reckoning" welfare cover. Not to mention Betsy McCaughey's unfair and unbalanced euthanasia of 1994's healthcare reform, and *TNR* regular Ruth Shalit's proven guilt of serial plagiarism and misattribution. Now, it turned out that their 24-year-old star columnist, Stephen "Shattered" Glass, had flat-out faked or embellished over *two dozen* of his feature stories for the magazine! More than *half* of his total output!

But in true late '90s style, instead of this being a cautionary tale, the very next year a journalist who knew far better than the young Glass, the plugged-in and middle-aged presidential biographer Edmund Morris, only kicked it up a notch. Morris cooked up a journalistically questionable "Official Biography" of Ronald Reagan called *Dutch,* that was *narrated by a fictional character*, and replete with that character's pop-psychology insights into Reagan's supposed mentality and motivations. (One can only guess at Morris' own psychological—or perhaps legal—motivations, for waiting until Reagan was pushing 90 and deep into Alzheimer's dementia, to publish his "definitive" biography.) And by the end of that year of 1999, Nina Tassler and Les Moonves at CBS were busy taking pitches for what would become *Big Brother* and *Survivor,* as the concept of "reality stardom" was about to go viral.

From Cronkite and Murrow to Snooki and Khloe

The emergence of the Internet posed a direct threat to traditional book, magazine, and newspaper publishing—and their business models—that movies and TV never could. O.J., Tonya & Nancy, JonBenét, and Princess Di had already taught the "real" newspapers and newscasts that it was the tabloid media—from *The National Enquirer, The Globe,* and to the nightly entertainment access strips and the trash talkers—that was now firmly in charge of the national narrative. You either got with the program, got out of the way, or got run over.

Noting the Reagan-on-steroids level of mass media consolidation during the Clintonomic '90s, legendary book editor and publisher Andre Schiffrin wrote in 1999, "Publishing in North America and Europe has changed more in the past decade than in the preceding 100 years, and not so far for the better. A major cause in the decline is the number of publishing houses absorbed by conglomerates whose managements have no experience—and often little interest—in books." (And this was *a full decade before* mainstream self-publishing, Kindles, e-books, and the 2011–12 bankruptcies of once-bulletproof businesses like Borders Books and Blockbuster Video.)

Schiffrin might just as well have been talking about newspapers and magazines, too. Already by 1999 and 2000, a new generation was coming of age, in high school and college, for whom waiting for the daily newspaper to get one's news would soon become as anachronistic and old-fashioned as a scene from *The English Patient.* The Internet was now the place to get your daily news fix, where you could comment and dish and react and interact about things in real time (and for your own customized tastes), without having to worry about being thought-policed by some snobby know-it-all editorial gatekeeper. When snarky Jon Stewart took over for sly Craig Kilborn on Comedy Central's flagship news satire, *The Daily Show,* just after the new year in January of 1999 (and just in time to wrap up the Monica Lewinsky scandal and get ready for *Bush vs. Gore*), fireworks ensued. By then, liberal comedian Bill Maher also had his nightly news satire, *Politically Incorrect,* ruling the ratings—his ABC late-night predecessor to HBO's *Real Time.*

Indeed, the Internet posed an occupational (and perhaps even moral) question not really addressed since the very origins of modern-day book and newspaper publishing in the 19th century. All civilized societies value freedom of the press and free speech—but who and what really constituted a "journalist" or "reporter" anymore? Was the 17-year-old stoner dude blogging on Geocities from his college dorm, in his open flannel shirt and wrinkled Phish T-shirt, really a "film" or "literary critic" the way that Roger Ebert, Tom Shales, Michiko Kakutani, Carolyn See, Gene Siskel, Richard Schickel, Digby Diehl, Manohla Dargis, or John Leonard were? But if the kid knew how to index Alta Vista, Hotbot, and Google searches, and used brand-new aggregation sites like Rotten Tomatoes (launched 1998) or Television Without Pity (1999) to grand effect, he might be able to start putting down almost as big a footprint. And just what separated a "blogger" from a real "reporter" in this brave new world? Could neo–Nazi hate sites denying the Holocaust and talking smack about African Americans and "wetbacks," or a "God Hates Fags" website, or a bunch of paranoiac conspiracy nutter-butters—could *they* all now gussy themselves up in the dress clothes of First Amendment "journalism," too?

More to the point: without a scandal-mongering, tabloid-addicted, 24-hour mainstream media with its ever-hungry maw to feed, crack-whoring for ratings, juiced-up circulation stats, and (by decade's end, web hits), most of these "wars" and "scandals" would have been like the philosophy professor's tree that falls alone in the forest. Without the desperate-for-content, 1990s media buzz-saw to enable them, would they have really made a sound?

It was this no-gatekeeper atmosphere that became the most thrilling aspect to early

Millennials and late Gen-Xers, raised as they were on a diet of nonstop irreverence and post-politically correct 'tude, from SNL to Spike Lee, from Bart Simpson and Cartman to Beavis and Butt-Head, from MTV and Letterman to Tarantino and Eminem. The "Comments" sections on many otherwise-respectable news websites by the end of the 1990s (and often continuing through today) were jam-packed with personal attacks and no-nos like "bitch," "nigger," "faggot," "ho," and "fuck"—making them seem spicy, naughty, and even somehow hip compared to the pre-screened "Letters to the Editor" in the print versions. Internet discussions were the true "marketplace of ideas" where everybody's opinion carried equal weight—*especially yours!*

The late 1990s also became the moment when newspapers and magazines started to feel the initial pinch of advertising as it slowly began to migrate online. "Alternative" free weeklies of any cache like the *LA* and *OC Weekly* (let alone the standard-setting *Village Voice*) were now often just as college-choosy and status-conscious for whom they would hire for paid positions as their most Establishment colleagues. Book publishers began demanding all submissions come through a known literary agent or a referral from a name author, to protect against frivolous "idea theft" lawsuits. (And also to ensure that they weren't swamped by a bunch of Blogspot or Geocities fanboys and housewives, now convinced that their Internet writings made them "writers" just like Mary Higgins Clark or Margaret Atwood.) During the following decade, the century-old job description, and the very cultural role of writers, journalists, and critics, would be sent to the "Rewrite!" department.

When Monica Lewinsky was caught with her Gap dress in 1998, that was the moment when blogging and do-it-yourself, primitive (pre–Twitter) social media-driven, often low-or-no paid online journalism emerged from its remote, stanky, Gen-X man-cave and roared across the finish line. The sex scandal that led to the impeachment of a sitting president was broken not by some big-name Establishment news source, but by a young Internet muckraker and tabloid stringer named Matt Drudge, with his spicy and too-hot-for-the-news Drudge Report (which also aggregated headlines from other newspapers around the world, as well as just North America). The very idea that some smart-mouthed nerd like Matt Drudge—running his Internet blog or radio webcast from home, with no staff, no departments, no printing press or network newsroom—the *idea* that he could bring the almighty *Newsweek* or *Time* to heel! That Someone Like Him could upstage and "scoop" the *NBC Nightly News* or *The New York Times* was almost unthinkable to the respectable world of establishment journalism circa 1997–98.

Until it actually happened. And that cold, hard news fact sent shudders and shooting left-arm pains throughout the newspaper, magazine, and book publishing worlds. Suddenly, the days not too far off in the future, when leading intellectual lights like Kim Kardashian, Snooki, Pamela Anderson, Paris Hilton, and Nicole Ritchie would be signing book and lecture deals the size of Maya Angelou and Toni Morrison's, started to become visible on the horizon. The near-future when snarky web magazines like *The Daily Beast,* aggregation sites like *The Huffington Post,* or even hot bloggers like Nikki Finke and Perez Hilton, could eat century-old behemoths like *Newsweek* or *Daily Variety* for breakfast, suddenly didn't sound like science fiction anymore. By the end of 1999, the hottest and most buzzworthy battle in the New York media status-sweepstakes wasn't Tom Brokaw vs. Peter Jennings, or *Time* versus *Newsweek.* It was Slate versus Salon.com.

In 2009, David Frum told this author that the average or median age of Fox News' audience was 65-plus (as well as overwhelmingly white). The Big Four broadcasters had all spent the 1990s and early 2000s conducting a veritable *pogrom* of all viewers over the age of 55—and of any shows that disproportionately appealed to them, in search of young adult and high-income-professional demographics above all else. As such, it only made sense that addictive and comparatively cheap-to-produce news-network shows—which even at their best could not compete with a buzzy drama or top sitcom—would now deliberately target TV's most loyal captive audience: housebound older folks. If that meant taking a reactionary stand against young whippersnappers or degenerate liberals or race/gay activists of all and every stripe (you know, those weird "other" people who mean to take away and irrevocably change the America that you grew up in), then so be it. You were just targeting *your* key audience.

As for younger viewers, they would spend the coming decade bidding all the "serious" news shows goodbye. By the Obama era, it was said that more Millennials got their "news" from Jon Stewart's *Daily Show* than from any one of the Big Three networks' 6:30 nightly newscasts. The old-fashioned rules of old-fashioned writers and newsmen who'd played by the rules had now become, quite literally, "yesterday's news." Over the next 10 to 15 years, the triumph of online reporting, cable screamfests, and talk radio (and their angry, snarky, in-your-face aesthetics) would become complete, absolute, and total.

By the time O.J.'s murder trial had ended, as Haynes Johnson noted, Americans were conditioned to witnessing a succession of scandalous real-life soap operas on the news. "No sooner did one end than another one took its place." They offered "a convenient running plot line of scandal and suspense." Joan Didion added that by the end of the '80s, most major news organizations were all about constructing a "narrative" to their stories—just like a screenwriter plot-twisting a sexy box-office thriller or a prestigious Sunday drama. "Tree it, bag it, defoliate the forest for it," she sarcastically noted, so long as whatever facts at hand could be placed into a continuing and preferably suspenseful storyline, with any and all inconvenient or off-message truths to be left on the cutting-room floor.

* * *

We'll leave it to the lovable 1970s talk-show titan Mike Douglas to have the last word on this chapter of media history, taken verbatim from his 1999 memoir, *I'll Be Right Back.* Commenting on the horror of the 1995 Jenny Jones show murder, he said, "I'm sure the last thing Jenny Jones ever wanted was to see anyone come to harm as a direct or indirect result of her TV cash cow—but it doesn't do any of us any good to pretend it didn't happen. There's a price for reckless irresponsibility on television, and there's a limit to what you can do for ratings." The late Mr. Douglas then added a finishing kick aimed at Jenny Jones—but which could have been applied to all of the hysterical media pants-wetters of the '90s—no matter how many ruined lives and shattered political institutions they left in their oblivious wake: "What happened to Jenny Jones was the worst nightmare of any media personality, and I sympathize, but the honorable thing would have been for her to sign off the day after it happened. That she stayed on the air says something chilling about Jenny Jones—*and her audience...*."

6

"Must-See TV"

I've been around too long. "She's still alive? Who cares—we're interested in the young hot ones!" They don't have any respect for longevity or talent, they really don't.
—*Lauren Bacall*

To be over 40 years old is [now treated] like having a disease. It's become really bizarre.... Growing old is not a leper colony where an unfortunate few are sent to die. It is a precious gift given only to some lucky human beings.
—*Dick Van Dyke*

Politics and advertising—which, as any viewer or reader of the works of Aaron Sorkin, Paddy Chayefsky, Norman Lear, Matthew Weiner, or Budd Schulberg knows, have much more in common with one another than they are separate—have always, at times, zeroed in on one group over another, depending on the product (or politician) that they're pushing. But the 1990s upped the ante to a level of *dividing* "target audiences" by race, class, income, education—and above all, by age, "hipness," and generation—instead of uniting them, to a degree that was almost unfathomable in American popular culture until then. It was the decade when the ABC chief Bob Iger would say that his sales department told him "that being No. 1" in general circulation "mean[t] absolutely nothing to them" anymore. His rival, NBC's Warren Littlefield, echoed the paradigm shift in even stronger terms. "The message loud and clear is *demographics.*"

With fragmented, audience-targeting cable TV exploding into one channel lineup after another—including "news" channels from left, right, and center—and "independent films" morphing from blaxploitation and slasher cheapies to buzzworthy Oscar bait, Littlefield's research chief David Rubens would say it best: the 1990s were the era when television, films, book publishing, and virtually all forms of advertising joined popular music in going from "mass market" to what Rubens called "UN-mass appeal."

Indeed, today's era when a niche cable show that appeals to a dream demographic (like *Mad Men* or *Game of Thrones*) receives far more media attention and buzz than a top-rated but downscale or "un-intellectual" show (like *NCIS*), truly began in the branding-buzzword 1990s. The era when indie films, niche releases, and cult TV shows like *Xena* and *Buffy the Vampire Slayer* would get parsed, analyzed, autopsied, and have near-dissertations written and blogged about them, also started with the passionate fanboys (and fangirls) on the World Wide Web.

But Joan Walsh of *Salon* underlined that it wasn't just snobby TV and movie execs who believed that new nostrum. American politics also went from a "big tent" to a narrow target, especially in the 1990s "third party" era of Ross Perot and Ralph Nader—using "focus groups," "Q scores" and "poll testing" as obsessively as the most show-bizzy Hollywood publicist, in order to survive. And the Democratic Leadership Council, whose greatest triumph would be the eight-year reality show known as the Clinton Presidency, was epitomized by a political environment that would, from then on, in Walsh's apt words, "define itself more by what it *wasn't* than by what it *was*."

"Everything that had a tree in it"

Once the three-network system was truly established in TV, the mathematics for success vs. failure was so simple, even a child could understand it. CBS and NBC were the top rated networks (in that order), with ABC usually bringing up the rear. (Occasionally ABC would have a true hit—Lawrence Welk, *Bewitched, Peyton Place*, even *Batman*, but until the Aaron Spelling/Garry Marshall 1970s, they were few and far between.) As such, in a three-way horserace, the passing grade for a show was at least 30 percent of all "sets in use"—a "30 share," for a show on CBS or NBC to survive. (On ABC, a show might usually get passed with a 25 share—and it could on CBS or NBC too, but *only* if it was opposite a couple of Top Ten megahits on the other channels, like *Laugh-In,* Dean Martin, or *Gunsmoke.*) Just like high school or college, if you made the grade, you got passed—and if you didn't, you were flunked out.

But that kind of Truman/Eisenhower simplicity was one of the many things to get reevaluated in the sturm und drang of the late '60s and early '70s. As Vietnam, civil rights protests, and cultural revolution took hold in the late 1960s, much of the small screen remained in a state of denial, except for the all-too-real nightly newscasts. Indeed, to many critics and intellectuals, the prime-time entertainment programming of the era offered an almost grotesquely disassociated contrast from the "real world" shown during the evening news. Nowhere was this more true than at top-rated CBS, which had always considered itself the "Tiffany Network." A decade earlier, CBS was the home to the most sophisticated (for its day) fare on the air, like *The Twilight Zone, Alfred Hitchcock, Perry Mason, The Defenders, The Dick Van Dyke Show, Dragnet,* and *Playhouse 90.* But now, it was now coasting on its early to mid '60s, pre-counterculture slate of country cousins and Western corn.

While young soldiers were being blown to rack and ruin in Vietnam, CBS was pickin' and grinnin' with *Gomer Pyle, USMC.* When African Americans were fighting for equal rights in the streets, CBS was a-servin' up *The Beverly Hillbillies, Green Acres,* and *Mayberry RFD.* Matters weren't helped when the network summarily axed its only program aimed squarely at hip, city-dwelling youth—the "dangerously funny" (as critic David Bianculli put it) and outspokenly anti–Vietnam War *Smothers Brothers Comedy Hour.* By the end of the decade, top TV and film critics were humiliating the former Tiffany Network, calling it the "Country Broadcasting System." To uber-influential, outspoken critics like John Leonard, Harlan Ellison, Richard Schickel, and Pauline Kael, CBS was no longer synonymous with the Golden Age brilliance of Brando, Newman, Leonard Bernstein, Rod Serling and Alfred Hitchcock—but with *Hee-Haw* and Hooterville.

The reaction came swiftly in 1971, in what Wikipedia rightly called the "Rural Purge" of that year. As *Green Acres* star and B-western movie legend Pat Buttram lamented, "That year, they cancelled everything that had a tree in it." It was goodbye *Green Acres, Beverly*

Hillbillies, Family Affair, and *Hee-Haw*—and hello *All in the Family, The Mary Tyler Moore Show,* and *Sonny & Cher.* Even Ed Sullivan (and over at ABC, Lawrence Welk) was forcibly retired, although both Welk and *Hee Haw* would make new shows for weekend syndication for several more years. Within another year or two after that, CBS would add the perennial classic *M*A*S*H,* Bea Arthur's feminist comedy classic *Maude* (followed by its ghetto spin-off *Good Times*), and the detective dramas *Cannon* and *Kojak* to their newer lineup of hard-boiled urban crime shows, like *Mannix* and *Hawaii Five-0.*

It would be another three full decades, until the summer of 2001, before CBS would ever go through a housecleaning as dramatic as that one again. But much more fatefully, back in the early 1970s, CBS and ABC weren't the only ones intent on conducting a "purge" of downscale viewers—or voters.

The Selling of the Presidency

After the infamous virtual meltdown at the 1968 Chicago Democratic convention, with open war breaking out between Mayor Richard Daley's police department and throngs of hippies and protestors, where Daley himself called anti–Vietnam Senator Abe Ribicoff a "dirty Jew bastard!" on live TV, where Dan Rather was punched in the stomach (also in front of the cameras) by a bunch of the mayor's Mafia-like "thugs," while outraged anchors like Walter Cronkite and David Brinkley turned red with anger and contempt, everyone in the Democratic Party knew that *something* had to be done. They could never afford to go through anything like *that* again—especially in that their candidate, Vice President Hubert Humphrey, had lost that year to the Democrats' worst nightmare, Richard M. Nixon.

Not long afterwards, with the smoke of the battle having replaced the smoke of cigars in the politicians' smoke-filled rooms, a "commission" was appointed to redesign and reboot the next (1972) Democratic presidential convention. And the chair of that commission would be the man who would end up being the next Democratic standard-bearer—the outspokenly antiwar South Dakota Senator George McGovern. Aided and abetted by intellectual California university leader Fred S. Dutton and a rising assistant named Gary Hart (who during his own 1980s presidential drives would give birth to the phrase "yuppie," a phrase which he himself defined), McGovern enacted floor-to-ceiling changes. Delegates would be awarded proportionately in each state, instead of "winner take all." Strict quotas for minorities and women would be put into place, and there would be a specific outreach to the overwhelmingly anti-war, "youth vote" hippies (especially after the 1971 Constitutional amendment lowering the age of adulthood to 18 in all holdout states).

Those changes weren't exactly welcomed by the non-youthful, all-white, and all-male power structure that they were intended to replace. Just look at those old, white-haired, turn-of-the-century-raised jockstraps like union boss George Meany, big city mayors Sam Yorty and Richard Daley, Sr., or their mobbed-up power pallies like Jimmy Hoffa and Sidney Korshak, or those corrupt "bosses" who'd even committed murder like Tony Boyle. Even now they could barely stop themselves from saying "nigger," with "colored" about the best they could do. And their attitudes towards women were downright antediluvian—get me a cuppa coffee honey, with a fanny-pinch to go! They believed in simple slogans for simple-minded people. They were so tired-blooded, so Depression-era, so yesterday's news…

Meanwhile, with racial minorities, women, antiwar hippies, and even "open fags!" (as an outraged George Meany put it) allowed in to fight the old bosses, the 1972 gathering turned out to be just as much of a disaster as 1968's partial-convention abortion. African American firebrands like Shirley Chisholm and Jesse Jackson and their cheering audiences (some of them wearing robes, dashikis, husa-shakos, and mega-Afros) got ratings almost as high as McGovern did. McGovern was tagged anonymously (by his first choice for running mate, Sen. Thomas Eagleton, no less) in a famed Robert Novak column as the "Triple-A candidate—Acid, Amnesty [for Vietnam draft-dodgers], and Abortion." As John Wayne might have said, there was only room for *one* of those two teams at the top, pardner. And the Democratic Party had just decided which group that would be.

When fair-mindedly liberal *Salon* doyenne Joan Walsh asked the noted labor historian Jefferson Cowie if there was any one movement or moment (besides the start of the Vietnam War itself) where the post–FDR Democratic Party came undone, she initially "expected him to fudge like a good academic." Instead, his answer was swift and to the point: "The 1972 decision by organized labor to destroy George McGovern." Cowie said that proved once and for all to the New Left and anti–Vietnam voices (let alone the emerging feminist, black, and Latino power structures) that "we can't work with the unions," period. It underlined forever that "organized labor is just about guys like George Meany and Mayor Daley, it's really the same [right wing, reactionary] monster, and we can't deal with them. And that created a natural alliance between the New Left and the New Democrats, who were much more sympathetic to important issues of diversity than to labor."

(Of course, Cowie's own telling is a veritable riddle of his own academic and elite sympathies. Regardless of who was right or wrong morally or ethically in this tete-a-tate, in the minds of aging Democrat "bosses" like Daley, Yorty, Meany, it was *they* who were the legitimate power brokers and decision makers at the Democratic table. They were there first, after all—before anyone had ever heard of Vietnam, "black power," the Stonewall Inn, or "women's lib." Fairly or unfairly, in their minds it was the Libbers and the Fags and the Commie Pinkos and the Flag-Burning Hippies and the Niggers and Spics who'd made a decision to "destroy" *their* power base, who'd decided that they wouldn't "work with" *them.)*

Whatever the case, the die was now cast. As Walsh continued, "McGovern's campaign manager [and future 1984 and '88 presidential candidate and Clinton mentor] Gary Hart, would pioneer the idea of 'New Democrats' who owed no allegiance to labor." When Hart ran for Senate in the 1974 "Watergate babies" election, he chose as in-your-face a stump speech as possible: "The END of the New Deal." That same year, Hart downright libeled the most iconic living Democrat of the Roosevelt tradition, when he said that his generation of educated, professional Dems weren't just a bunch of cheesy, vote-pandering "little Hubert Humphreys." It was a purposeful "slander" of "labor's longtime champion," as Walsh recalled.

However, that didn't matter—because the Republicans had already been refocusing for quite some time on appealing to that very same demographic. In his landmark 1969 book, *The Emerging Republican Majority,* young Republican strategist Kevin Phillips (who would later dearly regret the outer extremes that the Gingrich-Cheney-Rove era brought to the strategy he first outlined) said that while the Democrats were now going full-force after minorities, the real bada-bing jackpot was in downscale, "Negro-phobe" whites, who feared ghetto culture, affirmative action, and forced school busing. Religious conservatives—boiling over after the push for 1972's so-called "anti-family" Equal Rights Amendment and *Roe vs. Wade*, not to mention the Stonewall/Harvey Milk initial effort for gay and lesbian rights—added another crucial new demo that could be reaped for votes. What could be more "conservative" than a push for "conservative" family values, after all? And right-wing think tankers like Paul Weyrich, Richard Viguerie, Phyllis Schlafly, and Pat Buchanan wrote the roadmaps on just how to do it.

As early as the mid 1970s, TV icon Norman Lear saw where the future was headed. On his landmark *All in the Family,* working class hero Archie Bunker was about as far from the stereotype of an old-money "country club Republican" or a doctor/lawyer as it got— and yet he was second to no one in his admiration for Richard Nixon and Ronald Reagan. His pushy, "liberated" cousin *Maude,* played to perfection by Bea Arthur, lived just outside tony Scarsdale, had a successful appliance store-owning husband (and herself worked in real estate and politics) while wearing outrageous '70s threads, and leasing Mercedeses and Cadillac Eldorados. And just like her real-life counterparts on which she was based—educated, well-off, middle-aged feminist matrons like Betty Friedan, Bella Abzug, Rosalyn Carter, Dianne Feinstein, and Lear's own wife Frances—she voted a straight Democratic ticket, the more liberal and left-wing, the better. It was a narrative that would only double (and triple) down in the Culture War '90s, as labor-sympathetic liberals like Thomas Frank, Rick Perlstein, and Michael Moore would lament, again and again and again.

This turnabout cannot be emphasized strongly enough when it came to Bill Clinton's single-handed agenda to post-modernize the Presidency. In 1980, 1984, and 1988, despite having two of the oldest and most conservative candidates ever to run for the White House in modern times (69-year-old Ronald Reagan and 64-year-old George Bush, Sr.), the Republicans had actually *won* the 18–34 year old youth vote. College-conscious white yuppies simply weren't going to vote for a Democrat party that pandered to proletarians in Big Labor (let alone a Dem party whose "face" was Jesse Jackson or Al Sharpton, shaking their fists in street rallies). And the hippies of the '60s had become the parents of Gen-X and Millennial children by the '80s. Suddenly, drugs, sex, and rock 'n' roll didn't sound so groovy, when you had a junior high-schooler who was at risk for pot, AIDS, molestation, or gangsta rap.

Bill Clinton had single-handedly changed all that. Clinton's priority one in early 1992 was to create a generational distinction between himself and outdated, fusty old Bush Senior, who was old enough to be his own father—and just as importantly, between himself and gray, gaunt, desexualized gloomy-gusses like Mario Cuomo, Paul Tsongas, Ralph Nader, and Michael Dukakis within his own movement. He did so by making *Saturday Night Live,* Arsenio Hall, Jay Leno, and MTV into campaign must-stops, working to literally "Rock the Vote." Clinton would have probably lost the Presidency, both in 1992 and 1996 (when he enjoyed a 19-point lead among first- and second-time voters, versus his 73-year-old opponent, grumpy Republican Senate grandpa Bob Dole), had it not been for his enormous margins among younger voters, while being able to totally consolidate his fellow Boomers— especially high-income, educated, professional ones in upscale suburbs and on the coasts. Just like Barry Diller, David Geffen, Barbra Streisand, Harry and Linda Bloodworth-Thomason, Julia Phillips, and the other Hollywood moguls whom he partied and hung out with, Bill Clinton knew the importance of zeroing in on his target key demo.

Youth, More Than Anything Else

While 1980s TV had plenty of game-changers, from *Hill Street Blues* and *Miami Vice* to *The Cosby Show* and *Dynasty,* probably no event reshaped the grammar of American popular culture—not just on the boob tube but in pop music and motion pictures, too, as when MTV signed on the air on August 1, 1981. No network or TV show, not even *The Smothers Brothers, American Bandstand, SCTV,* or *Saturday Night Live,* had ever so targeted teenagers and young adults more than the first channel for edgy, sexy, outrageous music videos did—with its cutting-edge cinematography and editing, up-to-the-minute graphics and SFX, and youthful sexuality. But a close second had come five years later in 1986, when Rupert Murdoch launched the first for-real "fourth network" since the Dumont days of the early '50s. Many industry observers initially laughed at the upstart Fox Network, thinking that not even mighty Rupert could succeed where so many others had failed.

Just six short years later in 1992, it was Rupert Murdoch who was the only one still laughing—all the way to the bank! The other networks were too busy weeping, over the abysmal youth numbers that Fox had illustrated they had. No matter what one thinks of Murdoch's politics, he didn't get to be where he was and is by being stupid, or by not knowing how (and to whom) to sell his products. Seeing the smashing success of MTV (and its sister network in those early formative years of cable, Nickelodeon), Fox had come up with a mandate not so much to try and steal a slice of NBC, ABC, or CBS's pies—but to bake an entirely *new* pie altogether.

When the other networks were offering happy-ending, "awww!" family sitcoms like *The Cosby Show, Family Ties,* and *Full House*—Fox would offer the raunchy *Married ... with Children.* When other networks had given up variety shows for dead after Carol Burnett, Lawrence Welk, and Barbara Mandrell, Fox would reboot the format with edgy English comedienne Tracey Ullman (and her cartoon neighbors, *The Simpsons*), followed by the urban rap and hip-hop of the Wayans Brothers and *In Living Color.* When 65-year-old Johnny Carson and Ed McMahon were still presiding over late night TV like a couple of aging, lifetime-appointed judges, most Fox affiliates first snagged famously uncensored Joan Rivers, and then hit it out of the park with the hip, young, and black Arsenio Hall. When nighttime soap operas were busy with the trials and travails of *thirtysomething* (and forty-something) grownups on *Knots Landing, LA Law, Sisters, Dallas, Dynasty,* and *Falcon Crest,* Fox would set one at Beverly Hills High, in the most famous zip code in the world—90210. And while venerable Jessica Fletcher and Ben Matlock kept the rest of prime time safe from crime, Fox preferred to have smokin' hot, 20-something Johnny Depp on their case, at *21 Jump Street.*

Newly appointed NBC president Warren Littlefield, who was still in his late thirties when he made the big jump in 1991–92, was the first to notice Fox's recipe for success, among Madison Avenue advertisers who craved the impressionable and peer-pressured, first-time consuming, moving-target audience of youth and young adults that Fox and MTV mainlined. The same year as Bill Clinton's generation-war "change election" against Bush Senior, in 1992 Littlefield ordered a complete housecleaning at his network—one that was almost as ruthless as CBS's "Rural Purge" of 20 years earlier. In a year that was already scheduled to see the departure of Nielsen-rating royalty like Bill Cosby and Johnny Carson, and with the top-rated *Cheers* set to go only one more season, Littlefield also dropped the axe on *Matlock, In the Heat of the Night*, and took a pass on the revamped *Golden Girls* sequel, *The Golden Palace.* Every last one of those shows was still either first or second place in their NBC timeslots, with healthy ratings, name stars, and millions of loyal fans.

Littlefield's move made national newspaper headlines and was *the* talk of Hollywood that spring, just as he no doubt intended it to be. It was designed to "send a message" to the other studios and networks in Hollywood as knowingly as a raised eyebrow at Tony Soprano's dinner table. Why would a network that was already about to lose its two signature shows, its biggest moneymaking hits and most profitable anchors, go ahead and deliberately cancel *even more shows*, when they didn't have to? Wasn't NBC already risking enough loss for one year?

Nope. Not where Warren Littlefield was concerned, anyway, as he remorselessly rebooted the near-sole focus at NBC from total circulation to target demographics. From now on, the NBC chief decided, NBC was going to define itself just as much by what it *wasn't* than by what it was—by who WASN'T watching their "must-see TV" shows, as well as by who was. In a major interview, Littlefield spelled out his strategy for all of Hollywood to see. "We set some very specific goals. Continue the successful transition from households to demographic focus," and underlining that his new de-seniorized schedule "clearly satisfies our objectives." In other words, the newspaper article went on, "NBC will not try to reclaim the overall ratings lead that it held throughout the [mid to late] 1980s but lost to CBS [that] year. Instead of trying to attract a large general audience, NBC is specifically targeting those viewers most desired by advertisers—18 to 49 year olds."

Both ABC and CBS initially pounced like Tom seeing Jerry come out of his mouse-hole, at the gleeful chance to snag the proven, ratings-grabbing hits that NBC was canceling for no apparent good reason. CBS renewed *In the Heat of the Night* for two more years and used the *Golden Girls* follow-up as the anchor of their revamped Friday lineup for a year. Not to be outdone, ABC solved the mystery of what to counter-program NBC's hot Thursday sitcoms with, when it gave *Matlock* a full three-season pass into 1995. Hey, if NBC was *stupid* enough to give up three healthy shows just because some radical-chic, tragically hip programmer was off on a tangent, then why not assist our rival's professional suicide a little?

But the image-conscious and hip decision-makers of Wall Street and Madison Avenue couldn't have agreed more with Warren Littlefield's philosophy, especially in light of MTV, cable in general, and Fox. If a show had a large audience whose main members were frugal, stubborn, set-in-their-ways children of the Depression—the real-life counterparts to Grandpa Simpson—that was only proof positive of how tragically un-hip, outmoded, and out-of-date the show was. If a show was the hit of the party at Shady Pines, then how valuable could it really be? NBC was, according to *The New York Times*, "giving up bulk numbers for good," because, after Fox and MTV's success, "what advertisers want more than anything else is youth. The drive for young viewers is behind virtually every move made by NBC." And in another year or two, it would be "behind virtually every move" at virtually every network, studio, and ad agency from then on.

Indeed, as one CBS executive ruefully recalled in Bill Carter's seminal book *Desperate Networks,* in the fall of 1994, CBS's decade-old Sunday-night standard bearer, *Murder, She Wrote,* was posting far higher ratings (still in the Top Ten) than its ABC competition *Lois & Clark* or Fox's iconic *Simpsons.* "But they were getting FAR more than we were with

Angela Lansbury!" the CBS exec lamented. While Jessica Fletcher had the most eyes watching her, apparently too many of those eyes had glaucoma and cataracts for the youth-conscious, trendy sponsors of the coming dot-com era. ABC's Ted Harbert and Robert Iger told *The New York Times* that even though mass-audience CBS had finished the 1992–93 season as Numero Uno in total circulation, "It's not worth being No. 1in the household ratings if you're No. 3 in profits."

The rebooted TV schedule for the fall of 1993 illustrated the new narrative. Fox's youth-oriented hits *Beverly Hills, 90210* and *Melrose Place* were hotter and hipper than ever, as were its smart-mouthed sitcoms *The Simpsons* and *Married ... with Children.* Now they added the stylish, scary, and suspenseful supernatural drama *The X-Files,* which defined the word "buzzworthy" from its first telecast. The show was soon breaking ratings records for the upstart, perennial fourth-place network, which wouldn't remain in last place for much longer—especially in the key 18–49 and 18–34 age demographics that were their sole standards of success.

ABC was the next to play follow the leader. ABC had scored an even bigger hit than Agents Mulder and Scully that year, both critically and commercially, with *NYPD Blue,* Steven Bochco's sequel to his definitive '80s "quality television" NBC masterpiece, *Hill Street Blues.* The new show showcased its nude scenes, R-rated language (including the shit-word and the N-word), graphic gang violence and violence against women, plus conflicted and tortured cops who often didn't know right from wrong themselves, against the mean streets of early Giuliani (and later on, 9/11-era) New York, alongside NBC's longtime by-the-book counterpart, *Law & Order. NYPD Blue* would rank behind only *The Sopranos* and *The West Wing* as the most critically acclaimed game-changer drama of the 1990s, in American prime-time.

Not to be outdone, the January after their 1992 de-seniorization campaign, NBC launched a show that, while it would never achieve the ratings success or cultural buzz of *NYPD's* Detective Sipowicz or *The X-Files'* aliens and supernatural serial killers, would still have just as much of an effect on how critics and intellectuals viewed the "boob tube." Produced by a dream team of feature director Barry Levinson, bestselling journalist David Simon, *Quiz Show* (and future *House*) screenwriter Paul Attanasio, and *St. Elsewhere* vet Tom Fontana, *Homicide: Life on the Streets* became a Friday-night fixture on NBC for the remainder of the decade. (Fontana, Simon, and Levinson essentially made a sequel to the show with their HBO hit *The Wire*—President Obama's all time favorite—from 2002 to '08.) And nobody confused THIS one with *Matlock!*

Those three shows also marked a turning point in grownup television beyond their own orbits. Because of these shows' movie-level sex scenes and violence, there were also the by-now predictable sponsor boycotts by Religious Right groups and even station blackouts in the most conservative Bible Belt markets. But this time, those threats just didn't work anymore. Despite the blackouts and smears, *NYPD Blue* hit the Top 20 from its first season, and remained a smash until its end nearly a dozen years later—especially amongst educated, discriminating, cable-type viewers. Agents Scully and Mulder weren't far behind. Less than four years later, Ellen DeGeneres would "come out" on her sitcom, followed a year or so after by *Will & Grace.* The era when Phyllis Schlafly, the Reverend Don Wildmon, Jerry Falwell, Focus on the Family, and the Parents Television Council inspired leg-crossing fear in "liberal Hollywood" network executives was coming to an end. And the continued rise and visibility of cable only accelerated the change. The recent era of thorny and nov-elistic, flawed antiheroes like Tony Soprano, *The Good Wife,* Don Draper, Jack Bauer, Walter White, Dr. House, *The Mentalist,* Dexter, *Damages'* Patty Hewes, *How to Get Away with Murder's* Annalise Keating, and *Scandal's* Olivia Pope, would have been flat-out impossible without this 1990s game-change.

But one network hadn't yet gotten the memo. The same year that *NYPD Blue, The X-Files,* and *Homicide* were rewriting the rule book, CBS's big news in the hour-long drama department for the fall of 1993 was a delightful, lighthearted whodunit, starring the 68-year-old Disney movie, Broadway musical, and sitcom icon Dick Van Dyke. It was called *Diagnosis: Murder.* (Their two biggest new hits the previous season were even more Red State in their sensibilities: *Dr. Quinn, Medicine Woman* and Chuck Norris's all-American *Walker, Texas Ranger.*)

The following year, the contrast would become even more dramatic. The fall of 1994 may be best known for witnessing the Newt Gingrich "Republican Revolution" at the ballot box, but a revolution that targeted the exact opposite audience as Gingrich's core demo was going on in Hollywood—courtesy of Warren Littlefield's New NBC. The hottest new show that fall was the definitive Gen-X classic, *Friends,* the seminal sitcom about a group of young adults hanging out in a trendy Manhattan coffeehouse and living as roomies in the apartments above. *Friends* kicked off the Thursday night "must-see" lineup at 8pm, and an equally white-hot hit ended the night at 10. It was a Michael Crichton-created, Steven Spielberg-produced drama that made previous hospital standard-setters like *St. Elsewhere* and *Marcus Welby* look as slow and sedentary as a daytime soap opera—with its Quentin Tarantino camerawork, MTV-editing, and graphic procedures and jargon that left little to the imagination. (Not to mention a handsome and charismatic young star named George Clooney.) *ER* immediately sent any and all competition to the morgue, becoming TV's highest-rated hour-long drama since the heyday of *Dallas* and *Charlie's Angels* ten or fifteen years earlier, across all demographic groups. (It would run for 15 full years, until 2009.)

With the decade-defining *Seinfeld* already anchoring Thursday nights at 9, the defin-itive "must-see TV" lineup of the mid–1990s was now established: *Friends* at 8, *Seinfeld* at 9 (with two other trendy, upscale sitcoms about big-city professionals padding things out), and *ER* at 10. Fox, meanwhile, followed up its *90210* and *Melrose Place* soapy successes with the definitive mid-to-late '90s Gen-X family drama, *Party of Five.* If workplace and room-mate comedies like those '70s shows, *Mary Tyler Moore, That Girl, Alice, Rhoda, Laverne & Shirley, WKRP in Cincinnati, Taxi,* and *Three's Company* had sent the message that one's friends were the new family during the era of liberation, than these programs drove home the same point for the raised-in-daycare Gen-X children of the Me Decade. Comedies about hip young city-dwellers awkwardly (or selfishly) stumbling their way through adult life, and thirtyish professionals who despite being physically attractive, still always ended up with Mr. or Ms. Wrong, would become the default staple for comedy—from *30 Rock* and *The Big Bang Theory* to *Girls, New Girl,* and *The Mindy Project.* And shows like *Party of Five* and *Dawson's Creek,* with their hot, gender-and-preference-diverse casts of teens and early 20-somethings dealing with existential and dating dilemmas, wrote the blueprint for the later "mumblecore" independent films of Noah Baumbach, Andrew Bujalski, and Mark Duplass.

ABC's 1990s strength was, even more so than NBC's, in its bumper crop of standup-starring sitcoms—the blue-collar comedy of Roseanne, Ellen, Tim Allen, Drew Carey, and Brett Butler, plus their "TGIF" Friday family comedies (*Full House, Boy Meets World, Family Matters*), and some upscale, NBC-style shows (like *Spin City, The Naked Truth, Dharma & Greg,* and *Sports Night*). Now, in light of NBC's success, ABC decided to embrace demographics over ratings just as totally. It dropped *Matlock* like a wrinkled hot potato at the end of the 1994–95 season. (That was the year they also dumped *The Commish,* a crime show as lovable, down-to-earth, and mass-audience as its star Tony Chiklis' later cable cop drama *The Shield* would be controversial, anti-heroic, and ultra-violent.)

By the spring of 1995, primetime TV's extreme makeover of All (White Upscale) Youth, All The Time was nearly complete. But CBS was still doing business as usual. Amidst all these trend-setting, star-making, barrier-shattering Generation X groundbreakers, the Eye Network's longest-lasting and highest-rated hit of the Youth Fall of 1994 was the heartwarming Hallmark-style classic, *Touched by an Angel.*

Vampire Slayers, Log Ladies, Warrior Princesses, and Freaks and Geeks

In January of 1995, the United Paramount Network (UPN) and the much more successful WB (now The CW) network launched across independent and UHF channels from coast to coast. Both networks had a rocky start, but The WB would soon copy Fox's strategy of going after high school and college-age viewers and early 20-somethings, and enjoy almost as much success. Also in January of 1995, Universal Studios launched a first-run syndicated series for the weekend market, a gleefully historically inaccurate, swords-and-shirtless-men saga starring Kevin Sorbo as *Hercules.* Ted Raimi (whose indie-filmic brother Sam was the showrunner) costarred as the human-punching-bag comic relief, with the typically un-subtle (especially given the show's enormous gay subtext) name of Joxer. The show was such an instant success that in September of 1995, it spawned a spinoff that was even more iconic, *Xena: Warrior Princess.*

Starring the gorgeous New Zealand glam-azon Lucy Lawless as a breast-plated female mercenary in ancient times, the ultra-campy adventure became a lesbian must-see thanks to its barely coded subtext between Xena and her cute-as-a-button young female sidekick and "companion" Gabrielle (Renee O'Connor). And in early 1997, USA Network would also launch a Canadian co-production of the film (made originally in France and then remade with Bridget Fonda in 1992), *La Femme Nikita,* starring Peta Wilson as an up-from-the-streets young hit woman working for a ruthless female rogue-CIA boss (Alberta Watson). All three shows would run through the spring and summer of 2001.

Although without a doubt, the biggest LGBT moment in 1990s TV was when sitcom star and standup icon Ellen DeGeneres came out, both in real life and in her alter-ego TV character, in the spring of 1997. (Roseanne paved the way with a famous lesbian kiss scene, and acknowledged in her iconic "blue collar woman" speech during her 1997 series finale, that her butch sister Jackie was indeed gay.) With A-list guest stars Oprah, k.d. lang, and Laura Dern, Ellen announced (hilariously and by mistake, into an airport's public-address system), "I'M GAY!" She made the cover of most serious newsmagazines as well as the TV and movie trades, and deservedly so. Until 1997, the mere presence of regular and likable gay supporting characters on shows, like *Soap, Dynasty, LA Law,* and *thirtysomething,* had been enough for ultra-right action groups to call for sponsor boycotts (for endorsing such "perversion" and "immorality.") Immediately after going public, Ellen was condemned and called "Ellen *Degenerate*" by Jerry Falwell and other fundie royalty. Though Ellen lost her sitcom the following year, she rebounded better than ever with her top-rated daytime talk show in 2003. And Ellen's shattering of the glass closet directly opened the door for 1998's big sitcom hit *Will & Grace,* and the December 2000 and May/June 2001 launches of *Queer as Folk* and *Six Feet Under.*

The ultimate '90s example of heterosexual small-screen Grrrl Power was unquestionably *Buffy the Vampire Slayer.* Launched in March of 1997 on the struggling WB channel (and based on a 1992 Kristy Swanson movie of the same name), *Buffy* starred the beautiful and talented Sarah Michelle Gellar as a blonde suburban teen queen who finds out that she's the "Chosen One" to battle the evil undead. Created by *Buffy's* original screenwriter Joss Whedon, who would later go on to make one cult TV sci-fi classic after another (*Firefly, Dollhouse,* the *Buffy* spin-off *Angel*) in the 2000s, as well as directing mega-million studio films like 2012's *The Avengers,* Buffy Summers and her sexy gang of "Scoobies"—which included star-making performances by Alyson Hannigan, Seth Green, Michelle Trachtenberg, David Boreanaz, and Eliza Dushku—literally put The WB "on the map" culturally speaking. And Buffy found her perfect companion piece when *Scream* screenwriter Kevin Williamson set sail on *Dawson's Creek,* starring James Van Der Beek, Joshua Jackson, Katie Holmes, and future Oscar-nominee Michelle Williams, the following January.

The success of Buffy, Dawson, *Party of Five,* and *That '70s Show* was so great among desirable demographics that even top-rated NBC tried to cash in on the formula in 1999, with a one-season wonder still beloved to this day, about a group of suburban high-school misfits in the last days of disco, called *Freaks and Geeks.* And as for being a star-maker—the show was James Franco, Seth Rogen, Linda Cardellini, and Jason Segel's big break in front of the cameras, and writer-director Judd Apatow's big break behind them. (And teenage "star" John Francis Daley went on to become one of Hollywood's hottest young comedy screenwriters, with credits like *Horrible Bosses* to his name.) Meanwhile, the WB continued doubling down, launching shows like *Charmed, Popular,* and *Gilmore Girls,* each with more hip meta-media references and camp classic set pieces than the next—while no less importantly, giving Gen-X showrunners by the names of Ryan Murphy and JJ Abrams their first big Hollywood credits.

Buffy and *Xena's* influence lasted far beyond their home decade. It would be almost impossible to imagine girl-power young adult novels (and blockbuster film franchises) like *Twilight* and *The Hunger Games* without Buffy and Xena to have first paved the way. And when combined with the Internet, these shows and the sexy Fox soap operas and trendy young NBC sitcoms like *Friends,* created the phenomenon of (relation) "shipping" and "Fan Fiction," where Internet bloggers and passionate fans would write steamy and sexy stories—and post and share them online with other "fanboys" and "fangirls"—about their favorite characters' after-hours adventures. The popular and long-running "Television Without Pity" website (which ran from 1999 to 2014) largely started with this kind of thing, and one of the most passionate writers of TV and movie fan fiction went on to publish a novel of her own, years later. (It was called *Fifty Shades of Grey.*)

But all of these quirky groundbreakers, and indeed virtually all of the upscale dramas of the past quarter-century (and not a few magical-realist, dark-comedy feature filmmakers—we're looking at you, Wes Anderson and Charlie Kaufman) owe their lives to underground and indie film godfather David Lynch's subversively surrealist small-screen masterpiece, *Twin Peaks*. Premiering on April 8, 1990, and telling the story of a dead teen queen named Laura Palmer, savagely raped and strangled to death outside a small logging town in the Pacific Northwest named *Twin Peaks,* the town (and the show) was populated by a middle-aged lady who had a pet lumber log that sent her psychic messages, mute dancers and dwarves, S&M-tinged Asian women and teeny-boppers who still dressed like Fonzie or James Dean. (Not to mention hometown diners with "damn fine cups of coffee" and meal prices last seen around 1973 or so.) Starring Lynch veteran Kyle MacLachlan as existentialist, Nixon-suited FBI agent Dale Cooper, and '70s TV and B-movie heartthrob Michael Ontkean as Sheriff Harry S Truman (yes, that was his name), as tall and redoubtable as the spruce and fir trees that surrounded him, the hottest pop-culture question of the summer of 1990 was "Who Killed Laura Palmer?" (It was her own father, of course, after he was possessed by a shape-shifting demon named BOB.)

Earlier TV groundbreakers like *All in the Family, M*A*S*H, The Defenders,* and *Hill Street Blues* had redefined the limits of what you could get away with showing on TV, in terms of sexual or violent or political subject matter. But *Twin Peaks* redefined what you could literally DO on television. Picking up where the manically self-referencing, fourth-wall-breaking *Moonlighting* had left off less than a year earlier (when it met its premature end, also on ABC), *Twin Peaks* redefined the boundaries of what you could do in terms of pacing, feel, and style. Roughly a decade before Tony Soprano, Jack Bauer, *The West Wing,* and original-recipe *CSI* (and years before *ER,* or *Peaks'* most stylistically similar successor, *The X-Files*), *Twin Peaks* was the first TV drama to be truly thought of and executed in feature-film terms, with film school grammar and intellectual storytelling. It didn't bother to explain to you what was going on ahead of time, or tell you who the good guys and bad guys were upfront. Other TV shows you could *watch.* With *Twin Peaks,* you had to simply *experience* it. *Juno* screenwriter and *United States of Tara* creator Diablo Cody told PBS in 2011 that over twenty years later, *Twin Peaks* still remained the standard in virtually all the writers' rooms of truly quality TV drama.

(And CBS, of all networks, had launched two multiple Emmy-winners that were conceived directly as homages to *Twin Peaks,* albeit more traditionally televisual ones—*Northern Exposure,* the 1990–95 Rob Morrow dramedy about a handsome young New York Jewish doctor repaying his med-school tuition by federal service in a quirky, remote Alaskan town; and *Picket Fences,* David E. Kelley's sly, subversive, and unforgettable 1992–96 skewering of small-town suburbia, where ripped-from-the-headlines moral and religious dilemmas were faced by the residents of fractious yet indivisible Rome, Wisconsin. Would that our real-life culture wars of Clinton's first term could have had such happy and touching endings every Friday night at 11!)

TV's Second Golden Age

In the 1960s, '70s, and into the '80s, it was something of an upper-bourgeois status symbol to theatrically declare that you "never watched television," except for news and sports events, and maybe PBS and *Saturday Night Live*. It was the "idiot box," the "boob tube." It was so lowest-common-denominator, so crassly commercial, such a waste of time. By the end of the 1990s, however, the roles were reversed. Now, it was bizarre for a yuppie professional NOT to know what was happening on NBC's 1999–00 Wednesday-night lineup of *The West Wing* and (original recipe) *Law & Order*, let alone over at Tony Soprano's house on HBO Sundays. There were no intellectual brownie points to be gained by saying you "never watched" *Seinfeld* or *The X-Files* or *Homicide*. Quite the opposite, in fact. Someone who completely ignored Jon Stewart and David Letterman, or *The Simpsons* and *South Park*, would look just as pathetic in 1999 and 2000 as someone who confessed a burning passion for *Supertrain, The Brady Bunch Variety Hour*, and *The $1.98 Beauty Show* would've looked 20 or so years earlier.

And it should also be noted that the 1990s brought a new wave of dishy, sexy, sly, and wry post-feminist "girls' shows" to the fore, from *Ally McBeal* in 1997 to *Sex and the City* and *Will & Grace* the following year, culminating in the mid–2000s with the likes of *Desperate Housewives* and *Grey's Anatomy*, and the "rom-coms" of Julia Roberts, Meg Ryan, Reese Witherspoon, and Kate Hudson. These shows were the perfect examples of the Clinton and Bush II era's two most fetishized target political demographics: upscale suburban "soccer and security moms" with high incomes, stable lifestyles, and well-to-do hubbys; and their fashionably faboo, sexy and single professional sisters in the glamorous big cities. Indeed, NBC's 1990s must-sees like *Seinfeld, Frasier, Will & Grace*, and *Just Shoot Me* were practically the epitome of what *New York Times* cultural satirist David Brooks famously called "Bobos in Paradise"—both in their fictional characters on one side of the screen, and in their real-life target audiences watching on the other side.

Perhaps the biggest difference between 1990s TV dramas, and those of the Obama (and later-Dubya) era, was the pendulum-swinging evolution and revolution from star-driven shows to ensemble dramas and back again. By the 1990s, the era of "star vehicle" shows like *Kojak, Columbo, Rockford Files*, and *Magnum PI* were considered hopelessly old hat. Only a small handful were launched during the decade—and only a few of those, like *Nash Bridges, Xena, Ally McBeal*, and *Buffy*, could be considered true ratings (let alone artistic) successes. The new mandate was the "ensemble" or "workplace" drama, pioneered by *Hill Street Blues* in the early 1980s. *Homicide, Law & Order, ER, NYPD Blue*, and eventually *CSI* and *The West Wing* were shows where the setting itself was the "star." Major supporting characters (and sometimes even *lead* characters) could come and go, but the basic structure—a hyped-up cinema verite of life at a Chicago county hospital, a Vegas crime lab, the district attorney's office and urban police precincts, or backstage at the White House—*that* would remain.

Starting with Tony Soprano in January of 1999, followed by *24's* Jack Bauer in late 2001, the trend began moving back towards star-driven programs—usually with a morally compromised, flawed, and often anti-heroic (and usually alpha male) lead character. But even then, the postmodern dramas of the Bush II and Obama years would borrow a significant twist directly from the 1990s: From Tony and Jack, to Don Draper of *Mad Men*, Meredith Grey of *Grey's Anatomy*, Walter White of *Breaking Bad*, and Alicia Florrick of *The Good Wife* (and all of their modern spiritual successors—*Scandal, How to Get Away With Murder, Game of Thrones, The Walking Dead, Empire*), the show itself would revolve around the lead character's personal demons and struggles against the novelistic (and sometimes soap-sudsy) continuing backdrops of their lives, families, and co-workers. It wasn't just about what self-contained mystery Ben Matlock or Columbo would unravel this week or what disease Marcus Welby would cure, or what urgent social issue Quincy and Lou Grant would bring to the fore.

And all of this underlined the Fox-MTV-Warren Littlefield strategy. The WB/CW's path to success was ensured by copying *Friends, 90210,* and *Party of Five*—NOT by copying Jessica Fletcher and Dr. Quinn! The youthful ratings mandate that Fox and MTV's young upstarts had pushed from the sidelines, and that NBC had doubled down on in 1992, had now officially taken over all of Hollywood. Mass-audience ratings were officially out—they were literally "so ten minutes ago!" In the book *Selling Electronic Media,* Warren Littlefield proudly crowed his success. "The message loud and clear is demographics!"

Show Me the Money!

By the time Clinton reached his second term, CBS had been making the argument that at least the 55-to-64 year olds, if not the 55-to-74 year olds (the people who were *older,* but not nursing-home *elderly*) were the most valuable target audience of all—even as un-hip, retro, Depression-era frugal, and brand-loyal as they were. They had the paid-off homes, money in the bank, stable pensions and Social Security/Medicare—and the comparatively "younger" ones who were still working were at the height of their salary scales. For the first few years after NBC and ABC joined Fox and MTV in their All Youth All the Time campaign, the Eye Network was politely but firmly ignored. But by 1997, the CBS argument was no longer falling on deaf ears.

Yet instead of *widening* their demographic nets in response to CBS's plea, the other networks brutally *narrowed* theirs even further. In 1997 and '98, they conducted a virtual bargain-hunting holocaust of shows that featured or appealed to blue collar viewers. *Roseanne, Married ... with Children, Coach,* and *Grace Under Fire* were all summarily pink-slipped from the factory, and even the top-rated *Home Improvement* didn't have much time left. Many quality shows that portrayed casts of color, like *Martin* and *Living Single* were also given the axe, and the ones that remained were sent to marginalized C-list networks like UPN in those not-so-dark days before Shonda Rhimes, Lee Daniels, and Tyler Perry. (And virtually none of the urban comedies that still remained by the end of the decade came even close to the Emmy-winning writing, top ratings, or high visibility of a *Good Times, Sanford & Son, Cosby Show,* or *Jeffersons.*)

That was no accident.

Now, let's have a look at the new shows that *replaced* those oldies but goodies, from 1997 to 2000. There were the shoe-shopping career gals and faboo gay BFF's of *Sex and the City, Will & Grace,* and *Ally McBeal.* (Not to mention their designer knockoffs like *Suddenly Susan, Gilmore Girls,* and *Veronica's Closet*). There were the Ivy-educated, fast-walking and faster-talking, high powered pros of *The West Wing* and *The Practice.* There were the mostly white, hyper-articulate high schoolers of *Dawson's Creek, Buffy the Vampire Slayer,* and *Popular,* and the college-educated high techies of *CSI.* All bright, all high income, all good looking and glamorous—and almost all white. Even blue-collar-raised tough guy Tony Soprano lived in a palatial pool home, drove a brand-new black Lexus, and had weekly appointments with a high-priced analyst, plus two materialistic, spoiled-rotten teenagers at home. And every last one of NBC's "must-see" sitcoms was set in a trendy location like Manhattan, Seattle, Miami, or San Francisco, with plenty of upscale Jewish and gay characters to go around.

And THAT was no accident, either.

Now, an audience's income profile and education level was to become almost as important as ratings size itself, along with the decisive "18–49s," "18–34s" and "25–54s" in a TV show's sales portfolio. For the most part, working-class shows would disappear from primetime, in exchange for shows that fit the demographic profile of what was now the networks' uber-target audience. These hip new hits also (not coincidentally) tended to fit the pattern of the most powerful film and TV columnists and critics at the high-paying, high-profile national magazines and top-traffic Internet websites. To say that this trend mirrored the late 1990s goal among politics and politicians, especially the "Dick Morris Democrats" of the later Clinton-era—to fetishize economically upscale, socially liberal "swing voters" in the 35-to-49 and 25-to-54 year old age groups—would be a gross understatement. To anyone working in media research or as a political "fixer," it was as clear as a neon sign in Las Vegas.

Critical Condition

By 1999, ABC and NBC were battling it out for 18–49 and 25–54 supremacy, while Fox, NBC, and even young upstart The WB were adding one hit after another to their line-ups, and becoming THE launching-pads for hot new actors and producer-directors about to make the transition to feature films and edgy cable. George Clooney, Jennifer Aniston, Courteney Cox, Lisa Kudrow, Michelle Williams, Neve Campbell, JJ Abrams, Judd Apatow, Ryan Murphy, James Franco, Jason Segel, Seth Rogen, Eliza Dushku, Alyson Hannigan, Jennifer Love Hewitt, Sarah Michelle Gellar, and more. (Even Oscar-winner Hilary Swank got her big break with a recurring role on *90210*.)

Indeed, the year 1999 defined the coming decade's most important dramatic game-changes. Already *Sex and the City* and *Will & Grace* had brought a flip, cheeky new sexual sophistication to primetime, on the two hippest networks for "quality TV" back then, HBO and NBC. In January of 1999, the eight year saga of *The Sopranos* would begin, redefining the boundaries of TV drama like nothing since *Hill Street Blues, Twin Peaks,* or *The Twilight Zone,* with its Scorsese-influenced story of a New Joyzey crime boss trying to modernize the mob while holding on to his loyal friends (you don't wanna know what happened to his DIS-loyal friends, *capisce?*) and dealing with his spoiled and not-ready-for-*crime*-time teenage kids. *The Sopranos* is almost universally recognized as the most important TV show of the post–*Seinfeld* era, and was the training camp for the runner-up, *Sopranos* staff writer Matthew Weiner's modern retro classic, *Mad Men.*

The following fall, NBC elected Aaron Sorkin's artistically near-equal, cinematic saga of the behind-the-scenes at *The West Wing,* a fitting capper to a decade where White House functionaries and press secretaries had become real-life superstars thanks to 24-hour cable, elite opinion journals, and the Internet. *The West Wing* was also the door-opener for today's slate of high-IQ political TV shows—*Scandal, The Good Wife,*

Homeland, Madam Secretary, House of Cards, even the HBO spoof *Veep*—only with one notable difference. *The West Wing,* as intricate and dramatic and filled with moral quandaries as it was, presented a basically idealized portrait of a White House, of Big Guv'mint at its best—and its president, Josiah Bartlet, was conceived of by Sorkin, largely by his own free admission, as Clinton *minus* the scandals and appetites. In that, it was a healing balm for liberals (and some open-minded conservatives—Republican royalty strategist Mary Matalin worked on the show) who wished for a president who had genuinely altruistic policies, but who could also keep it zipped, and who had more of a sense of old-school class and innate dignity, someone who didn't act as though the White House was the *Big Brother* house in disguise. Running through 2006, it also served as an alternate-reality love song for liberals and progressives who realized—some of them too late—just how good they had it under Bubba, once George W. Bush had taken over the Oval Office cockpit.

Looking back, as over-the-top and sudsy as later shows like *House of Cards* and *Scandal* are, they are also a probably more realistic portrait of post–Clinton (and Bush II and Obama) era politics. As these newer dramas (including the considerably more grounded *Good Wife* and *Homeland*) continue to show, maybe you *needed* an ethically challenged, hypocritical, morally compromising, deal-making, in yo' face, ruthless son-of-a-bitch who would stop at nothing—if you actually wanted to get your "compassionate" and "liberal" and "diversity-sensitive" policies *passed* into black-letter law. (Which of course, may have been the main media lesson of both the Clinton and Obama eras all along.)

Meanwhile back in 1999, CBS was just hanging on, like a jilted lover in denial, to its all-but-capsized ship. As Derek Kompare and Victoria Johnson illustrated in Kompare's book on *CSI*, "CBS's late 1990s schedule of safe, middlebrow fare like *Dr. Quinn Medicine Woman, Promised Land,* and *Touched by an Angel* had cemented its status as a conservative, 'heartland' network—at the expense of critical acclaim, popular buzz, and enough of the critical 18–49 demographic favored by advertisers." And its late '90s crime and legal dramas, like *Diagnosis Murder, Nash Bridges, Walker, Texas Ranger, Martial Law, Judging Amy, Family Law,* and the just-concluded *Murder She Wrote* seemed like "staid, formulaic relics" that were "totally out of synch."

These kinds of predictable dramas, with their 1970s-style storytelling and bland cinematography, were now officially the face, the very "brand" of CBS, just as much and just as devastatingly as their outdated country comedies had been 30 years earlier. As Bill Carter taunted in *Desperate Networks,* CBS chief "Les Moonves' kids still weren't watching his network." (Carter also added phrases like "antediluvian," "totally outmoded," and a bunch of "refugees from Lawrence Welk reruns" to describe CBS at this time.) Aside from their Monday megahit *Everybody Loves Raymond,* CBS still had nothing that could approach demographic or pop-culture competitiveness with a *Friends, Sex and the City, Buffy the Vampire Slayer, X-Files, The Daily Show, South Park, Simpsons, Ally McBeal, Sopranos,* or *Seinfeld*—or even a *Will & Grace, Dawson's Creek,* or *That '70s Show.* By decade's end, it looked as though the former Tiffany Network had passed the point of no return. The network's younger executives were wondering how—or if—they could ever dig themselves out of their demographic death panel. And then, just like a sudden plot twist on a top-rated soap opera—the answer suddenly appeared!

Making Your Own Reality

Contrary to popular belief, "reality TV" has been a part of the television landscape ever since the first flicker of the cathode rays. From Ralph Edwards surprising everyone from Hollywood icons to Holocaust survivors to hometown heroes on *This Is Your Life* from 1948 to 1961 (and again from 1970 to '73), to Allen Funt grinning "Smile! You're on *Candid Camera!*" in TV's earliest days (most famously from 1960 to '67, and again in syndication from 1974 to '79). And who can ever forget "Chuckie Baby" Barris presiding over the madness and mayhem of the definitive disco-era program, *The Gong Show*, from 1976 to 1980? There was also the intellectual must-see, cinema verite "parent" to modern reality, in the form of the groundbreaking and ultra-controversial 1973 PBS documentary series, *An American Family.*

The current brand of "reality TV," however—an oxymoron if ever there was one, considering how manipulated to the point of being near-rigged much of it is, came into full force in the same year as Bill Clinton's election. Premiering on MTV in 1992, *The Real World* was originally intended by its producers (both of whose backgrounds were in daytime soaps), Jonathan Murray and the late Mary-Ellis Bunim, to be a scripted MTV answer to trendy FOX shows like *Beverly Hills, 90210* and the then-premiering *Melrose Place.* Unfortunately, the concept was willing—but the budget was weak. So instead, Bunim and Murray struck on the idea of "casting" their show with a representative group of all-too-real Gen Xers, from different backgrounds but with similar goals in life, to live together as roomies in a house—wired with cameras and sound.

Featuring dream-demographic, glam, and visual locales (New York, San Francisco, Hollywood, London, Miami, Hawaii, Paris, New Orleans—don't hold your breath for a *Real World* Wichita or Podunk), *The Real World* took off like a rocket. It was one thing for Gen X to escape into the fantasy world of FOX and WB soaps, of vampire-hunters and rich young execs; but *these* were people "just like us!" The brilliant Bunim/Murray team (who would go on to be one of the top production houses in Hollywood reality fare) used their soap background to ensure that there would be at least one person (nerd, jock, bitch, slut, bully, gay/lesbian, minority, "good girl," "nice guy," etc.) for each kind of viewer to love—or hate.

And the show proved as cutting-edge in its topicality as the hottest 10 o'clock drama, with every hot button you could think of, from sex, prejudice, religion, abortion, politics, alcohol, drugs, gay issues, and AIDS—often in politically incorrect and very "real" terms. By 1995, after the show's landmark 1994 season featuring quintessential Gen-X grunge slacker David "Puck" Rainey and terminally ill (with AIDS) young gay activist Pedro Zamora, the show surpassed *Beavis & Butt-Head* as MTV's most-watched regular series. It was even given a barely disguised spoofing in Ben Stiller and Winona Ryder's iconic 1994 indie, *Reality Bites,* and was a clear influence on grunge-era cinema like *Clerks.*

As far as the Big Four networks were concerned, the real reality turning point happened in the summer of 1999, with the unexpected success of a British-designed reboot of the old 1950s classic, *The $64,000 Question,* called *Who Wants to Be a Millionaire.* Not since the days of "Vanna-mania" in *Wheel of Fortune's* 1980s heyday, or Richard Dawson's kissing-and-telling on *Family Feud,* had a game show become as inescapable in popular culture as that one, which ran as often as 3 or 4 times per week in prime time wherever ABC had a weak spot, when it returned in the spring of 2000. Even though the show's first host, talk show icon Regis Philbin, was himself in his late sixties, the show's round *Dr. Strangelove* set with its doomsday lighting, special effects, and avant-garde camerawork, and its cheering, edge-of-your-seat audience, all ensured that it would bring in a healthy number of young viewers each week, at least until the initial novelty wore off.

Now, thought younger CBS execs, as they struggled to update their network's image from TV's old-age home, a show like *The Real World* was something that a generation of Generation Xers and high school/college age early Millennials WOULD watch! People who had come of age watching handheld-camera classics like *Clerks* and *The Blair Witch Project*. (*The Real World* was by now a corporate sister of CBS, as parent company Viacom also owned MTV as well.) VH1, A&E, and E! were also rakin' it in by the late 1990s, with their dishy, Oprah-fied, personality-driven *Biography, True Hollywood Story,* and *Behind the Music* franchises. And Fox and MTV had gotten where they were *not* by trying to play catch-up with the establishment. No, they'd "pantsed" the rest of Hollywood by going outside the box, hadn't they?

Now, if CBS could find a way to raise the stakes, to add the million-dollar competition and drama of *Millionaire* to the proceedings, then young people wouldn't just *watch* these new kinds of shows—they'd make appointments, have parties for them, and message-board one another on the Internet! Best of all, the tragically hip movie and TV critics, especially the younger ones—the ones who would sooner slam their fingers in a piano lid than write anything other than smart-assed snark about *Touched by an Angel, Walker, Texas Ranger, Family Law,* and *Diagnosis Murder*—why, they'd go frigging nuts! *They'd be all over this!*

At last, CBS got its "final answer" in the spring of 2000, when some alert and youthful programmers took the pitches for two shows that would change the game not only for their network—but for all of American culture itself. They were called *Survivor* and *Big Brother.* (The envelope-pushing Fox network had already spoofed the genre by then, with a prime time game show in the spring of 2000 stolidly titled *Greed,* and an appallingly sexist and tasteless Jerry Springer–like competition special, rightly blasted by media critics from coast to coast, called *Who Wants to MARRY a Multi-Millionaire?*) If the summer of '99 had belonged to *Millionaire,* the sexy summer of 2000 sizzled with the latest plot twists and turns of the real-life castaways of *Survivor,* with its shirtless men and skimpy bikini-wearing women, and its politically incorrect female truckers, manipulative gays, and ex-military seniors. That, and the Orwellian voyeurism of the even raunchier *Big Brother* house, which literally "peeked through the keyhole" at a hormone hothouse of scantily clad young hardbodies from all and every sex, race, and preference. While each "reality" show or competition on each network would have a new wrinkle here and there, almost all of them would stick to the pattern established by *Survivor* and *Big Brother* (and a soon-to-come hit called *American Idol* in 2002). There would be lovable and innocent "heroes" and evil, mustachetwirling "villains"—*and they'd be real-life people, too!* And just like an exciting crime show or a nighttime soap opera, we the viewers would be let in on the secrets, but the unsuspecting victims would never know until it was too late.

Reality TV directly anticipated the rise and importance of "social media" in the coming decade, where "bloggers" and "vloggers" (video bloggers) on YouTube and Vimeo, and where Twitter, Myspace, and Facebook-addicted Millennials would keep their friends—and the rest of the world—up to the minute on their personal dating games and love connections. The late Andy Warhol didn't know just how short he was selling the future when he famously predicted that one day, everyone would have at least "15 minutes of fame." From now on, book publishers, magazines, Internet sites, blogs, cable shows, YouTube, Facebook, and Twitter would focus on rebooting people's real lives into an online reality show.

Follow the Evidence

Sure enough, *Survivor* and *Big Brother* set youthful demographics and Internet message boards on fire, beyond even the wildest hopes of their creators or the CBS brass. So much so that by September of 2000, NBC and Fox themselves were burning with jealousy—and at "old and stodgy" CBS, too! Who woulda thought? Maybe CBS *wasn't* TV's electronic nursing home after all…

Not for much longer it wasn't! That same fall, the very last (but certainly not the least) pilot that CBS development exec Nina Tassler had commissioned made the schedule, produced by action movie maven Jerry Bruckheimer. A new drama that followed a group of hip young scientists who solved crimes in Sin City using up-to-the-second digital technology, and featured music video editing and feature-film visual effects. Premiering on the demographic graveyard of Friday night on October 6, 2000, just one month before the Bush vs. Gore game-changer, *CSI* was the most visual, kinetic, action-blockbuster stylish show ever attempted by a network—even including pay-cable, and most certainly including CBS—since the premiere of *ER* six years earlier.

Now, all the CBS sales department had to do was "follow the evidence." By November of 2000, *CSI* was racking up the highest Friday-night numbers any network had seen since the heyday of *Dallas* and *Miami Vice* over a decade before. No Friday night show on any network, ever since *The X-Files* had moved to Sundays in 1996, had come close to *CSI's* regular scores of 19, 20, and 21 million viewers a pop. Best of all, it had a larger audience of 18–49 viewers than any other show on the CBS network, except perhaps for the blockbuster *Raymond*. And that was in spite of the show's slot on Friday's "date night." If it could do this well sandwiched between their one-season, one-note *Fugitive* revival and Don Johnson's retro classic *Nash Bridges,* what could it do if it was put right before its most stylishly and stylistically compatible show (NBC's *ER,* of course) at 9 p.m. Thursdays? Especially if it had *Survivor* to back it up at 8? *Survivor* might not be able to equal *Friends,* but it was the only show on any network or cable channel that could give Monica, Ross, and Rachel a run for their money.

(It was almost too-perfect an irony that the show which *Survivor* displaced on Thursday nights was *Diagnosis Murder,* which moved to finish the 2000–01 season back to Friday nights at 8. Sure enough, *Diagnosis* won its Friday timeslot in total viewers to the very end—but it also remained network TV's oldest-skewing scripted show.)

Pulling the Plug on Grandma

In the summer of 2001, CBS head Les Moonves decided that the time had finally come—now that he also had the kind of shows where the future really "lied," in a literal sense—manufactured reality and explicit drama, on his frontline. In the biggest game change at CBS since the 1971 Rural Purge exactly 30 years earlier, CBS completely "death paneled" its senior shows in one fell swoop. And the De-Seniorization of 2001 was just as deadly as its predecessor.

Dick Van Dyke's lovable ol' Dr. Sloan would finish practicing in May, and he hung up his regularly scheduled stethoscope for good (aside from a couple of reunion TV movies), once the summer network reruns finished in September of 2001. In addition to *Diagnosis Murder's* euthanasia, *Walker, Texas Ranger* got karate-chopped and *Nash Bridges* drove off into the sunset in July of 2001, after only eight weeks of summer replays after their final first-runs in May. (The contrast couldn't have been starker, as by far the two hottest and most acclaimed new scripted dramas to premiere on TV that spring and summer were the R-rated cable duo of *Queer as Folk* and *Six Feet Under*.) A few months later in the spring of 2002, shows like *Family Law* and *That's Life* were history. As the highest rated of the bunch, *Touched by an Angel* held out the longest, but it too would go to heaven in April of 2003.

Indeed, while plenty of liberals (or at least Democrats) almost surely also loved shows like *Dr. Quinn, Touched by an Angel, Walker, Texas Ranger,* and *Diagnosis Murder*—and a few Midwestern and Southern conservatives no doubt watched *The West Wing, Seinfeld, The X-Files,* and *The Sopranos*—it didn't take a film school grad or an "elite" sociologist to see a veritable Red State/Blue State divide forming across 1990s TV. On the one hand, there was the coalition of the ascendant: HBO (and Showtime) cablers with their R-rated dialogue, edgy sexual scenes, and indie-film hip cache like *The Sopranos* and *Sex and the City*, plus network TV equivalents like *Homicide, NYPD Blue, Party of Five, Buffy the Vampire Slayer, Ally McBeal, The X-Files, Will & Grace, CSI, ER,* and *Seinfeld*. On the other hand, there were comfort-food classics like *Matlock, Murder, She Wrote, Touched by an Angel, 7th Heaven, Promised Land, Dr. Quinn, J.A.G.,* and so on, with their traditional storytelling and nonthreatening main characters.

Soon, the major newspapers and online entertainment sites would no longer list the "Top 20" or 25 shows of the week in order of their general audience size—as they always had. From now on, they would be listed by the *only* standard that mattered: Adults 18–49 (and occasionally 25–54).

Network ad sales and publicity departments would now regularly keep "two sets of books"—one showing just the 18–49, 18–34, and 25–54 scores, and the other one showing the top shows in those key demographics among households with $100,000 incomes or more. The era of "broadcasting" was officially out. The era of "narrow-casting" was in— and it would only continue to be more so as digital, online, cable, YouTube, and do-it-yourself digital platforms mushroomed in the coming years.

The fact that today, CBS's recent lineup of procedural shows skews slightly older and stodgier than the other Big Four networks, now only underlines just how totally, madly, single-mindedly, and completely the emphasis on youth, youth, and more youth became in the aftermath of the 1990s, and CBS's 2001 Senior Purge. (Interestingly, by 2014, the major networks would begin slightly toe-dipping into the water of 60-plus performers again, like aging Baby Boomers Mark Harmon, Robin Williams, Tom Selleck, and Kathy Bates, who had been the prime demo in the '80s and early '90s—while still lusting after young viewers when they could get 'em—because Netflix, TiVo, Redbox, and online were starting to make the very idea of watching scheduled TV at home into an anachronism for Gen Xers and Millennials. Still, as late as 2012, NBC cancelled their highest-rated scripted hour, Oscar-winner Kathy Bates' *Harry's Law,* because it appealed to too many people in Ms. Bates' age group and older.)

And in fairness, it also underlines just how acutely aged CBS's audience had become by the time that the purge happened. If a procedural like *CSI* was the network's "youngest and hippest" drama back in 2000, that showed just how utterly and completely dependent CBS had become on the most elderly and traditional segments still alive at the end of the '90s—the Greatest Generation, and the oldest of their Silent Generation brothers and sisters, plus old-fashioned rural viewers. Conan O'Brien cracked in May of 2001 that CBS had finally decided to cancel *Diagnosis Murder* because "network research had shown that the average viewer had passed away four years earlier." As offensively disrespectful to one's elders as the 2001 purge was, CBS had held out the longest of any of the Big Four, until it finally had perhaps no other choice but to give in and "pull the plug on Grandma"—or at least, on Grandma's favorite TV shows. If the network hadn't de-seniorized as remorselessly as it did and when it did, once those World War II and Korea veterans and their "sweethearts" faded over the white cliffs of Dover, it might have been "So long, Soldier!" for CBS primetime itself.

An almost fashion magazine level of snobbery now became the hallmark of what shows did—and pointedly *didn't*—get paid attention to by hot bloggers and "name" film and TV critics. (Though tellingly, even today's cheesiest and sleaziest "reality shows" receive gushing media coverage equal to the most serious, Emmy-worthy developments on *Mad Men, The Good Wife, Empire, Orange Is the New Black,* and *How to Get Away with Murder*—underlining that it's outré cultural hipness, NOT just intellectual or cinematic quality, that's really calling the shots.)

And the lessons of the demographics mania that swept the 1990s in Hollywood (and Washington) would redefine American culture forevermore. No longer would TV shows, motion pictures, traditionally published books and magazines, or even political candidates judge their success by how wide, far, and all-encompassing their appeal and reach was. Uh-uh—no way. The real winners would now set their standards almost as much by which audiences they *intentionally* weeded out, which people they *wanted* to throw under the bus—so as to keep their all-important "brand," their target demographic and image, as pure as the driven snow.

* * *

Just as the late nightclub impresario Steve Rubell had proven once and for all, with his velvet rope made of iron outside of Studio 54 from 1977 to '80, the more exclusive, restricted, and unattainable something was, the more desirable it became. Being "hip" and "in" was far more important than being a place that "just anyone" could get into, right? In book and magazine publishing, TV, feature films, music, anything whatsoever to do with advertising—and certainly in politics—the name of the game was no longer "how many," but "who?" The real-life "Mad Men" in both advertising and political consulting would now play the tune that Joan Walsh had named: defining oneself, one's products, and one's political candidates by what they—and their target audience—*weren't*, as much or more as by what they *were*.

Forget about uniting. From now on, it was all about *dividing*.

7

Indie-Pendent's Day

*It is in the humble opinion of this narrator that this is not just "something that hap-
pened." This cannot be "one of those things." This, please, cannot be that! And for
what I would like to say, I can't. This was not just a matter of chance. These strange
things happen all the time.... We may be through with the past—but the past is not
through with us!*
—Ricky Jay *(in voice-over) in Paul Thomas Anderson's film* Magnolia *(1999)*

What do Quentin Tarantino, Steven Soderbergh, David Fincher, Spike Jonze, Spike
Lee, David O. Russell, Kevin Smith, Richard Linklater, M. Night Shymalayan, the
Wachowskis, the Coen Brothers, Wes Anderson, Todd Haynes, Gus Van Sant, Sam Mendes,
Alexander Payne, Bryan Singer, Danny Boyle, Charlie Kaufman, Alan Ball, and Paul Thomas
Anderson all have in common?

If you say that they are among the most important, influential, and both artistically
and financially successful voices in film working today, you'd be right. And if you also said
that every last one of them had their cinematic coming-out party in the 1990s decade, you'd
be right as well. (OK, Steven Soderbergh and Spike Lee first broke out in '86–89, and the
Coen Brothers and Gus Van Sant had a couple of early hits in the mid '80s, but they were
all far from the Hollywood "A-list" until at least the start of the '90s decade. All of the rest
of them made their cinematic debuts that decade—and most of them quite unforgettably.)
If the recent Sunday and Thursday-night smorgasbords of sumptuous, multi-flavored, and
complex HBO, AMC, and Shonda Rhimes dramas are TV's Second Golden Age, then the
1990s were without a doubt the American big screen's Third Golden Age. (Its first being
the '30s through the early '50s, of course, that grand Studio System heyday of Mayer, Gold-
wyn, Warner, Zanuck, Hughes, Hitchcock, Ford, DeMille, and Huston—and its second the
New Hollywood of the '70s.)

The same can be said of the era's pop music soundtrack, bursting as it was with hard-
core rap, Gen-X grunge, auto-tuned house music and trance, New Country, sunshine rock,
Grrrl Power, glammy (and Grammy-winning) divas and power ballads, where one flick of
the radio dial or the remote control could get you to *Sessions at West 54th* and *Austin City
Limits* to VH1's Motown and Disco Divas Live!, or to MTV's videos of Kurt, Tupac, Biggie,
Alanis, and Madonna. From to Country Music Television and The Nashville Network to
Lilith Fair to BET's R&B slow-jams and urban gangsta grooves.

All moved along at a fast clip until a young computer nerd (and future Facebook
founding father) named Sean Parker whipped up a little concoction called Napster, that
allowed file-sharing of individual songs and singles, free and a la carte (instead of having

to buy full album CD's or cassette tapes). Parker got in legal hot water for copyright infringement (but boy did he ever bounce back, when he became Mark Zuckerberg's spiritual big brother and early consigliere!) And Parker's success planted a seed in Steve Jobs' fertile imagination, which bloomed into I–Tunes and the I–Pod—and the entire rebooting of the record industry's business model over the past 10 or 15 years, from an album-based into a singles-and-download-based medium. (Not to mention the mid–2000s deaths of Sam Goody, Wherehouse Music, and other similar "record store" hangouts of the '80s and '90s.)

In many ways, 1990s American film and music culture was the perfect cinematic metaphor for its political culture as well. A young (by political standards) couple—who not insignificantly built their initial political foundation *outside* the Wall Street-Washington mainstream—hits the jackpot when they are given that once-in-a-lifetime golden ticket. They then spend the rest of their movie racking up rock-ribbed friends who'd stand by and even take a bullet for them, no matter what, and pissy enemies who were, like Inspector Javert of *Les Miserables*, always on the lookout for the slightest slight, for one single mistake, always ready to strike. All while the couple busily redefined, rebooted, and postmodernized the Presidency as they went along, rearranging Washington's old clichés to fit their own auteurist style.

A Blockbuster Reaction

The late historian Arthur Schlesinger's famous "pendulum" theory was the social sciences' and psychology's version of hard science's "for every action, there is an equal and opposite reaction." It posits that history is a never-ending cycle, swinging back and forth between progress and reaction, left and right wing, innovation and tradition. And a good case can be made that the history of American film aesthetics is the perfect example of a pendulum-swinger. Most of the seeds for the great vitality in American film in the '90s came in direct reaction against the excesses of Hollywood's 1980s corporate-blockbuster mentality.

The 1970s era before that, of maverick, colorful directors doing whatever their artistic muses led them to do—people like Robert Altman, Hal Ashby, Terence Malick, Sam Peckinpah, and even to some degree Martin Scorsese, Woody Allen, Brian De Palma, and Francis Ford Coppola, seemed well and truly over by the early to-mid 1980s. The studio chiefs and agents who had likewise indulged those colorful directors, actors, and screenwriters who had defined New Hollywood 1970s cinema—Robert Evans, Sue Mengers, Bert Rafelson, Julia Phillips—found themselves now slipping from Hollywood power. The swingin' pool parties at Hugh Hefner, Aaron Spelling, Robert Evans, Warren Beatty, and Dominick and Lennie Dunne's mansions, back in pre–AIDS Tinseltown were starting to give way to frigid international business boardrooms. The new breed of hands-on 1980s film executives epitomized by Barry and his "Killer Diller" protégés from Paramount, like Michael Eisner, Jeffrey Katzenberg, Don Simpson, and Sherry Lansing, were now ruling the Hollywood roost. They were sick and tired of being sick and tired of dealing with air-quote "colorful" ascot-wearing and navel-shirted "auteurs," and their diva-like temperaments and pretensions (and their indifference to going over budget). It was high time to put the *business* back in show business.

The media-deregulation trend that had begun under Ronald Reagan—and would reach what Mel Brooks' *Spaceballs* would call "ludicrous speed" under Hollywood's own favorite, Bill Clinton—was starting to result in a veritable domino chain of mega-mergers, leveraged buyouts, and hostile takeovers. The '90s began when 77-year-old Universal Studios giant Lew Wasserman semi-retired by selling his studio (and pocketing a $300 million "pension annuity" for himself) to Matsushita. After a few years, they offloaded it to Seagrams, who then sold it to France's Vivendi, which then merged it with its best TV client and partner, NBC—owned by General Electric (who then sold half of NBC-Universal to cable conglomerate Comcast!) CBS was forced to spin off its syndication division, Viacom, in 1971, which grew by leaps and bounds syndicating reruns *(Lucy, Honeymooners, Andy Griffith, Dick Van Dyke, Perry Mason)* and game shows *(What's My Line, Family Feud)* and by investing in 1980s cable powerhouses MTV and Nickelodeon. A decade or so after Sumner Redstone's National Amusements theatre chain acquired it (snapping up publisher Simon & Schuster along the way), Viacom purchased Paramount Studios, and by 1999, Paramount-Viacom had so much bling, they were able to buy *back* their former parent, CBS! And Rupert Murdoch had already captured the crown in 1985 when he bought not only 20th Century Fox Studios, but the Metromedia TV stations group, to launch his own Fox TV network in 1986 (and the cable news giant Fox News a decade after that).

It should be noted that virtually all of the above media mega-mergers would have been as blatantly illegal as dealing crack and heroin outside of a junior high school, under the anti-trust laws that ran from FDR through Carter—until both Ronald Reagan AND Bill Clinton had begun deregulating the media. (Even Clinton's one and only attempt at major anti-monopoly enforcement, the Microsoft anti-trust lawsuit of the late 1990s, was interminably delayed and appealed until after Clinton left office. Of course, the George W. Bush justice department shut it down like a crashed hard drive.)

Everybody knows that the 1990s was the decade when the "Global Economy" truly came into its own. And Tinseltown was no exception to the rule. Eager for the prestige, glamour, and cultural footprint of America's most visible export, foreign and international companies began buying up the Hollywood movie studios like so many jeweled baubles or gourmet chocolates in a box. In addition to Matsushita/MCA, Columbia Pictures was selling out to Sony—not coincidentally, Japan's premiere maker and importer of TV's, VCR's, and CD systems in the North American market, while Japanese investors bought controlling interest in NBC's New York headquarters of Rockefeller Center over 1991–92.

One of the first things these new Hollywood power players recognized was that, when it came to making a film a financial (if not artistic) success, *it's the marketing, stupid.* As the "I Want My MTV!" era took hold, and as computer technology began (literally) altering the face of what was possible in film, more and more movies of the later 1980s became (as an aging and contemptuous Pauline Kael angrily put it) like "recruiting posters that were not so much concerned with recruiting, as they were with being a poster!" Indeed, *Entertainment Tonight, Entertainment Weekly,* and *People Magazine* had made predicting box-office scores almost as much fun as betting on sports in Vegas—so that if a movie failed to meet its already hyped-up expectations within the first couple of weeks, it wouldn't be just a private embarrassment, but a public disaster.

But the creative pendulum was about to swing back, thanks not so much to the major studios, networks, or moguls—*at least at first*—but to a bunch of scrappy Gen Xers and their slightly senior "Generation Jones" older brothers, who were sneaking in through Hollywood's back gate. The '90s would start with the auteurist indies on the fringes, and end up with the most talented and promising of those filmmakers being folded as effortlessly as a Martha Stewart soufflé into The System. Their films would do what their later Sunday night cable children would—tell sophisticated, intricate-character stories with a style and a flair that simply couldn't be found anywhere else. There really was nothing like them in mainstream Hollywood fare up to that time.

It was a decade-long saga that was years in the making. *In a world …* of penniless young auteurs desperate to change the system they loved—only for the system to end up changing *them*…. Why, it was just like a Hollywood movie!

Straight Outta Compton (and Seattle)

Film wasn't the only place thriving with diversity and a truly independent, do-it-yourself spirit in the '90s. When it came to the top of the pop charts, few decades were as multi-polar as the '90s decade, which offered everything from the downbeat grunge of white Seattle rockers like Nirvana and Nine Inch Nails, to the hard core anger of South-Central LA and Harlem-based rappers like Body Count, Public Enemy, N.W.A (Niggaz Wit' Attitude), Suge Knight, The Notorious B.I.G, Tupac Shakur (and unctuous white wannabes, like the lip-synching Milli Vanilli), as well as genuinely talented white rappers like Marky Mark (Wahlberg) and Eminem. There was the thought-provoking, existentialist rock of Oasis, Pearl Jam, Morphine, Soul Asylum, the Devlins, Everlast, Semisonic, and the Smashing Pumpkins, and the feel-good sunshine of Smashmouth, Sugar Ray (and, God help us, the Brady Bunch/Partridge wannabe preteen rock of Hanson), plus innumerable thumpa-thumpa gay "house" and "techno" tracks.

Women rocked and ruled the decade, from the Lilith Fair concerts and "Riot Grrrls," to artists like Alanis Morrisette, Joan Osborne, and Aimee Mann. Established ultra-divas like Cher, Barbra, Bette, Aretha, Whitney, Diana, Donna, and Madonna still packed' em in, along with newer divas-in-training like Celine Dion and Mariah Carey. And thanks to Loretta, Conway, Barbara, Kenny, Dottie, and Dolly, country had become cool by the 1970s and '80s— but the '90s truly brought that horse into the stable. The Nashville Network rode high on the hog during the late '80s and early '90s, segueing into Country Music Television by decade's end, while sexy, edgy, crossover-friendly performers and crowd-packers like Garth Brooks, Shania Twain, Lee Ann Rimes, and Dwight Yoakam put a good sting on the country charts.

Without a doubt, the most tragically iconic moment in 1990s music happened in April of 1994, when Nirvana founder and frontman Kurt Cobain committed suicide, while dealing with severe depression, an on-again/off-again relationship with his performance artist wife Courtney Love, and substance abuse issues. (Like Janis Joplin, Jimi Hendrix, and Jim Morrison, Cobain was the magic number of 27 years old when he died.) Nirvana had been at the cutting edge of the Seattle-based "grunge rock" movement, along with Pearl Jam, Stone Temple Pilots, Soundgarden, and Alice in Chains. Nirvana first hit it big with their 1989 album, *Bleach,* with its late '70s punk-style album cover, and self-aware songs like "Negative Creep" and "About a Girl." But they hit true pop-culture nirvana in the fall of 1991 with their release of *Nevermind,* with an album/CD cover that soon approached *Sgt. Pepper* in its iconic status, of a baby in a swimming pool grabbing after a dollar bill—a perfect fuck-you-very-much to the end of the "greed is good" 1980s. The album featured the group's signature song, "Smells Like Teen Spirit." The handsome Cobain with his long (if stringy and unwashed) blond hair and soulful blue eyes, was both butch and dangerous enough for white jocks (and even many African American and Latino fans), while sensitive enough for the artsy-intellectual girls and suicidal and alienated young dudes, who felt the acute hopelessness and "what's the use?" attitude of the early '90s to their core.

Just as the sweaty, funky, Salvation Army/homeless look of grunge rock was a deliberate, punk-soul rebellion against the 1970s era of "glam" and "glitter rock" and disco, and MTV's 1980s "hair bands" with their pyrotechnic special effects and strobe lighting, the other signal sonic trend of the decade was also bursting with rebellion and attitude—this time of a political and racial nature.

No other musical movement had more importance or longer-lasting cultural legs than the mainstreaming of gangsta rap and hip-hop in the late 1980s and early 1990s. The music became the veritable soundtrack to urban America during that dark time of crack, daily drive-by shootings, gang warfare, unprecedented urban decay, and the Rodney King riots of 1992. With song titles like "Fuck Da Police" and "Cop Killer," these songs and artists were straight from the streets, courageously and daringly peeling off the veneer of the other world that didn't get paid attention to (except on the nightly news when yet another gang shooting took place) in the 1980s era of Nancy Reagan, Barbara Bush, Leona Helmsley, Robin Leach, Joan Collins, and Elizabeth Taylor on *Entertainment Tonight*.

Love it or hate it, classic rap was a much-needed exposure of the hopelessness and institutional racism oppressing the 'hoods of late '80s and '90s urban America. (Though nothing could justify the war-on-women lyrics of many early hits—with titles like "One Less Bitch" (to worry about), "A Bitch Is a Bitch," and even "She Swallowed It," glamorizing rape and fist-punching violence against bitches and 'hos—that is to say, young women.)

As rap and hip-hop increased its popularity, driven by a mixture of the hard core ghetto 'tude of N.W.A., Tupac Shakur, Public Enemy, Body Count, and the like—plus the considerably more sunshiney stylings of DJ Jazzy Jeff and the Fresh Prince (aka Will Smith, who got his own NBC sitcom in 1991, launching him to later film stardom), as well as a few female rappers like the former Dana Evans (Queen Latifah)—it was inevitable for violent rap music to become its own battleground in the culture wars. Ironically, what really caused cultural conservatives to clutch their pearls was rap's initially unexpected success among well-off and white suburban teenage softies, who wanted to prove how "hip" and "tough" they were by listening along. An outrageous 1991 cover of *The New Republic* showed a preppy high schooler with blond highlights in his styled hair, wearing a brand-new walkman (at what appeared to be a country club) and a yellow polo shirt, with the caption, "The REAL Face of RAP!" Greatest Generation Hollywood legend (and Republican and NRA stalwart) Charlton Heston read the lyrics to "Cop Killer" at a shocked shareholders' meeting of Time Warner, with the movie, TV, and theatre icon demanding that major media labels disassociate themselves from this supposedly immoral—but also quite lucrative—new market.

Tragically (if somewhat predictably) the rap world also had its Kurt Cobain and River Phoenix moment in 1996–97, when arch-rival rappers Tupac Shakur (in September of 1996) and The Notorious B.I.G. (in early 1997) were murdered in gang-related shootings. (Indeed, one of the premier rap labels of the time was called Death Row Records.)

Sex, Lies ... and Sundance

The pioneering first-generation independent filmmaker Samuel Z. Arkoff, who worked with low-budget godfather Roger Corman to make American International Pictures the premier non-studio movie company from its 1954 founding until its sale in 1980, said that his target viewer was the "19 year old male" out on a date. He proved his point, with spooky American versions of Britain's Hammer horror films (starring people like Vincent Price and Peter Lorre in their later careers) and Frankie Avalon and Annette Funicello's beach-bunny and surfer romps. Leave it to the big studios to make "meaningful" message pictures about racism, anti–Semitism, existential alienation, social satire, and urban crime, or romance against the backdrop of exotic foreign locales, or Westerns and war movies with Cinemascope battle scenes.

But by the '80s and early '90s, with the major studios bursting with a never-ending lineup of Top Guns, Red Dawns, Red Octobers, Navy SEALS, Total Recalls, Rambos, Terminators, and Aliens, the roles were well and truly reversed. Now it was the big studio films that were being sold on TV-style high concepts, graphic violence, computer effects, and hard action. And made-for-TV movies of the week and miniseries had largely devolved from adaptations of prestige literary novels and biographies (*Roots, Sybil, Rich Man Poor Man, North & South, Chiefs, Lonesome Dove*) to so-called "disease of the week" pictures, with one-dimensional characters designed to illustrate a shocking social issue, or ripped-from-the-headlines true crime tales.

When it came to year-end Oscar bait, you had high-quality but sentimentalized "weepies" featuring all-star casts: *Cocoon, The Whales of August, Driving Miss Daisy, Fried Green Tomatoes, Steel Magnolias, For the Boys, Forrest Gump.* (Not coincidentally, these movies came during the last lap around the demographic track for small-screen senior faves like *Matlock, Murder, She Wrote, Golden Girls, Diagnosis Murder* and *Touched by an Angel.*) While they were mostly of high quality, like those elder-skewing and simply plotted shows, they were also the kind of stories that most cynical Gen-Xers (especially young straight guys) wouldn't be caught dead going to—unless they were dutifully taking Mom or Grandma out for the night. The other "prestige" pictures of the late '80s and early '90s were a bevy of hoary and overacted legal dramas and thrillers, complete with self-righteous speechifying and hard close-ups. Pretentious updates of *Lou Grant* or *Quincy,* with a John Grisham script and a John Williams or Hans Zimmer score.

It would be hard to imagine a more different cinematic path than the one blazed by a self-consciously "arty" and unconventional filmmaker named Steven Soderbergh, who became the toast of both Cannes and the Sundance Film Festival with his feature debut, in early 1989. It told the tale of a handsome, thirtyish, red-haired male voyeur (James Spader, of course), who got women to open up to him about their most intimate details while he video-recorded them—after which he would furiously masturbate himself to orgasm while watching the playback footage. (The irony being that this ethereal, fey, stereotypically gay-acting young man was impotent with women away from his candid camera, no matter how young or gorgeous they were.)

This steamy and sordid story of *sex, lies, and videotape* (complete with the pretentious uncapitalized title, then also used on the most intellectually upscale of late '80s/early '90s nighttime soaps, *thirtysomething*) received so much buzz and critical attention that even people who never set foot in an "arthouse" movie theatre heard of it. There had been, of course, equally steamy thrillers, like *Fatal Attraction, Body Heat,* and the soon-to-come *Basic Instinct,* but Soderbergh neither wanted nor needed a murder-mystery McGuffin to keep his threadbare plot rolling along, or keep his double and triple love triangles thickening. Especially since the possibility of murder, suicide, or nervous breakdown seemed to silently wait in his film, like a coiled serpent, around every hidden corner. Back when "the Internet" was barely a word, *sex lies and videotape* pre-visioned a world where 1–900 "phone sex" and Internet-era "cyber sex" would become the hottest thing, where people would have emotionally charged, erotic encounters with other people who were really no more than voices on a phone, or photographs and Instant Messages on a computer screen.

Without a doubt, the three biggest and most colorful characters, and the two companies most responsible for midwiving indies from minor-league to mainstream, were Harvey and Bob Weinstein of Miramax, and Robert Shaye of New Line/Fine Line Cinema. Interestingly, both of these companies—which would define edgy, prestigious, awards-bait filmmaking during their '90s heyday—were founded on the bloody carcasses of exploitation films. New Line's first big distribution success was 1974's proto-splatter drive-in classic, *The Texas Chainsaw Massacre* (and several early John Waters and Divine films), and the company truly came into its own a decade later, on the launch of the original *Nightmare on Elm Street* series from 1984 to 1991. And if New Line Cinema was the house that Freddy Krueger built, than the seeds for Miramax Films were first fertilized by the blood of the shrieking college-student victims of the hedgeclipper-wielding, finger-and-hand-chopping, deformed maniac Cropsey, in the "shear" insanity of 1981's *The Burning.*

Miramax and New Line Cinema (and their spinoffs, Dimension Films for Miramax and Fine Line Features for New Line), which partnered with biggies Disney (Miramax) and Warners (New Line), would be Hollywood's golden gatekeepers, between the grungy gravel roads of independent filmmaking, and the Oz of studio success and theatrical and home video distribution. The overwhelming majority of the films and filmmakers covered in this chapter came to the public's view from either one or the other.

And both Miramax and New Line's greatest cinematic grazing ground of the 1990s was the former Utah/U.S. Film Festival, co-founded by Robert Redford and his longtime business associate Sterling Van Wagenen in 1978. It was held near Redford's famous Utah mountain getaway, which he named in tribute to his most famous role—Sundance. *Sex, lies, and videotape* truly put Sundance on the cultural map in early 1989, and with the one-two punch of Richard Linklater's debut film in January 1991's fest, followed by the debut of Quentin Tarantino one year later, the festival began to achieve iconic status, perhaps second only to Cannes as THE most important and chic film festival on the circuit, at least in the 1990s.

Kevin Smith, David O. Russell, Richard Linklater, and Todd Haynes were only scratching the surface of the filmmakers of the '90s and beyond who owed their careers to Sundance shining on them.

Slackers, "Queers," and Boyz N the Hood

The other most important indie film to truly launch the independent film movement of the '90s was the near-antithesis of *sex, lies, and videotape* in style, attitude, and setting—

Spike Lee's *Do the Right Thing.* After breaking out in 1986 with the sexy and sassy '80s urban fable *She's Gotta Have It,* Spike Lee took whatever money and credibility he had, and went full-throttle on making a devastating, up-to-the-minute cultural photograph of the gang/crack era in New York. Coming just after the Robert Duvall/Sean Penn gang-violence groundbreaker *Colors,* and just before that movie's spiritual sequel *Falling Down* (also costarring Duvall), *Do the Right Thing* was the definitive cinematic autopsy of the simmering tensions between lower-middle-class white "ethnics" (symbolized by Danny Aiello's Italian restaurant owner), barely hanging on to their own crumbling slice of the American pie, and the young black men and their girlfriends who weren't able to get a slice at all—unless they brutally grabbed it for themselves.

(Minor historical footnote: It was also the first film that a black Harvard Law student in his late twenties took his fellow young attorney, Michelle Robinson, out to on a date. The post-film coffee and in-depth discussion of the movie that Michelle had with her new boyfriend—some dude named Barack Obama—helped to cement their new courtship.)

Do the Right Thing and Spike Lee in general, plus Robert Townsend's early movies like *Hollywood Shuffle* (a devastatingly nifty satire of racial discrimination and glass ceilings in movies and TV), and Keenen Ivory Wayans'1988 blaxploitation spoof, *I'm Gonna Git You Sucka!* were that much more of a welcome corrective to the prevailing winds in late '80s and early '90s "mainstream" cinema. After making serious (and seriously overdue) gains in the late '60s and '70s, black people had all but disappeared from the silver screen by the middle-to-late 1980s. There was Eddie Murphy making high-concept comedies, plus Oprah, Whoopi Goldberg, and Whitney Houston (and Bill Cosby every Thursday night on TV)— and then there was … *ummm??* Blaxploitation stars of the '70s, like Pam Grier and Richard Roundtree, were now busying themselves with TV guest shots and low-profile supporting roles in film and onstage. Sidney Poitier was all but semi-retired, and Rudy Ray Moore and Richard Pryor's feature film careers were essentially over, certainly compared to their swingin' and pimpin' '70s heyday. (And while the day would happily soon come for the likes of Jennifer Lopez, Salma Hayek, and Antonio Banderas, at the end of the '80s and the start of the '90s, for every Ricardo Montalban, Edward James Olmos, Rita Moreno, or Jimmy Smits who'd crashed the salsa ceiling, there were countless talented Latino actors and actresses trapped in roles as denigrating gangstas and 'hos, and barrio moms shrieking "No speaka de Ingles!")

Bottom line: there was virtually no way that an unapologetically urban, confrontational African American or Latino filmmaker from the wrong side of the tracks—like Spike Lee, Robert Townsend, or Robert Rodriguez—could have gotten the backing of a major studio or network, without first going the indie route. Not until they *already* proved themselves as critical and commercial commodities, by hitting their initial indies out of the park. And it wasn't exactly easy street for an eager-beaver white boy (let alone girl) to break into the ever-more bureaucratic and consolidated new media world, either. If they didn't have a degree from a prestigious "good" school, the odds got even longer. But thankfully, that didn't stop some of the most talented filmmakers to emerge in the '90s from going all the way. To wit:

Richard Linklater was a 26-year-old film geek and artist/musician in Texas who filmed his debut sociological comedy on hand-held cameras with no-name actors (although future comedy legend Louis Black makes an appearance) during the summer of 1989, for a total budget of less than $25,000. The name of his movie would soon become synonymous with the generation born between 1965 and 1980—it was called *Slacker*. The plot of *Slacker* was that it didn't have much of a plot; just a random collage of colorful teens and 20-somethings staring out the twilight windows in buses and taxis, talking to other people who are so busy doing their own thing they might as well be talking to themselves, preaching conspiracy theories about JFK, UFO's, and the nuclear apocalypse, drinking and doing drugs, trying and failing to commit robberies, and trying to peddle an authentic pap smear of Madonna's (who, of course, never appears in the picture). One almost doesn't need to see the movie to imagine it, with its credit-crawl cast of characters billed only by names like "Bush Basher," "Sadistic Comb-Game Player," "T-Shirt Terrorist," "Hand-Stamping Arm Licker," "Old Anarchist," "Cadillac Crook," "Scooby Doo Philosopher," and even "Papa Smurf!"

When *Slacker* was released on the festival circuit in July of 1990, culminating at the following January's 1991 Sundance Festival, it did more than make an underground impact; it served as a stylistic template for almost all the quirky, low-budget, first-time filmmaking efforts ever since—from *Clerks, Kids, Spanking the Monkey, Reality Bites,* and *Kicking and Screaming* in the '90s through *Funny Ha Ha, The Puffy Chair, Hannah Takes the Stairs* and more in the 2000s. Linklater himself moved on immediately for the equally iconic Gen-X snapshot, *Dazed and Confused* (with a breakout role for a young actor named Matthew McConaughey), and then launched his *Before* trilogy starting with *Before Sunrise* in 1995 (not to mention the sort of spiritual capper, 2014's much-nominated, and in Patricia Arquette's case, Oscar-winning, coming-of-age drama *Boyhood*). With that future pedigree, *Slacker* was easily the godfather of "mumblecore" moviemaking.

Another important and influential early '90s breakthrough came by way of directors like Todd Haynes and Gus Van Sant. Van Sant epitomized the so-called "New Queer Cinema" movement of the AIDS era in 1991, with his poignant, lyrically dreamlike, gay-grunge drama starring River Phoenix and Keanu Reeves, *My Own Private Idaho*. The love story between two gay runaway-hustlers (Phoenix's dreamy and ethereal character was appropriately afflicted with narcolepsy), rejected by their fathers (Keanu's family is rich and influential, and he'll cash in when his dying father finally goes), it was a heartbreaking yet uplifting mood piece on the nature of love in general, and young gay love in the "alienated" early 1990s specifically. (And just six months before his spiritual brother Kurt Cobain met his premature death, River Phoenix—already being touted, and not without good reason, as perhaps the most talented and promising English-speaking actor in the under-30 category, based on his roles in *Idaho, Running on Empty, Stand by Me,* and more—tragically OD'd on Halloween night in 1993, outside his pal Johnny Depp's nightclub in West Hollywood, The Viper Room.)

After making a genuinely touching but controversial student film in 1987 about the life (and tragic death) of the lovable, intelligent, and talented singer Karen Carpenter (with voiced-over Barbie dolls playing Karen and her family and associates), proudly gay director Todd Haynes helmed a trilogy of Queer-themed stories in 1991's *Poison*, winning multiple awards on the growing and rising film festival circuit. The thirtyish Haynes then established his first of several fruitful collaborations with rising young actress Julianne Moore in *Safe*, a stylish metaphor for claustrophobia, suburban shallowness (and perhaps the closet and/or female oppression), with Julianne's passive, disassociated housewife character wasting away from "multiple chemical sensitivity," with mainstream medicine unable to cure her. (In some ways, *Safe* was like an artier dramatic version of Lily Tomlin's 1981 satire on household products and consumerism, *The Incredible Shrinking Woman*.)

Like *Slacker*, these films weren't really "about" anything, as much as they were about an existentialist escape, the pseudo-suicidal impulse of drugs, suicide, or just giving up, of someone desperate to go somewhere, to be anywhere but here. In American cinema, their most obvious antecedents were dreamy, hallucinatory 20-year-old pictures cleaning up the mess that the late '60s and early '70s had made—*Midnight Cowboy, Five Easy Pieces, Play It as It Lays, Nashville.* Yet for a generation that was a day late and more than a few dollars short of all the fun of the go-go '80s, and for which the Microsoft/AOL/Yahoo/Google late '90s boom hadn't happened yet, these films spoke on an almost primal level to what it meant to be a teenager or young adult at that time and place, especially if you were a "sensitive" or "alienated" young man, whether gay or straight.

And for more macho straight dudes who may have also been sensitive and alienated, but also had a lot of Kurt Cobain or Eminem-style pent-up anger and testosterone rage that needed venting, the ultimate indie writer-director geek was about to save the day.

The Video Store Film School

Picture it: you're a testosterone-crazed, white hipster high school student or college kid, anytime between, say, 1987 and 1996. You're sniffing around the local Wherehouse, Blockbuster, or indie Econo Video shack. You see all the old Important Oscar Pictures of days gone by—*To Kill a Mockingbird, The Best Years of Our Lives, Boys' Town, Mildred Pierce, All About Eve, Gentleman's Agreement, Doctor Zhivago, Kramer vs. Kramer, Coming Home, Ordinary People....* Are you really gonna bring *those* back to the frat house for the pizza, beer, and pot party with the guys this Friday or Saturday night?

But then you detour over into the "Urban Action" section—and you get an eyeful of the likes of *Cleopatra Jones, Foxy Brown, Dolemite, The Human Tornado, Superfly, Coffy,* and *Scream Blacula Scream!* Then you look across the aisle and see those movies' white-faced spiritual sequels: *Prom Night, Friday the 13th, Halloween, The Toolbox Murders, Phantasm, The Exorcist, Terror Train, Maniac, Don't Go in the House, Don't Answer the Phone, The Texas Chainsaw Massacre, Jaws, The Seduction,* and *Sleepaway Camp.* And over there are the kung-fu karate-choppers of Bruce Lee, Sonny Chiba, and Angela Wong, plus "white-sploitation" classics like *Big Bad Mama, Jackson County Jail, Angel, Avenging Angel, The Big Bird Cage, Reform School Girls,* and just about anything starring Chuck Norris or Burt Reynolds.

Now you're talkin,' dude! They've got the action, they've got the chills and thrills, they've got the hot Charlie's Angel-type chicks taking their clothes off and playing with themselves or running around naked and jiggling and screaming. Who needs those "serious," turgid soap operas from the so-called "Golden Age" of Hollywood, those B&W and "Technicolor" oldies that nobody but old great-aunt Mitzi back at Shady Pines cares about? *These* movies are so much *cooler,* so much friggin' FUN! *Ya know what I mean, bro?*

Now combine that with the local, non-network-affiliated and UHF TV stations that ran "The 8 O'Clock Movie" (in those pre–WB/CW days), plus the growing late '80s and early '90s cable market. Most of those local and cable stations ran the same kind of slasher-blaxploitation-karate fare, plus former TV-movies of the week (*Calendar Girl Murders, Sins of the Past, Personals, Golden Gate Murders, Winter Kill, Revenge of the Stepford Wives, Someone's Watching Me!, The 11th Victim, The Babysitter, Buried Alive,* etc.) that clearly came from the same sensationalized wheelhouse. On the local or cable station's nightly movie, and at the video store, all movies were essentially equal. You didn't have some know-it-all New York intellectual like John Leonard, Pauline Kael, Richard Schickel, Stanley Kauffmann, or Vincent Canby (or even Siskel and Ebert, for that matter) telling you which new films were Important. You didn't have big studios looking for Oscars pushing prestige-fare broccoli in your face. Browsing at the video store, or remote-flicking to the TBS Super-station or local station's movie—*you* were the boss. You decided it all for yourself! Video stores and midnight movies were the ultimate "democratization" of the art of film.

The grammar of the 1990s cinematic revolution would be shaped by passionate "film geeks" largely by their discovery and rediscovery of what they thought was cool, what got their limbic regions workin' and blood pressure pumpin', the kinds of films that they viscerally responded to during their cinematic Wonder Years. The fact that these B-pictures and TV-movies were all made on the cheap, without the resources that an A-list director or producer took for granted, only made them even *more* attractive and invaluable as points of reference for their upcoming, do-it-yourself, indie cinematic crews. The Gen-X movie brats who came of age in the "whatever" decade, with their post-postmodern styles and meta-media aesthetics, would whip up a master celluloid concoction for the 1990s. Their recipe was one part the auteurist arthouse "seriousness" and gritty paranoia of John Cassavetes and Francis Ford Coppola's 1970s classics, combined with an equal part of the cheesy crowd-pleasing and in-joking instincts of the George Lucas/Spielberg blockbusters. They frosted the cake with film student plagiarisms and jazz musician riff-quotes of scenes from iconic movies and TV shows of the past. All combined with the knowing, winking self-awareness that they (and their media-hip audience) knew exactly what they were doing when they were doing it.

And no greater example of this aesthetic existed than the former video shack clerk who made his first major film debut in 1992. Quentin Tarantino famously said that he didn't go to film school—he watched films instead. Yet his movies became such instant sensations and so immediately iconic to film and communication students around the globe precisely *because* of their hyper-stylization. Tarantino spent the late 1980s working at the locally famous Manhattan Beach movie rental outlet Video Archives, while trying to pursue a career as an actor. Not the conventionally handsomest man in Hollywood (by his own admission), the hyper-energetic video clerk got the break of his life when longtime Martin Scorsese pallie Harvey Keitel got a look at Tarantino's script for an ultraviolent "heist" movie with double- and triple-crosses, machine-gun fast pop culture riffs and nods to kung fu, early Scorsese-style Mafia and street-gang movies, old-school slasher cinema, and *Cannon/Kojak*-style TV detective shows. Keitel attached himself to the project, enabling Tarantino to break the "no name stars" blacklist and get $1.2 million in financing. It was called *Reservoir Dogs*.

Filmed in 1991, the movie was released—where else—at the Sundance Film Festival of January 1992. It was almost immediately picked up by Miramax, and the rest as they say is history. *Empire* magazine claimed *Reservoir Dogs* as the single most important independent film of all time—the career-maker for Tarantino and the next biggest hit (besides *sex lies and videotape*) to come out of Sundance, underlining its status as THE place for hot new cinema hits. Featuring a cast of characters known by their gang code names (Mr. Pink, Mr. Blonde, Mr. White, and so on) and jarring scenes of torture (the most iconic bit has a young man getting his ear sheared off to the '70s jam-rock classic "Stuck in the Middle With You") and exploding pellet slo-mo shootings, the movie was the most stylishly bloody and violent non-horror and non-karate movie since *The Wild Bunch* or *Apocalypse Now*. Whether they loved it or they hated it or didn't know what to make of it, film and TV critics (and serious cinephiles from the most adrenaline/testosterone fanboy to the most intellectual film-theory deconstructionist) couldn't stop talking about it.

Now there was no stopping him. Tarantino immediately put his sadomasochistic screenplay *True Romance* (starring early '90s cinema brats Christian Slater and Patricia Arquette) into production, and began work on a gangster classic about two hit men (one Italian and one African American) and a sexy, campy, seen-it-all femme fatale who was as tough as any man. Starring John Travolta, Samuel L. Jackson, Bruce Willis, Uma Thurman, and a passel of celebrity cameos, *Pulp Fiction* is almost universally regarded by film and TV critics and historians as the definitive, single most important movie of the '90s decade, both stylistically and artistically.

What critic Thomas Harvey later called the "childlike sadism" of Tarantino, combined with the movie's gleeful mixing of genres, comic-book-style set pieces, and ultra-profanity (with ultimate no-no's like "fuck" and "nigger" being used in the script arguably more than anything besides "and," "the," and "hello"), *Pulp Fiction* rewrote the rules for the next two decades of film. When Spike Lee used the F-and-N words (and bitch and cunt), it was to make a political point; when *Platoon* or *The Deer Hunter* or *Roots* or *Schindler's List* used obscene violence, it wasn't just torture-porn. But Tarantino also wanted to make his own statement: that the old rules no longer applied, that the torch had been passed, and a new era was here. Indeed, he wanted to go beyond that—to say that there *were no rules* (even as he subverted them), that *anything* could happen. Few filmmakers of the post-modern age had the sense of sheer, rollercoaster-ride *fun* in their movies than Quentin Tarantino had. Like a naughty child (or really, more like some kind of Benny Hill or Pee Wee Herman *playing* a naughty child in an adults-only comedy skit), Quentin Tarantino welcomed everyone into his carnival funhouse.

Another example of a proud graduate of The Video Store Film School was a struggling young gay screenwriter, trying to find his calling card to break into the business, just as Tarantino and Spike Lee were hitting the big time with their macho, testosterone-fueled action epics and social satires. His name was Kevin Williamson, and while he initially wanted to work on "serious" and expressively personal films of the Soderbergh/Van Sant school, while pounding the Tinseltown pavement, he realized that perhaps the most personal expression of his art could come from writing the kind of movie that he responded to the most when he was a budding young cinephile. Williamson had loved coming of age with the cheesy slasher movies of the late '70s and '80s—with their campy, *Charlie's Angels* plotlines of jiggling young eye candy, virtually motiveless serial killers, and empowered "Final Girls" who'd tap into their reservoir of alpha-female strength, and give the baddie a taste of his own medicine at the end.

But the golden days of slasher cinema seemed to have just come to an end—*Friday the 13th* and *Halloween* had brought their nearly annual sequels to a (temporary) halt after 1989, and Freddy Krueger and Hannibal Lector made (what looked like) their final appearances in 1991. Then, Williamson had a masterstroke. What if he added in the meta-media, self-aware hipness and snarky style of Tarantino and Oliver Stone, and played the horror for laughs as well as chills? What if he wrote a movie where the characters were more realistic, post-feminist, and three-dimensional than the usual virgins, cheerleaders, jocks, nerds, and sluts to be found in "classic" horror films, and then used them to satirize the "rules" of predictable, by-the-numbers, slasher movie clichés?

Williamson's December 1996 debut (which created a "trilogy" and a decade-delayed sequel in 2011) was a real *Scream,* and not only snagged a deal with Harvey and Bob Weinstein via Miramax's boutique label Dimension Films (for which *Scream* and similar type horror and gross-out comedy movies would be the standard bearer), but it had the honor of being directed by horror maven Wes Craven himself! And following the lead of Joss Whedon with *Buffy the Vampire Slayer*—the closest small-screen corollary to *Scream's* hip, girl-power sensibility (Buffy star Sarah Michelle Gellar even cameo'd in *Scream 2,* and starred in Williamson's other big slasher franchise, *I Know What You Did Last Summer*)— Williamson knocked it out of the park when The WB came calling soon afterward, with the chance to run his own TV show. It was called *Dawson's Creek.*

Scream relaunched the young-adult horror genre, as *The Blair Witch Project, Final Destination* (and its sequels), *Halloween: H20, Freddy vs. Jason,* and so on rose from their graves, not to mention the Wayans Brothers' *Scary Movie* (*Scream's* original title) spoofs of the spoof, which made almost as much money for parent Miramax/Dimension as the mothership had. (And a director of the *I Know What You Did Last Summer* series, Danny Cannon, left to produce a stylish and horror-influenced series for CBS and Jerry Bruckheimer, called *CSI.*)

For both *Pulp Ficton* and *Scream,* their true cultural calling cards were their self-referencing hipness. Look at *Buffy, Clerks, That '70s Show, The Simpsons, South Park, Dawson's Creek, Party of Five, Action, Will & Grace,* Comedy Central, SNL, even *The West Wing*—with their quick witted comebacks, nonstop pop-culture references, show-stealing supporting characters, and cheeky, flip media-centeredness. Few things conveyed the essence of mid-to-late 1990s movies, TV, and music than that sort of knowing-you're-in-on-the-joke, self-aware, snarkily teasing humor about yourself, your friends, and the "tropes" and clichés of popular entertainment.

Pictures at a Revolution

The 1994 Sundance Festival, held from January 20 to 30 of that year, was perhaps the ultimate apex of the "indie film" movement (and moment) of the '90s. It not only boasted a lineup that stood on a par with some of the best and most challenging of New Hollywood's late '60s and '70s renaissance; it directly launched the careers of two of the most distinctively voiced and important directors in current film, right through today.

Shot in April and May of 1993 on a shoestring budget of less than $30,000, *Clerks* was the unlikely but genius cinematic calling card of a 23-year-old New Jersey aspiring filmmaker named Kevin Smith. (He was working a recessionary day job as a—you guessed it— convenience store cashier, while he wrote and filmed the screenplay.) *Clerks'* grungily artful non-aesthetic was a respectful near-plagiarism of Richard Linklater's *Slacker* (complete with equally colorful characters billed in the credits as "Cat-Admiring Customer," "Woolen-Cap Smoker," and "Burner Looking for Weed.") Smith openly gave a shout-out to Linklater and fellow indie groundbreakers Hal Hartley, Spike Lee, and Jim Jarmusch "for showing the way" in *Clerks'* end credits. But Smith's genius alteration was to keep the story (and its never-ending parade of bizarro-world customers) anchored by the two lovably short-tempered and potty-mouthed young counter jockeys who supervised the convenience store and its next-door video shack: the friendly but frustrated cashier Dante Hicks, and his best friend and next-store neighbor, the cynical and snarky video geek Randal Graves.

With its white-working-class but hyper-articulate 20-year-olds talking about money, movies, TV, music, sex disguised as love, and love disguised as sex, Dante and Randal could well have been Roseanne Connor, Peg Bundy, or *Grace Under Fire's* oldest and highest-IQ kids. Dante's inferno happened on a not-so typical workday when, in the span of one 16-hour shift (Dante even smells his armpits towards the very end), one girlfriend breaks up with him, another one has a nervous breakdown after going into the men's room to make love to Dante (and instead finds a naked 70-year-old man who'd died of a heart attack *in flagrante* while looking at a porno magazine), and Dante and Randal have a knock-down drag-out before eventually patching things up. The kicker is, this was supposed to be Dante's day off, a fact which he bemoans repeatedly with the battle cry, "I'm not even supposed to BE here today!"

Another masterpiece of Gen-X male alienation and mood came from a somewhat "older" first-time director (this senior citizen was all of 35 years old) named David O. Russell, whose debut film sported the transgressive title, *Spanking the Monkey.* (It refers to male self-release; you can figure it out.) Originally titled *Swelter,* it told the story of a handsome but introverted and depressive, well-meaning 19-year-old premed student named Ray Aibelli, who comes back to his wooded suburban Berkshires home for the summer, after his first year on scholarship to MIT. Only this was no ordinary summer vacation; Ray was forced to surrender a prestigious internship in Washington to care for his depressed, passive-aggressive, and still-sexy fortyish mother Susan (played to the hilt by the marvelous Canadian stage and screen star Alberta Watson). Susan was bedridden after a fall down a flight of stairs, which happened after she'd taken too many tranquilizers (possibly attempting suicide), and his unwanted role as caregiver leaves Ray with no outlet for his normal young-male urges in the small town he was only too happy to leave behind. Except that is, for a flirty and teasing high school girl, who's been crushing on the dreamy "older" Ray forever—though she's not quite ready to cash in her V-card to him just yet—and also, his ever more dependent, intimacy-starved, sensuous, and manipulative mother, who becomes a "MILF" in the most literal sense of the phrase, in the movie's most shocking scene.

In many ways, *Spanking the Monkey* was the perfect coming-of-age capper for later Generation Xers, and their left-to-their-own-devices, day-care upbringings by selfish careerist and divorcing dads, and "finding ourselves" moms who'd given up the career track for the mommy track and lived to regret it. In any case, few American films ever took on the subject matter of mother-son incest or teen-suicide feelings to begin with, let alone in anything that could even charitably be described as tasteful or humane. But that was to be expected from David O. Russell, given his later filmography ranging from *Flirting with Disaster* and *I Heart Huckabees,* to *The Fighter, Silver Linings Playbook,* and *American Hustle* in the years ahead.

More to the point, both Ray Aibelli and Dante Hicks were clearly raised to be suburban "good boys" in spite of all their superficial grunge-slacker affects. They wanted to be responsible employees, good sons, concerned citizens—yet instead of being rewarded, they got punished Coen Brothers-style, by the ironic hand of Fate. Both films were veritable Gen X-rays of high school and college students and recent grads, who were finding out the hard way that they had been promised a helluva lot more than life was prepared to deliver. (Perhaps the ultimate example of nice-young-white-dudes-pushed-to-the-breaking-point came a few years later in 1999, in the uncaring hands of the dependably cold, clinical, and cynical David Fincher, with his take-no-prisoners adaptation of Chuck Pahlaniuk's signature novel, *Fight Club*. This story of a mild-mannered junior exec [Edward Norton, fresh off his triumph as a repentant, working-class neo–Nazi in *American History X*] who is encouraged to work off his repressed anger and primal male violence, and to rebel against stifling corporate-speak conformity by his alpha-bad-boy friend, Tyler Durden [Brad Pitt], said more than a Ph.D. dissertation about post gay-visible and post-feminist, straight male "code" and masculinity. It was like a Clint Eastwood or Charles Bronson movie for their liberal-ish, college-educated grandsons.)

Fortunately, Sundance's focus on the likes of Dante Hicks and Ray Aibelli didn't mean that there also wasn't equal time for three-dimensional, intricate female characters. Following the feminist lead of 1991's box-office topper *Thelma & Louise* and small-screen heroine Murphy Brown, there was the lesbian-themed *Go Fish*, adding a much-needed feminist slant to the New Queer Cinema archives of the early '90s. Sexy stage ingenue Karen Sillas held her own opposite Broadway star and movie villain Tom Noonan (best known as the savage rapist and family annihilator "The Tooth Fairy" in the amazing 1986 William Petersen thriller, and retrospective *CSI* test-run, *Manhunter*), as he reinvented himself as a nervous romantic lead, in the stylish and witty minimalist date-drama *What Happened Was...* (And Kelly Reichardt offered the closest thing going to a working-class, low-budget cross between *Thelma & Louise* and *Play It as It Lays* with her ironic post-feminist "road movie" and salute to going nowhere, *River of Grass.*)

And while all of the above existed in a world almost as white as the snowcapped small-towns of Utah, racial and cultural diversity was on the menu thanks to perhaps the most skillful film of them all shown at Sundance '94—the searing and only too-real, inner city basketball documentary, *Hoop Dreams*. These movies were on the cutting edge of the culture. Just as rap music and grunge rock was speaking to a rising –and ever more diverse—generation of young people that the previous mainstream culture had been ignoring (and wouldn't have known how to speak to anyway), these do-it-yourself indies were channeling the zeitgeist, in a way that none of the mindless robo-flicks and prestige legal eagles of the big studios even knew how to. Not until this new generation of New Hollywood film brats showed them the way.

Slowly, the studios were starting to learn the lesson. With the Weinstein Brothers and Bob Shaye and Tarantino being given media coverage by film and TV critics worthy of Madonna, Princess Di, Meryl Streep, or any of Hollywood's true superstars, the big studios were starting to get hip to the necessity of tapping this new generation of new talent. As Peter Biskind noted, the 1994 and perhaps 1995 Sundance festivals were both the ultimate apex of the "indie film movement" and their last major hurrah. (At least for another decade, until the low-fi, "mumblecore" moviemakers, who again broke out on the indie circuit and then crossed over into studio films and TV shows—the Duplass Brothers, Andrew Bujalski, Miranda July, Brie Larson—following the format of their '90s forbearers.) The 1994 to 1996 period was also the first time that the major studios truly took notice of the indie aesthetics (and the formerly indie auteurs)—when the Spike Lees, Tarantinos, and Steven Soderberghs went from being the exception to almost becoming the rule.

The major studio films of the summer and fall of 1994 opened the picture. Along with the blockbuster release of *Pulp Fiction,* there was it's even its sleazier and seamier step-sibling, Oliver Stone's take-no-prisoners satire of true crime and tabloid TV, *Natural Born Killers.* Gay-friendly stoner dude Keanu Reeves reinvented himself as a buffed-up action hero in the macho, stylish, and ultra-suspenseful *Speed,* which transcended what could've been a routine action flick with its portrait of slowly rebuilding, post–*Colors* and *Falling Down,* "under construction" urban Los Angeles, and a breakout role for Sandra Bullock as his female lead. And while the year's biggest commercial hit, Tom Hanks' other 1990s Oscar-winner *Forrest Gump,* was as sentimental as *Pulp Fiction* and the Sundance indies were edgy, in some ways it deserved to be the definitive film of the Clinton era: a Southern-fried sequel to *The Big Chill,* as fortysomething ex-hippies and yuppies, now dealing with their first grey hairs and kids going off to college, looked back on the roads they'd traveled. (While Bill Clinton had a considerably higher IQ than the mentally challenged Mr. Gump, even Forrest himself could have probably seen the parallels—a good-natured 1945-model boy from the rural South, raised by an indomitable single mother, who somehow found himself careening from the center of Vietnam, civil rights, and Watergate to feminism and the AIDS era, with classic rock booming on the soundtrack.) Rounding things out was *Quiz Show,* Sundance founder Robert Redford's very own searing indictment of social class, anti–Semitism, self-hatred, and advertising corruption—as timely in 1994's rising era of tabloid TV, early "reality," and 24-hour cable as it was in its late 1950s setting.

Generation Next

Splitting the difference between the amped-up (and often camped-up) heightened realities of Quentin Tarantino, Oliver Stone, and Spike Lee, and the self-conscious artistic deconstructions of *sex lies and videotape* and *My Own Private Idaho,* were the ultra-aestheticized cinematic "constructs" of Wes Anderson, who made his premiere in 1995 (along with a couple of handsome, unknown actors in their mid-twenties named Owen and Luke Wilson), in a movie called *Bottle Rocket.* Anderson's surrealist and self-consciously intellectual film vocabulary was reflected by his frequent collaborator Noah Baumbach. The son of academics (literary and film critic Georgia Brown and novelist and professor Jonathan Baumbach), Noah also debuted in 1995 at age 25 with the bohemian Gen X *crie d' couer, Kicking and Screaming.* (Think a very special episode of *Friends,* as co-directed by Woody Allen and David Lynch.)

With Quentin Tarantino having resurrected the plasmatic ethos of "Bloody Sam" Peck-inpah, putting low-budget slasher and blaxploitation riffs and chop-socky Chinese/Japanese martial arts ultra-violence in big-budget, name-starring blockbusters (along with more "niggers" and "fucks" than any filmmaker in history), and with *sex lies and videotape, Fatal Attraction, The Silence of the Lambs,* and *Basic Instinct* having already pushed the limits of sex and violence in A-pictures, the new auteurs of the mid '90s needed to go to the edge of the envelope to stay on the cutting edge. Future Best Picture winner (*Slumdog Millionaire*) Danny Boyle broke out in 1995–96 with his grungy study of young drug addicts and slackers trying to keep themselves from being Generation X-ed out, in the hilariously graphic *Trainspotting*, with Ewan McGregor and Jonny Lee Miller in their breakout roles.

Todd Solondz reflected John Waters (without the camp) and anticipated (white versions of) *Precious* and *For Colored Girls* with his darkly comedic 1995 entry *Welcome to the Dollhouse*, and 1998's ironically titled *Happiness*. *Dollhouse* picked up where 1989's seminal *Heathers* left off in examining a nerdy junior-high age girl who gets abused and neglected at home and bullied at school (Sofia Coppola would also plough the same field five years later with her ethereal, dreamlike adaptation of *The Virgin Suicides*). *Happiness* starred Philip Seymour Hoffman leading an ensemble cast exploring suicide, rape, murder, obscene phone calls, and even the ultimate no-no—an almost sympathetic pedophile.

But for borderline pedophilia on parade, nobody could top Generation X's postmodern Pasolini, the punk screenwriter Harmony Korine, whose first film (at age 21) in 1995, bluntly titled *Kids*, told the story of a young "virgin surgeon" (who unfortunately shared his first name with the author of this book, and was around the same age as the author at the time) who casually infected his never-ending supply of bitch-and-'ho girlfriends with HIV. The only positive about this inhumane, flatly uncinematic (it made 1970s episodic TV or slasher films look like Kurosawa) farrago in Gen-X "whatever" nihilism was the screen debut of the lovely Chloe Sevigny, playing one of the young man's victims, and the only to have any real humanity in her character. Korine would go on to push the limits of celebrating-while-mocking white trash culture with his next film, *Gummo*, rightly considered by many critics to be one of the most hateful, morally repellent and artistically bankrupt films of all time, with its nearly subhuman-seeming adolescent freaks murdering cats and stalking tween females in pseudo-sexualized "arty" film imagery (thank God, the animal deaths were faked), turning off a helpless old woman's respirator, and having implied underage sex experiences that would be illegal in most states, including one character offering his developmentally delayed sister for prostitution. (Korine cast *Gummo's* lead while watching a *Sally Jessy Raphael* show about teenage drug abuse. He then moved on to such 2000s epics as *Trash Humpers* and reached perhaps his artistic peak, if you can call it that, with 2013's music videoesque James Franco-phile, *Spring Breakers*.)

On an infinitely higher artistic plane, the Coen Brothers knocked it out of the park with their modestly budgeted, wintry study of greed in a just-folks Midwestern city, the Best Picture-winning *Fargo*. Starring Frances McDormand, William H. Macy, and Steve Buscemi (none of whom were "name" stars before the film), *Fargo* was one of the last cinema blockbusters to go all the way without needing an A-list superstar to "open" the picture. (The Coens then moved on to perhaps the ultimate '90s celebration of slacker irony where "The Dude" abides, with *The Big Lebowski*, in 1998.) Another indie that turned their then-minor stars (Hilary Swank, Peter Sarsgaard, and Chloe Sevigny again) onto the Hollywood fast track was the fact-based and haunting *Boys Don't Cry*, starring an Oscar-winning Swank as the murdered transgender auto mechanic Brandon Teena.

But the biggest example of a no-budget indie to hit the box-office jackpot happened in the summer of 1999. The only film to equal that summer's spookiest big-budget classic, M. Night Shymalayan's breakout *The Sixth Sense* (wherein a little boy comes to grips with his ability to "see dead people!") in buzz and impact (or to even come close with regards to horror artistry) was the hand-held camera shot, deliberately lo-fi, zippo-budget chiller, *The Blair Witch Project*. Pioneering what would become known as "found footage" indie cinema, *The Blair Witch Project* was a devilishly ingenious witches' brew of shot-on-videotape, poorly lit and edited "footage" of a team of young thrill-seeking documentarians who'd gone into the woods to discover and/or debunk the legend of the deadly Blair Witch. *The Blair Witch Project* was also notable for being one of the first indie movies (or really any kind) to truly owe its publicity and media buzz to going "viral" on the Internet—and at least at first, the "allegations" that the footage may have been true. Six years before YouTube, mad fans were posting videos both respectfully copying and/or mocking the shaking, badly angled, nose-running, teeth-chattering moments from *Blair Witch*. (There was even a camp parody of the film using outtakes from that definitive '80s *Facts of Life* material girl, called "The Blair Warner Project.") Rather than sue for infringement, the net-savvy indie filmmakers basically encouraged this—as the online buzz and message-board discussions only drove the PR and box office up, up, and away. (The film also put actor Joshua Leonard on the fringe Hollywood map, and he would later partner up with other mumblecore masters like Mark Duplass and Lynn Shelton, and Hollywood actresses Vera Farmiga and Mindy Kaling, on future indies and TV gigs in the years ahead.)

And for some desperately needed diversity, Forest Whitaker's directorial debut, *Waiting to Exhale,* starring Whitney Houston, Loretta Devine, Angela Bassett, Gregory Hines, and Dennis Haysbert, became a sensation as one of the first major women's pictures to revolve around contemporary, professional and articulate women of color, and the first black women's picture to truly break the blockbuster glass ceiling since the slavery-days *The Color Purple* itself. On the other end of the sophistication spectrum was Mike Myers' gloriously campy, sexist-to-the-point-of-parody (which of course, it was) spoof of swinging '60s and '70s spy movies—with a master twist. Instead of being a sleek, chic, Hardy Amies-suited dry martini on ice like Sean Connery or Roger Moore, *Austin Powers: International Man of Mystery* was a crude, coarse, Beatles-wigged British superspy who dressed like he just got out of the costume department at *Laugh-In* or *Let's Make a Deal*. Powers raced around Britain and Europe with one "shag-a-delic" babe after another, all of whom the buck-toothed stud would (well … it rhymes with "buck"…) in between shootouts and explosions arranged by his bald, albino arch-nemesis, Dr. Evil (also played by Myers, of course). It was the SNL-comedy version of Tarantino and Kevin Williamson's humorously hip homages to '60s and '70s action movies and pop-culture. And as such, it was a "smashing" fit with the 1990s' meta-media, self-referencing style.

Perhaps the most talented filmmaker of all to emerge in the 1990s, and the only true artistic equal of the Coens, Spike Lee, and Tarantino to debut that decade, was the young son of the veteran Hollywood variety and game show announcer (and former Cleveland TV personality) Ernie Anderson. Ernie's young son, Paul Thomas, broke into Hollywood working as a PA on game and talk shows and for Nickelodeon-type kids' TV, until making his first indie about an aging professional gambler called *Hard Eight*, starring the veteran character actor Philip Baker Hall. *Hard Eight* put P. T. Anderson on the map as a 25-year-old to watch, but it was his next two features, the star-making and all-starring *Boogie Nights* and *Magnolia* (made with Robert Shaye's New Line Cinema) which would define the end of 1990s American film culture as indelibly as the early Sundance, Tarantino, and Spike Lee joints defined the "It's the Economy Stupid" beginning of the decade.

Boogie Nights deservedly catapulted the daytime soap veteran, New York theatre actress, and film ingénue Julianne Moore from edgy indies like *Vanya on 42nd Street* and

Safe, and scene-stealers in commercial films like *The Hand That Rocks the Cradle* and *Nine Months,* into the Meryl Streep, Helen Mirren, Glenn Close, and Jane Fonda pantheon. It veritably created the big-screen careers of Philip Seymour Hoffman, John C. Reilly, Heather Graham, and a talented young African American TV veteran (*Picket Fences, Golden Palace*) named Don Cheadle. And it brought the ultimate '70s movie star, Burt Reynolds, back into the Oscar-contender spotlight after years on TV sitcoms. A gloriously indulgent spectacle about the LA Valley porno industry of the late '70s and early '80s, *Boogie Nights* had all the references and stylings of the '70s New Hollywood films that were contemporary to its setting. And on that note, it (and *Austin Powers* and its sequels) helped to kick off a veritable retro rollerama of '70s nostalgia in pop culture. People lined up to watch *Boogie Nights, Austin Powers* (and its sequels), *(Studio) 54, Velvet Goldmine, The Ice Storm, Girl Interrupted,* and *Almost Famous* at the theatres, before racing home to catch that week's installment of *That '70s Show*—all while partying down with that weekend's "Disco" Friday or Saturday nights on the top big-city radio stations. The better to accompany VH1's *Behind the Music* and E's *True Hollywood Story,* plus reruns of *Flip Wilson, Laugh-In,* and *Sonny & Cher* on TVLand, and *Match Game, Joker's Wild, Newlywed Game,* and *The Gong Show* on Game Show Network.

Anderson's next and even more ambitious feature, ranked by many critics as behind only *Pulp Fiction* and perhaps *Schindler's List* as the greatest studio film of the 1990s decade, was his spiritual sequel to his main mentor Robert Altman's 1993 study of vacuous LA status/media and singles-bar culture, *Short Cuts.* Titled *Magnolia,* it was succinctly summarized by *The New York Times'* TV listings as the story of "pop culture victims." It was the pinwheeling tale of a dying game and talk show producer (Jason Robards), his much younger, hyper-medicated and guilt-ridden ex-model trophy wife (Julianne Moore), for whom he'd left his first wife when she was on her deathbed twenty years earlier (and when Julianne was barely into her twenties), his now-grown son (Tom Cruise) who channeled his abandonment by his dying mother and rejecting father into a career as a hateful, misogynistic "motivational speaker" (who meets his nemesis in the form of a black woman, played to perfection by April Grace, interviewing him for an *A&E Biography*-type show). And Robards' biggest hit, an exploitative game show that pits child prodigies against adults, hosted by Jimmy Gator (Philip Baker Hall), who has some dark paternal secrets of his own hiding in his Holmby Hills mansion—and who epitomized the Johnny Carson/Bob Barker type TV icon, worshiped by fans as a gruffly lovable 70-year-old grandpa on camera, but who wasn't always as nicey-nice behind the scenes. (Perhaps even shades of Bush Senior?)

Magnolia was the perfect film to kiss off the 1990s and kick off the 2000s, with its psychological autopsy of a world where the lines between reality-show pop entertainment and our real lives was fast becoming as blurred as a TV or computer screen. (And it was second only to *Harold & Maude* in its artfully haunting singer-songwriter pop soundtrack by Jon Brion and Aimee Mann, with plangent titles like "Wise Up," "Save Me," and "Nothing Is Good Enough.") It even had a magical-realist rain of frogs as its near-capper, the better to satirize all the "Y2K" and apocalyptic Rapture twaddle that was going around in real life, as the decade, century, and millennium wound up to its real-life series finale. (Philip Seymour Hoffman, who played Robards' angelic male nurse in the film and who himself would die far too young, penned a tribute to Robards for *TV Guide* when Robards died in December of 2000, less than a year after *Magnolia's* premiere, noting that the Broadway and film legend had taken the role of the terminally ill producer knowing it would be his last; he was dying of cancer in real life.)

Art Imitating Life

While the World War II early 1940s, and the Cold Warring late '40s, '50s, and early '60s, had plenty of films that held up a sometimes sentimental (*Mrs. Miniver, Battleground, The Best Years of Our Lives, From Here to Eternity*) or satirical (*The Manchurian Candidate, Dr. Strangelove*) mirror to the larger world, the 1990s had a conspiracy-theorist's heaven of films that prefigured and anticipated the world we were *about* to live in.

The Truman Show (1998) and ED TV (1999): No other silver-screen star defined 1990s blockbuster comedy more than Jim Carrey, who knocked it out of the park with the triple-headers of *Ace Ventura: Pet Detective, Dumb & Dumber,* and the gayish-stalker-themed black comedy *The Cable Guy,* from 1994 to '96. He'd scored these roles just after leaving his spot as the rubber-faced "token white guy" on the Wayans Brothers' 1990–94 urban variety show *In Living Color.* But with the charming, touching (and yes, very funny) *Truman Show,* a thoughtful warmup to his greatest "serious" roles in *Eternal Sunshine of the Spotless Mind* and *I Love You Phillip Morris,* Carrey proved he could do more than just make faces and take beatings. He played an Everyman named Truman who finds out that his entire life and known universe was the controlled fodder for a nationally televised (and rigged) reality show and psychological experiment. The following year's considerably more manic *Ed TV,* starring Matthew McConaughey in the title role, combined *The Truman Show* with *Network* by exploring the same idea—only with "Ed" as a willing and eager subject who signs on for 24–7 surveillance of his own free will.

Barely a year or two after all this, CBS redefined itself from its '90s role as the nursing-home's favorite network, with the young, sexy, and Gen-Xey *Big Brother* and *Survivor* duo, in the scintillating small-screen summer of 2000. (*Big Brother* in particular copped *The Truman Show* and *Ed TV's* feel, by having its real-life cast of characters living in a house and grounds with 24–7 security monitor surveillance—including the bedrooms.) The era of Kardashians, Snooki, Paris and Nicole, Sarah Palin, Donald "The Apprentice" Trump, and *American Idol* (not to mention the likes of Anna-Nicole, Honey Boo Boo and Duck Dynasty) was as pre-visioned by *The Truman Show* as surely as a reading from the Psychic Friends Network.

Wag the Dog (1997): Only the ugliest "torture porn" horror movies of the late '90s and early 2000s, like *Se7en, The Bone Collector, Final Destination,* and *Saw,* were as horrific as the fallout from this light-as-a-feather political satire—which told the story of a charismatic (and sociopathic) president who incites a war crisis to distract the nation's attention from his sex scandal. Barely a year after its release, Osama bin Laden went on world TV issuing his "fatwa" against America, and to prove he wasn't kidding, murdered dozens of American embassy employees in Nairobi and Kenya immediately after. Bill Clinton struck back—barely—but he completely failed to follow through on getting Osama or destroying his terrorist training camps. Clinton's political hands were tied; he was then facing the political fight of his life after Monica Lewinsky showed off her DNA-stained dress. Despite Osama's 24–7 calls for intifada and jihad, both isolationist Vietnam-leftover peaceniks on the left, and Clinton's usual right-wing critics, accused the president flat-out of quote "wagging the dog"—that is, of cynically going after Osama as nothing more than a rally round-the-flag distraction from his coming impeachment. Traumatized by this accusation, Clinton held back from ever again going full-throttle after Osama and al-Qaeda, even after a deadly October 2000 attack on the *USS Cole*. The deadly results of this situation were tragically witnessed in September of the very next year.

***Dave (1993), The American President (1995), Bulworth (1996),* and *Primary Colors (1998)*:** *The American President,* played here by Michael Douglas and scripted by Broadway playwright and *A Few Good Men* screenwriter Aaron Sorkin (who put the showstopper line, "You can't handle the truth!!" in Jack Nicholson's circa-1992 mouth) further underlined the reciprocal fascination that Hollywood had towards the institution of the Presidency during and after the run of Tinseltown's favorite pre–Obama president. And its success was undoubtedly the door-opener that got *President*-ial scribe Sorkin his pitch meeting at NBC and Warner Brothers, for a little TV number called *The West Wing* in 1999, starring longtime Douglas buddy Martin Sheen as President Josiah Bartlet. (Oliver Stone also famously borrowed and used some of *The American President's* sets and things, on his over-budgeted and all-star 1995 epic, *Nixon,* starring an incongruously cast Anthony Hopkins as the embattled president, who'd died the year before.)

Bulworth told the story of a veteran politician going on his final bid for re-election with nothing left to lose (he thinks!) by telling the truth, with Warren Beatty in his last (to date) top-line role, while *Dave* cast Kevin Kline as a middle-class small businessman who happens to be the lookalike for the current president, and who takes over for him after the Prez is incapacitated by a stroke. While the first was hip satire and the second a heart-warmer, both romanticized the Ross Perot/Sarah Palin philosophy that what the Beltway needed was straight talk, out-of-the-box thinking, and common-sense solutions from every-day people. (As to *Primary Colors,* we've already discussed the thinly disguised, John Travolta-starring *roman a clef* about a sexually insatiable and electrically charismatic Southern "bad boy" governor, who rewrites the rules of media politics.)

***Groundhog Day (1993)*:** This lovable frustration-comedy starred Bill Murray as a man who ends up reliving the same day over and over again, until he can figure out a way to move forward—if indeed he ever can! *Groundhog Day* was a rather perfect preview of the retro-rific and remake-happy late 1990s, where the forty-something baby boomers then in charge of the studios and networks erased the embarrassment of picking out those gray hairs, plumping up those sagging body parts, or sucking in that beer belly, by greenlighting glorifications of their younger and sexier salad days, like *Boogie Nights, Almost Famous, Velvet Goldmine,* and *That '70s Show.* (Not to mention ramping up Nick at Nite, VH1, TVLand, and Game Show Network.) On a darker note, it could also be taken as something of a fable about a world where all the lessons we *should* have learned from the past were constantly swept aside, so that our political leaders could continue making the same kinds of mistakes over and over (and over) again....

***Election (1999)*:** Director Alexander Payne and source novelist Tom Perrotta's charmingly sly satire of a virtually all-white Midwestern high school's popularity contest, boasted the considerable talents of Reese Witherspoon, Matthew Broderick, and Chris Klein. As future Cato Institute intellectual Gene Healy put it on a 2000 blog entry, Reese Witherspoon plays the "grotesquely ambitious," smirkingly superior, demagogic high school sweetheart

Tracy Flick, whose "ravenous lust for power" appalls her hapless teacher (Broderick). He recruits a kindly and devoutly Christian, but dumb-as-a-brick football jock (Klein), beloved by both nerds and jocks alike, to run against her for class president. Tracy is already burning with pseudo-feminist resentment that not everyone recognizes her "hard work" and achievements—and it chaps her skin something fierce that someone else has decided to challenge her on the grounds that he's just more goshdarn likable than she is. And all because his Daddy is the biggest and richest of all the school's parents, owning a prosperous GMC dealership, while *she* grindstoned it and *earned* all her expertise the hard way! What right does he have, after all, to try and play in her league? Why, it'd be a disaster if that *dummy* got in, and we all know it!

Anyone who can't see the parallels between this hilarious "Election" and the all-too-real (and very unfunny one) that immediately followed with Al Gore fighting George W. Bush, should head straight for their Netflix queue to get a clue. (And you just *know* Tracy had a framed picture of Hillary Clinton somewhere, like her later-on soul sister Amy Poehler did in *Parks & Recreation*.) Filmed during the climax of Monicagate, the movie's ending shout-out has a collegiate Tracy working in Washington as (what else?) an efficiently sexy *intern*. Also notable is that a single-parented young female, trying to advance herself on her own merits and break the glass ceiling against a male teacher and a rich jock who purposely threw obstacles in her way, is considered the ball-busting comic villainess. Talented tea leaf readers of the Left, like Thomas Frank and Rick Perlstein, could probably write their own "movie review" about what this kind of comic demonization of uppity, lower-middle-class strivers (who didn't Know Their Place against necessary "gatekeepers") said about the Ivy League-fetishizing, Human Resources-screening, neoliberal late '90s New Economy.

The Matrix (1999): The Wachowski Brothers first hit it big with this sci-fi fantasy about life in a series of alternate realities that can change at a moment's notice. (Andy Wachowski, and his brother and now sister Larry Wachowski, who revealed that s/he transitioned into Lana Wachowski just before the 2012 release of their *Cloud Atlas* adaptation.) Not since Ah-nold first strapped on the *Terminator* suit, and perhaps not even since the glory days of Harlan Ellison, Gene Roddenberry, and Philip K. Dick, did we have a better cinema-metaphor for an era where new technology kept on rewriting the rules and remaking our reality, a world where everything we thought we knew ended up changing or being wrong, seemingly every ten minutes.

Independence Day (1996) and True Lies (1994): *True Lies* was a winning combination of action-movie bangs and thrills with Carol Burnett-style comedy, starring Arnold Schwarzenegger as a seemingly typical suburban husband and father who actually works for The Company (and we *don't* mean General Motors or General Electric). His initially unknowing wife (a fabulous and funny Jamie Lee Curtis, who gives her all in a hilariously sexy striptease scene) thinks that her often-traveling and distracted husband is having an affair, and explores the possibility of having one too—only to find herself neck-deep in her hubby's latest spy shenanigans. Looking at it today, what casts a pallor over the fun and games is the film's big climax—featuring a plane hijacked by a Middle Eastern terrorist (albeit a much smaller 'personal' aircraft, rather than a gigantic commercial jetliner) being flown straight into a high-rise building. *Independence Day* was an all-star actioner featuring the latest in (circa 1995–96) CGI technology, with Bill Pullman as a somewhat clueless president faced with an army of hostile aliens who plan on blowing up the Earth bit by bit, targeting its symbolic landmarks and nerve centers. Sufficed to say, when people recalled turning on their televisions on the morning of September 11th, 2001, many of them said that initially, they thought they were watching a movie just like *Independence Day*.

Natural Born Killers (1994): This Oliver Stone directed adaptation of an early Quentin Tarantino screen treatment about a modern-day Bonnie & Clyde named Mickey & Mallory Knox (Woody Harrelson and Juliette Lewis) was transformed by the politically oriented Stone into a thrillingly deranged satire of media-whoredom, as the two criminals were pursued not only by law enforcement, but by a *Current Affair*–type tabloid anchorman (played to the hilt by Robert Downey, Jr.). Without a doubt, the most memorable scene was a Stone-written flashback sequence called "I Love Mallory," which depicted a level of abuse, domestic violence, and sexual assault that made later films like *Precious* and *For Colored Girls* (and the past standard-setter, *Mommie Dearest*) look downright subtle—as they *deliberately* played it for laughs, in the fashion of a raunchy early '90s sitcom. (Complete with canned laugh track and campy *Ozzie & Harriet* music, and comedy legends Rodney Dangerfield and Edie McClurg perfectly cast as Mallory's white-trash parents.)

As the scene begins, Daddy dearest yells at Mallory (wearing a skimpy black lace slip for a dress), "What the *(bleep)* are you wearing, Mallory—a broomstick and a trash bag? You'll end up peddlin' your ass, you stupid bitch!" *(The "audience" roars with canned laughter.)* Mom halfheartedly defends her daughter. "Now honey, you shouldn't yell at Mallory like that!" she caringly finger-points, wearing a purple fright wig. "Don't worry," Dangerfield winks at the camera. "I'll show her a little *tenderness* ... after dinner. When I get up there, she won't see my face for an hour!" *(More hysterical laugh-track.)* Then, when Mallory finally runs away with delivery-man Mickey ("Are you a big 'meat-eater,' Mallory?"), Daddy fumes as the "credits" roll to more canned guffaws. "Oooh, that meat-man cocksucker! I broke her in—and he grabbed her! Call the cops, honey!!"

What was so brilliantly disturbing and disturbingly brilliant about the scene *wasn't* that it was so outrageous or over-the-top, *but rather the exact opposite*: To many conservative or senior viewers, a "show" like *I Love Mallory* was only the slightest exaggeration of what proudly lower-class sitcoms like *Roseanne, The Simpsons,* and *Married ... with Children*— then at the height of their popularity—were really like. The next logical step, if you will. (Just think of *Beavis and Butt-Head*, or a few years down the road, *South Park*.) And did any film or comedy sketch paint a better picture of the aesthetic of daytime talk shows like *Springer, Ricki Lake, Jenny Jones, Maury Povich* (and the godfathers of them all, *Geraldo* and *Morton Downey, Jr.?*) Did any movie, from *Network* on down, ever so anticipate a world where viewers would find themselves hooked on "exclusive, probing interviews" with the likes of Charles Manson, Jeffrey Dahmer, Ted Bundy, plus various and assorted surviving Nazi war criminals and Third World genocidal dictators, on inescapable primetime "newsmagazines" like *Dateline, 48 Hours Investigates, 20/20 Downtown, Prime Time Live, Eye to Eye with Connie Chung,* and so on? (Even Osama himself eagerly sat down for *20/20* in 1998.)

(And if 2001 counts, then honorable TV mention must go to the Fox Network, which actually managed to surpass their Fox News sister with perhaps the most politically charged scripted TV event of the year, just after the '90s decade met its end. In the spring of 2001, Fox was filming a red-hot pilot starring Kiefer Sutherland as a fearless federal agent named

Jack Bauer, counting down the "24" hours of one of the worst days of his life in real time, as he raced the clock to stop a monumental terroristic and assassination threat. The nail-biting pilot—aired not six weeks after 9/11 in November of 2001—capped off with a hijacked airplane being blown out of the sky by Islamic terrorists.)

It's also interesting to note that for every pseudo-patriotic, testosterone music video like *Top Gun, The Right Stuff, Red Dawn, The Hunt for Red October, Navy Seals,* or TV's *The A-Team* during the supposedly militaristic Reagan-Bush era, there was another haunting, harrowing look back at the true horrors of war, like *Platoon, Born on the 4th of July, JFK,* and *Casualties of War.* Likewise, as the "liberal" Clinton era began inching towards the end, the Baby Boomers who then controlled Hollywood finally began to have second thoughts, as their World War II or Korea veteran parents began heading towards the exit. *Saving Private Ryan* brought back the 1940s-style, unabashedly patriotic and heroic war movie, followed soon after by the artistically far inferior but equally big-budgeted and hyped *Pearl Harbor.* Like *Private Ryan,* which was also directed by Spielberg, Sir Steven's most important serious drama of the decade, *Schindler's List,* reminded people of the moral necessity to intervene and go to war when faced with ultimate evil—a theme to which both humanitarian interventionists like Madeleine Albright and Leon Wieseltier, and unflinching neo-cons like Donald Rumsfeld and Charles Krauthammer, would have given two thumbs up. And *Forrest Gump* earned mega-millions and a Best Picture Oscar by reframing Vietnam, the protest movement, and civil rights through the innocent eyes of a developmentally delayed, racially tolerant, eternally cheerful Southern man.

Book-Endings

In light of the thriving and up-to-the-minute vitality in 1990s pop music, motion pictures, and even TV sitcoms and dramas, it's kind of depressing to move our pop-culture camera over to the book publishing industry of the decade. What is most notable about '90s book publishing wasn't so much its energy and influence, but a rather coldly foreshadowing absence of the book world's once-mammoth cultural footprint. David Foster Wallace, Jhumpa Lahiri, Nick Hornby, and Jonathan Franzen were probably the decade's most notable "serious" grownup-literary discoveries, along with Dave Eggers and Zadie Smith at the decade's very finish line. Talented and worthwhile novelists to be sure—but a far cry from the midcentury heyday when Mailer, Bradbury, Vidal, Buckley, Capote, Vonnegut, Roth, Updike, Cheever, Bellow, Didion, Dunne, Sontag, and Kael were all packing the bookstores with their "Have ya got the latest?" offerings.

As with today (at least regarding highly promoted, English-as-a-first-language writers) most of the 1990s' most notable and highest quality commercial fiction came from 1970s and '80s legacy authors like Toni Morrison, Maya Angelou, Joyce Carol Oates, Margaret Atwood, Haruki Murakami, and Stephen King. The biggest chart-toppers at '90s bookstores were the formulaic legal and spy thrillers from '80s stalwarts like John Grisham, Scott Turow, and Tom Clancy, with thirty- and forty-something yuppie professionals trying to untie some knotty social dilemma or past history, wrapped around a crackerjack present-day courtroom or spycraft drama. Female writers continued to make strides, with authors like Sue Grafton and Sara Paretsky finding ever greater success with the hardboiled female detectives they launched in the '80s, like Kinsey Millhone and VI Warshawski. But those novels' hard feminist edges were somewhat blunted with the emerging new genre of decidedly post-feminist "chick lit." *Bridget Jones' Diary* was the league-leader, which was followed quickly by *Sex and the City* (both the 1997 Candace Bushnell book and its iconic 1998–2004 HBO adaptation) and *Ally McBeal*, and reached their summit with the *Desperate Housewives, The Devil Wears Prada*, and *Eat Pray Love* a few years later in the 2000s.

The other big news, of course, was the trouble with Harry. In 1997 (in Great Britain) and in 1998 (North America), a divorced, thirtyish British single mom named JK Rowling set the publishing world on fire with the first of her internationally bestselling tales of sorcery and skullduggery, inspiring an a cult of young mad-fans not seen since *Star Wars* and *Star Trek*.

Rowling had been suffering through a particularly bad time before her life-changing success, dealing with the loss of her mother, a short-lived marriage and divorce (complete with single parenthood), living on assistance and occasionally teaching night school language classes before making her first book deal in late 1995, after nearly five years of writing the first story, *Harry Potter and the Sorcerer's Stone.*

Harry Potter was a nerdishly handsome young lad poised on his teens, who learns that he is one of the chosen with inborn magical powers, and begins his apprenticeship at the Hogwarts School of Witchcraft and Wizardry to learn how to harness and use them. Harry Potter, and his concurrent TV sensation, the enormously and deservedly popular 1997–2003 cult classic *Buffy the Vampire Slayer,* would completely define the next two decades in fiction publishing. Their massive successes and fan bases were directly responsible for more recent books and franchises like *Twilight* and *The Hunger Games*. These books turned "Young Adult" or "YA" literature into THE hottest trend by the end of the decade, only building throughout the next two decades, with even sophisticated-literary grownups proudly addicted to their empowering and stylized coming-of-age tales. Many childless and/or empty-nesting forty- and fifty-year old adults, who in the past would have considered it almost "pedo" (or embarrassingly immature and guilty-pleasure at the very least) to confess a passion for teenage-designed young adult literature, now stood in line to gobble up these stories for themselves.

Back to the Future (or, Fade to White)

As we've seen, from 1989 through '96, America's big screens had unspooled gritty, uncompromising, and culturally relevant indie (and mid-level studio) films that would not have been out of place during the very best of the "auteurist" New Hollywood of the '70s: *Boyz N the Hood, White Men Can't Jump, Do the Right Thing, Reservoir Dogs, Slacker, My Own Private Idaho, Sling Blade, Falling Down, Speed, Hoop Dreams, Nowhere, Clerks, Spanking the Monkey, Natural Born Killers, Clean/Shaven, Swoon, Go Fish, Poison, Trainspotting,* and *Pulp Fiction.* Each of these movies was distinguished by thrillingly intelligent writing, stylish direction, and intricate and unforgettable characters. Almost all of them were up-to-the-minute, holding up a veritable cinematic mirror and showing an often harsh reflection of what was then going on in society. And the big-budget dramas of the time, like Spike Lee's *Malcolm X,* Oliver Stone's *JFK* and *Born on the 4th of July,* Steven Spielberg's

Schindler's List, and Tom Hanks' Oscar-winning gay groundbreaker *Philadelphia,* dealt with themes—racial separatism, genocide and "ethnic cleansing," vast political conspiracies, AIDS—that were as relevant and contemporary as the headlines.

But a funny thing happened on the way to the end of the '90s, on screens both big and small. During Bill Clinton's "peaceful and prosperous" second term, from 1997 thru 2000, the most prestigious studio movies fell back into a pattern of historical costume dramas: *The English Patient, Shakespeare in Love, Titanic, Gladiator.* Even *Saving Private Ryan* and *The Cider House Rules* went back half a century to World War II. Class acts, but also a sharp contrast to the street stories and jump-cut stylishness, the "queer" and "slacker" vibes, and the gritty, grungy, and gangsta attitudes of early '90s cinema and pop music.

The test pattern ran parallel on the small screen, and in popular music, too. The biggest TV sitcoms from 1991 to '94 were shows like *Roseanne, The Cosby Show, The Fresh Prince of Bel-Air, Married ... with Children,* and *In Living Color*—shows that dealt with racial diversity, or life on the lower rungs of the white socioeconomic ladder. (Not to mention *The Simpsons,* and the ultra-raunchy *Beavis and Butt-Head.*) In the mid-to-late '90s, however, the comedy must-sees became *Friends, Seinfeld, Everybody Loves Raymond, Sex and the City, Frasier, Spin City,* and *Will & Grace.* And just how many lower-middle-class, economically struggling people did you see on *Will & Grace, Ally McBeal, The Practice, Sports Night,* or *Sex and the City?* How many African Americans, Latinos and Asians—even successful ones like the Huxtables or the Fresh Prince or the Jeffersons—were regular characters on *Friends, Seinfeld,* or *Raymond?* Or were fellow high school and college students on *Buffy, Party of Five, Popular, 90210,* and *Dawson's Creek?*

And as we noted, at decade's end, *Boogie Nights, Velvet Goldmine,* and (Studio) *54* hit the jackpot on the big screen (and TVLand, Game Show Network, and *That '70s Show* equaled them on the small). Not that there's *anything* wrong with remembering the glory days of disco dancing, variety shows, broughamy cars, and game shows a-go-go, mind you. But as American pop culture drove its DeLorean (or better yet, its brand new cordovan Lincoln Versailles or Mark V Cartier with the Corinthian leather and Astroroof) back twenty years from our 1999 or 2000 vantage point, with all this sudden glamorizing of the recent past, one has to ask the question: *Was this a society that was STILL "thinkin' about tomorrow??"*

Now that "tomorrow" had come, with all the stressful up-to-the-minute game changes of the Internet, cell phones, job retrainings, and a financially sophisticated, zippity-doo-dah Wall Street bubble, it seems that late 1990s culture was hitting the rewind button on the 8-track of life, auto-tuning for the predictable comforts of yesterday's biggest hits. As the racial and economic tensions of the early '90s recession temporarily eased, the racial and class diversity that was the trademark of early '90s edgy indie movies, working-class sitcoms, grunge rock, and urban hip-hop began to disappear. After things got better in the second half of the '90s, America's movies, music, and TV shows arguably became *less* diverse, *less* inclined to talk about modern-day social or political issues, *less* inclined to feature unapologetically urban content or people of color.

At decade's end, edgy director Mary Harron adapted Bret Easton Ellis' postmodern masterpiece *American Psycho* (with Christian Bale definitively embodying the part of horrible yet lovable yuppie-scum killer Patrick Bateman). What was most interesting about the stylish film was that, although it (and the book) was set in 1988, it didn't really come across like a period piece at all when it was released a decade or so later. The satiric portrait it painted of status-obsessed Ivy League twenty-somethings, shallow post-feminist princesses, too-sexy secretaries, campy gay interns, bullying business world braggadocio, and *Lifestyles of the Rich and Famous* wealth-porn was no longer dated. By 1999 and 2000, it was once again as fresh as the morning's CNBC or Fox News breakfast report. The sight of a smirking, metrosexual, white thirty-year-old exec with a personal trainer-toned bod underneath $500 shirts and Calvin Klein bikini briefs, pulling down a seven-figure paycheck at his old-money father's firm, blithely putting his feet up on his desk to while away his "workday" listening to headphones, looking at porn, and watching *Jeopardy!* on TV, could have been just another day at the office for a cashed-out young Netscape or Pets.com hotshot, a young late '90s Hollywood "playah," or successful stock market day trader.

By 1998, '99, and 2000, the gangsta rappers that had been saying "Fuck the Police" and calling for social justice were now all about the "bling," while—with a few notable exceptions like Eminem, Rage Against the Machine, and Fred "Limp Bizkit" Durst—the hard-edged, grungy anger of Kurt Cobain and Trent Reznor was replaced by the easy-livin' optimism of Smashmouth, Sugar Ray, Sheryl Crow, Fatboy Slim, and thumpa-thumpa gay "house" and auto-tuned techno music. Shoe-shopping single gals, unsentimental sitcoms about trendy white New York yuppies, dramas about rich mob bosses and even richer White House staffers, plus highly educated and highly paid lawyers, crime scene investigators, and ER doctors now ruled the TV roost. And the movies had gone back to the future with prestige period pieces and costume dramas. For inequality and/or identity-politics watchdogs looking at the big picture on the big screen, watching what they were watching on TV, and who were *really* listening to the music, the "movie" of the late 1990s was having a very unhappy ending.

Crossover Appeal

At least there was a silver lining on this increasingly glitzy new golden age. For one brief and shining moment, it seemed that Hollywood had finally figured out the formula to balancing arthouse Oscar dramatics with crowd-pleasing blockbuster popularity, in a way not seen since the height of the New Hollywood of the '70s. In his post-mortem, *The Best of Times,* historian and journalist Haynes Johnston repeatedly remarked about the thrilling vitality and renewed vibrancy in American film at the very close of the millennium.

He wasn't kidding. In just eighteen months between July of 1999 and December of 2000, Hollywood released a veritable Murderer's Row of contemporary classics. *Magnolia, American Beauty, The Sixth Sense, Fight Club, Erin Brockovich, The Green Mile, The Perfect Storm, O Brother, Where Art Thou?, American Psycho, The Talented Mr. Ripley, The Matrix, Girl Interrupted, Boys Don't Cry, Being John Malkovich, Three Kings, The Insider, Almost Famous, Requiem for a Dream, Before Night Falls,* and *Traffic.* Movies that were both of exceptionally high artistic quality AND could still pack 'em in, just like the latest formula blockbusters. Movies that became almost as referenced and important to the coming filmmakers of today's Millennial generation as the '70s classics were to the people who made these '90s films. These pictures also set the template for the literate, amped-up yet nuanced dramatics of today's most intricate "must see" TV shows and cable dramas on Thursday and Sunday nights. (The small screen also rose to the challenge back then, too. Between June of 1998 and June of 2001, *Sex and the City, Will & Grace, The Sopranos, The West Wing, CSI, Queer as Folk,* and *Six Feet Under* all launched, to both massive critical and commercial success.)

Most amazingly of all, virtually all of these non-franchise, non-superhero, stand alone, no-sequel films had major studio backing, plus generous TV and newspaper (and Internet) ad campaigns, and big budgets with bankable name stars. What *wasn't* a surprise, however, was that almost all of those postmodern classics of 1999 and 2000 were directed and written by people—Steven Soderbergh, David Fincher, David O. Russell, Mary Harron, M. Night Shymalayan, Cameron Crowe, the Wachowskis, Spike Jonze, and Paul Thomas Anderson— who had directly emerged from the "indie scene" of the early to-mid '90s. It was literally the climactic "Hollywood ending" to the decade where edgy indies resurrected the social consciousness and satirical commentary that was utterly lacking in the late '80s/early '90s mainstream studio fare, and then worked their way into those same mainstream studios.

* * *

It was inevitable that crossing over to mainstream success and bling-a-ding-ding fame and money would permanently change someone, especially someone who'd been working outside of or even *against* yesterday's establishment—and then suddenly found themselves sold or seduced into becoming a part of tomorrow's. Whether it was the grunge guru or Slim Shady who went from their *Breaking Bad*–like upbringings to mansions and Mercedeses, the ghetto or barrio rapper or ball player who suddenly found himself with more money and fly girls than he ever thought he'd see in a lifetime, or the indie filmmaker making movies on credit cards and parental loans one minute, and rubbing shoulders with Spielberg and Scorsese the next, the 1990s movie and music hit parade was as interesting and dramatic behind the camera as in front of it.

For some in the music and movie worlds, the end of the 1990s was a happy ending. (And just as sadly for others—River Phoenix, Kurt Cobain, Tupac and Biggie—the '90s were just The End.) But for those directors, writers, and singer-songwriters who made it through the gauntlet, who survived and thrived, the supposedly indifferent, "whatever, never mind" decade marked the beginning of the very best of what we have on our silver digital screens and up-to-the-minute iPods today.

8

A Holiday from History?

What's the point of you saving this superb military, Colin, if we can't use it?
—Madeleine Albright to Colin Powell, 1993

In 1918, Americans had just finished fighting what the government publicists and newly minted historians called "The Great War," or even "The War to End All Wars." (Unfortunately, somebody forgot to tell the guards over at Auschwitz and Buchenwald about that one....) Never fear, however—once Adolf Hitler was finished, as the war song "(There'll Be Bluebirds Over) The White Cliffs of Dover" noted, there would be peace in the world at last, when it was free! (But wouldn't ya know it—ol' Uncle Joe Stalin just wasn't in any hurry *at all* to pack up his crushing tanks, his torturing secret police, or his military troops, and leave the Eastern European "buffer states" alone.)

Then came Vietnam, when singers like Judy Collins, Joan Baez, Mary Travers, Melanie, and John and Yoko hopefully sang of how "Peace Will Come" someday. After that, movies and TV shows like *M*A*S*H* and *The Deer Hunter* reminded people of the incalculable waste and futility of war. But while there wouldn't be a full-on, open war on the level of World War II, Korea, or Vietnam until the Twin Towers fell 25 or 30 years later, the true peaceniks were appalled by the countless interventions and skirmishes led by Jimmy Carter (Afghanistan, the Iranian Embassy fiasco), Ronald Reagan (Libya, Grenada, Nicaragua, Beirut, Iran-Contra), and George Bush, Sr. (the first Iraq War, Panama, the beginnings of Bosnian intervention). *When will they ever learn? When will anyone listen!* the peace advocates wondered, all while the business of war and "police actions" went on uninterrupted.

Now, as the 1990s began, the gum-flappers were at it again, for perhaps their most eye-rolling turn yet. To the joy and jubilation of just about everyone in the civilized world, the Berlin Wall had finally fallen in November of 1989, just two and a half years after Ronald Reagan had famously "dared" Soviet premier Mikhail Gorbachev to "tear down this wall!" By December of 1991, Gorbachev's successor, Boris Yeltsin, had essentially disbanded the Soviet Union, allowing former "buffer states" like Czechoslovakia, Poland, Hungary, Romania, Yugoslavia, Bosnia, and the like to establish their own governments with some degree of independence. After 50 years of living in the shadow of total war—first with World War II, then with the Cold War—it finally looked like it was over at last. The good guys had won, once and for all.

These were all monumental accomplishments, but the initial jubilation over these triumphs led to some otherwise respectable historians and academics predicting what the esteemed right-wing honey Francis Fukuyama best-sellingly called *The End of History*. Other foreign policy hardliners said that the 1990s—the first decade since before World

War I to not be in the shadow of Hitler or the Soviet Union, and before 9/11—was a "holiday from history." In the wishful-thinking fantasy island (er, we mean Serious Projection of Future Trends) that sprung up after the fall of the Berlin Wall and the worldwide shaming of China following the Tiananmen Square atrocities, it was said that the triumph of Western freedom was so total, and that people were so prosperous and advantaged and had so little to worry about, ennui and boredom and aimless purposelessness would become the major "enemies" of the coming century. *What could possibly go wrong now?*

Isn't it funny how Osama bin Laden, Yassir Arafat, Saddam Hussein, Muammar Khadafy, Kim Jong-Il, Mahmoud Ahmeninijad, Hosni Mubarak, Vladimir Putin, Syria's Bashir al-Assad, and ISIS still managed to continue "making history" for the two decades since? Sadly, America's 1990s foreign-policy schizophrenia, multiple-personality disorders, and gross negligence and missed opportunities, fit the pattern of everything else in that decade's domestic culture war.

So Long, Soldier!

Back in 1992, every president going back to Harry S. Truman had served in uniform. Truman and Dwight Eisenhower had both served on the battlefield in World War I, and Truman was in the Senate (and at the end, vice president and then president), while Eisenhower was Supreme Allied Commander, during World War II. All the rest, from John F. Kennedy through George H.W. Bush, had served in one capacity or other during World War II. Many if not most of the losing candidates in those years' elections had also come from World War II (even including 1972's famously anti-war activist George McGovern, who had been an Air Force hero as a young flyer), or had come of age in the early Cold War/Korea era, like Walter Mondale and Michael Dukakis. Even most of the A-list Baby Boomers who were near the top of the mainstream political pyramid had served in Vietnam when it was "their turn." Dan Quayle and George W. Bush had served in the National Guard (though Bush's service was undistinguished, and that's putting it kindly), while Bob Kerrey, John Kerry, John McCain, Max Cleland, Colin Powell, and Al Gore had served in Vietnam itself (although Gore was in a non-combatant role).

But as with so much else, Bill Clinton was the game-change. He had gone out of his way to avoid military service in Vietnam "while maintaining [his] future political viability" (as a smoking-gun letter he'd written to a highly placed Arkansas official, after his student deferments had run out in 1969, would read). As far as that went, Clinton's opposite number, Dick Cheney, the Secretary of Defense under Bush Sr., and the future vice president under George W. Bush, had infamously told the 1989 Congress that he had quote, "other priorities" during Vietnam. Unlike the far-right Cheney, however, Clinton had actively protested against the war, had lived a full-on hippie lifestyle, and had cut his national-political teeth working for antiwar presidential candidate George McGovern in 1972.

The sexy and swingin' Clinton and his liberated, feminist, career-holding wife Hillary already painted a sharp enough contrast to the patriarchal, old-fashioned, 1950s-retro Presidencies of Ronald Reagan and George Bush. And Clinton's first major act in office only drove all those old stereotypes home. Instead of humbly deferring to the macho military brass, he forced the issue of allowing Gays in the Military as his very first policy initiative after taking the oath of office. Conservative Bible-belt states, still clinging to the "anti-sodomy laws" that made being gay itself a crime, never mind gay marriage (laws that had long ago been repealed or struck down on the coastal and Northeastern states), now hit the roof. Why, it was as if that "godless" draft dodger was throwing down the gauntlet! First he takes the coward's way out, after going to Russia as an exchange student, when it was his turn to serve. And then, sure enough, his very first act upon taking office is to theatrically diss the old-fashioned, masculine ethos of the military!

For those Millennials who think that the worst bigotry directed against President Obama (photo-shopping his head on a bone-wearing African witch doctor, portraying him as a monkey or ape, etc.) is something new or shocking in American politics, it would be useful to rewind to how the cultural Right first reacted to President Clinton. On Memorial Day 1993, when Clinton visited the Vietnam Memorial to lay a wreath, more than 100 military veterans in full dress "swiveled in unison," as the *New York Times* reported, and pointedly *turned their back* on this new Draft Dodger-in-Chief, right in front of the TV and magazine cameras! It was a culture-war picture worth more than a thousand words. Cries of "He's not MY Commander-in-Chief!," "COWARD!," and "Where Was Bill?" were commonplace. This time, it wasn't the hippies who were protesting with picket signs; it was the all-American conservatives. "Hypocrite," "For Shame!," "Never Trust a Draft Dodger," and "Dodge the Draft, Smoke Dope = Become President!" were some of the more colorful ones.

We've all heard of people who deny the Holocaust and deny climate-change. Well, this Hippie-in-Chief's very presence in office was so disturbing, so appalling, such an infamy to the all-American right of the early 1990s, it was as if they were trying to *deny* his very Presidency. They were helped along by many of Clinton's fellow Southern and rural "Blue Dog" Democrats, eager to curb this "ultra liberal" (on social issues) Democrat's enthusiasm before he ruined the Democratic brand for all of them. And the hard Republican ultra-right, desperate to deny this cultural game-changer his legitimacy, always reminded him that "57 percent of America" had voted *against* him in the 1992 election. It must be a dream … something this outrageous *simply* couldn't have happened!

As the late, great character actor Strother Martin might have said, what we had here was a failure to communicate. No wonder African American intellectuals like Toni Morrison and Maya Angelou said (in those pre–Obama years) that it was as if Bill Clinton was the "first black president." Just like a black man, Bill Clinton was being judged not so much for what he had done (or at least for what he was doing currently) but for *who he was*, and *what he had been* in the past.

While Steve Kornacki and other political journalists have debunked it since, the persistent myth of 1993–94 across all of official Washington was that Bill Clinton's subpar 43 percent victory was thanks to the crew-cut, "Yes Sir! No Sir!" Texas reactionary and billionaire businessman, H. Ross Perot. Surely if Perot hadn't run, Old Bush would be back where he belonged, and we wouldn't have to deal with any of this gay and feminist and Vietnam-leftover nonsense, especially in the armed forces. Our old Kansan sculptor friend bluntly but succinctly summarized what many on the social-right thought of the Clintons' power aesthetic, when he created his statue of (to use Rush Limbaugh's old phrase) our "Femi-Nazi" first lady, whom the sculptor called *Hitlery* Clinton.

But while all this culture war was going on at home, as oblivious media mavens blathered about a future where The Market would solve every problem as effortlessly as Jessica

Fletcher figuring out who dun it on that week's *Murder She Wrote,* a would where we had reached "the end of history," very literal wars were still going on. The bloody roadmap to 9/11 and today's conflicts in Iraq, Afghanistan, Syria, Israel (and an economically dominant China and India) were all under open construction in the 1990s. Right under the Congress and the White House's noses.

A Tangled Web

"Anti-Semitism," at least as we think of it today, "is a fairly recent innovation in the Middle East," said the Jewish and British-born Middle Eastern scholar and retired Princeton professor, Dr. Bernard Lewis, in a PBS documentary on the roots of Middle Eastern terror. "There were normal frictions before that," but it was largely the Middle East's alliance with Hitler, followed almost immediately by Israel asserting its statehood in 1948, that really sealed the deal. (Indeed, Professor Lewis called Iraqi dictator Saddam Hussein's Ba'ath Party a veritable "clone" of the Nazi party.) And in those early days, it wasn't just paranoid hatred of the "Jooz!" that motivated them. "Many Arabs [saw] Israel as an extension of European colonialism and imperialism," said Prof. Fawas Gerges of Sarah Lawrence College—a Western intervention that was "flaunted in the heart of the Arab world." *Newsweek* and CNN foreign-policy guru Fareed Zakaria agreed, telling PBS that "People in the Arab world largely allied themselves with the fascists" during World War II, because they were itching to get out from under the colonial, racialist, imperial grips of Britain and France. It was the oldest principle in the art of war: "the enemy of my enemy is my friend." The Nazis skillfully exploited both their built-in hatred of the colonial powers, as well as the rising tensions in British-run Palestine, where the machinery for what would become the Israeli Jewish state was already in motion.

Great Britain, at the height of its Victorian/Edwardian colonial dominance, had said during World War I that it would relinquish control of Palestine within thirty years' time, in response to the pleas of ardent Zionists who were intent on re-establishing a Jewish ancestral homeland, in 1917's famous Balfour Declaration. After the *next* world war, the horrors of the Holocaust only underlined the desperate need for the Jewish people to have a safe haven, and a government they could truly call their own. In May of 1948, the country of Israel was founded, with President Harry S. Truman immediately recognizing the new authority (and that other great superpower, the Soviet Union, formally recognizing within the week). Needless to say, many of the Islamic states surrounding the country of Israel weren't very keen on this new interloper. A fierce war for Israeli independence was already at hand, but thanks largely to Western support (as well as the courage of the Israeli fighters), Israel was able to declare victory.

Within the humiliated and beaten-back Muslim countries, the mood wasn't so joyous. Almost all of the heads of Arab governments that participated in the "fiasco of 1948," said Prof. Lewis, "were either deposed or assassinated." The new leaders created authoritarian police states—a trend which repeated itself in even more horrific fashion twenty years later, after Israel won the famous Six Day War in 1967, under famously no-nonsense Israeli generals like Moshe Dayan and Ariel Sharon, vastly expanding Israel's occupying territories and settlements. "It is out of the ruins of 1967 that emerge[d] the worst dictatorships that the modern Middle East has ever seen," Middle Eastern scholar Kanan Makiya told PBS' *Frontline*. Embarrassed and desperate to prove how tough they were, in light of their governments' impotence against the Israeli (and American-backed) forces, Makiya recalled that the new leaders mounted "tyrannies that exceeded the brutality of anything" that had come before. These new authoritarian regimes came with secret-police intelligence networks that were directly patterned after the worst excesses of the Soviet Union and Nazi Germany. The next stepping stones on the road to 9/11 would be laid a decade after this—but they were steps that were over thirty years in the making.

Shah Mohammed Reza Pahlavi's father was the founder of the post-colonial, post–World War I version of Iran. A visionary military leader, the elder Shah Reza patterned his reforms directly after the legendary modernizer Ataturk in Turkey—insisting on modern, Western styles of dress, beginning to secularize (by Middle Eastern standards) the schools and government, and—horrors galore!—insisting on literacy and employment opportunities for women. As historian George Hassan noted in his study *Iran: Harsh Arm of Islam,* Iran grew by leaps and bounds during the elder Shah's guidance in the 1920s and '30s. But unfortunately for the first Shah, his cozy business relationships with Adolf Hitler and Nazi Germany ensured that Winston Churchill, backed by the U.S. and Russia, would invade and occupy Iran, fearful that the Shah might open up Iran's ports (and its bottomless oil and fuel supply) to the Nazi armies.

However, there *was* a clever way out. Roosevelt, Churchill, and Stalin didn't want to risk having to manage a possible, insurgent-style Iranian uprising by removing the Shah totally, by installing some outsider puppet from Britain or America. They already had enough to deal with in World War II without creating a *new* war zone! So they allowed the first Shah to save face, by "agreeing" to go into a paid-for exile and pass the dice over to his 22-year-old, Western-educated son, Mohammed Reza—provided that the young Shah-to-be understood who was *really* in charge, at least for the duration of the war effort.

Far more book-educated and sophisticated than his father (though not nearly as natively intelligent or politically savvy), the young crown prince eagerly accepted the deal. A fortune in oil revenues and purchases from the Allies soon flowed the new Shah's way, and continued with little stop following the successful conclusion of World War II, as the American and Canadian auto industry hit its zenith, not to mention the booming plastics industries in postwar America and Europe. (The eventual rebuilding of Toyota, Honda, Hyundai, Mitsubishi, Nissan, Mercedes, BMW, Jaguar, Rolls-Royce, Saab, Volvo, Volkswagen, and so on across Western Europe and free Asia, along with their own petroleum industries, only made him richer.)

The only serious challenge to the Shah's power came in the early 1950s, when the Iraqi Parliament's then Prime Minister Mohammed Mossadegh attempted to mount a popular revolution to overthrow the Pahlavi royal family. (It was kind of a credit to the Shah that he maintained the surface appearances of democratic government, like the Western administrations that supported him and whom he admired, no matter how hollow those pretensions were.) The CIA and British forces helped the Shah's own army and secret police crush the popular uprising without mercy. Not only was Shah Reza a much-loved and loyal figure in global high society, but Mossadegh was pro–Soviet when the Cold War was at its hottest, while the Shah had proven himself to be a soundly pro–American and pro–Western leader, even after President Truman's 1948 recognition of the State of Israel.

Now restored fully to power, the Shah held Iran in his nearly complete control for the next 25 years. "Pomp and pageantry were essential ingredients of" the Shah's rule, said his all-too-accurate obituary in the 1980 Funk & Wagnall's Almanac. Unfortunately, the *Dynasty*-like atmosphere and old-time "regal" trappings of the now inconceivably wealthy Shah couldn't help but inspire as much resentment and jealousy as they did loyalty and reverence, amongst his basically Third World general population. By 1978, the now middle-aged Shah was one of the longest-running rulers in the entire Middle Eastern world, dating his reign to when he was practically a teenager back in 1941. Before the founding of Israel, before Nasser or Sadat in Egypt, before Iraq's Saddam Hussein or Libyan warlord Muammar Khadaffy or Palestinian Liberation Organization topper Yassir Arafat … before them all, there was Shah Reza. His government was tired, outdated, and increasingly out-of-touch. A Nixonian paranoia began forming, with the Shah increasingly relying on the brutal tactics of his secret police, the dreaded torture/execution-employing SAVAK, to maintain his grip. He was also in failing health, though he kept that a literal state secret. (He'd already been treated for cancer in France once. And now—unbeknownst to even the CIA or MI-5—it had come back.)

The exiled radical Muslim cleric known as the "Ayatollah Khomeini" was already in his late seventies by then. His long white beard and black, glowering eyes made him look like a cartoon of an aged evil mastermind (or a terroristic Santa Claus). Khomeini had spent much of his life in exile after having been expelled for fomenting revolution from his native Iran. After years of communicating with his sympathizers (many of whom were idealistic young university students) via the underground and recorded cassette tapes, at last Khomeini saw his chance. Starting at Christmastime in 1978, Khomeini's loyalists brutally overthrew the Shah's government. By February of 1979, they had finally ended the 38-year reign of the man who had been the most omnipotent and high-profile Middle Eastern leader up to that point, as the all-powerful Shah now fled into exile.

Sure enough, like something out of *The Handmaid's Tale,* once the Ayatollah took over, long-discarded traditions like burkas or veils, legal sexual experiences and arranged "marriages" for barely pubertal children, and other such outrages now returned from history's garbage dump. The Ayatollah launched a very literal war on women and children that included using "martyr" children in suicidal terror missions and to ferret out land mines, during its long war with neighbor Iraq. In November of 1979, desperately craving revenge for all the years America had propped up the Shah, radical Islamic students took over the American embassy in Iran and held it hostage for over a year, dooming then-President Jimmy Carter. Even Soviet and Red Chinese leaders expressed outrage at the brazen, proud support and protection the Ayatollah gave to the gun-wielding hostage-takers. It was almost like the antithesis to civilized government. However, with the motherlode of oil and gas supplies now at his disposal, the fanatical Khomeini couldn't have cared less what the rest of the world thought of him—indeed, he reveled in the contempt he inspired from the "infidel" world. A picture in the 1980 Funk & Wagnall's almanac said it all. Outside the seized embassy, the hostage-taking Islamic students put up a mural of a crying, white-haired President Carter, complete with Hitler mustache, with (in English language) "U.S. CANNOT DO ANYTHING!" written above. The Shah, meanwhile, was now completely ravaged by the cancer that he could no longer keep in the medical closet. He died in exile in Egypt, in July of 1980, at age 61.

Less than two months after the embassy seizure, at Christmas of 1979, the Soviet Union—paranoid as always about controlling its satellite and "buffer" regions—invaded Afghanistan, wanting to clamp down hard on the region, now that there was all this Islamic revolution in the air. Both Jimmy Carter and Ronald Reagan instantly understood the possibilities. This was the chance to give the Soviets "their Vietnam," as many foreign-policy mandarins would later put it. A war that would sap the Soviets' already breaking-point resources, and would be vastly unpopular among rank-and-file Russian citizens. With newly elected President Reagan and his ex-CIA chief Vice President George Bush already planning to defeat the Soviet Union by driving it into financial ruin as they accelerated the arms race, what better bankruptcy-helper than to turn Afghanistan into a bottomless money pit for Mother Russia? The CIA zeroed in on Afghanistan, helping to train an army of young jihadists, including the radical son of a vastly wealthy Saudi family named the bin Ladens, to fight the "godless," "infidel," and "imperialist" Russkies for the next nine years. Bin Laden christened his unit "The Base"—which translated in Arabic to "al-Qaeda."

Unfortunately, these revolutions only encouraged fundamentalist Islam around the world. Finally, someone had the "guts" to stand up to the Great Satan (America), and even Mother Russia on the other side. Egyptian Premier Anwar Sadat was brutally murdered in 1981, for his "offenses" like signing an historic peace accord with Israel in 1978, and offering safe haven for the Shah when he was on his deathbed—and above all, for continuing to "modernize" his society. (He was succeeded by the iron-fisted army general Hosni Mubarak's government for the next thirty years, until the "Arab Spring" uprisings of 2011.)

The "mother of all" wars

With the Afghanistan war starting to drain the Soviet Union's already skimpy cupboards, Presidents Carter, Reagan, and Bush (Sr.) all focused their attentions on payback for the Iranian hostage crisis. Iran and its neighbor Iraq declared war on one another in September of 1980, and it would be a struggle as long-lasting and destructive as the Afghanistan mess. The United States helped sponsor Iraq, providing it with money and weapons (even as the Reagan administration later made arms-for-hostages deals that ultimately came to light as the notorious "Iran-Contra" scandal). One especially ironic bit of news footage shows former (and future) Defense Secretary Donald Rumsfeld, acting as an envoy for the Reagan-Bush administration, shaking hands with Iraq's dictator in 1983. That dictator's name was, of course, Saddam Hussein.

By 1988, a spoiled-rotten and egomaniacal Saddam Hussein had enjoyed a free hand to do whatever he wanted in running Iraq for the past 20 years. This included Nazi-like atrocities such as developing germ warfare and using nerve gas on the Kurdish and Marsh Arab civilian populations (including women, children and the aged) to perform genocidal ethnic cleansing. His only global smackdown had come in 1981, when the Osirak nuclear reactor he had been building was bombed by Israeli pilots on the orders of hard-line Israeli Likud prime minister Menachem Begin. (The United Nations, including Ronald Reagan, Canada's Pierre Trudeau, and Britain's Margaret Thatcher, condemned Israel for over-reaching—taking Saddam's side, as it were. It was later revealed that Israel was entirely correct in suspecting that Saddam was planning on using the reactor as a headquarters for an atomic bomb.)

Saddam had first come to power as an army general, taking the second-chair spot as vice president of Iraq at age 30 within the Ba'ath Party's junta, after it took power in 1968. He assumed complete control in 1979 after a series of Stalin-like purges and show trials of officials he felt posed a threat to him. Saddam now patterned his government on two of his favorite role models, Hitler's Germany and the Kim Dynasty in North Korea. He established an idolatrous cult of personality, with grotesque landmarks like Saddam International Airport, Saddam University, Saddam General Hospital (and so on), plus countless authoritarian-art statues and gigantic murals of the Great Leader presiding over his country. He even had bricks installed in new buildings stamped with the logo, "Made in the Era of Saddam Hussein."

Saddam maintained absolute control of all media—books, newspapers, magazines, radio, TV, and films. (There wasn't really an Internet back then.) He published "poems" and "novels" and "screenplays" that were rapturously received by the state media, and exercised total censorship of the science and history curriculum from kindergarten through college. He prided himself on the ruthlessness of his secret police, and his willingness to kill, torture, or mentally hospitalize anyone who dared to speak out against him. (And that went for their families and/or closest friends or girlfriends and children, too.) His mentally unstable and self-indulgent sons, Uday and Qusay, were even more vomitous—the former was known behind his back as "the Devil" of Iraq for his sick sexual perversions, and for kidnapping and abusing Iraq's young women at will.

By August of 1990, it must have seemed to Saddam Hussein that he could do *anything* and get away with it. Instead, that month, Saddam got a crushing lesson in what his real place was in the global power hierarchy, when he had the temerity to invade his next-door neighbor, the tiny oil-rich country of Kuwait. Aside from its oil fields, Kuwait was nothing special in the global economy—but the truly influential Saudi Arabia was not far away, and their Royal Family hit the panic button, thinking (with good reason) that they might be next on Saddam's hit list. More importantly, with the Soviet Union about to disband and the Berlin Wall already having come down, the Western powers wanted to send a message that Hitler and Stalin-like takeovers of sovereign countries were now a thing of the past. Margaret Thatcher's Britain (in the final year of her reign) and George H.W. Bush's White House marshaled a global appeal to put Saddam back in his cage.

Now insane with power and ego, in the fall and winter of 1990, the tough-talking Saddam seemed eager for war, promising to give the U.S. "another Vietnam" and the "mother of all" battles. It was a dream that many peace activists in America were only too afraid might come true. Less than a dozen Democrats in the majority-Dem Senate of 1990–91 voted with the Republicans to authorize the first Gulf War, and only after Bush agreed to move his lips on his famous "Read My Lips—No New Taxes" pledge of 1988. One of those Democrats was a young, socially conservative Tennessee senator, who was pilloried by left-wing Democrats for his "betrayal"—and then skillfully turned that around to show moderate and conservative swing voters that he was tough enough to stand up to left wing hippies and peaceniks within his own party, while running for vice president in 1992. His name was Al Gore.

One of the first major Middle Easterners to volunteer to take the lead in repelling Saddam was the hero of the successful Afghan campaign against Soviet Russia—none other than Osama bin Laden. The Soviet goliath, now on its death bed, had finally given up the ghost in Afghanistan in 1988–89. For the first time since the 1940s, a country—a tiny, technologically backward, impoverished desert country at that—had managed to thwart the gigantic, nuclear-powered Soviet Union! "As Osama bin Laden and his followers see it, the collapse of the Soviet Union was not a Western achievement but a [specifically] *Muslim* achievement. It was a result of the guerilla warfare in Afghanistan," said Bernard Lewis in a *Frontline* documentary. Roham Gunaratna, the author of *Inside al-Qaeda*, added in a *National Geographic* miniseries on terrorism, that "If not for the anti–Soviet, multi-national Afghan jihad ... muhajadeen from all over the world would not have united to defeat one superpower [Soviet Russia] ... and then turn their guns on another superpower."

So why did Osama (and his friends) "turn his guns" on the United States? That happened largely because, instead of a hero's welcome and embrace, the Saudi Royal Family was apparently shocked and awed (and not in a good way) by their public's ecstatic reception to Osama the War Hero. Osama was bigger than the Beatles when he returned to his native Saudi Arabia, as far as rank-and-file Islamic citizens went. Truly he was proof that God— that Allah—was on our side! Middle Eastern intellectuals noted that Muslims were naming their sons after Osama at a far higher rate than they were after Saudi Prince Bandar (who was so close to America's Bush family, his nickname was "Bandar Bush.") If anyone could pose a real threat to the Royal Family's rule, could command the limitless money and fierce public loyalty to mount a successful revolution, could marshal the loyalty of the Saudi military to take over the country from the House of Saud's iron grasp—it would be Osama bin Laden.

The Saudis' nervousness accelerated into panic after Kuwait. Outraged by this affront from a formerly pro–Western state (Iraq) invading a sovereign Muslim country (Kuwait) next door to his own Saudi homeland, Osama patriotically volunteered to form a militia, to fight and protect the holy Saudi lands. But to Osama's horror, he learned that the House of Saud's distrust of him (and their loyalty to the Bush family) was so great, they flatly refused his offer. Instead, the Saudi Royals practically *begged* President Bush and Prime Minister Thatcher to save and protect them—with their armies of overwhelmingly Christian and Jewish, pro–Israel, Western-educated, mixed male and female soldiers, soon to be veritably crawling all over Islamic holy lands. Why, it was as if the Saudi Royals were *asking* to be "invaded" by the Christian and Jewish conquerors!

That was the last straw. Osama rebelled openly and violently, just as the House of Saud knew he eventually would. Like a global Judge Judy putting a smart-ass contestant in his place, the Saudi royals' response was just as final: "Put him out!" Barely a year or two after winning the greatest single triumph in modern Islamic history—beating the Soviet Russian colossus—a humiliated Osama bin Laden was brutally expelled from his homeland, like a no-good criminal, like he was nothing but a bum. It was clear the royals wanted to make an example of him, to show anyone else within Saudi Arabia what would happen to anyone who'd dare talk back to the power structure.

This ultimate betrayal changed Osama bin Laden's life forever, and crystallized the very worst assumptions that he and his radical Islamic cronies had about pro–Israel America. "It was that personal humiliation that led him to become the No. 1 terrorist in the world," sighed Middle Eastern scholar Rohan Gunaratna. No, Saddam Hussein and Osama bin Laden weren't directly working with each other (as the later George W. Bush administration would eventually try to claim). But it *was* true that Osama was now effectively on

Saddam's side, instead of Saudi Arabia's (which is to say, America's) side. And he was already plotting his revenge. "Bin Laden's genius was to say to these people, don't blame the Egyptians or the Saudis," said *Newsweek, Daily Beast,* and CNN foreign policy expert Fareed Zakaria. "Let's go for the head of the snake!"

After having been effectively thrown out of his homeland, Osama set up al-Qaeda housekeeping in the notoriously bloodthirsty Sudan, while maintaining terrorist training camps in relatively nearby Pakistan. In early September of 1992, one of al-Qaeda's best bomb-making experts, Ramsi Yousuf of Pakistan, flew into New York along with his partners. It was a classic bait-and-switch operation—Yousuf flew in on the same flight as a partner of his from al-Qaeda, who came off the plane belligerently, carrying duffel bags that were later discovered as containing bomb-making supplies. Meanwhile, Yousuf was clean-cut, respectful, and possessing a perfectly faked Iraqi passport, posing as a pro–Westerner seeking political asylum. "The Mozart of Terror," as author Peter Lance referred to Yousuf, was now in the United States, where he took a taxi to his contact, the head of the Al-Farouk mosque of Brooklyn, headquarters of the notorious "Blind Sheik," a close personal friend of Osama bin Laden. Yousuf and the Blind Sheik put together a staff of volunteers and started "cooking up" their plans—literally.

"Blood must flow. There must be widows, there must be orphans ..." intoned a cleric in a December 1992 "conference" of radical Islamic leaders, under the banner of the "Muslim-Arab Youth Association," infiltrated by journalist Steven Emerson, who later recounted his harrowing journey in the book *American Jihad.* (Interestingly, this conference was held in the unlikely locale of Oklahoma City, site of the non-affiliated Timothy McVeigh catastrophe two and a half years later.) Emerson had read about many of these radical and "Wahhabi" (warrior) Islamic sects, but later told the National Geographic Channel that he "never suspected" such violent fanatics "were in the United States." The speakers called for a jihad against the United States, even to the point of selling children's books encouraging them to become martyrs. Emerson called a contact of his at the FBI's counter-terrorism unit, but according to him, they poo-poohed his tip, and the documentary later revealed that "no known action" was taken against the conference by FBI. Their alleged non-response was a sad portent of things to come.

Barely two months after this, on February 26, 1993, a rented Ryder truck jam-packed with explosives ripped a seven-storey gash through the core of the World Trade Center in Manhattan. Six people were killed, and dozens more injured. Yousuf had escaped across the Hudson River by the time the explosion hit, and he watched the plumes of smoke rising from the Twin Towers—with a sense of disappointment. Not that he especially feared being caught, or that he had any regrets; he had simply been hoping that the bomb would cause one tower to fall over, domino-style onto the other, so as to kill thousands, even tens of thousands of people at once. (Especially all of those New York Jews.) Sadly for him, the WTC remained standing—though Ramsi Yousuf vowed, not for long.

If Ramsi Yousuf were Captain Ahab, the World Trade Center had now become his Moby-Dick. A dejected Yousuf flew first-class back to Pakistan, leaving behind a note where he promised that "next time," his "calculations" would be much more "accurate"—and deadly. Yousuf was also the nephew of Osama bin Laden's old friend, the notorious Khalid Sheik Mohammed, who would be universally recognized a decade later as the "mastermind" of 9/11.

Vietnam vs. the Holocaust

For most of the long, bloody, and largely pointless parade of warfare and conflicts throughout the ages, being a pacifist and opposing all war was certainly a morally justifiable position, to say the least. What greater point or moral purpose was there besides pure greed, megalomania, jealousy, and power-grabbing, for the vast majority of wars up to and including the Napoleonic wars, and even World War I? It was these kinds of wars for greed, and the Napoleon/Teddy Roosevelt notion of war as merely a manly "sporting event," that Quakers, Mennonites, and other pacifists were rightly revolted by. Ditto Vietnam, a war that may have been well-intentioned to begin with, but quickly escalated into an unwinnable quagmire, and other so-called "imperialist" and "proxy" wars, where small countries and their helpless peoples were used as mere disposable chess pieces in the real battles between superpowers.

But there were also times when the act of passive non-intervention could fairly be seen as immoral, and even indirectly encouraging far worse violence and depravity. When plantation slaves were being tied to trees and whipped while their wives were forcibly raped, when the ovens were being filled to capacity at Auschwitz, was hiding behind the Bible or holding hands and singing really that much more of a moral option than going to war, even if it meant fighting and killing people?

While it was arguable that Bill Clinton's greatest legacies as president were the peace accords he brokered in Northern Ireland, a war against genocidal warlord Slobodan Milosevic where virtually all U.S. soldiers came back alive, and other such "humanitarian interventions," Clinton's counterculture origins trapped him in the media and public's perception of these achievements.

By the time Bill and Hillary Clinton were in Yale Law School during the tail end of the Vietnam era, overt flag-saluting patriotism and "proud to be an American" sentiment had lost all respect among self-styled sophisticates and intellectuals in American liberalism. (Not for nothing did conservative hipster Tom Wolfe call his most famous book "Radical Chic and Mau-Mauing the Flak-Catchers," in 1970.) Going all mushy and sentimental and teary-eyed about the flag, about God and country—it was so gauche and tacky, so uneducated, so *not* Our Kind of People. It was so Archie Bunker, so Richard Nixon, so hopelessly middle-American muddle. Sentiments fit only for a special episode of Lawrence Welk or Ed Sullivan, something for Bob Hope and Perry Como's latest Christmas special—or better yet, for the next John Wayne, Charles Bronson, or Clint Eastwood shoot-em-up.

Right wing media conservatives very pointedly acted as if this kind of counterculture-chic attitude was still as true in 1992 as in 1972, as valid in 1999 as in 1969. To most straight-ahead Democrats, particularly in the Congress, Senate, and major governorships, nothing could have been further from the truth. (Keenly aware of the possibility of being thought of as less than a Real 'Murican, most Anglo red state Democrats made a point of trying to be as flag-waving and Mom/kids/apple pie as possible. Although tellingly, Bill and Hillary never made that much of an effort—and were rather unconvincing when they did.) But the academic-leftists and provocateur columnists and filmmakers of the '80s and '90s—who had the buzziest magazine, cable, and forthcoming Internet megaphones (and at the height of "political correctness," too) would give conservatives a limitless treasure trove of outrageous pull-quotes and revisionist theories—which conservatives could then turn around an use as "proof" of how degenerate, Commie, and anti–American ALL liberals and/or Democrats supposedly were.

Finally, there was the real issue, the key issue. Whether or not Vietnam was a moral or immoral war, if Bill Clinton had acted like it was merely his "choice" back then, had dodged the draft when it was "his turn," then what right did he have to order men and women close to his daughter Chelsea's age, people young enough to be his own grown children, into harm's way now that he was in office? Right wing conservatives said this as a trump-card—and on this score, left-liberals could only agree. Why wasn't Clinton still clinging to the ideals of the '60s, how could *he* of all people assume that America always knew best, that we had a "right" to interfere wherever and whenever we wanted, to impose our values and culture on them?

This was what people were really talking about when they were talking about foreign policy under Bill and Hillary Clinton. The peace movement and paleo-liberals were furious that Bill had once dodged the draft and protested an immoral war, yet was now coming across as a "keen militarist" (in the words of *American Conservative* columnist Daniel McCarthy, looking back in early 2009). These peace liberals' fury was akin to the anger of a Hollywood Ten screenwriter at a former colleague who'd "named names." *He was one of us—and now he's on THEIR side!* And yet, because the Right never allowed themselves to realize that Bill Clinton had changed a whit since the '60s (because of his social and religious liberalism), as Daniel McCarthy put it, Clinton "looked to the 1990s Right like just another [George] McGovern."

Nobody in their right mind had any real trouble telling who the good guys and who the bad guys were in America's struggles against Nazi Germany or the Soviet Union. And in both of those epic battles, perhaps just as importantly, the good guys and bad guys were evenly matched. But before the 9/11 attacks, the very *idea* that a piddling little country like Iraq, Somalia, the Sudan, Rwanda, Bosnia, or Afghanistan, could pose a true life-or-death threat to the United States and North America seemed ridiculous. That, however, wasn't the point. The point was to establish a 21st century new foreign policy, to deal with the new threats and moral quandaries that had risen up once the old ones collapsed. And because so many people believed that we were now on a "holiday from history" (as neo-conservatives contemptuously called the '90s), Clinton's crew would have to largely create this new doctrine from the ground up, making it up while they were going along, improvising as furiously as a jazz saxophone player or rock guitarist.

Perhaps the most interesting irony of 1990s foreign policy prescriptions was that people on both the farthest right AND the farthest left often ended up more in agreement with *one another*, while neoconservatives (who cared mainly about the balance of power and "creating" democracies) and neoliberals (who cared mostly about protecting against human rights crimes within nations) were forced to forge an uneasy alliance of convenience.

Exhibit A, submitted for your approval: The legendary novelist, screenwriter, essayist, and public intellectual Gore Vidal occupied the pinnacle of left-liberal dialogue in the United States from the 1960s until his death, and had been literally "born to rule" (senator grandfather, World War I ace and airline-founding Amelia Earhart-boyfriend father, international socialite mother, Kennedy relatives). Openly atheist, Vidal mocked observant Christianity and Judaism (calling neoconservative royalty Midge Decter and Norman Pod-horetz "Israeli fifth-columnists"), while bragging about having possibly fathered an illegitimate daughter and scoring well over 1,000 different sexual partners of men and women alike. When he died of old age in 2012, at his sumptuous Hollywood Hills estate, he left behind a net worth of well over $30 million.

The almost equally legendary dean of super-hyper-ultra right punditry, Pat Buchanan—the man who'd coined the phrase "culture war" to begin with—had served as one of Richard Nixon's youngest consultants, worked as an ideological police dog while in the Reagan White House (including *opposing* sanctions to punish South Africa's racist regime), and admired Adolf Hitler's "leadership" qualities. Buchanan was so far-right, he thought that Reagan's loyal vice president and ex–CIA head George H.W. Bush was too *liberal,* once Bush ascended to the top job in 1988. While Buchanan had been livin' large since the 1970s (writing for major newspapers and magazines, *TV Guide,* and as a fixture on cable and PBS), he never stopped acting the part of the lower-middle-class, lace-curtain Irish Catholic street fighter that he'd been raised to be.

And yet both of these men—as far apart ideologically, religiously, and intellectually as two white men within the boundaries of ruling class Western civilization could be—they were in *almost perfect agreement,* when it came to the major thrusts of American foreign policy. Around the time Bill Clinton was preparing to send his moving vans toward 1600 Pennsylvania Avenue, Vidal wrote in a widely publicized essay and address called *Monotheism and Its Discontents,* "The word 'isolationist' has been revived to describe those who would like to put an end to the National Security State [Vidal's disaffectionate term for Cold War America] that replaced our Republic a half-century ago, while extending the American military empire far beyond our capacity to pay for it.... Pat Buchanan [was] causing great distress to the managers of our National Security State by saying that America must abandon the empire if we are ever to repair the mess at home."

Although Vidal not incorrectly dismissed Buchanan as a "classic Archie Bunker type, seething with irrational prejudices and resentments," he felt that it was unfair that the mainstream media had written off Buchanan as an anti–Semite, because of Buchanan's belief that maybe America might have been better off sitting out World War II. (Vidal would know. Despite the fact that his live-in partner of fifty years was a New York Jew, Vidal mentioned the Holocaust not even *once* during a single-spaced, double-columned, two-page essay on "why" America fought World War II, in a January 1993 issue of *Newsweek.* That issue had a 1940s picture of a returning GI, and the headline, "So Long, Soldier!"—a blatant kiss-off to the first Bush White House, in favor of the first baby boomer-in-chief.)

David Frum snarkily noted in his 1994 book *Dead Right* that "the conservatives who took over the [Republican] party" in the post–Watergate invisible bridge of 1974 to '80 (after Nixon and before Reagan's administration), "were occupying recently vacated ground." The first modern generation of what we now call neo-conservatives (people like the Podhoretzes and *Commentary* legend Irving Kristol) had largely started out on the right wing of the Cold War-era Democratic Party. As far as their domestic concerns went, they basically approved of Social Security, Medicare, unemployment and workman's comp pay (and were largely in favor of equal rights for women, and some of them even quietly for gay rights). But they also agreed with Lyndon Johnson and Richard Nixon's chief domestic policy intellectual, future Senator Daniel Patrick Moynihan, and his famous late '60s assessment that (now that the voting rights and Great Society reforms were here), it was up to Black America (and Latino America) to sink or swim on their own. They abhorred affirmative action quotas, forced busing, housing projects, and the glamorization of thug and ghetto lifestyles with rap music and hip-hop.

Once the Democratic Party began courting the Age of Aquarius counterculture, with George McGovern's candidacy for president in 1972, followed by watching Jimmy Carter helplessly overwhelmed by the virulently anti–Israel Ayatollah of Iran, they didn't know what to do. Leading neoconservative intellectual Gertrude Himmelfarb wailed that there was "no place for us" left in the Democratic Party. (She and others only ran faster for the exit doors, as the "face" of the Democratic Party became more allied with ghetto-style demagogues like Jesse Jackson, Maxine Waters, Marion Barry, Willie Brown, Johnnie Cochran, and Al Sharpton.) The Reagan/Bush Republicans, keen to take a hard line in winning the Cold War and to intervene in the Middle East and Latin America, were only too happy to roll out the welcome mat. By the time that Bill Clinton entered the White House, all of the above (plus the next generation, like Irving Kristol's columnist son Bill Kristol, who'd worked as an assistant to Bush's VP Dan Quayle, plus rising stars like Charles Krauthammer and David Brooks)—all had become fixtures in the post–Reagan Republican Party.

The newly Republican neoconservatives' now reached the ideological intersection with the '80s and '90s neoliberals, keen on reforming and updating the Democratic Party from within. The goal of neoliberalism (as promoted by Marty Peretz, Michael Kinsley, Andrew Sullivan, Terry McAuliffe, and the DLC) was to take the liberal and Democrat movements away from their New Deal roots and modify for the coming post-industrial, college-and-electronics-based, international information economy. Likewise, the goal of neoliberal foreign policy was to establish a robust, interventionist foreign policy whose focus would be on stopping humanitarian disasters like ethnic cleansings, and would act as a "referee" in civil wars between small countries. And while there was certainly a big difference between the autocratic, nakedly authoritarian foreign policy of Dick Cheney and Co. during the Bush II regime, versus the United Nations-based Clinton approach, it was often mainly a question of degrees and goals. Both sides were passionately committed to a constant, interventionist global approach, and felt America had no choice but to play world policeman. To wit, Exhibit B.

Madame Secretary

Until the 1990s, in the liberal imagination, it was cynical, power-wielding "militarist" leaders like Teddy Roosevelt, Woodrow Wilson, Winston Churchill, Lyndon Johnson, and Richard Nixon who were regarded as the principal cause of war and death in the free world. Think of General George "Blood 'n' Guts" Patton, or ultimate Cold Warrior General Curtis LeMay—or for a much worse example, think of Lt. William Calley of My Lai Massacre fame in Vietnam. Think of Sterling Hayden and George C. Scott's demented generals in *Dr. Strangelove,* or Dan Rowan's comically bombastic "General Bull Right" on *Laugh-In* (whose catchphrase was "Remember—make war, not love!") Or *Apocalypse Now's* Robert Duvall crooning, "I love the smell of napalm in the morning!" Card-carrying "male chauvinist pigs" all of them, men who regarded the madness and violence of a World War II or Vietnam as some kind of character-building, straight-male-bonding ritual, like playing football or hockey in high school and college. Something necessary, even desirable, to turn spineless hormonal jellyfish into Real Men, ready to take the mantle of leadership in business, medicine, law, law enforcement, and their communities.

Why, if only we could get American foreign policy away from all those dreadful, hateful, racist, bullying *men*, then, maybe there was a chance that peace would *really* be at hand! Despite notable exceptions like Margaret Thatcher, Indira Gandhi, and Golda Meir, many feminists claimed that if only we had more *women*, more nurturers and mothers at the highest levels of government, maybe someone would finally stand up and say "No!" to all this Freudian dick-measuring, to the cruel prize-fighter dominance that people like LBJ and Nixon lived for during the deadliest days of Vietnam. (One of the premier '60s mainstream peace organizations for non-radical people over age 25 was called "Another Mother for Peace," whose figurehead was none other than America's definitive sitcom and movie mom, Donna Reed.)

This grand experiment finally came during Bill Clinton's term in office. On one side, we have General Colin Powell, a masculine and macho, bodybuilding African American career military officer, who proudly served in Vietnam, worked for Ronald Reagan to finish off the Sovietskys, and ran Gulf War I for Bush Senior. On the other, we have Madeleine Albright, clad in pearls or gold necklaces, basic black dresses, hosiery and polished heels, lipstick, manicured hands, and a tinted bouffant hairdo—the quintessentially "elite" academic intellectual and socialite. Why, it's already such an unfair fight, it's practically no contest. How could the cool-headed, motherly, middle-aged woman ever stop the warmongering, butch, macho militarist from going completely out of control?

Except for one thing: it was the matronly intellectual woman who couldn't wait to lay down her law at the point of a gun, and it was the career military warrior who was horrified by what he viewed as the reckless, almost promiscuous use of military interventionism that she advocated.

Born Marie Jane Korbelova in 1937 in Prague, Czechoslovakia, Madeleine Albright's father was press attaché at the Czech Embassy in Belgrade. Both he and Albright's mother were Jewish, but they converted to Catholicism as they made their escape to Great Britain, in exile. (Many of her relatives weren't so lucky; three of her grandparents were killed in the Holocaust.) Albright's parents had high hopes for a return to Czech international society when Hitler was defeated, but Josef Stalin crushed all those dreams under his iron tanks. By 1948, a barely middle-school aged Madeleine had been ping-ponged back and forth between eastern Europe and Britain for virtually all her young life, until her father was able to emigrate to America that fall. With her father safely installed on the tenure track as a professor at the University of Colorado at Denver (one of his future students was named Condoleezza Rice), Madeleine spent the rest of her growing-up years attending the poshest private schools, including the Kent Denver Prep Academy and ultimately graduating from Wellesley in the class of 1959, moving to Washington DC's ultra-elite Georgetown district in 1962.

After years of working on private school and charity boards, receiving her Ph.D. from Columbia in 1975, teaching at Georgetown University, and working for Jimmy Carter, Walter Mondale, and Michael Dukakis, Bill Clinton chose Albright to shatter one of the thickest-reinforced glass ceilings, when she was appointed as the first female Ambassador to the United Nations in February of 1993. Less than four years later, when seventyish San Francisco Democrat fixture and attorney Warren Christopher retired from his post as Secretary of State, Madeleine Albright was the natural choice for the top job—another all-time first for a woman—in whose footsteps Hillary Clinton would herself follow, under Barack Obama from 2009 to 2014.

It's no wonder with a background like that, that Madeleine Albright later famously said that while most of her generation's mindset was stuck in Vietnam, "My mind-set is Munich!" Perhaps without even knowing it, Albright defined the REAL domestic battle that all American foreign policy would boil down to, under the Presidency of William Jefferson Clinton.

The "enemy of the month club"

That dripping-with-contempt term (another Gore Vidal confection) was perhaps the perfect description of how both right-wing isolationists and '60s-style peaceniks regarded the Clinton Administration's foreign policy of "humanitarian interventions." Scanning the globe for hot spots, ever ready to run errands for the United Nations in this or that Third World hellhole, to play what an August 1993 *Newsweek* cover called "GLOBO-COP."

Globo-Cop's first shift on Clinton patrol was in the African country of Somalia, focusing on its capital city of Mogadishu. In the final days of George H.W. Bush's administration in November and December of 1992, Bush had responded to United Nations Secretary General Boutros-Boutros Ghali's pleas for a U.S.-led international peacekeeping force to restore some kind of order to the failed state, now under the de facto control of various tribal warlords, the most virulent being Mohammed Farrah Aidid. The U.S. effort was titled "Operation Restore Hope," but it certainly seemed that hope was in short supply, as the Somali warlords fought the UN do-gooders with everything they had, including land mines, surprise machine gun attacks, terrorism, and bombings. To the leader went the casualties—53 American soldiers were killed and 153 wounded, more than all of the other countries participating in Operation Restore Hope put together, with the exception of Pakistan.

More blood was shed in the fall of 1993, during "Operation Gothic Serpent," which resulted in the Battle of Mogadishu, and the infamous "Black Hawk Down" incident, where a Black Hawk helicopter, *Super Six Four,* was shot down by the forces of warlord Mohammed Farrah Aidid, with almost all the crew killed (including, eventually, two Delta Force snipers), and the remaining pilot, Michael Durant, taken hostage by Somali forces. Following the battle (which included a devastating mortar attack after the Black Hawk fiasco was concluded with Durant's eventual rescue), a humiliated Bill Clinton pulled out. He'd had enough, especially of defending in the media why one soldier after another had to die "running errands" as it were, with the United Nations, instead of in a place where there was a direct and tangible American interest. (Osama bin Laden, watching the action and avidly supporting Mohammed Farrah Aidid, couldn't have been more pleased: seeing Clinton pull out only convinced him that the Americans were weaklings, that they lacked the stomach for battle. And likely, it was trying to overcompensate for this that partially led the Bush II neo-cons to keep pushing, pushing, pushing, no matter how many deaths and injuries resulted, in their 2000s' wars in Afghanistan and Iraq.)

Next on Globo-Cop's international agenda was Haiti, a year later in 1994. Once again, to the horror of America First paleo-conservatives, President Clinton was using the U.S.

military to enforce United Nations goals and agendas, instead of limiting America's fighting forces to specifically North American and Western concerns. This time, the goal was to reinstate democratically elected Haitian President Jean-Bertrand Aristide, who had been exiled following a 1991 coup that placed a military junta in power. For exactly six months from September of 1994 to April of 1995, "Operation Uphold Democracy" engaged in a nation-rebuilding effort after the junta's fall and the restoration of Aristide's administration. (Unlike Somalia, there was no major armed combat; the junta, realizing they would be crushed, all but stepped down voluntarily when the U.S. entered the fray.)

But towering above it all was the situation in Bosnia. Slobodan Milosevic had governed much of the former Yugoslavia from the late 1980s onward. Yugoslavia, under the legendary General Josip Broz Tito, had been perhaps the most independent of the Soviet buffer states during the Cold War, conforming its government to basic communist ideologies and goals, but not merely acting as a straight-ahead puppet regime from Moscow. Now it had split into several ad hoc "states" revolving around ethnic and religious factions (which included Muslim, Catholic, and Orthodox populations), with Bosnia and Herzegovina being the major new establishments.

From early 1992 through December of 1995, Bosnia degenerated into all-out civil war, with tens of thousands of both military and civilian casualties. Rape and horrific sex crimes against women and the underage were commonplace. An "ethnic cleansing" campaign occurred in 1992 in the districts of Prijedor, Foca, and Visegrad, with Vietnam-like burnings of entire homes and apartment buildings, ransacking and looting of goods, and sadistic beatings and killings. Later that year and continuing into 1993, a murder campaign was carried out against Bosniak citizens in the Lasva Valley, with mass rape and political imprisonment and torture once again a key feature. (Even victims as harmless and innocent as a three-month-old baby and an 81-year-old woman were not spared.) Perhaps the worst genocidal "cleansing" of over 8,000 people was deliberately carried out in Srebrenica, in the summer of 1995.

Barely one month after Bill Clinton took office, the United Nations passed Security Council Resolution 808, establishing an international criminal tribunal (commonly known to some as "World Court"), patterned directly after the post–Holocaust Nuremburg trials and international courts to try Nazi war criminals following World War II. By 1995, the ICTY had set up operations in The Hague in the Netherlands, and had already begun issuing "arrest warrants" and indictments for top Bosnian army and political leaders.

The grand prize, Slobodan Milosevic, however remained in power. By 1998, war had returned to the area (not that it had ever exactly left), with the Kosovo War of 1998–99. This time, the United Nations, with the strong backing of U.S. Ambassador Richard Holbrooke, initiated a bombing campaign to take de facto control of the region, until a peaceful settlement could be reached. By the late spring of 1999, Milosevic had backed off from overseeing the worst excesses, and accepted the NATO-led Kosovo Force as a peacekeeping instrument. Milosevic held onto power for another 18 months, but was voted out of office in a referendum election he held at the end of September of the following year, and retired on October 6, 2000. (He was arrested six months later by UN forces to stand trial in The Hague for crimes against humanity, and was still undergoing appeals when he died of a heart attack in prison, in 2006 at the age of sixty-four.)

The Haitian, Bosnian, and Somali interventions were all the more poignant in that when it came to perhaps the worst state-sponsored violence of all in the 1990s, the U.S. had stayed all too "peaceful." There had been worldwide jubilation at the beginning of the '90s, when the noxious apartheid tradition was finally abolished in South Africa, and when black leader and intellectual Nelson Mandela was finally released from his decades-long stay in political prison. But the thrilling optimism that order and freedom might spread across the larger continent of Africa was soon extinguished by some of the worst human-rights catastrophes in modern history.

From April through July of 1994 in the African country of Rwanda, a veritable holocaust took place at the hands of the fanatical and power-mad Hutu tribal junta governing the country, following the shooting down of an airplane carrying Burundi tribal leader and district president Cyprien Ntaryamira and several of his top staff. Between 500,000 and 1 million Rwandans were mass-murdered by the military authorities in the span of barely 100 days' time. Rape and sex crimes against women and children happened on a round-the-clock, almost unprecedented scale—many of the victims of which were forcibly infected by HIV at the hands of their rapists. As with Adolf Hitler, the "final solution" was to try to kill every Tutsi in Rwanda. (Tutsi leaders were implicated in the October 1993 assassination of Hutu Burundi President Melchior Ndadaye, which may have been the final impetus for the genocide that came six months later.)

The United Nations had, of course, been aware of the rapidly deteriorating situation in Rwanda, and created the United Nations Assistance Mission for Rwanda (UNAMIR) after Melchior Ndadaye's assassination. However, UNAMIR lacked legal jurisdiction or a mandate to intervene with force when the genocide began to happen. Many columnists and academics found the entire exercise pointless, with the UN reduced to having such a "bystander" role (and in any event, their peacekeeping forces were completely overwhelmed).

According to documents later declassified and revealed in Britain's *Guardian* newspaper in March of 2004, Bill Clinton's administration knew that Rwanda was being "engulfed by genocide" in April of 1994, but "buried the information to justify its inaction," having already "decided not to intervene." Alison des Forges of Human Rights Watch fumed that the documents were "powerful proof that they knew" all along what was happening—and chose to do nothing. William Ferroggiaro of the National Security Archive confirmed that all members of the diplomatic and CIA/intelligence food chain had "provided timely information."

In all likelihood tragically misreading the reality of domestic politics in America, des Forges speculated that she thought Clinton "feared" that if the American public knew the truth, the public would "demand some sort of action, and they [Clinton's crew] didn't want to act." Des Forges was correct that the documents clearly indicated that Team Clinton knew what was going on and had decided not to act. But in reality, it seems far more likely that Clinton was probably "fearing" the exact opposite: that the conservatives who were out to get the Draft Dodger in Chief at any costs, that the Pat Buchanan/Gore Vidal style paleo-isolationists and the reflexively antiwar liberals, would all greet the Rwandan holocaust with a public shrug, so to speak. That it was terrible and unspeakable, yes—but that it was *also* none of our business, and certainly no place that was worth funneling thousands of American soldiers in to be killed or maimed. That Africa was a literal big muddy that could only bleed American forces out, never to achieve any real, lasting results. One can almost hear the thinking: *What strategic interest did America have in bloody Rwanda, after all? Why should my son or daughter have to go risk his or her life in some Third World hellhole nobody here cares about? Look at what had just happened in Somalia! If those colored people down in Africa want to go ape and kill each other, that doesn't mean that MY son or daughter should have to get killed defending them, too—does it?*

Clinton's harshest enemies on both the hard-right and extreme-left would have probably regarded Rwanda as, while tragic, just another tired contestant in Bubba's "enemy of the month club." Remember, this was at the height of the "Clinton Wars," as Sidney Blumenthal later rightly called them, over healthcare reform, gun control, gays in the military, the 1993 tax increase, NAFTA, and all the rest. The right wing noise machine was already sounding the alarm about "black helicopters" from the UN, about Clinton trying to establish some kind of one-world government, subservient to the Third World-coddling United Nations. Barring a direct threat to the United States, a full-on U.S. invasion of Rwanda (the only thing that would have probably stopped the killing) might have stretched the already-failing Congress and Senate of early 1994 past the breaking point, pushed the already boiling culture war melting pot into a total meltdown.

The other most epic foreign policy "fail" of the era—and one that would lead right towards 9/11—was Clinton's remorseless continuation of hard core sanctions against Saddam Hussein's Iraq, following the 1991 Gulf War and a (thankfully aborted) Saddam attempt to assassinate retired President Bush, Sr., in 1993. (Indeed, well before George W. Bush put the policy into lethal effect, "regime change" was a stated official goal of Clinton's Iraq policy.) Saddam mercilessly used what little resources and infrastructure were left within his country after the devastating 1991 war, to reward his loyalists, family, and military. When United Nations Ambassador Madeleine Albright (less than a year away from her promotion to Secretary of State) was asked by Leslie Stahl about this tragedy on *60 Minutes* in May of 1996, Stahl noted that some statistics (later disputed) claimed that around 500,000 children had died in Iraq after the imposition of sanctions, a figure "worse than Hiroshima." Ambassador Albright didn't flinch. "I think this is a very hard choice, but the price—we think the price is worth it," she infamously replied. (Albright later repeatedly and publicly said how much she regretted the statement—one that came to define North American and Western European callousness to the Middle Eastern and Muslim worlds, especially in light of America's later adventures under Bush II and Cheney).

Osama bin Laden must have also been watching that night, and he cited what he called "the greatest mass slaughter of children mankind has ever known" (the Jew-hating bin Laden probably couldn't have cared less about the victims of the Holocaust) as a principal motive for his later attacks. "You, the USA, together with the Saudi regime, are responsible for the shedding of the blood of these innocent [Iraqi] children." And Osama himself would soon be making his very own American newsmagazine TV debut.

Ignoring the Signs (or, Ready for Prime Time)

9/11 Commission member Jamie Gorelick told the History Channel that "the US government didn't really understand the threat [of Osama and al-Qaeda] until around 1997, 1998." That was all too true. But that didn't mean that there weren't any warning signs: the first 1993 WTC attack and Osama's approval of the "Black Hawk Down" shootings in Somalia being cases in point. Tragically, it's clear looking back that both Bill Clinton and George W. Bush demonstrated an almost willful defiance to face the facts.

By 1994, the CIA had given the Clinton White House a briefing calling Osama bin Laden and al-Qaeda, "The Ford Foundation of Sunni Islam," giving grants for terrorist projects around the world. "[Osama's name] seemed to be coming up everywhere!" said formidable Federal prosecutor Patrick Fitzgerald. By early 1995, Osama's training camps in Pakistan and the Sudan were, as the National Geographic Channel put it, "terrorist assembly lines." The following summer in 1996, Osama moved to Afghanistan, after the Clinton Administration successfully pressured the bloodthirsty Sudanese government to expel him. Meanwhile, original WTC attacker Ramsi Yousuf was finally caught by U.S. intelligence. But it was hardly a victory—Yousuf's capture alerted his mentor, 9/11 master-mind Khalid Sheik Mohammed, to go on the run. He headed straight for the safety of Osama's headquarters, to finish plotting what would become 9/11.

Finally, in the spring of 1998, Osama bin Laden considered himself "ready for prime time." He now spent most of his days commuting like a CEO or landlord, inspecting his various "properties" from 9 to 5, before going home to his wives and children at one of his many militia-guarded compounds. The only difference was that terror was his business, and business was booming. But Osama had just enough global leeway left to manage to get a *20/20* news crew, and ABC reporter John Miller, for the literal interview of a lifetime. The crew was whisked off to a tent somewhere in outer Afghanistan for a face-to-face with the man himself. Now, with the cameras rolling, Osama bin Laden declared war on the United States.

"We do not differentiate between those dressed in military uniforms and civilians. They are ALL targets," Osama announced. "We anticipate a black future for America ... if the present injustices continue." (These injustices included propping up corrupt pro–Western authoritarian regimes in Egypt and Saudi Arabia, sanctions on Iraq, and America's open-ended support of Israel.) If these situations continued, "it will inevitably move the battle to American soil." With Osama already an icon of intifada and jihad in the Middle East, ABC correspondent Miller rightly called the program Osama's "coming-out party to the United States."

Irish "Troubles" and Israeli Terror

For roughly a quarter century, through the 1970s, '80s, and early '90s, Northern Ireland had been a literal war zone, with what were euphemistically known as "The Troubles" between overwhelmingly Protestant and British-loyalist Union fighters, and Irish "Repub-licans," who were just as overwhelmingly Catholic and wanted political autonomy from Great Britain. The Troubles hit their all-time worst in the late '70s and early '80s, with the March 1979 car bombing of British war hero and Member of Parliament, Airey Neave (a mentor and best friend to Margaret Thatcher), and a spring 1981 hunger strike that killed IRA spokesman Bobby Sands and several others.

Conservative Party leader and soon-to-be Prime Minister Thatcher's eulogy for Neave was satirized in the Irish Republican Army newspaper *The Starry Plough*. "Airey Neave got a taste of his own medicine when the INLA pulled off the operation of the decade and blew him to bits…. The nauseous Margaret Thatcher sniveled on television that he was an 'incalculable loss.' And so he was—to the British ruling class!" After that kind of insult, a furious Lady Thatcher showed no mercy at all to the hunger strikers. "Despicable!" roared the Iron Lady. "And cowardly!" Lady Thatcher and her husband Denis were later targeted at a horrific hotel bombing, and a (fortunately unsuccessful) assassination attempt was even made on Queen Elizabeth, within just a few years of all this.

As staunchly allied with Margaret Thatcher's Britain as Ronald Reagan and George Bush, Sr., were, both presidents saw no point in inviting or creating an argument over Britain's treatment of Ireland, when far greater issues were at stake in winding down the Cold War. But now that all that was over, Bill Clinton (who, though Baptist and not Catholic, had primarily Irish ancestry, and was seeking the backing of many well-off Irish American Democrats and businessmen in 1992), made a priority of trying to negotiate a peaceful settlement, and bring both sides to the table in a "civilised" manner. Clinton reached out to both sides almost immediately, and told his State Department to make brokering some kind of peaceful solution into a top priority.

Clinton's efforts paid off with interest. By December of 1993, Thatcher's successor, Prime Minister John Major, issued the "Downing Street Declaration (of Peace)" jointly with Albert Reynolds, the head of the Irish Republic's government. In April of 1994, the IRA announced a temporary cease-fire, and by February of 1995, a "framework" for a peacefully united Ireland was published. At the end of November of that year, Clinton visited the epicenter of The Troubles, the Northern Ireland capitol of Belfast, and announced that terrorists were "yesterday's men," while ensuring both sides remained at the negotiating table. The peace process continued throughout 1996 and 1997, into Tony Blair's new Labour government in Britain. And on Good Friday, April 10th, 1998, a permanent agreement—brokered largely by Bill Clinton on continuous conference calls, running a sort of end-game interference between the two sides, was signed. The agreement was ratified by election in both Northern and Southern Ireland the following month. After nearly thirty years of battle, Bill Clinton had helped bring a stable government, if not full peace, to one of the First World's hottest hot spots.

However, as those greatest of world historians the ancient Greeks might have noted, as the Fates giveth, the Fates taketh away. As rhapsodic a relief as the peace settlement in Ireland was, just as shocking a setback would occur over the same time period, for the ultimate peace process—that of Israel and Palestine. On November 4, 1995, an assassin's gun took the life of 73-year-old Prime Minister Yitzhak Rabin of Israel, in Tel Aviv. The liberal Rabin had earlier been Prime Minister from 1974 to 1977 (succeeding a retiring 75-year-old Golda Meir, four years before her 1978 death), but his long-reigning Liberal Party had unexpectedly lost the Knesset (Parliamentary) elections in 1977 to the hard-line Likud Party leader, Menachem Begin. (Interestingly, it was Begin who co-signed the historic 1978–79 peace treaty between Israel and Anwar Sadat's Egypt, in a sort of Nixon-goes-to-China moment.)

Now finally returned to power, Rabin's Liberal Party was considerably more amenable to the idea of doing a peace deal, and perhaps even making some concessions to Palestinians and Muslims, than the Likud faction had been. Rabin had already signed off on the Oslo Accords, with President Clinton mediating the way between Rabin and Palestinian leader

Yassir Arafat, which guaranteed the Palestinians partial control over the Gaza Strip and West Bank (where numerous post–1967 Jewish settlements had taken place). In September of 1993, Rabin sent Arafat a letter officially recognizing the Palestinian Liberation Organization as a legitimate form of authority. Clinton pressed on, stimulating Rabin and Jordan's King Hussein to come together for a sort of "sequel" in 1994, with the Israel-Jordan Peace Treaty.

While both Rabin and Arafat would receive a Nobel Prize for these achievements, hard-liners on both sides of the Israeli/Palestine fence were outraged. What was most depressing about Rabin's assassination was that it *hadn't* been carried out by some anti–Zionist Palestinian or Iranian terrorist, some jihad-spouting mouthpiece of Saddam or Arafat or Osama. No, Rabin had been murdered by a religiously fanatical, Jewish Israeli hard-liner named Yigal Amir, whose main intent was to sabotage any peace process or settlement with (let alone any concessions to) the Palestinians and Islamists. In other words, he'd been killed by an "enemy within."

England Swings and China Opens

No sooner had Bill Clinton begun his second term than he received what was possibly the best news from Britain that he'd had since the start of the Irish Peace Accords. When Labour Party leader Tony Blair was elected Prime Minister that spring, Bill and Hillary finally had an almost equivalent "partner in power." Blair was Bill Clinton's closest political corollary outside the U.S.—in many ways, closer to Clinton in style and ideology than Clinton was even to many of his own fellow Democrats. The youthful, athletic, media-hip, and handsome Blair had ascended to the top of the Labour Party pyramid by highlighting the need to adjust to post–Thatcher Britain. Blair forced Labour to accept the fact that, whether one liked it or not, many if not most of Margaret Thatcher's conservative reforms would be a permanent part of English society for the forseeable future. It was a perfect mirror for Bill Clinton and the neoliberal columnists' mission. Just as social liberals wanted the hard core cultural right to accept that *Roe vs. Wade* and gay rights and feminism were here to stay, Clinton and the neoliberals wanted liberal Democrats to accept that most of the economic changes and deregulations that Reagan and Bush Sr., had forced through back in the 1980s were now settled into permanent law. Like it or not.

Dovetailing perfectly with the neoliberal theme of the '90s, the other top tune on the charts was finally folding the People's Republic of China into the free-trade landscape. Passionately committed to global free trade as a cornerstone of the New Economy, Clinton sent U.S. Trade Representative Charlene Barshefsky to Beijing in 1999 to begin serious negotiations to allow China full status in the World Trade Organization that Clinton was already the veritable mascot for—despite China's notorious human-rights abuses and dreadful pollution and worker conditions. Clinton had been meeting with top Chinese leaders ever since the beginning of his government, and had stepped up his economic diplomacy every year (including involving Al Gore in an embarrassing scandal revolving around a Buddhist temple on the border of Orange County, with strong connections to Chinese governmental leaders). He met with Chinese President Jiang Zemin at a summit in October of 1997, where the goals were forthright. World Trade admission was the name, and the

New Economy was the game. Noting that it had been barely a decade since the notorious Tiananmen Square crackdowns on Chinese students and youth demanding freedom of speech, Democrat Congressional royalty Nancy Pelosi roared (opposing the Clinton deal every step of the way), "More people today are [in political prison] than at any time since the [1966–76] Cultural Revolution!"

Pelosi's cries fell on deaf ears. In May of 2000—with votes that came mostly from the Republican majority in the Congress and Senate, and despite passionate opposition from both labor and peacenik Democrats (according to *The New York Times,* only 73 out of 211 Democratic congressmen had voted in favor; in other words, two-thirds of the Democrats had *opposed* him)—Clinton lifted the curtain on his crowning achievement: free trade normalization with China, with China to be successfully admitted to the World Trade Organization by no later than December of 2001. The China victory happened just days after Clinton had gone to Vietnam, on the 25th anniversary of the fall of Saigon to Communist forces, five years after he had normalized relations with the communist Republic of Vietnam in 1995. Cultural and military conservatives on cable and talk radio hit the roof. Dodging the draft and being an anti-war hippie wasn't enough for him, scolded Clinton's working-class critics. Now he had to make sure that the Commies had yet another victory (with a July 2000 Bi-lateral Trade Pact frosting the cake)—even if it meant the prospect of more possible outsourcing, too.

Wagging the Dog (or Collateral Damage)

Yitzhak Rabin's violent death in late 1995 shook the world, from North America and Western Europe to the entire Middle East. Few things so coldly demonstrated just how deep the mistrust, rebellion, and hate had grown on both sides. To his credit, Bill Clinton was determined that the Israeli peace process would continue, that Rabin's killer would not succeed in derailing things, that his death would not be in vain. One of Clinton's top foreign-policy priorities, if not his very top after Slobodan Milosevic was deposed (and later captured), was to bring together Israel and Palestine to discuss a final permanent settlement and/or two state solution. After nearly five years of intense negotiations with Yassir Arafat and Rabin's successors, Benjamin "Bibi" Netanyahu and Ehud Barak, the impossible was finally starting to happen, in the very last weeks and days of the Clinton administration. But as President Clinton and his teams of diplomats were nervously counting down the remaining minutes before time ran out, another Middle Eastern figure was running down a different kind of clock with his team. A countdown … to oblivion. What makes this part of the story so tragic is that, while he was certainly not expecting anything near what 9/11 turned out to be, Bill Clinton knew there was real danger ahead, too—but he felt that his hands were tied. And just what was it that had tied his hands?

It was the Culture War, stupid. Around the same time as Osama's horrifying *20/20* segment in 1998, the CIA and military went through a "dress rehearsal" of a plan to kidnap Osama and spirit him away to a location under American control. But satellite footage of Osama's latest hiding place revealed a swing set and playground, clearly indicating that Osama had surrounded himself with small children, perhaps to use as human shields in case of attempted capture. Since either an air strike or Scud missile/drone-targeted assassination, or a ground invasion and capture, were the only feasible ways to get him in hostile Afghanistan, the CIA and the Clinton administration concluded that the U.S. collaterally murdering small Muslim children was too great a risk. Just the image we needed in the Muslim world, especially with the furore over mass deaths due to sanctions. The last thing that Bill Clinton wanted on his record (especially after the 1993 Waco disaster that already cost so many innocent children their lives here at home) was to become an international "baby killer" with CIA and Special Ops snipers collaterally machine-gunning or blowing up tiny tots to get Osama. Rush, Bill-O, Pat Buchanan, Ann Coulter, Oliver North—why, they would have a field day! And if anything could have convinced the antiwar, 1960s-style Left to bail on Clinton during the coming impeachment battle, that would have been it!

In August of 1998—just after his "coming-out party" on *20/20*—Osama sent al-Qaeda hit men to bomb the U.S. embassy in Nairobi, Kenya. The same day, over in Dar Es-Salaam, Tanzania, another bomb smashed the U.S. embassy there to bits. Over 200 people total were murdered.

After the embassy attacks, President Clinton finally began bombing suspected terrorist installations in both countries. But by then, the Monica Lewinsky scandal was at its frenzied apex. Both right-wing voices out to impeach Clinton for his "sexual immorality," and '60s-style lefties who were already sick of Clinton's "keen militarist" police actions, now accused Clinton of cynically playing a game of Wag the Dog. They said that the Osama strikes were little more than a rally round-the-flag distraction to take people's minds off of Clinton's sex scandal. Bill Clinton couldn't afford alienating the Republicans any more than he already had, and he needed the entire American Left united that summer and fall to protect him against the threat of impeachment.

By early 1999, with the impeachment trial winding down, Bill Clinton finally authorized lethal force against Osama. However, the best chance to get him would have still resulted in an estimated 200 or more civilian casualties. Osama was also seen pallin' around with a crown prince from the United Arab Emirates, which had a relatively good relationship with the United States. "They decided not to shoot because it might have killed the Arab prince. Well, the world is lousy with Arab princes!" laughed former CIA bin Laden unit head Michael Scheuer. Having dodged these bullets, a smug and invincible-seeming Osama (now probably more convinced than ever that the unseen hand of Allah was protecting him) devoted himself full-time to overseeing what he and Khalid Sheik Mohammed now called "The Planes Operation."

He and KSM swore a group of young "muscle hijackers" and pilots-in-training, headed by young engineer Mohammed Atta, to a loyalty oath, and began arranging funds for flight training in the USA. Osama and KSM spent the rest of 1999 training the terror crews, including chief hijacker Atta, a young Egyptian engineer who'd studied in Hamburg (and thereby spoke German and English) whom they had cherry-picked in 1998. The hijackers-to-be received detailed lessons on decadent American culture, on how to go stealth and blend in with the crowd, on how best to live in the belly of the American beast. By the early summer of 2000, Atta and several of his better-educated top lieutenants had arrived in the U.S. for airline pilot training in Florida, while the "muscle hijackers" were being put through one of Osama's many boot camps back home.

Just one month before the Bush vs. Gore election, on October 12, 2000, Osama bin Laden sent President Clinton a very special thank-you note for sparing his life a year or two before. That day, two men piloting what appeared to be a small fiberglass supply boat sidled up alongside the naval ship the USS *Cole* in Yemen, waving a friendly hello to the sailors, who waved back. The "supply boat" crew bashfully apologized for getting too close, and put on a show of trying to turn things around. An instant later, an earth-shattering explosion destroyed the U.S. destroyer, as hundreds of pounds of explosives on the small dinghy ignited, blowing a mammoth charcoal hole in the battleship's gray hull. Seventeen USS *Cole* crewmen died at the scene, and 40 more were injured. The gigantic ship itself was almost sunk.

President Clinton went on TV and promised to "hold the perpetrators accountable." But with his Administration now in the 59th minute of the 11th hour, Clinton was all talk and no action. Once again, Bill Clinton held back, even though it was obvious that Osama was guilty. After all of the media's 1998 "wag the dog" trash-talk, the newscasters and columnists might now accuse him of trying to upstage both Al Gore and George W. Bush out of sheer Clintonian ego, or planning to somehow alter the coming election (which of course had his own vice president on the ticket).

The Last Peace Song

At least this time (as opposed to chickening out during the self-inflicted wound of Monicagate) there was a morally defensible reason for why Clinton refused to strike back. Just before the attack, in July of 2000, Clinton finally held a weeks-long Camp David Summit with Israel's Ehud Barak and Palestinian topper Yasser Arafat, trying to hammer out a roadmap to a two-state solution. After Clinton's monumental success brokering the peace deal in Ireland, somehow even this most impossible-seeming of dreams seemed possible. Clinton hoped that it would be his crowning foreign policy achievement before leaving office. Still traumatized by the murder of his old ally Yitzhak Rabin (Rabin's widow, Leah, would soon die of cancer at the age of 72, in November of 2000), Clinton threw everything he had into trying to broker at least some kind of basic roadmap or framework at Camp David with Arafat and Barak. But every time, according to Clinton, Arafat kept moving the bar, changing the rules, finding an excuse not to sign....

Finally, Arafat came out with it. "His people" would simply never accept a negotiated peace with the Jews of Israel. Oh some of them, indeed maybe *most* of them, would. But look what happens to any A-list Islamic leader who overtly makes peace with Israel or the Jews. (Just ask the Shah of Iran or Anwar Sadat ... at the cemetery!) If Arafat signed off on the deal, he'd be as good as signing his own death warrant. "You are a great man," Arafat tried to console Clinton. But Bubba was having none of it. Livid with betrayal, Clinton snarled back at Arafat, "No, I am a colossal failure—and you have made me one!!"

On July 25th, 2000, the Camp David effort ended without an agreement. The USS *Cole* disaster happened less than 90 days later. And just before the *Cole* attack, right-wing Likud Party leader Ariel Sharon staged a deliberately provocative visit to the Temple Mount, the holiest site in the world to Jews and the third-holiest site in Islam. The decorated, retired Israeli Army warrior promised that the site would always remain under Jewish control, in a blatant attempt to undermine "liberal" Ehud Barak for talking peace with Arafat to begin with. Unsurprisingly, riots broke out soon afterwards.

Now, if Clinton had attacked or killed Osama on the spot, what with bin Laden's enormous following in the Middle Eastern and Islamic worlds, Clinton could probably kiss any chance of good-faith negotiations with the Palestinians goodbye—as well as ruining it for either Al Gore or George W. Bush before their administrations even began. So instead, he and his foreign policy team began drawing up detailed plans and strategies for the next administration, mapping out how and why to nail bin Laden. (Plans which were sadly all but thrown in the trash initially by the incoming Bush government—especially by Bush's new Attorney General John Ashcroft, handpicked by Karl Rove as a payoff to the cultural right, who was preoccupied with homegrown moral issues like drugs, Internet porn, and whatnot before 9/11.)

If President Clinton felt like a "failure" after this, one can only guess what Prime Minister Ehud Barak felt like, when he too returned home empty-handed. By early 2001, Barak was booted out in favor of aging Israeli warrior Ariel Sharon, who would run an iron-fisted foreign policy that would often go beyond even the excesses of the Bush II crew, until Sharon became incapacitated by a massive stroke five years later. It was sadly ironic that after the solid successes in Ireland, Haiti, Bosnia, and the end of the Cold War and the first Iraq War, that the 1990s would end with this missed opportunity.

And speaking of missed opportunities: By August of 2001, there had been so much unforgivable inaction from both the recently departed Clinton and the newly arrived Bush crews (especially when it came to striking the head of the al-Qaeda snake), that what was about to happen next was probably inevitable. Still, that same month, Condoleezza Rice and other top-level Bush foreign policy chieftains were treated to a classified intelligence report with the not-very-ambiguous title "BIN LADEN DETERMINED TO ATTACK WITHIN THE U.S." Yet not even *that* red-alert warning was enough to make Osama *the* Number One priority in Washington. (When President Bush was given the notorious report from central intelligence, while he was summering down at his ranch in Texas, he was later quoted by Ron Suskind as having dismissed the delivery courier with, "Okay—you've covered your ass now.")

"I don't think anyone who worked on this problem expected anything less than what happened on 9/11," said Clinton-era CIA bin Laden unit chief Michael Scheuer in a 2006 National Geographic documentary. "If it surprised the policymakers, then shame on them!" "This is Osama bin Laden's legacy," added Abdel Bari Atwan, the editor-in-chief of Al-Quds Al-Arabi news services, in the same Nat Geo documentary. "The man who dared to say to the Americans, 'You interfere in our business, we will interfere in *your* business. You are killing *our* people—I am killing *your* people!'"

Looking back after the fact, a virtual victory garden of conspiracy theories arose, suggesting that Bush, Cheney, and company suspected or knew that bin Laden was about to strike—and instead of moving to stop it, allowed him to go forward as a pretext for global war and clamping down at home. Others even thought that Bush and Cheney had brought down the towers themselves (which would have taken some doing indeed, since the hijackers were already well at work on what would be called the "Planes Operation" way *before* Bush or Cheney got elected). Yet as morally offensive and treasonous as it would be if those things had been actually true, in many ways the arrogance and petty-mindedness of much of Bush II's Washington was as shocking as any spooky conspiracy theory. As Bush's own reaction indicated, the Osama attack report was greeted with what was essentially a bureaucratic shrug. *Well, of course Osama would LIKE to strike inside America—if only he could! But not even the Nazis and Communists had been able to seriously strike within the U.S. homeland. Who does Osama bin Laden think he is, anyway? Him and what army?* After all, didn't Osama know that we were living at the "End of History?"

The Project for a New American Century

These conspiracy theories were sadly given just enough of a patina of credence by a soon-to-be notorious document produced by an ad hoc think tank founded in the spring of 1997 by neoconservative royalty Bill Kristol and Robert Kagan. Like a mean high school or college athletics coach, they felt that Clinton-era America had gotten *soft*, that its foreign policy lacked a "compelling vision." They advocated a "more elevated vision of America's international role" to ensure a stance of "benevolent global hegemony."

So far, it sounded just like Bill Clinton and Madeleine Albright. But the Project was largely put together because Kristol and company felt that the Republicans had no coherent strategy with which to *criticize* the enemy Clinton, no bible to build their own foreign policy prescriptions on. Except of course, for the Pat Buchanan-style "isolationist" conservatives, and the old World War II and Korea veterans who were already disgusted with all of Clinton's United Nations errands-running with soldiers their grandchildren's ages—so unlike their own morally crystal-clear battles against Nazi Germany and the Iron Curtain.

To Washingtonians in the know, the Project's opening feel-good phrases were as obvious a coded appeal as a political ad starring Willie Horton or O.J. Simpson. The red meat came when the Project called for America to put its foot down hard, as the "world's preeminent power"—one that should intervene practically at will in other countries' affairs if need be, to actively "shape" situations directly "favorable to American principles and interests." The founding statement was signed by a veritable Who's Who of neoconservative and right-wing interventionist Washington society, many of whom would go on to serve at the highest levels in the Bush II government. (Signatories included Donald Rumsfeld, former Vice President Dan Quayle and future VP Dick Cheney, *End of History* academic Francis Fukuyama, Midge Decter and Norman Podhoretz, Scooter Libby, and Paul Wolfowitz.) The Project was seen by its opponents as a thinly disguised mandate for America to essentially act as Great Britain and France did at the turn of the previous century: as an unabashed global empire, one that would take an overseer's role in virtually all the major financial, oil, and food economies of the world. One that would not allow ANY potential challenge to its economic or pop-cultural and technological dominance to stand, and that would remorselessly crush any country or entity that tried to play the economic or military match game with the good ole U.S. of A.

As such, the Project became a conspiracy theorist's wet dream, especially in light of the 9/11 attacks and Bush-Cheney's reaction to them. The money quote that proved to be a veritable smoking gun for so-called "9/11 Truthers" (who believed that Bush and Cheney actively took part in September 11th), was that the Project acknowledged that the world-bending "transformations" of American policy that it was calling for, even demanding, were not likely to come without a great deal of public resistance. Unless there was, and we quote: *"some catastrophic and catalyzing event—like a new Pearl Harbor."*

However, this was no surprise to academics like Phillip Hammond, who felt that this was "exactly what one would expect" neo-con interventionists to believe. As *New Republic* stalwart Leon Wieseltier said in the unambiguous title of a later Obama-era essay, to both neoliberal humanitarians and neoconservatives alike, the post Cold War default mode had become "WE INTERVENE." Once again, right wing isolationists and quote-unquote 'paleo-conservatives' (who often held the most ultraconservative stances on women, gays, and racial minorities) had more in common with the peace-song set and ultra-liberal pacifists, than either the Left had with neoliberal, nation-building Democrats, or the mind-your-own-global-business Right had with neoconservative, global-empire Republicans.

*   *   *

Leave it to the odious Osama bin Laden to have the last word on America's 1990s foreign policy, which he literally *did have* on the September day that almost all historians and journalists agree that the '90s *really* ended. "We love death. The U.S. loves life. That is the big difference between us." Or, as 9/11 Commission Chairman Thomas Kean sadly eulogized, the 9/11 attacks (and indeed much of what preceded them) represented "a failure of policy, management, capability—and above all, a failure of imagination."

No, there was no "holiday from history" during the 1990s, as the neoconservatives who fumed that Bill Clinton hadn't gone far enough, hadn't been assertive and interventionist *enough*, called that decade. As we've just seen, the 1990s were jam-packed with round-the-clock foreign policy and global game changes; indeed, this chapter only scratches the surface. But it was that deluded thinking—that Clinton was both a hippie and a militarist, that we were acting as though were on a "holiday" where history had "ended" (while we were actually intervening from Africa to Asia to the former Soviet states to Israel and Iraq and Ireland on a continuous basis), that we were doing both too much and not enough at one and the same time … it was that bipolar mentality that made the real foreign policy successes of the '90s that much more impressive, and the real failures and missed opportunities of the '90s that much more tragic.

9

Identity Politics

Standing in the middle of the road is most dangerous. You get knocked down by the traffic from both sides.

—*Margaret Thatcher*

"Can't we all just get along?"

—*Rodney King*

In the 1971 cult classic *Harold & Maude,* one of the most memorable scenes saw the unlikely couple of a superficially suicidal 20-year-old man and a vivacious 80-year-old woman in a field of sunflowers and daisies. (A perfect cine-metaphor for the movie that defined the end of the "flower power" era.) What's so special about the flowers, Harold wonders? They're all alike!

"Oh, but they're *not!*" Maude protests. Some grow to the left, some grow to the right, some have petals torn off, some are fat, some are thin… "You know, Harold," Maude muses. "I feel that much of the world's sorrow comes from people who are *this*" (she indicates an individual flower) "and yet, allow themselves to be treated as *that*" (she sweeps her hand over the faceless, "all alike" field).

For all the group activism and sit-ins and "movements," especially as the Vietnam and civil rights eras began to wind down, the 1970s and early '80s were all about celebrating the beauty of the Individual. Not for nothing did Tom Wolfe call the '70s and '80s the "ME Decades." David Frum likewise called them the "Let's Talk About Me!" society, noting the trendy growth of "encounter" groups, psychoanalysis, and things like EST and Scientology. Mass audiences lined up to watch idiosyncratic, personalized films by only in-the-'70s directors like Robert Altman, Robert Downey, Sr., Bert Rafelson, and *Harold & Maude's* own Hal Ashby, when they weren't devouring existentialist novels about "alienated" loners and dissatisfied suburbanites.

Top-rated TV shows featured colorful and charismatic individualist detectives like Columbo, Kojak, and Jim Rockford. And by decade's end, upper-middle-class white families were trying to sort out the meaning of their lives, in movies and TV shows like *Family, Ordinary People, Kramer vs. Kramer,* and the start of *Knots Landing.* Variety and game shows featured lovable lost-soul types like Tiny Tim, Truman Capote, Monti Rock III, Gilbert O'Sullivan, Joey Heatherton, Andy Gibb, Rip Taylor, and Paul Lynde. Even children's shows like *Sesame Street, Mister Rogers,* and *Captain Kangaroo* constantly reminded self-esteem-deprived youngsters that "You're Special!" and "Everything I Am Is Me (Totally Terrific!)" and that they were "Free to Be You and Me!" in catchy songs. A 1979 book by educational psychologist Betty Osman on teaching children with *Learning Disabilities* cautioned that parents and teachers must think of a child with ADHD, autism or Aspergers, or dyslexia as "a[n individual] child with a learning difference first," NOT a "disability with a child attached." People were encouraged to "look beyond" allegedly superficial constructs like Labels and Skin Color, and to "evolve" to a more personalized understanding of things and other people. Books, Broadway plays, and TV shows from *Hair* to *Company,* from *I'm OK ... You're OK!* to *Jonathan Livingston Seagull,* and from *Sesame Street* to *Sonny & Cher* rhapsodized about a near future where we would all "live in harmony" with one another.

But as African American comedy legend Flip Wilson's sassy black honey child Sapphire might have retorted, "That's easy fo' YOU to say, honey!" What about the people—no matter how nice, polite, life-affirming, brilliant, and even "special" they were as individuals—who would always be judged first and foremost as being a faceless What, not an individual Who. You know who we're talking about: The "Faggots." The "Wetbacks." The "Spics." The "Niggers." Judged—and often hated for it. And what good was there in being "colorblind" anyway—if "colored" people were thereby prevented from proudly expressing their diversity and differences? What good was there in being admitted to the country club, if the price of admission was having to constantly pretend that you and your family had the exact same common culture as white America, as straight heterosexual America, as native English-speaking America? That you really were "just the same" as everyone else—and nothing more?

Diversity Daze

By the 1980s and '90s, most colleges were already offering "ethnic studies" programs. First were Afro American and Womens' Studies. They were soon followed in the ACT UP era of AIDS activism and visibility by Queer Theory programs. (And all were predictably vilified as a campy, pretentious, and useless waste of money, if not much worse, by movement conservatives.) School systems were already requiring social science textbooks from kindergarten through high school to go out of their way to feature and sidebar the accomplishments of both specific individuals of color and pioneering women, as well as to highlight them in the context of what those groups had accomplished against all odds. By 1983, even conservative Ronald Reagan had signed into law the Martin Luther King holiday in January, with February decreed Black History Month. And by the late '90s, in honor of the June 1969 Stonewall rebellion, there would be a Gay Pride Month added to the calendar.

While all of this was laudable and good, the end result was to get people to think of themselves and to derive their pride from whatever racial or gender *group* they belonged to. The real message of 1990s-style "Diversity" celebrations was NOT a '70s-style celebration of the diversity and uniqueness of *individual human beings*—but a celebration of *specifically defined groups.* And how the individuals assigned by race, gender/preference, or class to those groups should get out from their own narrow-focused selves, and celebrate the larger "team" that they found themselves playing on. To derive your self-worth from your larger *group's* accomplishments and identity—*not* just your own individual talents and personality. To not allow yourself to be "white-washed" or "straight-washed."

Art Imitates Life

The same dynamics were at play in the 1990s cries to cut funding for the National Endowment for the Arts, which had spent the latter Reagan and George Bush, Sr., era giving out funding for (among other projects) AIDS-era gay artists who were making deliberately S&M tinged photos and paintings to vent their rage at the Religious Right, hypocrisy, and homophobia. (This reached its all-time low with the revoltingly hateful "Piss Christ"—a crucifix in a bottle of urine.) Not long after, PBS, which had always tilted to the left (at least in conservative eyes) ran an Olympia Dukakis-starring, A-list miniseries of gay novelist Armistead Maupin's *Tales of the City* chronicles. The new Newt Gingrich Congress immediately called for PBS and NEA funding to be cut, and cut again.

Shrieks and cries of "Censorship!" and "McCarthyism," of "Thought Police" and "Fascism" rose up from Hollywood, Broadway, and the political left. They had a point, in that this wasn't about money, but about persecuting and smothering left-of-center ideology and expression. Bemused Midwestern liberal Thomas Frank recalled the 1990s NEA and PBS wars in his *What's the Matter with Kansas,* where he laughed that "some artist decides to shock the hicks by dunking Christ in urine," and all of a sudden that must mean that all federal support of the arts and humanities had to end. Yet in that very sentence, Frank gave away the game: the whole point of that kind of so-called art *was* indeed, to "shock the hicks." That was it. So who can blame those "hicks" for being shocked, for being livid— *when the artist had deliberately intended that.* Who can blame them for being angry that their hard-earned tax dollars were being spent to subsidize such "free expression," when it was designed to *provoke* their anger in the first place?

While it may be hard for those of us who support artistic freedom and free speech to concede that maybe the Bill O'Reillys and Rush Limbaughs of the world had a point, let's put the shoe on the other foot. After all, let's say that your tax dollars were being spent on a non-ironic mural of grinning and apron-wearing black "pickaninnies" and mammies? Of fish-eyed, hysterical yentas and fat, cigar-waving Jewish businessmen demanding a pound of flesh? Or how about one depicting lazy, sombrero-sleeping Latinos and woo-wooing, war-hooped cartoon Native Americans? Or buck-toothed, "so sorry pr-ease!" Asians with coke-bottle glasses? No doubt the liberal community would be up in arms—as well they should be.

So why the double standard? If it would be outrageous to spend tax money on gutter racism or anti–Semitism—then how was it somehow OK, if not *tres sophistique,* to spend tax dollars on "art" that was specifically designed to offend conservative Christians? The reason was, of course, because conservative Christians were largely regarded as superstitious, unscientific, uneducated, unsophisticated, prudish, intolerant, bigoted small-town "hicks" who *deserved* hip mockery, unlike the *truly* oppressed politically correct identity groups.

As the esteemed critics and authors Richard Schickel and the late William A. Henry III have noted, the art and practice of criticism, curatorship, and connoisseurship both implies (and perhaps even *requires*) a strong sense of intellectual "elitism" and outright snobbery—a sense that my educated, cultured values ARE in fact superior to yours, whether you want to agree with me or not. And that I *should* enjoy a sort of "judicial review" right-of-way in calling the cultural shots, in being an arbiter and decision-maker. And yep—that means that *you'll have to pay for it,* too! Just like the pro-lifers have to pay for the pro-abortion lesbian judge's six-figure salary, just like the Vietnam-era peacenik still has to pay for Henry Kissinger and Dick Cheney's gold-plated retirements. Tough cookies, Buster!

And this, *this* dynamic was what all of the players on both sides understood deep down, but nobody (outside of perhaps Ann Coulter or Bill O'Reilly) wanted to say out loud. That all these hyped-up "censorship" controversies were really coded battles about socio-educational *class* and "I'm smarter than you are" intellectual snobbery. About the authority of "gatekeepers" and "arbiters" in a fast-democratizing, soon-to-be Internet-besieged critical culture.

Speaking in Code

Another reason that Identity Politics and "censorship" were such sexy stories in the '90s was because of the *reductio ad absurdum* arguments that served to publicize both extremes in the culture war. For example, Lani Guinier was a prominent African American intellectual who was bigoted against both white people in general and black Republicans specifically, while the Black Muslim Rev. Louis Farrakhan was virulently anti–Semitic. Ergo, that "proves" that ALL black liberals are hatemongers and reverse-racists—right, Rush and Ann?

Pat Buchanan, Lee Atwater, and Karl Rove blatantly used "law and order," "war on drugs," and fear of "crime" as code words for putting urban black and brown people in their so-called place, back during the heyday of the Southern Strategy. So that must mean that if a 75-year-old widowed white granny tells her congressman or senator how terrified she is to walk to her Town Car at night—well, we all *know* what the old bitch *really* means, don't we? She's just a code-speaking racist—isn't she, Professor Guinier and the Reverend Farrakhan?

An academic feminist and "Womyns' Studies" Professor would give one of her "ovulars" (instead of semin-ars, you know) where she described marriage as rape, child-rearing and homemaking as slavery, and opined that all women were lesbians at heart. Count on it to be front-headline on *The Bill O'Reilly Show* as smoking-gun proof of how nutty and anti-family ALL feminists were. A shirtless Queer Theory professor or tattooed ACT UP activist would go to a gay pride parade wearing nothing but ass-less chaps or a black Speedo thong, or dressed as a rosary-swinging Mother Superior, carrying a picket sign that announced "GOD is GAY!" Guess what's gonna be the lead story on *The 700 Club* or *John Hagee Today*—as proof of how degenerate and pedophilic and predatory ALL gay people are.

In his later book *Pity the Billionaire,* Thomas Frank quoted reactionary tax-cutter Grover Norquist as saying to the effect that, just between you and me, he almost *liked* it when some transgressive artist decided to shock the hicks with anti–Christian art, or when PBS broadcast some Queer-radical Larry Kramer play or a science documentary that mocked Christianity, or whatever. Because that discredited the public-taxpayer funding of these things, *which was Norquist's real goal all along.* A lovely fountain outside the library or museum, or public statues of John F. Kennedy and Ronald Reagan, wouldn't incite anyone to call for cuts in government subsidies to artists. But "Piss Christ" and Robert Map-plethorpe photos sure would! Most conservatives had no problem with Big Bird, Elmo,

Barney, and Mister Rogers during the week, and reruns of Lawrence Welk and Ed Sullivan, old Brit-coms, and *Masterpiece Theatre* showcases on the weekends. But envelope-pushing gay indie films, or lefty Bill Moyers/Noam Chomsky interview programs, would have them attacking their local PBS stations with the surgical shears—*which is what people like Norquist wanted in the first place.*

To briefly recap, back in the idealistic, pop-psychology '70s, it was the crew-cut, reactionary, Nixon-voting, 1950s leftovers who still clung to the ideals of Cold War "conformity." It was the liberals and ACLU-types who were all about celebrating individual freedom— the right of a woman over her own body and career, the right of a man to be with another man if he wanted, the right of an Andy Warhol or Yoko Ono to express themselves artistically, the right to smoke pot or take cocaine if you wanted. It was the grim-faced Robert Borks, Ronald Reagans, and G. Gordon Liddys who wanted to push everyone back in line, to acting just like one of the herd. During the sunshiney "do your own thing" era of disco dancing, self-enlightenment, and *The Dating Game,* liberals could afford to blithely celebrate the beauty of individuality—because the momentum, the cultural undercurrent, still seemed to be with them.

Not so after 12 years of Reagan/Bush. Helped along by iconic 1980s movies and TV shows like *Wall Street* ("Greed is good … it clarifies, it sets things right!"), *Dallas* ("Power ain't somethin' that's *given* to you, boy—real power is somethin' you TAKE!"), and *thirtysomething* ("What about MYYY needs, Michael?"), focusing on the Individual had now morphed from being a cheerful celebration of life into looking like "code" for the most greedily self-centered Ayn Rand or Milton Friedman fantasies.

Indeed, the worst examples of "political correctness" and the campiest excesses of academia came largely *in direct reaction against* the Reagan/Bush era. Energized black firebrands like Jesse Jackson, Al Sharpton, Henry Louis Gates, and Kweisi Mfume, and AIDS-activist writers like Larry Kramer and Tony Kushner, led the opposition to the Reagan/Bush era's mainstreaming and acceptance of fire-breathing culture warriors like Jesse Helms, Pat Robertson, Rush Limbaugh, Robert Bork, Pat Buchanan, the Moral Majority, the Christian Coalition, Focus on the Family, and the like. Indeed, a perfect example of this cultural plate-shift was an African American law professor who published his first book in 1995, called *Dreams from My Father.* His name was Barack Obama.

Andrew Sullivan picks it up from here. In 2012, Sully noted how much President Obama had in common with the gay community, in that almost all gay people are born into straight families, but then have to break away from them to discover their own kind and their own separate culture. As a black child who grew up first with his white mother and Indonesian stepfather, and then in Hawaii with his white grandparents (where the dominant racial conflict, if any, was between Polynesian and Asian natives vs. white "haoles")—Obama as a teenager and young adult "had to discover his [culturally] black identity." Indeed, most of Obama's memoir regards his journey of having to conform to and embrace the richness, wisdom, and flavor of African American culture, in order to function effectively as a communicating, relatable black politician. In other words, the lesson young "Barry" Obama learned was that he needed to conform to and celebrate the accomplishments of the larger *group* that he found himself a part of—*on the GROUP'S terms, not on his own*—before he had any right to expect that very oppressed and courageous group to indulge and celebrate his own beautiful individuality.

The roles were now well and truly reversed. When Kennedy-era Democrat historian Arthur Schlesinger published a book in 1991 called *The Disuniting of America*, attacking things like "Afrocentrism" and Latinos who refused to learn English, the novelist Ishmael Reed compared liberal icon Schlesinger to white supremacist leader David Duke. Harvard's Henry Louis Gates said that Schlesinger's book was nothing less than a call for minstrel-like "cultural white-face." Three years later, just in time for the "Republican Revolution," sociologist Charles Murray (and his recently deceased colleague, Richard Hernstein) found himself temporarily elevated to the kind of front-cover and TV newsmagazine superstardom of a Madonna or Julia Roberts, when he published *The Bell Curve,* a grotesque bestseller which argued for genetic and racially based differences in human intelligence. (Naturally, to the detriment of the "darker" races.) All this proved once again that Alanis Morrisette didn't christen the 1990s the "Isn't It Ironic" era for nothing. *The Bell Curve* was published at the very height of academic demands for cultural separatism and for maintaining separate and "unassimilated" racial identities. Enemies of the book who quite rightly wanted to debunk the gutter racism of it were also forced to argue that yes, people *were* all scientifically just alike, and that there were no *real* genetic or objective differences among us—while at the same time making the demand that people form their identities based around racial and sexual identity group-pride above all else.

One of the reasons for this renewed emphasis on team-playing, identity politics, and groupthink was that there was still no other way to fight to maintain (what should *always* have been) one's "individual" rights to wholeness, without first joining a movement for strength in numbers. How could African Americans and Latinos have stood their ground or protected their hard-won gains against high-powered reactionaries like Newt Gingrich, Tom DeLay, Pat Buchanan, or Dick Cheney, without standing tall by standing together as a group, and voting in bloc-like numbers for the Party, rather than for the Person? How could national healthcare or educational reform ever work without some degree of high-handed "mandating" from above? And just look at the AIDS crisis of the '80s and '90s. How could the gay community have even *survived* if everyone in it had just kept blithely going about their self-centered, "individual" lives and affairs?

The 1990s era of Political Correctness and college campus "speech codes" was when we had to re-learn the lesson that David Fisher succinctly summed up in an early episode of *Six Feet Under,* aired the summer when the '90s era finally came to its close, just before the 9/11 attacks in 2001. "You didn't make the choice [to be gay or straight]—God made the choice for you!" And a later president named Barack Obama didn't choose to be a black male in America, with all the wonderful, and at times ominous, cultural baggage that entailed. God had made that choice for him. Now, *their* only choices were to show team-player loyalty and embracing support to their larger groups—or to "self-hatingly" diss and distance themselves from them.

North and South: Book II

A famous joke of Ronald Reagan went, "The most terrifying words in the English language are, 'I'm from the Government, and I'm here to help!'" A decade or so before that, Reagan's fellow Western-conservative icon Barry Goldwater warned liberals, "Remember—

the government that's big enough to give you everything you want, is also the government that's big enough to take it all away."

Even all these years later, those words are still a whiplash rebuke to the ears of liberals and progressives. Yet while nobody likes government red tape or paying taxes, one of the great mysteries of the late 20th century culture wars is how the American middle class's long love affair with a patriarchal, paternalistic, New Deal government flipped to the instinctive distrust, even hatred, of "Big Guv'mint" that ran from Ronald Reagan right through the recent Tea Party.

It's quite simple, really. Generally speaking, the vast expansion of government from FDR's New Deal through Truman, Eisenhower, and Kennedy, was a no-strings giveaway to the overwhelmingly white working and middle class. "Modern" air-conditioned school buildings with football and baseball fields, band equipment, and science labs. Libraries and public parks with filtered swimming pools and baseball fields, public golf and tennis courts, and county hospitals for the uninsured. Low-cost or virtually free state universities and community colleges, modern freeways and shopping malls, and of course, Social Security, Medicare, and public employee (or generous corporate and union) pensions for retirement.

Who could ever object to any of that? From the end of World War II through 1980, income taxes for the truly super-rich ranged between two-thirds to as high as 90 percent (after deductions and interest). Yet as Thomas Frank, Michael Moore, and others point out, all but the last five or six years of that era represented the high water-mark for North American middle-class prosperity. It was only when Big Government came to collect—and we don't just mean on property taxes—that things finally went over the cliff.

For the first decade or so of the modern civil rights movement, the focus of the war on racial apartheid and bigotry remained almost 100 percent focused on the rural Confederate South. From *Brown vs. Board of Education* to Rosa Parks getting on the bus, from the Freedom Marches in "Bloody Selma" and the "Mississippi Burning" to Martin Luther King's first speeches, the white newspaper-readers and Cronkite/Murrow/Brinkley-watchers of the Northeast and West could feel smug, secure, and superior in their comparative enlightenment and tolerance. Why, WE would never allow public lynchings or "Black" vs. "White" drinking fountains, or assault helpless young colored girls trying to get a public education! *We're BETTER than that!*

Then in 1964–65, the game changed. Following Kennedy's assassination (as well as the horrifying murders of 4 black girls in a church bombing, the killing of civil rights activist Medgar Evars, and the Klan-inspired 1964 murders of young Jewish civil-rights workers in Mississippi), JFK's successor Lyndon Johnson courageously leveraged the outrage over these atrocities and the "fierce urgency of now" to get the Congress to pass the Civil Rights Act, the Voting Rights Act, and eventually, the Fair Housing Act. A century after the Civil War ended, Jim Crow laws were finally lynched.

Yet less than a year after all that progress, the worst race riots in modern history (up to that point) broke out. This time, however, they weren't in the Confederate South—they were in the urban Watts ghetto of Los Angeles, California. And the smoke hadn't yet dissipated from the assassin's gun that had murdered Malcolm X, in New York City earlier that year. With the jarring force of a hand-held camera being jerked around during a riot, the focus of the Civil Rights struggle instantaneously flipped from Down South to Up North. Urban ghettos and barrios in the inner city slums of Chicago, Detroit, Baltimore/DC,

New Jersey, New York, Oakland, Boston, Vegas, and Los Angeles became the new go-to destinations for Martin Luther King, Bayard Rustin, Thurgood Marshall, Willie Brown, and Jesse Jackson to make their speeches and rallies—as well as the focal point of race riots, especially in the wake of Dr. King's assassination in 1968. The places where African Americans had previously *escaped to* during the "Great Migration," to get out from under Southern oppression.

Now, "social justice" and "economic opportunity" became the new watchwords for the civil rights struggle. The focus now shifted in academic and legal circles from colorblind laws to reparative treatment—they'd been oppressed; they had it coming—as a legal "remedy" for years of past discrimination. Suddenly, shocked white people in states and cities that had always regarded themselves "the good guys" in the civil rights struggle, now found an angry and accusing finger pointed at *them*. School districts and zoning commissions in large Northeastern, New England, and West Coast cities and suburbs found themselves being accused of nefarious crimes like "de facto segregation"—as if *they* had been no better than those white-sheeted Klansmen and demagogic governors down in Mississippi and Alabama.

The dam broke in the fall of 1974, when a federal court ordered a busing plan to "desegregate" the public high schools of that bastion of Dixie-flag, Old South Confederacy—Boston, Massachusetts. Along with the brand-new trend towards "quotas" and "set-asides" in hiring and college admissions, wags and pundits called these new trends "A Harvard Plan for the Working-Class Man." Their sarcastic snark revealed a harsh point: The Al Gores, George W. Bushes, Mitt Romneys, John Kerrys, and Donald Trumps of the world would never have to worry about one of *their* slots at a prestige college or a white-shoe law firm, at a Texas oil company or a Wall Street brokerage, being taken away from *them* to satisfy a diversity mandate. But an anonymous white male trying desperately to claw his way up from working or middle class status certainly *would* have good reason to worry. The most outspoken supporters of "forced busing" like Boston federal judge Arthur Garrity, Sens. Ted Kennedy and George McGovern, and newly elected liberal California governor Jerry Brown, all sent their children to elite (and virtually all-white) private academies or lived in insular rich districts (or were childless and single, like Brown).

Even more shamefully, as the brilliant documentary *A Day Without a Mexican* later underlined in the mid–2000s, the truly rich business moguls and campaign-financers of the last 20 or 30 years absolutely *loved* illegal immigration, outsourcing, and sweatshop conditions at vegetable farms, textile mills, and factories—the better to undercut and destroy the clout and bargaining power of America's home-grown labor movement. (Why, the Binkys and Muffys of the world *simply* couldn't get along without Manuel and Concepcion to do their laundry, tend their hedges and swimming pool, and change their childrens' diapers, don't you know?) With the Archie and Edith Bunkers of the world (or their children and grandchildren) forced to shoulder the burden of racial and diversity balance alone—even as the truly rich and privileged whites said "Not in MY back yard!"—it was not only natural but inevitable that a Hurricane Katrina-sized electoral backlash would come.

Even more upsetting to religious conservatives were the rulings that had outlawed school prayer, and made Christmas and Hanukkah and Ten Commandments displays at city halls and libraries into something "controversial"—while *also* making evolution, sex-ed, Freudian psychology, and feminism an absolute mandate to be taught in schools, regardless of parental or local objections. (We won't even bother here with gay marriage or *Roe vs. Wade*.) Then there were "eminent domain" zoning laws, ever-stricter pollution and traffic laws, and the forced downsizing of luxury and sports cars and family sedans to meet new fuel efficiency and air-quality standards, and all the rest.

When Ronald Reagan made his famous (or infamous) Inauguration Day speech in January of 1981, saying "In our present crisis, Government is not the solution—it's the *problem!*," he hit the sweet spot like Arnold Palmer. To many working and middle class white Americans, "Big Government" had gone from being their protector and bulwark into insinuating itself into every aspect of their day-to-day lives and local communities, hovering like a stern Nurse Ratched over all the decisions that businesses and banks, city halls and school boards, libraries and state colleges had previously made on their own, thank you very much—without any "outside interference."

Whatever Happened at Ruby Ridge?

In medicine, there is a term, *iatrogenic,* which, roughly translated, means "the cure that's worse than the disease," and/or denotes situations where perhaps unexpected and serious side effects happened as a result of medication or treatment. And no matter what side one was on, it would be hard to come up with a more perfect example of something politically *iatrogenic* than the August 1992 Federal raid on Randy Weaver and his family.

Randy Weaver was a Vietnam-era veteran and former factory worker from Iowa. He and his wife Vicki were religious fanatics, expecting the Second Coming and the Apocalypse any day now, and they had likewise moved themselves and their small children to an out-of-the way hillside homestead named Ruby Ridge in rural Idaho, in order to "homeschool [their] children and escape what he and Vicki saw as a corrupted world." The children's home education, unfortunately, went way beyond reading, writing, 'rithmetic, or even religion—a notable family picture portrait had their young son Sam wearing a shirt warning people about the dangers of "ZOG" (Zionist Occupied Government). In other words, those dirty Joooz!) A year after relocating to Idaho, in 1984, Weaver sued a neighbor named Terry Kinnison in small claims court. Kinnison lost, and in obvious tit-for-tat retaliation, he wrote letters to the FBI, Secret Service, and local law enforcement claiming that Weaver had made terroristic threats against President Reagan, Idaho Governor John Evans, and even the Pope! The FBI and Secret Service investigated the claims and found them to be baseless—but one of them was tipped off that Weaver *was* apparently a member of the virulently racist and anti–Semitic hate group, Aryan Nation.

Whether or not Weaver was an Aryan Nation-ista in 1985 was a question mark, but by the late 1980s Weaver had indeed become a regular at Aryan Nation meetings. What he didn't know yet was that the local Aryan chapter had been infiltrated by an informant, who barely legally (if not downright illegally) entrapped Weaver into allegedly selling him a sawed-off shotgun. The gun charge, of course, wasn't the jackpot; the real goal was to have something concrete on Weaver as leverage to force him to act as an informant—to "name names," if you will—against other Aryan "brothers" who possibly *were* into violence, guns, and hate crimes or terror threats. Weaver told the Feds to pound sand. And the Feds, realizing that they had been outed and the jig was up, now set out to prosecute Weaver to the fullest extent of the law, apparently even threatening him and Vicki with having their children taken away from them by Family Services, in the obvious hope of making an example out of them.

If one has a strong enough stomach, one can easily imagine the hate-filled interior dialogue of a racial separatist like Randy Weaver (or skipping ahead a bit later, perhaps of one of Timothy McVeigh's homeboys), during something like this. All of their most para-noiac fantasies about a Federal government worming its way into everything, like some kind of Nazi or Commie secret police, seemed to be coming true. And what must they have thought as they watched rioting 1992 Los Angeles explode into flames, or the so-called Central Park "wildings" and the Willie Horton and Rodney King footage on television in the late 1980s and early 1990s? In these people's (disturbed) minds, all they wanted was just to say goodbye to all that. To go off the grid, to go to a place where Big Guv'mint, and all its interfering ministrations (which they of course blamed for those situations) would just *leave them the hell alone*. But it was as if Big Government had answered them back in return. To quote Howard Beale in *Network,* "Well, I'm *not going to* leave you alone!!" The Feds came down on the Weavers like a ton of bricks, finally sending undercover agents out into the forests surrounding the Weaver "compound" in order to try and find a way to ambush and capture them. And that's when things *really* got out of hand.

On August 21, 1992, six federal marshals—dressed in camouflage like some kind of demented *Rambo* or *Apocalypse Now* outtake, complete with *Silence of the Lambs* green night-vision goggles, formed a "Recon" team with the name "Operation Northern Expo-sure." (All this for one wing-nut.) Eventually losing their patience, one of them tried to smoke the family out by throwing rocks at the front door. Unfortunately, it was young Sam Weaver, then 14 years old, who followed his beloved dog Striker out to investigate. Accounts vary at this point, but almost all the varying testimonies agree on these basic facts: Despite the agents scurrying away to secure "defensive positions," that ole huntin' dog Striker hit pay dirt, and prepared to attack Marshal Arthur Roderick, who shot and killed the dog in front of its horrified 14-year-old master.

"You shot my dog, you son of a bitch!" the hysterical youth cried, reaching for his gun. Sammy Weaver, no doubt thinking that he was merely defending himself and avenging the killing of his dog, shot at Agent Roderick. But Roderick's partners, Agents Bill Degan and Larry Cooper, were there for backup. They blew the teenager away, shooting him through the elbow and fatally in the back. Randy Weaver's best friend, Kevin Harris, had accom-panied young Sammy and Striker, and witnessed the confrontation. He shot and killed Agent Degan on the spot before himself being shot at by the other agents. Harris managed to escape (apparently with Sammy's body) and make it back to the Weaver cabin, where he gave a horrified Randy and Vicki his eyewitness news report.

By the second day of the siege, with the news that one of the federal law enforcement team had been murdered, the FBI and ATF sent SWAT-type snipers out to the compound with what the snipers themselves described as a green-light to "shoot on sight." One of them, Lon Horiuchi, shot Weaver in the armpit when he got a bead on the grieving father going into a shed to visit the body of his dead son. (That was an accident, Horiuchi revealed—he'd meant to shoot Weaver in the spine to paralyze or kill him—but darnit, Weaver had moved at the last minute.) As Weaver and his 16-year-old daughter Sara (who'd accompanied him) realized they were under sniper fire, they ran back to the main house. There, Horiuchi had better luck with Vicki Weaver, killing her when daughter Sara opened the front door to the main house. An unarmed Vicki was holding her 10-month-old baby Elisheba in her arms, when Horiuchi blasted her to kingdom come. Finally, by the last day of August 1992, the remaining Weavers (and Harris) had surrendered. Not surprisingly, Randy and Sara Weaver were acquitted of almost all of the trumped-up charges against them, except for the crime of missing Randy's original court date, escape, and failure to surrender. He served a total of four months beyond time already served waiting for trial.

Alas, the very literal overkill at Ruby Ridge was barely a warmup for another bigger, badder siege that the supposedly kinder and gentler, "liberal" new Bill Clinton government would oversee just six months later. Randy Weaver's wife, son, and dog hadn't gotten cold in their graves when another pressing militaristic-cult problem came to the fore, several hundred miles southeast near Waco, Texas. And this time the villain was a lot creepier than a bearish, bullying dad and a holier-than-the-Bible mom.

David Koresh was a youngish and handsome cult leader who headed the immodestly titled "Branch Davidians," a Jim Jones/Guyana like cult of entire families who lived with their children on a large compound called the Mt. Carmel Ranch. Once again, the pretext was the allegation that Koresh had been stockpiling weapons in excess of gun-control laws, perhaps also preparing for the Apocalypse—while other law enforcement officials suspected Koresh of child abuse and statutory rape, or group sex involving the cult's teenagers as well as the grownups.

Whatever the case, many people who didn't even sympathize with Koresh or Weaver thought that these accusations were clearly a coded a smokescreen for the real "crime"— the ballistically politically incorrect, anti-government, and hate-mongering beliefs of these child-raising patriarchs. After all, even if Randy Weaver had been innocent of violating gun laws, even if David Koresh had never laid a hand on the children of Waco, can you imagine the kind of skin-crawling racism and homophobia, the Nazi-like anti–Semitism and hate, that their innocent, impressionable children were being force-fed and indoctrinated in each day? From Mommy and Daddy, or from their cult "father" figure? Why, it was essentially mental child molestation. Somebody HAD to do *something!* This is a civilized, 21st Century society, and We Just Don't Allow People to do things like *this* anymore!

Shakespeare and Hitchcock couldn't have written it better. The more determined these batty, paranoid separatists were to be left alone in their world of hate (and to raise their impressionable children in these questionable environs), the more determined that the snoopy federal do-gooders were to invade their private world. And they would apparently stop at nothing.

When Koresh's people refused to recognize a search warrant to inspect for weapons violations and other possible crimes, an ATF raid ensued, killing four federal agents and six Branch Davidians. As if in a rerun of Ruby Ridge, the FBI under director Louis Freeh and newly minted Attorney General Janet Reno, initiated a siege at the compound, including playing eardrum-bursting "music" and recorded sound effects of animals screaming. (God only knows how they got *that* footage!) Finally, Reno ran out of patience. A tear gas assault was launched to smoke the Branch Davidians out, on April 19, 1993—only that phrase took on a literal meaning, as a fire swept through the buildings, killing not only David Koresh but many of the children that the federal officials were there to supposedly "protect." At least the horror was finally over....

Like hell it was!

Hate / Crimes / Laws

Timothy McVeigh was a 23-year-old, multiple-medal-winning veteran of the (first) Gulf War, who left the U.S. Army after over 4 years' service, honorably discharged during the post–Cold War military downsizings on the last day of 1991, after he had just barely failed to make the cut as a Special Forces soldier. The year 1992 was a searching time for him, as he was becoming more and more disillusioned about government, his own military past—and more mentally disturbed. Despite being handsome and buff, he'd also largely struck out with the ladies, as his post-traumatic depression and anger began setting in even more. As he aimlessly traveled around, McVeigh began taking solace and comfort in white supremacist literature, including the noxious modern-day *Birth of a Nation*-like white separatist novel, 1978's *The Turner Diaries,* about the backlash against a tyrannical, "well-meaning" U.S. government that had turned on its citizens.

McVeigh was beyond horrified at witnessing the Waco and Ruby Ridge attacks. Not only did they bring back traumatic battle memories of the Gulf War—they seemed to him like literal military attacks where American citizens (like Randy Weaver and David Koresh and their families) were now The Enemy. McVeigh apparently witnessed the Waco catastrophe firsthand—he'd traveled down to Waco to protest the siege and distribute pro-gun literature and bumper stickers. Wikipedia revealed that for almost six months after Waco, McVeigh found work touring the gun show circuit, handing out free business cards with Ruby Ridge sniper Lon Horiuchi's address on it, "in the hope that somebody in the Patriot Movement would assassinate" Horiuchi.

But by the end of the following year of 1994—as anti-government rhetoric hit its zenith during the Hillarycare backlash and the "Republican Revolution"—McVeigh and his best friend and fellow "Patriot," Terry Nichols, had decided that the time had come to make a statement that would equal the media coverage and force of the Waco and Ruby Ridge sieges. Justifying the unjustifiable deaths of innocents to himself, McVeigh would later claim that innocent civilians, including children and the elderly, were routinely bombed and killed in acts of war, as if that made what he was about to do somehow OK, if not even honorable. And that's just what he considered his next plan to be: fighting back in the "war" he considered the Federal government had declared on its own citizens.

On April 19, 1995—the two-year anniversary of the Waco disaster—a Ryder truck filled with fertilizer explosives destroyed the Alfred P. Murrah Federal Building in Oklahoma City. (This was not unlike the method used by the unrelated Osama bin Laden terrorist Ramzi Yousuf in his February 1993 bombing of the World Trade Center garage, which had coincidentally happened just after the Waco siege had begun.) The Murrah building was primarily a Social Security and disability office that catered to the old and to disabled workers—and even worse, the building housed a day care center for the infant and preschool-age children of its federal employees. 168 people died horribly in the blast, many of them children and seniors, and countless more were physically injured and/or permanently traumatized. It was the worst act of domestic terrorism in American history to date, and the worst terror bombing since Pearl Harbor, until September 11, 2001.

Newsweek stalwart Jonathan Alter told Michael Takiff that Oklahoma City was a "real turning point." People began to realize that all the "right-wing nuttiness" that had animated the 1994 Republican Revolution wasn't just mere rhetorical argument. "People could actually *die* from this right-wing nonsense." Barely a month after the Oklahoma City bombing, Clinton warned in a speech, "There is nothing patriotic about hating your country, or pretending you can love your country but despise your government." While Bubba would still have to deal with a "vast right wing" that would stop at nothing this side of actual violence to destroy him (and Hillary), the tide had slowly begun to turn. Just two years after reaching his bottom in 1994, Clinton would be re-elected in 1996, and the 1998 mid-terms would be a resounding victory for liberal Democrats.

Voyage of the Damned

Aside from the Jonestown-like mass suicide presided over by pop-eyed, white-crewcutted southern California cult leader Marshall Herf Applewhite in 1997, the late 1990s were thankfully free of another cult-led catastrophe or Feds-versus-fanatics confrontation on the same level. Free that is, until a five-year-old Cuban boy named Elian Gonzalez washed up on the shores of Miami in late 1999, after having watched his mother drown in her pursuit of freedom. Elian's late mom had taken her little boy away with her from Elian's apparently Castro-loyalist dad, who had no intention of "escaping" to *Los Yanquis*. Perhaps under pressure from the Castro regime, Elian's father demanded his son's immediate return, while Elian's late mother's Miami relatives wouldn't even consider returning their nephew to the Commies, after his mother had literally given her life for her son's chance at America.

Perhaps the most sensible resolution was the one initially proposed by Governor Jeb Bush's administration—that the matter be resolved by Child Protective Services in the Florida family courts, where the standard of evidence would be whatever was proven (by educators, social workers, and child psychiatrists) to be in the best interests of the child: reunion with a loving father on one hand, or a life in America with his mothers' family on the other. That wasn't acceptable to Janet Reno and Bill Clinton. What if some American boy was snatched away by his radical Islamic father to go live under Saddam or the Taliban, against his Americanized mother's wishes? If we decided we could keep a child away from his biological and custodial father, then what was to stop another enemy country from doing the same thing if the tables were turned?

Supporters of Elian's Miami relatives pointed out that if this were Nazi Germany, Soviet-era Hungary or Romania or Czechoslovakia, Pol Pot's Cambodia, Kim Jong-Il's North Korea, or Saddam Hussein's Iraq, we wouldn't even be *having* this discussion. Supporters of Elian's father pointed out that Castro's Cuba *wasn't* any of those Gold Standard of Evil regimes—no matter how much the Cuban exiles might want to pretend that it was. Of course, right on cue, one didn't even need to tune in to hear Rush Limbaugh and Bill O'Reilly bringing back the days of Che Guevara T-shirts and Ho-Ho-Ho Chi Minh, and of radical-chic Westerners like vintage Jane Fonda or Canada's Pierre Trudeau almost "sympathizing" with The Enemy, back in the day.

The Castro government also considered the idea of allowing a Florida state court to decide the issue to be completely off the table. What chance did Cuba have, in a Miami court of law under a Republican governor, to get a fair shake? Castro demanded Elian's return at once, and rumors were circulating that if Clinton didn't comply soon, Castro might send another "Mariel" boatlift (of criminals, junkies, homeless, and the mentally ill "discards" of Cuban society) to swamp American shores with, as he had in 1980. (Clinton had temporarily lost the Arkansas governorship that year largely in reaction to the Mariel disaster, many of whose refugees ended up in and around Arkansas.)

As all this drama spun around him, little Elian was living in a safe house with his Miami relatives. They still refused categorically to turn him over to his father—at least not without a fair hearing at a custody trial. The situation escalated to a minor civil war when Vice President Gore entered (or was forced to enter) the fray, during his campaign for president. Gore was then at the apex of his desperation to "distance himself" at all costs from Bill Clinton, following the Monica Lewinsky fiasco—and not by pandering to the Ralph Nader Left, but by trying to draw off George W. Bush's vote from the Joe Lieberman Right. Predictably under the circumstances, Gore sided with Elian's Miami relatives, and against Clinton and Reno. As one of the Democratic Party's staunchest anti–Communist cold warriors during the Reagan/Bush era Congress, easily the most rightist and hawkish Democrat in his age group (and a strong supporter of Bush Sr.'s 1990–91 Gulf War), Gore might just have been returning to his roots. (Then again, he might just have been shamelessly pandering to a crucial voting demographic in what would turn out to be the swing state of swing states in 2000. But that's no excuse for cynicism.)

In any case, Al Gore's views carried about as much weight as a feather with the Clintons at this point. Reaching into her old bag of Waco-era tricks, Attorney General Janet Reno decided to forcibly raid Elian's house early on Easter Sunday in 2000, for a "show of force" to put the family in its place once and for all. As the mess played out before the news cameras, Ann Coulter and Bill O'Reilly couldn't have designed it better as a screenplay: The worldwide-circulated photograph of a SWAT-vested, fatigue-wearing federal agent pointing an automatic weapon's barrel just inches from a shrieking, six-year-old Elian's face, while his relatives hid him in a clothes closet—followed immediately by other federal agents brutally tearing the six-year-old away from his relatives and carrying him into the van, was a picture worth more than the proverbial thousand words. Some of the Feds even wore ninja-style balaclava masks, just like the killer in the classic slasher movie *Prom Night*. (Wonder how a six-year-old child who'd just lost his mother would react to seeing *that!*) And on Easter Sunday, no less.

Once again, all of the ugliest "black helicopter" fantasies, all of the mind-numbing conspiracy theories that Randy Weaver and Timothy McVeigh had been babbling about, had almost seemed to come true. Especially as you could count on the Eyewitness News media to run with the most sensationalized, tabloidized, and shocking up-to-the-minute footage from the scene. And naturally, Al Gore had barely been consulted or warned by President Clinton about the shocking raid. (Not that Clinton needed to ask for Gore's input, much less his permission, of course. But the fact that Clinton didn't certainly said volumes about how appallingly far apart that his and his vice president's non-relationship had grown by then.)

And just like clockwork (if not more like *A Clockwork Orange*) came self-righteous Attorney General Reno, just as cat-with-the-cream smug as she had been seven years earlier during her death victory at Waco, banging on about the "rule of law." To outraged conservatives, it was as if she were bringing things full circle, so to speak. As for Elian himself, he was promptly turned over to his father (and the Cuban state police who accompanied him), and back he went to Castro with his Papi. It was all too eye-rolling in its predictability, when *60 Minutes* caught up to an adolescent Elian Gonzalez a decade or so later, to find that Elian was being groomed on the fast track for a local-level leadership role in the Communist state, talking eagerly about his "buddy," Unca Fidel. His father apparently couldn't have been more pleased with the results.

Back in Miami, Elian's still-traumatized American relatives had turned the safe house that had proven to be anything but, into a sort of borderline-grotesque "museum" of the 1999–2000 struggle, complete with shrines, framed pictures, and pseudo-Catholic imagery of the Innocent Child having been taken and corrupted by The Enemy. It was yet another perfect irony that Elian Gonzalez's Florida would become, just seven months after his forced departure, ground zero for the ugliest and most divisive presidential election in modern American history.

Massacre at Central High

No matter what side one was on during these terrors, the one terrible fact that was beyond dispute was that, in each of these literal battlefields of the 1990s culture war, it had been innocent children who had taken the biggest beating. From Randy Weaver's junior-high-age son lying dead, filled with Federal bullets, to the children of the Koresh compound burned and suffocated to death in the tear-gas fires (who might very well have been molested and abused by Koresh even before their deaths), to a shrieking Elian Gonzalez being home-invaded months after watching his mother drown before his very eyes, to the bombed-out babies and preschoolers of the Alfred P. Murrah building's day care center. Every one of these stomach-churners brought the ugliest meaning to the phrase "suffer the children."

For the ugliest hate crimes against young adults, it would be hard to top the bloody one-two punch of gay bashings to receive national attention that occurred in 1993 and 1998. The first was when the transgender-male auto mechanic Brandon Teena (a reversal of his biologically female birth name; Teena was hoping for final surgical transition into a man at the time of death) was brutally beaten, raped, and eventually shot to death, after his 'secret' was found out. No less gruesome was when gay and out 22-year-old Matthew Shepard was tied to a post after being sadistically beaten, and left to die slowly of exposure in the barren Wyoming outback. Both killings were carried out by doped-up, heavy-drinking, white-trashy youths and young adults, their testosterone and male insecurities boiling over with hate and fear.

Although if we move our focus away from young people for just a bit, perhaps the ultimate hate crime of the '90s happened when a middle-aged man named James Byrd was chained by white supremacists to the back of a car and dragged to death on a gravel-and-blacktop road at high speed. His "crime?" Being an African American male. (These murders led to another more comprehensive federal Hate Crimes Act, under President Obama in 2009.) There were also a number of high-profile bombings of abortion clinics during the 1990s, with the radical anti-abortion group Operation Rescue distributing Old West style "Wanted" posters with abortion providers' names and personal info on them. No doubt the killers and bombers would say that they were acting to "protect" innocent children and babies from the abortionists' scalpel, but that doesn't take away the fact that Drs. David Gunn (a subject of a "Wanted" poster), John Britton and James Barrett were murdered in 1993 and 1994 in two separate incidents in Pensacola, Florida (with Barrett's wife injured in the latter one).

Receptionists Shannon Lowney and Lee Ann Nichols were killed in a Massachusetts clinic attack on New Years' Eve week in 1994, while off-duty policeman Robert Sanderson was murdered while moonlighting as a guard at a Birmingham, Alabama clinic three years later in January 1998 (and his colleague, nurse Emily Lyons, lost an eye in the attack). Abortion providers Drs. Calvin Jackson, David Gandell, and George Tiller were all shot or injured in separate attacks during the '90s. (A man named Scott Roeder finally finished the job with Dr. Tiller, killing him in May of 2009, sixteen years after Tiller had first been shot and later recovered.) In an article on anti-abortion violence, the Anti-Defamation League's website noted that the early 1990s were replete with "dozens of arsons, bombings, [and] murders."

But abortion clinics weren't the only literal battlefields in the 1990s culture war. Some of the first of today's modern-day epidemic of terroristic school and church shootings were also inaugurated during the later decade. While most of them were less wantonly sadistic than the Teena, Shepard, and Byrd murders on an individual basis, the very last hate-crime horror shows of the pre–9/11 era would add an even more perverted new twist. Children and young people would continue to be the ones to take the worst of it, both physically and emotionally. But now, it wouldn't be just the kids who were the *victims*. Now they would be the *perpetrators* as well.

To wit, the killers who notoriously opened fire on their teachers and fellow classmates in Jonesboro, Arkansas, in March of 1998 weren't college or even high school students, but *junior*-high schoolers: Andrew Golden, just two months shy of his 12th birthday, and his partner in crime, Mitchell Johnson, then all of 13 years old. They killed four girls (all aged 11 and 12 years) and a 32-year-old female teacher, at their middle school. Ten others were injured. The two miscreants had loaded up one of their mother's minivans with enough weapons to mount a sequel to *Pulp Fiction*: nine guns total, including rifles, carbines, and several .38 handguns. Apparently they'd stolen them all from Golden's grandfather's home. (That dear ole Gramps had so many weapons just lying around his house made a statement about America's gun control laws—or perhaps it's *lack* of them—that was bolder than a *New York Times* headline to many anti-gun liberals.) Indeed, Andrew Golden was apparently given his first firearm to use by his father when he was only six years old.

Like so many white youths trying to act tough, Johnson and Golden (while having no discernible respect for African American or Latino males in their own right) coveted the bad-assness of urban gangsta and "thug" culture. Trying to act like their idols, they bragged to their friends about wanting to belong to the notorious street gangs the Crips and the Bloods, listened to hardcore rap, and viciously bullied other students. A year prior to the shooting, 12-year-old Johnson had attempted to perform sex acts on a 3-year-old toddler, while Golden had deliberately murdered a girl's cat with his BB gun. (Perhaps they were warming up, so to speak.) Johnson also liked hanging out with older high school and college boys, and claimed openly to have "a lot of killing to do."

And if you're wondering why no parent, teacher, or counselor picked up on these outrageous, head-bangingly obvious warning signs of severe mental illness and aggression, if you're wondering why no grownup staged a full-on intervention with those two kids before it was too late … well—*you're not the only one.*

A few months earlier, in December of 1997, a 14-year-old high school freshman named Michael Carneal murdered three students and injured five others in a campus prayer meeting (held before classes) on the grounds of Heath High School in Paducah, Kentucky. Carneal was found to be a paranoid schizophrenic, and unlike Golden and Johnson, had been more on the receiving than giving end of bullying and mistreatment. But though the lyrics had changed, the song remained the same. Carneal was able to get 5 rifles, a Ruger .22 pistol, and plenty of ammunition just by breaking into his neighbor's garage, while his own father's household had yielded two more rifles.

Less than two years later in the summer of 1999, a severely mentally ill adult man named Buford Furrow opened fire on a Jewish day care center in the upper San Fernando Valley in Los Angeles. Thankfully no one was killed, despite Furrow getting off over 70 shots, but three small children, and two grownups—a teenage counselor-intern and a secretary—were injured. Furrow then murdered a mailman named Joseph Ileto after fleeing the scene, killing Ileto on the spot just because Ileto was a "Latino or Asian-looking" (Filipino) American, and an employee of the evil Fed'ral Gub'mint. That was all it took. Furrow eventually was caught and surrendered, after which it was revealed by *The New York Times* that he had been treated for mental problems while in Washington state. He'd evidently tried to seek further help, too, only to have been turned away by dubious authorities. (You know—*he's faking it … doesn't meet the criteria for state commitment …* that sort of thing.) Unsurprisingly, Furrow was a longtime white supremacist with ties to neo–Nazis and Aryan Nation.

Before we get to the final chart-topper on our literal "hit" parade, it's worth pointing out that at least a part of the horror and revulsion that Americans and Canadians (deservedly) had towards all these attacks, came from the fact that they had all struck in white, rural or suburban surroundings. Many ghetto and barrio high schools already had to have metal detectors, locker raids, and occasional airport-like pat-downs, because of the epidemic of inner-city gang and drug violence, starting in the whack-on-crack, drive-by shooting 1980s. It was not entirely unheard-of for teachers and students to be forcibly raped on campus by high school punks and gangstas, stabbed with switchblades or razors, or even shot at outside "hood" schools, well before the late '90s and 2000s epidemic of high school and college shootings got underway.

In April of 1999, the worst school shooting rampage of all occurred on the celebration of Adolf Hitler's 110th birthday, and only one day after the anniversary of the Waco and Oklahoma City catastrophes. Sure enough, this one struck not in some hillbilly heaven or crime-ridden urban metropolis, but in safe, white, upper-middle-class, tract-house suburbia, in a place where This Kind of Thing Just Doesn't Happen.

Jared Harris and Dylan Klebold were members of the so-called "Trenchcoat Mafia" of burnouts and outcasts at Columbine High School in suburban Colorado. But this dynamic duo went way beyond just playing Harris' favorite video game of "Doom" or hanging out in the basement and listening to hardcore grunge and death metal. While not overtly allied with white supremacist groups the way that Randy Weaver or Buford Furrow were, the two admired Adolf Hitler and other serial killers and mass murderers, and Harris in particular had caught the eye of concerned parents for posting what appeared to be death threats and hate language on his AOL personal website. While a joint suicide appears to have been part of their plan from the outset (or at least an option on their menu, along with what is laughingly called suicide-by-cop), the two made a series of videotapes of their pre-massacre adventures—target practice, the weapons they'd acquired, manifesto statements—to be discovered after their deaths or arrest. In case they *were* able to escape, the two fantasized about (among other things) hijacking an airplane and crashing it into a building in New York. (Unbeknownst to them, an even more ambitious mass murderer was already at work developing that same plotline.)

Harris and Klebold's journals indicated that they wanted (for reasons of revenge against the world and sheer ego, perhaps) to commit a terroristic crime to rival Oklahoma City. And in that they succeeded, as they planted and secreted homemade bombs throughout their school. They learned how to make them off the Internet. (Apparently the two needed a few more lessons, thank God—only a couple of them went off successfully, and the main bomb failed to ignite at full force. According to CNN, if it had, it could have killed as many as almost 500 people in the adjacent school cafeteria at one time.)

Entering the school at midday, with weapons strapped to themselves and carrying gym bags filled with yet more instruments of death, Harris and Klebold began their attack in earnest at 11:19 am. They spent 10 minutes shooting people on sight and terrorizing others in the hallways, classrooms, and exit points, until they arrived at the school library at 11:29. There they proceeded to murder 10 of their fellow students at close range, and injured several more. One of them, Cassie Bernal, deservedly became a heroine to evangelical Christians, in that in the seconds before her death, Harris sadistically taunted her, asking Bernal if she believed in God. A terrified (yet perhaps miraculously dignified) Cassie Bernal said, "Yes." In that case, Harris indicated, he was going to introduce her to God right now! He blew her brains out. Isaiah Shoels, the only African American victim to be killed, was likewise taunted with racial epithets before his murder.

Finally, after police had surrounded the school and it had been evacuated, Harris and Klebold accepted the inevitable, and killed themselves—their mission accomplished. Psychologists and psychiatrists spent months, even years trying to conduct a psychological autopsy of the two to figure out what drove them to kill on such an unspeakably and unbelievably violent scale. Was it *Natural Born Killers*–like media whoredom taken to its extreme, or was it the ultimate expression of Generation X nihilism and grunge-rock rage? Was it their flirting admiration for "bad boys" like Hitler and Manson and Tim McVeigh, or the plans of two alienated outcasts taking their final revenge against the world? Perhaps one, perhaps all—and perhaps that was best left as an academic question, like the old *Saturday Night Live* sketch where an aging Nazi war criminal whispers to several of his friends the "perfectly good reason" why millions of Jews had to die—the grim joke being, of course, that there could *never* be any good reason for such a thing, no matter what.

*   *   *

A few days after Columbine, like Oklahoma City before it, a national day of mourning and a worldwide-televised memorial service was held. The Rev. Franklin Graham (Billy's son) led the services outside the high school, which had a distinctly evangelical and even fundamentalist altar-call revival meeting flavor to them. Some commentators found this rather offensive and questionably intolerant. There was serious jibber-jabber among intellectuals as to why the service wasn't more multi-culti, more inclusive—especially for something that clearly had all the hallmarks of a hate crime. That the majority of the victims were from white, evangelical Christian households may have been a fact, but tellingly, in the therapeutic daytime talk-show world of 1999, that didn't matter anymore. And that was perhaps a sardonically fitting final twist to all of these politically incorrect horror shows of the 1990s, and the breathy media coverage and intrigue that surrounded them. In our PR-friendly, diversified, and politically correct world, it seemed that everyone else's tragedies had become our own, and our own tragedies had become everyone else's.

As the 1990s "identity politics" wars brutally reminded us, before anybody could be accepted as THIS (we hold up an individual, beautifully unique flower), they would first have to make themselves become a fully participating, aware, and proudly identifying part of THAT (we indicate the wide, long-shot of Maude's sunflower field...)

10

It's the *New* Economy, Stupid!

"…They reflected, almost uniformly, the perspectives of their class, the top 1 percent.… They had no patience with protectionism, found unions troublesome, and were not particularly sympathetic to those whose lives were upended by the movements of global capital. Most were adamantly prochoice and anti-gun, and were vaguely suspicious of deep religious sentiment.… The problems of ordinary people, the voices of the Rust Belt town or the dwindling heartland, became a distant echo rather than a palpable reality, abstractions to be managed rather than battles to be fought."

—Barack Obama, describing neoliberal or "New Democrat"
voters of means, in "The Audacity of Hope" (2006)

The oldest and strongest emotion of mankind is fear, and the oldest and strongest kind of fear is fear of the unknown.

—H.P. Lovecraft

Picture it. You're at a long-established investment house or bank (like say, Lehman Brothers or Bear Stearns, for example. Not one of those fly by-night places that rip off their customers' money or play fast and loose with their life savings; but a *respectable*, year-in year-out, decades-old trust firm, someplace where your money would always be as "sound as the dollar" itself, for the rest of your life and then some…) It's 1999, and a nervous yet bored-looking twenty-something junior broker is trying to explain to his inherited clients—a pair of recently retired, working- or middle-class Everybodys in their late fifties or sixties from the Silent Generation (or perhaps some Greatest Generationers now in their mid-seventies) about the hottest stocks on today's market, and the new companies that he's got his eagle eye on for the forseeable future…

"Well, we're all waiting with bated breath for Google to come on the market after the way they set the world on fire when they went online last fall," the eager young man brags. (*Google? What's THAT?*—the old clients' wrinkled noses clearly convey.) "But meanwhile, Yahoo is looking really strong. And there's this virtual online bookstore called Amazon. com, and I'm really keeping an eye on this brand new one that just started, that does the same thing for rental movies called Netflix…. Oh, and there's this great new company called E-Bay that's like a virtual auction site, and…."

Yahoo, Google, E-Bay, Netflix … what is this, *Mister Rogers' Neighborhood?* What kind of self-respecting companies use baby-talk for names? They don't sound like legitimate businesses—they sound like something from *Captain Kangaroo!* "You're gettin' ahead of yourself, Mister," the older man interrupts, in his "yawp, pardner" Duke Wayne Midwestern bass-baritone. "Just what is it that these companies actually *make?*"

"Well, uhh…" Pools of sweat start forming under the tall young man's armpits on his blue shirt. "They don't really *make* anything, they're on the…"

"They don't MAKE anything?!" the full-figured wife breathes, turning her head at a quarter angle, her saucer-eyes bulging accusingly. You'd have thought the young broker had just said the N-word or the F-word, or called her an old bitch to her face. He might just as well have told them that he was trying to throw their life savings into the trashcan!

"Yes, uhm, well you see, they're on the *Internet.* Like Yahoo and Google, for instance. They're called Search Engines—you know, like Hotbot and Alta Vista?" (Clearly, they *don't* know, like Hotbot and Alta Vista…) "Like if you go online and want to look up Limp Bizkit—er, uhm, I mean, uh…. Loretta Lynn—they'll direct you to every website on the Internet that has stuff on Loretta. And they also provide Email to people. That's why I keep telling you about this Time-Warner/AOL deal that's going to be coming up any day now. It's gonna make you a *fortune* if you get in now! It'll be the hottest thing since Pets.com went public…"

"Ohhh-kay," the husband says, still not entirely convinced, but willing to at least think about it. "What about these companies you're 'hoping will go public'—these things like Craigslist and Netflix and E-bay? And Dell Computers—isn't that the one with that dirty, stoned-out hippie kid on TV goin' 'Dude, you're gettin' a Dell.'"

"Well, yes, that's the company … but I assure you, the Dell Corporation is a completely respectable and businesslike firm…" *(The clients' facial expressions clearly indicate that they believe otherwise.)* "As to Amazon, it's this cool website that allows you to buy books online, without ever having to leave your home and schlep to the bookstore. And Netflix is the same thing, but for renting movies, and…" The wife interrupts. "But *why* would anybody want to spend good money on a book, or on renting a bunch of videos, if they didn't have a chance to look at them in the store first?"

"*Uhhhh….*" Now our tall young broker's Adam's apple is starting to play basketball, as he realizes too late that he could really use some breath mints about now. "Well, my boss did tell me that he had a mandate for us to introduce our old—er, I mean, our *longtime*— customers to these new companies … but, uhh … how about we, uhh … double down on our Whirlpool, Toyota, Daimler-Chrysler, Smith-Kline, Merck, and IBM for now?"

GOOD IDEA.

As you can probably tell from our little story, for every tech-savvy, highly educated embracer of the future and futurism, who embraced the *Star Trek* speed and so-called "convenience" of the Internet and cell-phone era on the cusp of the millennium, there were others who were shocked, awed, and as confused as all hell by what it meant. Unfortunately, if those people were looking for an explanation, for anyone who'd even slightly help them to navigate and make sense of the lightning-round game changes of the New Economy, they had better have looked a lot further than the Democrat and Republican parties of America. For all the futuristic talk and media hype about the "new economy," when it came to actually *explaining* what it all meant and *planning* for a fast-changing future, "Big Government" failed as badly as the worst Ronald Reagan fable. And Big Government's gross failure to explain and prepare for that fast-coming future wasn't entirely by accident.

Mr. Clinton Goes to Washington

As we know, in 1992, Bill Clinton ran on a platform of "Putting People First"—and by "people" he clearly meant working and middle class people who had borne the brunt of the early 1990s recession, and the Reagan-era shift to a Wall Street, financial-services based, multi-national economy. "Hard working Americans who play by the rules have no voice in Washington," Clinton noted in his 1992 campaign literature. Clinton also planned to create quote, "tougher trade legislation" to "crack down on foreign companies that manipulate our laws," and eliminate privileges for "companies that ship American jobs overseas and reward outrageous executive pay."

On October 11th 1992, in St. Louis, he added, "My first priority [will] be to pass a jobs program, to introduce it on the first day I was inaugurated." Clinton also bragged he'd "restore the dignity of blue collar work," and that he would never, ever "raise taxes on the middle class." Pouring on the gravy even thicker, he told blue and lower-white collar workers that the "forgotten middle class" would be "forgotten no more" under his government, and that "American companies must act like American companies again, exporting products—not jobs!"

That was when Bubba was *running*. Nine months later, after he'd actually been *elected*, Clinton got a hot steaming cup of Reality Check forced down his throat, by the kind of people whom author Tom Wolfe laughingly called the "Masters of the Universe." Legendary journalist Bob Woodward recalled the sweltering summer 1993 discussions about the upcoming 1994 budget, the first to truly bear Clinton's stamp (as opposed to Reagan's or old-Bush's). The main topic of discussion from Al Gore, Treasury Secretary (and former Dukakis '88 vice presidential nominee and multimillionaire Texas businessman) Lloyd Bentsen, past and future Goldman Sachs legend Robert Rubin, and self-proclaimed "deficit hawk" budget guru Dr. Alice Rivlin, all concerned only one thing: what Ross Perot had called in his Texas twang "The Daff'cit." They had made it clear—as had Wall Street and Alan Greenspan's Federal Reserve—that there would be no real recovery until the $300-billion-a-year shortfalls of the early 1990s were taken care of once and for all. Clinton's face turned red with anger and disbelief, according to Woodward. "You mean to tell me the success of the program and my reelection hinges on the Federal Reserve, and a bunch of fucking bond traders?"

You got it, Bubba—that was *exactly* what they were saying! After all, wasn't Clinton's very own campaign slogan, "It's the *economy*, stupid?" Well, those "fucking stock and bond traders" and Federal Reservists had apparently taken him literally. As Woodward noted, there was "not a dissent" from any of the Wise Men (and Women) in the room. Later on, Clinton famously and sardonically stated behind closed doors that he and his economic team were nothing but a bunch of quote, "Eisenhower Republicans." (That was a judgment that would be echoed by everyone from an approving Republican Federal Reserve chief Alan Greenspan, to a considerably less-pleased future liberal cable goddess named Rachel Maddow.)

Bill Clinton would never do anything as economically liberal as Franklin Roosevelt, Harry Truman, or Lyndon Johnson did—indeed, Clinton wasn't even as economically "liberal" as Dwight Eisenhower and Richard Nixon had been! (Just ask Thomas Frank, Ralph Nader, Matt Taibbi, or Michael Moore.) Bill Clinton only looked like a raving leftist to the

Rush Limbaugh/Ann Coulter right wing because of his religious and lifestyle liberalism, and his '60s hippie past. But only in the most fevered dreams of Richard Mellon Scaife, the Koch Brothers, Sheldon Adelson, or Bill O'Reilly would Bill and Hillary Clinton actually "punish" job-creating CEOs, or pursue "confiscatory" taxation methods. In the reality-based world of the mid-to-late '90s, "one percenter" corporate bosses and bankers, media and Wall Street conglomerates, and international big business would never have it so good.

"Since Bill Clinton was elected in 1992, the economic predilections of the Democratic Party have been completely remade," said Jonathan Chait in a December 2001 *American Prospect* post-mortem. After Clinton's come-to-Greenspan moment, his economic policy proved "far more fiscally conservative than anything a president *of either party* would have dared propose," including even Ronald Reagan. After Clinton "shunt[ed] public investment" (at least initially) for the sake of cooperating with Greenspan and those "fucking bond traders," Clinton drifted steadily rightward.

Meanwhile, Clinton's right wing opposition had worked itself into a Gordian knot of circular illogic. If times were bad (as they were from the tail end of 1990 thru '94) why, you cut taxes! Cutting taxes *always* stimulates the economy so much, everyone actually makes more in the end, and makes the "job creators" feel more secure. However, when the economy is in good shape, and the government is taking in a surplus (as it was in 1999 and 2000, when the Clinton era came to an end), whaddaya do? Why, *you cut taxes,* of course! All that a surplus means is that tyrannical, elite Big Government is taking in more money than it needs, just like a thief going bang-bang! (It's "our money," isn't it?)

The main intellectual or scientific credibility this thinking had came from the famous "Laffer Curve" of conservative economist Arthur Laffer in 1974, which drew a rather breast-shaped (or half-moon, if you prefer a less Freudian metaphor) curve purporting to show a happy medium between two taxation extremes—the key words here being *medium* between two *extremes*. Laffer's curve illustrated that when tax rates are top-outta-sight, they stifle growth and investment so much that government actually makes less income. Very true, but the Laffer Curve *also* illustrated the equally no-brainer fact that if government reduces taxes on the rich all the way down to 10 or 5 or zero percent, the government *also* won't make any money either!

The Laffer curve may have served as something of a useful corrective back in 1975, when tipppity-top tax rates were still at their Cold War levels of 65 and 70 percent, and when senior citizens in California and the upper East Coast were about to be threatened with property tax foreclosures for their inability to keep up with late '70s and '80s real-estate inflation. But after Ronald Reagan slashed top taxes to roughly half the rates that had prevailed from Kennedy through Carter, the hard-right voices now began *purposely misinterpreting* the Curve (and Reagan's tax cuts) as "proof" that Tax Cutting Is ALWAYS Good. By the later Clinton era, longtime right-wing royalty Grover Norquist and his crew would start forcing new Republican candidates for Congress and Senate and high-profile state governorships to sign a "pledge" promising Never To Increase Taxes Ever, as they ran in their primary campaigns. Now it was clear. Raising taxes, for any reason besides maybe all-out war, was now officially ranked alongside publicly saying the N-word, making fun of the Holocaust, or physically assaulting a woman, at least in Republican circles. Inexcusable for any reason, instant career suicide. Tax cuts for the rich had become the economic *religion* of the GOP.

The Head-On Collision (Everything Left to Lose)

NAFTA and the birth of the modern day World Trade Organization would do nothing less set the template for all economic discussions from Clinton to Bush II to Obama and beyond. Reagan-Bush Republicans had written those laws. And years later, it would be the health insurance lobby (along with corporate "George W. Bush Democrats" like Max Baucus, Joe Lieberman, and Ben Nelson) who would write Obamacare, dissing and shutting out the left-labor wings of their party every step of the way (just after they'd voted for the Big Auto and Bigger Bank bailouts of 2008–09). But it would be a "liberal Democratic Congress" that would finally pass all of those controversial laws—both times under intense pressure from game-changer Democratic presidents, desperate to assert their authority and scrape together whatever victory they could, before it was too late. And it would be those same Democratic presidents who would sign them into law. And it would be the Democratic Party that would then take the blame for everything that went wrong afterwards.

Neoliberal guru Michael Kinsley, who was as passionately free-trade and New Economy as any Republican he sat across from on *Crossfire* (and far more so than "isolationist" conservatives like Pat Buchanan and Ross Perot), once again bravely stepped up to take the bullet for his favorite president. Kinsley hit the nail on the head when he wrote in *The Los Angeles Times* in September of 1993 that "the person who will get a job because of NAFTA isn't even aware of it yet, [while] the person who may *lose* a job because of NAFTA is all too aware." Kinsley noted that maintaining an economy that "pays ourselves $16 an hour for work that foreigners are willing to do for $3" was untenable. But he also acknowledged that NAFTA wasn't going to be all sunshine, lollipops, and kittens. "There is also no doubt that it hurts certain individuals … when a $16 an hour American loses his job to a $3 an hour Mexican. And it will happen."

Kinsley also noted that NAFTA was so virulently opposed by the Democratic Party as a whole, nearly 3 out of every 5 House Democrats were still adamantly against it, and poised to vote a resounding "NO!" The *only* way that Clinton could get it to pass was by turning on all of his Southern saxophone-player charms, lovin' up the same Republicans who had just torn strips off of him during the budget battle and the gays-and-guns controversies, who were already sharpening their knives for Hillary Clinton's health care bill.

And that's exactly what Bill Clinton did. Michael Waldman said that "NAFTA was the first time [Clinton] stood up to the Democrats in a significant way and mounted a public campaign that was not hand in glove with the leaders in Congress." (Though it would certainly not be the last time!) But high-ranking Democratic lawyer David Bonior couldn't care less. "NAFTA undermined all the progressive legislation that it took a whole century to put together. It's really ravaged working people." The Michael Moores and Roseanne Barrs who had thought Bill Clinton would be a working class hero might well have needed the smelling salts, as Clintonomics 2.0 moved full-speed ahead. And needless to say, the lauded "jobs bill" Clinton was supposed to pass on Day One fell under the category of not-gonna-happen. Charlene Barshefsky noted, "Politically there was nothing to be gained, and there was everything to lose…. Clinton knew he was running head-on into the Democratic caucus—and I mean, *head on!*"

By the mid 1990s, an already besieged white working class was running out of what little patience they'd ever had with "quotas," "set-asides," and "diversity mandates." Not long after NAFTA, they successfully passed ballot-initiative affirmative action repeals in California (in 1996) and Florida (in early 2000), and the toxically anti–Latino Proposition 187. *Salon's* Joan Walsh rightly later noted that no sooner had "industrial unions [been] forced, whether by upstart organizers or federal intervention, to bring blacks and women into their ranks," than the Gerald Ford/Jimmy Carter era of gas shortages, federally mandated auto-mileage standards, and high inflation and interest rates had reared its ugly head. Now, with NAFTA and free trade, the anger level doubled down. "The decline of industries like steel, mining, and auto manufacturing created a zero-sum agony in which the worst nightmares of white unionists came true. Integration often came at the expense of white guys, as the number of overall jobs began to contract nationwide. The paranoia of the white working class [male, especially] in some cases, came true. Diversity arrived to American industry just as industry was leaving America." As the brilliant Ms. Walsh again rightly put it, in the big picture, "nobody won."

"A post-industrial revolution"

Longtime Clinton associate and journalist Sidney Blumenthal noted in his book, *The Clinton Wars* that, as the Clinton era dawned, "A new economy, based on microchips and the Internet—a post-industrial revolution—was in the making. [Yet] hardly any major politician except for the new vice-president, Albert Gore, Jr., had given it much thought." That was putting it kindly. In 1992, one of the iconic moments that proved how aging and out-of-touch President Bush, Sr., was, came when the First Shopper expressed amazement at a grocery store's laser barcode scanner—which had been a commonplace technology at major supermarkets and Walmart/K-Mart/Target-type megastores for the past 10 or 15 years. And many if not most of the old boys in the Senate and Congress (of both parties) had been little better at keeping up with all that newfangled computerized stuff in the '80s and early '90s.

Blumenthal also sadly noted that Bill Clinton simply could not turn to any of his predecessors for real help. There were three full decades between Clinton and a "usable Democratic past." Activist government "had been discredited," at least of a forthrightly liberal nature, as Lyndon Johnson's civil rights reforms fell under the dark shadow of Vietnam. And Jimmy Carter, the only Democratic president in the last quarter-century, complete with gas lines, auto downsizing, double-digit interest rates, and hostage crises, had only "added new disabling handicaps and cautionary tales." No, the 46-year-old Bill Clinton would have to quantum-leap all the way back to when he was still an apple-cheeked high school senior, to when his hero John F. Kennedy was still alive to shake his hand, to get even so much as a clue about a "useful Democratic past" to lean on.

Unintentionally underlining this, Blumenthal repeatedly crooned in *The Clinton Wars* about what a "meritocracy" the Clinton government was. Sadly (although completely predictably), Blumenthal's definition of "meritocracy" seemed solely and completely based on what snob college a person graduated from. One's experience in the grubbier regions of small business, door-knocking-and-petitioning local politics, or ink-stained below-the-line journalism, didn't even seem to register with him. (It didn't mean a thing, without that Ivy League bling.) Clinton's government was certainly 'meritocratic' compared to one stocked with nothing but blue-blooded Kennedys, Cabots, Lodges, Vanderbilts, Bushes, Harrimans, du Ponts, Rothschilds, Fords, and Rockefellers, who'd gotten in by their royalty-level names alone. But it was hardly a "meritocracy" in the eyes of say, a talented state college grad or an unglamorous, working-up-the-ladder striver from Kansas or Flint, or any other bastion of the fabled "white working class." (What a shame that with all his vaunted education and sophistication, Mr. Blumenthal never quite understood that…)

Inventing the Internet

According to the website InternetLiveStats.com, when Bill Clinton took office in early 1993, there were only 130 known websites on what was then called "The World Wide Web." That's right, only one hundred and thirty—in the whole world. By June of the following "revolutionary" year of 1994, it had grown—to all of 2,738. But in June of 1998, the 1994 figure had metastasized to more than 2,410,000! In other words, *it had multiplied by a THOUSAND TIMES* what it had been just four years earlier! And by June of 2001, just after Bill Clinton finished holding the housewarming party for George W. Bush at 1600 Pennsylvania, it had gone up more than *ten times* from the 1998 figure—to 29,254,000 and change!

The statistics for Internet users grew just as exponentially. Between the time of some of the first listed statistics for the "World Wide Web" in 1988–89 through June of 1994, there were only 25 million people in the entire (6–7 *billion* population) world—less than the populations of Canada, New York State, or California by themselves—who had in-home or office access to the Internet and/or Email accounts. Just seven years later, in June of 2001, that amount had gone up by almost *two thousand percent*, to 500 million (or half a *billion*) people—*more* than the entire population of the United States and North America, or just about any country besides China.

No question about it, the impact of the Internet and cell phones on the 1990s economy cannot be overstated. And even though sites like Facebook, Myspace, Twitter, and YouTube had yet to be heard from, a look at the websites that launched in the Clinton era is almost like looking at a Who's Who of the modern-day economy. Yahoo and Earthlink both began in 1994, followed by Amazon.com and Ebay (initially known as AuctionWeb) and the first beginnings of what would become Craigslist in 1995, while Google revved up its search engines in 1998. And Netflix, Zappos, and PayPal launched in early 1999. (And if you want to count January of 2001, that was the month that marked the first entry in Wikipedia's game change, while 1989–90 had inaugurated America Online and the Internet Movie Database in their earliest forms.)

However, there were just as many World Wide Websites that crashed and burned, mostly amidst the 2001 dot-com meltdown—after all of the above had launched, but a few critical years *before* Facebook, Twitter, YouTube, Myspace, Flickr, Tumblr, LinkedIn, Pinterest, the "Cloud," et cetera kicked it up to the next level. Until Google and Yahoo shoved them aside, for a time in the mid–1990s Alta Vista and Hotbot were the hottest search engines in town. Netscape was almost as popular as AOL, Yahoo, and Google were in their initial runs, while GeoCities became one of if not the first Internet providers to give everyday people the opportunity to create their own custom-themed websites, blogs, and homepages, where they could post pictures of themselves, chat with other Internet users, look for dates or sex, and talk about whatever was on their minds. Just after it launched, in 1995, GeoCities had 100,000 subscribers. That grew a factor of 10 to 1,000,000 homepages in 1996—only to go up *another* ten times to 10,000,000 in 1997! (By 2009, it was all over, after having been a shell of its former self since about 2003–04 or so.)

But these dizzying statistics told only half the story of the 1990s game change, in the minds of many an average American worker, or even a petit-bourgeois professional. Some 25-year-old kid whips up some "code" for an "app" or a "website," and suddenly he's paying cash for a house next door to Julia Roberts or Courteney Cox, or for the entire floor of a Park Avenue high-rise. Some smart-ass college kids are huffing on hookahs in their day-old boxer briefs and gym shirts, listening to Green Day and Smashing Pumpkins in a Stanford or Harvard dorm room one minute—and then heading off to the Mercedes, Rolls-Royce, and Porsche showrooms the next minute, while buying their trophy blonde girlfriends head-to-toe Vera Wang, Prada, and Donatella, and jewels from Bulgari and Harry Winston. And some hotshot "day trader" or stock speculator gets a whispered raised-eyebrow tip about how this hot Internet company or that is about to "go public." He refinances his house or dumps his 401K into their stocks on opening night to take the big plunge—and next year, he's propping his feet up with a color-tini at a vacation villa on the Cote d'Azur.

What the hell is going ON here? What about people like me, who bust our humps every day at the office or factory actually *making* things and *conducting* day-to-day business and *closing* sales deals? What about me, the civil engineer who took my degree to go work for the big company or at the city hall or county office, or to teach these kids at a public high school or state college, because of the "job security" and the "good pay and benefits?" And *this* is my portion, my reward, my share? To be "scooped" by a bunch of twenty-something nothings who used to be my students—the ones who used to intern for me and fetch me my coffee—with their hot new Something-or-Other Dot Com? Bad enough that no screenwriter over age 50 can get anyone to answer their calls, let alone get a staff gig on *Friends* or *Buffy* or write the next Kevin Williamson, Spike Lee, or Tarantino epic. What did these slacker-generation dipsticks do to deserve to "retire" at age 30? Why, they didn't even *make* anything!

That '50s Show

To many a (usually well-paid, plugged-in) neoliberal journalist of the later Clinton era, it was a mystery more confounding than anything on *Law & Order* or *The X-Files* why Bill Clinton apparently got so little credit for this brave new economy. After all, he had "created" over 20 million new jobs. The stock market more than TRIPLED in value from late 1992 to March/April of 2000 (when it hit a then all-time high), as new technologies and the Internet began to thrive. When Ronald Reagan pulled America back from the brink in 1984, he was rewarded with the biggest landslide in modern history. Less than a dozen years later in 1996, with the economy and stock market starting to zoom off in similarly stratospheric fashion (and with the deficit in decline for the first time since LBJ and Nixon),

Bill Clinton barely managed to break 50–50, against 66-year-old has-been Ross Perot and 73-year-old Grandpa Simpson Bob Dole. *What was going on?*

Everybody knows that left wing voices and liberals, from the 1990s right on through today, make sporting fun of conservatives for wanting to turn back the clock on social progress to the black-and-white days of Harry Truman and Dwight Eisenhower. But when it came to the checkbook and the job applications, it turns out that economic liberals were just as hopelessly addicted to reruns of *That '50s Show*. Just as the Religious Right and social conservatives would settle for nothing less than a return to 1950s morality and sex roles, much of the '90s and 2000s working and middle-class—from Green Partiers to future Tea Partiers—wanted nothing less than a return to *Pleasantville's* economy. If you couldn't buy a home in Orange County or Long Island for $25,000 at 5 percent fixed, if you couldn't pick up a reliably built Chevy sedan for $3000 (or a Cadillac for less than $10 grand), if Mom worked because she *had* to, instead of because she *wanted* to—that was simply Not Acceptable.

And of course, no media megaphone articulated this rage better than Michael "Roger & Me" Moore. Responding to a *FrumForum* book review of Moore's 2011 memoir (written by one of FF's many talented columnists), a reader-commenter wondered aloud, "What kind of economic Kool-Aid were we drinking?" to think that the mid-century, gas-guzzling, *Father Knows Best* and *Mad Men* economy that ran from 1945 to 1974 would be sustainable indefinitely? That almost mythical economy of easy employment, low-priced houses and cars, and dirt-cheap college, gasoline, and medical expenses. "We were handed the most unrealistic situation in the world," the commenter bitterly laughed, a world where the United States and Canada were virtually the *only* First World superpowers with massive technological, scientific, and manufacturing capabilities (plus stock-marketed, ready-for-prime-time banking economies) whose domestic infrastructure was still basically intact from World War II. (And for a bonus, we *also* weren't being held prisoner behind the Iron Curtain, like half of Europe and darn near half of Asia.)

Back then, America and Canada were the ONLY First World economies that were, as they might say on *Family Feud,* "ready for action!" The only ones *in the entire world.* "And yet," the *FrumForum* reader shook his head, "to this day" that midcentury Great Prosperity is what most Americans and Canadians "still regard as the benchmark of *normal.*" In his book *Holy Land: A Suburban Memoir,* city planner Donald J. Waldie said that "You could say that [this] was the American dream made affordable for a generation of industrial workers," not to mention the many others who occupied similar stations on the economic totem pole—policemen, elementary school teachers, nurses, salesmen, etc. Quoting Waldie, Joan Didion picked up on the subtext. The Great Prosperity that the World War II and Korea veterans (and their "sweethearts") had experienced in the '50s, '60s, and early '70s, after growing up in the Depression, "was a sturdy but unsupportable ambition [that had been] sustained for forty years by good times and the good will" of a benevolent, patriarchal, Franklin Roosevelt-style Big Government. It was a lifestyle, as Waldie added, that the working and lower middle classes "in the preceding generations could never aspire to." Unfortunately, by the 1990s, the working and lower middle classes were starting to get the memo that their current and future generations might not ever be able to "aspire to" that kind of long-term economic security again.

"I'm not even supposed to be here today!"
(or, Supersize Me!)

In Kevin Smith's iconic Gen-X classic, *Clerks,* Dante Hicks, the twentyish community college dropout and head cashier at a local QuickStop minimart in suburban New Jersey, memorably groaned after being pushed past the point of human endurance, "I'm not even supposed to be here today!!" It was only fitting that Smith's follow-up to *Clerks* was the Jason Lee and Ben Affleck comedy, *Mallrats.* Indeed, few things said more about consumer culture in the Reagan '80s and the Clinton '90s than the gaggles of aimless working-class (and showoffy upper-middle-class) young people who moved like bangle-earringed dust clouds through every Galleria, Towne Center, and Mega-Mall in America and Canada. Not to mention the more artsy and literary Gen Xers who made bookstores, record and CD stores, movie "multiplexes," and video-rental stores into virtual second homes—working at them, hanging out at them, cruising for sex at them, and just about everything else.

But by the Clinton era, there was a lot more to mall culture than just a place to shop till you drop. Indeed, Bill Clinton's entire economic prescription for getting lower-middle-class, non-college people out of the doldrums of the manufacturing-declined, *Roger & Me* and *Roseanne* economy that existed when he took office, was by doubling, tripling, and quadrupling down on a retail-based "service economy" of mallrats, fast food restaurants, and super-wuper-duper megastores—preferably from large national chains. (Remember, Hillary was on the board of Walmart and was like "this" with Tyson Foods by the time she was forty.) Indeed, it seemed like every other economic article in the '90s New York and Los Angeles *Times, Time, Newsweek,* and *U.S. News,* was blathering about the transformation from a manufacturing economy to a "service economy."

What less-charitable pundits called "McJobs" at fast-food places, big-box stores, chain coffeehouses and restaurants, and giga-bookstores and video outlets, all seemed like the logical replacement for the lower-middle-class manufacturing jobs that were being out-sourced to Mexico and South America under Clinton (and would be outsourced at an even more alarming rate to China and India under George W. Bush and Barack Obama). The jobs were similarly low-skill (repetitive and rote, not requiring of a bachelor's degree or some kind of DeVry-type technical institute training). And many of them actually had some potential for advancement. Even at stingy employers like McDonald's, Walmart, Target, and Radio Shack, an experienced and no-more-than community-college-educated store manager (let alone a district manager) could find himself eventually shopping for the split-level with a swimming pool, and leasing an STS Seville or a Lexus.

But there was a fly in the ointment. While the 1990s are remembered today by many (especially by Clinton Democrats) as what Michael Kinsley only half-jokingly called in 2000 "the best economy in the history of the universe," that certainly *wasn't* always true if you were a small businessman. Not if your local bookstore was put out of print by Borders or Barnes & Noble, or your local video shack was permanently rewound by Blockbuster or Hollywood Video. Not if your local donut shop was deep-fried by Starbucks or Krispy Kreme, or your family Italian ristorante was ground into sausage by Olive Garden and Dominos, or if your local home emporium was pole-sawed by Walmart or Home Depot. In those cases, the 1990s were anything but "prosperous" for *you!* (And it goes without saying that many of these "bitter self-made" small businessmen, as Thomas Frank memorably described them, went from eagerly sponsoring the Gingrich Revolution in the '90s to providing the backbone of the Tea Party in more recent times.)

In a seminal 1998 *Rolling Stone* feature article titled "Fast Food Nation," journalist Eric Schlosser served up some tasty food-for-thought to go, about the low-unemployment, super-sized Clintonomic economy—especially from the POV of the lower-middle-class. The fast food industry had ballooned from $6 billion a year revenues in 1970 to nearly $100 billion less than thirty years later. By 1998, Americans spent more at Mickey D's, Colonel Sanders, and Taco Bell than they did on movies, books, music, newspapers, and magazines *combined*. Schlosser noted that the "rapid growth of the fast-food industry has been driven by fundamental changes in the US economy."

The purchasing power of the average American worker peaked at the end of President Nixon's run in 1973–74 (the time of the first major oil crisis) and "had steadily declined" until 1997. (And even then, as Robert Reich later noted, it had only barely crept up, with what little slivers of progress there were in the late '90s soon crushed by skyrocketing health insurance and college education costs under Bush II and early Obama.) "Women entered the work force in record numbers—often motivated less by feminism than a need to help pay the bills," Schlosser continued, echoing Reich, noting that from 1975 to 1998, the percentage of mothers with young children who worked outside the home *doubled*, from one-third to two-thirds of them. "This increased demands for the types of services that housewives typically performed—cooking, cleaning, and day care." (Needless to say, many of the people employed in those takeover professions were immigrants, legal and illegal, and other poor women of all races, who were paid slave wages and often *still* had to use food stamps, Medicaid, and subsidized housing just to get by—even though they were employed.)

In 1968, McDonalds had a total of 1,000 restaurants in the U.S. and Canada. Thirty years later, that number had metastasized to 23,000. And that phototropic growth rate wasn't out of the ordinary. By 1998, "franchises and chain stores have gained in the last twenty-five years a 40 percent share of all retail spending in the United States. *Almost every aspect of American life has now been franchised*." Schlosser also gave a sad shout-out to the sort of "literate and civilized bookstore[s]" and cinemaniac-managed video and music stores that were being "forced out of business" by then-growing chains like Borders, Barnes & Noble, and Blockbuster. And in a karate kick to all the puffery about the "best economy ever" of the '90s, Schlosser noted—at the very summit of the Clinton boom in 1998—that "the fast food industry has created millions of new jobs *at a time when other industries have been FIRING workers*. It now employs some of the poorest, most disadvantaged members of society." (Our emphasis.)

Columbia professor Thomas Edsall wrote a 2015 *New York Times* editorial, after authoring a book stolidly titled *The Age of Austerity: How Scarcity Will Remake American Politics*. In it, he quoted a chart by Duke University professor Nir Jaimovich and University of British Columbia economist Henry Siu, that illustrated, quote, "how, starting during the recession of 1991, recoveries do not lead to revived job markets.... If the past 30 years is any guide ... jobless recoveries may be the new norm."

But the 1995–2000 "recovery" from the early '90s recession was anything but jobless, you say! Didn't Bill Clinton "create" a net of 20-some million jobs? Yes, but once again— *they weren't necessarily the same jobs* that had been put to sleep "during the recession of 1991." Jaimovich and Siu's study went on to describe in detail the trend of "job polarization" that they observed in both the Clintonomic dot-com bubble recovery (and the 2003–08 Bush/Cheney "recovery" after 9/11 and the dot-com bubble-burst). On one end, there was phenomenal growth in jobs requiring college educations and computer sophistication—writing "code" and engineering, top-level Hollywood and CEO "personal assistant" positions, search engine optimization, and the like.

On the other, just as a 1992 *Los Angeles Daily News* editorial predicted, the long-term future of the outsourcing, fast-technologizing New Economy would be predicated on "the trend toward a new, more independent work force that will become less reliant on the company to provide for them, and more inclined toward entrepreneurship." Joan Didion accurately translated that as code for meaning, "In other words, no benefits and no fixed salary." People working commission only, signature-gathering, door-to-dooring, waiter-tipping, or hourly clock-punching—and fingers-crossingly living from paycheck to paycheck. It was "a recipe for motel people." A popular late 1990s joke went, "Bill Clinton created 20 million jobs, and I oughta know—I have *two* of them!"

Susan Faludi continued in her book *Stiffed*—written during the height of the "peace and prosperity" economy in 1998 and '99—that a "categorical shift had occurred … a social pact between the nation's men and its institutions was collapsing. Productivity was now measured not by employee elbow grease but by how many employees the company laid off." And as the iconic 1990s office cartoon *Dilbert* brilliantly satirized, Customer Service meant "nothing more than consumer assistance, exemplified by a telemarketer trapped in a cubicle, phone glued to his ear, his have-a-nice-day conversations preformulated and monitored. Such a profound and traumatic transformation" affected everyone in the New Economy of the '90s, "whether they lost their jobs or *simply feared losing them*, whether they drowned or floated in the treacherous new currents."

Outsourcing and downsizing and the preference for cheap, desperate, and yes, often "illegal" proletarian labor by big businessmen (who then cynically wrote checks to demagogic politicians who'd rile up working-class whites with how illegal Latinos were "taking" their jobs) took quite a toll on the 1990s economy. But Charlene Barshefsky drove it home. "The irony is that probably 80 percent of the job loss in the US [was] *technology* driven, not trade driven." In *Inequality for All*, Robert Reich didn't flinch when he affixed blame for lower middle class America's pocketbook woes: "Globalization and technology."

If one looks a little closer at the map, one can see the unlovely bones of Red America and Blue America forming around all this. What young person in his right mind would stay in a ghosted steel town in Cleveland or Flint Michigan or Pittsburgh's "rust belt," when there were jobs to be found at stores, hotels, casinos, and whatnot in Vegas, Miami, Honolulu, or Seattle? Or when there *were* still factory jobs to be had—at the non–UAW, Toyota, Honda, Nissan, and Hyundai plants being built in the American South and rural heartland, so as to take the stigma off of buying "non–American" Asian cars.

Now that things had finally recovered, California and New York were back in business. But in the early '90s recession—when NYC was all crack, decay, and muggings, when LA and even ritzy Orange County were flat on their backs with high taxes, annihilated city hall and school district services, crime and unemployment—both of those states saw a veritable exodus of small businessmen and entrepreneurs, outsourced and downsized aerospace workers, and so on. Eric Schlosser added that towns like Colorado Springs, and plenty of other areas in exurban Nevada, Arizona, Texas, Oregon, the Research Triangle in North

Carolina, Virginia, Utah, and the like, were becoming "Californicated" (and "Manhattanized") with coastal refugees from the early '90s recession.

While plenty of people of color were among these pioneers, in most instances, this was a "white flight"—and this time it wasn't due to a symbolic lifestyle issue like forced school busing or fair housing mandates from back in the '70s. In many cases, it was simply a matter of pure economic survival. And birds of a feather flock together. As the coastal states lost their working and middle-class Anglo anchors, they became more visibly minority and immigrant at one end of the spectrum, and more high-tech and educated at the other. The South and Midwest likewise made up for their slower-growing immigrant and minority populations with this new influx of mostly white (and overwhelmingly conservative) new residents from the former industrial powerhouses. Three cheers for the red, white, and blue—or better, for the Red States vs. the Blue States.

From a purely amoral, macro-economic view, it made sense for 1990s politicians on both sides to furtively (if not openly) favor big-box stores, Big Macs, and big business, despite all the hand-wringing and TV tear-snuffling about the "heroism" of "job creators" and local entrepreneurs.

After many communities and states passed property tax limitations on residential real estate in the wake of California's famed Proposition 13 in 1978, by the 1990s many local cities were engaged in an almost *Hunger Games*–like frenzy of clawing and gouging for the next Walmart, Starbucks, Best Buy, Circuit City, Home Depot, Borders, Barnes & Noble, or Blockbuster superstore (or all of the above) to anchor their "redeveloped" new mega-malls, strip malls, and shopping centers. Even more elephantine environmentalist-nightmare "auto malls" sprung up alongside freeways and boulevards in one city after another, with Lexus and Cadillac and Lincoln, Honda and Hyundai and Toyota, Chevy and Dodge and Ford dealers side-by-side-by-side, each one offering their latest subsidized 36- and 48-month Smart Leases, or low-low financing blowout sales.

Not only was that commercial real estate valuable for tax assessment itself; those businesses would also create jobs and yield millions in sales taxes each year. How much better than a bunch of low-income Section 8 apartments, dilapidated ticky-tacky tract bungalows, or senior citizens' mobile home parks? (Indeed, by the late '90s some communities became so desperate for the big-box bling, they began eminent-domaining people out of house and home to install new malls and superstores in the community's "economic interest"—a principle that was eventually upheld by the Supreme Court itself, in 2005's dreadful *Kelo vs. New London*—the direct predecessor to 2010's *Citizens United* corporations-as-people ruling.)

In the end, all of this might have been justifiable if those places—and the Shannen Doherty-era economy that supported all those Mallrats and Valley Girls—had been built to last. But alas, the Internet and globalization, and new ways of online shopping, soon cashed in their chips. During the Great Recessionary final days of George W. Bush and the entire first term of Barack Obama, many if not most of the too-big-to-fail corporate icons of the 1990s "Service Economy" would meet one cruel death after another: Circuit City. Blockbuster Video. Borders Books. Hollywood Video. Mervyns. Even decades-established brands like Continental Bakeries (of "Hostess" and "Twinkies" fame), Polaroid, and Kodak headed for the exit door. All like old cars crashing off a cliff in a CGI action movie or video game. Even the ones that survived relatively intact, like Best Buy, Sears, Radio Shack, and

Barnes & Noble, announced massive closures and downsizings. (And that quintessential American car brand of '90s Gen-Xers, Saturn, which premiered in fall 1990 for the 1991 model year, was sent into total eclipse by the GM bankruptcy restructuring in early 2010.)

Indeed, they were almost lucky to have lasted so long. Remember Netscape or Alta Vista, Friendster and GeoCities? Wanna buy a computer from Packard Bell or Leading Edge or Commodore? Care to go shopping at Tower Records or The Good Guys? Topping it all off was perhaps the ultimate "mascot" of dot-com bubble overreach, Pets.com (with its lovable hound dog spokes-muppet truthfully named Sock Puppet), which got put to sleep in November of 2000 after a pumped-up, TV-advertised run in late 1998, 1999, and early 2000. The investors who hadn't cashed out early were left with a case of financial rabies. And the appalling Enron, Tyco, and WorldCom bankruptcies—from those other supposedly "can't miss" stocks of the late 1990s boom—were just around the corner in 2001–02.

During the 9/11 Commission hearings in 2003–04, chairman Thomas Kean said that the lead-ups to the 9/11 attacks were "above all, a failure of imagination." No less destructive in its own way was the utter and abject failure from both Democrat and Republican A-listers in the Congress and Senate of the late 1990s and early 2000s to imagine what and where fast-developing new technology was going to take us over the next decade or so. Bill, Hillary, and especially Al Gore tried to spell it out, but their game-changing techno truths were just a little too inconvenient. Like a woman who finds a lump in her breast but refuses to go to the doctor, the narrative-writers at the top of both parties seemed to believe, by the end of the "record-breaking prosperity" of the late 1990s, that if you just didn't pay any attention, all the future's problems would just take care of themselves.

"It wasn't until the Clinton Administration that there was a real opportunity to reverse all of this," Robert Reich kvetched. "And that was what was so damned frustrating! I mean, we had budget surpluses [from 1997 to 2001], and we might have been able to take those surpluses and invest them in education and job [re]training programs. To change the structure, ultimately, of the economy." But Clinton had already given his famous 1996 shout-out to Reaganites, that "the era of Big Government is over." A DailyKos article in 2015 recalled Reich being taken out to a full-course meal with Fed chief Alan Greenspan around 1996. At the table, Reich practically begged Greenspan to support his plans for massive investment in job retraining programs for workers whose jobs would soon be outsourced or obsoleted by new technology. (Essentially, the fabled "jobs bill" that Clinton had promised on his "day one.")

Greenspan however, *simply* wouldn't hear of it! An inviolate, almost fetishistic worship of "the market" had become a cult-like mantra for 1990s financial policy among both Republicans and New Democrats (and everyone else except for progressive Left leftovers like Reich). The Market would take care of all those things on its own, intoned the Fed Chief. No need for government interference (let alone Johnson/Nixon-style big government social programs). Greenspan cut off any further discussion, like the bossiest federal judge of them all, banging his gavel. Reich groaned years later, "There [just] wasn't the political will."

The Emailing and cell-phoning, Hi Def economy that was just another day at the office in 1999 and 2000 would have been only barely imaginable in 1985 or even 1990, let alone before. But by 1999, Amazon was selling books, Netflix was launched on the video scene, Google was Googling, movie studios were beginning to release DVDs as well as VHS videos, digital photos were first beginning to be snapped, and Zappos was selling designer threads and shoes in areas where there wasn't a Manolo Blahnik, Jimmy Choo, Christian Louboutin, or Ferragamo showroom for miles. And the Drudge Report, Slate, and Salon.com were the hip places to get your news fix, not some boring ink-stained newspaper—just as Monster.com (1999) and Craigslist (1995–99) would soon cause newspapers dependent upon classified advertising to go from black ink to red. While none of these companies were the behemoths that they would become by the time of Barack Obama, both the Democrats and Republicans wishfully acted as though these new businesses and business models would *forever* be consigned to the B-list. As though new technology would *always* exist side-by-side with old. Like someone nervously whistling past a graveyard, they "reassured" themselves that these new upstarts could never *really* grow to where they would rewrite the rules for entire, decades or centuries-established business models. *Could they?*

"All of the language, all of the framework, all of the understandings that we had created in 1992, the original Bill Clinton message that the economy is nothing but its people—which I think were absolutely correct and are STILL correct ... vanished from Democratic rhetoric" during Bill Clinton's second term, lamented Robert Reich. A frustrated Reich would leave the Clinton government at the end of 1996, with not a little distaste at what he had seen—and for what he rightly predicted would be Clintonomic policy from then on.

Inequality for All

In 1980, the last year of Jimmy Carter's reign, the typical male worker earned the purchasing-power equivalent of $48,000 (in 2010–12 era dollars), according to Robert Reich, in his 2012 film *Inequality for All.* By the time the Reagan-Bush era had ended, that had fallen to the equivalent of $40,000 a year. And after all the "record-breaking prosperity" of Bill Clinton, when he finished his eight-year rule and passed the dice over to George W. Bush, it had *fallen* yet again, to the equivalent of only $36,000 a year. And this was *before* all of George W. Bush's Enron-era abuses and tax cuts, or the 2008 economic meltdown.

So where did all that new money go? Reich's charts also showed that the Top 1 percent saw their purchasing power literally *double,* from the 1978 equivalent of $393,000 a year (averaged in constant dollar values) to the 2001 equivalent of $748,000 a year, adding over $100,000 of that power under William Jefferson Clinton. This was all the more dramatic in that from Franklin Roosevelt in the mid–1930s through the end of Jimmy Carter, the Top 1 percent of taxpayers' share of the total American economic "pie" had held steady. The Top 1 percent then owned between 10 and 12 percent of the net worth of the economy. Not bad—in other words, the uber-rich of the Great Consensus era controlled ten times their proportion to the population. When the "greedy" Reagan-Bush era was finished in early 1993, the top 1 percent had seen their share of the American "portfolio" increase from 10 percent in 1980 to about 14–15 percent–a very impressive 50 percent increase in their holdings.

But that was just for openers. By the time Bill Clinton wrapped up at the end of 2000, the Top 1 percent had skyrocketed to owning over *20 percent* of the U.S. economy's net worth—going from 15 percent before Clinton to 20 percent *after* Clinton—effectively *doubling* their share of the pie from when Democrat Jimmy Carter had retired twenty years earlier. Indeed, the graph line from the start of the Clinton era to the finish goes up at an almost continuous Mt. Whitney-like angle for the super-rich.

Reich further revealed that worker productivity had roughly doubled between the start of America's "Happy Days" in the postwar late 1940s through the end of Richard Nixon's government in 1974—again, roughly the time span almost every economist and journalist looks back on as the Great Prosperity for the North American working and middle class. And workers' wages matched the increases in productivity almost dollar for dollar during all of that time, with only minuscule gaps in favor of shareholders and "corporate America."

However by 1990, worker productivity had gone up by *another* 50 percent, from 100 percent of the 1945–50 baseline to 150 percent of it—but worker wages were now going *down* slightly, after being adjusted for cost-of-living. Thankfully, at that critical time, the era of "greedy" and "selfish" Reaganomics ended, in favor of the kinder, gentler, and fairer Clintonomics approach, right? Well, let's take a look-see: By 2000, productivity had gone up yet *another* 50 percentage points—roughly *double* what it had been twenty years earlier in 1980 (the last year before Reaganomics), according to the 2011 Bureau of Labor Statistics graph where Reich obtained his figures. Yet worker wages, adjusted for cost-of-living, had essentially flat-lined from late 1990 to '94 (in other words, during the "It's the Economy, Stupid" recession). Finally, Clinton did get the middle class a slight increase—but it was a comparatively pathetic one: 10 to 15 percentage points from 1995 to 2000—as opposed to a *nearly 50 percent increase* in productivity—again! The headline for the April 30, 1997, issue of *The New York Times* said it all: "Markets Surge as Labor Costs Stay in Check"— which lefty historian Rick Perlstein later translated as, "The Rich Got Richer, While the Poor Got Poorer..."

Irrational Exuberance

That didn't mean that there weren't good times to be had by all during the late 1990s. It's just that a helluva lot of it was charged on America's Visa card. Household debt exploded from 2–3 times one's income in the late 1970s to 5 times one's household income at the end of the go-go Reagan-Bush years—only to zoom forward to *seven* times household income in 2000, according to a graph (cited in *Inequality for All*) composed by the San Francisco branch of the Federal Reserve offices. (Debt, of course, continued to photon-torpedo upwards under the housing boom of 2002 to 2008, followed by the Great Recession, so that by 2010 the debt demon had grown to a dizzying factor of over 10 times household income.) And both Bill Clinton and George W. Bush would encourage this consumption for consumption's sake—terrified of a return to the stagnant early '90s economy, when people stopped buying stuff and businesses began laying off.

This did not come without a price. Bankruptcies *doubled* between the Carter-era recession of 1979–80 and the Clintonomic "prosperity" of 1997. Payday advance and auto title loan stores and "money store" home equity refinancing operations sprang up like mushrooms during that same time, and became inescapable on daytime TV. Newspapers were jam-packed with auto dealers encouraging people to take subsidized leases on new upscale cars, instead of buying to own and building to last. All this added up to a verdict that while the Clinton era had seen the only real growth in lower-middle-class purchasing power *at all* since Ford and Carter, those gains were so minuscule that Robert Reich lamented in 2012 that worker wages had essentially "gone nowhere for 30 years."

Wall Street II: Money Never Sleeps

George W. Bush might have talked a good game about creating an "ownership society" during his 2002–08 housing bubble reign, but the general concept dated right back to Bill Clinton, who used the 1977 Community Redevelopment Act as a carte blanche to require more and more marginal mortgage loans to be made to low income borrowers, in the aftermath of the grotesque level of 1970s and '80s double-digit inflation in East and West coast housing prices.

From Jimmy Carter through Ronald Reagan and (most of) Bush Sr., both the Paul Volcker and early Alan Greenspan Federal Reserves had pursued a "tight money" policy of high interest rates on borrowed debt—with correspondingly high rates of return on safe bank investments. As late as 1989 and '90, a depositor or retiree with $50 or $100,000 in their life savings could expect to get 8 or 9 percent interest each year, just from the safe and insured money-market account at their local bank or S&L. But as Matt Taibbi noted in his book *Griftopia*, all that changed during the early '90s recession. Greenspan suddenly began slashing interest rates to 1950s and '60s levels, so that people could begin refinancing their homes as housing values (especially on the coasts) plummeted, and to protect against what later happened in the even worse 2008–12 collapse. (People walking away en masse from their "underwater" houses, further glutting the market with foreclosures and repossessions.)

Greenspan also wanted to encourage the people who still had jobs or stable incomes to shop till they dropped to stimulate the rest of the economy. What better way to juice things than to make new and late-model used cars, consumer goods, and fashions into deals "too good to say no to," with low-low financing and EZ credit? Better, if interest rates were held down, the government would pay less debt duty on its mammoth national debt and deficit, which would allow for even more savings and a faster-track towards a balanced federal budgeting!

The fly in the ointment came when suddenly, nonworking retirees and 40- and 50-somethings who'd been dutifully saving their money and watching it balloon at 7, 8, 9 percent annual interest rates under Reagan-Bush (and far more under Carter), outpacing general inflation, now saw their rates of bank interest suddenly annihilated to minuscule 2, 3, 4 and 5 percent returns. Now, if these people wanted to get a "real" return on their money, they had no choice but to look to Wall Street. And that's just what they did.

Economic liberals like Matt Taibbi, Michael Moore, and Thomas Frank smelled a rat. What better way to force Greatest and Silent Generation members—many of whom were allergic to "gambling" their money on Wall Street stocks, after having grown up in the shadow of the Depression—into glutting the stock market with their lifetime-earned savings? When working people saw a business downsizing and outsourcing, to make even more bling for their already-rich investors, it used to incite outrage. But now, if *other* working middle-classers, small businessmen, and publicly employed teachers and policemen had their retirements and savings accounts invested in Wall Street, how could they complain anymore? If those outsourcings and downsizings were helping to raise *their* own portfolios?

According to Social Security's website, the percentage of Americans participating in traditional "defined benefit" pension schemes was literally *cut in half* between 1980 and 2008, going from 38 percent to only 20 percent of the adult workforce. What largely replaced them was "defined *contribution*" retirement plans like IRA's and 401k accounts, which ballooned from only 8 percent of the job market to over 31 percent during that very same time. One of the reasons for this was the usual deregulation and big-money mentality of the '80s and '90s. But another very good reason was because many employees—now made all too aware of just how shaky their foundation was, of how unlikely it was that they would only work for one or two or even three payers in a working lifetime—wanted the "portability" of individual retirement accounts.

Someone who went to work for General Electric or General Motors at age 25 or 30, and retired 30 years later at age 55 or 60, had it much better off under a defined-benefit traditional system. But if someone was forced (by outsourcing, downsizing, and the high-tech "creative destruction" of old businesses and business models) to pick up and work for 4, 5, 6, or 7 different employers or payers in their working lifetime—*then* which idea worked best?

In any case, so much money flooded the 1990s stock market in so short a time, that a bubble every bit as artificial, and potentially almost as dangerous as the 2000s mortgage bubble, began to inflate. In 1996, the famed NASDAQ stock index was still only around 600; less than four years later, at the peak of the dot-com bubble in 2000, it had exploded to over 5,000! According to the humorously resourceful Dotcombubble.com, it was said that in 1999 and early 2000, a new millionaire was created every 60 seconds in Silicon Valley and Wall Street. Everyone drank the Kool-Aid. *The New Republic* was writing articles like "Praised be Greenspan!" (a story later found to be fraudulent, cooked up by the notorious Stephen Glass, about a "cult" of Wall Streeters who "worshiped" Alan Greenspan in bizarre ceremonies). What was *really* scandalous, of course, wasn't that the story was made up and printed as fact. What was horrifying was that dreck like that could ever be thought to have had serious news credibility in the first place. But such was the atmosphere of the late '90s New Economy.

In 1995, *Newsweek* coined the phrase "The Overclass" to describe the status and education-conscious tastemakers beginning to prosper most under the Information Age. (Not surprisingly, they were the same hyper-yuppies that David Brooks satirized as "Bobos in Paradise" a few years later.) By the start of 1997, Alan Greenspan himself had weighed in with a verdict, famously (and quite rightly) warning of "irrational exuberance" as the dot-com era stock market first began reaching eye-popping, never-before-dreamed-of proportions. Yet knowing full well of this, instead of doing something to curb this "irrationality," neither Greenspan nor Bill Clinton so much as lifted a toe to apply the brake pedal. As Dick Cheney himself might have put it, it was Full Speed Ahead! The '80s mentality was making a comeback faster than you could say DeLorean.

De-"Human"-ization

On the first episode of the classic *Mary Tyler Moore Show* in 1970, a young lady named Mary Richards is interviewing for a job that she's just answered a want-ad for. Her would-be boss, Lou Grant, tells her point-blank that he was planning "to hire a man for it." Instead of screaming bloody murder, Mary casually accepts this, but she still has enough famous "spunk" to try to charmingly convince the man to hire her. Which he does—on the spot. About nine or ten years earlier, when the first episode of *Mad Men* was set, a 21-year-old gal named Peggy Olson does the same thing, fresh from her community college secretarial degree. She answered her ad, made her appointment, and filled out her application. And after the office manager and head secretary who ran the "steno" department met with Peggy and decided she'd work out nicely, Peggy was being shown around the office—to start immediately.

What's remarkable about those scenes, looking back, is that they largely *weren't* a Hollywood cop-out. Back when both of those scenes were set—at the height of the midcentury Great Prosperity—many if not most people *did* get jobs just like that. They saw the ad, called in, made an appointment, filled out an app, got an interview … and if they made a good impression on their future boss, *on the person for whom they would actually be working*, it was "Welcome aboard. You start work on Monday!"

Those days were very much over by the Clintonomic 1990s—whether in the recession-recovery beginning years or the booming final days. Bill Clinton most certainly did help "create" a record-setting 20+ million jobs. But just because there were a lot of potential jobs out there, that certainly didn't mean that *each individual job* was all that *easy to get* in the first place. Now, Mary and Peggy would first have to submit their resumes and applications to Human Resources, and wait a week or so to see if they "survived" the first round of "screenings" and cuts, like a pair of reality-show contestants. Then, assuming they got callbacks, they would come in for a meeting—not with the man or woman for whom they'd actually be working, but with Miss Priss, the "recruitment manager" from HR. And if *she* thought they made the grade during the "qualifying interview," *then* they might get a "hiring interview" or panel session with their prospective boss. And still after that, the actual hiring decision would be made by the department boss and Miss Priss together—with Miss Priss holding the trump card.

Indeed, one of the main reasons for the well-documented rapid rise in "human resources management" positions throughout the late 1980s and 1990s was to put a sort of federal judge-like iron curtain *between* the foremen, supervisors, and vice presidents that the people being hired would report to—and the people who were actually doing the hiring. Even aside from racial or sexist considerations, consider: In the old days, a boss might hire his drinking buddy or brother-in-law for a job when he was out of work or wanted to transfer, someone he personally liked and got along with as a crony, rather than someone who was objectively best for the given job. A Gordon Gekko or Don Draper–type boss *might* hire someone who was truly the best and most talented person overall—or he might just as well hire a hack whom he knew would never pose a "threat" to him from within, someone who was loyal and subservient and all-too-grateful for the work, perhaps even someone slightly desperate for the paycheck. And of course, when it was an "insignificant" job like a receptionist or secretary or restaurant hostess, in a contest between the pretty, bubbly Dolly Parton or Loni Anderson look-alike, and some far more qualified but wiry-haired, granny-glasses-wearing, ambiguously lesbian old maid—we all know who was gonna get hired or promoted *there*, don't we?

There would be so much less chance of "hostile work environment" and "employment discrimination" noise if the people in charge of hiring and firing were kept separate and sequestered from the rest of the office or factory's functions, people who had no real personal stake or day-to-day working relationship with the employees they "screened" and hired once they were out on the floor. We could focus on "headhunting" and "recruiting" for the very best person in each field in an objective, scientific, psychological fashion, rather than by the whims and likes and dislikes of each division-boss and supervisor. And when the IRS or the EEOC came by for a cup of coffee, we could show them on paper that everything was done using proper, apple-pie procedure (which is to say, we covered our assets with due diligence).

The angered reactions from many of the people who were actually applying for these jobs in the '90s—plentiful in the want ads but (from their point of view) often harder to get on an individual basis, with the process so much more mechanical, so DMV-bureaucratic, so unnecessarily prolonged—was a different story. *It's a secretarial job, for goodness sake!* An accounts clerk at City Hall or the school district! A library checkout clerk, a Kinko's or Fed-Ex delivery man! A cashier at Walmart or Ralph's or Home Depot, a theatre usher or headwaiter at the Krikorian or Olive Garden! Do they really have to "recruit" for and "screen" applicants, and go through centralized "hiring procedures" for *these* kind of jobs? As if they were looking for some high-tech laboratory scientist, some high-powered Marcia Clark litigator or Hillary Clinton hostile-takeover queen with an MBA or law degree? It was so ridiculous, it bordered on a scene from a John Waters movie. *Why can't my son or grandson just walk in and get a job already? He's not some unmotivated "slacker dude" high on drugs! My daughter or granddaughter isn't some "welfare queen" or trailer-trasher. It's like they're being punished for wanting to work! Why can't they just do things the way they always used to do, the way that I got my job, the way that made so much more sense?*

And that it should take weeks, even perhaps over a month, to fill these kinds of unremarkable, upper-blue-collar and lower-white-collar positions? *Heck, I'm already 2 payments behind on my car loan or mortgage or rent. Even if I do get the job, the first check won't come for another two weeks after that. What am I supposed to do while everyone goes through their Proper Personnel Procedure, their Equal Opportunity Affirmative Action Compliance Process?*

Class Dismissed

By the late 1990s, the economic left was so mad at Bill Clinton, you'd think they were ready to file a consumer complaint with Ralph Nader. (Oh, wait....) From economic lefties who wanted to resurrect the power and influence of the labor movement, to right-wing firebrands shrieking "class warfare!" whenever anyone talked about raising the minimum wage or taxing the rich, what was most interesting about what little talk there was in the mainstream media about social class in the 1990s was how ludicrously tone-deaf it all was.

The big difference was that the economic left defined "class" almost as a small child would, based solely on a person's net worth or income—while barely taking into account their social status, consumer tastes, religious beliefs, or media clout. The right-wing pundits likewise defined "class" almost entirely by a person's snobbery, if you will. Their fashion statements, what college they'd graduated from and where they lived, where they were in the media pecking order—and above all, whether they projected an aura of being "better than" the average American. If they insisted on designer labels and luxury or foreign cars, vacationed at all the right places, and paid attention to the latest trends. Whether it was Ann Coulter fulminating about secularist rich judges, senators, and professors forcing their beliefs down the heartland's throat, or whether it was David Brooks making fun of the snobbish affectations of the hyper-educated and trendy professional rich, it all came down to what their opposite number Thomas Frank would later call "the Latte Libel."

Certainly judging a person's class (let alone their "class interests") based on that person's snobbish attitude and affect by itself, with no regard at all to income or money, was ridiculous. However, to judge a person's class entirely—or even *primarily*—based on money and tax bracket was just as absurd. Roseanne Barr, Snoop Dogg, and Eminem might very well have just as much money in the bank, live at equally tony addresses, drive cars as nice, and own as many jewels and fashions as Gloria Vanderbilt, Brooke Astor, Happy Rockefeller, Betsy Bloomingdale, Diane von Furstenberg, Princess Margaret, and Katharine Graham. But would anybody seriously suggest that made Roseanne and Eminem the same *class* as the high-society divas? A rich socialite might find herself having to file for bankruptcy after the 1989–91 S&L crisis and the early '90s recession (let alone after the 2008 economic disaster or the 2001 dot-com crash). But does that mean that some Edie Wasserman or Leona Helmsley type would suddenly be reduced to the same "class" as the retired school-teacher or police officer, who had savings in the bank and a paid-off house?

Back in 1983, when Ann Coulter was still cramming for the bar exam, David Brooks was just out of college, and Thomas Frank was graduating high school, the noted historian and scholar Paul Fussell literally "wrote the book" on the peculiarly American *Class* system. Anyone who has ever read one word of the late Mr. Fussell's other writings would know that he was about as far away from the stereotypical right-winger as you could get—a card-carrying "Eastern elite" Princeton academic and intellectual all the way. (Fussell also had very little sympathy for conservative heroes like Ronald Reagan and the Bushes.)

Yet when it came to sorting out the lines and rhymes of social class and status in America and Canada—Fussell's system (although predictably a bit more nuanced) was virtually identical to the "constructs" of Ann Coulter and Bill O'Reilly. Lower-middle-class and working-class people are identified as such not because of their annual IRS return—but because of their gauche style of dress, their bodystyles that go between buff-body tattooed tough guys and fat 'n' flabby snack-food junkies. By the game and talk shows, simple TV dramas, country-style music, and good-guy/bad-guy feature films that they prefer. By the cars they drove, the non-architecture of their shapeless ticky-tacky tract houses, the Denny's and Red Lobster-style places they ate at, and so on. Likewise, upper-middle and upper-class people were identified as such by their tastes in all of those categories, too—and even more so by the things that they *avoided*: the TV shows and movies that weren't prestigious or intellectual enough for them; the cars that were too vulgar or showoffy or all-American; the high-end wines and chocolates and designer labels and private schools and colleges for their kids that they insisted on…

A professor at Harvard or Yale, at Princeton or Stanford, might make far less money than the "bitter self-made men" that Thomas Frank described as the backbone of the right-wing political backlash of the Midwest, which had enabled the Republican Revolution of 1994 and would help create the Tea Party of recent years. But that still doesn't mean that on a person-to-person basis, those self-made *petit bourgeois* businessmen had anywhere near the same cultural footprint as the "elite" professors and critics did. Did a book or film critic or an op-ed columnist at the New York or Los Angeles *Times* or for *Time* magazine have as much power, clout, and influence as Donald Trump, the Koch Brothers, or Warren Buffett? Certainly not. But compared to some rich Dodge dealer in Kansas, some pork-belly millionaire in Muskogee, or some linoleum tile king in Podunk—it's a whole 'nother story. Who would be more likely to be invited to black-tie soirees with Henry Kissinger or Madeleine Albright, to parties that Rupert Murdoch or Barry Diller might also be attending, at the MoMA or the Paley Center for Media, at the Guggenheim or Lincoln Center or the Dorothy Chandler? Which group of people were *really* more likely to run in the same circles as the Masters of the Universe, as the People Who Matter?

The fact that the aforementioned opinion journalists and academics, while all comfortably well-off, might not have as much money in the bank as the big-frog-little-pond "bitter self-made" winger-businessmen was completely beside the point. It's the *access*, it's the *platform*, it's the *prestige,* stupid. David Brooks drove it past the gate-guarded driveway with his decade-ending book *Bobos in Paradise,* based on his hilariously satirical late '90s *New York Times* articles about the "Resume Gods" marrying and domestically partnering with one another in fashionable big-city society columns. (You know, where the prep-school-educated, Yale-graduated WASP Episcopalian working as a $1,000,000 junior exec at Goldman Sachs marries the $500,000 Beverly Hills Jewish sitcom producer, with her MFA from NYU or USC, and her size-six Donna Karan sheaths. After which would come the inevitable debates over which ultra-exclusive preschool and Suzuki-method music or dance classes and soccer leagues they would drive their Gap Kids-wearing children to, in their new leased E-Classes and Range Rovers.)

No, what the left wing *didn't* want to talk about was *class*; what they clearly wanted to talk about was good old fashioned *income distribution*—perhaps with the prefix "re" attached to "distribution." And in particular, income inequality, and how grossly distorted it had become. The "class" aspect came into the picture in the sense of the Left wanting to create a "class consciousness," in the quasi-Marxian sense; to make the oppressed working and lower-middle classes realize that The System (especially as it is now) was largely rigged against them, that they had to band together as a people based on their shared economic interest. And to put that economic interest ahead of "values voting" and mindless flag-waving and so on, if they wanted any hope at all against truly monolithic and powerful, monopoly minded global corporations and consolidated Big Media.

However demagogic and destructive, the Ann Coulters and David Brookses had every right to construct their diagram of class relations based on tastes in TV, movies, music, reading (or lack of it), cars, fashion statements, "jobs" as opposed to "careers"—and above all, on what name-brand college (or prep school) and preferably post-graduate educational level one attained. Because that's how class IS, in fact, largely determined in the U.S. and Canada. The right-wing writers and radio-talkers simply found a way to channel the snobbery, chauvinism, thinly disguised racism, and condescension inherent in many of those "class constructs" to their advantage. (And boy oh boy, did they ever use it!)

"Corporate KILLERS" and Barbarians at the Gate

"There was a widespread sense of denial that the present was producing the greatest prosperity in the country's history," Sidney Blumenthal wrote in the summer of 1997, citing an August 29 Richard Morin feature in the *Washington Post* centered on a poll that "found wide pessimism about [the] direction of [the] nation." Blumenthal went on: "The public still had the mentality of the Bush presidency's recession, combined with a lingering suspicion of government from the Gingrich revolt against it. [The Democrats also] remained fractious, regardless of Clinton's proven politics in the reelection campaign, and often captive to strong currents of protectionism. This literally reactionary protectionism proved how deep seated was the grip of past political mentalities over fresh facts."

Yet if someone had just survived an economic near-genocide, as in gangsta Southern California during the "Bush presidency's recession," if you had spent the late '80s or early '90s in "Fuck da Police!" or *Do the Right Thing* era New York City, or in the Michael Moore "Rust Belt" with ladies raising bunny rabbits for "Pets—or Meat?," then who could blame these people for having "lingering suspicions," and a deep-seated sense of post-traumatic stress and insecurity? Especially if they *did* lose a job and have to go look for another one because of NAFTA, or fight to keep their current one with some class-conscious human resources screener? Even at the height of the '90s boom, there would be no Prince Charming to kiss-awake the hollow aerospace plants of Lakewood and Houston, of Seattle and Vegas. The spark-plug and transmission assembly lines and steel quarries and mills of Flint Michigan and Cleveland Ohio were as deathly still in the "unprecedented prosperity" of 1998 as they were when the first wave of Mexican and Central American outsourcing had struck a decade before.

Just as tellingly, in midcentury America, the companies that were considered the best investments were the ones that had proven themselves to be reliable and (to use the now-dated phrase) as "sound as the dollar." To use the infamous "pain" metaphor that scrub nurses and surgeons give ICU and cancer patients, in *Mad Men* era America, you wanted your company's growth to be "like a lake, rather than an ocean." Stable, predictable, and orderly were the watchwords of the three-martini economy. A company that had phenomenal growth one year and then fell behind the next, and then went all over the map, was as grotesque as a bipolar housewife mugging and gesturing in the supermarket or restaurant, like someone having a nervous breakdown, a compulsive gambler at the casino or track. That kind of leadership disgraced itself, made the company look unserious, ruined its "brand"—and practically sent a messenger-invitation to the IRS or SEC to audit them.

But then came the coke-snorting, "green is good" era of leveraged buyouts and hostile takeovers, followed quickly by international and ruthless Asian and Middle Eastern competition. Now, it was the stable, year-in year-out steady business that looked bloated, lethargic, financially diabetic, and in need of dialysis or transfusion. Like an athlete training for a prizefight or marathon, companies needed to be leaner and meaner each year, to "Just Do It!" and never settle for second best. Eat or be eaten, eat what you kill, have that killer instinct! *No mercy.* Thomas Frank defined the new aesthetic when he quoted an author named Gary Aldrich (who wrote one of the endless series of "where-have-all-the-values-gone?" right-wing bestsellers of the late '90s and early 2000s), complaining about the unprofessional, slovenly, "casual Friday" frat-house atmosphere of latter-day Clinton-era businesses. But as Frank wisely noted, Aldrich went wrong only in fixing the blame on the usual right-wing talking points. This new attitude wasn't because hippies had taken over the executive suites. It was because the cell-phoning, faxing, Power Pointing, instant-messaging, Microsoft/Apple/Google New Economy had no place left for an old-school, country-club exec like Aldrich anymore. And deep down, though he may have found the wrong people to blame, he knew it—and so did a lot of other people.

In 2009, longtime Ohio Representative Marcy Kaptur was memorably interviewed on camera by Michael Moore for his film *Capitalism: A Love Story.* There she referred to the ongoing 2008 economic collapse as a quote, "economic coup d'etat." She implied that the mortgage meltdown had been conspiratorially planned, right from the beginning, as the ultimate, deliberate, and on-purpose wealth transfer from Main Street to Wall Street by the ruling class. "It was all very carefully planned, to happen the way that it did, to happen *when* it did, and to involve the players that it did," she intoned. "It was like an intelligence operation!"

More than a decade earlier, President Clinton had gotten a hard lesson in getting on Congresswoman Kaptur's bad side—but more on that in a bit. A year after *Capitalism: A Love Story,* the Democratic Ms. Kaptur was re-elected in spite of the anti–Obamacare "back-lash" Tea Party election of 2010 (although it was a close shave). And it was actually Kaptur's opponent that year, the film producer and former grocery store executive Richard Iott, whose '90s life story provides an almost perfect "Exhibit A" of the rebooted realities of the 1990s New Economy, from the lower-middle-class' POV.

From 1996 to 2000, Rich Iott served as president and CEO of a Midwestern-based grocery store chain called Food Town. The corporate cash registers at Food Town toted up their biggest profits ever under his stewardship—according to Wikipedia, the chain reported it's best-ever third quarter profit in summer 1999, and unlike the stereotype of the "greedy" exec, the employees shared in the wealth—Food Town opened three new superstores in 1998 and '99 alone. Stock earnings skyrocketed 300 percent between 1994 and 1998. With this kind of stellar new record, not even Food Town's best triple-coupon sale looked like as big a "bargain" as the Food Town chain itself, to bigger and richer store chains who were worried about the competition. In 2000, Iott oversaw an immensely profitable merger/acquisition with the Spartan Store chain, immediately after which (in fairness to Iott, both FactCheck.org and the *Cleveland Plain Dealer* found no evidence that he personally advocated for this) Spartan immediately crashed down on Food Town like a warehouse fire door. 5,000 jobs were downsized at once, and just about as many Food Town stores were closed as had been opened during Iott's prosperous tenure.

The same tune had been sung five years earlier in 1995, when the West Coast's First Interstate chain of banks was gobbled up by the bigger and richer Wells-Fargo (not long after Crocker Bank similarly bit the dust in 1992–93). In many cases, only one branch (and its employees) would survive if there were two operating in the same suburb or general vicinity. And the 1990s career of future presidential nominee Mitt Romney, during his days as CEO of Bain Capital (which he left to successfully pursue the Massachusetts governorship in 2002) are a veritable Mother Goose storybook of "pump and dump" operations, companies that saw their profit margins and stock values temporarily skyrocket—for the sole purpose of selling them off to other, even bigger companies and concerns, who would then get out the fat-cutting shears and the euthanasia needles.

And how can we forget the booming late 1990s careers of such companies as Enron, Tyco, WorldCom, and the like, whose houses of cards came crashing down in horrifying bankruptcies the minute that the '90s decade was over—taking untold investors' retirements and college funds with them? And then there's the late Reed Slatkin, who, despite making oil company-level profits from co-founding Internet service provider Earthlink in 1994, still committed mail and tax frauds so outrageous that he wound up in Club Fed by 2003.

You would *think* that when a company was enjoying record profits, when everything looked so rosy and happy, that that company's employees would be as sunshiney and carefree as a Beach Boys concert. You'd *think* that—but you'd be wrong. By the late '90s, the American lower middle class had gotten hip to the game. They knew the drill. When the company they worked for was doing a little *too* well, when all the economic reports were upbeat and glowing, they could just hear the music from *Jaws* circling in the background, as '80s-style leveraged buyouts, mergers, and hostile takeovers made a comeback. In February of 1996, *Newsweek* ran a front-cover story luridly titled "Corporate KILLERS"—telling the dread tale of several top CEOs (with evidently well-earned nicknames like "Chainsaw Al"), who were brought in by their parent companies (or who mounted hostile takeovers of "inefficient" and "failing" companies on their own), only to launch massive downsizing and outsourcing initiatives—while rewarding themselves and their corporate boards to the max.

This was the last thing that Bill Clinton needed. Here he was, trying to build a "Bridge to the 21st Century," to remind people of how far we had come, to get people excited about the limitless possibilities of tomorrow. And here was the national media (and a fairly liberal publication at that) brutally reminding people to keep looking over their shoulders, that the nightmare never ends…

"The old rules seem no longer to apply"

As we briefly noted in our look back at the movies and grungy/hip-hop music of the 1990s, during the early '90s recession, many liberals allowed themselves to think that the Reagan/Bush era of "greed" and "selfishness" was finally over. The conspicuous-consumption culture of Donald Trump, Ivan Boesky, Leona Helmsley, *LA Law, thirtysomething, Less Than Zero, Bright Lights Big City,* Gordon Gekko, Alexis vs. Krystle, and Robin Leach was thought to have ended with Kurt Cobain, Nine Inch Nails, Public Enemy, Ice-T, Dr. Dre, Tupac, Biggie, *Clerks,* Roseanne, Michael Moore—and Bill Clinton.

Instead, the late 1990s boom proved that it had been the grungy anger and working-class 'tude of the early '90s that was the aberrant exception. The Nancy Reagan world of barely visible minorities and working-classers (and invisible poor people), of 1980s-style greed and self-indulgence, leased luxury cars, bling jewelry and shoe-shopping, had now *become the rule,* the New Normal.

The saddest irony is that many of the labor and populist-left voices actually seemed more at home in the grungy and gangsta, recessionary early '90s than they now did in the Clintonomic "prosperity" of the late '90s. Back in 1992 or '93, there was simply no way to avoid discussion of income inequality, minority poverty, or the white people who were on society's losing column, unless you didn't read newspapers or magazines and never watched television. But now that Wall Street was skyrocketing and unemployment figures were going down, nobody outside the trashy daytime talk shows was paying attention to these left-behind people, or to their vulgar, depressing stories anymore. As the memorable bank-protesting black man in *Falling Down* who was "Not Economically Viable" might have said, those people hadn't gone away—but they were not *demographically* viable. Who wanted to hear about them, when we could watch *Ally McBeal, Friends, Dawson's Creek,* and *Sex and the City,* listen to Celine Dion and Sugar Ray? Or go to the movies to see light as a feather, chick-lit rom-coms with Meg Ryan and Sandra Bullock?

The same Bill Clinton that economic liberals thought would *end* the Reagan-Bush mentality in the early '90s had instead *resurrected* the Reagan-Bush mentality by the late '90s. This is what people like Ralph Nader and Alexander Cockburn (and circa 1999–2000 Michael Moore) meant when they would say that there wasn't "a dime's worth of difference" between the Republicans and Democrats. "The stories of the underemployed, contracted-out, and laid-off men of southern California, and their counterparts in other regions, illuminated losses that the later 'boom' economy would to some extent conceal—but not cure," said Susan Faludi in 1999. "The economic improvement spelled little relief for the men I had come to know at job clubs, retraining agencies, family service centers, military bases, and outplacement offices. It was little relief for these men to find [new] jobs. Something had been broken inside them, and it wasn't going to be made right by a boom based on inflated stock prices and temporary personnel, a boom that yielded great wealth for the already affluent and deeded to the average man an insecure job, a rise in status anxiety, and a mound of debt."

This was what authors like the talented Gen-X pundit David Sirota were talking about when they said that the Reaganized 1980s never really ended, that the Reagan era was the definitive one for our age. He may have been right—but there's one important caveat: It was the *resurrection* of that shallow, label-conscious, showoffy, go-go mentality during the "dot com bubble" late '90s which *really* sealed the Reagan deal.

Taking note of all this, Sidney Blumenthal sent a memo to President Clinton by the end of summer in 1997, where he tried to do something of a psychological autopsy of the voters who just weren't feelin' the love, the ones who didn't feel so prosperous or peaceful about their place in the "booming" New Economy. "The old rules seem no longer to apply," Blumenthal rightly began. And the politicians' inability (or just unwillingness) "to describe reality is perplexing.... For the past five years, the Administration has endured the harrowing ordeal of conducting the transition from the old economy to the new economy.... If Ronald Reagan was the last president to ride the old economy (just as he was the last president of the Cold War) and George Bush was thrown by the transition to the new one (just as he was president of the transition from the Cold War), then Bill Clinton is the first president of the New Economy.... Global in dimension and driven by high technology, the new economy is constantly increasing efficiency; yet it requires equally constant investments in [re]education and training." Blumenthal then offered a telling demo reel of the Obama era's political conundrums. To wit:

> *Clinton's reelection did not give him a sense of relief that after the storms of the first term, he could let up a bit. Critics on the Left continued to construe his actions as overly cautious [and as] warmed-over Republicanism. A sizable contingent within the House Democratic Caucus blamed him for the Democrats' having failed to recapture a majority in the House in 1996.* [As well they should have, too, considering his and Gore's cynical reelection strategy that year.] *Many Congressional Democrats, writhing under Republican rule, were both passive and accusatory. They expected Clinton to rescue them without their having to do anything more than be lifted out of the morass. They saw him both as deux ex machina and as the source of their afflictions. Operating by*

district and constituency, they were incapable of developing a coherent national message on their own; still, they resisted presidential leadership. They had not really approved of the balanced budget, even though Clinton's policies had created solvency as a basis for new social policies, and they mostly opposed free trade.

When President Clinton tried to "sell" the House Democrats on the benefits of Fast Track—a NAFTA/World Trade sequel popular with Republicans and corporate lobbyists that would have indeed "fast tracked" and further streamlined even more globalization—who else but Congresswoman Marcy Kaptur came riding to the rescue! Treating the sitting president of the United States like little more than a contestant on *The People's Court*, Kaptur tossed back at Clinton, "Why should I believe you?" The bill was practically dead on arrival. Kaptur's boss of sorts, House Democratic Leader Richard Gephardt of Missouri, was even more uppity. Pointedly dissing Clinton's famous Triangulation strategy, Gephardt said Democrats "should have the confidence to be who we genuinely are—not just a slightly more compassionate version of the other side, or a constantly shifting combination of tactics and momentary calculation." An incensed Sidney Blumenthal later fumed in his book that Gephardt was "speaking as if he were President, or a presidential candidate."

*   *   *

President Clinton grimly noted a few weeks later in September of 1997 that "there's still a war in our own party." He then floated his own memorandum, as he and his staff began the arduous march of planning ahead for the January 1998 State of the Union Address: *In an industrial age, the progressive movement and the New Deal forged a social compact in which the success of the economy was premised on the security of working people. The twentieth-century social compact served us very well.* ***But it is not adequate to deal with the rapid change and energy of the Information Economy.*** *Therefore, it is up to us—to all of us—the generation of the computer evolution, to craft a new social compact for a new economy, a new understanding of the responsibilities of government and business and every one of us of what we owe to each other.*

It was a brilliant and completely truthful diagnosis, but one that would also require every ounce of Bill Clinton's platinum political skills to accomplish, plus the chessboard diplomacy of a Henry Kissinger or Mikhail Gorbachev. Like a no-nonsense doctor giving a terminal cancer or AIDS patient the bad news, Clinton would need to utterly destroy any wishful thinking that maybe we could still return to the old mid-century way of life, that we could go back to the future, that "That '50s Show" could go back on the air. But Clinton would also need to reboot our social safety net into a real "Netscape 2.0" that would protect small businessmen, commission-only salesmen and independent contractors, willing-to-work victims of outsourcing and computerized automation, start-up businesses and garage entrepreneurs, and hard working taxpayers—all in need of a for-real sense of retirement, healthcare, and job security. And he would need to explain in explicit, no-uncertain-terms how much was enough—and how much was *too much*, in terms of outsourcing production and manufacturing to other countries.

Unfortunately, what little chance there ever was of a true national conversation to really deal with and plan for these inconvenient truths, would be partial-birth aborted the very next year. A little black-haired intern with a little black dress, plus a "vast right-wing conspiracy" and a mad-as-hell, 24–7 monopoly media with an insatiable appetite for scandal, would see to that.

11

Political Pornography

Do you know there's not one kid who has died in Iraq who wouldn't be alive today if there never was a Monica Lewinsky? Monica Lewinsky changed the world. Had there been no Monica Lewinsky, Tipper Gore wouldn't have insisted that she didn't want her husband campaigning [for president in 2000] with Bill Clinton; [Gore] would have won two more states in the South.... I think Monica did more to change the world than Cleopatra.

> —Legendary 60 Minutes *head honcho Don Hewitt,*
> *interviewed by Carol Felsenthal in 2006*

Because I could, I guess.

> —Bill Clinton, explaining the deep moral and ethical
> reasoning that went into why he did what he did with Monica.

Because we can.

> —Newt Gingrich, explaining the deep legal and ethical reasoning
> that went into why his Congress impeached Clinton.

Richard Nixon once famously opined that Watergate was little more than a "third-rate burglary" that had gotten out of hand. If he was right about that, then the Monica Lewinsky scandal and the resulting 1998–99 impeachment drama was little more than a fifth-rate tabloid soap opera that had gotten out of hand. But in true 1990s fashion, it inspired the bloodiest feeding frenzy since Joe Dante and John Sayles finished lensing *Piranha* in 1978. Because of the un–PC and unmentionable culture war raw nerves it touched on, Monicagate actually *became* almost as important—if not more so in some ways—than Watergate had been. Before Monicagate, the Big Four broadcast networks and the major weekly magazines and "newspapers of record" thought of Internet journalism as the last refuge for scoundrels. It was as beneath them as a campy TV show was to an above-the-title movie star, as an illegal-immigrant maid was to an old money heiress.

After Monica, it was a whole different story—in every sense of the word "story." From now on, Brokaw, Rather, CNN, Fox News, *Time, Newsweek,* and *The New York Times* would be trying to keep up with the Matt Drudges and Nikki Finkes of the world, instead of the other way around. What Hillary Clinton called "the politics of personal destruction," the politics of anger and rage that had started in earnest with the Bork and Thomas hearings and the coded racial appeals of Willie Horton, Rodney King, and O.J., would now go from being the exception to *becoming the rule,* to becoming standard operating procedure. Monicagate and impeachment was the literal "climax" to all the '90s culture-warring, all of the "agonies over love and sex and marriage" (and racial culture), as Andrew Sullivan recalled in 2007.

CSI: Washington

Okay, for those of us who have no access to Google, Yahoo, or Wikipedia, and who have perhaps been living as occupants of interplanetary craft for the past decade or two (and/or those who are just too young to remember), *in precis,* here's what happened: In 1995, during the Newt Gingrich-incited Government Shutdown, President Clinton met an attractive 22-year-old White House intern named Monica Lewinsky. A child of a painfully divorced Beverly Hills yuppie career couple, Lewinsky apparently had more "daddy issues" than Little Orphan Annie, and made no secret of her desire to go after the biggest and the best. "I'd better get out my presidential knee pads!" she was famously quoted as having said to one of her friends upon meeting the dynamic and virile Clinton, and "flashing" him her panties. (Earlier, she had engaged in what some have described as the borderline-stalking of a former teacher.)

Monica and Clinton began what is euphemistically described as an "adult relationship," featuring all kinds of bizarre and vaguely kinky sexual encounters throughout late 1995 and 1996 (the nadir of which had Monica "smoking" a cigar Clinton had been using—but not with her mouth. Another equally reckless and tasteless session had taken place when Clinton was on the phone with the Joint Chiefs, debating military action and intervention.) After the initial excitement of the affair had waned (at least on Clinton's end), Monica now began to think of her onetime presidential paramour as "The Big Creep." Not knowing quite what to do, she made the dreadful mistake of confiding in a matronly, middle-aged Washington federal administrative secretary named Linda Tripp.

Linda Tripp, who had been married to a military man during the Vietnam era and was a staunch Reagan-Bush Republican, wasn't exactly president of President Clinton's fan club. She didn't like him, nor the new people he and that bossy wife of his had brought to town, or the general tone of their administration. With Internet "blogging" and "personal websites" just beginning to be developed, and right-wing authors cashing in with one vessel-bursting, Clinton-hating tome after another, Tripp was looking to parlay her longtime career behind the scenes in DC to a book deal, and was in contact with the veteran Washington literary agent Lucianne Goldberg. (Ms. Goldberg had worked closely, and that's putting it mildly, with Lyndon Johnson and Richard Nixon, and is the mother of famed conservative author and *National Review* fixture Jonah Goldberg.) Goldberg and Tripp detected a gold mine in the too-sexy confessions of Tripp's new best-girlfriend, and Tripp began surreptitiously (and as it turned out, illegally) taping her and Monica's telephone conversations, in which she would encourage Monica to open up about the affair to remember, that Monica more and more wanted to forget.

In late 1997 and just after the New Year of 1998, Tripp and Goldberg were starting to make their moves. Journalist Michael Isikoff of *Newsweek* was tipped off to the potentially explosive bombshell, but wasn't quite ready to print full chapter-and-verse without getting more corroboration. But another journalist of sorts, tabloid stringer Matt Drudge of the online *Drudge Report,* was also keeping an eye on the proceedings—and on Isikoff. And Kenneth Starr, the religious fundamentalist Special Prosecutor who had seemed to come up empty just a few months earlier in his years-long pursuit of the Clintons over Whitewater and of Paula Jones' sexual harassment case against the president, also apparently heard at least the rumors of Monica and Clinton's special friendship. Starr reasoned that if Clinton had recently instigated an inappropriate workplace relationship with yet another young and impressionable employee, who couldn't really have said "no" to him even if she wanted to—that would certainly be of pattern-establishing evidentiary value in the ongoing Paula Jones inquiry.

After Monica was dragged into Kenneth's "Starr Chamber" and brutally threatened with hindering prosecution and obstruction of justice if she didn't start talking, she slowly but surely began to comply. Who but Monica herself could know what the worst part of the ordeal was: the humiliation of being used and thrown away by Clinton? Being essentially mind-raped by a threatening, right-wing fanatic like Kenneth Starr? Or the grim revelation that her "friend" Linda Tripp had violated her as much as any sexual predator could, pretending to be a real gal-pal while actually gleefully setting a trap—as if Monica were no more important to her than the killer-of-the-week on that week's episode of *NYPD Blue*.

Of course, the real worst for Monica happened next, when Matt Drudge dredged out the whole sordid saga online, scooping everyone—and essentially forcing *Newsweek* and the rest of the "papers of record" from *Time, The New York Times, The Washington Post,* and the Big Three nightly network news shows, to finally come out of the closet. And nothing could compare to the way the scandal took off on content-starved, controversy-baiting 24-hour cable networks like CNN and the new Fox News, plus the top-rated magazine shows like *Entertainment Tonight* and *Dateline NBC*.

As the most media-savvy president in history (up until then), Clinton moved swiftly to try to head things off at the pass. Before the winter of 1998 had turned to spring, Clinton was already reaching back into his trusty bag of showbiz shtick—the reddened cheeks, the index finger pointed for emphasis like an "indicating" stage actor, the bitten lips while looking the camera right in the eye, the whole works. And then, he (in)famously denied it all. "*I did not have sex with That Woman* ... er, Miss Lewinsky," he enunciated, erasing George H.W. Bush's "Read My Lips—No New Taxes!" debacle of a decade before as the most groan-worthy political one-liner of the decade. (His record would be broken by George W. Bush's nauseous "Mission Accomplished" strutting, in circa-2003 Iraq.)

Meanwhile, Hillary went on the *Today* show and just as famously blasted the furore around Monica as nothing but the paranoid ranting of a "vast right wing conspiracy" out to get her and her husband at all costs. As if the charges themselves were so obviously untrue, they didn't even deserve to be dignified with a response. Probably the same kind of cuckoos who thought she'd casually murdered Vince Foster while coming home with one of her lesbian lovers. (Though Hillary was wrong about Monica, she was actually right about everything else.)

But what Bill and Hillary didn't know (yet) was that Monica had an ace in the hole. Early in their relationship, Monica had kept a dark blue Gap dress that she'd worn with Clinton during one of their encounters—and the president, shall we say, had made a mess of it when he finished. Like any Cinderella who actually got to live out her fantasy of making it with the handsome king, she decided to keep this little souvenir untouched in her closet. Not since O.J. himself had a DNA case become more of a national cause célèbre, as when Ken Starr's staff lip-lickingly seized The Dress for its "evidentiary" value (presumably delivering it into Starr's greedily clutching hands)—*after* Clinton had already claimed on world TV that "That Woman" Monica was nothing but a big liar, and had said so in the investigation statements. (He later tried to squirm out of admitting that he'd committed perjury with the famously deathless line, "It all depends on what your definition of 'is' is....")

Now that we've got that cleared up, it's time to get down to the *real* historical and cultural significance of the first time since just after the Civil War that a president was actually impeached by the Congress, and the first time since Nixon that it had been seriously considered. And like O.J., what is most striking about the case is how *little* who was actually guilty or innocent really mattered, how the who-dun-it aspect was beside the point. The true significance of impeachment wasn't whether Clinton "had sex with that woman" or sexually harassed Monica or even lied under oath. As feminist *Slate* columnist Amanda Hess recalled in 2014, Monica Lewinsky "forced America to bumble through an unprecedented national conversation about sex, power, and sexism." Anita Hill or Dan Quayle vs. Murphy Brown was nothing compared to this.

Steamy Seduction, or Statutory Rape?

On one side, it was both ridiculous and offensive for the sensation-seeking press (and the right wing noise machines) to infantilize a grown and relatively sophisticated adult woman for the convenience of their oh-so-outraged "narrative." Monica Lewinsky was a 22-year-old college-educated young woman who grew up around Hollywood—not some pop-eyed little girl on the playground being moved in on by Chester Molester. If anything, Monica was the "aggressor," actively pursuing a relationship with her sexy and charismatic boss on her own motion, coming on to him (if not, at times, actually throwing herself at him). Indeed, if Monica had stayed in her native Beverly Hills and Hollywood, and been a 20-ish aspiring actress, singer, or model instead of a political intern, and had made the clear-eyed decision to "audition" herself for a 50-year-old producer, director, or casting agent—not a single eyebrow would have been raised. Even if he had used her and thrown her away afterwards, just like a nighttime soap opera villain. Welcome to Hollywood, baby. Happens every day. Nothin' to see here, people. Move along.

On the other hand, as proud neo-feminists like Maureen Dowd, Camille Paglia, and the late Marjorie Williams noted, there is no real excuse that would make the kind of inappropriate relationship President Clinton encouraged with Monica into something that could be easily excused. "Since when did the President start using the interns as a dessert cart? Mmmm, she looks good!" sarcastically asked Paglia. "When did that become OK?" Even if the subordinate employee is the aggressor, it was still the wrong move for the supposedly older, wiser, and much more powerful man to give in and take the bait. There is a legitimate reason, after all, why a tenured college professor might lose his job if he started sleeping with one of his students, even if the student is over the age of consent. Many state medical associations would disbar a psychiatrist or psychologist who had (consensual) sex with one of their patients faster than you could say the word "malpractice." And yes, when a 16-year-old girl eventually "hooks up" with her steady high school (or even college student) boyfriend, it's no big deal to anybody but the most repressed and repressive parents. But if that same 16-year-old goes to bed with a 45 or 50-year-old man, then he's gonna have some serious 'splainin to do—in front of a sex crimes investigator or a District Attorney.

That is because, of course, in each of those instances, *It's the Power Dynamic, Stupid.*

In no way are the two players involved on a remotely equal footing or level of fairness. And how could there be *any* equivalence at all between a 22-year-old princess fresh out of school with daddy issues, and a fifty-year-old Yale law graduate who was *literally* the most powerful man in the world? As Marjorie Williams noted in her brilliantly sarcastic 1998 satire, *Bill Clinton: Feminist,* while Monica may have been the temptress who eagerly initiated the affair, once Bubba took the bait, there was no doubt about who was actually in charge from then on. Bill Clinton controlled the times, dates, and circumstances. He would summon Monica for sex, like a servant, whenever and wherever he could get away with it. Monica may have started out being OK with this arrangement, but that didn't mean that she was anything approaching an equal partner in it, no matter how much she may have wishful-thinkingly deluded herself at the outset.

An Affair to Remember

How could he have been so stupid? As that great connoisseur of irony, William Shake-speare, himself might have said, "That Is the Question" when considering Bill Clinton's end of the affair with Monica. He had already been through the wringer with Paula Jones and Gennifer Flowers before this. He already had all the rumors about state troopers and staffers having to "help" him cover up and conduct his dangerous liaisons. He was already being sued for harassment and pursued by the dogged Ken Starr. He already had a repu-tation as being less than truthful. As political strategist Elaine Kamarck later told Michael Takiff, "The Republicans were looking for a scandal—but he didn't have to give it to them!"

More to the point, Clinton also knew that no group of voters hated him with more personal fury and intensity than the "family values" folks, and the people who thought that the draft-dodger-in-chief had dishonored and betrayed the office of the presidency. So what does he do? How does he bring himself down? **With a sex scandal!**—proving that all of the things his worst enemies had been saying about him had been "true." Hoisting himself on his own petard. Playing right into their hands!

Noted John Hopkins psychologist and bestselling author John D. Gartner set out to answer that question once and for all, in his "psychological biography" *In Search of Bill Clinton* (which was pro–Clinton in the extreme, by the way—hardly a hatchet job like so many others of its ilk). According to Gartner's plausible theorizing, Clinton's affair was hardly the "irresponsible" spur-of-the-moment self-indulgence that both friend and foe (and Clinton himself) had painted it to be. Indeed, the groundwork for L'Affaire Lewinsky had already been planted before Monica herself had left her hometown of Beverly Hills.

The Year of Our Lord 1993 was supposed to be, by all rights, the greatest and most triumphant year of Bill Clinton's life—being inaugurated to take the office of the Presidency, the very first Baby Boomer to take the torch from his idol JFK's Greatest Generation. Instead, 1993 had been a nonstop *annus horribilis* for him. First came Gays in the Military, and the pot-stirring, manufactured controversies over nominees like Lani Guinier, Roberta Acht-enberg, and Zoe Baird. Then the (first) World Trade Center attack, followed immediately after by the Waco catastrophe. Then Hillary's hard-bitten father (Bill's father-in-law) dropped dead in April 1993, just before his 82nd birthday, after spending his final decade as a near-invalid in assisted living (following a severe heart attack at age 71 in 1982, and several mini-strokes afterwards). That was followed by the suicide of longtime friend Vince Foster. The down-to-the-wire budget battle was next. Then the global-economy NAFTA and World Trade and gun-control controversies that would ensure almost as many "angry and bitter" white working-class voters going to the Republicans as civil-rights had driven the white South to the GOP, back when Clinton was coming of age. And to frost the cake, his beloved wife, harshest critic, and staunchest supporter Hillary was taking the "wife-beating" of her life on Healthcare Reform, just as Bill's own mother and kid brother Roger had put up with abuse from Bill's stepfather, Roger Clinton, Sr. And he was just as powerless to protect or defend her.

And just when things couldn't possibly have gotten any worse—they did. Back home in Arkansas, Bill Clinton's feisty and lovable mother Virginia had just returned from a New Years Eve soiree in Las Vegas, where Barbra Streisand always saved her the best "guest of honor" seat in the house. (Babs openly called Virginia "my Southern mother!" much to Virginia's delight.) Still going a mile-a-minute just like the good old days, still radiant and "beautiful" at age seventy in her son's admiring eyes, refusing to let breast cancer get in the way of another good time. Virginia had just gone out to lunch with friends from her famous Birthday Club, of "rowdy old ladies" who liked to drink while playing cards and "the ponies," and she'd cheered on a televised Arkansas basketball game before calling it a day.

But suddenly that night, it all caught up to her. Early in the morning of January 6, 1994, Virginia Clinton Kelley went into cardiorespiratory arrest. According to Gartner, Virginia had always been Clinton's "elusive erotic ideal," his veritable template for womanhood. Clinton had spent his early years longing for Virginia, as his widowed young mother left little Billy in the care of her own mother—a stern, domineering taskmaster (with more than a passing resemblance in style to Hillary, Gartner noted)—while the bubbly and energetic Virginia left to earn her anesthetist's certification that would enable her to earn much more money as a nurse, and to set her hours so she'd be home when young Billy got home from school in the coming years. "I knew it was coming, but I still wasn't ready to let her go," Clinton recalled. "Clinton had lost his mother again," Gartner finished. "This time, for the last time."

The death of his quintessentially full-of-life mother and champion, Virginia, had been the worst thing that had ever happened to Bill Clinton, and it had topped off what had probably been the worst year of his life. And the nightmare wasn't over. Before 1994 ended, Clinton would suffer one of the worst mid-term electoral defeats in modern history. Not six months after that, Timothy McVeigh would decide to visit Oklahoma City, as payback for what the Feds—for what Clinton—had done at Waco. (As well as Ruby Ridge a year before, under Old Bush.) Now, as 1995 wrapped up, the government itself was getting ready to go into lockdown, with the government shutdown tax revolt.

And then, after three straight years of this nonstop hell—this radiant, beautiful young breath of fresh air walks into his life, just like something out of a Blake Edwards movie. A bouncy, bubbly, outgoing and sunny Beverly Hills babe with the same taste for heavy makeup, the same raven hair done up in late '60s poufy rolled falls, the same heart-shaped face, bosomy figure, and big eyes that the younger Virginia Kelley had always prided herself on. More than that, in fact. According to Gartner, when the news of Monica (and what she looked like) came out, many longtime Clinton intimates whispered and eyebrow-raised amongst themselves, "Marla." Campaign staffer Marla Crider had been Bill Clinton's most meaningful extracurricular friend during his 1974 Congressional campaign (which failed by a hair) and subsequent 1975–76 race for Arkansas Attorney General (which succeeded). Aside from his notorious long off-and-on with Gennifer Flowers, Marla was Hillary's only serious competition during their engagement and the early days of their marriage. While many of Clinton's friends thought Monica bore a passing resemblance to Clinton's dearly departed mother in her glory days, they thought Monica was a virtual *rerun* of Marla in the looks department.

It was also just plain the ultimate middle-aged male fantasy come to life, when Clinton was at his lowest personal moment: a younger, prettier girl who could provide some secret refuge and recreation from all the trauma and decay, and it would be just for him. Someone who worshiped the ground he walked on and idolized him totally, someone who practically threw herself at him, just like the Elvis-Beatles-Sinatra superstar that he'd always dreamed he was. Someone who clearly wanted him to be, in the Freudian sense of the term, "her *Daddy!*"

Now, let's flash forward a bit for a more recent example: No matter what President Barack Obama does or did, to the people who hated him the most (or at least to those people who had the biggest media megaphones), he would always be nothing more than—let's say it outright—a Kenyan Commie Nigger, hopelessly in thrall (as if in a Warner Bros. cartoon) to his "anti–American," "anti–Colonial," long-dead African father. In almost *exactly* the same way back in the '90s, to the hardcore "values voters" and to many traditional and older Americans, Bill Clinton would always be the man who symbolized a globalized, outsourced, racially and culturally diversified high-tech future that they didn't understand—and didn't want to. Bill and Hill's steadfast refusal to back down on abortion, their seeming disdain for stay-at-home moms, their near-relentlessness in pushing gay issues and feminism to the forefront, and their easy embrace of Hollywood and it's (im)morality only underlined it … again and again and again.

No matter how many times Bill Clinton "triangulated," no matter how many times he gave in to Gingrich or reformed welfare or eulogized Nixon or echoed Reagan or ordered a military invasion or deregulated this and that—it just didn't matter. In the end, to his enemies, Bill Clinton would always be a flag-burning hippie from the '60s, giving his finger to The Man. It was just that simple.

In light of that, Bill Clinton might well have thought to himself when he first "got a load" of Monica…. *It's not like Falwell and Gingrich, or Limbaugh and Karl Rove, are going to give me any extra credit for NOT sleeping around, for staying true to Hillary! (A woman they actively hate as much as they do me—if that's possible.) They've already tried and convicted me as some kind of sexual degenerate, because of how I (and half the people of my generation, by the way) lived back in the '70s.* "So you DIDN'T have sex with one of your secretaries??" *Well, what are they gonna give me for that? The Nobel Prize, or the Congressional Medal of Honor?*

No, looking back, Bill Clinton wasn't stupid. He wasn't even necessarily lacking in judgment. *They* already *think I'm a pervert and treat me like one anyway. So why not go ahead and take advantage of it, and get some fun out of life for a change!* What's the worst that could happen?

Making Their Own Reality

Amanda Hess couldn't have been more correct when she used the term "bumbling through"—it was the perfect phrase for just how appallingly abysmal, out of context, sensationalized, and just plain dishonest the mainstream media coverage of Monicagate would be. More and more, the hyped-up news dispatches, updates, and Sunday "debates" were not coming from anywhere in the reality-based world—but from some kind of Washington cocktail-party version of a Madeleine L'Engle or Arthur C. Clarke parallel universe. The scandal inadvertently and unintentionally revealed everything you didn't want to know about our supposedly "trustworthy" news media and were afraid to ask. For the first time since Vietnam, the conspiracy theorists and the Internet wingnuts (on both sides) seemed like the sane, fair, and balanced ones—while the respectable, established newscasters and columnists increasingly found themselves in a whacked-out alternate reality of their own creation.

After all, people like Bill O'Reilly, Ann Coulter, and Rush Limbaugh had never expected Bill Clinton to tell the truth. (They would have probably laughed in your face if you told them *you* had expected him to be honest!) When Clinton was finally "caught with his pants down" so to speak, while they strutted and sputtered their venom, none of them even pretended that they were *surprised*. In the same way, the defensive hard-left voices and the Clinton partisans knew the score. They understood what was at stake. They knew the name of the game. It was either Clinton or Gingrich. Clinton or George W. Bush and Karl Rove. Clinton or Antonin Scalia and Clarence Thomas. Clinton or the Christian Coalition and Focus on the Family.

But the supposedly fair, "objective," oh-so-mainstream media voices were acting like Aunt Pittypat from *Gone with the Wind,* hyperventilating and fanning themselves with pseudo-outrage and mock-panic. They were shocked, *shocked* I say, that President Clinton could do such a thing! *To lie under oath!* To a special prosecutor, *to all of us, to the American People!* To say that he "didn't have sexual relations with that woman!" looking us in the eyes with those same baby blues that had once felt our pain—and here all along, he actually DID have sex with that woman! Fuggedabout Hillary—these people acted as though Clinton had betrayed *them* personally. *He actually lied to us!* they collectively shrieked, wringing their hands as they manufactured their own poorly written and acted soap opera for the cameras and headlines and the blog posts. Heavens to Betsy! What will we do! How will we go on? *How could he do this to us?* What's it all about, world? Auntie Em! Auntie Em!

Hello! This is *Bill Clinton* we're talking about! The man who'd already said that when he smoked marijuana in the '60s, he "didn't inhale!" The man whose wife had miraculously turned a penne-ante investment into a six-figure jackpot (in Carter-era dollars) while he happened to be governor of Arkansas. The man who admitted to having an affair with Gennifer Flowers, and whose allegations by Paula Jones of sexual harassment and a hostile workplace environment had gotten this whole ball rolling in the first place.

Top pundits from Reagan-era broadcast baron Sam Donaldson to ex-Clinton press guru George Stephanopoulos (having left the Clinton Administration for a blingy sinecure at ABC News, where he still resides as of this writing) were making ever-more outrageous pronouncements off the top of their heads. In October 1998, Donaldson speculated that he thought Clinton was just about to resign from office, while admitting *in the very same paragraph* how well-liked Clinton still was by much of the centrist public. "If he's not telling the truth and the evidence shows that," Donaldson predicted that the public would insist on the "rule of law." Forget little trifles like gender politics, what it would do to the zoom-booming Wall Street stock market—indeed, forget the entire cultural footprint of the cynical, "whatever," Nirvana- and Eminem-listening, *90210* and *Sex and the City*–watching, Quentin Tarantino late 1990s. Nope, if Bill Clinton made a boo-boo, the American public would surely *demand* that he be thrown out on his banky wanky!

Sally Quinn returned to do Donaldson one better—she said flat out that Clinton should "resign" at once so as to "spare Washington any more humiliation." Notice that she said to "spare Washington," clearly meaning Washington high society. *He always was so vulgar, so crude, so beneath us, you know.* And George Stephanopoulos tossed off a one-liner worthy of Milton Berle or George Carlin when he said (as early as January 1998 in *Newsweek*) that if Monica was telling the truth, it would show that Clinton "failed to meet the standard of character he set for himself" and had "shattered the promises" he made to the public. (He also added how "livid" Clinton's behavior personally made him.) Could you please cite your source, Mr. Stephanopoulos? Just when did Bill Clinton *ever* advertise himself as having some kind of Dudley Do-Right "standard of character?"

Frosting the cake was neoconservative royalty Bill Kristol, who wishful-thinkingly prophesied "We are in the final days!" during the *first week* of the crisis—without an iota of evidence to support his claim. If it was proven that Clinton lied, "I think he's finished." Like a spoiled child hoping to make something true if he wished it often enough, Kristol and his fellow right-wing royalty William Bennett flat-out blamed the American public when they failed to deliver. "They're wrong!" Kristol wailed, while fundie honey Bennett later added that an ever-more diverse public's refusal to redo the 1996 election that was held just two years ago, was nothing less than America's "moral and intellectual disarmament."

Not until the Iraq War itself would the Washington media bubble be so grotesquely disassociated from the actual reality of the country it purported to observe. Monicagate was when the cracks in the greasepaint of our "respectable" anchorpersons and Sunday pundits, and our "objective" newspaper and magazine journalists, became visible for all to see. They harrumphed and camped, vamped and vogued for the cable cameras, forcedly trying to create a sense of horserace suspense (where to any thinking person, none really existed), with one eye on the circulation stats or the ratings Sweeps books.

Permanent Washington took on all the atmosphere of a bitchy sorority hazing or cheer-leaders' locker room during this time—and some of the most shockingly sexist work was written by women themselves. *New York Times* political doyenne Maureen Dowd regularly made savage fun of Monica's battles with the bulge, and her makeup and clothes sense. When Monica was asked to submit a handwriting sample to the FBI, Dowd wrote an article imagining Monica doodling things like "'Monica Clinton Lewinsky,' 'Mrs. Big Creep (frowny face),' 'First Lady Monica' (smiley face)," and dreaming of being seated in between Leonardo DiCaprio and John Travolta at state dinners—as if Monica were some kind of lovestruck middle-schooler writing her Dear Diary. (And do we even have to mention Ann Coulter at this point, for whom 1998's "Case for Impeachment" was her big break as a national best-seller?) Respectable news organizations, now frantically trying to compete with *Hard Copy, Inside Edition, EXTRA!, E! True Hollywood Story, Behind the Music,* and the Internet meme-machines—all outdid each other to see which ones could be the most outrageous. They called Monica things like the "Portly Pepperpot" and compared her to that other Beverly Hills Jewish "Malibu Madam" temptress, Heidi Fleiss. It was O.J. Simpson and JonBenét Ramsey all over again, this time in the hallowed halls of Washington, D.C.

Double Standards

As Maureen Dowd admitted in 2011, archconservative Ann Coulter had a point "when she said that feminists rewrote their own rules on sexual harassment to support Bill Clinton." To her credit, Dowd added, back at the time, that once you "decide that it's OK to sacrifice individual women for the greater good, you set a dangerous precedent." Sadly, Maureen Dowd and Ann Coulter were about the only high-profile media women who owned up to that painfully inconvenient truth when the Lewinsky scandal was still in progress. Indeed, it was all too clear whose "side" leading feminist spokeswomen were on in the battle—which hit a comical nadir when novelist Erica Jong was quoted as cooing, "Oooh, imagine swallowing the presidential cum!" to her high-profile Manhattan and Hollywood girlfriends, in a *New York Observer* article. Jong and Susan Faludi implied that Commander-in-Chief Clinton was more his 22-year-old secretary's *victim* than the other way around! And the founding mother of feminism, Betty Friedan, told reporters that she flat-out "didn't care" if the allegations against Clinton were true or not.

"It's plain enough why feminists want to keep Clinton in office," noted the brilliant Washington columnist Marjorie Williams. He was solidly pro-choice, and despite Don't Ask Don't Tell and Defense of Marriage, was far and away up until that point the most gay-friendly president that America had ever had. He had signed into law the Violence Against Women and the Family and Medical Leave Acts, he favored affirmative-action preferences to help women climb up the corporate ladders, and he finally made subsidized day care, afterschool programs, and education a top federal priority. (Not to mention his Cabinet, packed with strong executive women like no other president in then-history, including Ruth Bader Ginsberg on the Supreme Court, Attorney General Janet Reno, and Secretary of State Madeleine Albright.) And Bill Clinton's re-election in 1996 was due mainly to the "gender gap" between men and women (plus overwhelming margins among motivated African Americans and Latinos)—which now, for the first time (but certainly not the last) had *far exceeded* the actual margin of victory.

Above all, feminists defended Bill Clinton—because after the game-changing 1994 mid-terms, it was either "swallow it" (to pardon the pun) and give him a hall pass—or get a government of Gingrich, Scalia, Jesse Helms, and Greenspan, with no check or balance whatsoever, besides maybe a crippled, caretaker Al Gore, just waiting for Dubya or McCain or Gingrich or Cheney to run him over in 2000. (And of course, feminists defended Hillary for obvious reasons.) But how many high-profile feminists rose up to loudly protect and defend *Monica* herself? How many big media, magazine, or newspaper voices stood up and said that raking a barely 25-year-old woman over Kenneth Star's coals—running national headlines slut-bombing and body-image-insulting her, and making filthy jokes about her on *South Park, The Simpsons*, Leno, SNL, and Letterman—was just plain *unacceptable,* no ifs, ands, or buts?

No wonder that, in looking back in 2014 on her trial by ordeal, Monica said she felt like a real-life version of Hester Prynne from *The Scarlet Letter*. Her whole life as an adult woman from age 22 to 40—her prime dating and mating years—had been defined by an affair she'd had when she was just out of college, her family name reduced to a standup-comedy punchline. In recent interviews, Monica also (somewhat understandably) revealed that she had almost as much contempt as Religious Right icons like Anita Bryant and Phyllis Schlafly had, for movement feminists. *Where the hell were the feminists when SHE needed them?*

As Marjorie Williams noted, the consensus on Monica amongst media-intellectual women was that she was "unsalvageably tacky, a creature from an Aaron Spelling soap opera." (And unlike Ivy-educated, articulate academic Anita Hill, Paula Jones was an unglamorous and "uneducated" denizen of the lower-middle-class, not perhaps the woman that most feminists wanted to see as their role model, much less someone to openly sympathize with.) Feminists "only think bluestockings are worth paying attention to," sneered conservative speechwriter Lisa Schiffren. "You know, Important Women with important careers and day care needs." To Schiffren, the teachable moment was that modern feminists clearly thought that "Wellesley girls and Yale graduates are worth fighting for," but high-school and community-college graduates like hairdressers, lounge singers, waitresses, and secretaries "can be destroyed." Marjorie Williams sadly agreed in the end, noting that "Feminists have all along muffled, disguised, excused, and denied the worst aspects of the president's behavior with women."

Sadly, because of how just high the culture war stakes now were, even if Monica had started out as the "aggressor," she sure as hell ended up the victim in the end. Few feminists or female columnists dared to feel sorry for her. (Nor was there any particular outpouring of leaning-in solidarity for Paula Jones, who had allied herself with political right-wingers as she pressed her own case, which was later dismissed by district court judge Susan Webber Wright, who although a Republican appointee, had known Clinton as governor of Arkansas.) And the male columnists, of course, completely vaporized both Paula and Monica—or whatever was left of them after the standup comics had their say. By the late '90s culture war, *it was the Realpolitik, stupid!*

"We've just got to win, then!"

That was a direct quote from President Clinton, when talking to Dick Morris about what his strategy would be now that the jig was up. After The Dress "came out of the closet," so to speak, not even Johnnie Cochran, F. Lee Bailey, and Alan Dershowitz themselves could argue that Bill Clinton was completely innocent, that he "had never had sex with That Woman" and had never lied under oath. Once again, Bubba had played his most loyal constituents like his saxophone. First he got the white working class and the left wing voices to vote for him in 1992—only to sign NAFTA and deregulate the media. Then he courageously reached out to gay people like no other president before had ever dared, especially in the AIDS era—but he signed Don't Ask Don't Tell and Defense of Marriage just the same. He became the most beloved president that urban African Americans and Latinos ever had until Barack Obama, and proudly embraced their cultures—but welfare reform still bore his signature.

And now this! Forget about lying to Ken Starr or Monica Lewinsky—what about all of the pro–Clinton columnists and congressmen and senators who had been banging on about how this was just another paranoid nutter-butter from the "right wing conspiracy?" That this was all just another hoo-hah to keep ratings high, like Vince Foster's "murder" and the Whitewater mess, just another Big Lie from the right-wing noise machine? For months these poor saps had been defending Clinton as innocent, promising everybody that this was all just the made-up work of a vast conspiracy—and now Monica's dress has "Guilty, guilty, guilty!" written (in you-know-what) all over it.

Of course, some well-meaning intellectuals and academics, and some thoughtful and reasonable columnists, did try to staunch the damage. They would pontificate to the effect that, *Yes, err, President Clinton did do the wrong thing, but it doesn't really, you know, Rise To The Standard of Impeach—well, yes, true—you* do *have a point there, but still, this isn't really quite what our Founding Fathers had in mind—although what President Clinton did was very, very* naughty! *And I am personally VERY offended by it!....*

However well-meaning these "reasonable" voices may have been, they succeeded only in sounding like a limp satire of Peter Sellers' dithering President Muffley in *Dr. Strangelove*. Instead of helping to tamp down the culture war wildfire, they unintentionally reduced themselves into a Comedy Central self-parody of it. The much more common—and effective—Clinton-supporter reply to all this *geshrei* about how Clinton had lied, LIED (not only from the hard-right, but from the insufferably self-righteous and self-dramatizing media pundits) now shifted as effortlessly as an automatic transmission into pure, Sonny Corleone-style, fist-under-the-chin attitude.

"You betcha, President Clinton lied under oath and on TV, about his private, personal affair! *Wouldn't you have?* And if *you've* got a problem with it, then that's *your* problem, honey!" To use one of Kathy Kinney's signature lines as the immortal (and immoral) office manager Mimi on *The Drew Carey Show*, these Clintonites' new attitude was, "Oh yeah? *Whaddare you gonna do about it, pig?*" Kiss ma grits! Eat my shorts! *DEAL with it!*

Alas, this new attitude on the part of defensive Democrats (and especially feminists) only validated the worst stereotypes of the Limbaugh/O'Reilly club: that liberals were indeed nothing but self-righteous hypocrites. That when the chips were down, liberals were just as ruthless, double-standard, and results-oriented as Newt Gingrich and Dick Cheney were. "Principle is nothing to liberals," Ann Coulter would often remind her fan club. "Winning is everything."

Monica as Metaphor

Let's say you're a classic, 40-ish, upper-middle-class suburban white guy—say, Kevin Spacey in *American Beauty*. You're married and settled down; you've got the wife and 2.3 kids. You're one of Clinton's prized "swing voters," his New Democrats. You've got the split-level in Scarsdale, New Trier, San Jose, or coastal Orange County, complete with backyard pool, while the Dodge Caravan and the leased BMW 740i are parked in the driveway. And you really do love your wife and your family. But when you go away each summer to the party house in Martha's Vineyard, or stay at the Fontainebleu or the Honolulu Sheraton with the guys, or jet off to Convention Week at the Mandalay Bay every six months ... and there's that 20-something, stone-fox hottie who still thinks you've got it goin' on.... Well, what happens in Vegas *stays* in Vegas, right?

Unless Ken Starr is there too—hiding in your bedroom or behind your bathroom mirror with his candid camera! You're only five or ten years younger than Clinton, after all. You did the free-love thing at the discos and singles bars back in the day, you smoked a few bowls while listening to Pink Floyd in high school and college. How would you like it if some self-righteous, *Carrie's*-mother type, Bible-toting loony took it upon his or her self to tattle to *your* wife and kids about what went on? Because they thought it was their moral or "biblical" duty??

Or what if you were another kind of guy, someone who started out his career as a bright, eager-to-please young man working in the *Mad Men* offices of the late '60s or early '70s. A nice young guy—who just happened to like other nice young guys. (Or a nice young lady, who happened to be fond of other nice young ladies.) You remember all too well the crippling fear of how just one wrong move could spell total disaster, could cause you to get "caught." (Indeed, if you lived outside of the coasts, it's likely you *still* lived with that fear in the workplace or at school.) No, when these many diverse slices of American pie saw Monicagate unfold, they were shocked and awed all right—outraged and scared shitless that if it could happen to Mister President, it could happen to *me!* (Or maybe it already had.) *There but for the grace of God go I....*

And speaking of the grace of God, when religious conservatives saw all this, it wasn't so much a big surprise as it was their worst nightmare, a validation of their ugliest stereotypes come true. That President Clinton was the kind of man who was capable of screwing his young personal assistant in the Oval Office (no doubt grinning that Cheshire Cat grin of his), while he was on the phone debating whether or not to send American soldiers into harm's way ... this painted a picture of a man who was so fleshly, sinful, and callous that they hardly had a vocabulary with which to describe it.

To someone who believed in traditional family values, who still got teary and saluted at the sight of Old Glory, it was just so goosebump-rubbingly *wrong* that HE was still sitting behind Reagan and Roosevelt and Lincoln's desk. "Mommy, why do all the grown-ups laugh about President Clinton's *cigar?*" "Nannie, I'm confused—did President Clinton really wear somebody's *dress?*" So much for being a role model! (Indeed, if George Stephanopoulos had been channeling anyone when he wrote how Clinton had "failed" to live up to the "standard" that presidents should have, it was these people.) To values voters and traditionalist patriots, it was almost as if any conscience, or even the most rudimentary sense of decent and indecent, was gone from this White House. There was simply nothing left.

"Not since Vietnam and Watergate"

On October 28, 1998, nearly 500 predominately Ivy League, top-college, and published "Historians in Defense of the Constitution" took out a full-page ad statement in *The New York Times*. The most prestigious of them all, 81-year-old Kennedy-era icon Arthur Schlesinger, joined Sean Wilentz and C. Vann Woodward to hold a press conference announcing the manifesto. Not since Vietnam and Watergate had liberal and left-wing intellectuals "rallied in the political scene with such intensity," said Sidney Blumenthal. (Although considering the resurgence of liberal activism against the dark, "Fahrenheit 9/11" days of the "Cheney-Bush Junta" that were soon to come, it was quite a useful dress rehearsal.)

"Although we do not condone President Clinton's private behavior or his subsequent attempts to deceive, the current charges against him depart from what the Framers saw as grounds of Impeachment," the memo announced. Then came the blistering money quotes. *"The theory of Impeachment underlying [the current] effort is unprecedented in our history. The new processes are extremely ominous ... and if carried forward, they will leave the Presidency permanently disfigured and diminished, at the mercy as never before of the caprices of any Congress. The Presidency ... will be crippled.... Do we want to ... tie up our government with a protracted national agony ... or do we want to protect the Constitution and get back to the public business?"*

Clinton's "early difficulties," the ever-loyal Blumenthal continued, "had destroyed" many of the left wing's initial hopes. But Newt Gingrich's rise "began to alarm them," and they were downright "repelled" by self-righteous fundie Ken Starr and his supporters. When tele-evangelist John Hagee went on TV accusing Hillary Clinton of committing "WITCH-CRAFT in the White House!," when culture warriors like William Bennett and Oliver North asked, "Where is the outrage?," when up-and-coming author Ann Coulter wrote a bestseller making the point-by-point legal "case" for impeachment, it was all simply too much for them to take. No longer could liberal intellectuals, academics, pundits, and journalists "take for granted that the basic institutions and ideals of the American government" would survive the "attack" by a desperately reactionary right wing. Blumenthal warned, "Even the Constitution itself was endangered."

If Proposition 187 and the affirmative-action repeals of the mid '90s were the wake-up calls for voters of color, then impeachment was a *Silkwood* alarm to the entire liberal and academic community. Impeachment offered nothing less than the demo reel for the Tea Party, as well as for Sarah Palin, Michelle Bachmann, and the 2011 and 2013 debt-ceiling standoffs and post–Obamacare wars. Why, if we lost the White House, the racially bigoted, anti-science, ballistically homophobic and war-on-women right-wingers would have won! They'd own EVERYTHING!

No wonder that perhaps Monicagate's longest-lasting legacy was the founding of the liberal website and community MoveOn.org, which was initially founded to encourage America and its political system to do just that—move on from impeachment. (And they found plenty of other things to advocate that America "move on" from, during the Bush-Cheney 2000s.) Porno king Larry Flynt offered a ransom for anyone who could "out" any adulterous straight or closeted gay politician who was calling for Clinton's impeachment. (Indeed, some of Clinton's worst critics were toe-tapping closet cases like Mark Foley and Larry Craig, and of course Newt Gingrich was getting a bit on the side from a younger mistress, even as the impeachment trial unfolded. And Gingrich's successor, Dennis Hastert, later got into his own blackmail scandal for past sexual misconduct, in 2015.)

Get Your Hands Off Our President!

Okay, let's recap: You have a Southern White President, who has an extramarital affair with a Rich Jewish Girl from Beverly Hills 90210, while his Bossy White Lawyer Wife sits at home and stews in her White House mansion, angrily ordering around her armies of servants, while dripping with designer power suits and jewelry. So what is this drama really all about, you ask? Simple! Isn't it obvious?

It's about The Race Card, stupid. "Black intellectuals were the great exception," Sidney Blumenthal noted, to the punditocracy's noise machine that Bill Clinton was a "disgraced" president, how he was going to be "forced" to resign "any minute now," how he was so "controversial," yadda yadda yadda. From Maya Angelou to Henry Louis "Skip" Gates to John Hope Franklin, "they understood Clinton's political predicaments. Black intellectuals—like blacks generally—saw the assault on Bill Clinton as an assault on themselves." That was putting it mildly. The African American, Pulitzer Prize-winning literary lioness Toni Morrison was only the first and most outspokenly quoted on the subject:

> *Thanks to the papers, we know what the columnists think. Thanks to round-the-clock cable, we know what the ex-prosecutors, the right-wing blondes, the teletropic law professors, and the disgraced political commentators think.... African American men seem to understand it right away. Years ago, in the middle of the Whitewater investigation, one heard the first murmurs: white skin notwithstanding, this is our first black president. Blacker than any actual black person who could ever be elected in our children's lifetime.* [Remember, back in 1998, nobody outside of Illinois, Hawaii, or Harvard had heard about Barack Obama, except maybe as a memoir-writer and civil-rights lawyer—and Colin Powell had categorically refused to run for president in 1996.] *After all, Clinton displays almost every trope of blackness: single-parent household, born poor, working class, saxophone-playing, McDonald's-and-junk-food-loving boy from Arkansas. And when ... the president's body, his privacy, his unpoliced sexuality became the focus of the persecution, when he was metaphorically seized and body-searched, who could gainsay these black men who knew whereof they spoke.... This is Slaughtergate. A sustained, arrogant, bloody coup d'etat. The Presidency is being stolen from us.*

And when the esteemed Ms. Morrison said it was being stolen from "Us," she meant it both in the sense of "us" as in We the People, and "us" as in the African American community specifically. Civil rights hero and longtime Congressman John Lewis picks up the story from here, in Michael Takiff's 2010 book on the Clinton era:

> *There was a feeling on the part of a lot of people that there was some history here. Bill Clinton may have been the first [white] person since Robert Kennedy to have had that type of hold on the African American community. People though they were trying to impeach, to get rid of, to silence the voice of someone who was standing up and speaking out for the needs of the black community. When my mother, who didn't become a registered voter until the Voting Rights Bill in 1965 ... saw what was happening to Bill Clinton, she said to me, "Tell them to let him alone." At the time she was in her eighties, and I think she was speaking for a lot of people. "Let him alone. Let my president alone." It was ownership. You'd hear people saying, "Don't let them impeach MY president! He is my man."*

The African American (and proudly gay) film and media historian David Ehrenstein now brings our narrative into home plate, noting the grim environment that still existed in the pre–Obama era for all people who swam against the current, either sexually or racially. More importantly, Ehrenstein essentially agreed with Rush Limbaugh and Jerry Falwell that Clinton and Monica's consensual affair was anything *but* a "private matter" in this kind of political and politicized, 24-7 culture war. Except of course, Ehrenstein believed the affair shouldn't be "kept private" for the entirely *opposite* reason:

> *Elsewhere, things [hadn't] changed very much. Sodomy laws remained on the books in more than twenty states* [until 2003's *Lawrence v. Texas*, the "*Roe vs. Wade*" of gay rights], *gay-bashing incidents continued to occur with alarming frequency, gay and lesbian teenagers were still tossed to the mercy of the streets by disapproving parents, and antigay diatribes from politicians, pundits, and preachers of every stripe [hadn't] been stilled to any degree.* [Sadly, Matthew Shepard found that one out the hard way, later that very same year. In a chapter entitled, "The Further Decay of Lying," Ehrenstein continued his elaboration.] *As the nation contemplated*

the curvature of the presidential penis, pausing every so often to catch the latest variation of "I Married a Trans-sexual Lesbian Stripper" on the afternoon television talk shows, it only goes to show that sexuality, of any sort or variation, is no longer a "private" matter. For those who struggled through the decades that saw the emergence of the gay and lesbian civil rights movement, that's as it should be. If nothing else, the movement [and Monica] proved that the "polite" societal declaration that "I don't care what people do in bed so long as they don't push it in my face" was a lie.... People don't live their lives "in bed." [What] goes on there affects every aspect of "out of bed" existence.... It should give them an idea of the minefield that gays and lesbians in perfectly ordinary walks of life are forced to trip through daily...

And a canny Bill and Hillary Clinton team realized that this racialization and post-feminization had delivered them something of a secret *weapon* they could use at the 1998 mid-terms. Black and Latino voters in major cities started receiving targeted phone calls, fliers, and Emails, some recorded by Hillary herself or other high-level Friends of Bill, encouraging them to get out and vote against this right-wing attack ... on THEIR president!

It's the Culture War, Stupid

It worked like magic, too. In what the mainstream media voices (most of whom were still wondering when-and-if President Clinton was about to resign) had predicted would be a huge low-turnout triumph for right-wingers, the 1998 mid-terms boasted a veritable "March on Washington" from voters of color, and proudly pro–Clinton feminists and gays. While the Congress still stayed in Republican hands, the margin was now slimmer than ever. And it was the proudest and most diverse pro–Clinton defenders—*not* the hard-right Republicans—who made the biggest gains. For the first time since Reconstruction, the party in the White House made gains, instead of losses, in the mid-term correction. And that was only the start of it.

California went back to a Democratic governorship for the first time since *Quincy* and *Laverne & Shirley* were on the air. Republican Senator Alfonse D'Amato, who ruled New York since the last days of disco, was shoved aside for Chuck Schumer. Even in the Deep South, a handsome Democratic lawyer named John Edwards knocked conservative Republican Lauch Faircloth into next week, in North Carolina's Senate race. And that was just for openers. So intense was the backlash that by the end of the year, Clinton's biggest foe finally realized that it was all over, as Newt Gingrich announced his retirement from Congress just four years after marching to triumph with his so-called Revolution. (He was replaced as Speaker of the House by the considerably lower-profile Dennis Hastert.)

Things like Proposition 187, affirmative action repeals, "defense of marriage" theatrics, and welfare reform may have awakened the sleeping giants. But impeachment was the biggest four-alarm clock ringer besides the soon-to-come election of George W. Bush himself—that people like Gingrich, Tom DeLay, Karl Rove, and Rush Limbaugh really *weren't* kidding, that they weren't just bloviating cartoon-conservative entertainers. They really *were* deadly serious about pressing the cultural rewind button—and they could *only* be stopped by equally overwhelming ballot-box force.

In some ways, impeachment was the best thing that could have happened to the Democratic Party. The 1998 mid-terms were the official coming-out party for the "Coalition of the Ascendant"—empowered and energized black, brown, and LGBT voters; single women (and their upscale, pro-choice/pro-gay suburban sisters); and young people who voted on social tolerance issues above all else. In other words, *the exact voter demographics that would deliver Barack Obama his "game change" a decade later.* While the lame-duck House still went ahead with the impeachment, by the time that Clinton's trial (presided over by ultra-conservative Supreme Court Chief Justice William Rehnquist) began in the Senate in early 1999, the verdict was now a foregone conclusion.

As what Sidney Blumenthal would call the "Show Trial" started in earnest, Clinton's initial lip-biting contrition now returned more proudly than ever to his more typical middle-finger attitude. And Clinton's cheeky defiance, after his total vindication in the 1998 midterms, combined with the sacrificial loss of Gingrich, now drove his critics completely nuts. Could it be that in his Freudian-kinky, sadomasochistic way, that Bill Clinton was actually *enjoying* it? That he was actually getting his kicks from all this? It was as if he was *taunting* us, double-dog daring us, making fun of us, smirking at us! "That's right," they could just imagine Bubba defiantly grinning back at them. "Fight me with all you've got!" Despite the media columnists still desperately trying to manufacture some sense of forced-hype suspense about it—now with a crystal clear voter mandate to Get Your Hands Off OUR President! from the 1998 mid-terms—Bill Clinton was easily acquitted in a couple of weeks.

"I'm Fed Up!"

Leave it to the founding mother of the Religious Right, Phyllis Schlafly, to sum it up best. In April of 1999, after Clinton's inevitable acquittal, she offered her own inimitable post-mortem, bluntly if effectively titled, "I'm Fed Up!" And in so doing, she provided a psychological X-ray of where cultural conservatives, "values voters," old-fashioned patriots, and believers in "traditional morality" were, as America headed towards the 2000 election that would decide the fate of Clintonism and Clintonomics once and for all:

> I'm fed up with the sanctimonious liberals imposing their values on me.... The liberals have their nerve trying to enforce a "nonpartisan" rule on Republicans, while at the same time winking at Democratic senators who goose-stepped to a unanimous partisan vote to save Bill Clinton.... The Democratic senators know that Clinton, like O.J., was guilty. The Democrats called his behavior "disgraceful," "dishonorable," "reckless," "contemptible," "shameful," "inexcusable," "sordid," "deplorable," "immoral," "debased," and "reprehensible." But all the Democratic senators [still] closed ranks to impose their values on the country by defeating what Alan Dershowitz called "the forces of evil."
>
> I'm fed up with the liberals' ... absurd caveat that "everybody lies about sex." If it's just "he says, she says" and everybody lies, we should toss out all the sexual harassment cases, enjoy sex in the workplace, and then lie about it.... I'm fed up with the liberals telling us we must show forgiveness for Clinton's perjury, peculiar sex, and per-version of justice at the same time he spells reconciliation R-E-V-E-N-G-E. I'm fed up with the liberals falsely accusing Republicans and the so-called Religious Right of imposing their values on society, when the evidence proves that the liberals have been using the full powers of government, the media, and academia to impose THEIR values on us.

However tempting it may be to "elitely" dismiss Mrs. Schlafly and her ultra-homophobic and anti-feminist politics with a sophisticated wave of the hand, let's actually try to argue against what she said. The Democratic senators clearly *did* "goose-step" to a defense of Clinton, for obvious reasons—in laughably ham-handed spite of all their strutting moral bugle music and bloviating tut-tuttery about how "inexcusable," "deplorable," et cetera, they "personally" thought his conduct was. (Can we say "trying to have their cake and eat it, too?") And by the way, many of those preening adjectives came from the mouth of that paragon of Democrat values, Connecticut Senator Joe Lieberman, who famously made a take-no-prisoners denunciation of Clinton on the Senate floor, actually calling for his "censure" in September of 1998. At least the Al Sharpton, Bill Maher, and Alan Dershowitz attitude-pundits and activists were intellectually consistent.

Naturally and perhaps justifiably, Schlafly pounced on the double standard—that sex games in the office were bad until Bill Clinton did it, and now they were OK. Clearly, Mrs. Schlafly knew full well that this was an embarrassed desperation-move from feminists who thought that the price of losing Clinton would be far greater for American women than the price of his "getting away with" his offensive behavior. But of course, it wasn't hard for her to make this seeming hypocrisy seem like it was liberals' standard operating procedure all along.

The City on the Edge of Forever

Bill Clinton's long national nightmare was finally over—but his vice president's nightmare had only just begun. Perhaps no one from the most outraged religious fundamentalist to the most shocked and awed feminist or left-winger, was as psychologically shaken up by the impeachment ordeal as the man who would have taken over the reins of power had Clinton actually been removed. This was the moment Al Gore had been waiting for, had been preparing for, his entire life—yet he'd probably never imagined that it would turn out this way in his worst nightmare. At least he had the small comfort of knowing that the entire Democratic establishment was now fully in back of him; that with impeachment finally a thing of the past, the Clintons, the liberal columnists, the big-name donors, the hard-left MoveOn.org types, and their trendy Hollywood pallies would be focusing 100 percent on getting *him* elected, with no further distractions or scandals.

And then, just like a surefire punchline from *Seinfeld* or *Raymond*—the other shoe inevitably dropped.

No sooner had Bill Clinton's trial finished in the Senate, than the Democratic Party was hit with another kind of "trial" in that same chamber, when the seventyish New York Senator (and chief Johnson and Nixon domestic policy intellectual) Daniel Patrick Moynihan announced that he would be retiring at the end of his term in 2000. The wildly popular Republican New York mayor Rudy Giuliani made no secret of the fact that he wanted that seat for himself—and whatever Rudy wanted, Rudy got! Even before his shining hour (immediately post–9/11), Giuliani was known to many as "America's Mayor," having broken up the John Gotti crime family, and rebooted America's proudest city from the recessionary crime-and-crack cesspool it had been when he'd taken over, to the *Sex and the City* and New Broadway era we were now living in as the decade came to a close.

No billionaire businessman (from either party) who could've posed a credible threat, no Michael Bloomberg or George Soros or Donald Trump, had any interest in running against Rudy for the Senate. And the Democrats knew that every one of their current no-name state legislators and local congressmen would get flattened like a suicidal squirrel on the Long Island Expressway by Rudy's well-oiled machine. No, there was only *one* person who had the name, bank account, and game-changer qualities to credibly challenge Rudy for the New York Senate seat. (Despite the small quibble that she had never lived, paid income tax, or been registered to vote in New York.) *But isn't that where you and Bill want to go and live after your time in the White House is over, anyway? Why not file the papers for a dual residency in New York now, and give yourselves a head start?*

Hillary Clinton wasn't quite the type to spend the rest of her useful life being a "lady who lunches" at the country club. Still in good health at only 50 years old, Hillary couldn't quite see herself becoming a retired senior citizen just yet, sitting around the house all day in lounging pajamas and watching *The Price Is Right*. She practically jumped at the chance! Hillary could erase the humiliation of Monicagate by emerging triumphant against its "vast right wing conspiracies" in her own right. And Bill was only too happy to be the wind beneath her wings, after the way she'd "stood by her man" (and saved his bacon—*again*) during the impeachment horrors.

But this was finally supposed to be MY turn! a jaw-dropped Al Gore might well have thought to himself—the time when after eight years of loyal service, he would finally have the undivided support and resources of the high-level Clinton machine at his complete disposal. Instead, the only thing that the newspaper headlines, magazine covers, Internet sites, and Oprah/Barbara Walters type shows were saying was, "It's HER Turn Now!"

Once again, Bill and Hill had upstaged Al Gore, sucking all the political oxygen out of the Democratic room. And just *how was* Gore going to handle all of this, anyway? How could Al Gore tap and motivate socially liberal Generation X "slackers" without totally freaking out their parents and grandparents, who were already scared of what change they'd seen? How could he square the circle of people who wanted to see Clinton thrown out on his butt with the people who thought impeachment was an "evil" racially coded "Slaughtergate?" How could he express his personal (and sincere) revulsion at Clinton's personal conduct, while still saying what a bada-bing job Clinton had done on everything else? How could awkward Al Gore even *touch* such a giant culture war melting pot, now that its angrily licking flames and sizzling water were this scalding, without risking a trip to the ICU himself? To put it bluntly if not politely, Al Gore was as badly mind-fucked by the impeachment circus, and the radioactive cultural fallout from it, as Monica had been "fucked" in the literal sense of the term.

Compounding things, the new media myth du jour was that the general public was now suffering from a mysterious malady called "Clinton fatigue." This had even less truth to it than the old "Perot cost Bush Senior the election" meme. Bill Clinton left office with approval ratings every bit as high as Dwight Eisenhower and Ronald Reagan, *hitting his all-time high the week of impeachment itself!* (There certainly *were* plenty of voters who had Clinton fatigue—but most of them were the same ones who'd loathed him and Hillary from Day One, and who had already bid a permanent *bon voyage* to the Democrats back in 1994. In other words, they weren't gonna vote for Al Gore—period.) For every sufferer of chronic Clinton fatigue, the 1998 midterms had just conclusively proven that there were as many activated and energized people of color and pro–Clinton loyalists who were more determined than ever to cement the Clinton legacy, after the unprecedented impeachment assault. And they wanted—no, *demanded*—that Al Gore have as in-your-face an attitude as Bubba had.

But perhaps nobody in Washington was more "Clinton fatigued" than Al and Tipper

Gore. Once Hillary announced for the Senate, what little was left of the relationship between Team Clinton and Team Gore disintegrated completely. Gore didn't just double down; he *tripled* down on a strategy of "distancing himself" from President Clinton, with the genius-level Al now reducing himself to tossing Sarah Palin–like word salads, so as to avoid even *mentioning* Bill or Hillary's names in his speeches. Gore's post-traumatic stress would show only too well as Campaign 2000 really got going—something which George W. Bush, and his lethal campaign team of Karl Rove, Karen Hughes, and Dick Cheney, would take full advantage of.

*   *   *

In the definitive book on Barack Obama's election, the bestselling *Game Change,* authors Mark Halperin and John Heilemann remarked that "after the aching disappointments of 2000 and 2004, and the depredations Democrats believed Bush had inflicted on the country, the sense of urgency about taking back the White House was bordering on manic."

Replace the words "Democrats believed Bush had inflicted" with "Republicans believed Clinton had inflicted," and the years "2000 and 2004" with "1992 and 1996," and you'd have a pretty good X-ray of where most Republicans stood poised on the edge of the 2000 election. Their sense of urgency about taking back the White House indeed "bordered on manic," more than at any time since the days of President Carter's hostage crisis, gas lines, and 15 percent mortgage and car loan rates. And the thumpin' that Republican reactionaries had just taken from energized and empowered minority, feminist, and gay voters in the impeachment-backlash election of 1998, only made them more frantic—and desperate. A third Democrat election in a row, they quite rightly feared, would truly mark their Waterloo, their sell-by date. "We've just got to win, then," indeed! This time, the Republicans would do *anything* to win.

First came the O.J. trial (along with its made-for-TV spinoffs, "Tonya vs. Nancy" and JonBenét Ramsey)—a big box-office success and a game-changing ratings-grabber if ever there was one. Then came the sequel, *Monicagate: Bigger, Badder, More Uncut*—upping the stakes and taking the game to the next level. Now, all that was left was for the inevitable final act of this horror trilogy to be unspooled, one so shocking and exciting and packed with unexpected plot twists, that it would bring it all full circle, with a dramatic big finish that nobody would ever forget. Indeed, the script was already being written somewhere in the bowels of Development Hell, and it had a firm release date set on the calendar: The first Tuesday in November of 2000.

The working title was *Bush vs. Gore*

12

"The Seinfeld Election"

Who knew that [George W. Bush] would be blessed with an opponent so wooden and awkward and arch, that he would make people overlook Bush's abysmal lack of fitness for the highest office in the land?
—A quite-understandably unnamed high-ranking member
of the Democratic National Committee, as quoted to
Kitty Kelley in her book The Family *(2004).*

Ever since Richard Nixon was in office, and perhaps ever since his predecessor Lyndon Johnson morphed from liberal Medicare and civil rights hero to anti-hippie Vietnam warrior, conservative presidents and candidates for president have always complained that the "liberal media" openly favors the other side. And in almost every campaign since then, they were proven right. From Nixon vs. McGovern to Obama vs. Romney, the "mainstream media," outside of the most right-wing columnists and cable channels, has always been clearly more sympathetic to the liberal or Democratic candidate. (The only other possible exception was Jimmy Carter in 1980—and even then, it took block-long gasoline lines, worsening inflation, interest rates, and unemployment, and a hostage crisis in Iran to do him in.)

But not in 2000.

For the first time since the days of Thomas Dewey and Dwight Eisenhower, the mainstream media had a Republican candidate for president that they actually seemed to prefer. Or, more accurately, the media had a *Democratic* candidate for president that they at best barely tolerated—and many of them, quite frankly, just couldn't stand him. And while there were plenty of good reasons to dislike Al Gore, there were certainly just as many to disdain and perhaps even to fear George W. Bush (especially after he brought Dick Cheney on board!). But it was the *reasoning*, the psychology for both *why* Gore was so disliked by the people who disliked him—and why the very idea of a President Bush inspired such shock and awe in his opponents (a full year BEFORE 9/11 or the War on Terror) that told the real story of Election 2000. And how both the politics and pop culture of the 1990s finally reached their climax.

Ironically, nothing better summed up the attitude of the mainstream media towards Election 2000 than *Newsweek's* initial November 2000 summary of the campaign. They had christened it "The Seinfeld Election"—"a show about nothing." After all, we were still in what some pundits called a recession-proof surplus economy, with no (apparent) real global threats since the Soviet Union went out of business a decade earlier. The civil rights and women's rights battles were largely won—nobody went around saying "I'm only gonna hire a man for that!" or overtly refusing to hire blacks and Latinos anymore. And both Bush and Gore were nothing but a couple of spoiled-rotten preppies; the same age, the same social class, who'd only gotten to where they were because of their daddies. If Bush hadn't been President Bush's son, he'd be lucky to run a real-estate or oil lease office out in panhandle Texas. And if Gore hadn't been Senator Gore's son, he would have probably been lucky to anchor the LA or New York *Eyewitness News. So what difference did it make who actually won?*

That was the uber-narrative that was followed through thick and thin, from CNN to Fox News, from *Time* and *Newsweek* to the New York and Los Angeles *Times* and the *Washington Post*, from "snarky" Web blogs to late night talk shows—no matter how obviously, self-evidently untrue it became. Likewise, according to this narrative, the punditocracy was convinced that this was an election that would be decided by high-income, highly educated, job-secure technocrats on both coasts, or in the bigger and richer metropolitan markets. The voters who had prospered the most (and would continue to under Bush and Obama) in the transition to the New Economy. (Voters who were also, for the most part, as whiter-than-white as a Tide commercial.) The "swing voters." The "soccer moms." The "New Democrats." The "makers, not the takers." The people whom both the Republican fundraising structure and the Democratic Leadership Council unanimously identified as the "base" of their parties, as the 1990s came to their close.

Indeed, the more that activists from Ralph Nader's raiders and desperate Democratic base voters protested the 1999 G8 summit (and the "D2K" and "R2K" conventions the following summer), the more that televangelists and family values pastors preached a culture-war Armageddon, the more determinedly—even defiantly—the Mainstream Media became to portray Election 2000 as nothing more than a campy *divertissement,* as frothy and light as a Bridget Jones rom-com, or a classic rerun of *Hart to Hart.* At least, up until Election Day actually happened. And that gave them a disaster movie reality show that was so sexy and high-rated, it managed to top O.J., JonBenét, and Monica! *Son of a bitch! We struck the motherlode!*

As anyone who has ever worked in sales can attest, the more room you give a would-be customer to start making excuses, raising one objection after another, and procrastinating like a little old lady dithering and teasing herself with an "expensive" purchase at the department store, with no sense of urgency, the more likely that they'll back out and cut the deal when it finally comes time to write the check. And all you end up with is hours and days of time you wasted with them, when you could have possibly been going after someone who really *was* interested in what you had to sell. Because they never really wanted to write that check in the first place, or they just weren't convinced that it was worth the trauma and the expense, no matter how hard or how eagerly you tried to please them.

As such, this ultimate "swing voter" strategy of making the election hinge on the people who were *least likely* to be directly affected or impacted by its outcome, could hardly have been more deleterious or destructive. Not for nothing did Joan Didion call it a "fatal eddy," like an undertow pulling an unsuspecting swimmer to his death, this almost obsessive pandering to every supposed whim of the terminally undecided, hypersensitive, last-minute political bargain shoppers—at the expense of everyone else.

G8! Y2K! OMG! (Party Like It's 1999!)

After Bill Clinton won his impeachment battle (and vanquished that wingy hatemonger Newt Gingrich in the bargain) finally, many optimistic left-wing voices thought, *finally* Bill Clinton would now see the error of his "triangulating" ways. Finally, he would be forced to realize that no matter what he did, no matter how far he bent over, no matter how many times he appropriated and plagiarized from the Ronald Reagan playbook or declared the era of Big Government over, it would never be enough. He'd always be a filthy, degenerate, pinko, dope-smoking hippie to his enemies. So what could it hurt him now to actually start acting the part?

There were no more "permanent campaigns" to run, no jobs that could top this one left to audition for. A six-figure lifetime pension, Cadillac health benefits, and millions in book deals, lecture fees, and cable/PBS appearances awaited him and Hillary. Finally, many labor leaders and left-liberals thought, *finally* Bill Clinton will be able to be that transformative, FDR-or-JFK-like, inspirational progressive that he always wanted to be, and never quite knew how! Revenge was gonna be sweet!

But true to form, Bill Clinton was playing on a much larger chess board. Now that the crazies had well and truly emerged from the fever swamps, and had almost undone a sitting government—would self-interested, wealthy bottom-line businessmen who valued "stability," and socially tolerant, educated fiscal conservatives (especially ones under age 40 or 50) really keep voting for a Republican Party that was this reckless, anti-science, and fundamentalist? One that slut-shamed their own girlfriends, just because they "fornicated" before marriage or used birth control? People who believed that their nice gay friends from the office would burn in hell forever alongside Adolf Hitler, Jack the Ripper, and Charles Manson, and that maybe they even *deserved* to die of AIDS? Especially since, during Clinton's last few stock-market-booming years—why, they hadn't had it this good since Ronald Reagan himself! If not *ever!*

In his 2004 bestseller *What's the Matter with Kansas,* Thomas Frank picks up the narrative from here. "Just look at how Ronald Reagan's 'social issues' have come back to bite his party in the ass!" he imagined a Democratic Leadership Committee–type, New Democrat thinking with eager anticipation. "If only the crazy [culture-war conservatives] push a little bit more … the Republican Party will alienate the wealthy suburban Mods" (aka the coveted "swing voters" of 1999–2000) "and we will be able to step in and carry [them] along with all the juicy boodle their inhabitants are capable of throwing our way." Frank went on to add that by the late 1990s and early 2000s, the DLC-type Democrats (of which Bill Clinton was the founding standard-bearer) seemed to actually be "*looking forward* to a day when their party really is what David Brooks and Ann Coulter claim it to be [now]."

Sure, the hardest of the hardcores—the Koch Brothers, Richard Mellon Scaife, the Coors and Walton (Walmart) families, maybe Donald Trump and Rupert Murdoch—they would still prop up the Republican brand for years to come. But Clinton already had George Soros, Warren Buffett, David Geffen, Barry Diller, Ted Turner, Michael Eisner, and Steve Jobs, just like money in the bank. Now, if Clinton could truly close the deal with the coming-up-next generation of Ivy League millennial wizards who would soon be old enough to vote (like say, a 17-year-old heading-to-Harvard genius named Mark Zuckerberg, or a 16-year-old Orange County poly sci major named Ezra Klein…) if Clinton could convince young high-earners once and for all that their future incomes would be just as safe with tomorrow's Democrats as it was with Ronald Reagan—why, in just a few more years, it would be Game Over for the GOP!

The New Democrat dream could finally come true, the whole cookie, the full Monty. And best of all, it would be written that HE, Bill "Comeback Kid" Clinton, was once again the "game changer" who'd made it all happen! As his final act, Bubba could knock the head off of the Republicans' corporate fundraising monster, as victoriously as Jamie Lee Curtis at the end of *Halloween: H20*.

President Clinton wasted no time in seizing the opportunity. In the fall of 1998, during the impeachment furore, a blatantly illegal merger (due to antitrust and banking regulations, most notably the Depression-era Glass-Steagall Act) between Citibank and Travelers Insurance was proposed. But Alan Greenspan and Treasury Secretary Robert Rubin, both of whom strongly wanted to see *even more* deregulation in the financial industry, issued a temporary waiver—which would give the Congress just enough time to get to work, if things played out right. Sure enough, the Republican Congress (with the fervent support of President Clinton) repealed the Depression-era Glass-Steagall law that separated investment and standard banking, and the too-big-to-fail behemoth Citigroup arose. Not long afterward, Rubin left government service to cash in on over $100 million in cash and prizes from the private sector.

A regulator and attorney named Brooksley Born foresaw all too well what kind of financial weapons of mass destruction could come from this massive sweep of deregulation and lack of oversight—which went beyond anything Ronald Reagan or George Bush, Sr., had ever done. She had earlier tried to force the government to regulate the notoriously unstable financial derivatives market (which morphed into the "credit-default swaps" of the pre–2008-meltdown era), but Greenspan and Rubin utterly crushed her efforts, with President Clinton's full knowledge and approval. Realizing that she was hopelessly out-gunned, Brooksley Born submitted her resignation in the spring of 1999. Clinton accepted it, avidly. As Brooksley Born sadly packed up her things, the sexist and class-ist Beltway bubble did everything but sing "Ding Dong! The Witch Is Dead." The "Ivy-educated pun-ditocracy" (as Eric Alterman called it) was, to put it coarsely, creaming its jeans over these Clintonomic extreme makeovers. A February 1999 cover of *Time* said it all. It had Greenspan, Rubin, and future Harvard head Larry Summers billed as nothing less than "The Committee to SAVE the WORLD!"

Barely a year later, fundamentalist Texas culture-warrior and Reagan-era financial deregulator Senator Phil Gramm pushed through the Commodity Futures Modernization Act, which essentially banned federal regulation of the derivatives market, and (trashing the Republican principle of states' rights) overturned state insurance and banking regulators' abilities to enforce derivatives regulation at their level. (For all this, upon the 10th anniversary of these achievements in May of 2010, Gramm, Greenspan, and Rubin were given the dubious honor of placement on the left-wing Alternet.com's "Ten Most Corrupt Capitalists" list.) And while Clinton later expressed public regret about the 1999 and 2000 deregulation orgy (following the 2008 economic meltdown), back then, with the Wall Street/Silicon Valley economy booming, Bubba could hardly wait to sign. To use Dick Cheney's favorite catchphrase, "Full speed ahead!"

(In Clinton's defense, the Congress so overwhelmingly supported the financial industry's wish list, they could have overridden by a ⅔ supermajority even if Clinton had vetoed the things. And that *wasn't* just because of the right-wing Republicans, who were barely 50/50 in the Senate and not much more in the House. It was the staunchly "pro-business" Blue Dog Democrats like Joe Lieberman, Max Baucus, Harry Reid, and Ben Nelson—the same ones who would also personally strangle the Democrats' own much-promised Obamacare "public option" to death a decade later, who had said "no" to the liberals, and "your wish is my command" to Wall Street.)

But Bill Clinton had something even more urgent on his plate to attend to as the summer of 1999 opened: the global-economy World Trade Organization conference that he had practically founded himself during the days of NAFTA and GATT, being held that year in Seattle. The left-wing voices both here and abroad knew that they had no time to waste to express their outrage and anger at this latest round of what they thought was more worker-exploiting, enviro-polluting global-oney. The uprising and protests outside the conference soon turned violent. Even the most cynical members of the *Mother Jones*/Pacifica Radio left couldn't believe what they were seeing—a *Democrat* president, an *ex-hippie!*—as good as authorizing a head-cracking, arm-twisting police riot, just like right-wing Mayor Daley had done back in 1968! And these weren't antiwar radicals throwing rocks and spraying aerosol in the police's face; for the most part, these really were physically peaceful protestors, singers, poets, neo-hippies; the type of folks who would try to "Occupy Wall Street" a decade later. All this violence, to protect Clinton's "new world order," his "global economy," his "information age." *This is a joke!* This can't be happening under a *liberal Democrat*, can it?

And then, in May of 2000, just after the Community Futures Modernization Act and the Glass-Steagall repeals, Bill Clinton and Charlene Barshefsky announced full admittance of the People's Republic of China to the World Trade Organization, effective December 2001. The bill was passed over a two-thirds "No" vote from Congressional Democrats, thanks to corporate-friendly Republicans in the House and Senate. Working-class voters' blood ran cold at the thought of the outsourcings and downsizings that could (and in many ways *would*) affect them in the next decade or two. In a 2012 article for the *Huffington Post*, the author and cultural critic Jane White, who wrote a book titled *America: Welcome to the Poorhouse,* said that Bill Clinton's real domestic legacy would probably be as "Outsourcer in Chief."

You always hurt the one you love, and only love can break a heart. And Brother Clinton's Big Money Globalized Salvation Show in 1999 and 2000 was the credit default-swap that broke the camel's back, as far as the hard left was concerned. *Even when those people lose, they win!* Forget Lee Harvey Oswald or the Protocols of the Elders of Zion, or the Freemasons and Scientologists—if THIS didn't prove a "conspiracy" at work in the government, than what did? These are the same right-wing asshats who almost impeached Clinton from office barely a year ago—and now he's right back there hugging and partying with them! While we, the liberal voices who took to the radio, the blogs, the grocery store petitions, and the picket sign barricades to save him, to stay true to him, while *we* get the cold shoulder! People like Phil Gramm, Tom DeLay, and "Casino Jack" Abramoff get the high-fives—and we get the dog ditch! *How could he!*

Needless to say, both Bill and Hill saw things a bit differently. Who had single-handedly kept the Democratic Party in business while Republican governors ran California, New

York, Florida, and Texas? While Richard Riordan and Rudy Giuliani ran Hollywood and Wall Street? While Newt and his cronies controlled both houses of Congress, Alan Greenspan ran the Fed, and William Rehnquist and Antonin Scalia exerted "Supreme" authority? Who had brought the Democratic Party back to life out of its respirator coma, as if from a scene in *Awakenings* or *Touched by an Angel,* after the Carter era, and its even worse Mondale-Dukakis sequels? Who had taken all the beatings, survived all the torture, the audits, the subpoenas, the scrutiny, Rush Limbaugh once calling their teenage daughter Chelsea the "White House Dog," even impeachment and accusations of rape and murder, all to keep the Republican wingers from total control?

And how did all those self-righteous "social justice" leftists in the downtown LA activism shacks, the white Upper West Side and Marin County progressive cocktail parties, and the snooty college-town academic gatherings (talk about Clorox Country)—how did *they* treat Bill and Hill in return? Like a bunch of cooties, that's how—the way a person picks up a snail or cockroach, holding it at arm's length pinched between thumb and forefinger with Kleenex, wrinkled nose in the air, head turned away. The left wing voices had barely *tolerated* the Clintons; they had never *liked* or *respected* them.

Just after impeachment reached its climax in the spring of 1999, the A-list columnist Christopher Hitchens released a bestseller criticizing Bill and Hillary from the left, saying that they were so compulsively dishonest and disgusting, they had *No One Left to Lie to* anymore. His fellow witty Brit, Alexander Cockburn, was hard at work by then on a book-length attack on Al Gore—one that would have made Nancy Grace and Ann Coulter proud in its level of flamethrower viciousness—titled *Al Gore: A User's Manual.* (It was strategically scheduled for publication just weeks before the Bush vs. Gore election, and came complete with Gore wearing the most offensive, stereotypically autistic, blank-slate facial expression imaginable on the cover photo.) Barbara Ehrenreich was also hard at work whipping up a buzzy case study to remind Democrats how despite the "prosperous" 20-million-job surplus economy, the lower-middle and underclasses were still being *Nickel & Dimed.* And Thomas Frank had already snarkily satirized the "hip" corporate pretentions of the Clinton era, in 1998's *The Conquest of Cool,* and was about to mount a sequel called *One Market Under God.* And all that was just for openers!

George W. Bush, Newt Gingrich, Karl Rove, and Dick Cheney must have been pinching themselves to see if it was real—they *wished* Fox News and Rush Limbaugh were as hard on 1990s Clintonomics as these *liberals* and *Democrats* were! Nope, even *after* Monicagate showed what the hard right was capable of, these people's tired old protest song against Clintonism still stayed the same. One can easily imagine a conversation between the two sides, pared down to their essence:

"How *dare* you re-appoint Alan Greenspan and Robert Rubin!" (*Wall Street and Silicon Valley would've fucking panicked and rebelled, 2008-style, if I hadn't. Who'd you have wanted for Fed Chief—Michael Moore?*) "How could you ever 'reform' welfare and sign Defense of Marriage?!" (*It was either that or get a constitutional amendment against gay people, while watching Newt help President Dole or President Perot totally* destroy *the Great Society. How'd you have liked them apples?*) "How could you push for free trade!?" (*Hell, I should have them print me up a T-shirt saying "I Created the Best Economy Since the '50s—And All I Get Is Kvetching That This Shirt Was Made in China!"*) *Bitch, bitch, bitch!* In the multiplex of one's mind, it was now as if Bill Clinton borrowed Jane Fonda's newly liberated line from *9 to 5,* and told the always-complaining, never-satisfied lefty loudmouths like Thomas Frank, Molly Ivins, Barbara Ehrenreich, Alexander Cockburn, Robert Scheer, Jon Wiener, and Michael Moore, to "Hit the road, Buster—this is where YOU get off!"

No, the sincere left couldn't control Bill Clinton, any more than the hard right could have outsmarted or unelected him in 1992 or '96. But much to their fury, *he* could still control *them* with his little finger! (And unless they wanted to garbage-can the chance for overwhelmingly Democratic, socially tolerant, minority-diverse New York to elect its first female senator, even the biggest leftie purists knew they had to hold their noses for Hillary in 2000.)

But there *was* one person on whom the left-wing voices *could* take out all their mounting and volcanic frustration: A Democrat who'd had an 84 percent record from Right to Life during the Congress and Senate of the late 1970s and '80s, and was notorious for his hostility to gays and lesbians (until he "coincidentally" evolved towards tolerance as well as women's choice—the *instant* he became the Democrats' nominee for vice president), while his wife crusaded against immoral music and films. A proud Vietnam Veteran who'd supported all of Ronnie Reagan and George Bush, Sr.'s anti–Commie cold warring (and the first Gulf War) to the max, and who was later almost single-handedly responsible for "selling" NAFTA on cable TV. Someone whose whiter-than-white, tech-nerd affect seemed like the very antithesis of the soulful and spicy people-person who Feels Your Pain. Someone who had proven himself only too loyal to Clinton's so-called "corporate agenda," in his eight years as vice president.

And so it went with the Democratic Party's powder keg, now after eight years of Third Way "neoliberal" triangulating, just waiting to explode. When consumer-advocacy icon Ralph Nader—the man who'd never "sold out," who'd always stayed true to the ascetic aesthetics of the Jerry Brown/Joan Baez era, the man who'd dedicated his entire adult life to liberal activism … when Ralph Nader announced his Green Party candidacy for president, the activist Left found (to their initial delight) that he was not only willing and able, but downright *happy* to light the match!

It was kind of poetic, in light of all this *mishugas*, that the big news as the calendar 1990s ended was the spectre of a "Y2K Meltdown." Much of computerized date-keeping technology only used the last two digits of a year's date—like the person who dated a check 6/18/93 as opposed to 6/18/1993—with the "19" prefix of the four-digit year taken for granted. When the "19" would change to "20" and the two last numbers would revert to "00" and then "01," "02," "03" etcetera, there were fears that computers—including those handling the power grid, nuclear weapons and reactors, security and law enforcement systems, and high-level banking/finance and IRS records—that those computers would essentially freak out and go haywire, and either melt down or go into some kind of self-destruct mode. Technicians worked round the clock on many of these systems throughout 1999, as news broadcasts and newspaper and online stories gave a running account of the "Y2K Threat."

Fortunately, January 1, 2000, came and went without much incident—there were reports of centenarians and long-dead relatives receiving truancy reports from old school district files that had been previously uploaded to computers, and other human-interest trifles like that. American and Canadian TV networks and cable news channels (and America Online, Google, Yahoo, Geocities, and the like) covered the changing of the millennium via satellite from all the western world's great cities and capitals—Paris, London, Rome, Berlin, Athens, Moscow, Hollywood, Las Vegas, San Francisco, New York. Even several Asian and far-Eastern countries which used non–Western calendars, for which that day wasn't anything special in their worlds, recognized the significance, and managed something of a celebration. The fact that 1–01–2000 went off without a major hitch or meltdown only capped off the late 1990s' sense of invincibility—that we had indeed reached "the end of history," that we were in a "recession-proof" economy, that major league disasters and historical catastrophes were finally a thing of the past....

The Stolen Succession

Despite all this, one of the silliest yet most popular talking points of Election 2000 was how "easy" it was supposed to be for Al Gore to win. Never mind the fact that when Gallup, ABC, *The Washington Post* and other major organizations began seriously polling a hypothetical Gore vs. Bush race in the spring of 1999, Gore ranged between 9 and 17 full points behind Dubya. And this was at the very height of dot-com "peace and prosperity" and the surplus budget!

Indeed, it seems almost painfully obvious looking back, that in order to navigate the 24–7 culture wars and the economic, social class, and racial minefields of 1999–2000, Al Gore would had to have had a Dorothy Hamill or Mikhail Baryshnikov–like ability to perform political triple-axels in a single bound. He would have to up his game to a level of political skill and maneuvering that, in comparison, would make Bill Clinton's mid 1990s "triangulation" strategy look like a childish exercise.

For example, when Gore spoke out in favor of gun control, he was slitting his electoral wrists in NRA-controlled precincts and Southern states like his own Tennessee. And he knew it. But *not* speaking out in favor of gun control, or even playing cutesy or coy on the urgent need for it, was simply no longer an option for a Democratic candidate, either. Not after Columbine, Jonesboro, Paducah, the Jewish day care shooting in Los Angeles, and Timothy McVeigh! It was either throw the NRA under the bus, or get run over by a truckload of arms-folded Carol Brady and June Cleaver "Education Moms," to say nothing of Democratic trial lawyers and the ACLU.

Ditto environmentalism and health care reform. If Gore didn't dramatically stand up to Big Coal and strip-mining interests, let alone Big Tobacco (as Clinton had done), he would reduce his decade-long career and brand as the nation's most prominent environmentalist-politician to a bad joke for Leno and Letterman. But if he came out with more "Big Government regulations," that would only cement his Rush Limbaugh/Bill O'Reilly status as an out-of-touch "enviro-whacko" who was indifferent (at best) to how many jobs would be cut back or downsized because of them. Put simply, Al Gore was damned if he did—and damned if he didn't.

And once again, on the biggest issue of them all, the one that was supposed to put Election 2000 in the bag for Gore—the economy, stupid—Gore had also been painted into a corner. How could Al Gore go populist and address the people left behind by the New Economy, the ones who used to define the Democratic Party's "base," especially among white voters—without completely undercutting the most powerful Clintonian argument of all for his election: the "peace and prosperity," diverse-workplace, surplus budget?

In the ten years from 1989 and '90 through 1999 and 2000, nothing besides the final collapse of Communism itself had as profound and lasting an effect on the world—and nothing *period* had more of an effect on how Americans managed their finances, conducted office business, and got their information and news—than the Internet and cell phones. And one of the biggest Whoppers-with-cheese on 1999 and 2000's political menu was when some overeager columnists pounced on Al Gore's (completely truthful) humble-brag that, while in the Congress and Senate, he "took the lead in creating" what became the Internet.

The talking-pointers used it as more proof-positive of what an monomaniacal, truth-bending, nerd-on-steroids Gore was, laughing that an unutterably egotistical Al Gore was now taking credit for nothing less than "inventing the Internet!" Talk about "burying the lede!" In retrospect, the real story here wasn't whether or not Gore invented the Internet. (And it should be emphasized that Gore's arch-enemy Newt Gingrich, and the two people who *truly* "invented" the Internet—Apple founder Steve Jobs, who later appointed Gore to Apple's board, and 1960s technologist Vinton Cerf—*they had no problem whatsoever* with Al Gore claiming "credit" for the Internet.)

Ben Stein, the famous TV host and columnist, was once asked whether or not "Jews controlled the media," and he replied to the effect of, "Yes, we do. And considering how many people love to go the movies and watch TV, we must be doing a pretty good job of it!" In much the same way, Al Gore could have easily counterstruck all the press corps' piffle about how and whether or not he claimed to have "invented the Internet" by saying something like, *As a matter of fact, yes I did! And you should be glad I did, because you saw how much the Internet and cellular technology changed the world in the last 10 years. Well, it's just getting started! And we're going to need the president who "invented" and understands the Internet to make sure that we pull through the next 10 years—and make those changes work for us and our working families, rather than against us. Do you really think that George W. Bush, whose father didn't even know what a supermarket checkout-scanner was, is capable of overseeing the transition to a truly net-based, cell-phone economy? Heck, Bush probably doesn't know a Python code from Monty Python's Flying Circus!*

Even Ann Coulter and Bill O'Reilly themselves would have freely admitted that Al Gore was far and away more qualified than George W. Bush when it came to managing an economy of computer chips and cell phones. Yet instead of Gore using this ultimate trump card against the supposedly "stupid" Dubya, Gore chose to downplay and avoid discussing what should have been his Obamacare, his Clintonomics, his "Tear Down This Wall!," his signature policy achievement. So why didn't Al Gore take the one area that he had *every* advantage in—and make that THE "talking point memo" of Campaign 2000?

Because of the Narrative, stupid. If the famously awkward "Gore-acle" actually made the massive, floor-to-ceiling game changes that new technology had wrought in the past decade—*and would likely bring in the coming one*—the centerpiece of his campaign, he would be ripping open the barely healing wounds of the first transition to New Economy, Inc., that not even Bill Clinton could deal with without getting hurt. While unemployment was low and the economy—now irrevocably transformed from one based on manufacturing and production to one based on financial services, electronics, and new media—was humming, working lower-middle-class people had still had to sign up for job retraining at the daytime TV-ad tech institutes or the local adult schools in record numbers during the past decade to get, transition to, or to just plain *keep* their newly updated or created jobs. If Gore dared raise the stress level, while George W. Bush was talking about sunshine, lollipops, kittens, and "compassionate conservatism," Gore would be as good as inviting people to vote for Bush instead, in the hopes that Bush really would "take America BACK"—in every sort of way. To use the immortal line that political screenwriter *par excellence* Aaron Sorkin put in Jack Nicholson's snarling mouth in 1992's *A Few Good Men*, "YOU CAN'T HANDLE THE TRUTH!"

Indeed, by the end of the 1990s, it appeared to many voters (especially lower-information ones) that we had already reached the tipping point where "progress" and even science was now our most terrifying, *Terminator*-like enemy than our best friend. In 1997, headlines around the world announced that a sheep named Dolly had successfully been "cloned" from an earlier sheep's DNA and cells. Less than a year later, Australian scientist Craig Venter and his bio-tech firm, Celera Genomics, built a privatized piggyback on earlier government attempts to map the "Human Genome." Conspiracy theorists were smokin' like the iconic Cigarette Smoking Man on *The X-Files*, thinking that perhaps big government—or worse, big companies like GM, GE, Monsanto, Halliburton, Bayer, etc—might be able to actually "own" and "patent" human beings' DNA and genetic codes. Needless to say, when it came to trying to explain in layman's terms the benefits and moral quandaries of these centrifuge-speed advances to the American public (in the sound-byte and pull-quote American media, no less)—Bill Clinton, Al Gore, and George W. Bush all had nothing to offer now but a crashed hard-drive's worth of FAIL.

So instead, by 1999 and 2000, both Al Gore and George W. Bush (and their spin-doctors) very purposely moved the camera of the national economic conversation to non-threatening non-issues like whether or not to put the surpluses ("as far as the eye can see!") in a so-called "lockbox" to protect Social Security and Medicare (for retired, out-of-the-job-market seniors), or whether to rebate the supposedly "endless" surpluses to Hard Working Taxpayers. The idea that there might *not be* a permanent surplus, that the late 1990s economy might largely be based on a bubble, was literally *unspeakable*. Both talked about health reform (when they talked about it at all, which wasn't much) on almost as deferentially a state's-rights platform as William Rehnquist or George Wallace might have done, still in post-traumatic stress from Hillarycare '94. And Bush and Gore didn't just *walk* away—they *ran* away from Generation X young voters—preferring instead to focus on 35- to 55-year-old "swing voting" Baby Boomers who already owned homes, and drove nice cars with established credit.

Things reached their nadir (if not their Ralph Nader) by summer and early fall, when Bush gave what was rightfully criticized as "fuzzy math" make-up story projections on Social Security during the debates, while both he and Gore raced to the gutter on who could "Medi-Scare" vulnerable seniors the most. And in his nomination speech in August of 2000, Al Gore—millionaire "one percenter," Southern aristocrat and senator's son, St. Albans and Harvard graduate, and sitting vice president—finished off his nomination speech with the laughable battle cry, "*They* stand for the powerful, while I stand for the People!"

Well, welcome to the Symbionese Liberation Army to you too, Mr. Gore! Gore's plans were certainly better than the awesomely irresponsible policies Bush actually effected later on. But at the end of the day, even that Internet-inventor Al Gore's economic policy "innovations" were little more than a tired plate of country-club Republican leftovers from the days of Eisenhower, Nelson Rockefeller, and Richard Nixon. Gore only looked progressive or liberal because of just how far to the right that Republican revolutionaries like Gingrich, Limbaugh, and Cheney had pushed the Overton Window definition of "conservative."

In contrast to all that, all George W. Bush had to do was to sit back and relax, skimming off all the people who had objections (legitimate or not) to the Clinton/Gore era, as effortlessly as a backyard pool filter pulling leaves from the surface. If you were "fed up," to plagiarize Phyllis Schlafly's famous column, with the Clinton White House's so-called immorality and its tabloidy, self-righteous sleaze—come on over, the water's fine! If you were a downscale dad or a single mom who wasn't doing appreciably "any better now than you were eight years ago," if you were working at a no-bennies McJob, still struggling to pay the bills each month, still going to the payday-advance store—while everyone on TV and in the movies and magazines was shoe-shoppin,' bling-blingin,' and cell-phoning their oblivious way through life, just like the "greedy" Reagan 1980s—then what had Bill Clinton's New Democrats, and their oh-so-prosperous dot-economy, really done for YOU?

If you were a small businessman who spent the '90s watching your local bookstores and coffeehouses, your video spots and corner markets get swallowed whole by Starbucks, Blockbuster, Barnes & Noble, Borders, Circuit City, The Coffee Bean, Walmart, Best Buy, Target, Costco, Olive Garden, Red Lobster, Chili's (not to mention eminent-domaining judges and tax-and-spend county officials), as the *Ghostbusters* would say, "Who you gonna call?" And if you were a blue-collar or low-level office worker, or an aging retired senior, and you felt just plain *frightened* by all this New Technology 2.0, all of this "outsourcing" and "re-branding" and "globalizing" that people like Tony Robbins and Tom Peters kept yammering about on PBS and cable, were you *really* going to vote for the man Rush Limbaugh sarcastically called the "Al Gore-ithm?" The uncaring "Gore-acle" who was still defending quota-based affirmative action in 2000, and who'd started this whole Information Age ball rolling in the first place? (And let's not even get into the threat that a culture growing ever more uncontrollably diverse, ever more melanin-enhanced and proudly alternative-lifestyled, could pose to many of these peoples' senses of security.)

Hurricane Monica's Blowback

While the impeachment trial was over by the time that Election 2000 got under way, like a vengeful ghost in Dickens or Shakespeare, the open wounds that Monicagate had ripped open had only grown more infected and inflamed. In their mad dash to defend and protect Bill Clinton at any and all costs, many liberal intellectuals had inadvertently napalmed every remaining shred of old-fashioned, Truman/Eisenhower era standards of decorum for presidential conduct. Clinton's vices had officially morphed into his virtues.

After all, how could a stiff, science-nerd wonk like Al Gore ever compete with the raw "unpoliced sexuality" and seductive mystique (as Toni Morrison had so memorably put it) of Bill Clinton? When Gore openly condemned Clinton the day he kicked off his campaign, and later told Diane Sawyer and others how offensive Clinton's conduct was to him "as a father"—only months after Gore had vigorously *defended* Clinton as one of "history's greatest presidents"—it was a move that backfired like a ruptured car muffler, especially among the most target and choice Democratic constituencies.

If, as Alan Dershowitz famously suggested, the forces out to impeach Clinton were really the forces of "evil," then to purposely distance yourself from Bill Clinton while his wounds were still healing was—in that context—almost to deny the Clinton "holocaust" as it were—at the very least, to take the same side as the evil. If Gore was out there moralizing and tut-tutting about Clinton's behavior—well, you know what? The white supremacists and the "God Hates Fags" types were also doing the exact same thing. *So how does that make you any different from them at the end of the day, Mister Vice President?*

Internet blogger and 1990s Democratic activist Marc Perkel takes up the story from here. No sooner was the 1996 election in the bag than Perkel, a staunch Clintonite, started one of the first (and thanks to his expertise at indexing web pages in those early Yahoo-Google-AOL days) one of the highest-traffic "Gore 2000" websites on the World Wide Web. (It was even profiled in the *Washington Post* in September 1998, as one of the first major Gore-for-President internet sites.)

But then, after impeachment, Gore began distancing himself from Clinton, which Perkel found intolerable. Not only was it ungrateful in extremis, but fact check: Who had obliterated the glass ceiling for executive women as Attorneys General, Secretaries of State, Surgeons General, and as a second Supreme Court justice? Who was the first to appoint out-and-proud, open gay men and lesbians to power positions—despite the wailing and gnashing of teeth from Helms, Falwell, Hagee, Santorum, James Dobson, Ralph Reed, and their crews? Who was the best white friend racial minorities ever had, at least since Lyndon Johnson—the man who'd put African American and Latino unemployment to their lowest modern levels, who made a point of effortlessly enjoying the distinct 'flavah' of their cultures, who created 20 million jobs? Was Gore going to "distance himself" from all of those Clintonian accomplishments, too??

Perkel demanded that the Gore campaign start giving more credit to Clinton or he would close down or even start denouncing Gore on his high-traffic website. So resolute was Gore's strategy to distance himself from Clinton that his people refused. After Election 2000 ended, Perkel angrily addressed Al Gore on his webpage, with quote, "You're 'your own man' now—enjoy it, motherfucker!"

Joan Didion was expectedly more subdued, but no less vehement. She took a carpet-beater to Gore's camp in a highly publicized essay just days before the election, which she pointedly titled "GOD's Country." When Gore agreed to restore honor and dignity to the White House just the way Bush was promising to do, she wondered, how was that *not* just more coded dog-whistling for the submit-unto-your-husband sexism and thinly disguised homophobia that many of Bush's core supporters believed in? (Maureen Dowd added in a 1999 column that the "subtext" of Bush's campaign was that voters could count on him to behave with more dignity than Bill Clinton—and that "the subtext of Gore's campaign is the same.") By essentially allowing the voters fed up with Clinton to write the narrative, with the two campaigns "essentially telling the same agreed-upon story," how did that not "disavow" the entire Clinton legacy that Gore had been co-pilot on for the past 8 years?

By "distancing himself" from Bill Clinton to an almost ludicrous degree, only to be dragged kicking and screaming back to Bill when it came time to collect the campaign-finance checks from the Hollywood, Silicon Valley, and Wall Street Democrats who supported Clinton totally (or to rally African Americans and Hispanics), Gore made himself look exactly like what his worst enemies had been claiming he was all along: Mr. Flip-Flop. A hypocrite, a charlatan, a con man.

Not that George W. Bush was any better in all this. He was just more vicious and ruthless. He found the last man standing against him before the Gore battle to be "maverick" Senator John McCain, instead of one of the clown car fundies and free-market fanatics who'd competed with him in the 2000 primary (Alan Keyes, Steve Forbes, and the like.) And McCain posed a threat to Bush that none of those others could hope to match. A career military man and five-year veteran of the Hanoi Hilton torture chamber in Vietnam, elected to Congress in 1982, McCain could wipe up the floor with Bush in the target Republican demo of military vets and working-class Vietnam veterans. Especially since Bush had spent much of his own Vietnam-era "service" living an almost *Three's Company* lifestyle in Texas or studying for his MBA back East, while flying safe stateside missions in the Texas National Guard (when he bothered to show up at all).

While McCain was pro-life and not exactly Harvey Milk on gay rights, he wasn't fanatically *against* either, and openly dissed tele-evangelists like Jerry Falwell, Pat Robertson, and Ralph Reed as being "agents of intolerance." In other words, McCain could suck up economically conservative but culturally tolerant "swing voters" and gender-gapping women like a New Democrat vacuum cleaner. (By 2008 McCain evidently had a change of heart, taking an endorsement from John "Witchcraft in the White House" Hagee, until Hagee's virulent anti–Catholicism, homophobia, and "the Holocaust was God's will" beliefs forced McCain to back away.) Most threateningly of all, McCain was almost as adept at playing the New Media game as Bill Clinton was, going on Comedy Central, David Letterman, and *Saturday Night Live,* and effortlessly enjoying himself.

After narrowly winning his governorship in 1994 against formidable Ann Richards, only to watch the horror of brother Jeb's defeat that same year to liberal Lawton Chiles in Florida, Dubya was determined that this "maverick" wouldn't upstage him! (Jeb had finally won in 1998 against Chiles' would-be successor, and in a sad irony, Chiles died of a heart attack in his final month in office, just before Jeb's inaugural.) Bush pandered to the hard right at evangelical Bob Jones University (whose policy on race-mixing was unenlightened, to say the least). Even more disturbingly, during the South Carolina primaries, mysterious phone calls and Emails started surfacing that outrageously accused McCain of being a stereotypical bug-eyed, unstable, born-to-kill Vietnam veteran right out of a 1970s police show or a *Rambo* movie, and claiming that John and Cindy McCain's adoptive child was an illegitimate "black baby" she'd tried to cover up. Evangelical radio stations and media went all out for Bush, fearful that McCain was insufficiently committed to stopping abortion and the "gay agenda," and powerfully insulted by his "agents of intolerance" business.

Sadly, the dirty pool worked its magic, and as the surfers say, it was a w-w-w-wipeout for McCain at the hands of Bush (and his own ruthless black hand, Karl Rove). Now with the nomination all but his, Bush began running to the center, crafting a new narrative of being a so-called "compassionate conservative" who would try to heal the wounds that the hard core culture warring of the Gingrich era (and his own primary campaign!) had inflamed. If Bill Clinton and Al Gore had needed to convince Reagan-era yuppies, and Greatest and Silent Generation retirees that their money was safe with them, Bush now needed to convince voters more liberal than say, Pat Buchanan or James Dobson, that he wasn't going to be some kind of scourge of the unrighteous among us.

There was only one big difference. While Gore's flip-floppery and exaggerations were eviscerated by the media—even on such laughably trivial issues as whether or not he was the model for the Ryan O'Neal character in *Love Story* or whether his mother had sung "Look for the Union Label" to him as a child—Bush was largely given a free pass for his "triangulations." And that was largely because, in stark contrast to the open hostility and dismissiveness Bush would show the press corps once he was actually in office, Bush skillfully made himself seem like Charlie Charming, a breath of fresh air (especially for a conservative Republican) on the initial campaign trail. Al Gore, meanwhile, seemed by his very nature to bring out the worst and ugliest in those who were covering him.

He Thinks He's "better *than* us!"

If Oprah, Phil Donahue, Sally Jessy, Dr. Ruth, and Barbara Walters had given rise to a "Let's Talk About Me!" society, the pundit-journalists who hit the jackpot during the Lewinsky crisis had decided to start reporting "Let's Talk About Me" journalism. What they *personally felt* as a woman/straight man/African American/gay male/insert-target-demo here, how all of this drama had "affected them" and their families. They were writing supposedly serious political analysis, but it was really *all about the reporter covering the story*. Norman Mailer would have probably called their columns "advertisements for myself." Reporters would dish about how exciting it was for them to be on a plane with this-or-that big name anchorwoman or newspaper legend, and to be sitting next to the possible next president ... what Al Gore and Dubya's tastes in men's suits and haircuts were like this year ... whether the catered food on the campaign plane was *really* from Wolfie's or Martha Stewart (or wherever), or just tacky ding-dongs and no-name bottled water ... what they *personally* felt like being away from their families and children or girlfriends and boyfriends...

Maureen Dowd took to writing the Bush vs. Gore campaign saga as though it were a medievalist novel or play right from the get-go, and it wasn't hard to see why. Her landmark June 1999 column, "The Freudian Face-Off" set the melody that the media would play for the next year and a half. "Al Gore is the Tin Man," she said. "Immobile, rusting, decent, badly in need of that oil can. [He's] so feminized and diversified and ecologically correct, he's practically lactating. Al is the Good Son, the early achieving scion from Harvard and Tennessee who always thought he would be president. (So did his parents.)" Whereas Dubya was "all swagger, with macho campaign accessories and a Betty Crocker wife ... the late blooming scion from Yale and Texas who never thought he would be president. (Neither did his parents.)" And of course, who can forget Ms. Dowd's November 2000 pre-election column, "I Feel Pretty!," with a vainglorious Al Gore singing show tunes to himself in the mirror?

Certainly both candidates did nothing to disprove that narrative. "Positively Nixonian in his naked longing," as the perceptive left-wing critic John Powers later put it, Gore may have been raised with a silver spoon in his mouth, but he came across to many as just a more elegant, Rolls-Royce version of resentful grudge-holders like Nixon, Lyndon Johnson, Bob Dole, and John McCain. Powers went on to say that Al Gore seemed to have a "sense of entitlement the size of a cruise liner," and that Gore, "far more than Bush, fairly reeked of insider privilege." MSNBC fixture Chris Matthews was even rougher, saying on his show that Gore's ambition was so grasping, he would probably "lick the bathroom floor" to be president! *Slate's* Jacob Weisberg said in the fall of 1999 that Gore's pandering for votes was so desperate, so almost grotesque, he behaved "like some sort of feral animal." Forget about Fox News—this was what the high-profile *Democrats* in the press thought of Al Gore!

The 2000 Election was a veritable remake of 1992—only with one shocking difference. In this little remake, George W. Bush was presenting himself as a Republican Bill Clinton (without the scandals), and Al Gore seemed just as grimly determined to play a Democratic Poppy Bush (and at Bush Sr.'s oldest and grumpiest, too). Bush and Karl Rove absolutely plagiarized the Bill Clinton media playbook that had worked so devastatingly against Daddy. Instead of whining and bitching about the Lib'ral Media and its "biases," in 1999 and 2000 Bush skillfully romanced the yuppies and trendies in the press corps, playing to and manipulating their self-centered egos. No one knew those tricks and treats better than Dubya—after all, they were the same ones that Bill Clinton had used to beat Daddy!

Al Gore, by contrast, would visibly lose his patience at the debates—just as when Old Bush famously checked his wristwatch in a '92 debate, dripping with disdain, during an empathetic Clinton closing speech, Bush's already low support cratered. And as Joan Didion and Mark Perkel had grimly noted, instead of reaching out to young voters or the Ralph Nader lefties, Gore decided to play me-too-catch-up with the cultural right. (Hi there, Joe Lieberman!) Instead of Bill Clinton's Joe Cool, or Dubya's Regular Joe, Gore came across as a priggish, chauvinistic, condescending robot. (One outrageous *Atlantic* magazine cover "blood-libeled" Gore in a manner of speaking, portraying him as a fang-dripping Dracula, completely consumed by jealousy and ambition, like a zombie from that week's episode of *Buffy the Vampire Slayer*.) Other columnists merely used adjectives like "repulsive" and "repellent" to describe Al Gore.

Bush's campaign plane and buses were Party Central: the food was gourmet, the water was designer, the in-flight TVs were always on, the treatment was always red carpet. In shocking contrast to his smirking arrogance and Cheney-managed distance from the press during his actual government administration, Candidate Bush made a point of asking individual reporters about their families, how their aged parents were doing and what the kids were up to in high school or college—sometimes even mischievously setting some of them up on dates! He would give them nicknames like "Dulce" and "Panchito," telling jokes and gossiping with them—as Sarah Palin might have later put it, he "palled around" with them freely. And Laura was always the perfect hostess, every demure hair in place, always the warm and gracious Southern lady.

Perhaps Bush's most loyal booster in the major leagues was *New York Times* columnist Frank Bruni, who would write the bestselling narrative of Bush as an affable underachiever, harmlessly and even at times charmingly *Ambling into History*—while mercilessly savaging Al Gore. And the mutual-admiration society was not unrequited. Indeed, Bush practically "cruised" the openly gay Bruni, outrageously mouthing "I love you, man!" across a crowded room in full view of Bruni's fellow reporters, and affectionately telling lil' "Panchito" (his nickname for Bruni) how much "we all loved" him!

When one of those second-rate scribblers stepped onto Gore's campaign plane, though—look out! By almost every account from left to right, Gore treated the status-conscious columnists and prestige-minded TV reporters the way that Judge Judy treated her dumbest contestants. He was Mister Vice President to you, Buster! He didn't answer your questions, you answered his questions. (Indeed, top staffer Carter Eskew told *Vanity*

Fair's Evgenia Peretz in 2007 that Team Gore had practically used a "whip and a chair" with the press.) Now that it was finally *his* turn, Gore insisted on the same level of absolute, federal judge decorum and deferential fear-respect that his postmodernist boss Bill Clinton had spent the past eight years lampooning, *Saturday Night Live* or *Caddyshack*-style.

Alexander Cockburn called it right when he said that Gore was a closet case from the 1950s—not closeted gay, but closeted by the strictures of his duty-first-self-second, Old Washington upbringing. Still in post-traumatic shock from the Monica fallout and from Elvis Clinton's endless excesses, Gore had become *more* uptight and standoffish, instead of less. Instead of embracing the way Bill Clinton had rebooted the Presidency, a betrayed and resentful Gore stylistically rebelled against everything Bubba stood for.

Journalist Josh Marshall noted that, "I think deep down most reporters just have contempt for Al Gore—disdain and contempt." *Washington Post* columnist Dana Milbank hit the nail on the head when he said (looking back in 2002) that "Gore is sanctimonious, and that's sort of the worst thing you can be in the eyes of the press. He has been disliked all along ... because he gives a sense that he's better than us. Whereas President Bush is probably sure that he's better than us ... but he didn't convey that sense. He does not seem to be dripping with contempt for us [the way Gore was], and I think that has something to do with the coverage."

Gee—YA THINK? Just try to imagine an old school, World War II or Korea-veteran, Don Draper–type newsman—a Cronkite, Sevareid, Germond, Stone, or Novak ... a Breslin, Bradlee, or Brinkley—feeling *entitled*, even *expecting* to get lots of hand-holding, huggy-bear warm fuzzies from a president or vice president that they were covering on the campaign trail!

But all that was in the era BC: Before Clinton. For two full terms, Bill Clinton had successfully branded the Democratic Party as the hip, Hollywood, happening one, with sitcom stars and movie queens, pop singers and literary writers, soulful blacks and spicy Hispanics. It was the Republicans who were still supposed to be caught in a time warp, with their shirt-and-tie wearing, lily white Stepford youth, and their beehived Greatest Generation women. And yet Gore's whole personality (or lack of one) and affect seemed to undercut, even to mock, all that. Between Bush's right-wing cultural pandering and Gore's Joe Friday-style stiffness, if this so-called "Bridge to the 21st Century" election had gotten any more trapped in the 1950s, Gore and Bush would have probably staged their debates while smoking cigarettes in isolation booths, wondering how to get to *Twenty-One*.

It seems that above all else, the press corps hated Al Gore mostly because he committed the unpardonable sin of seeming geeky and square compared to the vastly more entertaining and charismatic Bubba. *Time* reported that during a 1999 debate between Gore, and his only serious rival for the Democratic nomination, Senator Bill Bradley, "the 300 media types watching in the press room at Dartmouth were, to use the appropriate technical term, totally grossed out." These "objective" reporters booed Al Gore openly when it was his turn to speak, "the room erupt[ing] in a collective jeer, like a gang of fifteen-year-old *Heathers* cutting down some hapless nerd."

Even Gore's halfhearted attempts to get with the program were met with derision. He hired post-feminist blogger and pop culture author Naomi Wolf (for $15,000 a month—more than Gore's own monthly VP salary) to give him advice on fashion and media presentation. Sadly, her most lasting contribution was spurring a media-manufactured controversy over whether Gore should start wearing "Earth toned" clothing or not. (*Hello*, didn't orange and chocolate brown go out of style in like 1979 or '80? Look at Mr. Internet Guru—and he's dressed like he fell out of a rerun of *The Rockford Files!*)

Alas, for all the bling that Naomi Wolf earned for establishing the aesthetic regime of Gore's politics (or just trying to give Gore a clue about film, TV, and musical developments of the last 20 years), Wolf was utterly helpless to fight what Camille Paglia called Gore's "prissy, lisping, Little Lord Fauntleroy" affect of Richie Rich entitlement, or his built-in aristocratic snobbery that "bordered on the epicene." Later on, Maureen Dowd was even more brutally to-the-point: Al Gore had "gone from being Powerful Second-in-Command of Prosperous Happy Country to Obsessive Loon Whose Monomaniacal Quest Has Led Him to the Edge of Madness." Dowd then gave Gore a finishing kick worthy of Jackie Chan: "The more you insist you're a winner who somehow found a million different weird ways not to win, the more you seem like a loser."

From Bill Clinton's perspective, watching the campaign of his longtime understudy as it unfolded must have had the frustrating suspense of watching a child who failed to master basic math skills at the cash register, of watching Gilligan and the Skipper again grab defeat from the jaws of rescue on a classic Nick at Nite rerun. *Al Gore couldn't close a car door, let alone close the deal, could he? What's going on here?*

The Amazing Race Card

For all his computer-era sophistication and digital futurism, Al Gore insisted on conducting his campaign as though he were still living back in the world of Louis B. Mayer or *The Ed Sullivan Show.* "Something for everyone!" and "Fun for the whole family!" He was so eager not to leave any potential demographic group *out* that he never truly brought anyone *in*—certainly nobody who wasn't already there. Gore was jumping as recklessly and randomly across the demographic game board as the Whammy on a classic cable rerun of *Press Your Luck.* First he finished a full-throated defense of affirmative action preferences during his debates with Bush—then he pressed the panic button when he found his support suddenly cratering among white Southern and Midwestern "NASCAR Dads." *Quelle surprise! WHO* could have predicted *that?*

He used Bill Clinton as—let's call it what it was, shall we—a Token, in black churches and Latino fiestas with de facto segregated audiences, and virtually never mentioned him outside of those. (And watching a preppy-elite, cardboard cutout like Gore soul-talkin' and signifyin' in Gospel churches, or speaking in flat unaccented Spanish, was like watching a 21-year-old MTV pop tart trying to act "dramatic" opposite Allison Janney and Meryl Streep. It was so humiliating it was painful.) But according to Jake Tapper's book *Down & Dirty: The Plot to Steal the Presidency,* Gore's campaign also took steps to ensure that blacks and Latinos would be kept *away* from the cameras at certain times on the campaign—lest they raise a stern eyebrow from those wealthy white "swing voters" that his consultants "lusted after so unattractively." Instead of telling us "Don't Stop," the name of his tune was "I'm Dancing as Fast as I Can."

Interestingly enough, George W. Bush's people were going in just the opposite direction in their media offensive, making sure that Dubya was constantly surrounded by a veritable

Sesame Street rainbow coalition of conspicuously diverse black and brown children to be used as props during his campaign photos and the Republican convention. (Not to mention Colin Powell, Condi Rice, Clarence Thomas, and several Spanish-speaking officials.) If this managed to actually snag some for-real black and brown votes on Election Day, then so much the better. But of course, in an almost Serling-esque irony, the real purpose was to show the same educated white "swing voters" that the Republican (who in Jesse Helms and Lee Atwater's day could have been assumed to be racially insensitive, at the very least) was just a big, tolerant, inclusive teddy bear. Just as Gore's aforementioned *omission* of voters of color at certain events was to send the message *to this same target demo* that the Democrat (who could have been assumed in George McGovern, Rose Bird, Jesse Jackson, and Ted Kennedy's day to be a pander-bear for "quota queens" and pushy street activists) was really non-threatening, that he was really One of Us.

Actual African Americans and Latinos weren't fooled for a minute. As Eric Alterman noted, "Bush enjoyed almost no support from the minority voters these children were obviously chosen to represent" during his first time out. When the final totes came in, an appallingly low 7 to 10 percent of African Americans voted for Bush. (Even Ronald Reagan and Richard Nixon had managed to score roughly double, if not *triple* those amounts.) And despite Bush's sorta-bilingual Texas pedigree, Gore beat Bush by an almost 2-to-1 margin with Latinos in 2000, and that's *after* including conservative Cubans still furious about Elian Gonzalez.

As Jake Tapper noted in *Down & Dirty*, "little of that was attributable to Gore," but almost all of it *was* attributable to Bill Clinton. People of color were definitely out to "remember in November" 2000 how the wing-nuts had almost undone the 1996 election that racial minorities had single-handedly delivered for Bill Clinton, during the impeachment furore. (Clinton won by 49 percent in 1996, and he had lost the white vote again, despite having aging throwbacks like Bob Dole and Ross Perot for his opponents. Along with gender-gapping career women, minority voters hadn't just made a difference—they made THE difference.) Sidney Blumenthal further revealed that a post-election study by Kent State professor emeritus (and Consumer Reports research director) David Gopoian had stated that Bill Clinton single-handedly delivered Al Gore his mega-landslide in the African American community. "Clinton's effect did more to secure nearly monolithic support for Gore than *any other single factor*. The net gain for Gore was approximately *34 percentage points!*" (Our emphasis.)

No, people of color had turned out in record-shattering numbers (in an otherwise ultra-low turnout election) not to vote *for* Gore, but specifically for the purpose of voting *against* Dubya, "and his Bob Jones University-visiting, Confederate flag-waving, itchy-death-row-trigger-finger-wiggling, South Carolina racist-pandering, cracker Texas ass." (To quote the colorful words of Jake Tapper.) Not to mention Dubya's brother, "Jeb Crow," rescinder of state-and-local-level affirmative action in Florida, and Poppy Bush, the senior author of the Willie Horton ads and the sitting president during the deadly Rodney King riots.

Once again, the grammar of Election 2000 was as easy to diagram as a sentence in junior high English class. Fuggedabout getting anyone motivated to vote *for* Bush or Gore; this election would hinge entirely on which side successfully instilled more hate and fear in the electorate, on which side could get more people up off their duffs to vote *against* the other guy. For all the happy-talk tittle-tattle about the "peace and prosperity," booming economy, surpluses as far as the eye can see, the underbelly of the closeout election to the '90s decade was as negative and nihilistic as a punk rock or gangsta rap record. It was the most negative of negative campaigns.

"It's a miracle!"

According to George W. Bush and Dick Cheney's own (self-serving) accounts of their meetings, it was actually Bush who charmed, connived, and all but begged the man in charge of his "search committee" for VP, the Halliburton CEO and former congressman and Secretary of Defense Dick Cheney, to take the role himself. One can hardly blame progressives for doubting this tale, and thinking that Cheney passive-aggressively engineered his own selection—even friends of the former veep note that Cheney isn't just power-hungry; he's power-*starving*. His Secret Service nickname as early as the Gerald Ford government was allegedly "Backseat (Driver)."

Whether this was Cheney skillfully playing hard-to-get over a job he really coveted, or whether Bush perversely wanted Cheney all the more, instead of the governors and senators who were actively begging him for the job, is something that only historians and psychologists will be able to guess. In the end it hardly mattered. "Honey, sell the house," Cheney advised his wife Lynne. "We're going back into politics." And back into politics he went—with a *vengeance!* Meanwhile, Al Gore was delivering a game-changer when, in complete defiance of the need to appeal to either Clintonites or the Ralph Nader left wing—he picked a vice presidential candidate almost as reactionary as Cheney was.

Astoundingly, considering Senator Joseph Lieberman's later voting record and behavior under Bush and Obama (and the fact that as far back as the late 1980s, he was conservative icon William F. Buckley's favorite Democrat), the main reason that Gore picked Lieberman was, according to *Newsweek*, Lieberman's sense of "loyalty!" (To whom and to what, one wonders?) Indeed, Lieberman's most famous moments up until then were his marked *disloyalty* to President Clinton, calling for Clinton's censure and voicing his temptation to consider voting for impeachment—just like Rush Limbaugh and the Koch Brothers would have done if they could have. So much for Lieberman's loyalty to the first two-term Democratic president since Roosevelt and Truman, to the Yale Law couple who'd helped campaign for Lieberman's first-ever political office (Bill and Hillary had worked on his November 1970 election at age 28 to Connecticut's state Senate.) And as famously hostile and nasty as the Bush vs. Gore debates got, the Cheney/Lieberman vice presidential debates were a veritable mutual-admiration love fest—as well they should have been, considering.

"It's a miracle!" Senator Lieberman was quoted as rejoicing, when informed of the good news along with his wife, Hadassah. And on that score, he was quite right. It was indeed a miracle that he had been picked over equally accomplished, high profile Jewish Democrats like Barbara Boxer, Russ Feingold, Paul Wellstone, Carl Levin, and Chuck Schumer, all of whom were also available that year—people who were truly "loyal" to the Democratic Party, and who had supported the progressive agenda (and Bill Clinton) completely. In his published letters, the Democratic historian (and for what it's worth, part-

Jewish) Arthur Schlesinger was horrified when Gore chose Lieberman, calling him "miserable," "sanctimonious," and "a hypocrite" to Hillary Clinton.

And there of course, you have the *real* reason why Lieberman had been pole-vaulted to the head of the class. Actress Loretta Swit once shared the credit for an Emmy win on her legendary sitcom *M*A*S*H* with the show's creator by saying that "all I have to do is toss off another Larry Gelbart line and win an Emmy!" In a similar, if much more cynical sense, it seemed that where Al Gore was concerned, all a major Democrat had to do was openly denounce Hollywood and Bill Clinton—and presto! He gets to be vice president!

Convention Craziness

While the Republican and most of the Democratic conventions were more-or-less exactly what one would have expected, the real buzzworthy activity was happening outside, 1960s style. Third-party candidates Ralph Nader and Pat Buchanan were left out in the cold, with both Bush and Gore having a "Don't Ask, Don't Tell" policy of ignoring the two. (Although Team Bush did everything they could to "help" Nader in the media, in markets where they felt he might draw off from Al Gore's vote.) Left-wing activists planned a street-theatre series of sequels to their famed G8 globalization protests a year earlier in 1999, with the "D2K" and "R2K" uprisings outside the convention halls—complete with primitive art, puppets and effigies, picket signs, chanting, busker musicians, the works!

On the inside, the Republicans, having learned their lesson from Pat Buchanan's 1992 "Culture War" barn-burner, played a careful and cheerful waiting game, concentrating on safe topics like idolizing Ronald Reagan and the elder President Bush, and showing off their multicultural, "compassionately conservative" lineup of people like Colin Powell and Condi Rice. And of course, condemning the sleazy Clinton, by using his very own catchphrase of 1992 against him: "It's time for them to go!"

Meantime, the Democrats were giving their vision for the United States—the *United States of Tara*, that is. One minute, there was a near-hagiographic sequel to 1992's *The Man from Hope*, a big-screen mini-biography of the peaceful, prosperous perfection that only Bill Clinton could give us. The next minute, Clinton scourge Joe Lieberman was giving a dour, finger-pointing condemnation of sexy and violent movies and TV shows, unwholesome pop and rap music, and Hollywood immorality that would warm a Bible-thumping preacher's heart. When closing night came, it was finally Al Gore's turn—and he delivered a game-changer that nobody was expecting. Taking center stage with his wife Tipper, he gave her an open-mouthed tongue kiss that had viewers' tongues wagging from coast to coast. (Take THAT, all you people who think I'm a robotic, autistic, obsessive-compulsive stiff!) And Gore's convention speech was no less of a shocker.

"This election is NOT an award for past performance!" Gore scolded, right from the start—throwing the entire dot-com economy, and three years straight of surplus-budgets into the trash. So much for the painstaking groundwork Clinton had earlier lain in his nominating speech, stressing the need to protect and defend where we were and how far we'd come. Just in case Bill and Hill missed the insult, Gore spelled it out plainly. "I'm *not asking you to vote for me on the basis of the economy we have.*" No, Gore would prefer you voted on the basis of the "better" (than Clinton?), "fairer" (than Clinton?), "more prosperous" (than Clinton?) "economy we can build together!" He finished by flourishing that "We're electing a *new* president—and I stand here tonight as *my own man!*"

The speech might just as well have been written by Ann Coulter and Rush Limbaugh. It was as outrageous a rejection of the past eight years (especially to Clinton loyalists) as anything George W. Bush had said. Can you imagine a Republican sass-mouthing Ronnie Reagan or Duke Wayne that way, or a Democrat directing that kind of smart-aleck backtalk towards the memories of JFK and Dr. King? But this was Gore's moment to at last grab that elusive center spotlight he'd always coveted for himself, after all those years playing second fiddle, the moment where all his press-induced psychological "issues" against the Bubba-meister were finally up on their legs and roaring.

And it did not go unnoticed. Leave it to marvelous Michael Kinsley to typify the elite press's horror when, just one week before voters went to the polls, he shot back hard against Gore, in a scathing editorial where he accused Gore of essentially saying to voters, "You've Never Had It So Good—And I'm Mad as Hell About It!" (He also called the Clintonomic dot-com bubble "the greatest economy in the history of the universe," and only half-jokingly.) For good measure, Kinsley had added back in August, around the time of the Republican convention, how "appealing" and "genuine" and even "non-neurotic" Bush seemed in contrast to Gore, an appetizing candidate whose "flavors mix superbly." Although Kinsley admitted to voting for Gore later that fall, you wouldn't have gotten that impression of his plans when he finished his Bush profile, beaming that Bush's "preppy disdain for vulgar ideological positions and grubby policy details is well-suited to a contented people in a prosperous economy."

It was as surely a coded appeal as a race-baiting Republican attack ad—except this time, it was coming not from Karl Rove or Lee Atwater, but from the Clintonites in the media, and the target was their own vice president. And the rough translation of the message was, *Don't you start dissin' on my Clinton, boyfriend!* Bill Clinton had spent the past eight years fighting against all odds to build a New Democrat party for the New Economy—for Our Crowd, for professional, educated, influential People Like Us. And now, you're trying to drag us back to the proletarian, cigar-chomping world of Ralph Kramden and Archie Bunker! Pander-bearing to those ungrammatical Walmart moms, and those unedumacated, insensitive NASCAR dads. It's called a *rebranding,* Al. Didn't you get the memo?

By now, watching Al Gore on the campaign trail began to take on all the perverse pleasures of watching a Droopy Dog cartoon or a classic rerun of *Columbo.* He so badly wanted the campaign to be about HIM, about what *he* could bring to the table, about how *he* would lead the country, but it simply was never to be. Like a shrieking victim in a Michael Myers *Halloween* movie, every time Gore tried to hide in the closet, look under the bed, or run out the front door—the Big Dawg was already there, just waiting for him. There was nowhere to run, and nowhere to hide. As Kitty Kelley put it in *The Family,* "Clinton was the dog's mess in the middle of the living room." The faster Gore tried to run away, the more determined both the Bush team *and* the hardcore Clintonistas in the Democrat party were to drag him back, and "rub his nose in it."

Indeed, a *Newsweek* poll taken just after Gore's convention speech showed him with a new 52–44 lead over Bush, a net gain of a jaw-dropping 23 points, as he had been trailing Dubya by a 15 point deficit before the big night. But a Gallup poll taken less than a week after that one showed Gore and Bush as neck-and-neck. Whatever the actual results, in typical Gore campaign fashion, no sooner did the confused and confusing poll data come in than Gore started to panic—*again*—having second (and third) thoughts about his new "populist" narrative, thanks no doubt to the high-profile columnists' and bloggers' second (and third) thoughts about *him*. Soon, Gore was backpedaling as furiously as an Exercycle, presumably to please the high-income media voices who were eviscerating him, and to suck up to the check-writing Clintonite/DLC New Democrats who insisted on writing the meta-narrative. Gore began dialing down the dreaded "class warfare" rhetoric, and reaching out once again to the comfy, white, professional, well-off, educated (do we even have to say it again?) swing voters.

By the time debate season kicked off in early October, whatever lead Gore may or may not have had over Bush had evaporated like the summer wind. But the pressure-cooker stress and confusion was just beginning to take its toll. Gore's dissing of Clinton at the Convention, and his face-sucking with Tipper, had already planted the seed that he was less-than-stable among both headline-hunting careerist reporters *and* his sworn enemies in the right wing noise machine. (To say nothing of the journalists on his personal campaign beat, who seethed under Gore's Katharine Hepburn–like demands for absolute respect and deference, compared to Dubya's aw-shucks, gratuitous "friendliness.") To them, Al Gore may or may not have actually *been* irrational, but he was acting more and more like he was, like he was really starting to lose it...

The "Great" Debates

As Vice President Al Gore and Texas Governor George W. Bush took the stage on Tuesday, October 3, 2000, for their opening debate in front of PBS journalism legend Jim Lehrer, a confident-seeming Al Gore delivered an orchestral performance. He went from Medicare and Social Security to Eastern European foreign policy and human rights in Kosovo and Bosnia to what to do with the budget surpluses that some economists rosily forecast "as far as the eye could see" back in those days. He graciously complimented Governor Bush, and said that "we ought to focus on the problems and not attack each other. I want to spend my time making this country even better than it is, not trying to make [Bush] out to be a bad person." Gore also had statistics at his fingertips for all and every issue, as painstakingly backed-up as a doctoral thesis.

Bush, for his part, responded with his patented folksy humor, scripted one-liners, and friendly accessibility, making sure that there would be little sign of the anti-gay, war-on-women culture warrior that the hard right craved, except for just enough coded nods and whistles so that the base wouldn't bolt from him as a sellout "RINO." In other words, both men had essentially played exactly the parts that the media had assigned to them—Bush the accessible, working-class-friendly Republican "who you wanted to have a beer with," and Gore the expert statistician and administrator. Only Gore, it seemed, had played his part a little *too* well.

Bush's buddy Frank Bruni, a former film and TV critic (not that there's *anything* wrong with that) reviewed Gore's performance as if it were an embarrassing Very Special Episode of a TV sitcom, or a self-righteously "relevant" Stanley Kramer social drama. Gore was "barely able to suppress his self-satisfied grin" as he "loped effortlessly through the Balkans,"

Bruni sneered, adding that "it was not enough for Vice President Al Gore to venture a crisp pronunciation of Milosevic, as in Slobodan.... [he] had to go a step further, volunteering the name of Mr. Milosevic's challenger, Vojislav Kostunica. Then he had to go a step beyond that, noting that Serbia plus Montenegro equals Yugoslavia." Bruni summarized that the "point of all the thickets of consonants and proper nouns was not a geopolitical lesson." No, Gore's pinpoint accuracy and flaunted intellectualism was nothing less than a mean-spirited, coded, and cruel attempt to "unnerve and upstage" poor, tongue-tied George W. Bush. Later on, in the final debate, when Gore and Bush had met on the stage, the tall and broad-shouldered Gore got right up in the physically somewhat smaller Bush's face, death-gripping his hand, in what some journos thought was an effort to psych Bush out. (Imagine that—trying to psych out your *opponent* in a *debate*! How mean of him....)

Much more damningly in Debate One, however, was that when Bush was speaking, the cameras sometime would turn to Gore for reaction shots and face-overs—and his reaction was a negative one indeed, openly sighing and eye rolling and shaking his head, clearly conveying impatience if not outright contempt for many of the things Bush said. Overnight, the media narrative became clear. Bush may have been thought of as an "amiable dunce" (to resurrect Clark Clifford's old saw about Ronald Reagan), but back then, outside of the usual solidly left suspects (*The Nation, Mother Jones, Counterpunch,* Pacifica Radio, NPR, MoveOn.org, *Democracy Now*) and Hollywood and Broadway, he wasn't yet thought of as a *dangerous* one.

Gore, on the other hand, saw his entire debate performance reduced by the punditocracy to little more than a cheap impersonation of Bette Davis in *Wicked Stepmother*. The eye-rolling, the sighing, the contemptuous body language, the getting up in Bush's grille … all that stayed in the headlines, the cable chatter, and the web hits long after the actual questions and answers had been forgotten. Like a Joan Collins or Lana Turner villainess being chauffeured to her latest murder trial, Gore's campy campaign shtick gave off the impression of someone who regarded this whole electoral-democracy process, this little thing called the U.S. Constitution, as nothing but a boring, tiresome inconvenience. At least, *that's* the way the all-important media narrative now went in columns, op-eds, late night talkers, and hot Internet blogs from coast to coast. (Shamelessly biased though it was, as liberal columnist John Powers noted, it also wasn't entirely unfair. If Al Gore could come across as this dismissive, and yes, "elitist" towards President Bush's son, if he could treat the two-term, multi-millionaire governor of Texas like "the help," a typical blue-collar or office-drone voter might wonder, then my God! *What must he think of someone like ME?*)

No surprise that by the next debate, Gore wildly over-overcorrected, this time coming on almost humble in his seeming deference to Bush. He even came right out and smiled, "I agree with Governor Bush," or the near-equivalent, again and again, as he began his rebuttals and arguments. (Just as Joan Didion had sadly predicted, Gore was now officially letting Bush define the election, even though—hello! *Gore* was the incumbent.) For left-wing voices flirting with Ralph Nader or staying home, nothing could have appalled them more—or motivated them less.

According to *Newsweek* (and other numerous sources), President Clinton's blood was also nearly boiling when he watched Gore's debates. Not only did Gore let Bush "get away" with one toss-off and non-answer or less-than-truthful fudge on the issues after another;

Gore had mentioned Bill Clinton's name not at all during the whole thing. Still run-run-running away from him, the same way candidates never mentioned Richard Nixon or Jimmy Carter on the campaign trail—an unmistakable dog whistle that (in Gore's mind, at least), Clinton was now just as *bad,* just as much of an embarrassment, as Nixon and Carter had been. Minimum!

By this point, the Washington press corps had abandoned all objectivity in their raging hate-on against Al Gore. Newspaper publishers had endorsed Bush over Gore by a two-to-one margin and voted for him by three-to-one, according to Sidney Blumenthal. Meanwhile, liberal columnists like *The Nation's* Eric Alterman, and "out" and outré gay advice guru Dan Savage, were freaking out at the thought that holier-than-thou, Nader-voting leftists might swing the election away from the disappointingly neoliberal Gore to the far-right Bush. Alterman wrote an October article screaming "NOT ONE VOTE!" of progressives should be wasted on Nader's kamikaze candidacy, blasting it as little more than a toffee-nosed conceit of white liberals and students that no black, Latino, feminist, or gay voters could afford. (Nader had zippo support among organized minority or feminist/gay voter leagues.) And Dan Savage lived up to his last name, with his satires of "typical" Nader voters as nothing but losers, unemployed slackers, hippies, and dummies. (For some strange reason, neither Alterman or Savage had drunk the Kool-Aid that was being offered from every "respectable" news outlet, from the straight-ahead desks at Fox News to the *Time* magazine editorial page. Hadn't they gotten the message that *Bush vs. Gore* was nothing more than a "muted coda to the Era of Bill," as *Newsweek* put it, verbatim?)

By the final debate, Gore at last managed to find his footing—while Bush, meanwhile, got a very unpleasant "October Surprise" when reports of a drunk-driving arrest from around the time of his 30th birthday, in the summer of 1976, suddenly made the news just days before the Election. (To the Bush family's horror, it flipped Maine, home of the Bush summer compound in Kennebunkport, to Gore, whereas Dubya had been firmly leading there prior.) As this Seinfeld Election, this highly rated, sound-and-fury show supposedly signifying "nothing" now mercifully wound down to (what we *thought* would be) its series finale, the candidates were once again neck-and-neck in all the major polls. But a strange cliffhanging plot twist, conceived by one of the most minor background characters in the drama—someone whom nobody had been paying any attention to before—was about to change the game forever.

13

Epic Fail

[Gore] ended up getting the blame for Clinton's blow jobs without receiving any of the credit for Clinton's economy—quite an achievement, when you think about it.
—Eric Alterman, "What Liberal Media?" (2003).

Theresa LePore had been overseeing elections in Palm Beach County, Florida, from the time that bell-bottom slacks were all the rage, Pink Floyd and David Bowie were on the radio, and *The Partridge Family* was a current TV show. And while there had been recounts and contested elections under her administration before, none had ever resulted in any kind of serious accusations of fraud or incompetence on her or her staff's part, in her many long years of reliable and courteous service. Indeed, she prized herself on her impartiality and efficiency in her work life, although she was a proud and open Democrat in her own political sympathies.

As she got to work crafting the ballot for Election 2000, though, she noticed one troubling thing. The font that she had to use to make all the names fit on one page—not just of Bush and Gore, but of Buchanan, Nader, the Libertarian Party's Harry Browne, and all the other various and sundry "third (and fourth … and fifth…) party" candidates who'd made their quota and whose names were legally required to be listed equally (no matter how flimsy their chance of winning)—the font was too small, in her opinion, for the many elderly voters with vision issues who'd retired to Palm Beach, and who would be showing up on Election Day. So she came up with what she thought was a genius idea, one that was apparently OK'd by the rest of the officials in her orbit who'd been paying any attention. For the presidential election, she would list the candidates in big, blown-up print on TWO pages, right and left. To avoid any confusion, she would place a big "arrow" pointing exactly to the hole that needed to be punched to correspond with the voter's chosen candidate.

There was just one teency little snag. The overinflated size of the names, and the "brackets" each of the names were printed into, to further separate one set of candidates from the next, overlapped the tiny punch-holes in the middle of the ballot. Since Florida tradition long held that the party which controlled the governor's office would get "top billing" on the presidential ballot (a tradition one assumes held extra weight given that this particular governor was the presidential candidate's own brother), Bush voters had no problem locating their choice. He was the top man listed, and therefore the top punch hole—easy-peasy!

Pat Buchanan and Ezola Foster's names were next, listed across on Page 2, followed by Al Gore and Joe Lieberman's, back on Page 1 and immediately below Bush/Cheney. But while the arrow for Buchanan-Foster clearly pointed to Hole #2 from Page 2, for voters accustomed to one-page ballots, Gore/Lieberman was the next name down.

It stood to reason, after all, that Bush would be first listed (because of Jeb being governor) and that Gore, the man with the next most likely chance to win, would be second-billed, just like stars in a movie or TV show. And most fatally of all, the Gore/Lieberman "bracket" also overlapped Hole #2 (which was really Buchanan's punch-hole) even though Gore's "arrow" clearly pointed to Hole #3 (the actual Gore/Lieberman ticket).

"I think I may have voted for a Nazi!" a prominent Jewish radio talk show hostess claimed, in light of Pat Buchanan's "paleo-conservative" right-wing intolerance, and his provocative statements about Israel and about Hitler's leadership qualities. Her comment brought perhaps the ultimate gut-churner resonance to the phrase "buyer's remorse." "Can you picture me, a liberal Democrat, voting for Pat Buchanan?" another recently retired, Jewish female voter sarcastically asked a *Newsweek* reporter. "The ballot was designed deliberately to confuse us!"

This may have the result of an honest mistake with tragic consequences, but there was a considerably less "accidental" quality to the other—literal—road blocks to voting that had been set up in Florida. "Don't forget to vote!" fliers had been circulated in heavily black areas—giving the wrong date for Election Day. Traffic jams and road work mysteriously sprang up at or near polling places in predominately African American areas, and once voters arrived, they faced inefficient long lines, outdated equipment, and wait-times often in hours, not minutes. And a Republican-leaning computer contractor had been hired by Secretary of State Katherine Harris, ostensibly to ensure that people who'd had felony convictions in the past were taken off the voter rolls. (Harris was also serving as chairwoman of Bush 2000 in Florida, in a conflict of interest so appalling that if it wasn't illegal, it certainly should have been.)

Unfortunately (and perhaps not altogether accidentally), the computers purged completely innocent people, who'd never been in jail a day in their lives, simply for having the same (or even a similar-sounding!) name to people who had been convicted. (And if you can guess what color most of those knocked-off voters were, you win the grand prize.) There was also the fact that many of the poorest (and racially blackest) areas were stuck with antiquated voting machines and technology—ones more likely to leave a scourge known as "hanging chad" (the piece on a paper ballot that gets punched out when a hole is penetrated by the voter). The wheels of the scanning equipment designed to speed through ballots by the gross would sometimes "punch back" the chad if it hadn't been gotten rid of and completely punched out by the voter—making the vote "read" as though it had never been cast.

The Butterfly Effect

Florida and Palm Beach weren't the only places where the battle was raging. The 2000 Election map gave us the now-ubiquitous catchphrases "red state" and "blue state," as those were the colors that all the major networks and cable channels used to distinguish between Republican (red) and Democrat (blue). (Kind of funny, too, in that liberal Democrats were often called "reds" in past days, for their supposed Commie sympathies, and Bush-Cheney's official campaign literature color was blue.) And the 2000 map proved to be a veritable Rorschach test or X-ray of the culture war that the 1990s had left behind. Depressingly, it was, as things in the 1990s always had a habit of being, all about the Race Card and the Religion Card.

Virtually every state in the South and Midwest had gone for the conservative George W. Bush and Dick Cheney—in most cases, it wasn't even close. The mid–Atlantic junta of New York, New Jersey, and Pennsylvania, and virtually all of New England, plus the three West Coast states and Hawaii, had all gone just as decisively for Gore, as had Illinois and Michigan. Both Gore and Clinton were horrified to learn that Gore had lost his own home state (the first Democrat since George McGovern to have that dubious distinction) of Tennessee, and Clinton's Arkansas—and by a virtual landslide, too, thanks to hopping-mad white Religious Right and NRA voters, who were just as determined to vote against the liberal Democrats as African American and Latino voters were in the cosmopolitan states to stop the Republicans. When people now talked about the "Two Americas," it unfortunately wasn't any longer a hyperbole.

But at the end of the day, while there were battles elsewhere, it was clear before the night had grown old that there was only one state that was going to decide this thing decisively. As veteran political correspondent, *Meet the Press* host, and MSNBC fixture Tim Russert famously held up a placard, he smiled that the election would turn on just three things: Florida, Florida, Florida! And Florida Florida Florida proved to be a veritable minefield of racial and religious warfare. It was a geographically Southern and heavily Christian and military state, but also one with tons of liberal refugees from New York, DC, Pennsylvania, and New England, and a sizeable amount of racial minorities. In other words, a foolproof recipe worthy of Julia Child or Martha Stewart for an election that would hit on every racial and cultural raw nerve in Uncle Sam's mouth.

For one, if black turnout in Florida had held at the pre–impeachment, pre-affirmative-action-repeal levels of 1996 or earlier, Bush would have vaporized Gore in the state's vote. It wouldn't have even been close. However, nationwide African American voter registration had increased by nearly *one million* in the four years of culture war and coded appeals since then, and even with all the literal and figurative roadblocks, it had still shattered previous records. Between February and October of 2000, the NAACP helped to register 60,000 African American voters in Florida alone—new white registration barely matched half of that total. And after impeachment, black turnout would increase by a staggering 50 percent margin in Florida, from 10 percent of the state's electorate in 1996 to 16 percent just four short years later. Although 2000 was virtually tied with 1996 before it as having the lowest total voter-percentage turnout in postwar America (nationally speaking), blacks turned out in Florida at perhaps their highest per capita margin EVER, up to that point. And over 93 percent voted for Al Gore. They "remembered in November" all right, just as Jebby Bush had apparently feared.

Then there were the Jewish refugees from those bastions of right-wing conservatism like Manhattan, Philadelphia, Washington, D.C., and Boston. One of the grimmest ironies in an election already jam-packed with them was that Bush's margin of victory (aside from Ralph Nader, who scored almost 100,000 votes in Florida, dozens of times enough to swing the election) might well have been decided by the disproportionate 3,500-odd votes that paleo-conservative Pat Buchanan received in Palm Beach County alone, thanks largely to the senior voters who were confused and upset by the infamous "butterfly ballot." Bush's Jewish American spokesman (and future Press Secretary) Ari Fleischer wasted no time in going on world television on November 10th claiming that this was no problem because—straight face intact—everybody knew that overwhelmingly New York Jewish Palm Beach was a quote, "Pat Buchanan stronghold!" (The assertion was so outrageous that Buchanan himself mocked it openly on cable.)

On the other side of that same Judeo-Christian coin, there were the mighty Christian soldiers of the military bases in the panhandle, and the evangelicals of D. James Kennedy's megachurch and of Pensacola Christian College (home of the "A Beka Book" textbook empire serving thousands of Southern Baptist, Assembly of God, and Calvary Chapel church schools and home-schoolers who didn't like the evolutionist and feminist, Freudian "secular humanism" found in mainstream textbooks).

Around 8pm Eastern time, it looked as though America was about to have its answer. Al Gore was declared the winner of Florida by the Associated Press, based on Voter News Service projections from exit polls—which all four networks and CNN quickly followed suit on. However, at that early date, the whole country (particularly the West Coast) hadn't come in yet, so nobody knew—yet—that it would be "Florida-Florida-Florida." And unfortunately, those exit polls may have indicated a Gore win because of all of the African Americans and liberal Jewish voters who were turning out in droves to stop Dubya, who had thought that their ballots would count—even if they'd *actually* voted for Pat Buchanan thinking they'd hit the Gore button, or if their "chads" hadn't been punched all the way through.

By the time it was crystal clear that it would be Florida (Florida Florida), around 9:30 or 10pm Eastern, a funny thing happened. The Florida panhandle vote, some of which was in an earlier time zone where polls hadn't closed yet during the earlier call, was coming in with votes overflowing for Bush, many from the fundamentalist and evangelical community and the military. (And while the "New York Jewish" vote of Palm Beach and Miami was overwhelmingly for Gore, that certainly didn't mean seniors in general were voting for him in such huge numbers—even Jewish ones. Indeed, Bush won ⅓ of the Florida Jewish vote, as opposed to just ⅕ of the national Jewish vote, all told, and Bush had pulled essentially even with Gore among Greatest and Silent Generation retirees nationally.) By 10:00, the networks had retracted their earlier prediction, and placed Florida into the column where it had always belonged—too close to call. Although by almost every prediction then, Bush was now in the lead.

And that's when, as if on cue, a relatively obscure Fox News functionary by the name of John Ellis made a fateful decision. Ellis was in "constant contact" with Governor Jeb Bush and with Dubya, but not just because he worked for a major news organization—his mother was George H.W. Bush's sister! Ellis later openly told the *Boston Globe* that he was "loyal to my cousin [George W. Bush], and I put that loyalty ahead of my loyalty to anyone else." He wasn't kidding. At 2:16 am, under direct orders from Ellis, Fox News called Florida for Bush, and with it the entire election. Not wanting to be "scooped" by their rival, all the other networks and cable channels (and many newspapers preparing to go to press and what little existed of their online editions) matched the call within just 5 minutes. (It was rumored that GE CEO Jack Welch personally ordered NBC News—at the time, General Electric owned controlling interest in NBC—to call it for Bush immediately, as soon as Fox did, though this hasn't been conclusively proven.) CBS icon Dan Rather summed it up best when he said that you could "Sip it, savor it, cup it, photostat it, underline it in red, press it in a book, put it in an album, and hang it on the wall!" that George W. Bush was the new president. By 2:30 am, Al Gore called Bush to offer his concession. It was finally over.

The HELL it was!

Back in the "boiler room" of the Gore headquarters in Florida, longtime Democratic Party operative Michael Whouley was noticing that while the very final remaining votes in Miami and Palm Beach were being counted (obviously they took amongst the longest, given their heavy populations), Bush's margin of "victory" was slipping by the second. There was also evidently a computer error in one county that had falsely or inadvertently given thousands of votes to Bush inaccurately. While there was no way of knowing who'd won yet, one thing was dead certain—the election was so close that a recount was mandated in Florida law.

But the media hadn't yet gotten the memo. Whouley nearly had a cow when he was informed that Gore had already conceded—based on the news media's call, without even bothering to check back at campaign HQ! Whouley called everywhere and anywhere to check his streaming statistics, and then the Gore team, only to learn that Gore was right that very second, en route to the Nashville War Memorial in his home state of Tennessee— a state that had unambiguously voted for Bush—to deliver his nationally televised concession speech. "Are you shuah?" Jake Tapper colorfully quoted Whouley as saying, in Whouley's cement-thick Boston Irish accent. They were "shuah," all right.

Now, Recount was the name, and Stop Al Gore was the game! If Gore went on world TV and gave his concession speech, it would be politically and perhaps legally impossible for him to ever retake the White House mantle, even if the results of tomorrow's recount wrote "Al Gore Wins" in Las Vegas neon.

The next few minutes took on all the high-wire tension of a *Bourne Identity* thriller in the final reel, and gave the most literal, nail-biting meaning to the phrase "playing phone tag." As Gore's limousine plowed ahead in the sprinkling midnight rain, up towards the War Memorial, Whouley and his team frantically tried to reach the vice president. Gore was in no mood to chit-chat on the phone, and his personal contact info was, of course, the tops of top-secret. Michael Feldman, Gore's chief of staff, was so consumed with grief and futility, he had also turned off his cell phone. Screw it—he'd deal with the knife-twisting reporters and TV gossip shows tomorrow. It was over, wasn't it? Gore had already conceded the bloody thing!

The hot potato now passed from Whouley's offices to Democratic operatives Nick Baldick, Jeff Yarbo (and the janitor for all we know), until finally Yarbo managed to get through to Feldman on his government-issued pager (in those days, only the James Bond types had built-in pagers or cameras in their Mobile Phones 1.0). Feldman then called Bill Daley, who delivered the "duh!" obvious line of the night: "We've got to stop Gore from getting onstage!" Feldman then realized that he was riding in the same van as Vanessa Opperman, the girlfriend of Gore chief bodyguard David Morehouse. The minute he got Morehouse's number and got through, he screamed, "You can't let [Gore] go onstage!" briefly explaining in *preci* the almost unbelievable situation.

But at that moment, Gore's limo had already curbed up. He and Tipper were being shuttled well on their way towards the world cameras and press notebooks. Morehouse, with a bad leg that gave out once, herked, jerked, and skedaddled through the rain-slicked bullpen, sucking wind, until he finally caught the Gores and physically blocked them just a few feet from the stage!

Huddled safely backstage while the crowds waited (and waited, and waited) in the rain shower, Gore then made what would go down as one of the most bizarre phone calls in the history of American politics (at least ever since Linda Tripp became Monica Lewinsky's mother-confessor figure). He phoned "President Elect" Bush a second time, and informed him that he was taking back his earlier concession. When Bush expressed his "utter incredulity," as Anna Quindlen no doubt rightly imagined it in her *Newsweek* column that month, Gore replied with a phrase that became as unfortunate a part of the dialogue of that time as Jimmy Carter's "malaise" had been in 1979 and 1980. "You don't have to get snippy about it!" Gore rather snippily shot back.

Bush was now truly angry, and informed Gore that Florida's own governor was certain that Bush had won the state. Gore upped the ante yet again. "Your brother is not the final authority in this!" "You do what you have to do," Bush clenched. (And though it may have been unspoken, there was no doubt that Bush was thinking to himself that *he'd do what HE had to do, too.*)

Now the narrative was officially set in concrete. Bush was the presumed winner—he'd been officially christened and anointed as such by almost all of the major print, online, and up-to-the-minute Eyewitness News organizations when America went to sleep that night. But then, when America woke up, as if from a bad dream, it had suddenly turned into The Election That Wouldn't Die, something out of an Ed Wood or a Body Snatchers movie. Al Gore was trying to "steal" the election from Bush! He had actually *taken back his concession speech!*—something no one in modern presidential history, not even ruthless Richard Nixon, had ever done. To say that the cards were now stacked against Al Gore in the PR war to follow was putting it mildly.

Hanging by a Chad

As befitting a "show about nothing," the 2000 Election more-or-less equaled its predecessor of 1996 as having the lowest per capita turnout in postwar history for a presidential election—although the voters who felt the strongest about the outcome, from racial minorities to religious conservatives, turned out in droves. Yet the one voting group that did live down to their worst expectations that they would diss and ignore both Bush and Gore was the group that would emerge a decade later as the nation's most coveted and key voting demographic—young first-or-second-time voters. The 2000 election (and 1996 before it) saw perhaps the lowest proportional turnout in the 18–29 and 18–34 demographics on record—the starkest possible contrast to the game-changing youth vote in 1992's Clinton election—let alone to the veritable "youthquake" of jut-jawed, purposeful, energized and activist Millennials who provided Barack Obama with his victory margins.

But blaming the "disaffection," "alienation," and "slacker" mentality of Gen-X for their ultra-low turnout in 2000 was almost as outrageous as blaming a rape or sexual harassment victim for how she was dressed. While they both bitched and moaned about the so-called apathy of young people, neither Al Gore nor George W. Bush made even the most token, slightest whiff of an attempt to reach out to youth *on their terms*, or to address their culture. Mario Velasquez of Rock the Vote, the organization that was crucial in Bill Clinton's successful 1992 MTV campaign and in Clinton's "branding" as the first postmodern presidential candidate, groused that "Young people were obviously not part of the Gore-Lieberman strategy," to author Danny Goldberg. Goldberg added that while Nader (and even Bush) went to college campuses, Gore for the most part refused. Clearly, Team Gore was terrified that the media sight of tattooed, grungy, pot-smoking, multi-racial Gen-X dudes and "whiny" lesbian-experimenting Riot Grrrl college chicks might offend the *American Beauty* demographic of established (*oh no ... not again!*) Swing Voters "that he lusted after so unattractively."

Bush, for his part, famously thought that the Number One rated TV sitcom *Friends* was a one-off feature film. And Gore was so illiterate in current movies, TV, and music, he made *Matlock* look like Madonna; he actually needed to pay "pop culture guru" Naomi Wolf the big bucks just to tutor him on the basics. (Never mind Tipper's finger-pointing against Hollywood immorality and rock/rap music.) When Gore finally deigned to come on MTV, instead of reaching out to Gen-Xers on their terms, the Southern white millionaire VP used the occasion to pick an on-air fight with a young African American man in dreadlocks, who was a fan of rap star Mos Def. An appalled MTV exec named Judy McGrath told Goldberg that Gore used the opportunity to "lecture" the young black man about the immorality of gangsta rap music! "He just squashed him. And our audience." Forget Mos Def—how about TONE deaf!

Indeed, the only campaign to aggressively court young voters and idealists was Ralph Nader's—which made Team Gore especially resent him for it, openly libeling Nader's young supporters as a bunch of ignorant, whacko hippie kids who needed to get off the grownups' lawn. And when it came to addressing head-on the concerns of those entering the "business end" (in the most literal sense) of a completely rebooted, ultracompetitive, and globalized New Economy, both Gore and Bush had their own policy of "Don't Ask—Don't Tell."

In keeping with their strategy of zeroing in on stable, Baby Boom and "Generation Jones" homeowners with children, and pandering to the fears of people who were oh-so-offended by Monica, neither side pretended to care about a generation who couldn't remember before "liberated" women had entered the work force or before divorce was a fact of life, people who'd gone to integrated schools and come of age listening to rap and Latin rhythms with no big deal. During the debates, Bush and Gore purposefully twisted a question from a young voter, about how they planned to address young people's concerns as president, to indicate how (in their opinion), securing *Social Security and Medicare* was the real priority of America's youth! Even when confronted with a real live 1975 or 1980 model, they just couldn't wait to shove him aside to speak in code to their fellow Boomers, if not to Grandpa Simpson. So grossly uncomfortable were both Bush and Gore with their own young adult children's generation, it bordered on Freudian child abuse.

Still, as a "New Democrat," when it came to the youth vote, the game was Gore's to lose, and effectively, he lost it. Bill Clinton had beaten Bob Dole in 1996 by 19 percentage points among first-and-second time voters under 25, according to Danny Goldberg. And a motivated youth vote clearly gave Clinton his victory margin in high-turnout 1992. (And we all know about the World Series-sized victories Barack Obama would command among the 18-to-30-year-old demographic, in both 2008 and 2012.)

In sharp contrast, Al Gore barely managed a statistical tie with the right-wing, reactionary Bush: 48 percent to 46 percent, with the few under-30 voters who bothered showing up at all. If Gore had managed to come within 100 miles of equaling Bill Clinton's youth appeal and energy (let alone Obama's), the 2000 election would've been in the bag for him, both in Florida and nationally. His campaign staff's "outreach to" (read: aggressive dissing on) Gen-X voters in the 18–34 demo was almost as fateful a miscue as if they had nearly lost black voters or single women.

*   *   *

As thuggish and nasty as much of the Republican operation became, for one moment early on in the spin cycle, the Democrats fatefully equaled their Cheney-Rove adversaries in scraping the bottom of the barrel, when they petitioned for a recount—ONLY of the four most hand-picked, overwhelmingly Democratic counties in Florida, rather than of the whole state. (There wasn't yet any set legal procedure for demanding a state-level recount in Florida. However, the Democrat-dominated Florida Supreme Court eventually *did* order a statewide recount—on their own motion, without even being asked. Unfortunately for Gore, they waited until the last minute. With 20/20 hindsight, it's clear that Gore should have sued for a statewide recount in the state Supreme Court the instant the election went into dispute.) As it was, with only the four most-Democratic counties being recounted, longtime Bush family attorney James Baker and Karen Hughes' reply was succinct—and lethal. "Al Gore doesn't want to count the votes. He only wants to count Al Gore votes!"

The Democrats also wanted included (and Republicans largely opposed) questionably marked ballots from Jewish voters who maintained part-time homes in Israel and were spending the fall in the Promised Land, voting by absentee. (They were, predictably, over-whelmingly for Gore or Nader.) But then, a cache of questionably dated and/or witnessed absentee ballots started coming in from overseas military officers—with just as overwhelm-ing a margin of victory for the tough-talking, flag-waving Texan Bush. Now it was the Democrats who protested against their inclusion, and the Republicans who shrieked like banshees. When asked about the latter controversy by Tim Russert on *Meet the Press,* Dem-ocratic VP pick Joe Lieberman gave his fellow Dems a sneak preview of his much-touted "loyalty" (on future issues like the healthcare "public option," the Bush tax cuts, his eagerly nominating Sarah Palin for vice president in 2008, the too-big-to-fail Bailouts, and the Iraq War, to name a few). Lieberman said that the disputed military ballots *should* be included—knowing full well this could lose Gore the election.

Yet the press corps was *still* trying to paint this Watergate-level story as a meaninglessly cheesy circus, by focusing on happy-talk news stories and "colorful" events produced explic-itly for the media's benefit: There was the "Brooks Brothers Riot," where Republican activists locked down and intimidated a ballot-counting center; the "Sore-Loserman" protests com-plete with a grown man dressed as a baby throwing a temper-tantrum (symbolizing Al Gore), while the Wicked Witch of the West flew an airplane banner reading "Surrender Gore-thy!" above. On the other side of the coin, African Americans and Jewish voters went to the barricades with masking tape over their mouths, to testify in cinematic imagery to their voices having been silenced.

Some nihilistic voices practically reveled in this carnage. The late ultra-left journalist Alexander Cockburn, who'd vocally supported Ralph Nader, openly said he preferred Bush over Gore just between the two of them, so lukewarm and contemptible did he find Al Gore. On his alt-news website *Counterpunch,* Cockburn beamed, "As for Nader holding the country to ransom, what's wrong with a hostage-taker with a backing of 2.7 million voters? He got them where it counted, and now the Democrats are going to have to deal with it!"

Finally, the air-quote "criminal" confessed himself at last. At a cheering appearance in the heart of conservative Orange County, Ralph Nader came right out and said that if he had to choose, he wanted Bush. Nader said he would rather have a "provocateur" (Bush) that would energize left wing voices to fight, rather than a namby-pamby, triangulating, calculating "anesthetizer" like Al Gore—someone who'd keep on compromising to accommodate Republicans, while betraying the truly liberal and progressive. (Of course, Gore supporters had to grimly swallow the irony that Clinton and Gore had only gone as far to the right as they had because of the necessities of governing against the law firm of Gingrich, Scalia, Greenspan, Rove, and Limbaugh, after the 1994 Republican Revolution. And this, *this* was their reward!)

Amidst this already Camp Snoopy atmosphere, the bizarre makeup and fashion statements of Florida Secretary of State Katherine Harris proved a particularly ripe and juicy target. (In fairness to the press, she would have been hard to resist.) Nearly a decade before Sarah Palin and Michelle Bachmann went national, the fundamentalist Ms. Harris openly fancied herself as an heir of Queen Esther, seeing her newly amplified role in world history as being biblically pre-ordained from above. Adding to the sense of governmental multiple personality disorder was the conundrum that while the lower courts, the offices of governor and secretary of state, and the state legislature were all controlled by the Republicans, the Florida Supreme Court was still jam-packed with overwhelmingly liberal justices appointed by Jeb Bush's predecessor, the late Clinton Democrat Lawton Chiles.

Before the ultimate Supreme Court's partisan *Bush vs. Gore* decision in December, both the entire judicial and state-executive systems in Florida abandoned all pretense of being impartial arbiters in the rule of law. Republican leaning lower-court judges like Sanders Sauls and Terry Lewis reliably ruled against Gore, as did, of course, Secretary of State Katherine Harris and Governor Jeb Bush. Then, as if on sitcom cue, the Florida Supremes not only reversed them almost every time, they also unilaterally extended and rescinded deadlines *that they themselves had come up with*—almost at will—so long as it would keep Gore's campaign alive a minute longer.

The most troubling aspect of the whole recount circus was that, 35 years after Jim Crow had finally kicked the bucket, the voting procedurals in Florida were still as laughably separate, disorganized, and unequal as the "machine politics" of Bull Connor and Tammany Hall. The only uniform state-wide standard memorialized in Floridian black-letter law was if "the clear intent of the voter" could (or could not) be discerned by the local county officials. A reasonable-sounding standard, but a dangerously vaporous and subjective one as well.

Now, it was truly a "horse race" in the worst sense of the term—or really, more like a cheesy sketch of a horserace from an old TV Land rerun of *Laugh-In* or *Sonny & Cher*. He pulls forward! He's caught back! It's with the lower courts! Now it's with the state Supreme Court! Now it's back to the lower courts again! The State Supreme Court says the Secretary of State gets to rule on November 26th! But wait—now the court's changed its mind! Now she *doesn't* get to rule on November 26th! These ballots over here in the white county are counted by the "intent of the voter" standard—but the ones from the walking-distance black county over there are counted by strict-constructionism! *It's here! It's there! It's everywhere!*

The Forrest Gump Election

Before November of 2000 was over, the likes of Fidel Castro and Saddam Hussein had made sarcastic offers to send in "election monitors" (just like the UN does in banana dictatorships) to ensure that Americans received the same "fair" elections that they promised everyone else. (How thoughtful of them!) The London *Mirror* summed it up best of all: Their front-page showed Bush and Gore's faces transposed on Forrest Gump-bodies and his park bench, with the headline, "Elections are like a box of chocolates—you never know what you're gonna get!" It was billboarded by "U.S. HUMILIATED IN PRESIDENTIAL SHAMBLES."

Yet as late as Thanksgiving, the talk from many if not most legal scholars and academics was that all this would, could, and should be worked out at the local Florida level, that it certainly wouldn't end up in the Supreme Court! *Perish the thought!* Gore's people themselves had ridiculed the notion, at least at first, whereas for those of us living in the reality-based world, the idea that it *wouldn't* end up in front of the Supremes was looking like the most ridiculous idea of all. Indeed, from the moment that the election went into serious dispute, it was not only natural but almost inevitable that Election 2000 would end up being resolved at the same place where the final legal word was also issued on all the sexual, cultural, religious, and racial culture wars that Election 2000 was *really* about.

Liberal justices like Ruth Bader Ginsburg and John Paul Stevens were indeed shocked, by many news accounts, that their fellow Supreme Court jurists had decided to meaningfully go hands-on in the case to begin with, when the Court finally did so in early December. Meanwhile, Justice Sandra Day O'Connor had already gotten her dose of shock and awe while watching news coverage at a party on Election Day 2000, back when it looked like Gore was going to win.

"This is terrible!" O'Connor was widely quoted as having said, with her husband explaining that his seventy-year-old justice wife was looking to retire in 2001, her 20-year anniversary on the Court, and clearly desired a Republican to name her successor, instead of a President Gore. (She actually waited another five years until her silver anniversary, handing in her notice in 2005 and retiring upon Judge Samuel Alito's confirmation in early 2006. O'Connor would also later express some degree of regret at the *Bush vs. Gore* fiasco, as opposed to her ultra-right colleague Antonin Scalia, who famously and repeatedly advised that people just "Get over it!" already.)

O'Connor was also furious at reports and/or gossip she had heard about voter fraud that the Democrats were allegedly perpetrating, like supposedly going into nursing and assisted-living homes and gathering votes from people who were legally or medically incompetent. (Indeed, one story told of a woman leading her doddering, 80-something father—obviously suffering the effects of Alzheimer's and senile dementia, or from a severe stroke—into the voting precinct and "helping" Dad cast his vote for the candidate he thought was Franklin Roosevelt, having reverted aloud to his young adult days during World War II. Although, in that particular case, the beneficiary was apparently Bush, and not Gore.)

And the complaints of the Palm Beach *bubbies* and *machers* who were confused by the butterfly ballot sounded a little too much like "excuses, excuses" to Justice O'Connor. If they couldn't or wouldn't follow clear instructions that a reasonably intelligent fifth-grader in Arts & Crafts class could be expected to follow, than what business did they have voting anymore in the first place? (Indeed, many of the elderly voters had offendedly brushed off overweening local precinct workers trying to help them—we've been voting longer than you've been alive, Kiddo! They could do it just fine, thank you very much—until they saw the redesigned ballot they were up against.)

It couldn't be simpler, Justice O'Connor noted, and on the surface, it was hard to argue with her. Why couldn't the voters simply punch the holes with enough "oomph" to do the job—or at the very least take one second to ensure that all their punch-holes had actually been punched through-and-through before they handed their ballots in? Why didn't they just align and point their little stylus pens at the big, honking arrows that said "vote HERE!" for Gore, Bush, Buchanan, Nader, etc? What was so hard about all that?? (Denis Leary's foul-mouthed version of Democratic operative Michael Whouley humorously and succinctly answered that question, in HBO's award-winning 2008 movie on the *Recount.* "When you're 80-something years old, you've got arthritis, and you're blind as a fuckin' bat—it's pretty goddam hard!")

On December 12, 2000—the latest in the never-ending series of "deadlines" prescribed and proscribed by Florida law and rulings (the "safe harbor" for when Florida's electors were to be decided for good), the only people left in America with the power to truly decide things went ahead and decided them. Once and for all.

By a 7-to-2 ruling, the Court found that the all-over-the-place, multiple, and often mutually exclusive county-by-county vote-counting catastrophes—or at least the way they were being conducted in the Florida fiasco—were a complete violation of Civil Rights laws and the Equal Protection Clause of the Constitution. A black man who voted in County #1 might get his "undervote" or "hanging chad" arbitrarily thrown away because his group of zippo-accountability, local-level officials didn't think it demonstrated his "intent" enough—while the one belonging to his white neighbor, who lived only a bike ride away on County #2's borderline, got his identically punched ballot counted, by a different set of no-accountability local yokels. The antiquated technology in one precinct versus the up-to-the-minute high-tech stuff in the next, the "butterfly" vs. standard ballots, the looming deadlines—like a group of mad scientists, nobody had planned or expected for a modern-day election to be this inconsolably divided, this down-to-the-wire close. And now, it was apparently too late.

But it was in Decision Two where the court really dropped the guillotine. By a completely partisan, 5-to-4 ruling, with the two Clinton appointees and the two most liberal Republicans voting no, and a panel made up entirely of Reagan, Bush I, and Nixon appointees carrying the day, the Supreme Court ordered a permanent halt of the entire recount circus, as their only "remedy" for the hopelessly corrupted situation. Since Bush was still ahead (albeit by the slenderest of threads) when the decision came down, once the legalese was properly parsed and sorted, there was no doubt about what the Court actually meant. As Regis Philbin might have said on that week's edition of *Millionaire,* after one and a half months of political street theatre, America at last had its "final answer."

It was Game Over for Al Gore.

In what struck many as a particularly outrageous irony, the same Civil Rights laws and courtroom precedents that had been put into place a generation earlier specifically to safeguard and ensure black, Latino, and Native American voting rights were now being used to strike down the candidate who'd won 9 out of 10 African Americans, and 2 out of 3 Latinos. (Well aware of this, the Court's majority issued the caution that their ruling—the most important Supreme Court verdict since *Roe vs. Wade*—specifically *could not be used as precedent in any other case*; that its scope was "limited to the present circumstances.") And speaking of precedents—without the precedents established during the battle to finish off Jim Crow, it is unlikely the Court would have, or even *could* have found the "Equal Protection" rulings and laws it needed to back up its dual decisions, or to interfere so decisively in the electioneering affairs of a state or local government.

But they could. And they did.

*   *   *

In her definitive book on the Jean Harris/Herman Tarnower murder trial, the late Shana Alexander said that, even though Mrs. Harris had physical evidence on her side to prove her innocence, "she was too much of a lady to [openly] admit that she was jealous of the office girl." At least not until the DA surprised her, and read her damning (attempted) suicide note aloud to the jury, which made that unseemly fact crystal clear. "She would rather have gone to prison for murder than admit" to something so ugly, "and so she did."

In much the same way, Al Gore had tried everything, had used every weapon in his arsenal that he could in order to win. Everything, except for the main thing. He couldn't bring himself to truly and convincingly embrace the rebooted rules of hip, hot, happening, postmodern, post-everything, snarky, raised-eyebrow, in-your-face media politics, in the post–Clinton-O.J.-Monica world—the world of *Entertainment Tonight,* 24-hour-cable, Oprah, Internet snark, Comedy Central, and *Survivor.* The irony of this was all the more painful in that Gore had indeed been the one, more than any other senator or congressman, to get the New Media ball rolling in the 1970s and '80s. (Newt Gingrich, Vinton Cerf, and Steve Jobs all said as much.) If Al Gore was the legislative "father of the Internet"—as he could absolutely and truthfully claim to be—then the 2000 election made a good case for a charge of first-degree patricide.

Maybe, like *Monk* or Rain Man, maybe he simply *couldn't* do it, couldn't extreme-makeover himself into one of the Cool Kids, and any effort to try and do so would be doomed to failure from the start. (The Kiss, the cringey attempts at self-parody, Naomi Wolf's fashion tips…) Or maybe—and more likely—he just couldn't bring himself to swallow his considerable pride and sense of dignity, and to *own* just how much the political-media game had changed in the past eight years. On some level at least, Al Gore would have rather lost an election for president than to truly embrace the legacy of Clintonism and Clinton-era culture.

And he did.

"Just moments ago, I spoke to George W. Bush and congratulated him on becoming president," Gore began, with a tears-of-the-clown smile on his face as he addressed the cameras the next day—a very unlucky December the 13th for him. "And this time, I promised I wouldn't call him back." One could practically hear the clanging of a bell on the mental soundtrack, the dramatic low guttural strings drawing across, see the curtains ringing down. It would be Gore's last major speech as an elected official, his final concession and farewell, and it would be universally acknowledged as the finest speech he ever gave.

This wasn't the way the movie of the 1990s was supposed to end! This certainly wasn't the "Seinfeld Election," with a snappy zinger and a laugh track, or even the snarky triumphs of a *Scream* or *American Pie* movie. We were supposed to be rockin' and rolling! Irrationally exuberant! Recession-proof! I've Got the Power! Fo' shizzle-dizzle! *What just happened here?*

When Barack Obama won against Mitt Romney despite an anemic, barely recovering economy and massive anxiety about the future in 2012, a famous feminist blogger rightly said that American women (who proved to be the decisive vote—especially minority and single career women, plus gay men and lesbian voters) had been "told" for a year by the media that, just like 1992, it would be all about "the Economy, stupid!"

Funny how women just don't do what they're told, she exulted, noting that—as dozens of other headlines in America and across the world correctly blared that day—it was Culture War, not "the economy," that had made all the difference, *stupid!* While Monica and O.J. may have been the dress rehearsals, it was Election 2000 when the mainstream media would truly earn the nickname that Sarah Palin would give them a decade later—the "lame-stream" media. They had spent a full 18 months telling the American people that this was just a corrupt comedy "show about nothing," that it was just a battle between two smarmy and entitled rich white preppies, people whom it might actually be fun to watch beating the shit out of each other. That it was merely a contest of two individuals and their personalities, instead of one about the *parties*, instead of about the specific constituencies and the symbolism that their parties represented (or at least claimed to). They told us that it was just a corporate showdown between two would-be, so-called "CEOs" who'd house-sit for us at 1600 Pennsylvania (while Bill Gates, Warren Buffett, Alan Greenspan, and Antonin Scalia really did the heavy lifting), that it was little more than a high school or fraternity-hazing popularity contest.

Funny how all those uppity blacks and Latinos, those proud Hollywood gays and Holocaust-surviving Palm Beach Jews—and even those family values evangelicals and bitter white working-classers—*funny how they just wouldn't do what they were told!*

As Marx might have put it (albeit Groucho, not Karl), this election might not have made any difference to the people whom it wouldn't have made any difference to—but for all the *non-swing* voters out there, for the passionately committed racial, gender, cultural, and religious bases of both parties, it made all the difference in the world. (As Tom Brokaw rightly said on Election Night, the so-called experts of the media world "didn't just have egg on our faces—we had the whole omelet!") For them, this was THE last chance of the millennium, either to cement the surplussy Clinton "Third Way" once and for all, along with his legacy of unprecedented glass-ceiling-shattering for women and people of color in executive positions, and the first real steps towards LGBT recognition. Or it was the last, desperate chance to say goodbye to all that, to take a bottle of electoral Spray 'n' Wash to the stains of Clinton's in-your-face immorality and attitude and his Jerry Springer sleaze, and try and reclaim that neighborly, proud, kindly, flag-saluting Our America before it was too late.

"And now," Al Gore laughed with an admirably forced mirth, as he concluded his brief and classy cable concession that wrapped up the election in a nutshell. "In words that I once directed towards others eight years ago.... It's Time for Me to Go."

14

Bright Shiny Morning

The last act is bloody, no matter how fine the rest of the play.
—Blaise Pascal

A house divided against itself cannot stand.
—Mark 3:25

"BUSH STOLE THE ELECTION!," "HAIL to the THIEF!," "YOU'RE NOT <u>MY</u> PRESIDENT!!" and "I KNOW YOU LOST!" screamed the picket signs and banners, as the black-stretched Cadillacs, Lincolns, and Mercedeses rode down the streets of Washington, surrounded by armed-to-the-teeth police and Secret Service motorcycles and barricades. Not since the very worst of the Vietnam/Watergate era had Washington looked this ugly. At times, the motorcade was even pelted with eggs and rotten fruit and vegetables. People gave the finger to the presidential limousine, shouting and screaming openly, shaking their fists on the news cameras as Bush and company rode by. The Rev. Al Sharpton led a march of outraged voters and activists across the Capitol to the Supreme Courthouse. And all of his protestors were the same color that day—red with anger, after not only the *Bush vs. Gore* verdict, but another, equally humiliating and racialized spectacle as well.

In the most sadistically cruel irony yet of Election 2000, not long after the Supreme Court verdict had come in, Al Gore was required to essentially preside over his own lethal injection ceremony, as (in his capacity as president of the Senate) he was forced to re-declare himself the loser in *Bush vs. Gore,* when the Electoral College roll call was certified. Gore had gaveled down almost the entire Congressional Black Caucus (and several other minority representatives) because not *one* of the old boys in the lily white Senate would cosign their protest petitions against formally certifying the election. The not-so-subtle racial imagery here had an acrid stench to anyone with the faintest memories of the Struggle. As Michael Moore succinctly if bluntly put it in *Fahrenheit 9/11,* "One by one, the black people were told to sit down—and shut up!"

Party Crashers

"*FUCK YOU!!*" screamed the white-haired, 75- or 80-year-old Jewish lady at the top of her lungs, as she raised both hands up and down on the chilly December blue night, vigorously giving her younger female assailant the finger. "Women are going to die in back alleys because of you!" Was this other woman in that argument a conservative or fundamentalist icon—an Ann Coulter, a Katherine Harris, a Sarah Palin?

Not even close! The reason our elderly feminist heroine was so angry was because she saw the happy, self-satisfied face of a young woman coming towards her—a young woman still proudly wearing an "Another Babe for NADER" campaign button, the day after the Supreme Court decided *Bush vs. Gore*. And now, this Lilith Fair–type, young ultra-liberal lady was being blamed for all the back-alley abortions and bullied gay teens about to commit suicide and wars against women to come, by her fellow feminist founding-mother. As if *she* had been as pro–Bush and right-wing as Bill O'Reilly all along!

Probably nobody had really expected Ralph Nader to win (except maybe for Nader himself), but most liberals were simply hoping that Gore would get the message, that he would stop trying to run as a Democratic Leadership Council business-neoliberal, and come out with a forthrightly progressive agenda for the future. Others were just too elated that there was a third option for all of us who found the first two choices to be, in *Consumer Reports* parlance, "Judged Not Acceptable." Many of the nation's youngest, first-and-second-time voters—who were completely and utterly dissed by both the right-wing, family values Bush and the arrogant and out-of-touch Gore, had found 65-year-old Ralph Nader to be the only candidate who was remotely interested in what they had to say. Michael Moore, Eddie Vedder of Pearl Jam, Susan Sarandon, Tim Robbins, and countless other celebs and author-activists made Nader's campaign look as refreshing and tempting as a sweltering glass of iced Dr. Pepper on a hundred-degree Vegas summer day.

But as a gloomy and justifiably nervous Eric Alterman noted just before the big day, "Elections are not therapy." Nobody would have liked for there to be an even more left-wing and liberal alternative to Al Gore, than longtime *Nation* intellectual Alterman. But as he and those other battle-scarred veterans of the Civil Rights Movement, *Roe vs. Wade,* and the AIDS era knew, under the current reality of 1999 and 2000 at least, they weren't going to get a better "deal" than the Democrats, at least not in the nick of time. The name of the game wasn't to support Al Gore blindly, but to use him as a tool to protect against another Reagan/Bush reactionary making his foreign policies and Supreme Court appointments, until something (or *someone*) better came along—from within an electable party structure.

The Republicans, meanwhile, had already learned that lesson all too well, still immovable in their belief that Ross Perot had caused Old Bush to fall in 1992. Towards the end of the Bush II era, Jonah Goldberg noted in *National Review* that Dubya himself (once in power) had deviated at will from orthodox conservatism: "big government" federal education and prescription-drug programs, unbelievable inefficiency and wishful thinking (Hurricane Katrina, the 2008 meltdown, the Iraq mess), the most flagrant and irresponsible deficit spending in history. Yet conservatives kept running back to protect and defend him, almost to the very end—because, after 8 full years of being trump-carded and outfoxed by Bill Clinton, if it was a choice between having Bush—or having a Hillary, Obama, Jesse Jackson, John Kerry, Elizabeth Warren, Howard Dean, Nancy Pelosi, etc., it was simply no choice at all. (Just as liberals and feminists who otherwise brooked zero-tolerance on office sex with young subordinates had come to Clinton's rescue in 1998.)

In the end, the post-traumatic effects of Election 2000 still cleave us today, and serve as the ultimate cautionary tale to voters tempted to go "off the grid" in every election since. To some, it still stands as the grimmest possible reminder of what happens when people let their idealism get the better of them, when they make the perfect the enemy of the good.

To others, it illustrates all the more desperately how the whole electoral system needs a Reboot 9.0, how in today's era of YouTube, Facebook, Twitter, Myspace, Tumblr, Netflix, Amazon, OnDemand, iTunes, Tablets, Hulu, Pinterest, Blogspot, Skype, and Kindles, just how disgustingly dated and dysfunctional the "two party system" has become, how desperately we need a real choice beyond just Curtain Number One and Curtain Number Two.

And they're both right. To this day, the lesson of Bill and Hillary, Bush and Cheney, Newt Gingrich and Rush Limbaugh—soon to morph into the lessons of Donald Trump and Bernie Sanders—would remain the most "inconvenient truth" this side of global warming, the most politically incorrect of topics besides the N-word. The battle between ideological purists and corporate Beltway insiders. Between what is wishfully possible and what is politically practical. Between a threatened and fading "Our America" trying desperately to hold on to its comfort zone, and a rising Diversity America that was just as determined to double down on the reboot button. Starting with the 1994 Revolution, continuing through *Bush vs. Gore*, and right on through to today, this would be the battleground that all other major American elections, from primaries to the Presidency, would be fought on ever since.

But the mainstream media, *still* not having learned their lesson from Monica and *Bush vs. Gore,* was just as blitheringly, obliviously out-of-touch as ever. Over the holidays of 2000–01, reporting on the possible presidential transition, *Newsweek* ludicrously hailed Dick Cheney in their December 11, 2000, issue as a quote, "savvy insider who will *nurture* ties to the Hill." Talk about assuming facts not in evidence! Whatever was there in Dick Cheney's long career—a career where Newt Gingrich had endorsed that Cheney had voted even more intractably to the right than *he* had, someone who had proudly defended virtually all of the Iran-Contra abuses, someone who'd dedicated himself 24–7 as Gerald Ford's chief of staff to restoring the "Imperial Presidency" that Nixon and LBJ had just discredited, someone who wore his contempt for the Congress on his sleeve even while he'd served in it during the '80s—how did ANY of that add up to ruthless Halliburton CEO Dick Cheney being a cheery, back-slapping Jay Gatsby, some kind of conciliating Congressional bridge-builder?

Indeed, not long after that in the reality-based world, Cheney was having a meeting with the "Mod Squad" of (what little remained after 1994) socially tolerant, economically pragmatic Republican senators, like Jim Jeffords, Olympia Snowe, Susan Collins, and Lincoln Chafee. The esteemed senators made the same mistake as the press had, offering their help in making a transition to a more uniting and less dividing, kinder-gentler administration. But their help wasn't wanted. Cheney practically threw them out of his office, making it clear that there would be *no* so-called "moderating" of the hard-right agenda under his and Dubya's government. *Crystal* clear!

This too came as a shocker to all but the most plugged-in movement conservatives, as the conventional wisdom (and of course the even more conventional pundits) had all predicted that because of the narrowness of the 2000 victory, Bush would have no other choice but to pursue a triangulated, centrist, largely uneventful, don't-make-waves style of government. Moderate liberals and conservatives from Andrew Sullivan on down would later gape with shock and awe as they watched Bush's actual governing style unfold. After all, how could George W. Bush, who squeaked over the finish line by the skin of his teeth, rule as high-handedly and uncompromisingly as if he had won Ronald Reagan's 49 states?

In one of the endless ironies of the 1990s culture wars, the razor-narrowness of Bush's victory was the very *reason* why he chose to pursue a hard-right agenda right off the bat. Bush's chief pollster Matthew Dowd was quoted in the DVD commentary to HBO's excellent 2008 movie on the *Recount*. Dowd said that because the 2000 election was *so* bitter, *so* divisive, *so* beyond the pale, the consensus soon became in Bushworld that it would be pointless to try to appeal to or pick up Democrat, liberal, or even "centrist" voters anymore. It was one thing for your preferred candidate to lose an election fair and square. *Too bad that stupid ole Bush won ... boo-hoo ... but hey—life goes on, right? Let's see if he's any good....* If Bush extended an olive branch and really reached out, maybe he could prove that he wasn't so bad after all, and get your vote the next time! Right?

But if you really believed that Bush "stole" the election from Al Gore—as if Bush were some kind of Augusto Pinochet or Fidel Castro, goose-stepping his way through with his "junta" (as Gore Vidal and others soon called it), if you thought that the 2000 Supreme Court verdict was a veritable "coup d'etat," that the election had been decided by smothering black voters just like old Jim Crow—then what could Bush *ever* do to win you back after *that?* Heck, if you really thought Bush was that guilty, that monstrous, he would have almost as little chance of you ever "forgiving" him as if he had been a Nazi guard or a child molester.

Yes, in another ugly irony, it was actually *because* of how inconsolably divided we now were, that Bush and his crew coldly decided to double, triple, quadruple down on the most deliberately divisive and ideological agenda in modern memory. As Andrew Sullivan later said, instead of seeing the horrid aftermath of Monicagate and *Bush vs. Gore* as a deep wound needing desperately to be healed, Team Bush just "poured acid on it." Karl Rove said his top priority for 2004 was to get even *more* "missing" (white) Evangelicals to turn out (which he successfully did, by ensuring parental-abortion-notification and anti-gay-marriage initiatives were on the ballot in most or all of that year's swing states). Never mind that one of Cheney's own daughters was a liberated career woman and power lesbian—gotta break a few eggs to make an omelet, right?

At least the mid-to-late 1990s era of almost sexually fetishizing the mythical "Swing Voter" finally came to its end. Matthew Dowd underlined the new reality with a concept analysis report that conducted a thorough study of both liberal and conservative voting patterns since the last election to be this close (1976's Ford vs. Carter, decided by less than 1 percent). Dowd produced a graph showing conclusively that the percentage of what he called "persuadable voters" (voters who voted for the *person*, rather than the *party*, voters whose minds weren't already made up from Day One) had completely collapsed: from 22 percent of the electorate in 1976 to less than 7 percent twenty-four years later! By the end of the Clinton years, 93 to 94 percent of the electorate "was going to be already decided" right off the bat.

Looking back on the 2004 election, Dowd told PBS's *Frontline* (while he also said he wouldn't have openly admitted it at the time) that "Base motivation is what we're going to do, and that's ALL we're doing." And in 2008 and 2012, when it was Barack Obama's turn, he likewise threw the mythical Swing Voter beast under the bus, building a brand-new "base" of socially tolerant and tech-savvy, futuristic and diverse Millennials instead. It was a twist-ending worthy of O Henry and Rod Serling. The whole Swing Voter fetish had really gotten going as a way for Bill and Hillary to protect themselves against a fickle public, after the 1994 Republican Revolution. (And in order for them to get elected as New Democrats in the first place, at the end of the Reagan-Bush era—back when "Democrat" was a code word for Jesse Jackson and Al Sharpton, for soft-on-crime judges, atheistic senators, and know-it-all bureaucrats, at least amongst *real* swing voters.)

By late January of 2001, *Newsweek* had effectively issued a retraction or a correction, when they made Religious Right pinup John Ashcroft their latest cover boy. On the strong advice of Karl Rove, Bush and Cheney had just appointed Ashcroft the new Attorney General, after he had suffered an appallingly humiliating and decisive defeat in his race for Senate the previous fall. More people in Ashcroft's state of Missouri had voted for his *recently deceased* opponent (Mel Carnahan, who'd died October 17, 2000, with his wife agreeing to take his place) than had voted for him! The Ashcroft move was as shameless a payoff to the hard right as anything Lee Atwater or Joe McCarthy had thought up. As environmentalist Harvey Wasserman summarized in *Common Dreams* in early 2001, Ashcroft was "pro-corporation (especially tobacco), pro-gun, pro-military, pro-death-penalty ... anti-black, anti-choice, anti-feminist, anti-gay, anti-poor, anti-green, and anti-labor. In short—a poster child for the Bush junta." Ashcroft was also a veteran of fundamentalist must-sees like *Praise the Lord* and *The 700 Club,* and so Victorian in his sexuality that he famously asked district officers to "cover up" the exposed genitalia of priceless classical sculptures in his neck of the Capitol.

Sore Winners

The Ashcroft pander was only the beginning. In May-June of 2001, Bush forced through a tax cut package (more on that shortly) to re-stimulate the economy, now in recession as the first wave of overhyped late '90s "dot com" stocks truly whooshed out that winter and spring. (Remember, this was a few critical years *before* the next-level Internet 9.0 reboot of the mid-to-late 2000s, when things like Facebook, Myspace, Twitter, Hulu, Tumblr, Kindle, YouTube, and the "Cloud" would appear.) Bush had planned on helping make up the difference with some cuts to Special Ed programs that were dear to the heart of moderate Vermont Republican Sen. Jim Jeffords. (The same Jim Jeffords who had earlier offered his hand of help to Dick Cheney and had gotten it swatted back, hard.) Jeffords protested, and asked if the comparatively small allotment could be restored.

To his credit, President Bush was then teaming with Sen. Ted Kennedy to launch a bipartisan "No Child Left Behind" initiative that established strict national education standards at each level for the globalizing, technologizing, Information Economy. (And Bush had been bragging all along about being an "Education President.") Surely in light of all this, they could find some other ways to cover the gap, since they would be risking deficit one way or the other. Especially since Jeffords was the ultimate "swing vote" that year in the Senate, now 50/50 after impeachment backlash and *Bush vs. Gore.* If he got into a huff and switched parties or bowed out, control of the Senate would flip to the Democrats. Why, any halfway decent administration would easily find a way to accommodate the senator...

They had Cheney instead. Showing the kind of conciliatory Old Washington Hand he really was, he convinced Bush that having a Janet Reno-style "show of force," to prove that the president would not be air-quote-intimidated into moderating his agenda just to pacify some kind of RINO-sellout senator or congressman, was actually *worth* the (temporary—

they got it back from 2002 to '06) loss of the Senate. Though he doubtlessly used nicer terms, Bush essentially told the polite, soft-spoken Senator Jeffords to F-off. There would be NO concessions on *his* agenda!

(Ironically, this was just a cruder and nastier riff on Bill Clinton's iron-handed strategy for dealing with "professional Left" Democrats and ultra liberals, especially after the 1994 Republican Revolution. The big difference was that Clinton was in 24–7 defense mode, with a virulently hostile opposition party in near-total control of the House and Senate, the Federal Reserve, the major statehouses, big-market talk radio, and the Supreme Court. Here, Bush *already* had the Republican world at his feet; he just wanted to purge the unfaithful!)

George W. Bush had learned all the wrong lessons from his father's traumatizing 1992 loss. Dubya had veritably guzzled the Koch Brothers-Richard Mellon Scaife-Ann Coulter "kool-aid." The narrative on the ultra-right was that Daddy Bush had lost reelection *not* because he was an aged-out, ultraconservative leftover from World War II and the 1950s, who found himself cluelessly trapped in an era of gangsta rap, grunge rock, AIDS awareness, racial identity politics, feminist career moms like Murphy Brown, and a rebooting New Economy. Nope. Poppy lost because he hadn't been "conservative" (which is to say reactionary) *enough*. Because he had RAISED TAXES! Because he hadn't declared all-out "culture war" himself. Because he hadn't "finished the job" against Saddam, hadn't taken over and occupied Iraq the first time. The future Tea Party's doctrine was already becoming inviolate: Republicans *only* lose elections in Real 'Murica when they're *not conservative enough*. There's no such thing as being *too* red-meat, indulging the base *too* much, going too far....

And any narrative that disproved that theory was going to suffer the consequences. A perfect example was Bush-Cheney's treatment of the seventh or eighth largest economy in the world, a state that held roughly one-tenth of the entire US's population. Unfortunately and perhaps not coincidentally, California was also the state that Karl Rove had reportedly spent something like $20 million of Bush campaign money on, to purchase newspaper and TV/radio ads in the two most expensive media markets (Los Angeles and San Francisco) besides New York itself, in hot pursuit of California's 50-odd electoral college votes. Votes which Papa Bush had easily won only a dozen years earlier, in 1988. California had voted for Richard Nixon three times, Ronald Reagan *four* times (twice for governor and twice for president), and had just come off 16 years straight of Republican rule under Governors George Deukmejian and Pete Wilson, from 1982 to 1998. The state had given us Orange County and San Diego, two places that were synonymous with "Republican" during their '60s and '70s heyday, and had given birth to the "Tax Revolt" in 1977–78.

However, after a decade of Proposition 187 immigrant bashing, the 1996 affirmative-action repeal, impeachment, slut-shaming Monica and dissing Hillary, and a successful initial anti-gay initiative (Prop 22, later revived as the eventually struck-down Prop 8), a firewall of motivated African Americans, Latinos, liberated single women and upscale suburban sisters, plus proud LGBT and liberal Jewish voters (in other words, the *exact voter coalition of Obama's later victories*) had all turned up in such determined force against Bush, it was like a tidal wave knocking out a pier at Huntington Beach.

The indispensable Steve Kornacki's decade-later diagnosis in *Salon* was right on the money. The same fulminating Dixiecrats and talk radio/cable Revolutionaries who had ensured Bush's solid Southern and rural Midwestern victories, had now absolutely repelled the big population centers, especially after impeachment. Because of the culture war cliches and coded racial appeals that people like Newt and Dickie simply couldn't get along without (not if they still wanted to keep their rage-addicted, fist-shaking "base!"), the diverse coastal states had now become almost *immune* to Republicanism. Unless an individual Republican was overtly and explicitly pro-gay, pro-diversity, feminist, pro-choice, and pro-science (like Arnold Schwarzenegger and Rudy Giuliani, for example), people like Gingrich, Rove, Jerry Falwell, Ken Starr, James Dobson, and Cheney had so damaged the GOP's blue-state brand, the big coastal states would slam their doors in the face of Republicans, barking "Not Interested!" before the GOP-er could even open his mouth. Al Gore would have lost the election in the popular vote as well as the Electoral College, if the Golden State (or New Jersey, Pennsylvania, or Washington State) had voted as they almost always had in the 1970s and '80s. But now, they had all spanked Bush so totally, they had given Gore his 500,000-vote popular victory.

Well, payback was gonna be a bitch! California had deregulated its energy trading market under Republican Governor Pete Wilson, now safely in retirement, with pseudo-liberal Jerry Brown protége Grey Davis now running the show. (A man who can best be described, in John Powers' apt terms, as "a cold fish who made a career out of being the lesser of two evils," a Democrat whom even liberals nicknamed Governor Cash Register, for his Lincoln Bedroom–like cynical obsession with corporate donations and fundraising.) The first three years after deregulation, everything had basically gone business-as-usual, but in the summer of 2000, some energy prices began spiking, just for a split second, almost like a con artist trying out a new gag to see if it would work or not, to see if the IRS or the cops would notice it.

They didn't—but as 2001 got underway, the taxpayers and businesses of California sure did! Energy prices suddenly went through the roof, during California's notoriously mild winter and early spring, doubling and tripling when (as it turned out) energy providers like Enron began deliberately shutting off power plants so as to "create" artificial energy shortages and drive up short-term prices. So outrageous were the abuses, by the summer, the once-omnipotent Pacific Gas & Electric (the gross-polluting corporate villain in last year's big hit *Erin Brockovich,* wherein a PG&E lawyer brags that the company was worth over $28 billion) was now reduced to receivership. "Rolling blackouts" started being implemented by cities and counties so as to manage the disaster without even more risk of hospital horrors and traffic-signal accidents, as the Southern California late spring and summer finally took hold.

The threat level in economic-bellwether California, already in a nationally declining economy, was now so great that even the biggest states-rights advocates recognized that it had to be handled at the Federal level. And who else but Dick Cheney was more qualified to "chair" a commission put together for the emergency, having run Halliburton and all? In the spring, Cheney began holding closed-door meetings with his usual oil, gas, and electricity cronies (including Enron, of course) to figure out what laws and regulations to force down states' throats, to best deal with this "crisis." (So determined was Cheney to keep the meetings' contents top secret, he later *literally* went to the Supreme Court to prevent the Congress from ever finding out what went on in them.)

The fact that the Texas-based Enron Corporation had been Numero Uno on the Bush-

Cheney campaign's list of big money contributors, and its CEO (who died in 2006) was such a close personal friend of Bush that he was nicknamed "Kenny-Boy" Lay ... well ... *this may or may not have influenced the process a little.* Enron traders were recorded on phone tapes as making obscene "jokes" that would not have been out of place at a Nazi party—*laughing* at ideas like helpless little old grandmas having heatstroke and heart attacks in their un-air-conditioned homes ("she couldn't even figure out the fucking ballot!"), or automobile smash-ups when signals went out. Real knee-slapping comedy, all right.

And that still wasn't enough. Back in Washington, supply sider Bush pointed to the declining dot-com stock market as proof positive that they needed to cut taxes to stimulate things, and they needed to do it *now.* (He also opted America out of the Kyoto Protocols against global pollution that spring, by executive order.) To grease the wheels, Alan Greenspan testified in January 2001 that (especially if the economy *did* bounce back) the government was paying down the Federal deficit *too fast,* that stock and bond traders might get nervous and start raising interest rates. To Greenspan's great credit, he refused to take the bait the second time, when more irresponsible cuts for the rich were forced through by Cheney and Rove (even as the Iraq War approached in late 2002)—against both Greenspan and Republican Treasury Secretary Paul O'Neill's strenuous objections, to say nothing of Democrats and progressives.

In direct, total, and complete defiance of the Republican Party's "revolutionary" rhetoric about the need to pass a Balanced Budget Amendment, one of the first things Bush and Cheney successfully petitioned the 2001 Congress to do was to repeal the early 1990s' "Pay-Go" pay-as-you-go budget system, which required spending increases beyond population and inflation to be matched by corresponding cutbacks elsewhere or tax increases. The Congress eagerly complied. They killed PayGo like a Texas death-row inmate who'd run out of appeals. After all those years of pent-up frustration under Clinton's vetoing pen, the Congress finally got to throw back its collective head and have that gushing, shivering, tax-cutting orgasm it had always wanted—aimed, of course, almost exclusively at the rich. (Or, in Dubya parlance, the "job creators.") The vote was bipartisan, too, as plenty of top Blue Dog Democrats—like future public-option killers Max Baucus, Ben Nelson, and "loyal" ole "Joe-mentum" Lieberman all shared in the orgy, gleefully giving the finger to their own party's left wing so as to go full speed ahead with Bush and Cheney.

The Times Square "deficit clock" that had been happily retired at the end of 1999 for having outlived its usefulness (after having run *backwards* for a year or two), would soon find itself revived from the dead as suddenly and frighteningly as a teen-lit vampire. Between the collapse of the dot-com stock market, the tax cuts, and something worst of all that was about to happen (though nobody knew it yet), the Days of Wine and Roses, the days of "surpluses as far as the eye can see" were now going over Thelma and Louise's cliff. All that work during the Clinton years, not to mention Reagan and Old Bush's controversial 1986 and 1990 tax adjustments to try and stem the debt-tide. And this, *this* is what it had all come to...

Liberal Democrats were shaken to the core by Bush/Cheney's brazenness. (Obviously, it had never *really* been about "balancing the budget" or "saving for a rainy day.") Maybe the left-wing voices had been right all along. The *second* that the supply siders came back into office (and we all knew they would, sooner or later), we were right back in Deficit Ditch again. And all those surpluses to be saved in a "lockbox," all that budget-balancing blather goes right down the drain. So why did that "Eisenhower Republican" Bill Clinton even *bother* with all his H. Ross Parrot-ing in the first place? The way he prioritized paying off the "daff'cit" and pleasing the bond traders as his Priority #1, like some Milton Friedman fanboy! When he could have been spending *even more* lavishly on schools, colleges, health-care, safety nets, retirement, forensic science, job retraining infrastructure, art projects, inner cities, and giveaways, while the good times still rolled? Heck, even if Al Gore *had* won for real this time, who's to say people wouldn't be sick of him and ready for a change by 2004? *It was only a matter of time before this happened.* Why did Clinton WASTE all that money on paying down the debt? *It was just gonna go back up again anyway!!*

No surprise that the deficit and national debt would reach cancerously metastatic pro-portions under presidents both Bush and Obama, and under Congresses both Democrat and Republican. Deficits beyond anything even *attempted* by Reagan and Old Bush, let alone by Lyndon Johnson's liberal Great Society. It was the one thing that everybody could "agree" on.

The Blame Game

With all this going on, as the protests about Bush "stealing" the election were just starting to die down, Washington certainly looked to many like a "crime scene." And like those sleuths on the hottest network drama of the 2000–01 season, *CSI,* a lot of people still wanted to know Who Dun It. How could all of this trauma, how all the left-wing's darkest, most paranoid-conspiratorial seeming fantasies of conservative rule during the 2000 elec-tion, have come true in such (seemingly) short a time?

Leave it to the late *Vanity Fair* legend Marjorie Williams to put all the pieces together. In her definitive 2001 essay, "Scenes from a Marriage," she revealed the real reason that Al Gore had gone to such ridiculous lengths to distance himself from Bill Clinton, almost surely losing the 2000 election largely because of it. Remember how, when Gore started to campaign for real in early '99, he was trailing prospective Republican favorite George W. Bush by double-digit margins? *How could that be?* Responsible, reliable, genius-IQ, loyal son, Vietnam veteran, devoted dad Al Gore, "Dudley Do-Right," someone untouched by scandal (except for the 1996 Buddhist temple hiccup) … how could *he* be getting his clock cleaned by a smirking, selfish, "un-intellectual" longhorn Texas bully like that George W. Bush?

There was only one explanation. *Clinton fatigue.* Had to be. The public was visiting its distaste for Clinton's immorality and attitude on an innocent Al Gore. At least, that's what Tipper and Gore's young-adult children were telling him, particularly eldest daughter Karenna Gore Schiff. (Karenna was also a bestie of Naomi Wolf, source of Gore's fashion follies and Wolf's almost Halliburton-level fees for "pop culture consulting.") It was one thing for the American public to grudgingly *accept* an undignified, sexually insatiable, appetite-eating president—as long as he brought home the bacon for them with a dot-com surplus economy. Especially if he was your only hope against grumpy old grandpas like Bush Sr., Reagan, Bob Dole, Ross Perot (let alone foaming-at-the-mouth wingers like Gin-grich, Cheney, Jesse Helms, James Dobson, Grover Norquist, Ken Starr, John Hagee, Ann Coulter, and Limbaugh). But surely, the public would *want* to have a professional, dignified president if they had the chance! *Wouldn't they?*

While there were significant differences between the two of them in substance, when it came to style, perhaps no two presidents in modern history (including Obama) had ever been as "gangsta" as Bill Clinton and George W. Bush. Whether it was the up-your-nose-with-a-rubber-hose defiance and "feel yer pain" shamelessness of Bill Clinton, or the over-compensating pubescent macho-swagger of Dubya. Bush articulated the rage of people who felt that his father's (and by extension, Ronald Reagan's) legacy had also been "stolen" by the vulgar, 43 percent-elected Clinton. Not to mention the religious conservatives, flag-saluting patriots, and pre–Tea Party reactionaries who'd had it up to here with the hip-hop, trash-TV culture, and Alternative Lifestyles of Clinton's Boomer Hollywood Rich and Famous. And by the same coin, Bill Clinton's defiant attitude had come as a liberating "You tell 'em!" valedictory validation for the racial minorities and AIDS-era gays whose voices had been pointedly silenced, ignored, and downright dissed by Permanent Washington up until then. Their styles were made-for-TV, print ready, and Internet compatible. And from that point on, both the hard left and the red-meat right would insist on a combative, Tony Soprano approach to the Presidency. The stakes were just too high for anything else.

Now, the you-know-what really hit the fan. Four days before Christmas of 2000, Bill Clinton and Al Gore finally had it out, face to face, at a closed door post-election meeting, called at Gore's request. *You wanna see attitude? You got it, baby!* After eight long years of almost Prussian-level repression and loyal service bordering on servitude, Al Gore finally let Bill Clinton know what he *really* thought of the last eight years, to his face. Former Gore campaign topper Tony Coelho euphemistically referred to the Gore/Clinton tete-a-tete as a "heated discussion," while Clinton staffer Larry Sabato characterized it to journalist Carol Felsenthal as "a screaming match ... filled with profanity."

And Bill Clinton evidently gave back every inch as good as he got. Bubba still took it as a very personal insult that Gore had distanced himself from him (and from Hillary, who'd won her Senate victory in a landslide. She was helped by the fact that Rudy Giuliani had to bow out due to a fortunately temporary cancer scare, leaving Hillary's opponent to be the relatively unknown Rick Lazio). As for Gore having to push the broom in back of Clinton for all his media-manufactured "scandals"—that fell under the category of Too Bad, Buster! Clinton pointedly reminded Gore that he had been handed a situation that virtually every presidential nominee since Calvin Coolidge—Democrat and Republican alike—would have cut off a finger for: No Herbert Hoover or Jimmy Carter-style recession. No race riots, hostage crises, gas lines, or Vietnam wars. No Nazi Germany, and no Soviet Union. No more deficits—instead, how about surplus money in the bank?

All that handed to him on a silver platter, plus an opponent who (to use libertarian author Gene Healy's tasty words) could barely string together a sentence without committing a syntactical hate crime. *And STILL you couldn't close the deal! Couldn't even win your own bloody state!* (Or the Clintons' Arkansas, for that matter.) Why, even a couple of loser-pants like Mondale and Dukakis had won their own home states!

Will Saletan of *Slate* rubbed it in even more when he wrote a June 2001 snark-article called "Clinton, Gore, and Darwin," postulating that the reason Clinton was able to keep winning (while Gore tanked) was because Bubba had spent his life indulging himself in one sexy sin-sation and shady deal after another, and then Southern-charming and fast-talking his way out of them. Awkward, dutiful, dorky Al Gore just never honed the ruthless "practice" of getting out of tight spots that Clinton had. (And as we all know—practice makes perfect!) Saletan quoted one White House staffer as summarizing, "The more stupid shit Clinton did, the more disapproving Gore got." Yet instead of the slightest penitence or apology, the source said, "Clinton's attitude was, 'Yeah buddy, and when *you* can do what *I* can do, *then* you can stand in judgment of me!'"

Now for the biggest question of all: had George W. Bush really "stolen" the election from Al Gore? As the filthy laundry of Election 2000 was unfurled for all the world to see, there was a good argument to be made that indeed Bush had. Black voters were absolutely racially profiled and harassed. Secretary of State Katharine Harris and Governor Jeb Bush had never once made a final ruling that wasn't a total Dubya victory. Every Supreme Court justice who'd ruled in Bush's favor had owed his or her appointment to Bush Senior, Ronald Reagan, or Richard Nixon. And did 3,400-plus, FDR-and-JFK-worshiping, New York Jews really make for a "Pat Buchanan stronghold" in Palm Beach?

Indeed, the only incontrovertible finding of the autopsy was that the 1990s may have started with one America, indivisible—but after the Republican Revolution of 1994, and certainly after *Bush vs. Gore,* we were Red and Blue America now. The Civil War 2.0 had risen again.

Alas, it wasn't just the most divisive election in modern American history that was officially over now. As Gore's decisive 2000 election loss in Tennessee clearly illustrated, Gore would probably have been lucky to have held on to his daddy's Senate seat during the Culture War '90s, in his ever-more Religious Right, proto-Tea Party, and NRA-controlled home state. (Never mind running for president, after his disastrous 1988 semi-try for the nomination.) Many a Clinton loyalist thought that if Bill Clinton hadn't picked him for VP in 1992, by now Al Gore would be such a political has-been, he'd make Mamie Van Doren and Brett Somers look like Jennifer Aniston and Angelina Jolie. They viewed Gore's loss not as a tragedy for *him*—but as a betrayal of *them.*

Clinton pallie and arch-fundraiser Terry McAuliffe (soon to become Democratic National Committee chairman) had absolutely "detested the way that Gore had distanced himself from the Clintons ... and dissed" on them, said lefty journalist Jeffrey St. Clair. McAuliffe "swiftly took his revenge" when the Democratic Party planned one final Clinto-nomic blow-out—an all-star farewell in January at Andrews Air Force Base, to wrap up the administration that had changed the grammar of domestic politics and media news forever. "Gore, naturally, expected to give the keynote farewell address," St. Clair revealed. "But McAuliffe refused to allow Gore even near a microphone," nor did he "permit [Gore] to speak a single word." A top DNC aide confirmed St. Clair's story as true to *The Washington Post.* "McAuliffe didn't want Gore to speak," the source said. "McAuliffe didn't even want Gore there. The send-off was about good memories, success stories. And the VP wasn't either!"

That same month, as Clinton and Gore attended to Bush's inauguration, the body language said it all—Clinton addictively grasping, glad-handing, and smilingly autographing his palace guards and staff to the very end, as he and Gore emerged from the White House halls; Gore solemn and self-contained, staring straight ahead, as distant and haughty as an old studio mogul or chief of surgery. The friendship and partnership of those two whip-smart, handsome, and youthful Southern men that had seemed so promising, dynamic, and even Obama-level "hopeful" back in 1992, back when they were ready to lead us rocking and rolling into Tomorrow, now seemed as cancelled as a bad television show.

Burying the Lede

With all of these trials and traumas going on in our all-too-real lives, wasn't it nice to know that, in true late 1990s style, our mass media was kind enough to provide us with plenty of things to take our minds off of our own personal troubles, by showing other people who had far worse problems than our own. Forget *Survivor, Big Brother, The Weakest Link, Fear Factor,* and *Who Wants to Be a Millionaire.* The newspapers, magazines, and nightly news shows were really launching that summer's popcorn-poppingest "reality shows," just in time for TV's legitimate dramas like *ER, CSI, The West Wing, Law & Order, NYPD Blue, The X-Files, The Practice,* and Tony Soprano to wrap up their exciting and excitable season finales. And all of these big-time scandals were buzzy sequels to the last decade's biggest crowd pleasers.

The disappearance of lovely and intelligent Congressional intern Chandra Levy added a scintillating whodunit angle to the proven Monica Lewinsky formula of "sexy young Jewish girl has what appears to be a barely closeted affair with an old-enough-to-be-her-father WASP authority figure." While the congressman she was working for, Gary Condit, ultimately proved to be cleared of her murder (once Chandra's body was eventually found some years later), the fact that Condit had *acted* as stereotypically guilty and shifty as a Mafia enforcer, added a provocative JonBenét twist to the narrative. But as far as "acting guilty" was concerned, Gary Condit had nothing on movie tough guy and TV legend Robert Blake. Blake's estranged wife Bonnie Lee Bakley was found shot to death in her and Blake's luxury car outside of their favorite Italian eatery, Vitello's in Los Angeles, in late May of 2001. Even a child could see the parallels to O.J. versus Nicole—a mean-tempered, jealous, over-the-hill tough guy and a too-liberated wife playing out the final act of their battle royale at the fringes of Tinseltown. The big difference was that Nicole was automatically sympathetic due to her having been a loving mother to O.J.'s two children (however rococo her personal lifestyle was).

By contrast, Bonnie Lee Bakley seemed to have lived her entire adult life as if she were auditioning to be the Victim of the Week on an episode of *Law & Order.* She tangled with Marlon Brando's violent-tempered son Christian, and took advantage of a dying 77-year-old Dean Martin in his final days before hitching her star to Blake, while running online porn businesses and "dating" type services off her own computer. Blake got a "not guilty" acquittal a few years later (only to go on to lose the now-inevitable "wrongful death" civil suit afterwards, being found "civilly liable" for Bonnie Lee's murder).

The worst of this trio of tragedy happened on June 20, 2001, when the ultimate "desperate housewife," a devout and horrifically misguided fundamentalist Texas woman named Andrea Yates, murdered all of her small children while in the grips of severe post-partum psychosis. If Chandra Levy was Monica plus murder, and Robert Blake was the white O.J., it somehow seemed inevitable that the often merciless hands of Fate would deliver us "another" Susan Smith, a Columbine massacre for the *Barney* and *Elmo's World* set, with Mommy chasing her preschool and elementary-school age babies around the house to drown or strangle them, one by one, in the bathroom. Yates had been undergoing psychiatric treatment, but her doctor had recently been scaling back her medication—while her not-in-the-least "Christian" cult-church taught a Taliban-like liturgy for women right out of *The Handmaid's Tale*: that Woman's worth in this life was to be a brood-mare (and a human housekeeping appliance) to endlessly populate God's kingdom, no matter how financially strapped, harried for time, or emotionally spent that woman might be.

By the time Yates snapped, she was convinced that Bugs Bunny and Big Bird were telling her through the TV to kill her kids, to save them from the flames of eternal hellfire that awaited them if they grew up to be "sinful" adults. (It was all too fitting that Andrea's murder rampage occurred within just days of the death of that other standard-setter for supposedly "justifiable" child murder, as Timothy McVeigh was finally put to sleep in the execution chamber of Terre Haute's maximum-security Club Fed.) It was also a testament to the insane and inane insanity laws of George W. Bush and Rick Perry's Texas that it took two full tries for the barely comprehending Yates to be adjudged "legally insane" and shipped off to the state mental hospital instead of prison. (What could a regular prison do with a near-catatonic schizophrenic who barely knew what planet she was on?) Of course, that was where Yates *should* have been all along—especially back when her children were still alive!

The Final Countdown

After all those tireless, 24–7 workdays he'd been putting in at the Oval Office during the first half of 2001—protecting Enron, passing tax cuts for the rich that risked ending our hard won-surpluses, trashing budget-balancing guidelines passed under Clinton (and his own father), temporarily losing the Senate in a "palace coup" with moderate and liberal Republicans, and all the leftover trauma from *Bush vs. Gore,* it was understandable that George W. Bush would need some "me time" to work off some of that awful stress. He took one vacation and then another in the late spring and summer of 2001, perhaps to get away from having to pay attention to the black clouds that were starting to hover over his government. He'd looked at those clouds from both sides, now—after all, he'd seen them forming over dear old Poppy's head, back when *he* was running at crunch time in 1992.

One thinks perhaps Bush was getting a bit of his own medicine. After mercilessly preying on Al Gore's awkwardness with the media, now it was Dubya who was trying to paint on the too-wide smile and keep a "confident" stiff upper lip before the cameras, as things started caving in around him. Despite Dick Cheney's best efforts at top-secrecy, the cracks in the Enron dam were now popping loose, and the dot-com stock market bubble continued its dizzying free-fall. More to the point, if anyone from Rush Limbaugh to Michael Moore to a young Illinois rep named Barack Obama—if *anyone* had asked voters in August 2001 the question, "Do you feel better about today than you did a year ago?" the answers from the vast majority of the public would have pointed in a horrifying direction for President George W. Bush. If things kept going the way they were going, his vacation back at Crawford might soon be made into a permanent one.

Indeed, by March of 2002, the stock market would have lost a total of $5 TRILLION in value—*enough to have paid off the entire national debt at that point*—compared to just two years earlier, in March and April of 2000. And though they would zoom through the ceiling in the 2002–06 bubble years, by the spring and summer of 2001, middle-class real estate prices in California and New York had only just recently recovered to the levels they'd been at a decade ago in 1989–90, just before the S&L crisis and the "It's the Economy, Stupid" recession had struck, and gotten this whole ball of wax going in the first place.

Amidst all this domestic chaos, hardly anyone noticed the activities of the group of young Middle Eastern men who'd by now gotten their pilots' accreditation, and were spending the late spring and summer of 2001 bivouaced in cheapo apartments and motel rooms, mainly in New England. (Although, perhaps in a warm-up session for all those "virgins" he thought would soon be his sex slaves in paradise, Mohammed Atta and his crew took a sortie to Vegas in July of 2001 to engage in round-the-clock sex with call girls in Sin City, as if in some kind of demented *rumspringa* from their dreary, disciplined, fanatical lives, before the main event.) While nobody knew just how far along their plans and plots had gotten, a White House messenger did deliver the now-notorious Condi Rice memo to Bush while he was on vacation in mid–August, with the not-exactly ambiguous title, "BIN LADEN DETERMINED TO ATTACK WITHIN THE U.S." President Bush went right to work—doing exactly what he was doing *before* he got the report.

* * *

Tuesday, September 11th, 2001 was a beautiful late summer's day, especially on the Eastern seaboard. New York and New England were enjoying the last of their lovely Atlantic beach summer, while the supposedly preferable climates of California, Florida, Hawaii, and Vegas baked in their "Indian summer" heat. The weather was perfect—not too muggy, smoggy, or sweaty, but balmy and blue, with skies as crystal clear as digital film.

First thing in the morning on that day, at an airport in Portland, Maine, an experienced ticket agent named Michael Tuohey was checking in a young Middle Eastern man in his late twenties or early thirties. Though the young man was not conventionally handsome, he could have been passably good looking, if it weren't for the way that his facial expression was contorted in a glaring rictus of malevolence and contempt. "He had the most hateful look, the most angry look on his face. I had never gotten a feeling like this," Tuohey shivered years later, for a National Geographic documentary. "He looked like the [skull and cross-bones] on a poison bottle.... I looked at him, and I'm thinking, 'My God, I sense *anger* here!'" *If that guy doesn't look like a terrorist....*

Tuohey initially denied the young man his boarding card for the transfer to Flight 11 out of Boston, which only made the young seethe even more. But Tuohey had no legal reason, nothing besides a gut instinct, to refuse the ticket—and he knew it. "That guy" was dressed like a businessman, like a young professional. He had a top-of-the-line first class ticket worth nearly $2500, for a commuter flight to Boston's Logan Airport, where he would connect to a cross-country flight to LA. Tuohey gave himself a "mental slap." If he denied this young man entry just because he didn't like the way the Middle Easterner looked, and the guy turned out to be an honest family man or executive (which he almost surely was, after all), *why, I would essentially be guilty of a hate crime, wouldn't I?* He'd have ruined someone's business or vacation, perhaps damaged their career and cost them money, just because he didn't like the way the guy looked, because the man looked like a cartoon-stereotypical "bad Arab." How was that any different or more defensible than the bigot who crosses the street to avoid African American or Latino youths, after all?

Against his better judgment, Tuohey processed the entry pass, and Mohammed Atta boarded the plane. And seventeen other men, from trained pilots to the "muscle hijackers" whose job it was to kill the pilots and key staff and subdue the passengers while protecting the terrorist pilots, all likewise boarded their planes, at airports across the Eastern seaboard.

A couple of hours later, around 8:45 that morning, almost two hundred miles to the southwest, two French filmmaker brothers were shooting a documentary on the New York Fire Department in lower Manhattan, completely unaware that they were about to inadvertently capture something far more important—as well as the NYFD in its finest hour. Alerted by the "whoosh" of a commercial jet flying dangerously low at top speed just above Manhattan's skyscrapers, they jerked their cameras suddenly to see American Airlines Flight 11 plowing straight into the middle of the World Trade Center's North Tower, with a gigantic orange explosion.

While the FAA was just now coming to grips with the fact that Flight 11 had been hijacked, thanks to the courageous phone calls of flight attendants Betty Ong and Amy Sweeney, the second plane, United Airlines Flight 175, was already now on its way, having made a grotesque U-turn towards Manhattan after the terrorists took over and murdered the pilots. (At that point, the FAA assumed the first hijacking was to hold the passengers to ransom, not to use the plane itself as a weapon of mass destruction.) And no one yet outside of the FAA loop even knew that much, not the media or even the Bush White House. During the next 15 or 20 minutes after the first towers' hit, most of Manhattan and the world on the ground simply assumed they were watching a horrific accident. Perhaps the pilot had suffered a heart attack or stroke, like these elderly people who suffer attacks behind the wheel and crash full-bore into a crowded intersection or street fair. Maybe he was drunk, or high on drugs. Perhaps there was a malfunction of the plane's GPS and air-traffic technology.

By 9 o'clock Eastern time, every major TV network and cable news channel had dispatched camera crews and tele-copters to hover above and watch the action. NBC, CBS, and ABC were just about to finish their *Today* and *Good Morning America* and *CBS This Morning* shows, and most simply stayed with it, while Fox News fed itself to over-the-air Fox broadcast affiliates. The syndicated *Live with Regis & Kelly* show was just getting started, and fed over to ABC coverage, as America nervously watched the rescue effort begin.

Then, at 9:03 a.m., cameras caught sight of another jet plane, flying even lower than the last one, remorselessly barreling straight towards the heart of the South Tower, as Flight 175 hit with a giga-fireball crash, even worse than the first one. Women's voices shrieked from the ground, helplessly watching the impact. "Oh my God! They did it on purpose!! It's terrorists! It's an attack!!" One horrified and depressed news anchorman grimly intoned, as the deathly black smoke choked the side of the jagged grey towers, "I think we have a terrorist act of proportions that we *can't even begin to imagine* at this juncture." Within a few minutes, people above the impact zone were forced to commit suicide against their will, or be burned alive in the towering inferno. Hardened reporters and police and firemen tried not to vomit at the sight and sounds of the "thuds" of people falling from the towers. (One young woman crossed herself, opening her arms to God before allowing herself to fall, as if from a high-dive, to escape the hell behind her.)

Condoleezza Rice was holding an executive meeting that morning at the White House with her staff. She had already been handed a note about the first plane hitting, but she'd largely dismissed it; she wondered to herself "what an odd kind of accident" that was, and on such a clear blue morning too. *Oh well—that was horrible, but it was probably the pilot having a heart attack or stroke behind the wheel, or some kind of mechanical malfunction....* Then an aide hurried in to tell her about the second impact. Rice recalled she momentarily froze, with the same chilling thought that virtually every sentient American and Canadian between the ages of 10 and 100 who'd heard or seen the news had pop into their heads. *THAT'S NOT AN ACCIDENT!!* Rice immediately ended the session and headed straight for the Situation Room, where she huddled in to hear word from President Bush.

President Bush, for his part, was on yet another vacation/PR junket, this time in Florida, in a photo-op visit with a bunch of ethnically diverse first-graders at the Emma E. Booker School in his brother Jeb's home state, the same state that had been the epicenter of the last national-level disaster, nine months earlier. Andy Card had given Bush a note about the first plane, but like Rice, Bush had dismissed it—he wasn't about to go running around with his head cut off, hysterically crying "Terroristic threat!" in front of a bunch of six-year-old babies, when it could just as easily have been a tragic accident. Now, as Bush received the second hasty ear-whisper, that America was, indeed, under attack, Bush's face froze and his eyes went dark with horror and indecision, as the adorable little ones continued reading *My Pet Goat* to him, innocently oblivious to the fact that something cataclysmic was now happening in their world.

As horrible as it was, very few people actually expected yet *another* plane to hit, let alone 250 miles south of the bull's-eye zone in Manhattan. But it was all about the cinematic imagery and symbolism to the media-savvy, CIA-trained, Western-educated Osama bin Laden. The WTC symbolized America's economic dominance (some might say arrogance). But Washington, D.C., was America's governmental heart, brains, and nerve center. The next plane, American Airlines Flight 77, hit the Pentagon at about 9:30 with such force that it crashed through four of the five concrete and I-beam reinforced "rings," completely disintegrating the jumbo jet in the process. The brightly lit, high-tech Pentagon offices and think-tank laboratories were instantly transformed on that crystal blue morning into the sooty-dark tunnels of a torture-porn horror movie—which is exactly what the inner Pentagon had now become.

And there was yet *another* plane that had been taken, this one United Flight 93, which had perhaps the most ironic story of all. United 93's pilots were warned from ground control to beware of any cockpit intrusions or signs of trouble on the flight. Barely seconds after the air-traffic controllers had issued the warning, though, the terrorists were forcing their way in, brutally stabbing, beating, and strangling the pilots and taking over the controls. Thankfully however, the time for the terrorists had also run out. When the hijacked passengers began making cell phone calls to their families on the ground, they realized that this was no ordinary hijacking, the way the terrorists wanted them to think. Their friends and relatives told them what had just happened to two other hijacked planes at the World Trade Center, and now the Pentagon. Flight 93's passengers immediately understood the situation. They weren't going to be held hostage; they themselves were going to be used as a weapon of mass destruction—probably against the Congress or Supreme Court, or even the White House itself!

A group of people who defined the term "ordinary heroes," like Todd Beamer and Jeremy Glick, ganged up on the "muscle hijackers" and knocked them out or killed them, and then smashed in the door to the cockpit. The terrorist pilots, realizing that they would never get the chance to make their crowning achievement in Washington, sent the plane heading virtually straight down as the passengers attacked, determined that if they couldn't assassinate President Bush or the Congress, they would at least wipe out all these ugly

Americans on the plane. Seconds later, a gigantic explosion and a horrific ashen sinkhole hit in the rural farmlands of Shanksville, Pennsylvania. The plane and its passengers had once again essentially disintegrated upon impact. Passengers who had no idea they were in for anything more than a routine plane ride an hour earlier, now had paid the ultimate price to save their country's nerve center. Thanks to these heroes, the institutions of American government—at least in physical terms—were still safe.

Back at the Pentagon, two incredibly heroic African American female Army officers named Sheila Moody and Marilyn Wills were banging futilely on tempered glass windows (Moody had an injured hand—she later recalled leaving a bloody handprint), choking on exhaust fumes, bacteria, and pollution. Despite the seeming futility, both women led not only themselves but their civilian and injured coworkers behind them to eventual safety, snaking through the blistering tunnels to daylight, and clapping and screaming until rescue workers and paramedics could hear them. Both the officers and their friends managed to get rescued—and just in the nick of time, too. Just before 10:00, a 75-foot section of the supposedly indestructible Pentagon collapsed, crumbling in on itself like a broken rag doll.

But a far deadlier collapse was about to happen back in New York. Canadian American financial executive Brian Clark had rescued his fellow WTC office worker Stanley Praimnath, who had just barely avoided being smashed to bits by the plane that had hit his floor. Now the two men had finally made it out into (what they thought was) the safety of the sunshine, after descending the endless choking staircases within the hundred-storey towers, and were now walking a couple of blocks away from Ground Zero. Suddenly, Praimnath heard a terrible, mechanically monstrous moan, and looked over his shoulder at the towering infernos. He told Clark that they'd better run for their lives, that the building was about to topple over. Clark almost laughed at the absurdity. "That's just drapery and carpets that are burning," he began to reply. *And then...*

Before Clark could even finish his sentence, both men heard the death-groan of snapping and creaking support beams, the South Tower's sides buckling in on themselves, like an old woman trying to rise from her chair and then falling back, as the building's massive upper weight began giving out on itself. The 2000-degree, porcelain-kiln heat of the planes' roasting diesel jet fuel was turning the building's iron and metal support cores as soft as satin, while the fireproofing had already been knocked off by the impact. As journalists and police gaped with shock, the tower began a compression collapse, the quarter-mile-high building pancaking from top to bottom, all the way down to street level.

The most evil and deadly clouds since Hiroshima and Nagasaki now began chasing the mobs of screaming and running New Yorkers around every corner, suffocating every nook and cranny, like some kind of demonic blob determined to smother and strangle them. Hundreds and thousands of tons of metal, concrete, glass, plumbing, furniture, paper, and gasoline exhaust were atomized by the explosions, fire, and collapse; the laws of physics now demanded that the displaced matter find its release.

Barely a half an hour later, just before 10:30 am, the now-inevitable final horror occurred. What was too horrific to contemplate an hour ago had now become what we were all grimly waiting for. The North Tower disintegrated too, folding in on itself like an inverted volcano, sending an even worse mushroom cloud of asphyxiation around every corner, huge chunks of concrete and glass smashing to the ground, crushing parts of surrounding buildings to bits, choking entire blocks of the bright sunlit morning into post-nuclear darkness.

While their life stories are no more or less important because they were celebrities, it seems only fitting in light of the celebrity-crazed '90s, that two of the biggest "names" to be murdered on 9/11 demonstrated ironies so great that if they were put in a fictional novel or movie, it would seem totally unbelievable. Berry Berenson was the socialite wife of the late Anthony Perkins, and mother of their two young adult sons, one of whom was the aptly named singer-songwriter Elvis Perkins. September was a grim month for the Perkins family; the very next day was the ninth anniversary of the Broadway and Hollywood legend's death from AIDS at age sixty, in 1992. But this year, both mother and son were finally going to erase the disappointment of that day, as Elvis was about to make his debut that very night performing at the legendary Hollywood nightspot The Troubadour. After summering on Cape Cod and the Vineyard, Berry eagerly boarded the plane from Boston to Los Angeles, hardly able to wait to see her son's upcoming triumph, a performer just like his father and grandparents, while Elvis anxiously awaited his mother's return back in Hollywood. But Mohammed Atta had other plans. Berry Berenson, and all her hopes and dreams, got crashed into the North Tower.

No less ironic or horrific was the fact that Barbara Olson—the bestselling author, attorney, impeachment-era cable firebrand, and wife of sitting Solicitor General Ted Olson—was also on her way to Los Angeles on Flight 77, to put lefty comedian Bill Maher in his place on a taping session of *Politically Incorrect,* with her Texas-twanged humor and bouncy attitude. (Indeed, without Ted and Barbara Olson, there might not have even *been* a second Bush presidency in the first place: Ted was the primary counsel who'd won the *Bush vs. Gore* case less than nine months earlier.) Barbara called Ted at his Washington office, and Ted Olson, who had been watching the news coverage and was being kept posted by high-level government staff, was now presented with the hardest closing argument he would ever have to make. Swallowing hard, he told Barbara about the other hijackings and the attacks on the WTC. "I told her because I thought I had to. So in a sense, I had to tell her how bleak the situation was." At some point the connection was broken, and Olson recalled, "I never heard from her again." That was just minutes before Barbara Olson was forced into the world's most unspeakable homecoming, her plane brutally reverted back into Washington, D.C., by the terrorist hijackers to crash into the Pentagon. It happened practically walking distance from her and Ted's household and offices.

Two other people, both of then top-level security experts who had led lives that were the opposite of high-profile or "celebrity" until Black Tuesday, deservedly found themselves thrust into the spotlight after death. Rick Rescorla, a former British citizen who emigrated to the U.S. in the mid 1960s to assist the American war effort as an enlisted soldier in Vietnam, had forseen the possibility of an attack on the World Trade Center, fully four years before the *first* WTC attacks in early 1993! Living in New Jersey, Rescorla felt after the December 1988 Locherbie airplane bombing outrage (orchestrated by Libyan terror warlord Muammar Khadaffy) that the greatest symbol of American capitalism and economic dominance would be just too irresistible a target to terrorists. Following the 1993 attacks, he was asked to become a security director at Dean Witter/Morgan Stanley's WTC corporate headquarters, after years in the Army and in private corporate security at the highest levels.

The other man who had "predicted" 9/11, John O'Neill, was a former FBI agent who had just retired earlier in 2001, after butting heads with his Federal superiors, who regarded him as an alarmist, with all the ruckus O'Neill kept raising about the threats he perceived of a domestic terroristic attack. Like a horror-movie doctor or Captain Ahab, O'Neill had been hotly pursuing Osama and al-Qaeda for years; he had been instrumental in the capture of 1993 WTC attack mastermind Ramzi Yousef. His last priority before taking early retirement from the FBI was investigating the October 2000 USS *Cole* bombing. (No surprise, he solved the mystery—Osama did it.) The bombing which neither an outgoing Bill Clinton nor an incoming George W. Bush thought worthy of avenging with anything for real. Now, O'Neill had become Director of Security at the WTC.

Both men were certain after the 1993 attacks that, like a monster in a slasher movie, the killer wasn't finished yet. To them, it was only a question of *when*, not if, the WTC would be attacked by terrorists again—though neither man could have anticipated in their worst nightmares just what a calamity of calamities that next attack would turn out to be. Both of these heroes died as they lived, crushed to death as they selflessly spent their last mortal minutes on Earth trying to help others get to safety. And as for the non-rich and less-than-famous, of the roughly 3,000 other people who would die that day (and the countless others physically injured and/or shell-shocked), how many everyday people's plans and dreams, how many other families and lives, were destroyed or warped or irrevocably shaken to their core, by that singular act of madness?

Newsweek told the harrowing story of a burn victim named Virginia Di Chiara, who was trapped in an elevator when the second plane hit. Horrific "raindrops" of fire and gasoline-rain from the plane's carcass above trickled down through the office ceilings, mingled with the misty water fanning out from the fire sprinklers. Di Chiara, having made her narrow escape from the elevator box-coffin suspended nearly a thousand feet above ground, ran for the stairwells. The adrenaline high was too much for her to feel pain or exhaustion— yet—but that would soon change, as she and a co-worker (whom she had recently rather brutally audited within her company) wind-suckingly made it down the tenth, twentieth, thirtieth set of stairs, in the desperate anticipation of finally reaching the ground floor.

Di Chiara had already been whisked away to the hospital by one of the army of ambulances at Ground Zero by the time the towers collapsed, but her ordeal was as horrific as if she'd remained trapped in the building. She had to undergo skin abrasion removal of scar tissue and have needles and pressure bandages applied to drain and relieve the swelling in her badly burned arms, which she had used to shield her hair and face (which thankfully remained intact). She recalled the "tank room" at the hospital, where burn victims were showered and cleansed and had to undergo dermabrasion therapy, to keep from being grossly disfigured scar-tissue zombies for life. "And the babies," she shuddered, recalling child burn patients she'd seen there—as if it were too horrible to even contemplate further, like something out of a concentration camp.

IRS worker Ling Young, who awoke in "the land of dead people" in the blacked-out smoke of her office after it had been hit, had barely made it out to safety before the collapse. She too had to endure years of skin grafts, bandage treatments, plastic surgery, and reparative therapy. Young recalled sitting home in the first few years of the aftermath, watching cable reruns of *Murder, She Wrote* as cozy comfort food to take the edge off, unable to work anymore and living on disability, all her plans shot or at least irrevocably altered. And "the man with the bandana," an amateur athlete and young broker named Wells Crowther, had met his end leading people to safety in and out of the stairwells, just like Rick Rescorla and John O'Neill had, although there was a chilling difference: Crowther was young enough to have been Rescorla's or O'Neill's son when he died—he was only 24 years old.

An entire book as big as this one itself could be written on just the survivors' stories alone, and it would barely scratch the surface. But the bottom line was that America had been attacked. For the first time since Pearl Harbor, a ragtag army of fanatical Third Worlders had done what Hitler and Stalin could not, tearing the iron curtain of security that had kept inland America safe, in both fact and mind. Air traffic was grounded entirely by mid-morning on 9/11, and remained so through Thursday, although there was one telling exception to the rule. The remaining bin Laden family members still in the States (who had completely disassociated themselves from Osama—*they said*) and several other prominent Saudis were allowed to fly back home to Saudi Arabia on private flights, at the strongest urging of the Saudi royal family and its diplomats, ostensibly so that those people would not be the victims of press harassment or hate crimes.

*   *   *

On Friday, September 14, 2001, George W. Bush presided over a ceremony which virtually all the living ex-presidents attended, at Washington's National Cathedral. (Ronald Reagan wasn't able to come, of course—by then he was 90 years old and completely senile, requiring 24-hour care, less than three years before his death.) It was surely George W. Bush's finest hour. For the first time since taking office, Bush truly seemed like a real "compassionate conservative," someone focused on uniting and not dividing. Al Gore himself told Americans that George W. Bush was "my president," and asked for total unity. This was something that went beyond party or person.

Suddenly, on that bright shiny morning, everything had changed—or so we thought. The partisan pettiness of the 1990s, the ugly hate speech of the Republican Revolution and *Bush vs. Gore* and the Monica Lewinsky impeachment battle—that all seemed so ten years ago, let alone ten months ago. Why, even Vladimir Putin's Russia, and Communist China were on Team America now. Both had ordered their state military bands to play The Star Spangled Banner in the days following 9/11. Maybe America would finally follow the advice that a post-beating Rodney King gave a decade earlier, when the '90s decade was just getting started: "Can't we all just get along?"

Cultural critics tut-tutted that the era of raised-eyebrow, automatic "irony" had come to an end, what with Rudy Giuliani hosting the first *Saturday Night Live,* and even Jon Stewart, Dan Rather, and David Letterman overcome by emotion. Surely, they prophesied, all the cheesy bread and circuses of the past few years (*Big Brother, Survivor, Millionaire, The Real World,* trashy daytime talk shows and cheesy cable programs, early evening gossip shows) would be headed for the exit door. Ditto comic-book feature films, blow-'em-up CGI thrillers, and death-porn splatter movies, things that trivialized terror, torture, and murder. We were going to be Serious and Mature again. America had had its "holiday from history." Now it was going to roll up its sleeves and get to work, with the old-fashioned, uncomplaining steel machismo of John Wayne or Marshal Dillon riding to the rescue, of Greatest Generationers like Charles Bronson and Clint Eastwood fighting back in World War II or Korea, when they were young.

Surely President Bush would rise to the occasion. What other choice did he have, after all? Surely he wouldn't—he *couldn't*—squander the worldwide expressions of good will from virtually every country that could reasonably be considered civilized. George W. Bush was no genius, granted, but nobody who could make it as high as the Presidency, let alone to have been the firstborn son of another president, CIA chief, and World War II hero … *nobody* like that could mishandle something like this! He couldn't just throw it all away … *could he?*

Perhaps the best epitaph for 9/11—and everything that's happened since—came via a simple, ordinary appointment calendar on Condoleezza Rice's desk. After the initial horror and those first panicked meetings at the White House upon Bush's return, she returned to notice the appointments and plans she'd made for the next several days, many of which were now pointlessly redundant, after this mother of all game-changes. Looking back on that moment, Rice made a statement to a TV documentary crew (which she famously repeated for the Council on Foreign Relations). "If you were in a position of authority on September 11th…" Rice began, starting to choke up. "Every day since then has been September the 12th."

Conclusion: Don't Stop Thinkin' About Tomorrow

What didn't cha like about the '90s—the peace, or the prosperity?
—James Carville and Paul Begala

So now then. If the 1990s really were our last great decade of fun and excitement before everything went to hell in a handbasket, then that rather begs the question—the big-money question, too, the one Regis Philbin might have asked on a 1999 or 2000 episode of *Millionaire:* Namely, if the '90s were so goshdarned peaceful and prosperous—then why weren't people feelin' the love at the time?

Instead, why did every news report, from print to online to TV, and every political bestseller keep hyperventilating and pulse-pounding, keep the ball rolling, keep frosting the cake? Why did a decade of such shiny, happy people end amidst worldwide pants-wetting about Y2K meltdowns, the impeachment of one president, and the most vicious, divisive, and blatantly hate-mongering presidential election in modern U.S. history?

Why was the tone for the decade set at the beginning with angry, in-your-face, cynical and sometimes violent filmmakers and musicians like Quentin Tarantino, Spike Lee, Tupac Shakur, Kurt Cobain, Public Enemy, and Trent Reznor? And why did the "peaceful and prosperous," go-go late 1990s end not with the sunshiney optimism of a Retro Reagan, but with the 1970s-style, where-the-sidewalk-ends existentialism of *Magnolia, Girl Interrupted, Almost Famous, American Beauty, The Ice Storm, Traffic, Boys Don't Cry,* and the premiere season of *Six Feet Under?* Why did the mid-to-late 1990s hit parade have songs with titles like "Anywhere But Here," "Save Me," "Nothing Is Good Enough," "Waiting," "Isn't It Ironic?," "Then You Might Know What It's Like," "What If God Was One of Us?," "Don't Look Back in Anger," "Still Haven't Found What I'm Looking For," "Can't Even Tell," and "Closing Time"—plus Lilith Fair, Eminem, Public Enemy, Limp Bizkit, and Rage Against the Machine?

The great poet and humorist Charles Baudelaire once wrote that the ugliest, most degenerate, and wickedest of all sins was "L'Ennui." Traditional Catholic and Talmudic Jewish teaching also stands that unmitigated, self-pitying despair is a sin that, if indulged in for indeterminate lengths of time, borders on the unforgiveable, the proof of a total lack of faith not only in God but in one's fellow man. If that was the case, then in some strange sense that they probably never even realized themselves, perhaps Jerry Falwell and Pat Buchanan were right about the 1990s after all, about how filthy and reprehensible our society had become. (Although their 24–7 culture-warring was also certainly among the leading causes of 1990's anger and malaise.)

323

The reason that many religions consider suicide a mortal sin (in more ways than one), and why constant boredom and/or total self pity is thought to be almost as wicked, is because of the profound ungratefulness they connote for the blessings of simply being alive in this world. Just think: all that surplussy money in the stock market bank ... all that post–Cold War and pre–9/11 peace ... four and five percent unemployment from 1998 thru 2000 ... highest homeownership since the days of *Ozzie & Harriet* or *Mad Men*.... And yet instead of veritably skipping through life, walking on sunshine, pinching ourselves with our good fortune, the popular culture and shrieking 24–7 noise-machine "news" headlines of right, left, and center just got meaner, angrier, and snarkier, just got more snide and smart-alecky and vicious. More preoccupied with nihilism, personal attacks, and point-lessness each and every year. "Nothing Is Good Enough" and "Anywhere But Here" indeed!

Nothing less than a return to 1950s sex roles and biblical morality would satisfy religious and cultural conservatives. Nothing less than 1960s-style pacifism and hand-holding would satisfy the peace advocates and "isolationists" horrified by Clinton-Gore's "enemy of the month club" of "humanitarian" interventions and sanctions—and nothing less than tyrannical, iron-fisted, Cheney-style policy would satisfy those who still thought of Bill and Hillary as a folk-singing, doped-up hippie and a "radical feminist" Commie mommie. Nothing less than a return to the *Make Room for Daddy* midcentury economy of easy credit, easy-to-get jobs, and pre-inflationary, pre-globalization easy living for the working middle class would truly satisfy the Michael Moore/Thomas Frank/Bernie Sanders left. And nothing less than a complete *pogrom* of those "uneducated" Labor hardhats and paleo-liberals, and those "ignorant" and "superstitious" sincerely religious voters clinging to their religion and guns, would satisfy the Bimmer-driving neoliberal pundits, the in-your-face atheist scientists, or the snarky, latte-sipping op-ed columnists.

"Time," that eccentric British minor-aristocrat Miss Marple once sighed, "really is a One Way street, isn't it, Inspector?" Quite so, madam. William F. Buckley said that one definition of the conservative philosophy was to "stand athwart History, shouting STOP!" But the next generation of Boomer conservatives who came after him, like Newt Gingrich, Karl Rove, Lee Atwater, Tom DeLay, Dick Cheney, and Rush Limbaugh, were too busy making and rewriting history in the 1990s and 2000s to worry about telling it to stop. And the Democrats who had bopped into the White House singing the mantra of "change" in 1992 were, by decade's end, reduced to blathering about Social Security "lockboxes" for out-of-the-job-market retirees, school uniforms and V-chips, and winning the sweepstakes to see who could be the most theatrically "offended" by Monicagate. Change—not just sun-shiney hopey-changey change, but oncoming and massive technological, financial, and educational change—was the last thing Al Gore or Joe Lieberman (let alone George W. Bush and Dick Cheney) wanted to talk about by the end. And every time Bill Clinton coura-geously tried to talk about it, like a game of whack-a-mole at the carnival, something else—O.J., JonBenét, Princess Di, Monica Lewinsky, Osama bin Laden, Saddam Hussein, Oklahoma City, Columbine, Whitewater, *Bush vs. Gore*—came up and stole the show. Like a woman who ignores the lump in her breast or a man who dismisses the stabbing left-arm pains when he works out, if we just ignored all that nasty stuff it would all go away—right?

Whether we knew it or not, this was our last chance. Tomorrow would be another day. Ready or not, here it comes. Part of it was, as that post '90s millennial whiz Ezra Klein diagnosed in 2007, "the creation of a scandal-obsessed media" that had well and truly "lost its mind" for a decade. To put it bluntly, as those incomparable late '90s feminist philosophers Daria and Debbie Downer might have put it, we had our "last great decade" all right—and it looks like we frickin' blew it! And we're still picking up the pieces today.

The great 20th century historian Arthur Schlesinger, Jr., was fond of explaining modern civilized history as being on a metaphorical "pendulum," which slowly swings from periods of progressivism and liberal public interests to conservatism and an emphasis on private concerns. If that was so, perhaps the 1990s and early 2000s can best be illustrated as the story of two elevators in a sky-high building, not unlike the World Trade Centers themselves. One was the America of midcentury—overwhelmingly white, working or middle class, suburban or rural, family oriented, proudly patriotic, observantly Christian or Jewish at least on the surface, and basically traditional. The other was the post–Obama "Coalition of the Ascendant"—proudly single women and gay men from the big cities, Mexicans/Latin Americans, Asians, and Middle Eastern immigrants, African Americans, computer-hyperliterate techno fanboys, and those whose religious beliefs can best be described as skeptical (if not nonexistent).

The terrific conservative historian and journalist Daniel McCarthy wrote an unusually soul-searching and self-critical feature piece in the January 12, 2009, issue of *The American Conservative* (a week before Obama's inauguration) with the deliberately provocative title, "McGovern Beats Nixon." It was a back-atcha at the George F. Will and William F. Buckley conservatives who liked to joke that Barry Goldwater "won" the 1964 election—it just took 16 years (until Ronald Reagan's victory in 1980) to "count the votes." Reagan's election, at least the first time (and a good case can be made that all the other conservative triumphs through at least the 1994 Republican Revolution if not *Bush vs. Gore*) owed itself largely to liberal overreach and systems-failure on the "pendulum" that had first swung left in 1932 with Franklin Roosevelt.

The 1990s and the early 2000s were when the "elevator" containing the old America of mid-century truly "met up" with, so to speak, the elevator containing the Coalition of the Ascendant, when things reached critical mass and began to boil over. The second car was indeed on the ascent, and the former one was on the way down—and by the time of William Jefferson Clinton, both sides knew exactly in which direction their car was traveling. And therein lay the real reason for the decade-long Culture War that overwhelmed just about everything in those years. The ones on the way down were doing something, anything, frantically pushing every button, jim-cracking every gear, desperate to stop their free-fall; while the ascendant box, sweltering and suffocating as if in a real elevator car, packed to the rafters with stale air and flat body odor, furiously frustrated by the *sssslllooowww* movement of change and diversity, was bursting with tension and repressed anger, equally desperate to rocket themselves up, up, and away.

Instead, this stalled elevator crash paralyzed the rest of the building. Because the other immutable fact of the 1990s, like a child impatiently waiting in the back of a minivan on a vacation trip, was that *we weren't there YET*. Not on either side. The "Our America" of the past, remembering the relatively wholesome entertainment and easy-street economy that had been taken for granted such a short time ago, still had what 1970s San Francisco columnist Herb Caen once called "the dying strength of the moribund," clinging to their last gasp of life as a real force to be reckoned with, gobsmacked by the sudden, impending loss of their old world in the face of massive technological, economic, and demographic changes.

But they *hadn't* hit rock bottom yet. There were still plenty of aging Greatest Generationers and Silent Generationers who could see the exit door up ahead, but weren't inclined to go gently into that good night, especially if it meant their whole world as they knew it would be joining them at Forest Lawn soon. And their completely understandable anger at being totally dissed by TV network and motion picture executives craving only the youngest, hippest, and richest (let alone the rap/metal/grunge music on the radio) only made them more resentful.

Ditto conservative Baby Boomer Vietnam veterans, Red State white businessmen, sincere religious conservatives, proud stay-at-home housewives, and bill-paying Walmart moms who had "jobs" instead of "careers." Riven by the founding modern culture wars of Vietnam and Watergate, feminism and civil and gay rights, too young to retire yet but too old to start their careers over again, they were mad as hell at each other—Andrew Sullivan rightly said in 2007 that the "Baby Boomer culture wars" had already nearly destroyed America from within—and that was *before* Barack Obama vs. the Tea Party, or Donald Trump and Ted Cruz for president. And the people relentlessly pushing change, change, and more change, from the right-wing "one percenter" venture capitalist performing leveraged-buyouts and strategic bankruptcies of flabby Old Economy businesses to hyperdrive their right-sized remains into the Global Information and Education Age, to the liberal civil-rights or AIDS firebrand who demanded full gay marriage and equality and total racial/feminist diversity in TV and movies RIGHT NOW—they also found themselves boiling over in frustration.

Because things just hadn't gotten that far *for either side*—yet.

As such, perhaps the Culture Wars of the 1990s were inevitable in that regard, as America began its long and painful rebirthing process, from the dying off of one kind of society and social contract into another. Maybe "Triangulation" was not only a genius political strategy but perhaps the *only* strategy for the decade. Nobody ever said that either dying or childbirth were painless. What *could* have been helped, however, was the will to truly learn from the mistakes and tragic injuries and injustices of that decade, as all of us were forced by Father Time to pick ourselves up, dust ourselves off, and start all over again.

Maybe in some alternate universe, we *did* learn our lesson, as we left the 1990s behind. Maybe President Al Gore really was elected after all, and perhaps he did everything all of his most passionate supporters believed he would've done, as they ruefully looked back on his loss from our post–Dubya vantage point of today. Surely he'd have preserved those never-ending surpluses, while paying off the national debt as blithely as Vanna White waving away a grand prize, plus pre-empting 9/11 right in the nick of time, just like a Jack Bauer or Jason Bourne, while ending global warming and thwarting Hurricane Katrina, too! (And for his exercise routine, he might have even lept tall buildings in a single bound...)

Or perhaps President George W. Bush went on to be that truly compassionate conservative he always promised he would be, respecting the right to privacy (including that of gays and lesbians to live their own lives with dignity), trying to keep abortion as rare as possible (while still ensuring it was safe and legal) and always respecting the equal rights of women and minorities. Perhaps this president's government would encourage a *truly* Christian, charity-based society that really did leave no child behind, and helped people help themselves to get back on their feet, a society that punished rather than rewarded corporate corruption, waste, fraud, and abuse. A president who, as he repeatedly said to the press in 1999 and 2000, didn't believe it was his job to engage in bullying and dictating orders to other countries just to show that he could.

But for any of this to have happened, we needed the biggest perhaps of all. Perhaps the narrative-writing mass media—from screens large and small and on computer laptops, to the threatened yet then-flourishing print magazines, books, and newspapers—perhaps *they* would have finally learned *their* collective lesson, too.

Maybe, even as late and after the fact as it already is, we can still actually learn something from having lived through the stressed-out yet peaceful, prosperous yet unequal 1990s—rather than simply living through them, and then immediately moving on to the next thing, as if they had never happened in the first place. Maybe.

Then again, as those great philosophers Oasis advised back in 1995—don't look back in anger. At least, not today...

Bibliography

The majority of the quotations from magazine articles, newspapers, Wikipedia, peer-reviewed journals, and websites are attributed directly in the text. When using facts from magazines, third-party sources, and personal memories of having come of age and lived through that decade as a reasonably aware and sentient kind of fellow, I have tried to draw upon over 15 years of working as a professional writer, researcher, movie/TV staffer, and critic. And I have used that sometimes exciting, sometimes tiresome, and always necessary experience sorting out the wheat from the chaff and eliminating questionable or unreliable information.

Alterman, Eric. *Sound and Fury: The Washington Punditocracy and the Collapse of American Politics.* Ithaca, NY: Cornell University Press, 1999.

_____. *What Liberal Media? The Truth About Bias and the News.* New York: Basic, 2003.

Biskind, Peter. *Down & Dirty Pictures: Miramax, Sundance, and the Rise of Independent Film.* New York: Simon & Schuster, 2004.

Blumenthal, Sidney. *The Clinton Wars.* New York: Farrar, Straus, and Giroux, 2003.

Carter, Bill. *Desperate Networks.* New York: Doubleday, 2006.

Clinton, Bill. *My Life.* New York: Knopf, 2004.

Cockburn, Alexander, and Jeffrey St. Clair. *Al Gore: A User's Manual.* New York: Verso, 2000.

_____. *Dime's Worth of Difference: Beyond the Lesser of Two Evils.* Oakland, CA: AK, 2004.

Didion, Joan. *Where I Was From.* New York: Knopf, 2003.

Ehrenstein, David. *Open Secret: Gay Hollywood 1928–1998.* New York: HarperCollins, 2000.

Emerson, Steven. *American Jihad: The Terrorists Living Among Us.* New York: Simon & Schuster, 2003.

Faludi, Susan. *Stiffed: The Betrayal of the American Man.* New York: HarperCollins, 1999.

Frank, Thomas. *The Conquest of Cool.* Chicago: University of Chicago Press, 1998.

_____. *What's the Matter with Kansas?* New York: Henry Holt, 2004.

Frum, David. *Dead Right.* New York: Basic, 1994.

_____. *How We Got Here: The '70s (The Decade That Brought You Modern Life, For Better or Worse).* New York: Basic, 1999.

Gartner, John D. *In Search of Bill Clinton: A Psychological Biography.* New York: Macmillan, 2008.

Gunaratna, Rohan. *Inside Al-Qaeda.* New York: Columbia University Press, 2002.

Hassan, George. *Iran: Harsh Arm of Islam.* Santa Ana, CA: Seven Locks, 2005.

Henry, William A., III. *In Defense of Elitism.* New York: Anchor Books/Random House, 1994.

Johnson, Haynes. *The Best of Times: The Boom and Bust Years of America Before and After Everything Changed.* New York: Harvest/Harcourt, 2001, 2002.

Kelley, Kitty. *The Family: The Real Story of the Bush Dynasty.* New York: Doubleday, 2004.

Kinsley, Michael. *Big Babies: On Presidents, Politics, and National Crazes.* New York: HarperCollins, 1995, 1997.

_____. *Please Don't Remain Calm: Provocations and Commentaries.* New York: W.W. Norton, 2008

McAuliffe, Terry. *What a Party! My Life Among Democrats ... and Other Wild Animals.* New York: Thomas Dunne/St. Martin's, 2007.

Powers, John. *Sore Winners.* Doubleday, 2004.

Sirota, David. *Back to Our Future: How the 1980s Explain the World We Live in Now.* New York: Ballantine, 2011.

Taibbi, Matt. *Griftopia: Bubble Machines, Vampire Squids, and the Long Con That Is Breaking America.* New York: Spiegel & Grau, 2010.

Takiff, Michael. *A Complicated Man: The Life of Bill Clinton as Told by Those Who Knew Him.* New Haven, CT: Yale University Press, 2010.

Tapper, Jake. *Down & Dirty: The Plot to Steal the Presidency.* Boston: Little, Brown, 2001.

Walsh, Joan. *What's the Matter with White People? Why We Long for a Golden Age that Never Was.* Hoboken, NJ: John Wiley & Sons, 2012.

Williams, Marjorie. *The Woman at the Washington Zoo: Writings on Politics, Family, and Fate.* New York: Perseus, 2005. [Published posthumously with forward, by Ms. Williams' journalist husband, Timothy Noah.]

Films and Video

Capitalism: A Love Story. Dir. Michael Moore. Overture Films/Weinstein, 2009.

Fahrenheit 9/11. Dir. Michael Moore. Lionsgate, IFC Films and Miramax Films, 2004.

Falling Down. Dir. Joel Schumacher. Warner Bros., 1992.

Inequality for All. Dir. Jacob Kornbluth. Starring Robert Reich. RADiUS-TWC, 2013.

Recount [DVD commentary]. Dir. Jay Roach. HBO Films, 2008.

Remembering 9/11. National Geographic, 2006.

The Road to 9/11. Frontline/PBS, 2005.

Roger & Me. Dir. Michael Moore. Dog Eat Dog Films/Warner Bros., 1989.

The War Room. Dirs. D.A. Pennebaker, Chris Hegedus. October Films, 1993.

Index